INTRODUCTION TO MIDDLEWARE

Web Services, Object Components, and Cloud Computing

INTRODUCTION TO MIDDLEWARE

Web Services, Object Components, and Cloud Computing

Letha Hughes Etzkorn

CRC Press
Taylor & Francis Group
Boca Raton London New York

CRC Press is an imprint of the
Taylor & Francis Group, an **informa** business

A CHAPMAN & HALL BOOK

CRC Press
Taylor & Francis Group
6000 Broken Sound Parkway NW, Suite 300
Boca Raton, FL 33487-2742

First issued in paperback 2020

ISBN 13: 978-0-367-57359-1 (pbk)
ISBN 13: 978-1-4987-5407-1 (hbk)

Visit the Taylor & Francis Web site at
http://www.taylorandfrancis.com

and the CRC Press Web site at
http://www.crcpress.com

Dedication

*To my husband and sweetheart, Dave, who always does so much for me
(he did most of the review of the proofs for this textbook), to the other centers
of my heart: Tricia and Chris, and to the memory of Daddy and Mama.
Mama always wanted one of her kids to write a book, although I don't think
a textbook was what she had in mind.*

Contents

SECTION I   The Different Paradigms

SECTION II   Enabling Technologies for Middleware

SECTION III   *Middleware Using Distributed Object-Oriented Components*

SECTION IV   Middleware Using Web Services

SECTION V Middleware for the Cloud

SECTION VI   Message-Oriented Middleware

SECTION VII   Comparison of Middlewares

Online Resources

The following Online Resources can be found at https://www.crcpress.com/Introduction-to-Middleware-Web-Services-Object-Components-and-Cloud-Computing/Etzkorn/p/book/9781498754071

Preface

What I am primarily interested in presenting in this textbook is a comparison of different middleware technologies and the overarching middleware concepts they are based on. My expectation is that students can come out of a course that uses (the major portions of) this textbook and be able to select an appropriate middleware technology to use for any given task, and also to be able to learn new middleware technologies as they appear over time without being greatly overwhelmed by any particular new concept. Middleware technologies come and go and have different advantages and disadvantages but many of the concepts overlap. They should also have sufficient background in the area to enable them to be critical thinkers when the next new middleware fads appear.

Also, students will become well-functional in a given middleware technology after they study the sections dealing with that technology in this textbook. One of my goals is that students will acquire some practical skills that can be used to acquire good jobs after graduation, that is, buzzwords on the resume that they actually deserve, based on real projects that they have actually done. These middleware technology sections can also be useful for practitioners in industry who are working to expand their skills.

I have taught the technologies in small enough chunks that I hope not to lose anyone along the way. I have also tried not to make too many assumptions about how much the student already knows. I have a substantial quantity of background material, but I put most of it in separate chapters or sidebars, so it can be skipped by better prepared students. I have provided sufficient portions of code that the students can run the examples without having to do such mundane tasks as, for example, web searches to figure out what library functions must be included to make the code run, as I have found that kind of grunt work greatly discourages students. I have also provided larger, more practical examples for when the students have become familiar with the technology (these are in separate chapters, Chapter 17 and 18, which are available with this textbook as online resources).

Also, to encourage students to actually read the textbook, I have adopted a somewhat informal and breezy tone throughout the book, used real examples from my past experience in industry, added a little extra (sometimes extraneous) detail at times to make projects feel a little more real to the students, and even tried to be mildly humorous on occasion. I tried to capture in this book the way I teach my own courses on a sleepy day right after lunch when students are having trouble keeping their eyes open. So many students nowadays google for the answer to questions rather than reading the class notes or the class textbook, and often the answers out there in the wild aren't very good answers. The easier and more fun it is to read the textbook, and the more they get out of it per unit time spent reading it, the more likely they will be to persevere.

There are several different courses that could be taught using this textbook. Suggested courses and how to use this textbook for these courses follow. (I teach Course A and Course B myself.)

Depending on how in depth you cover the material, and what kind of prerequisites you expect, most of these courses could be taught anywhere from sophomore level to graduate level.

Normally for Course A and Course B, I don't require a prior network course. An operating systems course is a suggested co-requisite. However, if you require a prior networking course and a prior operating systems course, you should be able to cover the material in more depth—possibly covering more sections of more chapters—and the course in that case would be more appropriate at the graduate level (or advanced senior level).

Course A: (senior level/graduate level—could be taught at junior level depending on prerequisites and chapters covered.)

Course Name: Client/Server Architectures or An Introduction to Middleware
This course examines different client/server architectures and introduces modern middleware technologies that can be used for each of the different paradigms. The different paradigms are compared.

Suggested Textbook use:
　　Chapter 1
　　Chapter 2
　　Chapter 3 (depending on course prerequisites)
　　Chapter 4 (depending on course prerequisites)
　　Cover portions of Chapter 5 if you want to examine security aspects of middleware
　　Cover Chapter 6 if you select one or more of the .Net technologies
　　Select ONE distributed object component technology from Chapter 8, this would be:
　　　　• CORBA, *or*
　　　　• .NET Remoting, *or*
　　　　• Enterprise Java Beans
　　Chapter 9
　　Select ONE non-RESTful technology from Chapter 10 (you must cover SOAP and WSDL), this would be:
　　　　• JAX-WS, *or*
　　　　• WCF
　　Select ONE RESTful technology from Chapter 11 or Chapter 12, this would be:
　　　　• AJAX, *or*
　　　　• Java Servlets and JAX-RS, *or*
　　　　• WCF-RESTful, *or*
　　　　• ASP.NET MVC and/or ASP.NET CORE 1.0
　　　　　　(NOTE: it's difficult to examine JAX-RS without a prior knowledge of servlets. You could cover servlets alone without JAX-RS, but if so you should thoroughly examine how they can be made RESTful along with ways in which they can be created in a less RESTful manner.)
　　Chapters 17 and 18 (available as online resources) provide larger, practical examples for each of the technologies in Chapters 8, 10, 11, and 12.
　　(NOTE: depending on how you set up the course, you can give an overview of cloud computing interfaces as examples of RESTful technology. If so, you would make use of either Chapter 13 or Chapter 14.)
　　Chapter 15
　　Chapter 16

Course B: (senior level/graduate level—could be taught at junior level depending on prerequisites and chapters covered.)

　　Course Name: Introduction to Cloud Computing
　　This course examines modern cloud computing, with an emphasis on open source cloud software.
　　Suggested Textbook use:
　　Chapter 1, Section1.3.6
　　Chapter 2, Sections 2.4, 2.5, and 2.6
　　Chapter 3 (depending on course prerequisites)
　　Chapter 4 (depending on course prerequisites)
　　Chapter 5 (depending on course prerequisites)
　　Chapter 7
　　Chapter 9
　　Chapter 11, Section 11.1 (just so they see a practical RESTful web service)
　　Chapter 13
　　Chapter 14
　　Chapter 15 (because clouds make heavy use of MOM)
　　Chapter 16, Section 16.3.2

Course C: (senior level/graduate level—could be taught at junior level depending on prerequisites and chapters covered.)

Course Name: Introduction to Web Services
This course examines modern web service architectures.
You may choose to use only RESTful architectures or a mixture of non-RESTful and RESTful architectures (nowadays it would be unusual to use non-RESTful only).
Suggested Textbook use:
Chapter 1
Chapter 2
Chapter 3 (depending on course prerequisites)
Chapter 4 (depending on course prerequisites)
Chapter 5 (depending on course prerequisites)
Cover Chapter 6 if you select one or more of the .Net technologies
Chapter 9
Chapter 10 (select one or more web services technologies as desired)
Chapter 11 (select one or more web services technologies as desired)
Chapter 12 (select one or more web services technologies as desired)
For technologies chosen from Chapter 10, Chapter 11, and Chapter 12, you may use the associated larger practical examples from Chapter 17 and Chapter 18, as desired. Chapters 17 and 18 are online resources.
Chapter 16 (Here focus only on web service architectures and architectural styles)

Course D: (This course is probably junior level or sophomore level depending on choices.)

Course Name: Introduction to Web Programming
This course examines how to program on the World Wide Web.
Requires supplementary material from w3schools on HTML, CSS, JavaScript, PHP.
Suggested Textbook use:
Chapter 1, Sections 1.3.4, 1.3.5
Chapter 2, Sections 2.4, 2.5
Chapter 3
Chapter 4
Chapter 9
Either Chapter 10 or Chapter 11 or Chapter 12 or selected portions.
  • Choose Chapter 11, Sections 11.1 and 11.2 if this is a sophomore course.
  • You may have to teach Java if this is a sophomore course.
  • You may use larger practical examples associated with the chosen technology from Chapter 17 or Chapter 18, as desired. Chapters 17 and 18 are online resources.

Course E: (This course is probably junior level or sophomore level depending on choices.)

Course Name: Advanced Object-Oriented Software Development in Java
This course examines advanced object-oriented programming including advanced use of Java libraries. Includes Java Graphics APIs such as AWT or Swing, and Java Middleware including Enterprise Java Beans and Java Servlets.
Suggested Textbook use:
Should be supplemented with web pages, etc., dealing in more depth with Java Graphics APIs. Note that the selected sections in Chapter 18 include a basic introduction to Java Swing libraries. Chapter 18 is available in online resources.
Chapter 1, Section 1.3.2
Chapter 2, Section 2.3
Chapter 3

Chapter 4
Chapter 8, Section 8.3
Chapter 11, Section 11.2 (can possibly also use Section 11.3)
Chapter 18, Sections 18.1 and 18.4 (possibly also Section 18.5)—this contains the Java Swing
    GUI examples as part of the middleware code (note that additional java swing material is
    included in Section 17.1.4, if you cover that section, stick just to the java swing material)
    Chapters 17 and 18 are available in online resources.

Course F: (This course is probably junior level or even sophomore level depending on choices.)

Course Name: Advanced Object-Oriented Software Development in C# with .NET
Suggested Textbook use:
    Should be supplemented with web pages (or a textbook) dealing in basics related to the C# lan-
    guage. Note that the selected sections include a basic introduction to Windows Presentation
    Foundation. Could be supplemented with web pages and materials with more extensive
    WPF or possibly additional aspects of .NET.
Chapter 1, Section 1.3.2, 1.3.4, 1.3.5
Chapter 2, Section 2.3, 2.4, 2.5
Chapter 3
Chapter 4
Chapter 6
Chapter 8, Section 8.2
Chapter 10, Sections 10.1, 10.2, 10.4
Chapter 12
Chapter 17, Sections 17.2, 17.3, and 17.4—this contains an introduction to Windows Presenta-
    tion Foundation as part of the larger practical middleware examples. Chapter 17 is available
    in online resources.

Other possible courses where this textbook might be useful:
- Course on advanced cloud computing
    - This course would focus on the internals of an open source cloud and how the open source
      clouds are actually implemented.
    - Would have to be supplemented by looking at the actual code from a particular open source
      cloud (OpenStack, CloudStack).
- Course on system administration in the cloud:
    - This course would focus on how to set up a cloud, and on standard system administration
      issues that would arise in a cloud, with a particular look at security issues.
    - Would have to be supplemented by web pages associated with specific open source clouds
      such as OpenStack or CloudStack.
- Course on virtualization:
    - This course would focus on various kinds of virtualization techniques, including hypervi-
      sors and containers, and how those can be used in practice.
    - Would have to be supplemented by web pages associated with specific open source hyper-
      visors such as KVM or Xen or on containers such as LXC or Docker.
- Course on analysis and design patterns
    - The idea is that this course would first teach general design patterns and analysis patterns
      and then focus on networking/middleware/cloud patterns as examples.
    - Supplemented by web pages such as www.vincehuston.org/dp
    - Supplemented by textbooks such as the Gang of Four design patterns book (Gamma, Helm,
      Johnson, and Vlissides) (possibly the Analysis Patterns book by Fowler).

Letha Hughes Etzkorn
The University of Alabama in Huntsville

Author

Dr. Letha Hughes Etzkorn is a professor in the Computer Science Department at The University of Alabama in Huntsville with more than 30 years of experience. She earned her master's degree and PhD in computer science from The University of Alabama in Huntsville, and bachelor's and master's degrees in electrical engineering from the Georgia Institute of Technology, Atlanta, Georgia. She is a registered professional engineer (Electrical Engineering, State of Georgia) and is a senior member of the Institute of Electrical and Electronics Engineers. She has graduated 16 PhD students so far. She has served as an associate editor/member of editorial board for several journals. Prior to her career in academia, Dr. Etzkorn worked in industry for several years, primarily in networking, modems, and embedded systems, for companies including Motorola, Hayes Microcomputer Products, and Lockheed-Georgia.

Dr. Etzkorn has published more than 100 peer-reviewed research papers. Also, she has received more than $3.9 million in grants and contracts as Principal Investigator or Co-Principal Investigator from federal agencies including the National Security Agency (NSA), the National Science Foundation (NSF), the National Aeronautics and Space Administration (NASA), and the U.S. Army. Some of her major research areas are in software engineering (software metrics, program comprehension), middleware, and cybersecurity within the Internet of Things. She has taught more than 28 different courses, including courses at both undergraduate and graduate levels. These include (among others) courses in software engineering, computer architecture, computer networks, computer security, and, of course, middleware and cloud computing.

Section I

The Different Paradigms

1 Introduction

We will begin by discussing the *Rendezvous problem*:

> Imagine a person trying to start two programs at the same time, on two separate computers, and wanting them to communicate with each other.

There are a few different ways that two programs on two different computers can handle their communications with each other. We will start with client/server, which is probably the best known way, and this will be what we primarily concentrate on in this textbook (although later on we will discuss some other ways as well).

The client/server model solves the rendezvous problem by determining that one side (the server) must start execution, and wait indefinitely for the other side (the client) to contact it.

- Server—a program that waits for incoming communication requests from a client. When the server receives a communication from the client, the server provides some useful service to the client, and sends the client the results.
- Client—a program that initiates communication with the server. The client has need of some service that the server can provide.

Clients are often easier to build than servers, and commonly require no special system privileges to operate. Servers often need to access data and/or routines or resources that are provided by an operating system and protected by the operating system. Therefore, servers often need special system privileges.

Servers are concerned with:

- Authentication—verifying that the client is who it claims to be
- Authorization—determining whether the given client is permitted to access any of the services the server supplies
- Providing services
- Data security—guaranteeing that a client is not able to access data that the client is not permitted to access, preventing data from being stolen

Servers typically come in two different versions:

1. Stateless—server does not save any information about the status of ongoing interaction with clients
2. Stateful—server saves information about the status of ongoing interactions with clients

In this textbook, we will examine lots of different ways in which software on one computer can talk to software on another computer across a network. As we saw before, we will especially examine how clients can connect with servers. We are going to compare (many of) the major paradigms by which this is done.

Our work doing this begins here in Chapter 1, where we will first introduce the different distributed computing paradigms. Then in Chapter 2, we will move into a review of the different kinds of architectures, architectural styles/patterns, and properties that various researchers have used in the past to examine distributed applications and to determine the quality of a distributed application. This will give us a background and some language that will allow us to begin comparing the various distributed computing paradigms as we go through the rest of the book.

In the following chapters, we will learn some background material needed to understand the different technologies that implement the different distributed computing paradigms that we will be examining.

Then we will learn how to use several different technologies related to the major distributed computing paradigms. Sufficient detail is provided on each of these technologies to make us reasonably functional in that technology. That is, after studying that technology we will be able to go to a company and begin doing real work using that technology, although we may still have quite a bit more to learn. ☺ While learning all these different technologies, it is important to keep in mind the architectures, properties, and patterns that we learn in Chapter 2, as of course we'll be comparing these technologies later on using this information!

Here in Chapter 1, after we have examined the different distributed computing paradigms at a high level, we will look at two projects that can be used to illustrate the practical use of middleware. One of these projects is a general distributed project that doesn't rely on the World Wide Web part of the internet, and the other project is a database project that is best implemented using the World Wide Web. (We distinguish the World Wide Web from the internet, in that the World Wide Web consists of websites connected through the use of HTTP and hyperlinks, which are implemented on top of the internet.) Then, as we go through this textbook, after we have learned how to use each technology, we will see an implementation of one of these two projects, chosen as the one of the two that is most suited to that particular middleware. These two projects are described below in Sections 1.4 and 1.5. The implementations themselves are provided in Chapters 17 and 18 (available as online resources with this textbook), except the implementations for ASP.NET MVC and ASP.NET Core 1.0, which are provided in Chapter 12.

Finally, in Chapter 16 we will examine the various technologies in depth in relation to architectures, architectural styles/patterns, and general performance considerations. We will look at how a framework for comparing distributed computing paradigms and the distributed computing technologies can be developed.

When we get done reading this textbook, we should know how best to select a particular paradigm and technology for a particular task. And we will know enough about several distributed computing technologies to be very dangerous. ☺

1.1   WHAT IS MIDDLEWARE?

Middleware is the focus of this textbook. So what is it? Let's look at a few definitions.

First of all, according to Oracle (2016a):

> Middleware is the software that connects software components or enterprise applications. Middleware is the software layer that lies between the operating system and the applications on each side of a distributed computer network. Typically, it supports complex, distributed business software applications.

The following definition from Techopedia (2016) is more comprehensive:

> Middleware is a software layer situated between applications and operating systems. Middleware is typically used in distributed systems where it simplifies software development by doing the following:
>
> - Hides the intricacies of distributed applications
> - Hides the heterogeneity of hardware, operating systems, and protocols
> - Provides uniform and high-level interfaces used to make interoperable, reusable and portable applications
> - Provides a set of common services that minimizes duplication of efforts and enhances collaboration between applications

The following definition from Apprenda (2016) is also good to use in the context of this textbook because it clarifies that in today's world, cloud computing is also considered to be part of middleware:

A simple middleware definition: software that connects computers and devices to other applications. It can also be referred to as the slash or connecting point in client/server. Another way to define middleware is to say that it is software that acts as a liaison between applications and networks. The term is often used in the context of cloud computing, such as public or private cloud.

So the meat of these definitions are that middleware is used to hide the lower level complexity of networks and operating systems from the application programmer. It can allow a client running on one kind of computer with one kind of operating system to talk to a server on a different kind of computer running a different operating system. Middleware allows the definition of clearly defined interfaces to servers, that clients can easily call.

In the next section, we will begin our examination of Middleware technologies by looking at sockets. Sockets can be considered an early form of Middleware by the definitions we're using. However, they have major drawbacks compared to many more modern Middleware technologies in that they require the application programmer who uses them to have a good understanding of networking and also of how bytes are stored on computers.

1.2 TECHNOLOGY REVIEW: SOCKETS

The Berkeley Software Distribution (BSD) of UNIX back in 1983 defined an application interface called *sockets*. This eventually became a Portable Operating System Interface (POSIX) specification. So, they're commonly known as BSD sockets or as POSIX sockets.

There is a Windows version of sockets, called Winsock that was originally based on the POSIX sockets. However, there are quite a few differences in terms of include files, names of library routines, etc. According to MSDN (2016) there are also some implementation differences based on differences in Windows compared to UNIX. However, it is usually possible to port socket applications between Linux and Windows.

In this section of the textbook, we will concentrate on POSIX sockets, since they are the sockets upon which other sockets are based. Also, we are primarily looking at sockets in order to show their limitations in regard to more modern middleware technologies, that is, that sockets require the programmer to know more about networking issues and how data is stored on computers than modern middlewares do. So we are anxious to get on to the modern middlewares! We're going to look at sockets in C++ (really in C although we're using a few C++ items), although they're also available in many other languages. They can be very powerful and are still very widely used.

1.2.1 SOCKET DATA STRUCTURES

With POSIX/BSD sockets, a socket is treated similarly to a file. Sockets are stored in the file descriptor table and thus, an application cannot have both a file descriptor and a socket descriptor with the same value.

To perform communication, sockets choose a family of protocols to use. Which family to use is defined in the *sockaddr* struct, which is defined in the file *sys/socket.h* as follows:

```
struct sockaddr
  {
    unsigned char  sa_len;    // length of address
    sa_family_t  sa_family; // the address family
    char sa_data[14];        // the address
  };
```

(note that sa_family_t is defined earlier as an unsigned integer)

There are several different address families supported—these are based on the kinds of protocols being used. Some of the predefined address families included in the sockets' specifications were for protocols that are not used a lot nowadays (remember that sockets have been around since the early 1980s), but some are still in existence. However, we will focus only on TCP/IP here, since these are the main protocols the internet is based on. There is another protocol that is often used on the internet, called UDP, but we will only talk about UDP in passing, since it is less commonly used with sockets than TCP/IP (although still very often used with sockets—but we're just getting started so why try to learn everything at once ☺).

If you haven't had a networking course, then it would be helpful to first read Chapter 3 for a brief introduction to networking and for a discussion of TCP/IP, UDP, IPv4 versus IPv6, and port numbers before you go on. If you don't want to read those, you can just try to skim over the network-related socket information in this section, then do monkey-see, monkey-do with the rest of the socket stuff, and you will probably be okay to get a socket working.

At a minimum, to go on working with sockets or any other middleware for that matter, you need to know that TCP/IP defines a communication endpoint to consist of an IP address and a protocol port number. There are two versions of IP on the internet, the old version IP version 4, usually known as IPv4, and IP version 6, usually known as IPv6. An example of an IPv4 address would look like: 69.84.132.16: 1132. Here the number "69.84.132.16" is the IPv4 address, and the "1132" is the port number. We will ignore IPv6 addresses for now, see Section 3.3 for a description of IPv4 and IPv6 addresses.

However, as mentioned earlier, if you want to really understand sockets you have to read the networking stuff first. The fact that you have to read the networking stuff in order to really understand sockets is one of the biggest drawbacks of sockets versus more modern middleware technologies, because the other middleware technologies are better at hiding the lower level networking stuff from the application programmer.

Let's continue by looking more at the data structures that you have to make sockets work.

If the address family being used is TCP/IP, then you use either the struct *sockaddr_in* or the struct *sockaddr_in6* everywhere you would otherwise (for different families) use the sockaddr struct. The *sockaddr_in* struct is used for IPv4 and the *sockaddr_in* struct is used for IPv6.

First of all, the sockaddr_in struct is defined in the file *netinet/in.h*. The sockaddr_in struct will contain the following members (at a minimum):

```
sa_family_t      sin_family;
in_port_t        sin_port;
struct   in_addr sin_addr;
```

The sin_family is set to AF_INET (AF_INET is a constant value defined as the number 2), which selects TCP/IP using IPv4 addressing. (This corresponds to a protocol family called PF_INET, that is, the internet protocol family for IPv6, which is also number 2.)

The sin_port is a port number, and the sin_addr is a typical IP address.

The sockaddr_in6 struct is also defined in the file *netinet/in.h*. The sockaddr_in6 struct will contain the following members (at a minimum):

```
sa_family_t      sin6_family;
in_port_t        sin6_port;
uint32_t         sin6_flowinfo;
struct in6_addr  sin6_addr;
uint32_t         sin6_scope_id;
```

The sin6_family is set to AF_INET6 (AF_INET6 is a constant defined as the number 28 in base 10), which selects TCP/IP using IPv6 addressing. (This corresponds to a protocol family called PF_INET6, that is, the internet protocol family for IPv6, which is also number 28.)

The sin6_port value is used to store an IPv6 port number (IPv6 port numbers happen to be the same as IPv4 port numbers, however, see Section 3.4 to read about port numbers).

The sin6_addr stores the IPv6 address. (This is quite different from the IPv4 address, see Section 3.3)

The sin6_flowinfo is for IPv6 traffic class and flow information, and sin6_scope_id is the set of interfaces for a scope. We'll be ignoring those otherwise because we're not going to look here at an IPv6 socket.

There is another value called "socklen_t," a 32-bit integer, that we will also see when we start looking at actual socket code. Among other things, this is the type used to define the size of an address.

Alternately, instead of using either sockaddr_in or sockaddr_in6, you could use *sockaddr_storage*. This can be used to hold and pass around either IPv4 or IPv6 addresses. Note however that if you wanted to implement a socket that would work with either IPv4 or IPv6 you're likely to have to do a lot of typecasting, since the various socket API calls (connect, accept, etc.) depend on the sockaddr struct.

1.2.2 SOCKET LIBRARY CALLS

An application calls a *socket* to create a new socket for network communication. The call returns a descriptor for the newly created socket.

Arguments to the socket call include: protocol family, type of service (stream or datagram). Stream means a data connection is being used where several blocks will be sent (this is how TCP/IP work), and datagram means a block of data is sent all by itself without a regular connection being established (this is how UDP works—remember we're not studying UDP for sockets here).

Summary of main socket calls:

- socket—creates a descriptor for use in network communications
- connect—connect to a remote peer (client)
- write—send outgoing data across a connection
- read—acquire incoming data from a connection
- close—terminate communication and deallocate a descriptor
- bind—bind a local IP address and protocol port to a socket
- listen—set the socket listening on the given address and port for connections from the client and set the number of incoming connections from a client (backlog) that will be allowed in the listen queue at any one time
- accept—accept the next incoming connection (server)
- recv—receive the next incoming datagram
- recvmsg—receive the next incoming datagram (variation of recv)
- recvfrom—receive the next incoming datagram and record its source endpoint address
- send—send an outgoing datagram
- sendmsg—send an outgoing datagram (variation of send)
- sendto—send an outgoing datagram, usually to a prerecorded endpoint address
- shutdown—terminate a TCP connection in one or both directions
- getpeername—after a connection arrives, obtain the remote machine's endpoint address from a socket
- getsockopt—obtain the current options for a socket
- setsockopt—change the options for a socket

The write() routine writes to an operating system buffer, and blocks when the buffer is full.

When read() is used with the TCP/IP protocol, it extracts bytes and copies them to the user's buffer. It blocks if there is no input data. When there is data, it fills the receiving buffer, then stops.

When read() is used with the UDP protocol, it extracts one incoming UDP message. If the buffer cannot hold the entire message, read() fills the buffer and discards all remaining data in the UDP message.

Note that you can also use a recv instead of a read, and you could also do recvmsg, recvfrom, sendmsg, sendto. These would allow you to send a message without waiting for a response to tell whether the message was received by the other side or not. This is datagram type operation, and uses the UDP protocol instead of the TCP protocol. Since this course does not require a prior network course, we're not going to do any more work with UDP here.

SIDEBAR 1.1   BYTE ORDER

Big endian – most significant unit of data is stored at the lowest numbered address.

Little endian – least significant unit of data is stored at the lowest numbered address.

The terms *little endian* and *big endian* are from the book *Gulliver's Travels* by Jonathan Swift. Little endians break eggs at their narrow ends, and big endians break eggs at the big end, and were unable to agree on which method to use. Danny Cohen used these terms in *IEEE Computer*, Oct. 1981, to call for data storage standardization.

Let's look at an example of big endian versus little endian for a 32-bit number. Let's choose the number 70A32C17 base 16, and assume it is stored starting at byte address 100.

In big endian this would be stored as follows:

    100: 70
    101: A3
    102: 2C
    103: 17

Whereas in little endian this would be stored as follows:

    100: 17
    101: 2C
    102: A3
    103: 70

A major example of little endian processors are the Intel x86 family. The PowerPC is an example of a big endian processor.

Some other processors, known as "bi-endian" processors, can be configured (on some by software, on some by hardware) to select either big endian or little endian operation.

1.2.3   NETWORK BYTE ORDER AND HOW IT IS USED WITH SOCKETS

TCP/IP specifies a standard representation for binary integers in protocol headers. This is called network byte order, and it specifies integers with the most significant byte first (big endian). Although the protocol software hides headers from application programs, a socket programmer has to understand network byte order, since some socket routines require arguments to be stored in network byte order. For example, the protocol port field of a sockaddr_in structure uses network byte order.

The socket routines include several functions that convert integers between network byte order and the localhost's byte order. Programs must explicitly call the conversion routines (and always should call them, even when not necessary, for portability).

Short conversion routines—operate on 16-bit integers (unsigned):

Host to network short (htons)
Network to host short (ntohs)

Long conversion routines—operate on 32-bit integers (unsigned):

Host to network long (htonl)
Network to host long (ntohl).

There is no POSIX-compliant version of htonl for 64 bits. So treat 64 bits as two 32 bit words.

1.2.4 GENERAL SOCKET OPERATION

The Flow of Operations example in Table 1.1 tries to show by relative placement of client socket calls and server socket calls more or less in what order things must happen. You can see that the server must be started first, and must be listening before the client connects. Then the client must send a connect message, after which the server would accept the connection. At this point, the client and the server can send data to each other via reads and writes.

Note that the client is closing the connection first. This helps avoid an error where the socket connection can be held by the operating system kernel for a while after the server terminates (you would get an error that the binding to the socket failed). Note that if you're having a lot of trouble with this binding problem, there is something called SO_REUSEADDR that you can google to help you find ways to get around it. However, there are a couple of things you can do. First, check to see if your server is still running, you can do a ps command, this shows which processes are currently running. See the example in Figure 1.1. If your server is still running, then unless you changed the address and port number somehow when you called that server again, this is why you got the error that the binding to the socket failed—because that address and port are really still in use!

You can also see from Figure 1.1 that your myserver process has the process identifier (PID) 3318. To get rid of it, do:

kill 3318

Then, if you do another ps command you can see that your myserver process is no longer running.

If your server isn't running and you're still getting the error that the binding to the socket failed, then most likely the kernel of your operating system hasn't given up that address yet. Just wait a little while.

TABLE 1.1
Socket Flow of Operations

Client Flow	Server Flow
	socket(…);
	bind (IP address, protocol port);
	listen(…);
socket(…);	while not end of time allowed
	{
connect(…);	
	accept(…);
write(…);	
	read(…);
	write(…)
read(…);	
close();	
	close();
	}

FIGURE 1.1   How to check if your server is running.

1.2.5   SIMPLE SOCKET EXAMPLE

In this section, we will look at a simple example of a socket server, shown in Listing 1.1 and a socket client shown in Listing 1.2. These follow the flow previously shown in Table 1.1.

LISTING 1.1   Simple Socket Server

```
#include <iostream>
#include <string.h>    // partly to get bzero function to clear char arrays
#include <string>      // we're using C++ strings also
#include <unistd.h>
#include <sys/types.h>
#include <sys/socket.h>
#include <netinet/in.h>
#include <stdlib.h>
#include <stdio.h>

using namespace std;

void PrintError(const string & message)
{
  cerr << message << endl;
  exit(EXIT_FAILURE);
}

int main()
{
    int server_socket_fd, client_conn_fd;
    int client_addr_size;
    struct sockaddr_in server_addr, client_addr;
    int port_number;
    char message_from_client[256];
    char message_from_server_to_client[256];
    int client_message_length, server_message_length;

    // Set the port number
    port_number = 1132;
```

```
// Create the socket for the server to listen on
server_socket_fd = socket(    AF_INET,
                              SOCK_STREAM,
                              0
                          );
if (server_socket_fd < 0)
   PrintError("ERROR opening socket");


// clear out the server address to make sure no problems with binding
// if the address is clear then it won't think the address has
// already been used by another socket
bzero( (char *) &server_addr, sizeof(server_addr));
// set the sockaddr_in struct appropriately
// note that this assumes IPv4
server_addr.sin_family = AF_INET;
server_addr.sin_addr.s_addr = INADDR_ANY;
server_addr.sin_port = htons(port_number);


// Bind the socket descriptor to the address
if (bind(    server_socket_fd,
             (struct sockaddr *) &server_addr,
             sizeof(server_addr))
                 <0)
             PrintError("binding to socket failed");


// Start the server listening on the socket
// limit the number of connections in the listen queue to 3
// (this is the backlog)
listen(server_socket_fd,  3);

while (1)
{
            // clear out the client address to make sure no problems with accepting
            // on this address
            // if the address is clear then it won't think the address has
            // already been used by another socket
            bzero( (char *) &client_addr, sizeof(client_addr));

            // accept a connection from a client
            // on the open socket
            client_addr_size = sizeof(client_addr);
            client_conn_fd = accept(    server_socket_fd,
                                        (struct sockaddr *) &client_addr,
                                        (socklen_t *) &client_addr_size
                                );

            if (client_conn_fd < 0)
                PrintError("the accept failed");
```

```
                    // Clear out the character array to store the client message
                    // to make sure there's no garbage in it
                    bzero(message_from_client, 256);

                    // read the message from the client
                    client_message_length = read(    client_conn_fd,
                                                     message_from_client,
                                                     255
                                        );
                    if (client_message_length < 0)
                      PrintError("unable to read from socket");

                    cout << "message is" << message_from_client << endl;

                    // Now write a message back to the client

                    // Doing a little mixed mode C++ strings and char buffers
                    // just to show you how
                    string mystring;
                    mystring = "Server received from client, then echoed back to client:";
                    mystring += message_from_client;
                    bzero(message_from_server_to_client, 256);
                    mystring.copy(message_from_server_to_client, mystring.length() );

                    server_message_length = write(    client_conn_fd,
                                                     (char *) message_from_server_to_client,
                                                     strlen(message_from_server_to_client)
                                        );
                    if (server_message_length < 0)
                        PrintError("unable to write to socket");

                    sleep(5);       // let the client close first, avoids socket address reuse issues

                    close(client_conn_fd);

        } // end while (1)

        close(server_socket_fd);        // this isn't reached because we used while (1)
                                        // but with a different while loop test condition
                                        // this would be important
        return 0;
}
```

In the server in Listing 1.1, let us look first at the call that sets up the socket:

```
    server_socket_fd = socket(    AF_INET,
                                  SOCK_STREAM,
                                  0
                        );
```

This *socket* call returns a file descriptor that represents the socket. From the Linux Programmer's Manual (2015b), the first parameter is the protocol family, the second parameter is the communication type, and the third parameter is the selected protocol. Since the protocol family (AF_INET) has only one associated protocol (TCP/IP), the selected protocol is set to 0 since no selection is necessary. The communication type selected is SOCK_STREAM, which means a two-way connection can have data going in both ways at the same time (this is called full duplex), and the data is treated as streaming data, that is, any record boundaries are not saved.

Next, look at the code that sets up the address and port number for this socket. This server is making use of the sockaddr_in data structure, so we know it's using TCP/IP. The data variables within sockaddr_in are set as follows:

```
server_addr.sin_family = AF_INET;
server_addr.sin_addr.s_addr = INADDR_ANY;
server_addr.sin_port = htons(port_number);
```

First of all, we see again that the protocol family is set to AF_INET, which means TCP/IP. Next it sets INADDR_ANY as the internet address, this means that the server will accept connections associated with any IP address that is associated with the computer hardware.

Finally, we set the port number. Earlier on in the code we see that the variable port_number was set to 1132, so that is the fixed port number we are using for this server. We call the htons routine to convert the local byte order to network byte order.

Next we bind the socket file descriptor to the *sockaddr_in* struct that we previously set up. In this case, the name of our sockaddr_in struct is *server_addr*.

```
bind(    server_socket_fd,
         (struct sockaddr *) &server_addr,
         sizeof(server_addr)
    )
```

The first parameter of the bind routine is the socket file descriptor. The second parameter is the address (server_addr) that contains our TCP/IP address and port number. We pass in the size of our sockaddr_in struct as the third parameter.

Next, we start the server listening on the socket at the appropriate IP address: port number for connect messages from the client. The second parameter of the listen routine is the number of connections in the listen queue—the backlog of connect attempts from various clients. These will be serviced by our server in order. Since we set the backlog to 3, if we get more than 3 in the queue then we will throw additional connect attempts away:

```
listen(server_socket_fd, 3);
```

When connect messages from the client come in, we accept them as follows:

```
client_conn_fd = accept(    server_socket_fd,
                            (struct sockaddr *) &client_addr,
                            (socklen_t *) &client_addr_size
                       );
```

The first parameter of the accept call is of course the socket file descriptor. Notice that we are accepting this (see the second parameter) using a different sockaddr_in variable than we used in the bind. We could have used the same one that we used in the bind. Doing it this way makes it clearer what's going on if we were to use a routine such as getpeername to find out more information about the connected client.

We read the data from the client as follows:

```
client_message_length = read(  client_conn_fd,
                               message_from_client,
                               255
                             );
```

This just reads the data from the socket and puts it in the 256 byte message_from_client buffer. We could have used a recv instead of a read as follows:

```
client_message_length = recv(  client_conn_fd,
                               message_from_client,
                               255,
                               0
                            );
```

As we mentioned earlier, the recv function has one more parameter than a read, that can specify some more advanced options about how to do message reception. We're ignoring this (because we don't need it) and setting it to zero.

Next we write some stuff from the server back to the client as follows:

```
server_message_length = write(  client_conn_fd,
                                (char *) message_from_server_to_client,
                                strlen(message_from_server_to_client)
                             );
```

This simply writes the buffer to the socket.

The accept, read or recv, and write are all in a loop. At the end of the loop, we close the connection from the client that we previously accepted. Note, however, that we continue listening on the socket (do not close the socket). That way, other clients can call the socket (or the same client can call again).

LISTING 1.2   Simple Socket Client

```cpp
#include <iostream>
#include <string.h>  // partly to get bzero function to clear char arrays
#include <unistd.h>
#include <stdlib.h>
#include <stdio.h>
#include <sys/types.h>
#include <sys/socket.h>
#include <netinet/in.h>
#include <arpa/inet.h>
#include <netdb.h>

using namespace std;

void PrintError(const string &message)
{
  cerr << message << endl;
  exit(EXIT_FAILURE);
}
```

```
int main()
{
    int socket_fd;
    struct sockaddr_in serv_addr;
    int port_number;
    char * IP_address;

    char client_message[256];
    int message_result;

    // Set the IP address (IPv4)
    IP_address = new char [sizeof("127.0.0.1")];
    strcpy(IP_address, "127.0.0.1");  // could instead have copied "localhost"

    // Set the port number
    port_number = 1132;

    // Create the socket
    socket_fd = socket(   AF_INET,
                          SOCK_STREAM,
                          0
                      );
    if (socket_fd < 0)
      PrintError("ERROR opening socket");

    // clear out the server address to make sure no problems with binding
    bzero((char *) &serv_addr, sizeof(serv_addr));

    // set the sockaddr_in struct appropriately
    serv_addr.sin_family = AF_INET;
    serv_addr.sin_port = htons(port_number);

    // Use the inet_pton function to convert the IP address to
    // binary
    if (inet_pton(  AF_INET,
                    IP_address,
                    &serv_addr.sin_addr
                 )
              < 0
       )
      PrintError("Unable to convert IP address to binary to put in serv_addr");

    // Connect to the server
    if (connect(    socket_fd,
                    (struct sockaddr *)
                    &serv_addr,
                    sizeof(serv_addr)
               )
            <0
       )
      PrintError("unable to connect to server");
```

```
cout << "Enter message to send to server:  ";
bzero(client_message,256);


string mystring;
getline(cin, mystring);  // read the line from standard input
cout << endl;


strcpy(client_message,mystring.c_str());


// Write the message to the socket to send to the server
message_result = write(   socket_fd,
                          client_message,
                          strlen(client_message)
                      );
if (message_result < 0)
  PrintError("unable to write to socket");


// Read the return message from the server
bzero(client_message,256);
message_result = read(    socket_fd,
                          client_message,
                          255
                      );
if (message_result < 0)
  PrintError("unable to read from socket");


cout << client_message << endl;
//   close(socket_fd);      // commented out because only close it if you
                            // don't want to do more calling the server from
                            // a run of the client


delete [] IP_address;  // return the memory to the heap


return 0;
}
```

The various socket calls in the Client in Listing 1.2 are very similar to those we saw in the server.

The socket, write, and read routines are pretty well the same. There are two new calls, however, that are needed here. The first one is:

```
inet_pton(     AF_INET,
               IP_address,
               &serv_addr.sin_addr
           )
```

This routine converts an IP address, which is stored in character format, to binary and puts it in a sockaddr_in struct for use in setting up the client's socket file descriptor.

The second new call is the connect call, which the client uses to call the server (the server would presumably then accept this call). This is as follows:

```
connect(    socket_fd,
            (struct sockaddr *) &serv_addr,
            sizeof(serv_addr)
        )
```

It has as parameters the socket file descriptor, address of the socket, and the size of the address.

1.2.6 SENDING DATA OTHER THAN CHAR DATA—PROBLEMS WITH ENDIANNESS

In the previous example, we sent character data. Let's look at sending another kind of data, as an example a double, defined on the client as follows:

```
double client_message;
```

We could send this from the client to the server using a write routine as follows:

```
client_message=123456789;
// Write the message to the socket to send to the server
message_result = write(    socket_fd,
                           &client_message,
                           sizeof(client_message)
                       );
```

We could then read it on the server as follows:

```
client_message_length = read(    client_conn_fd,
                                 &message_from_client,
                                 sizeof(message_from_client)
                             );
```

However, this has the problem that the client and the server may be different in regard to endianness.

This example uses a double, which is double precision floating point. The endianness problem can apply to both floating point and integers. In the past, somewhat oddly, a single machine might treat its floating point as having a different endianness than its integers. Nowadays, however, one can expect that if a particular machine is little endian then both its floating point numbers and its integers are little endian, and similarly for big endian.

However, if one is sending data between computers where one machine is little endian and the other machine is big endian, there is a problem. This is one of the problems that Middleware addresses. On most modern middlewares, this problem is handled transparently to the programmer. With sockets, however, the programmer has to take action.

By the way, if you want to figure out what kind of endianness your computer is using, you can do this by checking how a predefined constant is stored—you would do this by looking at each byte of the constant one by one.

To handle integer and unsigned values, you can use the appropriate htons, etc. routine.

It gets more complicated if you use a float, or a double, like we just saw. You can, of course, write your own routines to handle this. One way would be to convert a float to an unsigned value then use the htonl, routine, then cast it back to a float. Another way would be to look at your number as a collection of unsigned chars, and then swap the bytes yourself.

Also, the Microsoft Visual Studio compiler provides a few instructions for byte swapping and the GCC compiler provides some built-in byte swap routines. There's also a convenient x86 assembly language instruction called BSWAP.

Additionally, there are several software library routines that use External Data Representation (XDR) to handle transferring data between different (big endian/little endian) architectures for many different data types. XDR is an Internet Engineering Task Force (IETF) standard for data serialization that was originally developed at Sun Microsystems. It has been used by many different systems.

Remember that network byte order, used for TCP/IP headers, is big endian, so if you were sending headers from a little endian to a little endian machine, you'd have to convert to network byte order in the middle and then convert back.

1.3 BRIEF INTRODUCTION TO OTHER MIDDLEWARES

In this section, we are going to look briefly at the different kinds of middlewares, just to get ourselves started. We will look at most of these in considerably more depth later on. However, having a general idea what these are will help us later in this chapter, when we look at different kinds of ways that middleware can be organized (middleware architectural styles/patterns). Then later on in this textbook we can look at the details of various middleware technologies in the context of middleware architectural styles/patterns.

1.3.1 WHAT ARE REMOTE PROCEDURE CALLS?—ALSO INTRODUCTION TO SYNCHRONOUS AND ASYNCHRONOUS OPERATION

The first attempts at middleware were things like sockets and Open Network Computing (ONC) Remote Procedure Calls (RPCs).

Sockets write explicitly to the network on one side, and read explicitly from the network on the other side, so they are not doing a procedure call. With RPCs (such as ONC RPC), the idea is that you treat a call across the network the same as you would treat a call to a local procedure. So part of the idea is that data transfers to and from a remote computer are performed using a (fairly standard) procedure call. The other part of the idea is that the procedure that is being called, and the caller of the procedure, *think* that they are located on the same computer. We will see later on, when we talk about CORBA, that this concept is called *location transparency*.

RPCs are functionally oriented because they came along before the object-oriented paradigm was widely used in industry. Functionally oriented means they focused on procedure calls—data was separate. Note, however, that the way various technologies that employ Distributed Objects work is often also called, in a generic way, a remote procedure call. An object contains data, and the procedure that accesses that data. But if an object is located on a different computer from your client, then your client has to call a remote procedure (on that object) to do the appropriate task. In the next section, we will look at distributed objects. The way non-RESTful web services work is also sometimes called a remote procedure call. We'll look at non-RESTful web services in Section 1.3.5, and in Chapter 10.

ONC RPCs are a well-known RPC-based technology, originally from Sun Microsystems, which dates from the mid-1980s. With ONC RPCs, the remote procedures that are to be called across the network are defined in a file with a ".x" extension, for example, this could be called *mycalls.x*. Then a program called *rpcgen* is used to translate this .x file into handlers in the C language. At a minimum, there is a stub file created for the client side (mycalls_clnt.c), and a skeleton file created for the server side (mycalls_svc.c). The server itself is in mycalls_svc.c. After compilation, the mycalls_svc.c file is linked with the remote procedure call definition, and the mycalls_svc.c is linked with your client code. The stub and skeleton provide the necessary networking connections, etc., required to do the data transfer, so the application programmer doesn't have to worry too much about this, although there is some boilerplate code that is required to make this work, in the remote procedure definition and in the client code. Note that if more complicated data types are to be used, ONC RPC uses XDR format (see Section 1.2.6), and rpcgen automatically creates routines that employ XDR for the data transfer.

Other than what we just did, which is giving you the general flavor of how ONC RPCs work, however, we won't be going further into this particular technology. There are so many more modern ones where we can spend our time. ☺

Before we leave this section, however, let's briefly look at the concept of synchronous communication. RPCs typically use *synchronous* communication. In synchronous communication, the client calls the server, and then the client blocks and waits for the server to finish. The server starts work immediately as the client calls it, does the work, and then returns a reply to the client. When the client receives the reply, the client can finally go do more of its own work. See Figure 1.2 for an UML diagram that illustrates synchronous operation for RPCs.

The alternative to synchronous communication is *asynchronous* communication. In asynchronous communication, the client doesn't want to wait until the server gets done before it proceeds with doing its own work. An UML diagram illustrating this is shown in Figure 1.3. Here the client calls the server, but instead of blocking and waiting for the server's response, it goes on about its business. When the server receives the call from the client, the server goes ahead and does the work. When the server gets done, it notifies the client. The version shown in Figure 1.3 is one particular example of asynchronous communication named a *callback*. With a callback, the client previously told the server the address of a function located on the client that the server can call when the server finishes. Note that the diagram in Figure 1.3 sort of assumes that the server will immediately do the work required by the client when the call comes in. This is not necessarily the case; the server might instead queue up a message from the client and handle it later. Or there

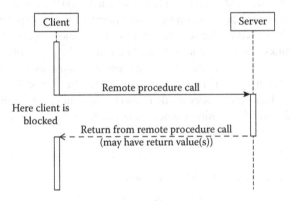

FIGURE 1.2   Synchronous communication in a remote procedure call.

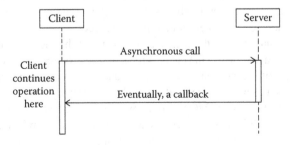

FIGURE 1.3   Asynchronous communication with callback.

might be an intermediate broker between client and server that handles all this—that is getting into something called Message-oriented middleware (MOM) that we will discuss later.

By the way, note that the arrowheads in Figure 1.3 are different from those in Figure 1.2. This is how UML distinguishes asynchronous calls.

1.3.2   What Are Distributed Object-Oriented Components?

So, as the industry moved toward using the object-oriented paradigm in the late 1980s and early 1990s, a need to have distributed objects talk to one another arose. In the object-oriented paradigm, of course data and procedure calls are encapsulated inside an object. So distributed objects just refer to objects that are located on different computers.

Generally speaking, component-based software engineering consists of combining loosely coupled components into systems. There have been arguments about whether there is, in fact, a difference between component-based systems and object-oriented systems. The general argument is that objects in an object-oriented system focus on modeling real world situations, whereas instead components in a component-based system are focused solely on combining existing components into systems. (But where do the existing components come from in the first place goes the other argument.)

Gomaa (2011) defines a distributed component as follows: "a distributed component is a concurrent object with a well-defined interface, which is a logical unit of distribution and deployment. A well-designed component is capable of being reused in applications other than the one for which it was originally developed." He further states, "because components can be allocated to different nodes in a geographically distributed environment, all communication between components must be restricted to message communication."

In any case, what we have with Distributed Object Components is a case where one or more server objects are located on a different computer from the client object. The client contains a local proxy object (often that was previously generated in a more or less automated way) that knows how to call a procedure on a remote object, without the application programmer having to know explicitly how to write to the network or read from the network. The idea is that this proxy object represents the remote object to the client. The client thinks it is doing a local procedure call on the proxy object, whereas in fact the proxy object translates that local procedure call to the network, and passes it on to that procedure on the remote object located on the server. Then the remote object replies across the network—the networking control needed to send data on the server side is also transparent to the application programmer.

Note that the Distributed Object middlewares we examine in this textbook handle both synchronous and asynchronous communication.

1.3.3   What Is Message-Oriented Middleware?

Message-oriented middleware is a form of middleware whose purpose is to provide a middleman between the client and the server, such that the client talks to the middleman and the server talks to the middleman, but the client doesn't have to talk directly to the server, and the server doesn't have to talk directly to the client. Nearly always the middleman uses a message queue to store the messages between the message producer and the message receiver.

This paradigm is asynchronous, so the message producer and the message consumer run independently. For example, if it is a case where the client is the message producer and the server is the message consumer, then the client runs independently of the server, and the server runs independently of the client.

In practice, if the client has a message that it wants the server to receive, the client would send the message to the MOM. Most likely the MOM would put the message on a queue. Eventually, the server will have time to receive this message, and the MOM will send the message to the server. There are a few variations on how this might work, we will look at these later (push model, pull model, publish/subscribe, etc.). Figure 1.4 is a general diagram of how this could work.

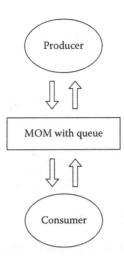

FIGURE 1.4   Message-oriented middleware with message queue.

The MOM might also do additional processing. For example, if the MOM is worried about quality of service, it might put higher-priority messages closer to the front of the queue (or possibly maintain multiple queues at different priority levels). Or perhaps a server can tell the MOM certain kinds of messages the server doesn't want to receive. In that case, the MOM can throw such unwanted messages away, and not bother the server with them. Clearly, both these MOM activities can improve performance.

1.3.4   What Are Service-Oriented Architectures?

According to the Open Group (a global consortium that develops open, vendor-neutral information technology (IT) standards), a *Service-Oriented Architecture* is an architectural style that supports service orientation. Service orientation is a way of thinking in terms of the outcomes of services, and how they can be developed and combined. In this definition, a *service* is a repeatable business activity that can be logically represented, the Open Group gives the examples: "check customer credit," and "provide weather data." Further, a service is self-contained, may be composed of other services, and consumers of the service treat the service as a black box.

So more colloquially speaking, an application that is in the form of a service-oriented architecture would call a service to perform a particular task. The application might call several different services to do parts of its task, and then provide some glue code plus maybe some extra processing to provide the whole needs of the task. This is illustrated in Figure 1.5.

However, so far you might not see the difference between a service and a library function. ☺

So, differentiating further between services and library functions, these services may be located on different computers from the application. It also may be that each separate service is on a different computer from the other services. Each service has a well-defined interface that should be well documented. Since these services are independent and are potentially reused by different applications, it is important for these services to be loosely coupled with any of the calling applications, and with each other.

A common way to implement services in a service-oriented architecture is through the use of web services. However, it is possible to implement a service-oriented architecture using distributed object components. Difficulties with a distributed object–component approach to a service-oriented architecture can include: (1) problems with firewalls, and (2) distributed object computing can be more tightly coupled than is desirable in a service-oriented architecture.

Some distributed object technologies, such as CORBA, have known difficulties working through firewalls. However, if you have an application that is going to run inside a single company, behind a

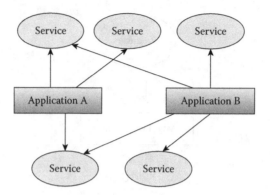

FIGURE 1.5   Service-oriented architecture diagram.

firewall, then a distributed object implementation can be a reasonable way to implement a service-oriented architecture.

However, distributed objects tend to be more tightly coupled than web services. For example, it is common in a distributed object architecture to have a client talking to a particular instance of a server object. This is significantly more tightly coupled than what would happen with a web service. However, as we will see later in Chapter 8, some distributed object technologies would allow stateless access of a pool of objects (such as Stateless Session Enterprise Java Beans). Similarly, it is common for a distributed object to be storing the state of an (ongoing) communication (stateful). Although stateful services are not strictly forbidden by the general definitions of a service-oriented architecture, this would be an uncommon implementation—normally in a service-oriented architecture one would expect the individual services not to store a state, and thus to be easily reusable between different applications.

So for these reasons, service-oriented architectures are commonly implemented using web services technologies.

1.3.5   What Are Web Services?

Web services are applications that typically expect to make use of the World Wide Web to provide application services. (Note that you might have a web service and client that both run only on your own computer. But they would be using technologies appropriate for the World Wide Web.)

We distinguish the *World Wide Web* from the *internet* in this discussion. The internet is connected using the TCP/IP protocols (see Section 3.2 for a discussion of TCP/IP).

The World Wide Web is a collection of information in the form of web pages that are connected using hypertext (clickable) links. These web pages are connected to each other and to web browsers (such as Chrome, Mozilla Firefox, etc.) using the HTTP protocol, which runs in a layer on top of the TCP/IP protocols (see Section 4.2 for a discussion of the HTTP protocol).

A web page consists of formatted text information along with images, videos, etc. A web page is typically stored in an HTML-type format (see Section 4.3 for a discussion of HTML and XML).

So basically a web service is a web page, that is treated like any other web page on the World Wide Web in that it is accessible using HTTP protocol messages. However, in this case, the web page performs some service that the client needs.

There are two kinds (architectural styles) of technologies that are commonly used for web services: non-RESTful web services implemented with WSDL and SOAP technologies (we will describe these more in Chapter 10) that use a remote procedure call-type interface that treats HTTP as an independent lower protocol layer, and the RESTful web services that use HTTP directly (we will describe these more in Chapter 11).

We will also discuss the RESTful web services when we discuss Fielding's RESTful architecture, first in Section 2.3 and then again in Chapter 11.

1.3.6 WHAT IS CLOUD COMPUTING?

IBM (2016) defines cloud computing as follows:

> Cloud computing, often referred to as simply "the cloud," is the delivery of on-demand computing resources—everything from applications to data centers—over the internet on a pay-for-use basis.

So the idea with a cloud is that instead of doing your own computing and storing your data on the computer on your desktop yourself, you hire a company to do the computing and store the data on their big computer servers that you access via the web. This is the idea of a *public cloud*.

A company can also implement its own *private cloud*. That is, instead of having computing and data storage on employees' desks, the company can buy its own big servers, then the employees do their computing and store their data on those servers.

Hybrid clouds are also possible, where part of a company's computing is provided by a separate cloud company, and part is done in house.

There are three different paradigms for cloud computing:

1. Infrastructure as a Service (IaaS)
2. Platform as a Service (PaaS)
3. Software as a Service (SaaS)

With IaaS, you or your company pays a cloud provider for computing resources. You provide your own operating system and application software.

With PaaS, you or your company pays a cloud provider for an environment provided by the company that provides everything you need in order to develop and run your applications. This environment includes operating system, development tools, website hosting, among other things.

With SaaS, you or your company pays a cloud provider for the use of their software application. You use this software application to do appropriate work for you.

Applications running on the cloud often employ a service-oriented architecture. We will talk about how this can work in Chapter 9.

1.4   ENVIRONMENTAL MONITORING PROJECT

The Environmental Monitoring Project is as follows:

We will use sensors to do temperature, air quality, and water quality monitoring of Lake Guntersville and send your data back to the University of Alabama in Huntsville (UAH) for analysis. We will implement appropriate servers at Lake Guntersville to handle your sensors, and we will implement appropriate clients at UAH to read these sensors. Oh, you thought you were going to send it back to wherever you are instead of UAH? Well, you can do that. It's just this is the way I've always worded this problem before. ☺

Using the UAH clients, we will be able to get and set all appropriate values on the sensor servers. There are two reasons we will be able to set these values, the first reason is that way we can set the (temporary) value read from the sensors to a known bad value (such as a large negative number) so that we will be able to tell when the sensor hardware is actually working because it will replace the known bad value. The second is the real reason: that way I can make sure you, the student, know how to send data as well as receive data.

Air quality and water quality will be represented in all cases as a double with a range between 0 and 1.

Our temperature sensor will set and read only one temperature value, but it will consist of both a temperature (stored as a double or equivalent) and temperature units, stored as a single character or a string: "F" for Fahrenheit, and "C" for Celsius. (HINT: think passing some kind of composite user defined data type as a parameter—perhaps a struct or a class.)

Our water sensor will set and read an array of four values of type double, representing water quality at the following depths: shallow, 6 feet deep, 20 feet deep, 100 feet deep. This set of four values will be set/read from one of four locations, each of those locations represents one quadrant of Lake Guntersville. These quadrants will be stored as a single character or as a string: "N," "S," "E," "W." For example, at the "E" (East) quadrant, you might have the values: 0.9, 0.3, 0.7, 0.5.

Our air sensor will read and set a value of type double. Since this is the simplest parameter we will be using, we will make this sensor more interesting by doing a small simulation. Each time the sensor is read, the sensor's server will read a new value from a file called *airdata.txt*, and send that value back to UAH. When all values in the airdata.txt file have been used, the sensor's server will start over again at the beginning of airdata.txt. However, if a client sets the air value, then the next read of the air value will return the value the client set it to. After that, however, subsequent reads will use the standard simulation values.

I have used variations on this project as a course project for a number of years in my middleware course. Back when I had more emphasis on CORBA in the course than I do now, I had different teams start with different ORB/operating system combinations then over the semester move to cross-team assignments making these different ORB/operating system combinations talk to teach other.

We will look at implementations of this project in the following middleware technologies: CORBA, .NET Remoting, Windows Communication Foundation (non-RESTful), and Windows Communication Foundation (RESTful). All these technologies could instead have been used with the Marina Database project (described in the next section).

For CORBA, I chose the environmental monitoring project because the Marina Database project is described as a web-based application, and CORBA is probably not the best technology to use over the World Wide Web (as opposed to the internet). (I'm distinguishing between the World Wide Web and the internet, see Chapter 4, Section 4.1 for more information about why and how I make this distinction.)

For .NET Remoting and Windows Communication Foundation (non-RESTful and RESTful), I chose the environmental modeling project because there seems to be a trend in Microsoft users toward ASP.NET MVC or (more recently) ASP.NET Core 1.0, particularly for web-based database applications (see Sneed 2016). There was already previously a trend that replaced .NET Remoting with Windows Communication Foundation (WCF). There are large established bases of both .NET Remoting and WCF, and I still hear of a lot new development in WCF in particular.

Note: One place in which WCF and .NET Remoting have an edge over ASP.NET MVC is that it is quite easy to set them running direct over TCP/IP (called using TCP binding instead of HTTP binding). So for my WCF (non-RESTful) example I used TCP binding. For my .NET Remoting example I gave a choice between TCP binding or HTTP binding. For WCF (RESTful), however, I used HTTP binding—it was RESTful so I sorta kinda hadda use HTTP. You'll understand why after you read the RESTful and non-RESTful discussions later on in this textbook.

Note that in this project as well as in the Sailboat Marina Project, I did very little checking for validity of input values. Of course this is important! But by adding complexity it makes it harder to see the various technologies in the code, so I left it out here.

Due to the size of the code, the various implementations of the Environmental Monitoring Project in the different technologies are provided separately in Chapter 17. After you learn each new technology, please go to Chapter 17 to see it in use. Chapter 17 is available in online resources.

1.5   SAILBOAT MARINA MANAGEMENT PROJECT

The Sailboat Marina Project is as follows:

This project is a web-based application that is used to manage a large sailboat marina that employs a database to keep track of sailboats, owners, whether the owners have paid their sailboat rental (and for what dates), and also handling any sailboat maintenance requests that come in from owners.

I have given various versions of this Marina project to my middleware course over several years for class projects. I got the idea originally right after my husband and I bought a 27-foot sailboat, and we rented a slip at a sailboat marina on Lake Guntersville to park it.

The idea is that a boat has an owner (string), a boat is of a particular model (string), and a boat is parked in a particular slip (parking spot next to the dock) identified by a number (integer) in the marina. The begin date and end date (in Date types, depending on your programming language) refer to the time period for which the owner has paid slip rental. (I thought about also storing the name of the boat but it seemed superfluous in terms of a computing problem, in that we're already handling a couple of items with a string-data type. However, that would be one way to expand the problem a little.) The marina also has one or more maintenance persons on staff to handle the maintenance problems of a boat; when a problem arises one of these persons should be assigned to the problem.

Note that to distinguish one record in the database from another record in the database we will use an integer called "id." Each record in the database should have a unique id number. We could also have used "slip" for this, since generally a slip will have room for only one sailboat, but I decided to allow for the possibility of having both a canoe and a sailboat in the same slip. ☺ I thought about doing this myself in the slip where I have my sailboat, because my husband and I also own a two-person canoe, which we have to lug down to the lake on top of our car, but unfortunately, our canoe is just too big and won't fit in the slip when the sailboat is there. We should probably trade that two-person canoe in for two individual kayaks, because the kayaks would probably fit on the deck on our sailboat. (And also my husband and I don't do well in a two-person canoe, because I do paddle-paddle-paddle all the time, whereas he likes to look at scenery and does paddle-paddle look around paddle-paddle look around. ☺) In any case, in some of the Marina project implementations in this textbook, I allow for deletion and display of records using either slip or id.

Note that in this project as well as in the Environmental Monitoring project, I did very little checking for validity of input values. Of course this is important! But by adding complexity it makes it harder to see the various technologies in the code, so I mostly left it out, except in a few places—for example, in the case of ASP.NET MVC, using it didn't add substantially to the complexity of the code, since it can be done with an annotation, so I used an example there. But sometimes in various figures you will see multiple records with the same slip number or the same id number. Don't worry about it; the code I've given you works either way. But it won't be a production-level system unless you add extensive input validity checking.

By the way, very small sailboats, called dinghies, don't have motors. Larger sailboats, called cruisers, do have motors. The larger ones also have onboard sinks and toilets and such. There's a lot to break! It works out to be a very large maintenance problem because new sailboats are very expensive so most sailors buy really old sailboats, which means there are a lot of 30-year-old and 40-year-old sailboats still in use! This means their motors and their toilets and their depth finders and all those things break a lot and someone has to fix them. Generally, there's a big waiting list for stuff to be fixed, so every sailboat marina needs someone or several someones to do maintenance. We're going to use this as an example of asynchronous behavior, because (believe me, I know this from experience) when you request maintenance at a sailboat marina you often have to wait a while!

So this is a very practical homework problem. At least, if you happen to be running a sailboat marina.

The Marina and the various slips remind me of a previous homework problem I had given my students involving (physical) books in a library. On the face of it there is no connection, but conceptually there is: for example, to compare the two, a boat model is a book title, a slip is the location the book is stored, the name of the boat owner is the library patron who is borrowing the book, the begin date and end dates of the slip rental are the begin dates and end dates of the allowed time before the book must be returned. So, once you have learned this problem, it's easy to modify it for other situations.

I used the Marina project for Enterprise Java Beans, for Java API for XML Web Services (JAX-WS), for AJAX/JavaScript/PHP, for Java servlets, for Java API for RESTful Web Services (JAX-RS), for ASP.NET MVC, and for ASP.NET Core 1.0.

For ASP.NET MVC and ASP.NET Core 1.0, their MVC-type support works very well for web-based databases, so this was an obvious project for those technologies.

For AJAX/JavaScript/PHP, JAX-RS, and even Java servlets, their web-based format also made using this project a clear choice, and the client would be easily created as html running in a web browser. Also, all these technologies have good database support.

Since JAX-WS is also intended primarily for web applications, this project was also a good choice, although with JAX-WS, since it is non-RESTful, the client does not run in a web browser. The database support for JAX-WS is the same as for JAX-RS, Java Servlets, and Enterprise Java Beans (I used JDBC), so that reason also made this project a good choice.

The choice of this project to exhibit the characteristics of Enterprise Java Beans (EJBs) is a little more of a stretch, as the traditional way to access it is through a separate client (similar to JAX-WS), but also EJBs is not truly a web service. However, after some thought, I decided that the Marina project was better to illustrate EJBs than the environmental monitoring service would be, since EJBs run in a container (that is part of an application server/web server), and it seemed just a little less appropriate to have an EJB talking to (simulated) sensor hardware than having an EJB talk to a database. I used JDBC to access the database with EJBs as well. However, I added the JDBC jar file in the GlassFish application server library (lib) directory instead of including it in a project, as I did with the web applications, so that was somewhat more difficult. We'll talk about this more when we get to the EJB technology.

Due to the size of the code, the various implementation of the Sailboat Marina project are provided separately in Chapter 18, except the implementations for ASP.NET MVC and ASP.NET Core 1.0 which are provided in Chapter 12. (Due to the characteristics of the ASP.NET MVC and ASP.NET Core 1.0 technologies, it just worked better to implement the project while we were learning the technologies, instead of creating it after we'd learned the technology.) After you learn each new technology, please go to Chapter 18 to see it in use. Chapter 18 is available in online resources.

EXERCISES

1. Why do you think stateless operation of a server, where the server does not save any information about the status of ongoing interaction with clients, might sometimes be attractive?
2. Why do you think stateful operation of a server, where the server saves information about the status of ongoing interaction with one or more clients, might sometimes be attractive?
3. Give two specific code examples as to why sockets might not be a good example of middleware.
4. Why are socket connectors treated as file descriptors in BSD sockets?
5. Full duplex connections have data going two ways simultaneously whereas half duplex means data is sent only in one direction at a time (the direction in which data is sent could swap at different times).
   Are there any situations when using full duplex might not be a good idea?
6. What is the purpose in using a separate file with a ".x" extension to define the remote procedure calls for ONC RPCs?
7. Think of a specific example when asynchronous communication might be preferred over synchronous (don't just tell me it happens anytime you have to wait on something).

8. Read Section 1.3.3 about message-oriented middleware (MOM). Can you think of an application for MOM?
9. What is the difference between a cloud and a distributed system?
10. Can you think of any possible situations where it might be better to access the network directly rather than use middleware?

CONCEPTUAL QUESTIONS

1. Think about middleware that might be used to implement a cloud—Would there be reasons for it to run in an asynchronous manner? What categories of middleware seem best for use in a cloud?
2. Why would a company ever use IaaS for a cloud when it could use PaaS or (even better) SaaS? Can you think of some reasons?
3. Why do you think servers usually tasked with authorization, rather than having the client do the authorization?
4. Is a cloud really an example of middleware? Why or why not?
5. What good is the internet if you're not using the World Wide Web?

BIBLIOGRAPHY

Adiga, H.S. 2007. Writing endian-independent code in C. http://www.ibm.com/developerworks/aix/library/au-endianc/ (accessed April 17, 2016).

Apprenda. 2016. Cloud middleware. https://apprenda.com/library/glossary/definition-cloud-middleware/ (accessed April 16, 2016).

Bittner, K., Spence, I. 2005. *Managing iterative software development projects*. Pearson Education, Boston, MA.

Buschmann, F., Meunier, R., Rohnert, H., Sommerlad, P., Stal, M. 2006. *Pattern-oriented software architecture: A system of patterns*. Wiley, West Sussex, UK.

Castro, E. 2003. Porting applications to IPv6. http://long.ccaba.upc.edu/long/045Guidelines/eva/ipv6.html (accessed April 16, 2016).

Cohen, D. 1981. On holy wars and a plea for peace. *IEEE Computer* 14(10): 48–54.

Dornsife, S. 2013. Message queues, background processing, and the end of the monolithic app. Heroku. https://blog.heroku.com/archives/2013/12/3/end_monolithic_app (accessed April 9, 2016).

Fielding, R. 2000. Architectural styles and the design of network-based software architectures. Ph.D. Dissertation, University of California, Irvine, CA. https://www.ics.uci.edu/~fielding/pubs/dissertation/top.htm (accessed April 2, 2016).

Fine, T. 2016. Bind: Address already in use, resources provided to the internet community. http://hea-www.harvard.edu/~fine/Tech/addrinuse.html (accessed April 17, 2016).

FreeBSD. 2014. Essential socket functions. In *Developers' handbook*. https://www.freebsd.org/doc/en_US.ISO8859-1/books/developers-handbook/ (accessed April 16, 2016).

Fu, J., Bastani, F.B., Yen, I-L., Hao, W. 2009. Using service patterns to achieve web service composition. *Proceedings of the IEEE International Conference on Semantic Computing*: 402–407.

Gamma, E., Helm, R., Johnson, R., Vlissides, J. 1994. *Design patterns: Elements of reusable object-oriented software*. Addison-Wesley, Reading, MA.

Gieseke, S. 2008. *Architectural styles for early goal-driven middleware platform selection*. GITO-Verlag, Berlin.

Gillies, A. 2011. *Software quality: Theory and management* (3rd edition). (Earlier editions were published by Chapman and Hall). http://www.lulu.com/shop/alan-gillies/software-qualitytheory-and-practice-3rd-edition-hardcover/hardcover/product-18848289.html (accessed April 22, 2016).

Gomaa, H. 2011. *Software modeling and design: UML, use cases, patterns, and software architectures*. Cambridge University Press, New York.

Henningsson, K., Wohlin, C. 2002. Understanding the relations between software quality attributes: A survey approach. *Proceedings of the 12th International Conference on Software Quality (ICSQ)*. American Society for Quality, Milwaukee, WI.

Homer, A., Sharp, J., Brader, L., Narumoto, M., Swanson, T. 2014. *Cloud design patterns: Prescriptive architecture guidance for cloud applications*. http://download.microsoft.com/download/b/b/6/bb69622c-ab5d-4d5f-9a12-b81b952c1169/clouddesignpatternsbook-pdf.pdf (accessed April 20, 2016).

Huston, V. 2001. Design patterns: The sacred elements of the faith. http://www.vincehuston.org/dp/ (accessed April 20, 2016).

IBM. 2009. How SOA can ease your move to cloud computing. http://www-01.ibm.com/software/solutions/soa/newsletter/nov09/article_soaandcloud.html (accessed April 9, 2016).

IBM. 2016. What is cloud computing? https://www.ibm.com/cloud-computing/what-is-cloud-computing (accessed April 19, 2016).

ISO (International Standards Organization)/IEC (International Electrotechnical Commission)/IEEE (Institute of Electrical and Electronics Engineers). 2011. Systems and software engineering—Architecture description. http://www.iso-architecture.org/ieee-1471/ (accessed April 22, 2016).

ISO (International Standards Organization)/IEC (International Electrotechnical Commission)/IEEE (Institute of Electrical and Electronics Engineers). 2016. Defining architecture. http://www.iso-architecture.org/ieee-1471/defining-architecture.html (accessed April 2, 2016).

IETF (Internet Engineering Task Force). 2006. RFC 4506: XDR: External data representation standard. https://tools.ietf.org/html/rfc4506.html (accessed April 18, 2016).

Jain, P., Schmidt, D. 1997. Dynamically configuring communication services with the service configurator pattern. *C++ Report*. http://www.cs.wustl.edu/~schmidt/PDF/O-Service-Configurator.pdf (accessed April 20, 2016).

Javed, A. 2015. Introduction to software architecture. http://www.lucemorker.com/blog/introduction-to-software-architecture (accessed April 2, 2016).

Kruchten, P. 2009. Software architecture and agile software development—An oxymoron? Presentation at the University of Southern California. https://pkruchten.files.wordpress.com/2009/07/kruchten-090608-agile-architecture-usc.pdf (accessed April 2, 2016).

Linux Programmer's Manual. 2015a. Getpeername. http://man7.org/linux/man-pages/man2/getpeername.2.html (accessed April 17, 2016).

Linux Programmer's Manual. 2015b. Socket. http://man7.org/linux/man-pages/man2/socket.2.html (accessed April 17, 2016).

Liu, Y., Gorton, I. 2005. Performance prediction of J2EE applications using messaging protocols. Component-based software engineering. 8th International Symposium (CBSE). In *Lecture notes on computer science 3489*. Eds. Heineman, G.T., Crnkovic, I., Schmidt, H.W., Stafford, J.A., Szyperski, C., Wallnau, K.: 327–334. Springer-Verlag, Berlin.

McCall, J., Richards, P.K., Walters, G.F. 1977. *Factors in software quality: Concept and definitions of software quality*. RADC-TR-77-369. Vol. I. http://www.dtic.mil/dtic/tr/fulltext/u2/a049014.pdf (accessed April 2, 2016).

Meier, J.D. 2008. What is application architecture? *Shaping software*. http://shapingsoftware.com/2008/10/26/what-is-application-architecture/ (accessed April 2, 2016).

Meier, J.D., Hill, D., Homer, A., Taylor, J., Bansode, P., Wall, L., Boucher, R. Jr., Bogawat, A. 2009. What is software architecture? *Software architecture and design*. MSDN. https://msdn.microsoft.com/en-us/library/ee658125.aspx (accessed April 2, 2016).

Melendez, S., McGarry, M.P., Teller, P.J., Bruno, D. 2015. Communications patterns of cloud computing. *IEEE globeCom Workshops*: 1–7. IEEE, San Diego, CA.

MSDN. 2015. _byteswap_uint64, _byteswap_ulong, _byteswap_ushort. Visual studio. https://msdn.microsoft.com/en-us/library/a3140177.aspx (accessed April 18, 2016).

MSDN. 2016. Porting socket applications to Winsock. https://msdn.microsoft.com/library/windows/desktop/ms740096.aspx (accessed April 17, 2016).

Open Group. 2016. Service oriented architecture: What is SOA? https://www.opengroup.org/soa/source-book/soa/soa.htm (accessed April 2, 2016).

Oracle. 2016a. Fusion middleware concepts guide. http://docs.oracle.com/cd/E21764_01/core.1111/e10103/intro.htm#ASCON109 (accessed April 16, 2016).

Oracle. 2016b. rpcgen tutorial. *ONC developer's guide*. https://docs.oracle.com/cd/E19683-01/816-1435/rpcgenpguide-21470/index.html (accessed April 19, 2016).

Presson, P.E., Tsai, J., Bowen, T.P., Post, J.V., Schmidt, R. 1983. *Software interoperability and reusability guidebook for software quality measurement*. RADC-TR-83-174, Vol. II. Boeing Company, Rome Air Development Center, Air Force Systems Command, Griffiss Air Force Base, NY.

Raines, G. 2009. Cloud computing and SOA. https://www.mitre.org/sites/default/files/pdf/09_0743.pdf (accessed April 9, 2016).

Schmidt, D. 1996. Acceptor-connector. *Proceedings of the European Pattern of Programs Conference.* http://www.cs.wustl.edu/~schmidt/PDF/Acc-Con.pdf (accessed April 20, 2016).

Schmidt, D., Buschmann, F. 2003. Patterns, frameworks, and middleware: Their synergistic relationships. *Proceedings of the 25th International Conference on Software Engineering,* pp. 694–704. IEEE Computer Society Press, Washington, D.C.

Schmidt, D., Stal, M., Rohnert, H., Buschmann, F. 2000. *Pattern-oriented software architecture,* Vol. 2, *patterns for concurrent and networked objects.* John Wiley & Sons, New York.

Shaw, M., Clements, P. 1997. A field guide to boxology: Preliminary classification of architectural styles for software systems. *Proceedings of the Twenty-First Annual International Computer Software and Applications Conference (COMPSAC '97).* IEEE Computer Society Press, Washington, DC.

Shaw, M., DeLine, R., Klein, D.V., Ross, T.L., Young, D.M., Zelesnick, G. 1995. Abstractions for software architecture and tools to support them. *IEEE Transactions on Software Engineering* 21(4): 314–335.

Shaw, M., Garlan, D. 1996. *Software architecture: Perspectives on an emerging discipline.* Prentice-Hall, Englewood Cliffs, NJ.

Sneed, T. 2016. WCF is dead and web API is dying—Long live MVC 6! Tony Sneed's Blog. https://blog.tonysneed.com/2016/01/06/wcf-is-dead-long-live-mvc-6/ (accessed October 11, 2016).

StackOverflow. 2008. How do I convert between big-endian and little-endian values in C++. http://stackoverflow.com/questions/105252/how-do-i-convert-between-big-endian-and-little-endian-values-in-c (accessed April 18, 2016).

StackOverflow. 2010. Floating point endianness. http://stackoverflow.com/questions/2945174/floating-point-endianness (accessed April 17, 2016).

StackOverflow. 2010. What's the difference between architectural patterns and architectural styles. http://stackoverflow.com/questions/3958316/whats-the-difference-between-architectural-patterns-and-architectural-styles (accessed April 9, 2016).

StackOverflow. 2012. API using sockaddr_storage. http://stackoverflow.com/questions/8835322/api-using-sockaddr-storage (accessed April 16, 2016).

StackOverflow. 2013. Understanding INADDR_ANY for socket programming. http://stackoverflow.com/questions/16508685/understanding-inaddr-any-for-socket-programming-c (accessed April 17, 2016).

Stal, M. 2006. Using architectural patterns and blueprints for service-oriented architectures. *IEEE Software* 23(2): 54–61.

Taylor, R.N., Medvidovic, N., Anderson, K.M., Whitehead E.J. Jr., Robbins, J.E. Nies, K.A., Oreizy, P., Dubrow, D.L. 1996. A component- and message-based architectural style for GUI software. *IEEE Transactions on Software Engineering* 22(6): 390–406.

Taylor, R.N., Medvidovic, N., Dashofy, E. 2010. *Software architecture: Foundations, theory, and practice.* Wiley, Hoboken, NJ.

Techopedia. 2016. Middleware. https://www.techopedia.com/definition/450/middleware (accessed April 16, 2016).

The Open Group. 1997. Internet protocol family. http://pubs.opengroup.org/onlinepubs/7908799/xns/syssocket.h.html (accessed April 16, 2016).

The Open Group. 2004. Listen. http://pubs.opengroup.org/onlinepubs/009695399/functions/listen.html (accessed April 17, 2016).

Thelin, J.A., 2003. Comparison of service-oriented, resource-oriented, and object-oriented architecture styles. Cape Clear Software, Inc. http://research.microsoft.com/pubs/117710/3-arch-styles.pdf (accessed April 2, 2016).

Young, W. 2016. BSD sockets compatibility, Winsock programmers FAQ. http://tangentsoft.net/wskfaq/articles/bsd-compatibility.html (accessed April 17, 2016).

Zhu, H. 2005. *Software design methodology: From principles to architectural style.* Elsevier, Oxford, UK.

2 Software Architectural Styles/Patterns for Middleware

2.1 JUST WHAT IS A "SOFTWARE ARCHITECTURE," ANYWAY?

This section is a bit abstract/higher level and perhaps also a bit argumentative in that we're going to discuss somewhat different views of what a software architecture is. Bear with me on this, if you don't have a grasp of these kinds of issues then you won't be able to fully understand the pros and cons of one middleware paradigm and its associated technologies versus other middleware paradigms and their associated technologies, which of course is the major goal of this textbook.

The term *software architecture* has not always been completely agreed on. For example, a team at MSDN, Meier et al. (2009), provides the following definition:

> Software application architecture is the process of defining a structured solution that meets all of the technical and operational requirements, while optimizing common quality attributes such as performance, security, and manageability. It involves a series of decisions based on a wide range of factors, and each of these decisions can have considerable impact on the quality, performance, maintainability, and overall success of the application.

Several web references cite the following definition, attributed to Booch, Bittner, and Reichman while at Rational Corporation in 1995, and mention that this is a follow on to an earlier definition by Shaw and Garlan. Bittner and Spence (2005), in their textbook on Iterative Software Processes, say that this definition was drawn from personal communication with Grady Booch, Philippe Kruchten, and Rich Reitman and was inspired and informed by prior work done by Mary Shaw and David Garland:

> Software architecture encompasses the set of significant decisions about the organization of a software system including the selection of the structural elements and their interfaces by which the system is composed; behavior as specified in collaboration among those elements; composition of these structural and behavioral elements into larger subsystems; and an architectural style that guides this organization. Software architecture also involves functionality, usability, resilience, performance, reuse, comprehensibility, economic and technology constraints, tradeoffs and aesthetic concerns.

Note that the MSDN definition is targeted more specifically toward meeting requirements, whereas meeting requirements is implied rather than stated in the Bittner and Spence definition. The MSDN definition is higher level in terms of the actual software organization, note that the Bittner and Spence definition mentions "structural elements," their interfaces, collaborative behavior, composition into subsystems, and that this should be driven by an architectural style, whereas the MSDN definition uses the simple term "structured solution." Both, however, discuss how quality factors must drive how an architecture is developed.

ISO/IEC/IEEE Standard 42010 defines a "system" architecture (as opposed to a "software" architecture, note that a software is one kind of system) as:

> Fundamental concepts or properties of a system in its environment embodied in its elements, relationships, and in the principles of its design and evolution.

ISO/IEC/IEEE have a further description of what is meant by an architecture. They say that a system architecture is what is *essential* to a system, not everything about a system. They say that there are two different philosophies of what constitutes an architecture: "architecture as conception" and "architecture as perception." Architecture as conception is a concept of a system in a person's mind, whereas architecture as perception is how the properties of a system are perceived. They differentiate these abstract ideas of what an architecture is from a separate term they call "architecture description" that refers to the artifacts used to describe and document architectures. They say that the abstract concept of architecture and the artifacts that describe and document the abstract architecture concepts are commonly confused with each other (they don't believe this is a good thing).

They further define an architecture as a system as it appears within its environment, related to the influences of the environment on the system. By this definition, "architecture" is distinguished from "design" because design is focused internally to the system (after the system boundaries have been determined), whereas the system architecture is focused outwardly toward its environment.

They say that what is essential or fundamental to a system are its elements, its external and internal relationships, the principles governing how it is designed, and the principles governing how it evolves over time. They mention that "software" architecture typically focuses on software components (elements) and their interconnections, while "enterprise" architecture focuses more on principles of how it is designed and how it evolves over time, whereas "system" architecture focuses on subsystems and allocation of requirements to these subsystems.

Let's examine the MSDN definition phrase by phrase in light of the ISO/IEC/IEEE discussion:

1. "Software application architecture is the process of defining a structured solution that meets all of the technical and operational requirements"
   - "structured solution"
     - Software components and interconnections, software components are a form of sub-system.
   - "meets all the technical and operational requirements"
     - Allocation of requirements into subsystems.
2. "while optimizing common quality attributes such as performance, security, and manageability."
   - This relates to principles for how the system is designed
3. "It involves a series of decisions based on a wide range of factors, and each of these decisions can have considerable impact on the quality, performance, maintainability, and overall success of the application."
   - This relates to principles for how a system evolves over time

Now let's examine the Booch, Bittner, and Reichman definition phrase by phrase in light of the ISO/IEC/IEEE discussion:

1. "Software architecture encompasses the set of significant decisions about the organization of a software system"
   - This relates to principles for how the system is designed
2. "including the selection of the structural elements and their interfaces by which the system is composed;"
   - Software components and interconnections—software components are a form of sub-system
3. "behavior as specified in collaboration among those elements;"
   - Principles for how the system is designed
   - Software components and interconnections—software components are a form of sub-system
4. "composition of these structural and behavioral elements into larger subsystems;"
   - Allocation of requirements into subsystems
5. "an architectural style that guides this organization."
   - Principles for how the system is designed

6. "Software architecture also involves functionality, usability, resilience, performance, reuse, comprehensibility, economic and technology constraints, tradeoffs and aesthetic concerns."
   - Principles for how the system is designed
   - Principles for how a system evolves over time

Hmmm, well at least we kinda, sorta have a feel now for what kinds of things might be involved in a software architecture.

Now let's ask ourselves, is there any software architecture definition that is more targeted toward Middleware? Or even better, particular software architecture definitions that are targeted toward particular Middleware paradigms?

A good place to start is the dissertation by Fielding (2000) that is usually mentioned when RESTful architectures are discussed (Roy Fielding is the person who coined the term "RESTful" architecture).

Fielding looks at the runtime characteristics of a software architecture rather than the source code structural design that is dependent on the implementation. He says that architectural design and the structural design of the source code are separate considerations. In this context, his initial definition of a software architecture is as follows:

> A software architecture is an abstraction of the run-time elements of a software system during some phase of its operation. A system may be composed of many levels of abstraction and many phases of operation, each with its own software architecture.

In this he is expanding on the work by Shaw and Clements (1997) who distinguish a software component by what it does at runtime, rather than the structure of the software system.

He states a Shaw et al. (1995) definition as follows:

> The architecture of a software system defines that system in terms of components and of interactions among those components. In addition to specifying the structure and topology of the system, the architecture shows the intended correspondence between the system requirements and elements of the constructed system.

However, he says that Shaw et al. (1995) think of a description of the software's architecture as if the description itself (the diagrams, boxes, and lines) were the architecture, rather than thinking that the software architecture exists within the software. He says that this definition is limited when describing network-based software architectures because many issues such as nature of elements, and the location and movement of elements within a network are often the most important determiner of system behavior, and the diagram-type method does not capture this information.

Fielding mentions that architectures typically include non-functional properties (quality attributes) such as reusability, efficiency, and so forth. He says that since these are an inherent part of an architecture, that therefore it can be difficult to directly compare the architectures of different systems or even compare the same system in two different environments. For example, a system that has a strong need for efficiency would likely look quite different from a system that has a strong need for reusability, since the two needs tend to pull in different directions. To provide comparisons, he discusses architectural styles, which are a mechanism for defining the common characteristics of architectures, and using these to categorize the architectures.

2.2 ARCHITECTURAL STYLES/PATTERNS

Fielding defines *architectural styles* as follows:

> An architectural style is a coordinated set of architectural constraints that restricts the roles/features of architectural elements and the allowed relationships among those elements within any architecture that conforms to that style.

In this section, we will look at distributed architectural styles, otherwise known as architectural styles for network-based applications. In the context of this textbook, we will be focusing on how these architectural styles could apply to various kinds of middleware.

Now let's look at other people's definitions of "architectural style" just to make sure we have a handle on the concept before we use it further. Shaw and Garlan (1996) define architectural style as follows:

> An architectural style defines: a family of systems in terms of a pattern of structural organization a vocabulary of components and connectors, with constraints on how they can be combined.

Another definition of architectural style provided by Gieseke is:

> An architectural style defines a formal family of component-and-connector views by providing a vocabulary of component and connector types and a set of declarative configuration rules. The common property of the formal family is the conformance to the configuration rules.

These definitions seem fairly similar if you say that "pattern of structural organization" is very similar to "formal family of component-and-connector views" and "allowed relationship among those elements," and if you assume that "rules" and "constraints" mean basically the same thing in this context.

In general, there is some discussion as to what the difference is between an "architectural style" and an "architectural pattern." In StackOverflow (2010b), there was a discussion of what is really the difference between the definition of architectural pattern from Taylor et al. (2010), which is:

> An Architectural Pattern is a named collection of architectural design decisions that are applicable to a recurring design problem parameterized to account for different software development contexts in which that problem occurs.

and the definition of architectural style, also from Taylor et al. (2010), which is:

> An Architectural Style is a named collection of architectural design decisions that (1) are applicable in a given development context, (2) constrain architectural design decisions that are specific to a particular system within that context, and (3) elicit beneficial qualities in each resulting system.

One person discussing this in the StackOverflow (2010b) article says that to the layman the terms are synonymous, and that he himself had always considered them to be synonyms. He said based on some googling he could differentiate the two as follows:

> An architectural style is a conceptual way of how the system will be created/will work.
> An architectural pattern describes a solution for implementing a style at the level of subsystems or modules and their relationships.

Another person discussing this in the StackOverflow (2010b) article says that:

> An Architectural Pattern is a way of solving a recurring architectural problem.
> An Architectural Style, on the other hand, is just a name given to a recurrent Architectural Design. Contrary to a Pattern, it doesn't exist to 'solve' a problem.

Yet another person in the StackOverflow (2010b) discussion differentiated the definitions as follows:

> An architectural style is a concept, theory (and how it's implemented is up to you). It can also apply outside of the software world.
> An architectural pattern describes a solution at the software system (or module) level.

Gomaa (2011) says:

Software architecture patterns provide the skeleton or template for the overall software architecture or high-level design of an application.

Gomaa further goes on to say that:

Shaw and Garlan (1996) referred to *architectural styles* or patterns of software architecture, which are recurring architectures used in a variety of software applications.

Gomaa's take on Shaw and Garlan (1996)'s definition thus appears to consider "architecture style" and "architecture pattern" to be synonyms.

2.3 ARCHITECTURAL STYLES/PATTERNS FOR MIDDLEWARE

As we will see in the following sections, Gomaa's work and Fielding's work taken together are good starting points for our discussions of the differences between different kinds of middleware technologies, since Gomaa and Fielding specifically address distributed/network-based applications. Fielding calls these "architectural styles" and Gomaa calls these "architecture patterns."

Although somewhat complementary in their viewpoints, which is why using both Fielding and Gomma's work for our discussion is a good way for us to look at middleware, there is some overlap between Fielding's architectural styles and Gomaa's architecture patterns. For example, Fielding refers to a "client/server" architectural style, which could be considered a subset of Gomaa's Multiple Client/Single Service pattern. Fielding refers to an "Event-based integration" architectural style which overlaps with Gomaa's group messaging notification patterns (broadcast and subscription/notification). So I don't propose, in this textbook, to worry overmuch about the differences between an "architectural style" and an "architectural pattern." When we're using Fielding's work, we will call it a "style" and when we're using Gomaa's work we will call it a "pattern." When we're contrasting or comparing between the two, we'll use whichever term seems most comfortable at the time.

Note that Fielding's work was done a good while ago now, so although it covers up through RESTful architectures (which Fielding invented!), it's lacking in a general discussion of service-oriented architectures since that concept hadn't been invented back in 2000 when Fielding wrote his dissertation. We'll extend Fielding's work a little later on when we do our actual comparisons of middlewares, both when we talk about web services and when we talk about cloud computing. However, Fielding's work on RESTful architectures maps well into how service-oriented architectures are used. Also, cloud computing typically makes heavy use of RESTful web services, and many distributed-type issues identified by Fielding fit very well into the cloud computing paradigm (see Fielding's discussion of Virtual Machine and Remote Evaluation, for example).

We will also extend Gomaa's work with some clarification about his terminology versus other terminologies in the area of group messaging and message-oriented paradigms.

2.3.1 GOMAA'S ARCHITECTURAL PATTERNS

Gomaa (2011) divides architectural patterns into two categories: structure patterns, which describe the static structure of an architecture, and communication patterns, which address dynamic communication among distributed components of an architecture.

A subset of the structure patterns Gomaa (2011) defined are applicable to middleware, these address different ways that client/server software can be structured. He describes one architectural pattern, called multiple client/single service, in which one service fills requests from more than one client. Another architectural pattern is multiple client/multiple service, where a client communicates with several services but a service may also communicate with other services. The client may call different services either sequentially or concurrently. Yet another is multi-tier client/server, where a client calls a server, but in order to perform the requested service, the server must itself act as a client to another server. For example:

Client → server (web page) → database

Here the middle tier is the web page, that performs a useful service itself, but in order to perform that service must read some data from the database.

However, in terms of middleware, we will focus more heavily on Gomaa's (2011) communication patterns. He specifies these in a general way in terms of producer of a message and consumer of a message. To help you understand it better, I have simplified Gomaa's definitions in most cases by calling the producer of a message the "client" and the consumer of the message the "server." I have put these communication patterns in a different order than Gomaa used, the order I selected is based on how middleware technologies are generally presented—the less complex to understand are described first. Additionally, not all Gomaa's patterns apply directly to middleware-type communications/interactions, I have only included the ones that do:

- Call/return pattern
  - Assuming distributed object-oriented software, a caller operating in the calling object invokes a called operation in the called object (located on another node), with input parameters passed to the called object, and output parameters and return value returned to the called object at the end of the operation. (This would just be a remote procedure call, when thinking generically in terms of distributed objects.)
- Synchronous message communication with reply (we saw this previously in Figure 1.2)
  - A client sends a request to a server and waits for a response.
  - Since several clients may send requests to the same server, a queue of messages can form at the server.
- Asynchronous message communication
  - The client and the server proceed at different speeds.
  - A client sends a message to the server and does not wait for a reply.
  - When the server receives the message, if it is busy, it queues the message.
    - The server alternately could request a message from the client, if there is no message available, the server would suspend itself until a message becomes available.
  - When the server completes handling the message, the client is notified.
- Asynchronous message communication with callback (we saw this previously in Figure 1.3)
  - This is a variation on the asynchronous message communication.
  - When the client sends a message to the server, the client includes a handle to a callback routine.
  - When the server completes the message, the server calls the callback routine on the client to pass its information to the client and thus complete its response.
- Broker patterns—a broker is an intermediary between client and server
  - Service registration pattern
    - The service must register with the broker, including name, description, and location.
  - Broker forwarding pattern
    - The client sends a message to the broker; the broker forwards the request on to the server.
  - Broker handle pattern
    - Instead of always forwarding each client message to the service, after the first message from the client, the broker returns a service handle to the client. Then for all subsequent messages, the client calls the server directly.

- Group communication patterns
  - Broadcast pattern
    - An unsolicited message is sent to all recipients.
  - Subscription notification pattern
    - This is a selective form of group communication where the same message is sent to members of a group. A component can subscribe and unsubscribe from a group, and can belong to more than one group.

The server can be designed to be independent of whether it is being accessed by a synchronous client or an asynchronous client, indeed in some cases the same server may be accessed by both.

Gomaa's group communication patterns, broadcast, and subscription notification, have similarities to other group communication paradigms, but there can be some distinctions. For example, Liu and Gorton (2005) describe Message-oriented middleware (MOM) as follows (we met MOM previously in Section 1.3.3, and we will look again at MOM in Chapter 15):

> MOM typically supports two forms of messaging: point-to-point and publish/subscribe (Pub/Sub). In the PTP model, the message producer posts a *message* to a *queue* and the message consumer retrieves the message from the queue. In the Pub/Sub model, a message producer publishes a message to a *topic*, and all consumers subscribing to the same topic retrieve a copy of the message. MOMs also define a set of reliability attributes for messaging, including non-persistent or persistent and non-transactional or transaction queues.

Note that Gomaa's broadcast pattern sends unsolicited messages to several receivers (servers).

So Gomaa's subscription notification pattern is the same as "publish/subscribe," if you define Gomaa's "group" as being associated with a "topic" and subscribing to the "group" as being equivalent to subscribing to a "topic." Typically the topic is maintained by a broker of some kind, so this is related to Gomaa's Service Registration patterns and Broker forwarding patterns.

Liu and Gorton's point-to-point sends one message to (one or more) consumers. In this case, the consumer retrieves the message. This is different from Gomaa's broadcast model where the message is sent unsolicited to the recipients. A more generic term for these two models would be the "message queue" model. In a message queue model, a producer sends a message to a broker that maintains a message queue. Then at some point the recipient retrieves the message from the queue.

Note that the message queue paradigm is also related to Gomaa's Service Registration patterns and Broker forwarding patterns.

In terms of retrieving messages from a queue, this can be done in a "push" manner or in a "pull" manner.

With a pull message queue, the potential message recipient periodically polls the message queue to see if it has a message. This makes more work in terms of polling for the recipient, but it also means that the recipient is never overwhelmed by having too many messages to process at the same time.

With a push queue, when the message reaches the front of the queue, the message recipient is notified. This works well when messages are fairly infrequent, and when the recipient needs to know as soon as possible when the message is available.

Gomaa (2011) also discusses different ways that components can be structured. He said that a component might be associated with a particular physical location or constrained to execute on or using specialized hardware. It may be important to design a component such that it is physically close to the data, based on data access speed. It may be important for a particular component to be able to operate autonomously, that is, independently of other components located on other nodes, in case the other nodes are temporarily not available.

2.3.2 Fielding's Architectural Styles

Fielding (2000) examines several architectural styles for network-based applications. As you will see, these could potentially apply to many different kinds of middleware.

The styles he examines include (among several others):

- Hierarchical styles, these include:
  - client/server
    - A server listens for requests, a client sends requests to the server.
    - The basic form of client/server is often called *remote procedure call.*
  - Layered system and layered client/server
    - Lower protocol levels are hidden from the main level.
    - Enhances the basic client/server style with proxy and gateway components.
      - A proxy forwards requests from one or more client components to a server component
      - A gateway appears to the client to be a normal server, but is actually forwarding the requests, which it may modify (for security, etc.), on to the server
  - client-stateless-server
    - Like client/server except that the server is not allowed to retain an application state.
      - A request from the client to the server is interpreted only in the context of the information included in that request, and is not interpreted using information stored on the server
    - Any session state is stored on the client.
  - remote session
    - The state of the application interaction is stored on the server.
  - remote data access
    - The application state is spread across both client and server.
- Mobile code styles, these include:
  - Virtual machine
    - The code is executed within a controlled environment.
    - When combined with remote evaluation, it is part of a network-based style.
  - Remote evaluation
    - A client possesses code to perform a service but lacks the resources.
    - The client sends the code to perform a service to a remote server that possesses the necessary resources, which then executes the code (in a controlled environment, one possible environment is a virtual machine).
    - The server then sends the results back to the client.
  - Code on Demand
    - A client has access to the resources needed to perform a service, but does not possess the code to perform the service.
    - The client requests a remote server to send it the code to perform the service, then the client executes the code locally.
  - Mobile agent
    - An entire computational component that contains the code needed to perform a service is moved to a location that possesses the necessary resources to perform a service, along with its state.
    - This can be considered either a derivation of either Remote Evaluation or Code on Demand, since the computational component can be moved from client to server or from server to client.
    - The computational component can be in the middle of processing when it is moved to the remote site.
- Peer to Peer styles, these include:
  - Event-based integration
    - Instead of invoking a component directly, a component can broadcast events.
    - Components register interest in an event, and the system invokes the registered components.

- C2 (see Taylor et al. [1996]; was called C2 because it was based on experience with the Chiron-1 user interface)
  - Combines event-based integration with layered-client-server.
  - A connector between components routes, broadcasts, and filters messages.
    - Receives asynchronous notification messages—notifications are announcements of a state change within a component
    - Sends asynchronous event messages
- Distributed Objects
  - Objects possess encapsulated data and have a well-defined interface, the interfaces define operations that may be used to invoke an object
  - An operation on one object may invoke operations on other objects
  - For one object to interact with another, it must know the identity of the other object
    - When the identity of an object changes, all objects that invoke it must be modified
- Brokered Distributed Objects
  - These include name resolvers that accept a service name from a client and return the specific name of an object that will satisfy the request.
  - He gives CORBA as an example of a brokered distributed object system.

Fielding mentions that Distributed Objects are not good in terms of efficiency compared to other network-based architectural styles, and that they would best be suited for invocation of encapsulated services such as hardware devices. This is an interesting statement in terms of what others have noted about the relative efficiency of distributed object systems (such as CORBA) compared, to, for example, a SOAP-based web service. We will revisit this issue later on in this textbook.

Fielding was the inventor of the Representational State Transfer (REST) architectural style, which applies to distributed hypermedia systems (of course, the World Wide Web is the primary example of this). We will examine the RESTful architectural style in depth later on in Section 9.2.

2.3.3 FIELDING'S ARCHITECTURAL PROPERTIES

Fielding also describes architectural properties that will allow one to differentiate between architectural styles. In Fielding's case, he is concentrating on architectural styles for network-based applications. In the context of our textbook, we further restrict this to architectural styles for middleware, but since middleware is a subset of network-based applications, Fielding's architectural properties make sense to use here. (We will discuss this in terms of client/server interactions.)

This comparison technique is important to us, since we will use this in a later chapter to compare all the different middlewares we have learned in this textbook. Stay tuned!

A summary of Fielding's architectural properties is as follows:

I. Performance—consists of three sub-categories:
  - Network performance, which consists of:
    - Throughput
      - Rate of transfer of information between components (includes both application data and overhead required by communication).
    - Overhead
      - Consists of initial setup overhead and per-interaction overhead.
        - This distinction is important when you consider that some communications can share setup overhead over several connections.

      – Bandwidth
        – Maximum available throughput on a particular network link.
      – Usable bandwidth
        – The portion of the overall bandwidth that the application can actually use.
    • User-perceived performance, this is how a user individually perceives performance as he or she waits for an application to get done. This consists of:
      – Latency
        – Time between initiation of a command and when the response arrives. In this context, latency consists of:

          i. Time required for the application to recognize the command
         ii. Time required to set up a communication between a client and a server
        iii. Time required to send a message from client to server (and separately, the time to send the response back from server to client)—this involves actual network interaction
        iv. Time to process a message on the client, and time to process a message on the server
         v. Time to complete sufficient message transfer and processing so as to render a usable result—this involves actual network interaction

      – Completion time—amount of time taken to fully complete a user action. This is different from latency because it is related to whether (and to what degree) the data is being reported to the user in chunks. That is, does the middleware wait until the entire quantity of data being transferred has arrived before it is reported to the user? Or are parts of the data reported as they come in. The user would likely feel that things are going better if s/he were getting some early results. That is, the early results represent a reduction in latency to the user. However, if on-the-fly processing is going on in order to present early results to the user, the completion time of the whole user action could actually be worse (because the on-the-fly processing required more time than after-the-whole transmission processing).
    • Network efficiency
      – What is the distance and network complexity between the client and the server? If they're in the same process it's a lot faster than if they're at widely separated spots on the internet.
      – Caching data can improve efficiency by reducing the amount of data that must be transferred over a network. Finding ways to reduce the number of network interactions can also improve efficiency.

II. Scalability—suppose suddenly the server must handle huge numbers of clients, how easy is it for the server to handle this suddenly large number of connections?
    • The amount of coupling between components affects this, so can a decentralized style as opposed to a centralized style.
    • How frequent the interactions are is an issue.
    • Synchronous operation versus asynchronous operation is also important.

III. Simplicity
    • Can small software components be created? If the software components are small, then they can be more easily understood and verified.
    • How easy to understand are the middleware connections between software components? If they are well defined in a general way, and you don't have to define a lot of specialized connections between particular software components, then the overall connectivity is simpler and thus more easily understood and verified.

IV. Modifiability
  - How easy is it to make changes in your distributed system? Is it possible to change components without stopping the whole distributed system from running?
  - How hard is it to configure your distributed system to run in the first place?

V. Evolvability
  - Do you have to change multiple software components in order to change one component? If so, how many of these do you have to change?

VI. Extensibility
  - How hard is it to add new functionality to an existing, running system.

VII. Customizability
  - How hard is it to (temporarily) extend the functionality of an existing component?

VIII. Configurability
  - How hard is it to change your configuration when the system is running?

IX. Reusability
  - Can software components (or connections) be reused in other software components (or connections) without modification?

X. Visibility
  - How easy is it to monitor the interactions between software components?

XI. Portability
  - Can the software run in different environments?

XII. Reliability
  - How likely is the software to fail?
    - Are there single points of failure, or is there some redundancy?
    - Can recoverable actions be implemented?

Fielding further discusses how network performance can be impacted by the distributed architectural style chosen. Architectural styles impact the number of messages between the client and the server and the size of the messages. So if a client and server are transferring large quantities of information, an architectural style that would tend to send small messages would be inefficient. Also, if an architectural style is targeted toward filtering (examining and perhaps blocking some data) large data streams, this would not map well to an application where small control messages are primarily being used.

Fielding looks at how the various architectural styles he examined affect quality factors such as network performance, user-perceived performance, etc. In Tables 2.1 through 2.3, we look at a subset of Fielding's architectural styles relative to his quality factors. I chose the particular subset of

TABLE 2.1
Architectural Styles versus Quality

Factors	Network Perf.	User Perceived Perf.	Efficiency	Scalability
Client/server				+
Layered client/server		−		+
Client-stateless-server	−			++
Remote session			+	−
Remote data access			+	−
Remote evaluation			+	−
Event-based integration			+	−
C2		−	+	
Distributed objects	−		+	
Brokered distributed objects	−	−		

TABLE 2.2
Additional Architectural Styles versus Quality Factors

	Simplicity	Evolvability	Extensibility	Customizability
Client/server	+	+		
Layered client/server	+	++		
Client-stateless-server	+	+		
Remote session	+	+		
Remote data access	−			
Remote evaluation	+/−		+	+
Event-based integration	+/−	+	+	
C2	+	++	+	
Distributed objects		+	+	
Brokered distributed objects		++	+	

TABLE 2.3
Yet More Architectural Styles versus Quality Factors

	Configurability	Reusability	Visibility	Portability	Reliability
Client/server					
Layered client/server		+		+	
Client-stateless-server			+		+
Remote session			−		
Remote data access			+		−
Remote evaluation			−	+	−
Event-based integration	+	+	−		−
C2	+	++	+/−	+	+/−
Distributed objects	+	+	−		−
Brokered distributed objects	+	++	−	+	

architectural styles that I did because I feel these are a good set of architectural styles to use to examine the middleware technologies that we see in this textbook. The relation of these styles to the various quality factors using + or − is the information provided by Fielding. Here, a + means that the architectural style improves the associated quality factor, whereas a − means that the architectural style makes the associated quality factor worse. Presumably, Fielding's notation +/− means that in some situations the architectural style can make the associated quality factor better and in other places the architectural style makes the associated quality factor worse (this was not explained in Fielding's dissertation).

Let's think about the degree to which we believe Fielding's table. There is something in it that surprised an old software quality researcher like me (I've got umpteen [technical term: "umpteen"] software quality publications). We see that in these tables, Remote Session, Remote Data Access, Remote Evaluation, Event-Based Integration, C2, and Distributed Objects all are said to improve Efficiency. However, we also see that Remote Session is said to improve Simplicity and Evolvability. Remote Data Access is said to improve Visibility. Remote Evaluation is said to improve Extensibility, Customizability, and Portability. Event-Based Integration is said to improve Evolvability, Extensibility, Configurability and Reusability. C2 is said to improve Simplicity, Extensibility, and Configurability and also to improve Evolvability and Reusability a lot. Distributed Objects is said to improve Evolvability, Extensibility, Configurability, and Reusability.

So what I'm saying is that it surprises me that using a particular architectural style can *both* improve Efficiency while also improving some other quality factor (such as Extensibility, Reusability, etc.)

The reason this surprises me is that it tends to go against a rule of thumb that has been long accepted in software quality: that is, something that improves efficiency generally hurts all other software qualities. For example, I refer you to Table 2.2-4 of the Presson et al. guidebook for Software Quality Measurement, which shows the relationship between standard quality factors. This shows that if all other quality factors they examined (Usability, Reliability, Portability, Flexibility, Reusability, Interoperability, etc.) are high, then Efficiency will be low. In Table 2.2-5 of the Presson et al. book, they discuss why this is. For example, looking at the Usability quality factor, they say that the additional code and processing required to provide more usable output and to ease an operator's task usually increases runtime and requires additional storage. For Reusability, they say that making software more generic, which is necessary to make it more reusable, increases overhead and thus decreases efficiency.

Note that others such as Gillies (2011), Zhu (2005), and Henningsson and Wohlin (2002) have also discussed how Efficiency is inversely related to other quality attributes such as Reliability, Usability, and Flexibility.

One of the things I want students to be able to do in this course is begin to think about quality, in particular, the quality of the middleware you choose to do your tasks. To think about quality, it's important to be open minded, that is, don't just accept what has been told to you without thinking whether it's correct or not. Whether or not someone important, perhaps someone in authority or someone with a big reputation, has decided that something is good or not is definitely important, but it shouldn't necessarily be the last word on any subject. Think about it yourself and make up your own mind, particularly in regard to your own situation. We'll come back to this toward the end of the textbook when I will give you various scenarios and ask you to evaluate various middleware technologies in the context of those scenarios. There may be cases, for example, where you will know more about a particular task or even a particular middleware than, say, I do. ☺

2.4 ARCHITECTURAL STYLES/PATTERNS FOR DISTRIBUTED OBJECT-ORIENTED COMPONENTS

Now that we've looked at patterns that could be applied to many different kinds of middleware, let's see if there are patterns that specifically apply to the kinds of middleware technologies we will examine in this textbook. We will start with Distributed Object-Oriented Components.

Schmidt and Buschmann (2003) examined patterns that could apply to The ACE ORB (TAO ORB), a CORBA ORB that was developed by Schmidt (CORBA is a Distributed Object middleware.) These include (among others):

- The Reactor pattern
- The Acceptor–Connector pattern
- The Component–Configurator pattern
- The Proxy pattern (originally from Gamma et al. 1994)
- The Adapter pattern (originally from Gamma et al. 1994)

The Reactor pattern allows an application to handle events that come at the same time from several different sources (timers, signals, etc.). In a distributed system, a server has to handle several different kinds of requests. So the server must be able to handle new events while waiting for other events to occur—a server shouldn't block indefinitely waiting on one kind of event. In servicing requests, it is important to address each separate request as quickly as possible (minimize latency) and it is also important to maximize the number of service requests handled per unit time (maximize throughput). Multithreading can handle this by having a separate event server for each event run on a different thread.

However, multithreading may not be available or it may be too time consuming (due to context switching) or may lead to complicated code. A single threaded solution can be created by using the Reactor pattern.

When using the Reactor pattern, each service should have its own separate event handler. Each event handler registers itself with an initiation dispatcher. A separate synchronous event demultiplexer waits for events to occur. When a particular event occurs, the synchronous event demultiplexer tells the initiation dispatcher about the event. The initiation dispatcher then calls the appropriate event handler.

The Acceptor–Connector pattern is used to separate the work of establishing connections from the work of handling a service. To do this, three components are used: a service handler, a connector, and an acceptor. The acceptor waits for connection requests (in a passive way), then establishes the connection and starts up the service handler. The connector works actively to establish a connection with a remote acceptor, and starts up a service handler on its side. After the connection is established, the two service handlers talk to each other without talking any more to the connector or acceptor.

The Component–Configurator pattern allows linking and unlinking of separate components at runtime without a need for static compilation or linking. Using Component–Configurator you might run a script that contains directives for how to link and unlink different components at runtime.

The Proxy pattern is described in Gamma et al. (1994). This extremely well-known book is also known as the Gang of Four book and was instrumental in popularizing the concept of design patterns. In any case, the Gang of Four book described three kinds of proxy patterns. The one that is primarily applicable to Distributed Objects is the Remote Proxy. Huston (2001) describes remote proxy as:

A remote proxy provides a local representative for an object that resides in a different address space.

As a peek ahead, we will later see the use of the Proxy object in all three Distributed Object-Oriented Components that we examine: CORBA, EJBs, and .NET Remoting.

The Adapter pattern also comes from the Gang of Four book. Adapter is used to convert the interface of an object to an interface that the caller desires. That is, an Adapter object that provides a particular interface, but delegates the work to a different object (that has a different interface). There is a runtime version of Adapter and a compile-time version.

2.5 ARCHITECTURAL STYLES/PATTERNS FOR SERVICE-ORIENTED ARCHITECTURES

Stal (2006) mentioned several patterns that apply to service-oriented architectures.

He says first that loose coupling in regard to interfaces is very important. The first pattern to achieve loose coupling that he mentions is Gamma et al.'s (1994) Bridge pattern. The purpose of the Bridge pattern is to separate the service interface from the service. It allows the implementation to vary independently of the service.

The next pattern to achieve loose coupling is another Gamma et al. (1994) pattern, the Proxy pattern. A Proxy object is used on the client side to represent the remote service. Thus, the Proxy does all actual communication with the remote service so that communication is transparent to the client.

He says further that it is important for the client and the server to be able to employ different technologies, and that thus the interface to the service must be implemented in a way that different technologies can use. The interface must be defined in a basic way that different technologies can use (the least common denominator that can be implemented by the different technologies that can be in use).

Also, the interface must be explicitly defined. Stal says that the Reflection pattern of Buschmann et al. (2006) can help employ and manipulate meta-information that describes a service's interface. With the Reflection pattern, meta-information is used to describe an application and allows the application to examine and know itself. This can allow the system to change certain aspects of itself. The idea in regard to service-oriented architectures is that this meta-information can be used to generate proxies and bridges.

Next, loose coupling in regard to communication is important. This can be achieved via the use of certain communication patterns. Several styles must be supported, including one-to-one, one-to-many, event-based, etc.

At the lower layers, clients and servers communicate by sending messages to each other. This message passing should be loosely coupled. Clients and servers must agree on a standard format for messages. In addition to data, (some of) these messages must include other kinds of information about security and quality of service.

Loose coupling and scalability improve when the messages do not preserve state information (when they are stateless). In regard to loose coupling, when it is not important to save state information, service instances can be kept in a pool with other service instances, and assigned to an incoming client request as needed. Since one object on the server is not always bound to the client, the coupling is reduced. Also, using a pool of already-created instances can improve the time taken for a client to access the service. This can help in cases where scalability is needed, for example, when a large number of clients are calling the server. Also in regard to scalability, when the message exchange is stateless, it is possible for the server to minimize resource usage by only activating a servant to handle a message at the time it is activated. Saving resources enables more clients to call the server, which improves scalability.

It is sometimes necessary, however, to preserve state information, for example, sometimes a session is necessary, in which one message depends on a preceding message. This can be important in situations where information is sent in chunks, particularly when what kind of information is sent next depends on some kind of processing of the earlier information that was sent.

It is best for service composition to be described at a high level, rather than with a low-level programming language. Service composition means forming a service-oriented application through combining existing services. Usually, service composition cannot be performed in an *ad hoc* way, it must be performed in a coordinated way, with certain services executing before other services. It may be that a way to roll back to the beginning of a series of services is necessary: In the case where one service fails, the previous services must also be rolled back to a previous state.

There are different ways to represent web services (as part of a service-oriented architecture) in order to coordinate the services they provide. Fu et al. (2009) suggested that coordination patterns (that they call service patterns) can be used within applications to help control the workflow of services and can be stored in a semantic representation language such as OWL-S. The idea is that the service patterns capture typical ways that services can be composed in order to attain certain goals.

OWL-S is an ontology of services that is based on the OWL semantic description language. OWL-S can be used to describe what a particular service provides, and how to access it, so that clients can discover whether that is the service they need to connect to, and then connect to it.

To summarize, the qualities that Stal (2006) thinks a good Service-Oriented Architecture should possess are:

- Loose coupling in regard to interfaces
  - Interface and its implementation can vary independently
  - Client talks to proxy instead of directly to remote service
- Client and server can employ different technologies (for example, programming languages, operating systems, middleware technologies)
- Interface must be explicitly defined
- Loose coupling in regard to communication
  - Done through message passing
    - Messages must be represented in a standard format
  - Stateless interaction between client and server is preferred
- Scalability is important
  - Stateless interaction between client and server is preferred
- Service composition must be coordinated

2.6   ARCHITECTURAL STYLES/PATTERNS FOR WEB SERVICES

If one takes a single web service being accessed by a single client, then the patterns are very similar to what any individual middleware communication would be, so we can treat it in some ways as a generic middleware and refer back to some of Fielding's architectural properties to determine quality.

The basic architectural style choice here is between non-RESTful web services and RESTful web services. I pretty much skipped those in Chapter 1, other than just mentioning that they exist, because you need quite a bit more background to understand them. We will hit that topic heavily in Chapter 9, and then we will examine non-RESTful middleware technologies in Chapter 10, and RESTful middleware technologies in Chapters 11 and 12.

However, briefly, just to be getting on with it: You can think of a non-RESTful web service as being yet another example of a remote procedure call. RESTful web services, however, use the HTTP protocol layer directly and employ HTTP messages such as GET, POST, etc., thus they do not follow the remote procedure call paradigm.

If we think of web services being used to implement a service-oriented architecture, we have already covered those issues in Section 2.5.

2.7   ARCHITECTURAL STYLES/PATTERNS FOR CLOUD COMPUTING

Melendez et al. (2015) first look at communication between a cloud client and a cloud service provider. They divide communication between cloud clients and cloud service providers into *interactive* and *non-interactive* based on the amount of user-interaction involved. They say that Software as a Service (SaaS) tends to be interactive and use a thin client (a thin client is a client that is kept small, with most processing performed on the server), whereas Infrastructure as a Service (IaaS) and Platform as a Service (PaaS) are often non-interactive because they offload a computational job to the cloud.

A non-interactive communication would often include large file transfers, because one or more of the application program itself, the input data, and the output data may be uploaded to the cloud or downloaded from the cloud (they assume the application program will actually be executed on the cloud).

With an interactive communication, a user would be sending data to the cloud interactively and receiving data from the cloud interactively. Because a user is waiting for a response from the cloud, the latency of the communication is important. Melendez et al. (2015) mention that, based on Human–Computer Interaction studies, a response time of less than 150 milliseconds is not noticeable, between 150 and 400 is acceptable, but above 400 milliseconds is unacceptable. In regard to throughput (bandwidth) requirements, there is an asymmetric traffic pattern in that data from the user working on the thin client to the cloud service provider is typically sent in much smaller quantities than from the cloud service provider to the user, so network throughput to the user from the cloud should be higher.

Next, Melendez et al. (2015) look at communication within a cloud data center. They say that client-to-cloud service provider traffic that leaves the data center is called *north-south traffic*, while traffic that stays inside the data center is called *east-west* traffic. The quantity of north-south traffic in a particular data center compared to the quantity of east-west traffic depends on the applications that use that data center. For example, data mining applications are mostly east-west.

A typical physical data center architecture consists of a rack of servers and storage devices, with a switch at the top of the rack. Then the racks are aggregated into groups, each with its own switch. Then the groups are aggregated into the main data center router, which connects the cloud to the internet.

Based on previous traffic studies, east-west traffic primarily stays within a single rack, and most communication occurs among adjacent servers, with the magnitude of traffic between servers decreasing as the physical distance between the servers increases.

A server is typically either a receiver of data or a sender of data. However, if a server is primarily a receiver, it will send back an almost equal number of data packets in the form of acknowledgement messages.

Homer et al. (2014) from Microsoft provide twenty-four design patterns that they feel can be helpful in an application that is hosted in a cloud. Note that they are not specifically talking about how the cloud itself is implemented. They divide their patterns into categories that are based on the main problem areas in application development for a cloud. These categories are:

- Availability—the amount of time the application is available
- Data Management—how can data hosted at different locations be kept synchronized
- Design and implementation—consistency, maintainability, reusability, etc.
- Messaging—asynchronous messaging is widely used because of the need for loose coupling between services (see service-oriented architecture on the cloud, Section 9.1.2)
- Management and monitoring—how does monitoring occur in a remote data center?
- Performance and scalability—throughput, response time (latency), scalability (ability to handle increases in workload)
- Resiliency—ability to gracefully recover from a failure
- Security—prevent malicious use of cloud resources. Preserve user data privacy

In keeping with our focus on middleware that provides the communication between different computers, we will prioritize here by discussing the patterns from categories that are most related to middleware first. For the most part, we won't talk about patterns that are more directly database-focused. (Also, note that I have made a decision about whether to include certain patterns based on my judgement of their general importance, particularly in an introductory course.)

The messaging patterns include:

- Competing Consumers—different servants receive messages on the same channel
- Priority queue—messages to servants are prioritized
- Queue-based load leveling—a service queues up tasks, so that intermittently heavy loads can be better handled
- Scheduler agent supervisor—coordinate actions across a distributed set of resources, be able to roll back the set of actions if necessary

The performance/scalability patterns include (among others):

- Competing Consumers—see above
- Command and Query Responsibility Segregation—use a separate interface to read data and a separate interface to update data
- Queue-based load leveling—see above
- Throttling—control resource consumption so that demand from one or more entities doesn't overrun resources

The security patterns include (among others):

- Federated identity—use an external identity provider to perform authentication
- Valet key—instead of a client having to re-authenticate (username/password, etc.) every time the client needs to access a resource, the application does authentication once and then provides the client with a time-limited token. The client then uses the token to access the resource

We will see later on when we examine cloud computing, that in the OpenStack cloud, the Keystone service acts as a federated identity provider. Also, Keystone provides a token to the client, that the client then uses to access other OpenStack resources.

EXERCISES

1. Think about the ISO/IEC/IEEE Standard 42010 definition of a system architecture that we saw in Section 2.1 (and remember that we have discussed software as one kind of system or at least as part of a system). This definition in part defines an architecture as a system as it appears within its environment, related to the influences of the environment on the system. Think of an example where a software package exists in one environment and must be ported to a different environment, where the influences of the new environment on the system require changes to the system.

2. In regard to the discussion about Fielding's view of architecture from Section 2.1, why does it say it is difficult to directly compare the architectures of different systems or even compare the same system in two different environments? Give an example.

3. Does it really matter whether you call something an "architectural style" or an "architectural pattern"?

4. Fielding refers to an "Event-based integration" architectural style and Gomaa discusses group messaging notification patterns (broadcast and subscription/notification). In Section 2.3, you were told that these overlap. How are they alike? How are they different?

5. Why do you think Gomaa divides architectural patterns into structure patterns, which describe the static structure of an architecture, and communication patterns, which address dynamic communication among distributed components of an architecture. In particular, Gomaa specifies an example of a structural pattern, called multiple client/single service, in which one service fills requests from more than one client. But…but…but, client/server is an example of communication between distributed components. Why does Gomaa call this a structure pattern? Why isn't it just yet another example of a communication pattern?!?

6. In the message queue paradigm, what are the advantages and disadvantages of push compared to pull?

7. What really is the difference between completion time and latency in terms of user perception? Give an example that illustrates this.

8. Can you think of any situation where scalability is important? Give an example.

9. Discuss how efficiency could be hurt when reusability is improved.

10. Why might it be important to design application software such that different middleware technologies could be used at different times?

CONCEPTUAL QUESTIONS

1. Do a detailed comparison of the Fielding architectural styles to Gomaa's architectural patterns. Where do they overlap? Where are the differences?

2. Where do the Fielding architectural styles and the Gomaa architectural patterns apply to Message-oriented middleware? Be complete.

3. Do a detailed comparison of the Fielding architectural styles and Gomaa architectural patterns to Homer's et al. (2014) cloud computing patterns. Where do they overlap? Where are the differences?

4. Do a detailed comparison of the Fielding architectural styles and Gomaa architectural patterns to Schmidt and Buschmann (2003)'s distributed object patterns. Where do they overlap? Where are the differences?

5. Consider the Fielding mapping of architectural styles to quality factors in Tables 2.1, 2.2, and 2.3.c. Look at where he has +, −, or +/− ratings. Do you believe his ratings? Why or why not? Do this for each of the +, −, and +/− ratings.

BIBLIOGRAPHY

Adiga, H.S. 2007. Writing endian-independent code in C. http://www.ibm.com/developerworks/aix/library/au-endianc/ (accessed April 17, 2016).

Apprenda. 2016. Cloud middleware. https://apprenda.com/library/glossary/definition-cloud-middleware/ (accessed April 16, 2016).

Bittner, K., Spence, I. 2005. *Managing iterative software development projects*. Pearson Education.

Buschmann, F., Meunier, R., Rohnert, H., Sommerlad, P., Stal, M. 2006. *Pattern-oriented software architecture: A system of patterns*. Wiley, New York.

Castro, E. 2003. Porting applications to IPv6. http://long.ccaba.upc.edu/long/045Guidelines/eva/ipv6.html (accessed April 16, 2016).

Cohen, D. 1981. On holy wars and a plea for peace. *IEEE Computer* 14(10): 48–54.

Dornsife, S. 2013. Message queues, background processing, and the end of the monolithic app. Heroku. https://blog.heroku.com/archives/2013/12/3/end_monolithic_app (accessed April 9, 2016).

Fielding, R. 2000. Architectural styles and the design of network-based software architectures. Ph.D. Dissertation, University of California-Irvine. https://www.ics.uci.edu/~fielding/pubs/dissertation/top.htm (accessed April 2, 2016).

Fine, T. 2016. Bind: Address already in use, resources provided to the internet community. http://hea-www.harvard.edu/~fine/Tech/addrinuse.html (accessed April 17, 2016).

FreeBSD. 2014. Essential socket functions. In *Developers' handbook*. https://www.freebsd.org/doc/en_US.ISO8859-1/books/developers-handbook/ (accessed April 16, 2016).

Fu, J., Bastani, F.B., Yen, I-L., Hao, W. 2009. Using service patterns to achieve web service composition. *Proceedings of the IEEE International Conference on Semantic Computing*: 402–407.

Gamma, E., Helm, R., Johnson, R., Vlissides, J. 1994. *Design patterns: Elements of reusable object-oriented Software*. Addison-Wesley, Reading, MA.

Gieseke, S. 2008. *Architectural styles for early goal-driven middleware platform selection*. GITO-Verlag, Berlin.

Gillies, A. 2011. *Software quality: Theory and management* (3rd edition). (Earlier editions were published by Chapman and Hall). http://www.lulu.com/shop/alan-gillies/software-qualitytheory-and-practice-3rd-edition-hardcover/hardcover/product-18848289.html (accessed April 22, 2016).

Gomaa, H. 2011. *Software modeling and design: UML, use cases, patterns, and software architectures*. Cambridge University Press, New York.

Henningsson, K., Wohlin, C. 2002. Understanding the relations between software quality attributes: A survey approach. *Proceedings of the 12th International Conference on Software Quality (ICSQ)*. American Society for Quality.

Homer, A., Sharp, J., Brader, L., Narumoto, M., Swanson, T. 2014. *Cloud design patterns: Prescriptive architecture guidance for cloud applications*. http://download.microsoft.com/download/b/b/6/bb69622c-ab5d-4d5f-9a12-b81b952c1169/clouddesignpatternsbook-pdf.pdf (accessed April 20, 2016).

Huston, V. 2001. Design patterns: The sacred elements of the faith. http://www.vincehuston.org/dp/ (accessed April 20, 2016).

IBM. 2009. How SOA can ease your move to cloud computing. http://www-01.ibm.com/software/solutions/soa/newsletter/nov09/article_soaandcloud.html (accessed April 9, 2016).

IBM. 2016. What is cloud computing? https://www.ibm.com/cloud-computing/what-is-cloud-computing (accessed April 19, 2016).

IETF (Internet Engineering Task Force). 2006. RFC 4506: XDR: External data representation standard. https://tools.ietf.org/html/rfc4506.html (accessed April 18, 2016).

ISO (International Standards Organization)/IEC (International Electrotechnical Commission)/IEEE (Institute of Electrical and Electronics Engineers). 2011. Systems and software engineering—Architecture description. http://www.iso-architecture.org/ieee-1471/ (accessed April 22, 2016).

ISO (International Standards Organization)/IEC (International Electrotechnical Commission)/IEEE (Institute of Electrical and Electronics Engineers). 2016. Defining architecture. http://www.iso-architecture.org/ieee-1471/defining-architecture.html (accessed April 2, 2016).

Jain, P., Schmidt, D. 1997. Dynamically configuring communication services with the service configurator pattern. *C++ report*. http://www.cs.wustl.edu/~schmidt/PDF/O-Service-Configurator.pdf (accessed April 20, 2016).

Javed, A. 2015. Introduction to software architecture. http://www.lucemorker.com/blog/introduction-to-software-architecture (accessed April 2, 2016).

Kruchten, P. 2009. Software architecture and agile software development—An oxymoron? Presentation at the University of Southern California. https://pkruchten.files.wordpress.com/2009/07/kruchten-090608-agile-architecture-usc.pdf (accessed April 2, 2016).

Linux Programmer's Manual. 2015. Getpeername. http://man7.org/linux/man-pages/man2/getpeername.2.html (accessed April 17, 2016).

Linux Programmer's Manual. 2015. Socket. http://man7.org/linux/man-pages/man2/socket.2.html (accessed April 17, 2016).

Liu, Y., Gorton, I. 2005. Performance prediction of J2EE applications using messaging protocols. Component-based software engineering. 8th International Symposium (CBSE). In *Lecture Notes on Computer Science 3489*. Eds. Heineman, G.T., Crnkovic, I., Schmidt, H.W., Stafford, J.A., Szyperski, C., Wallnau, K.: 327–334. Springer-Verlag, Berlin.

McCall, J., Richards, P.K., Walters, G.F. 1977. *Factors in software quality: Concept and definitions of software quality*. RADC-TR-77-369. Vol. I. http://www.dtic.mil/dtic/tr/fulltext/u2/a049014.pdf (accessed April 2, 2016).

Meier, J.D. 2008. What is application architecture? *Shaping software*. http://shapingsoftware.com/2008/10/26/what-is-application-architecture/ (accessed April 2, 2016).

Meier, J.D., Hill, D., Homer, A., Taylor, J., Bansode, P., Wall, L., Boucher, R. Jr., Bogawat, A. 2009. What is software architecture? In *Software architecture and design*. MSDN. https://msdn.microsoft.com/en-us/library/ee658125.aspx (accessed April 2, 2016).

Melendez, S., McGarry, M.P., Teller, P.J., Bruno, D. 2015. Communications patterns of cloud computing. *IEEE globeCom Workshops*: 1–7.

MSDN. 2015. _byteswap_uint64, _byteswap_ulong, _byteswap_ushort. Visual studio. https://msdn.microsoft.com/en-us/library/a3140177.aspx (accessed April 18, 2016).

MSDN. 2016. Porting socket applications to Winsock. https://msdn.microsoft.com/library/windows/desktop/ms740096.aspx (accessed April 17, 2016).

Open Group. 2016. Service oriented architecture: What is SOA? https://www.opengroup.org/soa/source-book/soa/soa.htm (accessed April 2, 2016).

Oracle. 2016. Fusion middleware concepts guide. http://docs.oracle.com/cd/E21764_01/core.1111/e10103/intro.htm#ASCON109 (accessed April 16, 2016).

Oracle. 2016. *ONC developer's guide*. https://docs.oracle.com/cd/E19683-01/816-1435/rpcgenpguide-21470/index.html (accessed April 19, 2016).

Presson, P.E., Tsai, J., Bowen, T.P., Post, J.V., Schmidt, R. 1983. *Software interoperability and reusability guidebook for software quality measurement*. RADC-TR-83-174. Vol. II. Boeing Company, Rome Air Development Center, Air Force Systems Command, Griffiss Air Force Base, New York.

Raines, G. 2009. Cloud computing and SOA. https://www.mitre.org/sites/default/files/pdf/09_0743.pdf (accessed April 9, 2016).

Schmidt, D. 1996. Acceptor-connector. *Proceedings of the European Pattern of Programs Conference*. http://www.cs.wustl.edu/~schmidt/PDF/Acc-Con.pdf (accessed April 20, 2016).

Schmidt, D., Buschmann, F. 2003. Patterns, frameworks, and middleware: Their synergistic relationships. *Proceedings of the 25th International Conference on Software Engineering*. pp. 694–704.

Schmidt, D., Stal, M., Rohnert, H., Buschmann, F. 2000. *Pattern-oriented software architecture, Volume 2, patterns for concurrent and networked objects*. Wiley & Sons.

Shaw, M., Clements, P. 1997. A field guide to boxology: Preliminary classification of architectural styles for software systems. *Proceedings of the Twenty-First Annual International Computer Software and Applications Conference (COMPSAC '97)*.

Shaw, M., DeLine, R., Klein, D.V., Ross, T.L., Young, D.M., Zelesnick, G. 1995. Abstractions for software architecture and tools to support them. *IEEE Transactions on Software Engineering* 21(4): 314–335.

Shaw, M., Garlan, D. 1996. *Software architecture: Perspectives on an emerging discipline*. Prentice-Hall.

StackOverflow. 2008. How do I convert between big-endian and little-endian values in C++. http://stackoverflow.com/questions/105252/how-do-i-convert-between-big-endian-and-little-endian-values-in-c (accessed April 18, 2016).

StackOverflow. 2010a. Floating point endianness. http://stackoverflow.com/questions/2945174/floating-point-endianness (accessed April 17, 2016).

StackOverflow. 2010b. What's the difference between architectural patterns and architectural styles. http://stackoverflow.com/questions/3958316/whats-the-difference-between-architectural-patterns-and-architectural-styles (accessed April 9, 2016).

StackOverflow. 2012. API using sockaddr_storage. http://stackoverflow.com/questions/8835322/api-using-sockaddr-storage (accessed April 16, 2016).

StackOverflow. 2013. Understanding INADDR_ANY for socket programming. http://stackoverflow.com/questions/16508685/understanding-inaddr-any-for-socket-programming-c (accessed April 17, 2016).

Stal, M. 2006. Using architectural patterns and blueprints for service-oriented architectures. *IEEE Software* 23(2): 54–61.

Taylor, R.N., Medvidovic, N., Anderson, K.M., Whitehead, E.J., Jr., Robbins, J.E., Nies, K.A., Oreizy, P., Dubrow, D.L. 1996. A component- and message-based architectural style for GUI software. *IEEE Transactions on Software Engineering* 22(6): 390–406.

Taylor, R.N., Medvidovic, N., Dashofy, E. 2010. *Software architecture: Foundations, theory, and practice.* Wiley.

Techopedia. 2016. Middleware. https://www.techopedia.com/definition/450/middleware (accessed April 16, 2016).

Thelin, J.A., 2003. Comparison of service-oriented, resource-oriented, and object-oriented architecture styles. Cape Clear Software, Inc. http://research.microsoft.com/pubs/117710/3-arch-styles.pdf (accessed April 2, 2016).

The Open Group. 1997. Internet protocol family. http://pubs.opengroup.org/onlinepubs/7908799/xns/syssocket.h.html (accessed April 16, 2016).

The Open Group. 2004. Listen. http://pubs.opengroup.org/onlinepubs/009695399/functions/listen.html (accessed April 17, 2016).

Young, W. 2016. BSD sockets compatibility, Winsock programmers FAQ. http://tangentsoft.net/wskfaq/articles/bsd-compatibility.html (accessed April 17, 2016).

Zhu, H. 2005. *Software design methodology: From principles to architectural style.* Butterworth-Heinemann/Elsevier, Oxford, UK and Burlington, MA.

Section II

Enabling Technologies for Middleware

3 Introduction to Internet Technologies

3.1 JUST WHAT IS THE INTERNET, ANYWAY?

The internet is a network of computer networks. Big networks connect to each other and also to lots of small networks (subnets). Connecting to small networks are individual desktop computers, laptops, switches, routers—and nowadays cell phones and smartwatches. And refrigerators and light bulbs. See Stables (2016) to help figure out the very best light bulbs you can control from your smartphone. ☺

The World Wide Web and the internet are not the same thing. The internet pre-dates the World Wide Web by 20+ years. The origins of the internet go back to the creation of the Advanced Research Projects Agency Network (ARPANET) by the United States Department of Defense back in 1969, whereas the World Wide Web dates from the 1989 to 1990 time frame.

Loosely speaking, the World Wide Web is a collection of documents that each possess a URL, linked by hypertext (we'll see more on the World Wide Web in Chapter 4). The World Wide Web runs on top of the internet and makes use of the internet to communicate.

The internet uses a protocol suite known as TCP/IP, where TCP stands for Transmission Control Protocol and IP stands for Internet Protocol. TCP/IP was created back in the early to mid-1970s and was formally adopted by ARPANET in 1983. There were many competing protocols back in the early days, and considerable reading material was created on how much better all these other protocols were than TCP/IP. Also, considerable reading material was created that said how TCP/IP did not truly obey the OSI seven-layer model and was thus destined to be replaced.

I haven't bothered to look these references up again—an exercise for the reader, in case you're really interested in the history of technology. ☺

But in any case, TCP/IP won.

(The Open Systems Interconnection model, see ISO/IEC 1994, divides networking into seven layers: physical, data link, network, transport, session, presentation, application. Loosely, it says that a different protocol should inhabit each layer and connect only in very well-defined circumstances to protocol layers immediately below it and immediately above it. The lowest layer is the physical layer.)

An example of a competing protocol was X.25 from ITU-T (formerly CCITT) standard X.25, ISO standard 8208. X.25 dated back to 1976. Another competitor was Systems Network Architecture from IBM, which dates to 1974. Yet another competitor was DECnet, from Digital Equipment Corporation, which dates to 1975.

I note in passing that the V.42 dial-up modem standard included a lot that was drawn from the X.25 link layer. I know this because back in the 1980s I worked for Hayes Microcomputer Products, creating an X.25 protocol stack for Hayes modems. I just found a fun press release (well, it's fun for me) at Totse (2015) from Hayes back in the old days that talks about the Hayes X.25 modem.

3.2 BRIEF INTRODUCTION TO TCP/IP AND UDP

The Transmission Control Protocol (TCP) is responsible for bidirectional data transmissions between two distributed applications on a network. It does this by:

- Breaking data streams into data chunks (known as packets) at the sender
- For making sure the packets haven't been mangled during transmission and causing any packets with problems to be retransmitted:

- It does this by using a checksum field in the packet
  - If the checksum that was sent doesn't match the newly calculated checksum at the recipient, then the data in the packet was mangled
- For making sure packets are reassembled in the correct order so that the data stream arrives correctly at the recipient:
  - It does this by numbering each packet with a sequence number. Then if packets arrive out of order, they can be rearranged before being sent up to the application.
- In order to do these tasks, TCP creates a connection (session) between the sender and the receiver

However, the Internet Protocol (IP) is responsible for actually making sure that individual packets get from the sender to a receiver. It does this based on IP addresses in the IP packet header (we'll learn more about what IP addresses look like in Section 3.3). Each IP packet is routed, based on its header, across the internet from the sender to the receiver. If some portion of the internet should require using packets that are smaller than the originally sent packet, then IP can break the bigger packets into smaller packets in order to get across that internet portion, then reassemble them into the original packet after all the smaller packets get through that portion of the internet.

Note, however, that with an IP packet you don't know whether the receiver ever got the packet or not. Also, the receiver doesn't know whether or not to expect any packets. IP leaves those tasks for TCP to do (TCP does those tasks by establishing a connection). So IP taken by itself is considered to be a connectionless protocol.

TCP is nested inside IP. That is, an entire TCP packet is encapsulated inside an IP packet, and the IP packet is responsible for delivering its data to the recipient. Then the entire IP packet is nested inside the local area network (LAN) frame, the LAN could be using Ethernet, for example. (The IP packet is nested inside the Ethernet frame when the packet is being transferred across an Ethernet LAN.) See Figure 3.1. After the recipient acquires the frame from the LAN it will strip off the LAN headers. Then the recipient has to interpret and handle the IP packet headers, and then extract the data from the IP packet before the TCP packet can be interpreted. This is also true of the User Datagram Protocol (UDP) which is used in some situations instead of TCP.

Another way of thinking of this is that the TCP packet layer lies on top of the IP packet layer. This is generally how the OSI seven-layer model works. In the OSI seven-layer model, it can be said that IP is at the network layer, and TCP is at the transport layer. (Also, UDP is at the transport layer. We'll talk about UDP a little later.) However, Frenzel (2013) provides a discussion of ways in which the TCP/IP protocol stack does not map well otherwise into the OSI seven-layer model.

To establish a connection between two distributed entities, TCP does a three-way handshake:

1. Host A asks Host B if it is willing to establish a connection
   - It does this by sending a synchronize (SYN) packet to Host B
2. Host B tells Host A that yes, it is willing
   - It does this by sending an *I am willing* packet (Synchronize Acknowledgement, or SYN-ACK) to Host A
3. Host A tells Host B: well, ok then, I'm ready to get going
   - It does this by sending an *okay then* packet (Acknowledgement or ACK) to Host B

LAN header	IP header	TCP header	Data (payload)

FIGURE 3.1   TCP packet inside IP packet inside LAN packet.

To make sure that individual packets get from the sender to a receiver, IP includes a source address and a destination address in its header.

When passing through the network, an IP packet normally must pass through several IP routers. The routers look at the IP address in the packet and forwards that packet on to a computer (or to another router) based on the IP address.

Note that port numbers are used inside the TCP header to make sure that the data inside the TCP packets gets to the correct application (we'll learn more about what port numbers look like in Section 3.4).

So loosely speaking, the IP addresses get the data to the correct computer, and the port numbers get the data to the correct application on that computer.

The UDP uses datagram service, that is, it doesn't specify a connection. It provides a checksum to make sure it's known whether or not the packet has been garbled during transmission (the checksum can be disabled when using UDP in IPv4), although it does not cause a retransmission if the packet is garbled. It includes port numbers so the data can get to the correct application on the receiving computer.

UDP is an alternative to TCP, both ride on top of IP.

3.3   IP ADDRESSES (IPv4 AND IPv6) AND SUBNETTING

TCP/IP defines a communication endpoint to consist of an IP address and a protocol port number. There are two versions of IP on the internet: the old version is IP version 4, usually known as IPv4, and the newer is IP version 6, usually known as IPv6.

3.3.1   IPv4 Addresses

An IPv4 address is 32 bits long, and is normally divided into four bytes. When each byte is represented as a decimal number that is called *dotted decimal notation*. For example, a typical IP address could be:

01000101010101001000010000010000

When this is broken into four bytes, you get:

01000101   01010100   10000100   00010000

When each byte is represented as a decimal number, you get dotted decimal notation:

69.84.132.16

A port number can be appended to an IP address, let's append port number 1132:

69.84.132.16: 1132

A few special IP addresses:

127.0.0.1—the loopback address, accesses your current computer
224.0.0.1—multicast address, addresses all hosts on the same network segment. Only devices which are members of the particular multicast group will accept packets from this address.
224.0.0.2—multicast address, addresses all routers on the same network segment
255.255.255.255—broadcast address of the zero network (0.0.0.0) which means the local network (this one is not forwarded by routers)

3.3.1.1   Private IP Addresses and Network Address Translation

RFC 1918, see IETF (1996), reserves the following ranges of IP addresses as private addresses that cannot be routed on the internet:

- 10.0.0.0 – 10.255.255.255 (10/8 prefix)
- 172.16.0.0 – 172.31.255.255 (172.16/12 prefix)
- 192.168.0.0 – 192.168.255.255 (192.168/16 prefix)

(See Section 3.3.3 below for a description of what the /8, /12, and /16 mean.)

Normally private IPs are mapped to one or more public IPs through the use of Network Address Translation (NAT). It allows a single device, perhaps a router, to interface between the outside internet and a local (private) network. In this way, only a single public IP address is required to represent an entire group of computers. Internal to the private network, those computers employ private IP addresses, which are then mapped to a public IP by the router.

3.3.2   IPv6 Addresses

Why was IPv6 necessary? Bradley (2012) says:

> The most obvious answer is that IPv4 is out of IP addresses. IPv4 has only 4.3 billion addresses, and with PCs, smartphones, tablets, gaming systems, and just about everything else connecting to the internet we've tapped the system dry. IPv6 uses 128-bit addresses and is capable of 340 undecillion addresses. That is 340 times 10 to the 36th power, or 340 trillion trillion trillion possible IP addresses.

IPv4 and IPv6 can run beside each other, there are so many IPv4 addresses in use in the world that it wasn't possible to ditch them in order to go straight to IPv6.

IPv6 addresses use 128 bits divided into eight sets of four hexadecimal digits. Here is an example of an IPv6 address:

$$3001:0B0E:3247:CEF1:0073:0000:0000:AF0C$$

There is a shorthand notation where leading zeros are dropped. For example, the following would be acceptable:

$$3001:0B0E:3247:CEF1:\mathit{73}:0000:0000:AF0C$$

Notice the "73" in italics in the middle, 5th set of 4 hex digits. This is shorthand notation for "0073."

Also, if at least two consecutive sets of 4 hex digits have the hex digits all zero, then you can use this shorthand notation, which replaces those with a ":", as in the following:

$$3001:0B0E:3247:CEF1:73::AF0C$$

Note that here there is a "::" just before AF0C, this double colon represents two sets of 4 hex digits (8 hex digits total).

Note the four sets of 4 hex digits in the following example:

$$3001:0B0E:0000:0000:0000:0000:32AF:AF0C$$

These can be replaced by a double colon:

$$3001:0B0E::32AF:AF0C$$

You can only use "::" once in an address.
You represent an unspecified address as "::" (it's all zeroes).
A few special IP addresses:

0000:0000:0000:0000:0000:0000:0000:0001—IPv6 loopback address
also shown as
::1—IPv6 loopback address
ff02::1—multicast, addresses all hosts on the local network segment

Note that all multicast addresses start with 0xFF.

3.3.3   SUBNETTING

Networks can be broken into chunks called subnets, based on their IP addresses. When you're using a subnet, an IP address is considered to consist of a Network Prefix followed by a Host address. It's the same format IP address as before, you just pick several of the most significant bits and call them a *network prefix* and the remaining bits will be the host address.

You can specify an IP address similarly to the following, this is called Classless Inter-Domain Routing (CIDR) format:

69.84.132.16/16

Here, the first 16 bits of the IP address are used to specify the Network Prefix.
A subnet mask that has 1s in every location in the first 16 bits would be ANDed with the raw IP address to extract the Network prefix.
The subnet mask corresponding to this would be (in dotted decimal notation):

255.255.0.0

Which corresponds to, in binary:

11111111   11111111   00000000   00000000

If you recall from Section 3.3.1, the binary address that corresponds to the dotted decimal notation 69.84.132.16 is:

01000101   01010100   10000100   00010000

So this number ANDed with the subnet mask would be:

01000101   01010100   00000000   00000000

or in dotted decimal notation:

69.84.0.0

which is the network prefix.
Note that we used an even number of bytes in the CIDR format example:

69.84.132.16/16

You don't have to use an even number of bytes, for example, the following would be acceptable:

69.84.132.16/12

For this one, the subnet mask would be:

11111111   11110000   00000000   00000000

Or in dotted decimal notation:

255.240.0.0

So if you AND this with the raw IP address (69.84.132.16) you get:

69.80.0.0

A router uses a subnet mask ANDed with an IP address to extract the Network Prefix. The Network prefix is then used by a router to route a packet to the appropriate subnet. The remaining host address can be used to route the packet to the appropriate host within that subnet.

You may have noticed, the examples we just saw all used IPv4 addresses

When using IPv6, the smallest recommended subnet is 64 bits (of its total 128-bit wide address) as the Network Prefix. So the 64-bit prefix is always used for a subnet, instead of having a variable prefix. You're not supposed to use a subnet smaller than that (that is, using more bits as the Network Prefix, and thus having fewer host addresses).

According to RIPE Network Coordination Centre (2015):

Currently, most ISPs assign /48 network prefixes to subscribers' sites (the End Users' networks). Because all IPv6 networks have /64 prefixes, a /48 network prefix allows 65,536 LANs in an End User's site.

3.4   PORT NUMBERS

An internet port number is part of an address. A server, when launched, will be listening for input on a particular port number. Port numbers range from 0 to 65535. Port numbers in the range 0 to 1023 are called "well known ports" or "system ports," and are preassigned by the Internet Assigned Numbers Authority, IANA (2016), to certain functions (by default).

Port number 80 is accessed by default using the http protocol. Port number 443 is accessed by default using the https protocol. So if you did the following and did not specify a port number, things would still work (assuming your server was previously set to listen on port 80):

http://myownplace/MyService

Since you didn't specify a number, but you're using http, this would default to using port 80. This is the same as the following:

http://myownplace:80/MyService

This works similarly for https and port 443, or for the other protocols (such as TCP) on their default assigned ports.

You can use other port numbers instead if you want to. For example, you could access port number 5731 using http, or you could access port number 5731 using https, or for that matter you can access port number 5731 using tcp (shown as net.tcp in WCF), or other protocols.

Note that port numbers are the same when you use IPv6 as when you use IPv4.

3.5 OTHER IMPORTANT NETWORK INFORMATION

We're going to look at a few other networking concepts you may run into along the way when we look at middleware in depth. You may especially find this useful when we get to cloud computing.

3.5.1 INTERNET CONTROL MESSAGE PROTOCOL

Internet Control Message Protocol (ICMP) is used to send messages back to the source IP address in cases where some sort of error occurred, or some sort of rerouting has taken place. For example, a typical ICMP message would be sent because an IP packet could not be delivered.

ICMP messages are sent as payload (data) inside IP packets but are typically handled separately from the IP protocol, that is, they are not treated as a special case of the IP protocol.

A *ping* that is used to see if a remote host is there and responding is done by sending an ICMP message containing an "echo request" type in the header. The remote host would respond with an "echo reply" type in its header.

A "timestamp" type in the header could receive a "timestamp reply" type response in order to allow two hosts to synchronize their times. They can be used to help determine network delays. However, attackers can potentially use a timestamp too, according to Mitre (2016):

> An attacker may be able to use the timestamp returned from the target to attack time-based security algorithms, such as random number generators, or time-based authentication mechanisms.

However, most other ICMP message types are related to error conditions. Destination unreachable is a common ICMP message, it could have subcodes that mean destination network unreachable, destination host unreachable, destination port unreachable, etc., in order to give more information about the problem.

3.5.2 LAN PROTOCOLS: ETHERNET AND WI-FI

When we're talking about TCP/IP and the internet, we're talking about Wide Area Networks (WANs).

When we're talking about the layers below the IP layer, we're generally talking about LANs.

A LAN, traditionally, is a computer network that connects computers that are located close to each other. Maybe in one building, or maybe just on one floor of a building, depending on the size of the building. Or maybe in someone's home. You might think of a LAN as consisting of devices that share a common communications line or wireless link.

Commonly used protocols for LANs are Ethernet and Wi-Fi.

Typically, one thinks of Ethernet being used when you have a physical connector (maybe twisted pair or fiber) and Wi-Fi being used for a wireless connection. The specifics can get pretty complicated, especially, if you also include cell phone networks. So since this isn't a networking textbook, we're going to discuss this in a slightly more generic way, and talk about a Media Access Control (MAC) layer rather than going into the details of different LAN protocols. (Strictly speaking, according to the OSI seven-layer model, a MAC layer is a sublayer at the bottom of the data link layer that forms an interface with the physical layer but we're going to ignore that.)

The primary tasks of a MAC layer are to form frames of data that can go between one device on a LAN and another device on that LAN, that is, from one Network Interface Card (NIC) to another. (A frame of data is just another name for a packet of data; it's just that frames are used at the data link layer and packets are used at higher layers.)

What we're primarily concerned with in the context of this middleware/cloud computing textbook are the addresses that are used on a LAN to identify individual addresses. We'll look at that in the next section.

3.5.3　Media Access Control Addresses

A Media Access Control (MAC) address is an address that is assigned to a physical device, normally at the time the device is manufactured. The Institute of Electrical and Electronics Engineers (IEEE) Registration Authority (RA) assigns blocks of MAC addresses to companies, in return for a fee, which the companies can then burn into their devices, see IEEE RA (2016).

Traditionally MAC addresses are 48 bits long in hexadecimal, with bytes divided by colons, as follows:

$$xx: xx: xx: yy: yy: yy$$

where x represents hex digits assigned to a company (an Organizationally Unique Identifier, or OUI) and the last several hex digits (y) are in a pool of addresses assigned to the company, that the company uses. So the OUI is 24 bits long. The OUI is purchased by the company from the IEEE RA.

Nowadays, there are two kinds of MAC addresses, a 48-bit Extended Unique Identifier (EUI-48) and a 64-bit Extended Unique Identifier (EUI-64) are globally unique identifiers used for identification of objects.

An EUI-48 is a string of six bytes in hexadecimal format. The IEEE Standards Association (2016) gives the following example of an EUI-48 address:

$$AC\text{-}DE\text{-}48\text{-}23\text{-}45\text{-}67$$

An EUI-64 is a string of eight bytes in hexadecimal format. The IEEE Standards Association (2016) gives the following example of an EUI-64 address:

$$AC\text{-}DE\text{-}48\text{-}23\text{-}45\text{-}67\text{-}AB\text{-}CD$$

The broadcast MAC for a 48-bit MAC is:

$$FF\text{:}FF\text{:}FF\text{:}FF\text{:}FF\text{:}FF$$

(Note that either colons or dashes can be used between bytes in a MAC address.)

Note that a MAC address on a Virtual Machine is typically assigned by the hypervisor. For example, the Xen hypervisor allows (see Xen Project Wiki 2016):

> When choosing MAC addresses there are in general three strategies which can be used. In decreasing order of preference these are:
>
> Assign an address from the range associated with an Organizationally Unique Identifier (OUI) which you control. If you do not know what this means then you likely do not control an OUI and this option does not apply to you.
>
> Generate a random sequence of 6 bytes, set the locally administered bit (bit 2 of the first byte) and clear the multicast bit (bit 1 of the first byte). In other words, the first byte should have the bit pattern xxxxxx10 (where x is a randomly generated bit) and the remaining 5 bytes are randomly generated. See Wikipedia for more details the structure of a MAC address.
>
> Assign a random address from within the space 00:16:3e:xx:xx:xx. 00:16:3e is an OUI assigned to the Xen project and which has been made available for Xen users for the purposes of assigning local addresses within that space.

3.5.4　Hubs, Bridges, Switches, and Routers

A hub is a layer 1 (physical layer) device. When data comes in one port of a hub, it is copied out to all other ports of the hub.

A Bridge is a layer 2 device that connects one layer 2 network segment to another layer 2 network segment. A bridge looks at the MAC address in a frame, if the destination is not on the other side of the bridge it will not transmit the data across. If the destination is on the other side of the bridge then it will transmit the data across. A bridge is very simple, it can connect one device to one other device, so it is not a practical device when trying to connect more than two devices. (One use would be to connect a bridge between two hubs, as that would allow connections between several devices.)

A Switch is a layer 2 device that acts as a multiport bridge and maps MAC addresses to ports. A frame would come in on one port. The switch then looks at the MAC address in that frame, and sends the frame to the port that is connected to that MAC address.

A Router is a layer 3 device that connects multiple layer 3 networks and uses IP addressing.

A broadcast domain is a network segment in which any network device can transmit data directly to another device without going through a router. So a router is the edge of a broadcast domain.

3.5.5 AUTOCONFIGURATION FOR IPv4: DYNAMIC HOST CONFIGURATION PROTOCOL

By "autoconfiguration" what we mean mostly is that a device is automatically assigned its IP address. However, a Dynamic Host Configuration Protocol (DHCP) server can also configure other parameters. Some examples include (see Study CCNA 2016):

- Subnet mask
- Default gateway
- Domain name
- Domain Name Server (DNS)

When you're using IPv4, without DHCP, a device on a LAN would have to have its IP address manually configured by the system administrator (this is called a *static IP*). Worse, any time that device was moved around the network, its IP address would have to be reconfigured. Consider the case of laptops or smartphones where you may want to use the Wi-Fi at home and also maybe at Starbucks. If it weren't for DHCP, you'd have to manually reconfigure the IP address on your laptop or smartphone whenever you moved it to a new location. Note that a version of DHCP can be used for both IPv4 and IPv6; we'll see the IPv6 version in the next section, although IPv6 has other options as well.

DHCP messages ride inside UDP packets, so DHCP is connectionless. The UDP port number for a DHCP client is 68, and the UDP port number for a DHCP server is 67.

A DHCP client requests an IP address from a DHCP server. A DHCP server gives a lease to a DHCP client for a certain amount of time. At the end of that time, the client must request a new IP address (or it can request to be assigned again its last known IP address).

The DHCP handshake is shown in Figure 3.2.

A DHCP client begins by broadcasting a DHCP-Discover message on its subnet. Assuming IPv4, its source address would be 0.0.0.0 and its destination address would be the broadcast address 255.255.255.255. The DHCP-Discover message will include the MAC address of the client. This is an address that uniquely identifies the client.

A DHCP server has a pool of available IP addresses. When a DHCP server receives the

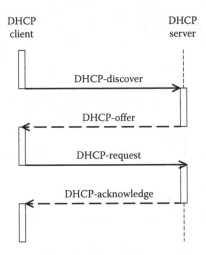

FIGURE 3.2 DHCP for IPv4 handshake.

DHCP-Discover message, it will reserve an IP address, and send back a DHCP-Offer message to the client. This message will include the client's MAC address, the IP address being offered, and the duration of the lease. This message will be sent to the broadcast destination IP address (255.255.255.255 for IPv4) and the source address will be the address of the DHCP server. Inside this message will normally be included a "server identification option"—this is a value that identifies this particular server in the case when multiple DHCP servers respond to a DHCP client.

The client then replies to the DHCP server by sending a DHCP-Request. The destination IP address of the DHCP-Request will again be the broadcast address (255.255.255.255 for IPv4), and the source address will be 0.0.0.0 (for IPv4). It will include the "server identification option" value that it previously received in the DHPC-Offer. Thus, the correct DHCP server will know that it is the one whose IP address was accepted by the DHCP client, and any other DHCP servers who also sent a DHCP-Offer will know that their offer was not accepted (they return the reserved IP address to their pool of IP addresses).

Finally, the DHCP server who's DHCP-Offer was accepted sends back a DHCP-Acknowledgement (ACK). This message will be sent to the broadcast destination IP address (255.255.255.255 for IPv4) and the source address will be the address of the DHCP server.

Linux and Windows Server can be configured to act as a DHCP for IPv4 server. Also, many routers can be configured to serve in this capacity.

3.5.6 AUTOCONFIGURATION FOR IPV6

Autoconfiguration for IPv6 can work quite differently than autoconfiguration for IPv4. There are several different methods available:

- Static addressing can still be used, only with IPv6 addresses instead of IPv4 addresses
- Static addressing—the IP address is assigned statically but other configuration information is assigned using (stateful) DHCP for IPv6
- Stateful autoconfiguration—the entire IP address is assigned and other configuration information is assigned using (stateful) DHCP for IPv6
- Stateless Address Autoconfiguration (SLAAC)—(see immediately below)

With SLAAC, an IPv6 network router sends out a Router Advertisement (RA) periodically. The RA includes:

- IPv6 subnet prefixes of length 64, that is /64 (see Section 3.3.3)
- Lifetime information for the prefix
- Default router to use
- Lifetime of default router

The device on the network that needs an IP address will use the IPv6 subnet prefix for the most significant 64 bits of the IPv6 address. Then, then bottom 64 bits of the IPv6 address are formed by using a manipulation of the device's MAC address using EUI-64 rules.

The EUI-64 rules work as follows, see RFC 4291 from Internet Engineering Task Force (IETF) (2006a):

- To transform an IEEE EUI-64 identifier to an interface identifier all that must be done is to invert the "u" (universal/local) bit. The universal/local bit is the seventh bit, counting from the top of the word.
- To transform an IEEE EUI-48 identifier to an interface identifier, insert the hexadecimal value 0xFFFE in between the OUI in the 24 bits at the top of the 48-bit MAC address,

and the manufacturer supplied identifier in the bottom 24 bits of the 48-bit MAC address. This makes it a 64-bit identifier (48 bits plus 16 additional bits equal 64 bits). Then invert the universal/local bit, which is the seventh bit, counting from the top of the word.

However, there are some privacy considerations with this. For example, if a person is traveling around with a laptop, and connecting to the internet from different locations then the bottom 64 bits of the laptop's IPv6 address will always relate to its MAC address, even though the upper 64 bits would change based on its current network location. This could be used to track a person's movements, through servers that log usage information (addresses used). This is particularly applicable to, say, a smartphone, because a smartphone is typically not shared with others. For these reasons, RFC4941 from IETF (2007b) allows generating a set of temporary interface identifiers (that would then be combined as before with the /64 subnet address to form IPv6 addresses). These pseudo-random sets of interface identifiers are generated using an MD5 hash, and depend on both the MAC address and a random component, in order that different nodes generate different sequences of interface identifiers. Periodically, the next interface identifier in the sequence is generated, new IPv6 addresses are formed, and the previous IPv6 addresses are no longer used. Some Microsoft OSes (for example, Windows 8.1) can be configured to work this way.

Of course, another way to preserve privacy would be to use DHCP for IPv6 (DHCPv6) instead of using the EUI-64 identifier.

3.5.6.1 DHCP for IPv6

DHCPv6 is the stateful address autoconfiguration protocol.

First of all, the DHCPv6 client creates an identity-association (IA) consisting of a set of related IPv6 addresses and assigns it an IA identifier (IAID). Each network interface that the DHCPv6 client will request an IPv6 address for must have at least one IA associated with it.

The client sends a Solicit message to locate any available DHCPv6 servers, the Solicit message includes the IA for each interface the client wants information for (this can include suggested IP addresses).

Any server that can meet the client's request sends an Advertise message to the client that includes IP address assignments plus additional resources.

The client chooses one of the servers and sends it a Request message, to request the configuration information (with IP address) from the server.

The server sends back a Reply message that includes the assigned IP addresses and the configuration information.

Note that DHCPv6 may or may not include IP addresses, the IP addresses could be assigned in a different way, perhaps using SLAAC or perhaps statically assigned.

3.5.7 Virtual Local Area Network

A Virtual Local Area Network (VLAN) is a set of devices that are logically isolated such that they act as if they are on a single LAN, even though they may be (somewhat) geographically distributed. All this happens at protocol layer 2.

According to Cisco (2016):

A VLAN is a group of devices on one or more LANs that are configured to communicate as if they were attached to the same wire, when in fact they are located on a number of different LAN segments.

A broadcast domain is a set of devices that can broadcast to each other at layer 2. A layer 3 router does not forward a broadcast frame, so it forms a boundary on a broadcast domain.

A VLAN is a group of hosts with a common set of requirements that communicate as if they were attached to the same broadcast domain regardless of their physical location.

On a switch that handles VLANs, ports are associated with a VLAN number. The switch then only allows data to be sent between ports that are on the same VLAN.

To have a VLAN connected between two switches, a VLAN tag is used in the layer 2 frame header (see IEEE 802.1Q for specifics on how this works). For an outgoing packet, a switch adds the VLAN tag to the layer 2 frame header. Then the receiving switch reads the VLAN tag and sends the data to the appropriate port.

A device on a VLAN is not able to connect to a device that is not on that VLAN without going through a level 3 router.

Advantages of a VLAN:

- Reduces the size of the broadcast domain, and thus results in less wasted bandwidth (frames don't get sent to [as many] computers that aren't interested in seeing them
- Increases security, the traffic on a VLAN is not visible to devices not connected to the VLAN
  - For example, could have a "company" VLAN versus a "guest" VLAN

3.6 UNIVERSALLY UNIQUE IDENTIFIERS

A Universally Unique Identifier (UUID) is an identifier that is most likely different from all other identifiers, in the area where you're looking at them. That is, the way a UUID is generated makes it unlikely that two separately generated UUIDs are the same.

Early versions were first created in the 1980s by a graphical workstation manufacturer (Apollo Computers) as part of a system called the Network Computing System (based on the Network Computing Architecture). Later it became part of the Open Software Foundation's Distributed Computing Environment (see Open Software Foundation 1995; the Open Software Foundation was a precursor to The Open Group). More recently, UUIDs were defined in an IETF Standard (see IETF 2005); this is the definition of UUIDs that we'll be following in this section.

We're looking at this last in this internet chapter, because although they're defined in an IETF standard, UUIDs apply more widely than the internet. They're sometimes used as record identifiers in databases, although this can be controversial (see Clayton 2016). They've also been used in Linux file systems (see Gite 2008), and to identify storage devices on Solaris (see Teguh Triharto Learning Center 2013).

A UUID is represented as a 128-bit number (16 bytes/octets). An example would be:

- abcd1234-fae3-*1*2cd-*a*4be-1234abcd4321

This example consists of:

- 8 digits, 4 digits, 4 digits, 4 digits,12 digits
- Lower case hexadecimal
- The digit in italics in the 3rd group shows the version # (1, 2, 3, 4, or 5)
- The first two bits of the digit in italics in the 4th group show the variant. "10" is the variant from RFC4122, so this digit would be 8, 9, a, or b

Table 3.1 shows all possible UUID variants. As you can see, the previous example is the RFC4122 variant.

There are five different UUID versions:

1. Time-based+MAC address
2. DCE
3. Name-based with MD5 hash
4. Random (what Keystone uses)
5. Name-based with SHA-1 hash

TABLE 3.1
Format of UUID Variants

MSB	MSB -1	MSB -2	Description
0	X	X	Network Computing System (NCS) Backward compatibility
1	0	X	RFC 4122 Variant
1	1	0	Microsoft backward compatibility
1	1	1	Reserved for the future

TABLE 3.2
Time-Based UUID Format

Byte #	0–3 Time_low	4–5 Time_mid	6–7 Time_hi & version	8 Clock hi & reserved	9 Clock low	10–15 Node (MAC) address
	abcd1234	fae3	*1*2cd	*a*4	be	1234abcd4321

For versions 3 and 5, just so you understand some of the terminology, in terms of the MD5 (Message Digest) and SHA-1 hashes, even small changes in the message will (usually) result in a mostly different hash. The MD5 hash is a 32-digit hexadecimal number, while the SHA-1 hash is a 40-digit hexadecimal number. SHA-1 considered safer than MD5. (We will see these in more depth in Chapter 5.)

However, we won't look at the DCE version, and we won't really look further at the name-based versions as we won't be using those in this textbook.

For Version 1, the Time-based UUID:

- The timestamp is a 60-bit unsigned integer (15 hex digits), Coordinated Universal Time, representing 100 nanosecond intervals since October 15, 1582 (date of Gregorian calendar reform).
- The clock ID is a 14-bit unsigned integer, initially (once in a system lifetime) initialized to a random number.
- The MAC address is a 48-bit unsigned integer, in 6 sets of two hexadecimal digits

Given the following time-based UUID example, see Table 3.2:

- abcd1234-fae3-*1*2cd-*a*4be-1234abcd4321

The time is: 0x2cdfae3abcd1234

- Time_hi = 0x2cd, Time mi=0xfae3, Time_low=0xabcd1234

The Clock ID is: 10 0100 1011 1110 base 2

- Clock hi is 10 0100 (MSB is version 10, gives a4) Clock lo is 0xbe

MAC address is: 12:34:ab:cd:43:21

For Version 4, the Random UUID (this is the version that the OpenStack cloud Keystone authentication component uses), an example is:

- xxxxxxxx-xxxx-*4*xxx-*a*xxx-xxxxxxxxxxxx

where the 4 in italics indicates the version number (as before).

The a in italics indicates the variant (as before, the first two bits are "10" which means this value can be 8, 9, a, or b).

The other hex digits, represented by x, are randomly generated.

An example OpenStack token, from Section 13.4 is as follows:

- 12ea1917464149dcad68d0dc1eb30842

Dividing it up according to the above UUID4 template, you can see it follows UUID 4 format:

- 12ea1917-4641-*4*9dc-*a*d68-d0dc1eb30842

EXERCISES

1. We saw in Section 3.2 that a TCP/IP handshake is three way: HostA: SYN, then Host B: SYN-ACK, then Host A: SYN. What happens if the third SYN is lost?
2. What is the purpose of a loopback address such as 127.0.0.1?
3. What is the purpose of private IP addresses?
4. What is the subnet mask that corresponds to 69.84.132.16/20?
5. When using a subnet mask of 255.255.252.0 with IP address 69.84.132.16, what is the range of addresses of the subnet?
6. How many possible addresses can you have on your subnet if you use 69.84.132.16/22?
7. What is the difference between IPv6 addresses:
   3001:0B0E:0047:CEF1:1273:AABB:1234:AF0C
   and
   3001:0B0E:47:CEF1:1273:AABB:1234:AF0C?
8. What is the default port for http? What is the default port for https?
9. How does a "ping" work?
10. How does a network card get its own MAC address?
11. What is an Organizationally Unique Identifier (OUI)?
12. Why might you care if someone else knows the MAC address of your notebook computer? And how does this work in regard to Stateless Address Autoconfiguration (SLAAC)?
13. Why do we care what UUIDs look like?
14. Why does the MAC address used by a virtual machine have to be assigned on the fly?
15. How is a computer typically assigned its IP address?

CONCEPTUAL QUESTIONS

1. Why do you think you need to know internet stuff in order to work with middleware? Didn't we see in Chapter 1 that middleware tends to hide the networking information from the user?
2. Think about the world of cloud computing. It's a bunch of virtual machines running on servers, right? Why do you need to know about the internet to work with that?
3. What kinds of technological kluges (ahem, accommodations) must occur for IPv4 and IPv6 to work together at the same time? Justify your answer with both Google references and formal journal and conference references (from the IEEE or ACM, or similar major publishers).
4. Consider privacy on the internet. Consider particularly the privacy issue that occurs when SLAAC is used. Just how bad is the privacy problem with SLAAC? Justify your answer.
5. Consider all you've learned in this chapter about the internet. Do you see any other privacy considerations?

BIBLIOGRAPHY

Bradley, T. 2012. *IPv6: Five things you should know*. PC World. http://www.pcworld.com/article/257037/ipv6_five_things_you_should_know.html (accessed May 15, 2016).

Cisco. 2016. Understanding and configuring VLANs. In *Catalyst 4500 series switch Cisco IOS software configuration guide*, 12.2(25)EW. http://www.cisco.com/c/en/us/td/docs/switches/lan/catalyst4500/12-2/25ew/configuration/guide/conf/vlans.html (accessed May 15, 2016).

Clayton, R. 2016. Do You Really Need a UUID/GUID? https://rclayton.silvrback.com/do-you-really-need-a-uuid-guid (accessed May 15, 2016).

Frenzel, L. 2013. What's the difference between the OSI seven-layer network model and TCP/IP? *Electronic Design*. http://electronicdesign.com/what-s-difference-between/what-s-difference-between-osi-seven-layer-network-model-and-tcpip (accessed May 15, 2016).

GestioIP. 2015. IPv6 Address Examples for Different IPv6 Address Representations and Types. http://www.gestioip.net/docu/ipv6_address_examples.html (accessed April 16, 2016).

Gite, V. 2008. How to Use UUID to Mount Partitions/Volumes Under Ubuntu Linux, nixCraft. http://www.cyberciti.biz/faq/linux-finding-using-uuids-to-update-fstab/ (accessed May 15, 2016).

IEEE (Institute of Electrical and Electronics Engineers). 2011. 802.1Q. Virtual LANs. http://www.ieee802.org/1/pages/802.1Q.html (accessed May 16, 2016).

IEEE RA (Institute of Electrical and Electronics Engineers Registration Authority). 2016. Home page. https://regauth.standards.ieee.org/standards-ra-web/pub/view.html#registries (accessed May 15, 2016).

Institute of Electrical and Electronics Engineers (IEEE) Standards Association. 2016a. Guidelines for 48-Bit Global Identifier (EUI-48). https://standards.ieee.org/develop/regauth/tut/eui48.pdf (accessed May 15, 2016).

Institute of Electrical and Electronics Engineers (IEEE) Standards Association. 2016b. Guidelines for 64-Bit Global Identifier (EUI-64). https://standards.ieee.org/develop/regauth/tut/eui64.pdf (accessed May 15, 2016).

IANA (Internet Assigned Numbers Authority). 2016. Home page. http://www.iana.org/ (accessed April 16, 2016).

IETF (Internet Engineering Task Force). 1994. RFC 1631. The IP Network Address Translator (NAT). https://www.ietf.org/rfc/rfc1631.txt (accessed May 18, 2016).

IETF (Internet Engineering Task Force). 1996. RFC 1918. Address Allocation for Private Internets. https://tools.ietf.org/html/rfc1918 (accessed May 18, 2016).

IETF (Internet Engineering Task Force). 1997. The Server Identification Option for DHCP, Internet Draft. https://tools.ietf.org/html/draft-ietf-dhc-sio-00 (accessed May 15, 2016).

IETF (Internet Engineering Task Force). 2003. RFC 3315. Dynamic Host Configuration Protocol for IPv6 (DHCPv6). https://tools.ietf.org/html/rfc3315#page-23 (accessed May 16, 2016).

IETF (Internet Engineering Task Force). 2005. RFC 4122. A Universally Unique Identifier (UUID) URN Namespace. http://www.ietf.org/rfc/rfc4122.txt (accessed April 26, 2016).

IETF (Internet Engineering Task Force). 2006a. RFC 4291. IP Version 6 Addressing Architecture, Appendix A. https://tools.ietf.org/html/rfc4291#appendix-A (accessed May 16, 2016).

IETF (Internet Engineering Task Force). 2006b. RFC 4632. Classless Inter-domain Routing (CIDR): The Internet Address Assignment and Aggregation Plan. https://tools.ietf.org/html/rfc4632 (accessed May 15, 2016).

IETF (Internet Engineering Task Force). 2007a. RFC 4862. IPv6 Stateless Address Autoconfiguration, https://tools.ietf.org/html/rfc4862 (accessed May 16, 2016).

IETF (Internet Engineering Task Force). 2007b. RFC4941. Privacy Extensions for Stateless Address Autoconfiguration in IPv6. https://tools.ietf.org/html/rfc4941#page-7 (accessed May 16, 2016).

ISO (International Standards Organization)/IEF (International Electrotechnical Commission). 1994. Information Technology—Open Systems Interconnection—Basic Reference Model: The Basic Model, 7498-1. http://www.ecma-international.org/activities/Communications/TG11/s020269e.pdf (accessed May 15, 2016).

Mitre. 2015. CAPEC-295: ICMP Timestamp Request, Common Attack Pattern Enumeration and Classification (CAPEC). https://capec.mitre.org/data/definitions/295.html (accessed May 15, 2016).

Open Software Foundation. 1995. OSF DCE Introduction to OSF, DCE Release 1.1. Prentice-Hall.

Popeskic, V. IPv6—SLAAC Stateless Address Autoconfiguration, How Does Internet Work. http://howdoesinternetwork.com/2013/slaac (accessed May 16, 2016).

RIPE NCC (RIPE Network Coordination Centre). 2015. Understanding IP Addressing and CIDR Charts. https://www.ripe.net/about-us/press-centre/understanding-ip-addressing (accessed May 15, 2016).

SearchUnifiedCommunications. 2015. DHCP (Dynamic Host Configuration Protocol). http://searchunified communications.techtarget.com/definition/DHCP (accessed May 15, 2016).

Stables, J. 2016. *The best smart bulbs for your connected smart home.* Wareable. http://www.wareable.com/ smart-home/best-smart-bulbs-for-your-tech-home (accessed May 15, 2016).

StackExchange. 2012. How Does IPv6 Subnetting Work and How Does It Differ from IPv4 Subnetting? http:// serverfault.com/questions/426183/how-does-ipv6-subnetting-work-and-how-does-it-differ-from-ipv4- subnetting (accessed May 15, 2016).

StackOverflow. 2008. How Do Ports Work with IPv6. http://stackoverflow.com/questions/186829/how-do- ports-work-with-ipv6 (accessed April 16, 2016).

Study CCNA. 2016. DHCP & DNS. http://study-ccna.com/dhcp-dns/ (accessed May 16, 2016).

Teguh Triharto Learning Center. 2013. How to Check Host ID, UUID on Solaris & Check Solaris Version. http:// teguhth.blogspot.com/2013/08/how-to-check-host-id-uuid-on-solaris.html (accessed May 15, 2016).

Totse. 2016. X.25 and V.42 Solutions for Data Communications. http://totse.mattfast1.com/en/technology/ telecommunications/x25v42.html (accessed May 15, 2016).

Wikipedia. 2015. List_of_TCP_and_UDP_port_numbers. https://en.wikipedia.org/wiki/List_of_TCP_and_ UDP_port_numbers (accessed July 7, 2015).

Wilkins, S. 2013. *Mastering IPv6 SLAAC concepts and configuration.* Cisco. http://www.ciscopress.com/ articles/article.asp?p=2154680 (accessed May 16, 2016).

Xen Project Wiki. 2016. *Mac addresses.* Xen Networking. http://wiki.xenproject.org/wiki/Xen_Networking# MAC_addresses (accessed May 15, 2016).

4 Introduction to World Wide Web Technologies

4.1 JUST WHAT IS THE WEB, ANYWAY?

As we previously discussed in Chapter 2, the World Wide Web and the internet are not the same thing. The internet pre-dates the World Wide Web by 20+ years. The origins of the internet go back to the creation of the Advanced Research Projects Agency Network (ARPANET) by the United States Department of Defense back in 1969, whereas the World Wide Web dates from the 1989 to 1990 timeframe.

Loosely speaking, the World Wide Web is a collection of documents that each possess a URL, linked by hypertext. Hypertext means that text in a document is associated with a link that, when clicked, points one's web browser to another web document or to a link inside the current document. You can look at the architecture of the World Wide Web in a more formal way—we'll do this when we look at RESTful architectures later on in Section 9.2. Note: a URL is the name of a web page, such as www.cs.uah.edu.

The web runs on top of the internet and makes use of the internet to communicate. Normally, web sites are accessed using the HTTP protocol. HTTP runs on top of the TCP/IP protocol that is normally used to communicate on the internet. As we previously saw in Chapter 3, when we talk about protocol A running on top of another protocol B, what we mean is that protocol A is sent as data inside protocol B, and protocol B doesn't generally know anything about protocol A.

Web documents (that are what web pages consist of) are typically stored in HTML format. Communication between web pages is done via HTTP. Data transferred in HTTP is often in XML format, or in JSON format. Different data formats can be sent using HTTP, if so the format of the data that is being sent is often described by Internet Media types (MIME types).

We will look below at HTTP and the various data formats that are used on the web. Then we will look at some web servers that are used to make web pages public on the web so that users can access them.

4.2 HYPERTEXT TRANSFER PROTOCOL

Hypertext transfer protocol (HTTP) assumes that you are using the client/server model. An HTTP client sends a request, and an HTTP server sends back a response. HTTP defines several methods (also called messages or verbs) that are included in an HTTP request to specify what action is being requested of the server.

The HTTP methods (verbs) are:

- GET—requests a resource (such as a web page). That is, download the web page.
- HEAD—return the same HTTP response headers as for a GET, but don't include the data. Sometimes information about the data (meta-information) is transmitted in the header, and the meta-information may be all you want.
- POST—accept the information in the request as a new subordinate resource of the URL. Exactly what happens depends on the server's purpose. This could be used to append a message to a newsgroup, or to append a new record to a database, for example.
- PUT—store the information in the request at the URL, if the URL already exists then modify it to store the new data, otherwise create it.

- DELETE—delete the specified resource. The server may or may not do this, it depends on the server.
- TRACE—echo back the message that the server actually received, so the client can tell anything that had been added by other entities along the path to the server.

With a GET request, any data you send will be included as part of the URL, and will therefore be visible in the web browser, and in the web browser history (so you don't want to send a credit card number this way). In the following example, the variables name1 and name2 will be passed in the GET request to the server named simple_server.php:

    simple_server.php?name1=value1&name2=value2

If you used a POST, then the same data (name1=value and name2=value) would be included in the body of the request, not in the URL.

Some important HTTP status messages that (among several others) might be returned in response to a request:

- 200—OK
- 201—Resource created
- 202—request accepted but processing not yet completed
- 400—request had bad syntax
- 401—unauthorized access
- 404—resource (web page) not found
- 500—internal server error

4.3   HTML, XML, AND HTML FORMS

XML (eXtensible Markup Language) is a standard for storing and sending data. It is intended to be human-readable as well as machine-readable.

HTML (HyperText Markup Language) is a standard for representing web pages (also called web documents, see the Document Object Model (DOM) in Section 4.10).

There are several tutorials on XML and HTML available on the web (see W3 Schools 2016a, 2016f, and 2016h), so we will just do an overview to get you started. We're putting just enough so that in later portions of this textbook you can look back here to see the background you need, instead of having to read through external tutorials.

Note: in the listings in this section, the indentation is added so you can more easily read them. The indentation is not needed in the web document.

We begin with a brief example of an XML document, shown in Listing 4.1.

LISTING 4.1   Example XML Document

```
<?xml version="1.0" encoding="UTF-8"?>
<racehorses>
      <horse>
            <name>Secretariat</name>
            <breed>thoroughbred</breed>
      </horse>
      <horse>
            <name>Dash for Cash</name>
            <breed>Quarter Horse</breed>
      </horse>
</racehorses>
```

There are a couple of ways this could have been done, however. In Listing 4.1, the breed of the horse is stored as an element:

```
<horse
  <name> Secretariat</name>
  <breed>Thoroughbred</breed>
  </horse>
```

But it would also be possible for the breed of the horse to be stored as an attribute:

```
<horse breed="Thoroughbred"
  <name> Secretariat</name>
  </horse>
```

An example HTML document is shown in Listing 4.2.

LISTING 4.2 Example HTML Document

```
<!DOCTYPE html>
<html>
  <body>
    <h1>Racehorses</h1>
    <h2>Thoroughbred Racehorses</h2>
    <p>Secretariat won the Triple Crown back in 1973.</p>
    <h2>Quarter Horse Racehorses</h2>
    <p>Dash for Cash won the Champion of Champions race in 1976.</p>
  </body>
</html>
```

Since Listing 4.2 contained "<!DOCTYPE html>," it means Listing 4.2 is using HTML5. HTML5 is the most recent version of HTML, it became a World Wide Web Consortium (W3C) standard in 2013. It is a superset of HTML4 (HTML4 dates from 1997) and also includes some offshoots of HTML that arose over the years (such as XHMTL, a reformulation of HTML 4 document types as applications of XML 1.0). HTML5 has added many new features, particularly features that support multimedia (video, audio, and animation).

HTML forms allow an easy way to input data to a web page, and send it to a server to handle it. There are several tutorials online for HTML forms (see Tutorials Point 2016; W3 Schools 2016b), so again we'll just look at enough to get us started.

Listing 4.3 gives a simple example of an HTML form. This is the same example we will use later on in Section 11.2 to interact with JavaScript, PHP, and AJAX.

LISTING 4.3 Example HTML Form

```
<form action = "simple_server.php"
    <p> Enter your name: <input type="text" name="myname"/>
        <button type = "button" onclick = "doAJAXstuff(this.form)">
        Paint part of the web page
        </button>
    </p>
</form>
```

This first creates an input block, as follows:

Enter your name: [   ]

And a button that looks something like (I didn't run the code here and capture a screenshot, I've just recreated the output with Word, so the look would be just a trifle different):

[Paint part of the Web Page]

Let's assume you run this. If you typed your name and hit enter, the *action* would call the PHP code to handle it: simple_server.php. If you instead clicked the button (Paint part of the web page), then what would happen is the JavaScript routine called doAJAXstuff would be called, and the form information would be passed to it. It would do some processing that we can't see here because here I haven't given you the JavaScript code, wait till Chapter 11. ☺

Let's look at a few more HTML items before we go on, this will be helpful when we get to ASP.NET MVC.

The HTML fieldset tag is shown in Listing 4.4. This is used, in a form, to group related elements. The *legend* tag gives the group of related elements a title.

LISTING 4.4   Fieldsets

```
<!DOCTYPE HTML>
<html>
  <body>
    <form>
      <fieldset>
        <legend>my wonderful stuff </legend>
        <p>my name is letha</p>
        <p> this is a great textbook</p>
      </fieldset>
      <fieldset>
        <legend>yet more wonderful stuff </legend>
        <p>my name is still letha</p>
        <p> If I say it myself, your textbook rocks! </p>
      </fieldset>
    </form>
  </body>
</html>
```

The HTML <div> tag is shown in Listing 4.5. The div tag defines sections in an HTML document that can be given particular characteristics. In Listing 4.5, we're setting one set of text to a red color and another set of text to a purple color.

LISTING 4.5   <div> Tag

```
<!DOCTYPE HTML>
<html>
   <body>
      <form>
         <div style="color:red">
            <p> jolly good stuff</p>
         </div>
         <div style="color:purple">
            <p> and more really good stuff</p>
         </div>
      </form>
   </body>
</html>
```

The next listing, Listing 4.6, shows both the div tag and the fieldset tag being used together in a form.

LISTING 4.6   Both div and fieldset in a Form

```
<html>
   <body>
      <form>
         <fieldset>
            <legend>my wonderful stuff </legend>
            <div style="color:red">
               <p>my name is letha</p>
               <p> this is a great textbook </p>
            </div>
            <div style="color:purple">
               <p> Seems like I heard this somewhere before: this is a great textbook </p>
            </div>
         </fieldset>
         <fieldset>
            <legend>yet more wonderful stuff </legend>
            <p>my name is still letha</p>
            <p> If I say it myself, your textbook rocks! </p>
         </fieldset>
      </form>
   </body>
</html>
```

The next listing, Listing 4.7, shows how to set styles that can be used by div tags.

LISTING 4.7   Using Styles with div

```
<!DOCTYPE HTML>
<html>
  <body>
    <style>
      div.mydisplay {
        background-color: blue;
        color:red;
        font-family: courier;
        padding:10px;
      }
      div.myotherdisplay {
        background-color: red;
        color:purple;
        font-family: verdana;
        padding:10px;
      }
    </style>
    <form>
      <fieldset>
        <legend>my wonderful stuff </legend>
        <div class="mydisplay">
          <p>my name is letha</p>
          <p> this is a great textbook </p>
        </div>
        <div class="myotherdisplay">
          <p>I am happy with the textbook</p>
          <p> Did I say it before? This is a great textbook </p>
        </div>
      </fieldset>
      <fieldset>
        <legend>yet more wonderful stuff </legend>
        <p>my name is still letha</p>
        <p> If I say it myself, your textbook rocks! </p>
      </fieldset>
    </form>
  </body>
</html>
```

The next example, Listing 4.8, shows how to create a table in HTML. The <tr> tag specifies table rows. The <th> tag specifies column headers. The <td> tag specifies data.

LISTING 4.8   Tables in HTML

```
<!DOCTYPE HTML>
<html>
    <style>
      th {
         padding: 20px;
      }
    </style>
    <body>
      <table>
        <tr>
          <th>Book Title</th>
          <th>Author</th>
        </tr>
        <tr>
          <td>Middleware</td>

          <td>Etzkorn</td>
        </tr>
      </table>
    </body>
</html>
```

The next example, in Listing 4.9, specifies a table, and then uses a textarea to describe one of the elements in the table. However, usually a textarea would be used to enter data rather than to describe an element. Usually you would enter data in a textarea, then press a submit button in the form to send this data to a web page to be handled. To do that, you'd have to specify a name for the textarea, which I didn't do here, something like: NAME="mytext".

LISTING 4.9   textarea Example

```
<!DOCTYPE HTML>
<html>
    <style>
      th {
         padding: 10px;
      }
    </style>
    <body>
      <table>
        <tr>
          <th>Book Title</th>
          <th>Author</th>
          <th>
            <textarea rows="1" cols="100">
                Johnson defined lexicographer as a 'harmless drudge.' Maybe textbook
                authors too?
```

```
            </textarea>
          </th>
        </tr>
        <tr>
          <th>Middleware</th>
          <th>Etzkorn</th>
        </tr>
      </table>
    </body>
  </html>
```

In Listing 4.10, we see an example that creates a radio button. Note that " " character, this makes a space in the web page output, it's called a *non-breaking space*.

LISTING 4.10   Radio Button Example

```
<!DOCTYPE HTML>
<html>
  <body>
    <form action = "simple_server.php" method="GET">
      <div align = "center">
        <p>Enter your current emotional state: </p>
        <input type="radio" name="mydata" value="Happy"/> Happy
        <input type="radio" name="mydata" value="Sad"/> Sad  
        <input type="submit" value = "Submit"/>
      </div>
    </form>
  </body>
</html>
```

HTML5 improved image handling considerably compared to the earlier versions of HTML. In Listing 4.11, we see a figure with a caption. The "alt" tag specifies the text that will print if for some reason the image won't display.

LISTING 4.11   Images and Captions in HTML5

```
<figure>
  <img src="prettyhorse.jpg" alt="A Very Pretty Horse" width="300" height="500"/>
  <figcaption>A Very Pretty Horse </figcaption>
</figure>
```

HTML5 also introduced the <canvas> tag, which creates a rectangle on a web page that you can use a scripting language (such as JavaScript) to draw graphics on. The code in Listing 4.12 draws a red and orange X across the canvas. In the body, the canvas rectangle is created (in this case it's a square) of 300 by 300 pixels. When the body is loaded, the onload command runs the drawX() JavaScript function. This uses the Document Object Model (DOM) to acquire a reference to the canvas. The beginPath() method is used to start a path. Then the first (red) stroke of the X is drawn from top left to bottom right, then the second (orange) stroke of the X is drawn from bottom left to top right. Then a green circle is drawn around the middle of the X. In this command:

ctx.arc(150,150,50,0,Math.PI*2);

the midpoint is (150,150). The radius of the circle is 50. The starting angle is 0 radians, and the ending angle is PI*2 radians.

LISTING 4.12   HTML5 Canvas Example

```
<!DOCTYPE html>
<html>
    <script>
        function drawX(){
            var mycanvas = document.getElementById("myCanvas");
            var ctx = mycanvas.getContext("2d");
            ctx.beginPath();
            ctx.moveTo(0, 0);
            ctx.strokeStyle = "red";
            ctx.lineTo(300, 300);
            ctx.stroke();
            ctx.beginPath();
            ctx.moveTo(0, 300);
            ctx.lineTo(300, 0);
            ctx.strokeStyle = "orange";
            ctx.stroke();
            ctx.arc(150,150,50,0,Math.PI*2);
            ctx.strokeStyle = "green";
            ctx.stroke();
        }
    </script>
    <body onload="drawX();">

        <canvas id="myCanvas" width="300" height="300"> </canvas>

    </body>
</html>
```

4.4   XML SCHEMA BASICS

An XML schema specifies the format that is required of an XML document that references the schema.

An XML schema allows an XML parser to determine whether the XML elements and attributes are defined appropriately in the XML document, whether attributes are optional or required, and if the content of the attributes conforms to the specified type of the data. This is referred to as *validation*. This can offload some input correctness checking from the application that is using the XML document onto an XML parser, such that the application does not have to write new code to perform the input correctness checking.

If you didn't fully understand that, perhaps you need a little more description of what an XML element and an XML attribute are. In the following two XML data definitions (here we are defining an XML document, we are not defining an XML schema) we define a horse named "Secretariat," the breed of the horse is "thoroughbred." In this first example, the breed of the horse is stored as an element:

```
<horse>
    <name> Secretariat</name>
    <breed>Thoroughbred</breed>
</horse>
```

In the second example, the breed of the horse is stored as an attribute:

```
<horse breed="Thoroughbred">
    <name> Secretariat</name>
</horse>
```

Whether or not an XML document conforms to the format specified by an XML schema is different from whether or not the XML document obeys basic XML syntax rules. For example, it is possible for an XML document to be a well formed XML document (obey all basic XML syntax rules) but still not conform to a given XML schema.

An XML schema would begin as follows:

```
<xsd:schema xmlns:xsd="http://www.w3.org/2001/XMLSchema">
```

This specifies that the basic vocabulary (elements and simple types) used in the XML document belongs to the XML schema language itself, rather than being defined new by the author of the particular XML document.

XML schema language simple types include: string, integer, long, unsigned long, short, unsigned short, float, double, Boolean, date, time, hexBinary, among many others.

The XML schema language also allows definition of complex types. Complex types can themselves contain elements and attributes, whereas simple types that are not allowed contain elements or attributes. An example complex type (as stored in the XML schema, as opposed to an XML file that would contain data that obeys the format of the schema) is the following:

```
<xsd: complexType name="horse">
  <xsd: element name="name" type="xsd:string"/>
  <xsd: attribute name="breed" type="xsd:string"/>
</xsd: complexType>
```

Here we defined a complex type and gave it as an element with a name. However, you can use <complexType> without a name, and define it inside an element, as follows:

```
<xsd: element name="horse">
  <xsd:complexType>
    <xsd: element name="name" type="xsd:string"/>
    <xsd: attribute name="breed" type="xsd:string"/>
  </xsd: complexType>
</xsd:element>
```

Some other items you might find useful to know:

The XML schema "list" element is a list of values of a specified data type. For example, you can have a list of integers or a list of strings.

The XML scheme "sequence" element specifies that the elements included inside the sequence must occur in the specified order.

Another useful namespace associated with XML schemas is the XML schema instance. This would normally be specified as follows:

```
xmlns: xsi =http://www.w3.org/2001/XMLSchema-instance
xsi:schemaLocation="myschema.xsd"
```

The first statement above defines some attributes that can be used in XML documents. These are defined in the namespace http://www.w3.org/2001/XMLSchema-instance.

In the second statement, xsi:schemaLocation tells your XML parser where to find your own schema that you created.

One way xsi is used to define an attribute called "xsi:type" that defines the type of an element (the type can be either simple or complex).

4.5 JAVASCRIPT OBJECT NOTATION (JSON)

JavaScript Object Notation (JSON) is a text-based and human readable data format. JSON is language independent, but has a structure that is familiar to users of modern programming languages such as C++, Java, Python, among others.

JSON is specified by two somewhat different standards, RFC 7159 and ECMA 404. JSON is similar to XML in that it is text-based and human readable. However, JSON is much less wordy than XML.

JSON has become very widely used. In AJAX, for example, JSON has replaced XML as the most used data format.

The basic types of JSON are:

- Object—a collection of string/value pairs, enclosed in curly brackets
- Array—an ordered collection of values, enclosed in square brackets
- Number—signed base 10 numbers, can be either integer or floating point
- String—represented in Unicode, enclosed in double quotes. Recognizes escape characters such as "\n" for line feed and "\r" for carriage return.
- Boolean True or False
- Null

Example of a JSON Object:

```
{
    "username": "topprogrammer",
    "password": "didntyouwanttoknow"
}
```

Examples of JSON Arrays:
First example: an ordered list of numbers:

```
[1, 2, 3, 4, 5]
```

If you stored this in, say, JavaScript or C++ in a variable called myarray, then myarray[0] would contain the value 1.

Second example: an ordered list of strings

```
["hi", "there", "to", "you", "all"]
```

If you stored this in, say, JavaScript or C++ in a variable called myarray, then myarray[0] would contain the value "hi."

Third example: an ordered list of objects (an array of objects):

```
[
    {
      "hi": "handsome"
    },
    {
      "where":"there"
    }
]
```

Fourth example: an ordered list of arrays (an array of arrays or multidimensional array):

```
[
    [
      "here",
      "we",
      "go",
      "again"
    ]
]
```

Other Comments:

A JSON object can contain arrays.

It is also possible to mix different kinds of values in JSON. For example, a JSON array could contain an array where one value is a simple data type such as a string, and another data type is an object.

The content-type (mime type/internet media type) for JSON is:

application/json

although other variations are sometimes seen.

4.6   INTERNET MEDIA TYPES (MIME TYPES)

Internet media types are often called Multipurpose Internet Mail Extensions (MIME) types (they were originally used in email).

The format of an internet media type/mime type is:

type/subtype+suffix

Here, "type" could be: text, application, audio, video, image, example, among others.
Then "subtype" (also called "media type") could be: xml, soap, plain, html, pdf, jpg, etc.
Note that a "vnd" prefix on a subtype indicates that the type is vendor specific.
The "+suffix" specifies the underlying structure of the subtype/media type.
Some common Internet Media Types are shown in Table 4.1.

4.7   BASE 64 ENCODING

Base 64 encoding represents binary data in an ASCII format, for the purpose of sending or storing the data using some technology that is not able to handle binary data, that is, some technology that must have its data in text format (one example of this kind of technology is email, where a file attachment needs to be in text format). Base 64 encoding handles this by representing the binary data in base 64

TABLE 4.1

Some Common Internet Media Types (MIME Types)

Internet Media Type/Mime Type	Associated File Type
text/plain	plain text files
text/html	HTML file
text/xml	XML file, SOAP 1.1 file
application/soap+xml.	SOAP 1.2 file
application/json	JSON file
application/pdf	pdf file
audio/mpeg	.mp3 file
video/mpeg	.mpeg file
image/jpg	jpeg graphics/image file
image/gif	gif graphics/image file
application/vnd. openxmlformats-officedocument. wordprocessingml.document	Microsoft Word 2007.docx file
application/vnd .openxmlformats-officedocument. spreadsheetml.sheet	Microsoft Excel 2007.xlsx file

(radix 64) and then translating that into ASCII. This kind of base 64 encoding is used with MIME, see IETF (1996).

Note first of all that it requires 6 bits to represent 64 (base 10) different values, counting from 0 (000000 base 2) to 63 (111111 base 2).

The way base 64 encoding works, you break a string of binary numbers into 6-bit chunks. Then you use a mapping table to map that to printable ASCII characters. The information in Table 4.2 came from MIME in IETF (1996).

For example, let's take three 8-bit binary numbers:

- 01010111 01101000 01101111

Put them next to each other (no spaces in between):

- 010101110110100001101111

Break them into 6 bit chunks:

- 010101 110110 100001 101111

Turn each 6 bit chunk into its equivalent decimal number:

- 010101 = 21 base 10
- 110110 = 54 base 10
- 100001 = 33 base 10
- 101111 = 47 base 10

Look each separate value up in Table 4.2, and you get the following:

- V2hv

TABLE 4.2

The Base 64 Value to Character Encodings

Value	Character	Value	Character	Value	Character	Value	Character
0	A	17	R	34	i	51	z
1	B	18	S	35	j	52	0
2	C	19	T	36	k	53	1
3	D	20	U	37	l	54	2
4	E	21	V	38	m	55	3
5	F	22	W	39	n	56	4
6	G	23	X	40	o	57	5
7	H	24	Y	41	p	58	6
8	I	25	Z	42	q	59	7
9	J	26	a	43	r	60	8
10	K	27	b	44	s	61	9
11	L	28	c	45	t	62	+
12	M	29	d	46	u	63	/
13	N	30	e	47	v		
14	O	31	f	48	w		
15	P	32	g	49	x		
16	Q	33	h	50	y		

Which is the base 64 encoding for the original number.

If you encode three 8-bit numbers at a time (three bytes in your message) because this ends up evenly with four 6-bit numbers. If you did one 8-bit number you'd have 2 bits left over, etc. In cases where the number of bytes in the message being encoded is not divisible by three, then at the end of the message the remainder, up to three bytes, is padded with zeros. Each 6-bit chunk that is all zeros is represented by the "=" character.

For example, if you had only 1 byte in your message, that would be one 6-bit value plus 2 leftover bits.

- 01010111

So if you were to break this into sections of 6 bits you would get:

- 010101 with 11 left over, so this won't work

Instead, you make the value three bytes long by padding with zeros:

- 01010111 00000000 00000000

Then breaking this into 6-bit chunks, you get:

- 010101 110000 000000 000000

Which then converts to:

- Vw==

4.8   URL ENCODING (PERCENT ENCODING) AND URL BASE 64 ENCODING

IETF (2005) lists the reserved characters of a Uniform Resource Identifier (URI) as follows:

gen-delims = ":" / "/" / "?" / "#" / "[" / "]" / "@"
sub-delims = "!" / "$" / "&" / "'" / "(" / ")"
   / "*" / "+" / "," / ";" / "="

Because we don't want to delve deeply into the formal notation of a URI, we'll ignore the difference between gen-delims and sub-delims and just call them all *reserved characters*.

A percent encoded character is shown as the "%" character followed by the hexadecimal representation of the character.

For example, a space character in ASCII is the number 32 (base 10) or 0x20 (base 16). So its percent encoded representation would be %20, and so forth.

Sometimes you need to URL encode data that has been previously base 64 encoded. For example, if you look back at Section 4.6, you'll find that standard mappings from MIME use characters that URI has reserved: "=" and "+" and "/." You have to URL encode these before you can send this data with, say, an HTTP GET.

The "/" character is 47 (base 10) or 0x2F (base 16) from an ASCII table, so its percent encoded representation is %2F.

A "+" character in an ASCII table is the number 43 (base ten) or 0x2B (base 16). So its percent encoded representation would be: %2B.

An "=" character in an ASCII table is the number 61 (base 10) or 0x3D (base 16). So its percent encoded representation would be: %3D.

4.9   DOMAIN NAMES AND DOMAIN NAME SERVERS

You're used to domain names, they're just the URLs that you use on the web. Two examples:

1. www.amazon.com
   - a good choice for this textbook because we'll look at Amazon Web Services later on
2. www.cs.uah.edu
   - my home university and department. ☺ Check it out!

You can't use just any string as a domain name. I mean, it would be awkward if another retailer suddenly wanted to use Amazon's URL, right? Or if another university wanted to use UAH's URL.

World oversight of domain names and IP addresses is done by the Internet Corporation for Assigned Names and Numbers (ICANN) and a department of ICANN called the Internet Assigned Numbers Authority (IANA).

The Internet Numbers Registry for Africa (AFRINIC) describes the work of ICANN and IANA as follows:

ICANN
The Internet Corporation for Assigned Names and Numbers (ICANN) is a non-profit organisation coordinating the Domain Name System (DNS), Internet Protocol (IP) addresses, space allocation, protocol identifier assignment, generic (gTLD) and country code (ccTLD) Top-Level Domain name system management, and root server system management functions.

IANA
The Internet Assigned Numbers Authority (IANA) is responsible for the global coordination of the DNS Root, IP addressing, and other Internet protocol resources such as IP numbers or addresses. IANA manages the global pool of Internet numbers (Internet Protocols IPs and Autonomous System Numbers ASNs) and distributes them among the five regional Internet registries (RIRs).

TABLE 4.3
Root Servers

Hostname	IP Addresses	Manager
a.root-servers.net	198.41.0.4, 2001:503:ba3e::2:30	VeriSign, Inc.
b.root-servers.net	192.228.79.201, 2001:500:84::b	University of Southern California (ISI)
c.root-servers.net	192.33.4.12, 2001:500:2::c	Cogent Communications
d.root-servers.net	199.7.91.13, 2001:500:2d::d	University of Maryland
e.root-servers.net	192.203.230.10	NASA (Ames Research Center)
f.root-servers.net	192.5.5.241, 2001:500:2f::f	Internet Systems Consortium, Inc.
g.root-servers.net	192.112.36.4	U.S. Department of Defense (NIC)
h.root-servers.net	198.97.190.53, 2001:500:1::53	U.S. Army (Research Lab)
i.root-servers.net	192.36.148.17, 2001:7fe::53	Netnod
j.root-servers.net	192.58.128.30, 2001:503:c27::2:30	VeriSign, Inc.
k.root-servers.net	193.0.14.129, 2001:7fd::1	RIPE NCC
l.root-servers.net	199.7.83.42, 2001:500:9f::42	ICANN
m.root-servers.net	202.12.27.33, 2001:dc3::35	WIDE Project

As this description says, IANA is the coordinator of the Domain Name Server (DNS) root, the top level of the DNS Hierarchy; these root names (top level domain names) are the last segment of a domain name, for example: .com, .nz, .gov, etc. Then there are subdomains, for example, in the address: www.cs.uah.edu, .edu is the top level domain name, and "cs.uah.edu" is a subdomain of "uah.edu."

But how are domain names assigned, other than specifying the possible root names? There is a service of ICANN called InterNic that enforces unique domain names, however, commercial domain registrars do the actual domain name registration. A list of accredited commercial registrars is available at InterNic (2016). So you or your company can pay to use a domain name for a certain length of time.

For the domain name system to work, servers must be available to translate between names and IP addresses. The IANA (2016) gives the hostname and associated IP addresses, and the Managers for the root servers as of 2016. This is shown in Table 4.3.

There are numerous domain name resolvers that receive URLs (domain names) and must translate them into their associated IP addresses. According to InterNIC FAQs (2016), the way this works is: the domain name resolvers previously had connected to the root servers, so they know what kind of root domain name (.com, .org, etc.) a particular root server handles. So when they receive a URL (domain name) from a user, they can pass it to the correct root server that handles the registry for the appropriate top-level domain (.com, etc.). Then the domain name resolver queries the correct top-level domain registry to get the IP address for the URL. Then it queries a local computer at that address to get the final IP address for the URL.

At the lower levels, your company can maintain an internal DNS. Your Internet Service Provider (ISP) can maintain a DNS. DNS lookups start at the lower levels, often they don't have go much further up because recent URLs accessed have been cached locally, along with the IP address they are mapped to. However, if necessary, when the URL mapping is not available locally, the DNSs can access the root servers to try to track down a domain.

In terms of IP addresses, according to the IANA (2016), internet service providers (ISPs) assign IP addresses to users. The ISPs themselves acquire IP addresses from a local or national internet registry, or from an appropriate Regional Internet Registry (RIR). As of 2016, there are five regional internet registries:

1. AFRINIC—Africa
2. APNIC—Asia/Pacific
3. ARIN—Canada, USA, and some Caribbean Islands

4. LACNIC—Latin America and some Caribbean Islands
5. RIPE NCC—Europe, the Middle East, and Central Asia

4.10 DOCUMENT OBJECT MODEL AND BROWSER OBJECT MODEL

The Document Object Model (DOM) is a set of Application Programming Interfaces (APIs) that manipulate a web document (that is typically located at a URL). According to W3C (2015):

> In its original sense, "The DOM" is an API for accessing and manipulating documents (in particular, HTML and XML documents). In this specification, the term "document" is used for any markup-based resource, ranging from short static documents to long essays or reports with rich multimedia, as well as to fully-fledged interactive applications.
>
> These documents are presented as a node tree. Some of the nodes in the tree can have children, while others are always leaves.

Because of the DOM's object-oriented nature, it partakes to some degree of both an API (in terms of methods) and a data structure, or one could call it a model (organization of data in a document, in terms of an object hierarchy). This is because an object implies both data and the methods that access that data. I've seen some different descriptions of a DOM online, where sometimes the data structure side of the DOM is emphasized more than the API and sometimes the API is emphasized more than the data structure side. However, the *purpose* of the DOM is to change a web document in the ways that the programmer needs, whereas the *manner* it does this uses a hierarchy of objects (an object model). So if one is forced to be strict in the definition of a DOM, it is more accurate to call the DOM an API than it is to call it a data structure or a model. The name "Document Object Model" is perhaps a little misleading in this regard.

There are three levels of the Document Object Model:

1. Core Document Object Model—associated with all web documents
2. XML Document Object Model—has more specific interfaces for XML documents
3. HTML Document Object Model—has more specific interfaces for HTML documents
   - The XML DOM and the HTML DOM are sub-classes of the core DOM (inherit from the core DOM) that have more specific behaviors

There are several good online tutorials for using the DOM available, see W3 Schools (2016c, and 2016g), Tutorials Point (2016). So we'll only do a brief overview here.

Every item in the document tree is a node object. A node has a name, an associated URI, and a type. It has attributes, and can have parents and children. The node object methods allow one to add or remove children, to set or get the data associated with the node, to compare whether two nodes are equal, etc.

Some important data types include:

- Document—root object of a document
- Element:
  - In the XML DOM, the Element object represents an element in an XML document
  - In the HTML DOM, the Element object represents an HTML element
- nodeList—an array of elements
- Attribute:
  - In the XML DOM, an Attribute object represents an XML attribute
  - In the HTML DOM, an Attribute object represents an HTML attribute

A few important API calls:

- document.getElementById(id)
- document.getElementsByTagName(name)

- document.createElement(name)
- parentNode.appendChild(node)
- element.innerHTML

Just to give you the flavor of the DOM, a small example of a couple of these API calls using JavaScript:

```
<h1 id="myheader">original name of block in web page</h1>
<script>
    document.getElementById("myheader").innerHTML = "a better name for block in web page";
</script>
```

We won't look at it here anymore ourselves, because you're better off using those online tutorials. However, there are several more examples using the DOM later on in Section 11.2, when we look at AJAX.

The Browser Object Model (BOM) is the set of APIs that is supported by a web browser such as Chrome, Mozilla Firefox, Microsoft Edge, Safari, Opera, etc. Its purpose is to manipulate how a browser displays one or more web documents. There is no standard for a BOM (unlike the DOM which is standardized through W3C). However, modern browsers implement mostly the same set of objects with their associated methods, although there can be some differences.

There are several online tutorials about the BOM, see W3 Schools (2016d) and Home and Learn (2016). So we'll just give you a quick overview to get you started.

The window object is the base object in the BOM. It is the browser's displayed window. It can have global variables and functions, which are properties of the window object.

A few example BOM objects and functions:

- window.document—allows access to the web document inside the window
- window.open(), window.close()—open and close a window
- window.innerHeight, window.innerWidth—height and width of the window
- window.screen—the screen seen by the user, contains properties about the display
  - screen.height
  - screen.width
- window.navigator—contains information about the browser
  - navigator.cookieenabled—tells you whether or not cookies are enabled

4.11   POPULAR WEB SERVERS

The purpose of a web server is to make web pages accessible over the web. It does this by receiving HTTP requests, and responding to these using the appropriate content from web pages. Web servers also support server-side scripting languages, such as PHP, ASP.NET, Perl, Python, server-side JavaScript (note that originally JavaScript was only implemented in a web browser), etc. They can also do a lot more than that.

Originally, there was a distinction between web servers and application servers. A web server was responsible for handling HTTP and web page things, whereas an application server handled business applications. The two concepts have mostly merged today, partly because web type interfaces have become widely used even for applications that are not intended for public use on the World Wide Web itself, and partly because web pages have become much more powerful than back in the early days of the web.

Thinking in general terms, the extreme form of an application server would be cloud computing itself. Or if you're thinking in a more application-specific way, you could have an application server that runs on a cloud. In either case, a web server would be a sub-part of the cloud that would provide the web facing interface. But in any case, we're not looking at cloud computing just yet, that's for Chapters 13 and 14. Right now we're focusing in on the web server side of things.

4.11.1   WEB/APPLICATION SERVERS: LAMP VERSUS WINDOWS/ASP VERSUS JAVA

There have traditionally been some competing technology "worlds" in regard to providing web server solutions. Some of the major ones are LAMP, Windows/ASP.NET, and Java EE Middleware/GlassFish.

The LAMP solution to web servers consists of the technologies: Linux, Apache HTTP web server, MySQL, and PHP. So in the LAMP world, all your web servers run on Linux, use the Apache HTTP web server to process HTTP requests, handle all databases working with MySQL, and do all dynamic web page processing in the PHP scripting language.

It is possible to substitute other technologies for the original four technologies, and still be considered to be using LAMP. For example, Python or Perl are often used instead of PHP. The major example of this is probably using the MariaDB instead of MySQL. When Oracle acquired Sun Microsystems in 2010, there was some concern about the future of MySQL as freeware under the GNU GPL. One of the original developers of MySQL forked off MariaDB from MySQL. MariaDB is intended to remain highly compatible with MySQL.

Internet Information Services (IIS) is a web server provided by Microsoft. When you're using IIS, it has traditionally meant that you're using Microsoft Windows, the IIS web server, the SQL server database, and ASP.NET scripting (originally just ASP but now ASP.NET).

IIS supports PHP as well as ASP.NET, although it must be separately installed. In the past, I've noted an occasional incompatibility of my own PHP code when moving from LAMP to IIS, but it mostly has worked well. It's possible to use other databases with IIS than SQL server, for example, it can also work with MySQL.

The mono project, sponsored by Microsoft, among other things supports the use of ASP.NET on Apache web servers. Several of my students have used this off and on over the years, back in 2010 we had some problems with a project, but more recently it has seemed to work well.

On the Java side of things, there are several application servers available. GlassFish is the reference server for the Java Enterprise Edition, and supports many aspects of Java EE: Enterprise JavaBeans, Java Messaging Service, Java Server Pages, Java servlets, among many more. However, in 2013 Oracle announced that it was going to cease support for GlassFish, and try to get commercial customers to move over to their commercial Oracle Web Logic Server.

Another available open source Java server is Wildfly (formerly JBoss), which is as of 2016 supported by RedHat.

Other notable servers include:

Apache Tomcat—in this past this has been known for being primarily a Java servlet container, although it also supports several other Java EE specifications.

nginx—this is a widely used server known for its performance. It supports Perl scripting, Lua, and nginScript (server-side JavaScript).

We're going to be moving around through numerous web server technologies in this textbook. For our AJAX stuff, which uses PHP and client-side JavaScript, we could use an Apache HTTP Server (this is what I use when I teach this in a course). For WCF, we will be using self-hosting, which doesn't require us to separately start up an application server (otherwise we would have to use IIS). For Enterprise Java Beans (EJBs), we'll be using the GlassFish Application Server. For Java Servlets and JAX-RS, we'll be using GlassFish. For JAX-WS, we'll be using the Endpoint Publisher (otherwise we'd have to be using something like GlassFish).

Since we'll be using GlassFish a lot, we'll go over how to use it in Section 4.11.2. But first, let's take a look at MySQL since we use it for various examples in this textbook (see the Sailboat Marina project, Section 1.5 and Chapter 18, available in online resources).

4.11.1.1   MySQL—The M in LAMP

As we learned in the previous section, the LAMP solution to web servers consists of the technologies: Linux, Apache HTTP web server, MySQL, and PHP. Although each of these technologies in the LAMP world sometimes has another technology substituted, and MariaDB is a notable replacement for the MySQL database, MySQL is still widely used. We use MySQL for the Sailboat Marina projects in this textbook (see Section 1.5 and Chapter 18), so we will examine here how to use it. Chapter 18 is available in online resources.

Note that the steps we follow here must be done before the Sailboat Marina project implementations will work for all the non-Microsoft technologies (for Microsoft technologies we will not use the MySQL database) because all of them are dependent on a database named "thething" containing a table named "marina" set up as in the following.

First of all, log in to mysql as root:

```
mysql -u root -p
```

Then at the mysql prompt, create a database named "thething" and get it ready to use:

```
show databases;
create database thething;
use thething;
```

Next create a user with a password, here the user will be "myownstuff" and the password will be "mypassword." (Substitute the username and password you want to use here.):

```
CREATE USER 'myownstuff'@'localhost' IDENTIFIED BY 'mypassword';
GRANT ALL ON thething.* to 'myownstuff'@'localhost';
FLUSH PRIVILEGES;
```

Lastly, use Ctrl-C to exit the mysql prompt.
Now log in to mysql as user myownstuff:

```
mysql -u myownstuff –p
```

Then MySQL will prompt you to enter your password.
Inside MySQL, to create a table in the thething database, type:

```
use thething;
CREATE TABLE marina (name VARCHAR(50), model VARCHAR(30), slip INT, begin_date DATE,
end_date DATE);
SHOW TABLES;
```

Now, to enter data in the marina table in the thething database, type:

```
DESCRIBE marina;
INSERT INTO marina VALUES ('Etzkorn','Catalina27',17,'2013-07-10','2016-07-19');
INSERT INTO marina VALUES ('Smith','Hunter25',16,'2012-02-05','2016-08-17');
INSERT INTO marina VALUES ('Smith','ODay37',3,'1985-05-09','2016-08-17');
```

Now, to see all the contents of the marina table (this shows all rows and all columns in marina), type:

```
select * from marina;
```

Now you can see portions of the marina table based on your queries, as follows:

```
select name from marina where slip=3;
select model from marina where end_date='2016-08-17' AND name='Smith';
```

4.11.1.2   Using Java Database Connectivity (JDBC) with MySQL

In this textbook, when we are using Java, we will use JDBC to connect to MySQL and control MySQL. We're only going to cover the bare minimum here that we need to do the various Sailboat Marina (see Section 1.5 and Chapter 18, available in online resources) projects in Java, as this is a middleware textbook, not a database textbook, although it is common for database control code to be accessed using a middleware.

You must import the following libraries:

```
import java.sql.DriverManager;
import java.sql.Connection;
import java.sql.*;
import java.sql.SQLException;
```

The remaining code will be inside a Java class.
Then set up the JDBC driver and the url of the database:

```
static final String JDBC_DRIVER = "com.mysql.jdbc.Driver";
static final String DB_URL = "jdbc:mysql://localhost/thething";
```

Then create strings to contain your database username and password

```
static final String myUN = "myownstuff";
static final String myPW = "myownpassword";
```

You must register the JDBC driver:

```
Class.forName("com.mysql.jdbc.Driver");
```

Then to create the connection to the database, you do:

```
Connection conn = DriverManager.getConnection(DB_URL, myUN, myPW);
```

To create a query for the database, you do something like the following:

```
String mysql_Query;
Statement stmt = conn.createStatement();
mysql_Query = "SELECT name, model, slip, begin_date, end_date, id FROM marina";
ResultSet rs = stmt.executeQuery(mysql_Query);
```

Note that the data types of these items in the query are as follows:

- name, model—type string
- slip, id—type integer
- begin_date, end_date—date

As you can see, the results of the query are stored in a variable named "ResultSet."
You can iterate over this result set as follows (note that rs.next() will return "null" when there are no more items in the set of results):

```
while(rs.next())
{
    // do useful processing such as extract certain items from the results
}
```

To extract a data item of type string from the ResultSet rs, do:

```
String thename = rs.getString("name");
```

To extract a data item of type integer from the ResultSet rs, do:

```
int theslip = rs.getInt("slip");
```

To extract a data item of type Date from the ResultSet rs, do:

```
Date theenddate = rs.getDate("end_date");
```

You can also extract a date as a string from the ResultSet rs as follows:

```
String thebegindate = rs.getString("begin_date");
```

Our select statement above performed a query consisting of a single statement on the database. As an alternative to this, we can instead use a "prepared statement." The advantage of a prepared statement compared to a typical statement is that, as the PreparedStatement object is being created, the statement stored in the object is being precompiled by the database. Therefore, the PreparedStatement object will contain a precompiled statement, so when the statement is (eventually) executed by the database it doesn't have to be compiled again first. So if you plan to execute a statement over and over again, it improves the execution time of your code if you use a PreparedStatement object.

Next we will insert an item into the MySQL database using a PreparedStatement object. First, to set up the query, do the following—note that this leaves 6 values specified with "?" that we will replace with real values inside the PreparedStatement object:

```
String mysql_QueryA;
mysql_QueryA = "INSERT INTO marina (name, model, slip, begin_date, end_date, id) VALUES
(?,?,?,?,?,?)";
```

Now create a PreparedStatement associated with the query:

```
PreparedStatement statement = conn.prepareStatement(mysql_QueryA);
```

Now inside the PreparedStatement object, replace the "?" with values, in order starting at the count of 1 for the first "?":

```
statement.setString(1, "Etzkorn");            // replaces first "?" in the query
statement.setString(2, "Catalina27");         // replaces second "?" in the query
statement.setInt(3, 18);                      // replaces third "?" in the query
// Prepare a date for insertion
SimpleDateFormat sdf = new SimpleDateFormat("MM-dd-yyyy");
Date thedate = sdf.parse("1979-01-07");
java.sql.Date sqlbegin_date= new java.sql.Date(thedate.getTime());
// Insert the date
statement.setDate(4, sqlbegin_date);          // replaces fourth"?" in the query
// Prepare a date for insertion
thedate = sdf.parse("1980-07-12");
java.sql.Date sqlend_date= new java.sql.Date(thedate.getTime());
// Insert the date
```

```
statement.setDate(5, sqlend_date);        // replaces fifth "?" in the query
statement.setInt(6,100);                  // replaces sixth "?" in the query
```

Then finally update the database according to the statement:

```
int rows_inserted = statement.executeUpdate();
```

Afterward, check to see if the number of rows inserted is greater than zero. If so, the database update was successful.

Now let's again use a PreparedStatement, in this case to delete a record from the database:

```
String mysql_stmt;
int whichid=300;          // Arbitrarily select an item with id = 300
mysql_stmt = "DELETE FROM marina where id="+whichid;

PreparedStatement stmt = conn.prepareStatement(mysql_stmt);

int rows_deleted = stmt.executeUpdate();
```

Afterward, check to see if the number of rows deleted is greater than zero. If so, the database update was successful.

To finish up the statement, result set, or connection when you're done, do as appropriate:

```
stmt.close();
rs.close()
conn.close();
```

Note: to deploy JDBC in a war file along with your web application, you should put its jar file in a lib directory under the WEB-INF directory.

To deploy JDBC so it was accessible by an EJBs application, I installed it in GlassFish itself: to make the JDBC library available to all applications in a domain, put it in the lib directory under the GlassFish domain directory then restart GlassFish.

4.11.1.3 Using MySQLi in PHP with MySQL

In this textbook, when we are using PHP, we will use MySQLi to connect to MySQL and control MySQL. We're only going to cover the bare minimum here that we need to do the Sailboat Marina (see Section 1.5 and Chapter 18, available in online resources) project in PHP, as this is a middle-ware textbook, not a database textbook, although it is common for database control code to be accessed using a middleware.

To create a connection to a MySQL database using PHP, do the following:

```
$username = "myownstuff";
$password = "myownpassword";
$dbname = "thething";
$conn = new mysqli($servername, $username, $password, $dbname);
```

To check whether connecting was successful or not, you could do:

```
if ($conn->connect_error) {
        die("Connection failed: " . $conn->connect_error);
}
```

To do a query reading various items from the MySQL database, do:

```
$sql = "SELECT name, model,slip, begin_date, end_date, id FROM marina";
$result = $conn->query($sql);
```

This puts the results of the query in the variable "$result."

Before you look at the contents of the result, first check to see if the $result was empty or not. To do this, check to see if "$result->num_rows" is greater than zero.

Next, to iterate through the items in the result, do:

```
while($row = $result->fetch_assoc())
{
        // extract items
}
```

From inside the above while loop, to extract a data item from the $row variable, do something like the following:

```
$thename=$row["name"];
$theslip=$row["slip"];
$thebegindate=$row["begin_date"];
```

To create a new record in the database, you could do something like:

```
$name='Etzkorn';
$model='Catalina27';
$slip=18;
$begin_date='2013-07-23';
$end_date='2030-08-29';
$id=100;
$sql = "INSERT INTO marina (name, model, slip, begin_date,end_date,id) VALUES ('$name', '$model',
        '$slip', '$modified_begin_date', '$modified_end_date', '$id' )";
$success_or_not=$conn->query($sql);
```

To check if the creation of the new record was successful, do:

```
if ($success_or_not=== TRUE)
{
        echo "New record created successfully";
}
```

To delete a particular item in the database, do:

```
$id = 300;                    // arbitrarily select an item with id = 300
$sql = "DELETE FROM marina WHERE ";
$sql = $sql."id=" .$id;       // this appends "id=300" to the whole string making the query:
                              // DELETE FROM marina WHERE id=300
$success_or_not=$conn->query($sql);
(again, you should check to see whether $success_or_not is true)
```

To close the connection, do:

```
$conn->close();
```

4.11.2 GLASSFISH APPLICATION SERVER

GlassFish is an application server for Java EE. It works with both the NetBeans and Eclipse IDEs, or it can be used with Java EE command line (which is what we do in this textbook). GlassFish supports the reference implementation of Java EE including: Enterprise Java Beans, Java Server Pages, Java Messaging Service, servlets, Java Persistence API, and so forth.

GlassFish is Open Source and was supported by Oracle after Oracle bought Sun Microsystems in 2010. However, in 2013 Oracle announced future termination of commercial support for GlassFish. Oracle is attempting to have commercial customers move over to Oracle's proprietary WebLogic Server. Oracle stated that GlassFish will continue to be the Java EE reference implementation.

There is a fear among developers that lack of commercial support for GlassFish will end its viability as a commercial product. As of this writing (in early 2016), however, support for Open Source GlassFish is continuing. The most recent release was in October 2015.

There are other alternatives that support Java EE, one is the WildFly application server (from RedHat; it was previously known as JBoss).

Next we will look at how to run GlassFish. This is included because we are using GlassFish for our Enterprise Java Beans (EJBs) and servlet examples.

4.11.2.1 How to Start GlassFish and Run an Application on GlassFish

First we have to start the GlassFish application server. Go to the GlassFish bin directory and type:

./asadmin start-domain

This will start the GlassFish application server. See Figure 4.1 to see how this command looks.

FIGURE 4.1 How to start GlassFish.

Now if you go back to the console window and type:

ps

then you will see something like this:

```
PID    TTY    TIME      CMD
2239   pts/0  00:00:00  bash
2318   pts/0  00:00:29  java
2397   pts/0  00:00:00  ps
```

the "java" at 2318 is the GlassFish application server (you will probably have a different number here).

Next we will go to the administration console. In your browser, go to:

http://localhost:4848

See Figure 4.2 for what this will look like. We will select "Deploy Application" to deploy a JAR file.

We have to select a particular JAR file to deploy. We will select a local file that we previously created ourselves (this might be an EJB or it might be a servlet). See Figure 4.3 for what this looks like.

Okay, now we have navigated through the menu to the directory that contains our very own JAR file. Select this JAR file as shown in Figure 4.4

After you choose the JAR file, you must go down to the bottom of the page and select OK before the deployment starts. Note that this can be off your screen (especially if you're using Linux inside a VM such as VirtualBox), so you'll have to scroll down. See Figure 4.5 to see what this looks like.

Finally, our JAR file has been deployed! We see a deployed file named helloworld in Figure 4.6

Note that you can do prints to the server log file from your EJB. Just do System.out.println and the results will be printed to your server log file.

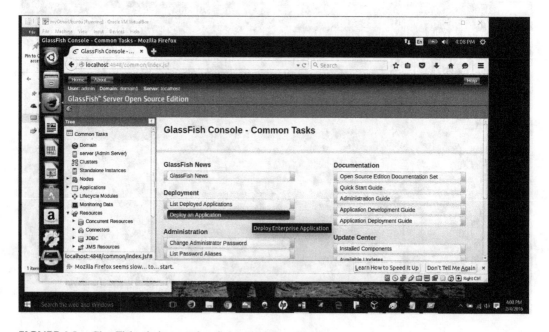

FIGURE 4.2   GlassFish admin console—Select deploy application.

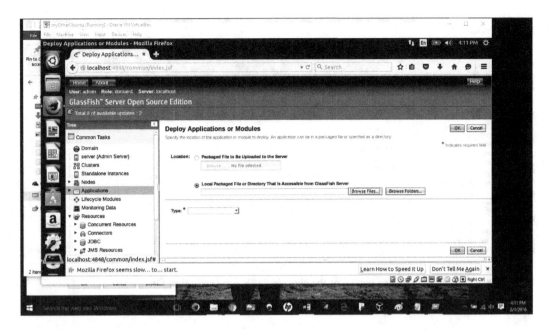

FIGURE 4.3 Deploying GlassFish application—Select local packaged file.

FIGURE 4.4 Deploying GlassFish application—Choosing the JAR file.

To see the server log file in the admin console, click on server. You will get the screen shown in Figure 4.7

Now, to see the contents of the server log, scroll down. See Figure 4.8 (if you want to show a subset of the contents, you can do a search instead). Note that Figure 4.8 shows that an EJB, in this case one of the Stateless Hello World examples, has been deployed. Note that it also has "top of getcount." This was a print statement I put at the top of a remote procedure call named "getcount"—my print statement looked like this:

System.out.println("top of getcount");

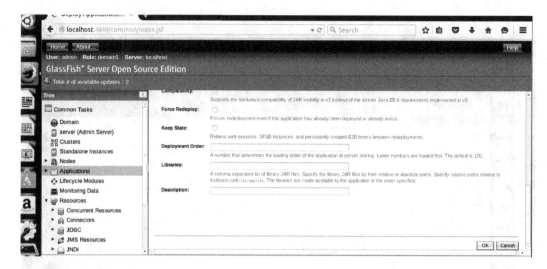

FIGURE 4.5   To deploy—Go to bottom of the choosing JAR page and select OK.

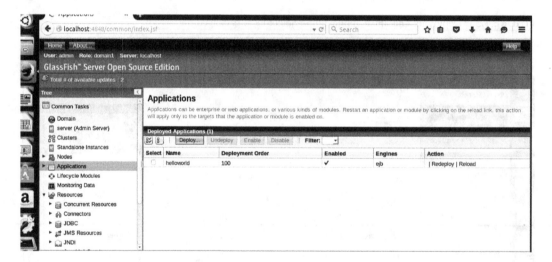

FIGURE 4.6   Now the application is deployed on GlassFish.

Alternately, we could have deployed our file without using the administration console menus: go to the GlassFish bin directory and type:

      ./asadmin list-applications

to see which applications are currently running.
    Then to deploy your own application, do:

      ./asadmin deploy yourjarfile.jar

Later, if you want to undeploy it, do:

      ./asadmin undeploy yourjarfile

FIGURE 4.7 How to select GlassFish server log.

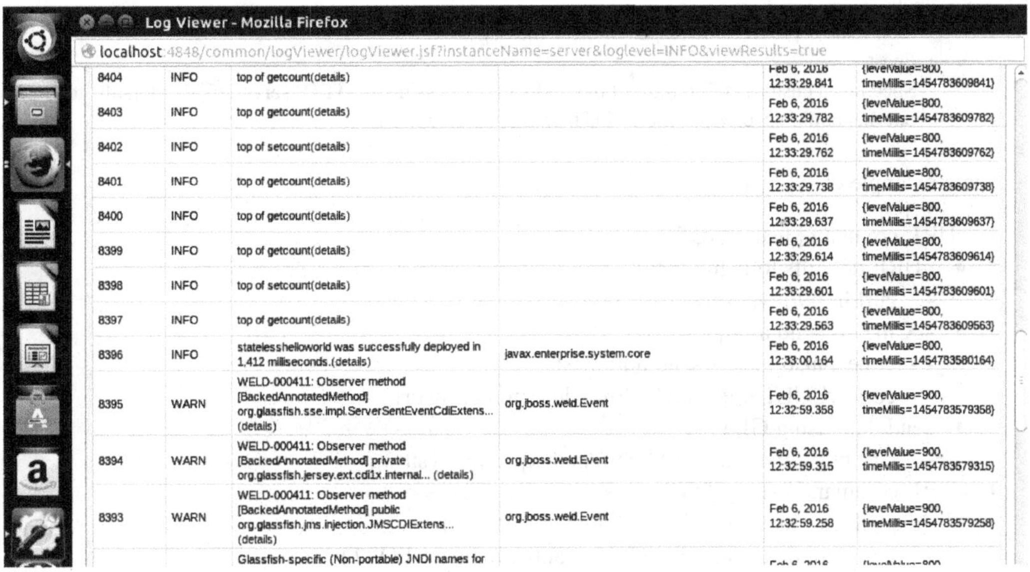

FIGURE 4.8 Example of GlassFish server log contents.

to check if it was really undeployed, do:

    ./asadmin list-applications

4.12 cURL

libcurl is a library that supports numerous web protocols, such as HTTP (GET, POST, PUT), HTTPS, LDAP, IMAP, among many others. It is intended to be used on the client side, and can be used (has bindings for) many programming languages, including C, C++, Python, PHP, Java. Libcurl is available on Windows and on Linux, as well as iOS and Android, among numerous other platforms.

cURL, which uses libcurl, is a command-line tool (runs on a console window) that accesses URLs. Using cURL, one can access a URL (such as a web page) and send/receive data to/from the URL, for example, using HTTP.

Both libcurl and curl are open source software.

Some cURL command-line options include:

> -d or –data
>> sends a POST request that contains the specified data to an HTTP server
>
> -d @filename or –data @filename
>> sends a POST request containing the data from the specified file to an HTTP server
>
> -h –help
>> lists command-line options with description
>
> -H or –header
>> Specifies an extra header to include in the HTTP request that is being sent to an HTTP server
>> for example: curl -H "X-My-Header-Name: NewHeaderData" myURL
>
> -H "Content-type: application/json"
>> says that the data being sent in the request will be in JSON format
>
> -H "Content-type: text/xml"
>> says that the data being sent in the request will be in XML format
>
> -i --include
>> include the HTTP header in the output
>
> -s –silent
>> don't show progress messages or error messages
>
> -X --request
>> Specifies a custom HTTP request method when accessing an HTTP server. cURL defaults to GET, but this could specify the use of PUT or DELETE instead.

Some example cURL commands:

- cURL command using GET:
  - cURL defaults to using get:
    - curl http://myhelloworld.com
  - –X means send a request
  - - - request also means send a request
    - curl –X GET http://myhelloworld.com/helloworld
  - send data using GET:
    - curl http://myhelloworld.com/path?query=mystring
- cURL command using POST:
  - –d send data using POST (-d defaults to POST)
  - - - data send data using POST (- - data defaults to POST)
    - curl –d "arg1=mystring&arg2=myotherstring" http://myhelloworld.com/path
  - cURL command using PUT:
    - –d send data using PUT
      - (-d defaults to POST, override with –X PUT or – - request PUT)
      - curl –X PUT –d "arg1=mystring&arg2=myotherstring" http://myhelloworld.com/path
  - - - data send data using PUT
    - (- -data defaults to POST, override with –X PUT or – - request PUT)
    - curl – - request PUT - - data "arg1=mystring" - - data "arg2=myotherstring" http://myhelloworld.com/path

- cURL/libcurl can handle both xml format and JSON format:
  - –H means send an HTTP header
  - HTTP clients use the HTTP "Accept" header to tell the HTTP server what kinds of data types they will accept (in the response body)
  - HTTP servers (when sending a response) use the "Content-Type" header to tell the client what data format the response contains.
  - However, HTTP clients can also use the "Content-Type" header. This is important when the HTTP client is actually sending data to the server as part of the request, for example, in a POST or a PUT request. It tells the server what format the data is in the request.
    - Set XML format:
      - curl –H "Accept: application/xml" –H "Content-Type: application/xml"
    - Set JSON format:
      - curl –H "Accept: application/json" –H "Content-Type: application/json"

EXERCISES

1. If you're using TCP/IP, does that mean you're not using the World Wide Web?
2. What is a security problem associated with sending your data in an HTTP GET?
3. When you get a 404 message from your browser, technologically speaking what does that mean?
4. Create an XML document that specifies the names and class standing (freshman, sophomore, junior, senior) of students in a Middleware course.
5. Create a JSON object that specifies the names and class standing (freshman, sophomore, junior, senior) of students in a Middleware course.
6. If the HTML document you are examining starts with "<!DOCTYPE html>," then which version of HTML are you using?
7. Create an HTML5 document containing a table that specifies the names and class standing (freshman, sophomore, junior, senior) of students in a Middleware course. Make the headers for the document purple and make the data in the document red.
8. Create a complex type for an XML Schema that specifies the names and class standing (freshman, sophomore, junior, senior) of a student.
9. If you wanted to send a JSON file to a server, what Internet Media Type (MIME type) would you use? What if you wanted to send an XML file to a server?
10. Given the base 64 encoded value: V2hv. Convert this back into its original binary number and explain each step.
11. Uniform Resource Identifiers (URIs) have "+" signs reserved. If you're sending a space character as data in a URI, how would it be encoded?
12. Why are both a Document Object Model (DOM) and a Browser Object Model (BOM) needed?
13. Why can't we just use our browsers to send GETs to our servers? Why do we have to use cURL?

CONCEPTUAL QUESTIONS

1. Why are Internet Media Types (MIME types) needed? Can you think of some alternative methods to sending a type field in an HTTP header?
2. When would JSON be preferred and when would XML be preferred? Use some web references to acquire various opinions and discuss this in detail.
3. Remember what you read in Chapter 3 about protocol layers. HTTP is in a layer that is on top of the TCP layer. Could what HTTP does be done instead inside, as a part of, TCP? Give reasons.
4. What are some alternatives to using cURL to send HTTP commands, especially if you drop the requirement that you're using the command line (the console)?

5. We've looked at the Internet Engineering Task Force, the World Wide Web Consortium, and the Internet Corporation for Assigned Names and Numbers. Are these connected in any way? Where do they derive their authority? Are they in any way connected with the International Standards Organization (ISO)/ International Electrotechnical Commission (IEC) or the International Telecommunication Union (ITU) or the Organization for the Advancement of Structured Information (OASIS) or the Object Management Group (OMG)? If not, do these authorities clash in any way? Use both web references and a formal literature review in your answer.

BIBLIOGRAPHY

AFRINIC (Internet Numbers Registry for Africa). 2016. Home page. https://www.afrinic.net/community/ig/icann-and-iana (accessed May 20, 2016).

Brain, M. and Crawford, S. 2016. How domain name servers work, how stuff works. http://computer.howstuffworks.com/dns3.htm (accessed May 20, 2016).

cURL. 2015. Home page. http://curl.haxx.se/ (accessed July 28, 2015).

Digital Ocean. 2013. What is nginx and why might I want to use it over apache? https://www.digitalocean.com/community/questions/what-is-nginx-and-why-might-i-want-to-use-it-over-apache (accessed May 21, 2016).

Digital Ocean. 2016. How to install MySql on Ubuntu 14.04. https://www.digitalocean.com/community/tutorials/how-to-install-mysql-on-ubuntu-14-04 (accessed June 22, 2016).

Ecma International. 2015. The JSON data interchange format. http://www.ecma-international.org/publications/standards/Ecma-404.htm (accessed August 29, 2015).

GlassFish. 2013. GlassFish server open source edition: Application deployment guide. https://glassfish.java.net/docs/4.0/application-deployment-guide.pdf (accessed February 4, 2016).

GlassFish. 2015. World's first Java EE 7 application server. 2015. https://glassfish.java.net/ (accessed February 4, 2016).

Hacking on HTTP from the Command Line. 2015. 9 Uses for cURL worth knowing. http://httpkit.com/resources/HTTP-from-the-Command-Line/ (accessed July 28, 2015).

Home and Learn. 2016. The Browser Object Model. http://www.homeandlearn.co.uk/JS/browser_object_model.html (accessed May 21, 2016).

IANA (Internet Assigned Numbers Authority). 2015. Media types. https://www.iana.org/assignments/media-types/media-types.xhtml (accessed August 29, 2015).

IANA (Internet Assigned Numbers Authority). 2016. Root servers. https://www.iana.org/domains/root/servers (accessed May 20, 2016).

Internet Corporation for Assigned Names and Numbers. 2016. Home page. https://www.icann.org/ (accessed May 20, 2016).

IETF (Internet Engineering Task Force). 1996. Multipurpose internet mail extension (MIME) part one: Format of internet message bodies. https://tools.ietf.org/html/rfc2045 (accessed May 3, 2016).

IETF (Internet Engineering Task Force). 1999. Hypertext Transfer Protocol—HTTP/1.1 RFC 2616. https://tools.ietf.org/html/rfc2616 (accessed May 21, 2016).

IETF (Internet Engineering Task Force). 2005. Uniform resource identifier (URI): Generic syntax, RFC 3986. https://tools.ietf.org/html/rfc3986#page-12 (accessed May 3, 2016).

IETF (Internet Engineering Task Force). 2014. The JavaScript Object Notation (JSON) data interchange format, RFC 7159. http://www.rfc-editor.org/rfc/rfc7159.txt (accessed August 29, 2015).

InterNIC. 2016. InterNIC—Public information regarding internet domain name registration services. https://www.internic.net/ (accessed May 20, 2016).

InterNIC FAQs. 2016. The domain name system: A non-technical explanation—Why universal resolvability is important. https://www.internic.net/faqs/authoritative-dns.html (accessed May 20, 2016).

JSON. 2015. Introducing JSON. http://www.json.org/ (accessed August 29, 2015).

Krill, P. 2014. Nginx has big plans for JavaScript, InfoWorld. http://www.infoworld.com/article/2838008/javascript/nginx-has-big-plans-for-javascript.html (accessed May 21, 2016).

Microsoft. 2008. Register the 2007 office system file format MIME types on servers. https://technet.microsoft.com/en-us/library/ee309278(office.12).aspx (accessed August 29, 2015).

Microsoft. 2016. Running PHP on IIS. https://php.iis.net/ (accessed May 21, 2016).

Mono Project. 2016. Cross platform, open source, NET project. http://www.mono-project.com/ (accessed May 21, 2016).

Oracle. 2016. MySQL 5.6 Reference manual. https://dev.mysql.com/doc/refman/5.6/en/connecting-disconnecting. html (accessed June 22, 2016).

Sysoev, I. 2015. Launching nginScript and looking ahead, Ngnix. https://www.nginx.com/blog/launching-nginscript-and-looking-ahead/ (accessed May 21, 2016).

Tutorials Point. 2016a. HTML forms. http://www.tutorialspoint.com/html/html_forms.htm (accessed May 21, 2016).

Tutorials Point. 2016b. XML DOM tutorial. http://www.tutorialspoint.com/dom/ (accessed May 21, 2016).

Vaughan-Nichols, S. 2013. *Oracle abandons commercial support for GlassFish JEE server, Linux and Open Source* ZDNet. http://www.zdnet.com/article/oracle-abandons-commercial-support-for-glassfish-jee-server/ (accessed February 5, 2016).

W3C. 2004. XML schema part 0: Primer second edition. http://www.w3.org/TR/xmlschema-0/#CreatDt (accessed August 29, 2015).

W3C. 2004. XML schema part 1: Structures second edition. http://www.w3.org/TR/xmlschema-1/#Instance_Document_Constructions (accessed August 29, 2015).

W3C. 2015. W3C DOM4. https://www.w3.org/TR/dom/#introduction-to-the-dom (accessed May 20, 2016).

W3 Schools. 2016a. HTML(5) Tutorial. http://www.w3schools.com/html/ (accessed May 21, 2016).

W3 Schools. 2016b. HTML forms. http://www.w3schools.com/html/html_forms.asp (accessed May 21, 2016).

W3 Schools. 2016c. JavaScript HTML DOM tutorial. http://www.w3schools.com/js/js_htmldom.asp (accessed May 21, 2016).

W3 Schools. 2016d. JavaScript window—The Browser Object Model. http://www.w3schools.com/js/js_window.asp (accessed May 21, 2016).

W3 Schools. 2016e. JSON tutorial. http://www.w3schools.com/json/ (accessed May 21, 2016).

W3 Schools. 2016f. What is HTML? http://www.w3schools.com/html/html_intro.asp (accessed May 21, 2016).

W3 Schools. 2016g. XML DOM tutorial. http://www.w3schools.com/xml/dom_intro.asp (accessed May 21, 2016).

W3 Schools. 2016h. XML tutorial. http://www.w3schools.com/xml/ (accessed May 21, 2016).

5 Security Basics

5.1 JUST WHY SHOULD ANYONE CARE ABOUT SECURITY, ANYWAY?

Once upon a time, the internet was innocent.

The first computer virus that was released outside the lab was the Elk Cloner virus, written by high school student Rick Skrenta back in 1982 for Apple II computers (see Leyden 2012).

Those of us who have, *ahem*, been around computing for a long time remember those innocent days. It all reminds me of Tom Bombadil from *Lord of the Rings*, the book not the movie ☺:

Eldest, that's what I am... Tom remembers the first raindrop and the first acorn... He knew the dark under the stars when it was fearless—before the Dark Lord came from Outside.

Sigh. Nowadays hackers steal your cloud credentials to generate bitcoins (see Rashid 2014).

You can just never be absolutely sure your data is secure. ☺ As an example, a few years ago a lecturer in my department told me the following story: he was teaching a junior level computer science course and they happened to talk about computer security one day. He had recently spent a good bit of time setting up his work desktop, with an emphasis on security. He dared his students to hack his computer. Two of them hacked it in less than an hour.

Do I have to say more?

Let's jump into some things that can sorta, kinda help you keep your data secure.

Just don't trust it all too much. ☺

5.2 SYMMETRIC KEY CRYPTOGRAPHY AND ASYMMETRIC KEY/PUBLIC KEY CRYPTOGRAPHY

Symmetric key cryptography uses the same key to encrypt the text and to decrypt the text. This has the problem that both sides have to have some way to know the key (which is where public key cryptography comes in).

With public key cryptography, two mathematically related keys are produced: a public key and a private key.

A message that is encrypted using the public key can only be decrypted by its associated private key. A message that is encrypted with the private key can only be decrypted by the public key. So this method is also called asymmetric key cryptography since different keys are used by the encryptor and the decryptor.

Public keys are often used to provide a secure connection between two entities, so that the two entities can use this connection to negotiate the use of a Symmetric key. This is done because encryption of data using a typical symmetric key algorithm is less computationally intensive than using a public key algorithm.

5.3 HASH (MESSAGE DIGEST) FUNCTIONS

A hash function creates a fixed-length compressed value from an arbitrary-length digital message using a mathematical function. The hash value is much smaller than the original digital message, so a hash is often called a "digest."

Well-known hash functions include:

- Message Digest (MD)
  - MD5 has been widely used—128 bit (16 byte) hash value
    - Others include: MD6, MD4, MD2

- In 2004, successful attacks on MD5 were reported, so MD5 was no longer recommended for use
- Secure Hash Algorithm (SHA)
  - SHA1 has been widely used—160-bit (20 byte) hash value
    - Successful attacks reported in 2005, SHA1 will be replaced in major browsers by 2017
  - SHA2 family SHA256, SHA512, etc., based on number of bits in the hash value
  - SHA3 released by National Institute of Standards in 2015

Message Digest algorithms are used to create Digital Signatures and Message Authentication Codes (MACs).

5.4 DIGITAL SIGNATURES AND MESSAGE AUTHENTICATION CODES

Digital signatures are used to tell the recipient of a digital message that the message really came from the person it was supposed to come from, and that the message hasn't been tampered with since that person sent it.

To create a digital signature, the digital message is first hashed, using an algorithm such as SHA-1 or etc. Then the sender's private key is used to encrypt the hash. The reason only the hash is encrypted is that the hash is a fixed-length value whereas the original message may be an arbitrary length.

Then the message is sent to the recipient along with the digital signature.

The recipient of the message and digital signature uses the sender's public key to decrypt the digital signature. Then the message itself is hashed. The hash from the message is compared to the hash from the decrypted digital signature. If the two are the same, then the recipient accepts the message.

A Message Authentication Code (MAC) is different from a Digital Signature in that it uses a secret (symmetric) key that is shared by both sender and receiver, whereas a Digital Signature is encrypted using a private key and decrypted using a public key.

With a MAC, since both sender and receiver must both have access to the same secret key, any receiver that can verify a MAC value is able to generate MAC values of its own. So it is possible that the receiver could later "pretend" to be the (original) sender to some third party.

With a digital signature, it's possible to have messages verified by a receiver (with access to the public key) without having that receiver being able to later "pretend" to be the (original) sender to some third party.

One well-known MAC is the Hash-based Message Authentication Code (HMAC) that combines a hashing function (MD5, SHA1, SHA256, etc.) with a secret key. It is calculated generally as follows:

```
HMAC (key, message) =
    hash (
               (secret key XOR outer-padding) concatenated with
                   hash(
                           (secret key XOR inner padding) concatenated with message
                   )
            )
    where
    outer padding = 0x5c0x5c...0x5c (block long hex constant)
    Inner padding = 0x360x36...0x36 (block long hex constant)
```

5.5 PUBLIC KEY INFRASTRUCTURE AND CERTIFICATE AUTHORITIES

When a client wishes to connect to a server on a network, a third party that is trusted by both client and server verifies the server's credentials so the client will know that the server is who it says it is. The trusted third party is called a *Certification Authority*.

The server's credentials are actually verified in advance of any desired communication. At some point, the user who owns the server issues a Certificate Signing Request including the user's credentials and the server the user wants to have verified to a Certification Authority. The Certification Authority then verifies the user's credentials—it may run some outside checks about the user's business in order to do this.

Once a user's credentials have been verified by the certificate authority, the certificate authority will issue a certificate. The certificate contains the name of the user (as well as other information) and the user's public key. The Certification Authority digitally signs this certificate.

Note that the user's public key and associated private key can have previously been generated by the user and the public key sent on to the Certification Authority, or the Certification Authority can generate the public key and private key, and send both keys separately to the user (as well as including the public key in the certificate).

Once the user has a certificate, the user's server can present that certificate to any client that wants to connect to the user's server.

When a client wants to connect to that server, the server sends the certificate to the client. The client then verifies the issuer of the certificate to its own list of trusted Certification Authorities.

To the client who receives this certificate, the certificate says that the certification authority vouches that the user who is named in the certificate truly owns the private key that is associated with the public key in the certificate.

The Certification Authority is called the *root of trust*. That is, the Certification Authority itself is the trusted third party. A Certificate issued by the root Certification Authority itself is called a *root certificate*.

Note that the root certificate is itself signed, it is self-signed by the Certification Authority. Often there is a separate *signing certificate* that is signed by the root certificate—in this case the Certification Authority may take the root certificate offline and store it. Then the signing certificate will be used to sign server certificates.

The Certification Authority can also certify other entities, called Registration Authorities (or subordinate Certification Authorities or intermediate Certification Authorities), to issue certificates—or the Certification Authority can issue certificates itself.

So if a given Certification Authority issued the certificate, and the client finds that particular Certification Authority on its own list of trusted Certification Authorities, then all is well, the client believes that the server is who it says it is.

However, if the given Certification Authority is not on the client's own list of trusted Certification Authorities, then the client must look at the given Certification Authority's (the issuing Certification Authority's) own certificate and see if that was issued by a trusted Certification Authority. (If this is the case, then the issuing Certification Authority was a subordinate Certification Authority to the original trusted third-party Certification Authority.) If so, then all is well. If not, then the certificate is not accepted.

Note that web browsers come with the signing certificates (or root certificates) of many Certificate Authorities already installed inside them.

To make this procedure work, a Certificate Database is needed on the Certificate Authority that saves the certificate requests that have been issued and whether or not they were later revoked.

A Certificate Store is necessary to save certificates that were issued to the user, on the user's local machine.

How to do public key infrastructure is specified in standard ITU-T X.509, also see IETF RFC 5280.

Contents of a typical digital certificate are as follows:

- Serial Number: identifier number that identifies the certificate (can later be used for revocation)
- Subject: The entity (for example, server belonging to a user) that is being identified
- Algorithm used to create the signature
- Signature itself
- Issuer: trusted third party that issued the certificate
- Validity period
- Public Key: public key of the entity being identified
- Thumbprint Algorithm: algorithm used to hash the public key certificate
- Thumbprint (fingerprint): the hash of the public key certificate itself

A digital certificate can also include other information about the user.

If a certificate must be revoked, then the Certification Authority creates a Certification Revocation List (CRL) that is digitally signed by the Certification Authority and that identifies revoked certificates by certification identification number. CRLs are typically issued periodically and can become quite large.

5.6   TRANSPORT LAYER SECURITY AND SECURE SOCKETS LAYER

According to Information Security Stack Exchange (2011):

> HTTPS is HTTP-within-SSL/TLS. SSL (TLS) establishes a secured, bidirectional tunnel for arbitrary binary data between two hosts. HTTP is a protocol for sending requests and receiving answers, each request and answer consisting of detailed headers and (possibly) some content. HTTP is meant to run over a bidirectional tunnel for arbitrary binary data; when that tunnel is an SSL/TLS connection, then the whole is called "HTTPS."

Both Transport Layer Security (TLS) and Secure Sockets Layer (SSL) are intended to provide confidentiality and message authentication over a network link (TLS is a follow on to/descendant of SSL). In the network protocol stack, TLS and SSL run on top of TCP/IP, but below network protocols such as HTTP.

SSL dates from the mid-1990s, it had gotten up to SSL version 3.0 by 1996. TLS is the follow on to SSL, with TLS version 1.0 dating from 1999, however, it was different enough from SSL 3.0 that they couldn't talk directly to each other. However, TLS does allow downgrading to SSL 3.0 via negotiation. TLS 1.2 is the most recent version of TLS at this writing, it dates from 2008. RFC 6175 (see IETF 2011) prohibits TLS 1.2 from negotiating the use of SSL 2.0.

RFC 6175 lists the deficiencies of SSL 2.0 that should prevent it being used as follows:

- It uses MD5 which is no longer considered secure
- It is subject to man-in-the-middle attacks that select weak cryptography algorithm choices because it does not protect handshake messages
- The same key is used for message integrity and message encryption (a problem if the cryptography algorithm choice is not strong)
- It is subject to man-in-the-middle attacks that can terminate a session, and the communicating entities cannot determine whether the session was ended legitimately.

5.6.1   BUT HOW DOES TLS WORK?

TLS achieves confidentiality through encryption, authentication through the use of public key certificates, and integrity through the use of MACs.

Let's assume you're using a web browser as a client, connecting to some kind of web server.

TLS consists of several sub-protocols, see RFC 5246, IETF (2008b):

- Record protocol—this protocol takes a message, breaks it into blocks, compresses the data (optional), adds a MAC, then encrypts the whole and transmits it
- The following protocols operate on top of the Record layer:
  - Handshake protocol negotiates what algorithms, etc., will be used during a session
  - Alert protocol—sends error messages, can be warnings or else fatal errors (with connection terminated). Some possible errors are:
    - Bad certificate
    - Certificate revoked
    - Decryption error—unable to verify a signature or validate a message
    - Record overflow
  - Cipher spec protocol—changes cipher strategies/signals the beginning of secure communication
  - Application data protocol—data messages from the application are carried by the record layer and treated as transparent data

At the beginning of a connection, the handshake protocol does the following:

- Hello message from client to server, hello response from server to client:
  - Used to negotiate:
    - TSL or SSL version to be used,
    - Session ID,
    - Cipher Suite
      - Cipher suites are combination of cryptographic algorithms for:
        - Key exchange (Diffie-Hellman, RSA, etc.)
        - Cipher (AES, etc.)
        - MAC (SHA256, etc.)
    - Compression Method
  - As part of the Hello exchange, the server sends a certificate to the client, this includes the server's public key (for example, RSA)
- The Client then does the following:
  - Generates a premaster secret—see Information Security Stack Exchange (2014b):
    - This 48-byte premaster secret is generated by concatenating protocol versions with some randomly generated bytes.
    - The client then encrypts the 48-byte premaster secret with the server's RSA public key (from the certificate).
  - Sends it to the server
- The Server decrypts the premaster secret using its private key.
- Both client and server generate a master secret using the premaster secret, then immediately delete the premaster secret.
- The client and the server use the master secret to generate the session keys—these are symmetric keys used to encrypt and decrypt data transferred during the session (AES, for example).
- The client can now send the server a message that is encrypted with the session key and authenticated with the MAC (for example, HMAC with SHA256).
- The server determines that the MAC was authentic, and similarly sends back an encrypted message with a MAC that the client also determines is authentic.

5.7   CRYPTOGRAPHIC MESSAGE SYNTAX

Cryptographic Message Syntax (CMS) is used to support certificate-based key management in X.509 Public Key Infrastructure (among others). CMS supports various architectures for certificate-based key management by providing an encapsulation mechanism that supports encryption and digital signatures.

It allows one encapsulation envelope to be nested inside another, and it allows encapsulated data to be digitally signed.

In CMS, the data that is encapsulated (this is called the content) is associated with an identifier that describes its type (this is called the content-type). Although CMS can support many different specialized content-types, normally the content-type is specified using Abstract Syntax Notation One (ASN.1).

ASN.1 is a formal notation that describes data that is transmitted by communications protocols.

Kaliski (1993) and MSDN (2016a) list a few basic types and string types that are defined in ASN.1. Basic types listed include (among others):

- BIT STRING—an arbitrary string of 0s and 1s
- BOOLEAN
- INTEGER
- NULL
- OBJECT IDENTIFIER—a sequence of integers that uniquely identify an object
- OCTET STRING—an arbitrary string of 8 bit values

String types listed include (among others):

- IA5String—an arbitrary string of International Alphabet 5 (ASCII) characters
- PrintableString—an arbitrary character string that contains only printable characters
- UTF8String—a string with characters in UTF-8 format
  - Uses Unicode Transformation Format 8 (UTF-8)
    - UTF-8 is the most widely used character encoding on the internet
      - Uses 8 bit blocks to represent a character
      - UTF-8 encoding is recommended by the W3C for XML and HTML

The CMS values are encoded using Basic Encoding Rules (BER encoding). These were the original rules specified in the ASN.1 standard to encode data into a data stream. Using BER, information is encoded using Type-Length-Value (TLV) encodings, which consist of a Type identifier, a Length field, the data value itself, then (where it's needed) an end-of-data marker. cn_equals_directory_manager (2006) gives the following example of ASN.1 BER encoding:

- The OCTET STRING "Hello" is represented as:
  - 04 05 48 65 6C 6C 6F
    - 0x04 is the Type identifier for OCTET_STRING
    - 0x05 is the length field (specifies 5 bytes)
    - 48 65 6C 6C 6F are the IA5 (ASCII) characters for "Hello"

A digital envelope uses two layers of encryption. The message itself is encoded using symmetric encryption. The symmetric key to use for decryption is sent over the network, but it is itself encoded (and decoded on the other end) using public key encryption. Thus, no plain text communication of the symmetric key takes place.

The six basic types provided by CMS are as follows:

1. Data—arbitrary strings of bytes, usually encapsulated in one of the other types
2. Signed-Data—includes the data plus zero or more digital signatures

- More than one digital signature is possible, from different signers
  - Any number of signers can sign any type of content
- A hash (message digest) is computed on the content
- The hash (message digest) is digitally signed using the signer's private key
3. Enveloped-Data
  - A digital envelope includes:
    - Data encrypted using a symmetric key
    - The symmetric key to decrypt the content is separately encrypted for each recipient using the recipient's public key
4. Digested-Data—includes the content plus a hash (message digest) of the content
5. Encrypted-Data—the encrypted data itself, keys are sent in some other way
  - A method for key management MUST be used! CMS does not define any particular key management method
6. Authenticated-Data—this consists of the content, MAC, and encrypted authentication keys for one or more recipient

The Data format looks like:

- Content-type=DATA
- The data itself

The Signed-Data format looks like:

- Content-type=SIGNED-DATA
- Hash (Message Digest) algorithm (can be more than one)
- The data itself
- Digital signatures (can be more than one)

The Enveloped-data format looks like:

- Encrypted-data

The Authenticated-data format looks like:

- Content-type=AUTHENTICATED-DATA
- (optional) Information about the recipient—may contain digital certificates, etc.
  - Present only if needed by key management algorithm
- MAC algorithm used by the originator
- (optional) Message Digest Algorithm
  - Author attributes field must be included if Message Digest Algorithm is included. Contains:
    - Content-type of information being authenticated
    - Message digest of the content
- MAC itself
- Encrypted Authentication Key for one or more recipients

An MAC is a value created by a message sender using the message and a secret key (symmetric key). The calculated MAC is sent along with the message to the recipient.

Then the message recipient uses the message and the same secret key to regenerate the MAC. If the MAC value is the same as the MAC value received from the sender, then the message is from the correct sender. Hash-based MACs that use a secret key together with a hash function (such as MD5 or SHA1) have become common. Other techniques such as DES encryption were used in the past.

In this case, however, according to RFC 5652, if any information is being authenticated in addition to the content, then a message digest is calculated on the content, and the message digest of the content plus the other information are authenticated together using the authentication key—the result is used as the MAC.

EXERCISES

1. What is the primary advantage of public key cryptography over symmetric key cryptography?
2. What is the difference between a Digital Signature and a Message Authentication Code?
3. How does a client find third parties to trust?
4. How might one actually do a SHA1 hash? Is there any way to do it without writing your own code?
5. Is using a Certificate Authority always safe?
6. TLS uses Public Key Cryptography to authenticate, but then it uses MACs for integrity. Why didn't it use MACs to authenticate?
7. Given the following example of ASN.1 BER encoding:
   04 05 48 65 6C 6C 6F
   What data is actually being sent?
8. Encode "STUDY" in ASN.1 BER encoding.
9. What is International Reference Alphabet, otherwise known as International Alphabet 5 (IA5)?
10. What is Unicode?
11. Why do you think a certificate authority might revoke a certificate?

CONCEPTUAL QUESTIONS

1. How might HTTPS and TLS/SSL apply to middleware? What can middleware do to affect security that HTTPS and TLS/SSL don't do?
2. In depth, what are the primary advantages of public key infrastructure certificates using asymmetric key cryptography compared to symmetric key cryptography? Are there any disadvantages, that is, is there anything that symmetric key cryptography gets you that PKI certificates and asymmetric key cryptography don't?
3. Why do you think a standard like ASN.1 is needed?
4. Google for Certificate Authorities, that is, "trusted third parties" who issue digital certificates. Several big commercial companies do this kind of work. Who are these certificate authorities, and why should anyone trust them? Do you trust them? What steps do they take to make people trust them?
5. What is the difference(s) between International Reference Alphabet (International Alphabet 5) and Unicode?

BIBLIOGRAPHY

Antivirus Ware. 2016. History of computer viruses. http://www.antivirusware.com/articles/history-computer-viruses.htm (accessed May 7, 2016).

cn_equals_directory_manager. 2006. A quick introduction to ASN.1 BER. https://blogs.oracle.com/directory-manager/entry/a_quick_introduction_to_asn (accessed March 24, 2017).

Dewan, M. 2002. An idiots guide to public key infrastructure. https://www.giac.org/paper/gsec/2171/idiots-guide-public-key-infrastructure/103692 (accessed April 30, 2016).

Forouzan, B. 2008. *Introduction to Cryptography and Network Security*. McGraw-Hill Education, Columbus, OH.

Indiana University. 2015. What are signing and root (digital) certificates of authenticity? Knowledge Base. https://kb.iu.edu/d/auaw (accessed April 30, 2016).

Information Security Stack Exchange. 2011. What's the difference between SSL, TLS, and HTTPS. http://security.stackexchange.com/questions/5126/whats-the-difference-between-ssl-tls-and-https (accessed May 7, 2016).

Information Security Stack Exchange. 2014a. How does SSL/TLS work? http://security.stackexchange.com/questions/20803/how-does-ssl-tls-work (accessed May 7, 2016).

Information Security Stack Exchange. 2014b. How is the premaster secret used in TLS generated? http://security.stackexchange.com/questions/63971/how-is-the-premaster-secret-used-in-tls-generated (accessed May 7, 2016).

IETF (Internet Engineering Task Force). 1992. The MD5 message-digest algorithm. https://www.ietf.org/rfc/rfc1321.txt (accessed May 1, 2016).

IETF (Internet Engineering Task Force). 1999. The TLS protocol, RFC 2246. https://www.ietf.org/rfc/rfc2246.txt (accessed May 7, 2016).

IETF (Internet Engineering Task Force). 2008a. Internet X.509 public key infrastructure certificate and certificate revocation list (CRL) profile, RFC 5280. https://tools.ietf.org/html/rfc5280 (accessed April 30, 2016).

IETF (Internet Engineering Task Force). 2008b. The Transport Layer Security (TLS) Protocol Version 1.2, RFC 5246. https://tools.ietf.org/html/rfc5246 (accessed May 7, 2016).

IETF (Internet Engineering Task Force). 2009. Cryptographic message syntax (CMS), RFC 5652. https://tools.ietf.org/html/rfc5652 (accessed May 1, 2016).

IETF (Internet Engineering Task Force). 2011. Prohibiting secure sockets layer (SSL) version 2.0, RFC 6176. SANS Institute. https://tools.ietf.org/html/rfc6176 (accessed May 7, 2016).

International Telecommunications Union. 2012. Recommendation X.509. https://www.itu.int/rec/T-REC-X.509-201210-I/en (accessed April 30, 2016).

International Telecommunications Union (ITU)-Telecommunications Standardization Sector. 1988. X.208 specification of Abstract Syntax Notation One (ASN.1), CCITT Recommendation X.208. International Telecommunications Union Publications, Geneva, Switzerland..

International Telecommunications Union (ITU)-Telecommunications Standardization Sector. 2002. Information technology—ASN.1 encoding rules: Specification of basic encoding r(BER), canonical encoding rules (CER) and distinguished encoding rules (DER), X.690. http://www.itu.int/ITU-T/studygroups/com17/languages/X.690-0207.pdf (accessed May 1 2016).

International Telecommunications Union (ITU)-Telecommunications Standardization Sector. 2016. Introduction to ASN.1. http://www.itu.int/en/ITU-T/asn1/Pages/introduction.aspx (accessed May 1, 2016).

Kaliski, B.S. Jr. 1993. A layman's guide to a subset of ASN.1, BER, and DER. An RSA laboratories technical note. http://luca.ntop.org/Teaching/Appunti/asn1.html (accessed May 1, 2016).

Krawetz, N. 2007. *Introduction to Network Security*. Charles River Media/Thomson Learning, Boston, MA.

Lawton, S. 2015. Introduction to public key infrastructure (PKI), Tom's IT Pro. http://www.tomsitpro.com/articles/public-key-infrastructure-introduction,2-884.html (accessed April 30, 2016).

Leyden, J. 2012. The 30-year-old prank that became the first computer virus. *The Register*. http://www.theregister.co.uk/2012/12/14/first_virus_elk_cloner_creator_interviewed/ (accessed May 7, 2016).

McKinley, H. 2003. *SSL and TLS: A Beginners Guide*. Sans Institute InfoSec Reading Room. https://www.sans.org/reading-room/whitepapers/protocols/ssl-tls-beginners-guide-1029 (accessed May 7, 2016).

Microsoft Support. 2016. Description of symmetric and asymmetric encryption. https://support.microsoft.com/en-us/kb/246071 (accessed May 1, 2016).

Morton, B. 2011. Is it SSL, TLS or HTTPS? Entrust. https://www.entrust.com/is-it-ssl-tls-or-https/ (accessed May 7, 2016).

MSDN. 2016a. ASN.1 type system. https://msdn.microsoft.com/en-us/library/windows/desktop/bb540789(v=vs.85).aspx (accessed May 1, 2016).

MSDN. 2016b. Managing certificates with certificate stores. https://msdn.microsoft.com/en-us/library/windows/desktop/aa386971(v=vs.85).aspx (accessed April 30, 2016).

MSDN. 2016c. Public key infrastructure. https://msdn.microsoft.com/en-us/library/windows/desktop/bb427432(v=vs.85).aspx (accessed May 1, 2016).

Rashid, F.Y. 2014. How hackers target cloud services for bitcoin profit. *Security Week*. http://www.securityweek.com/how-hackers-target-cloud-services-bitcoin-profit (accessed May 7, 2016).

Schlawack, H. 2014. The sorry state Of SSL. https://hynek.me/talks/tls/ (accessed May 7, 2016).

SearchSecurity. 2016. Message authentication code (MAC). http://searchsecurity.techtarget.com/definition/message-authentication-code-MAC (accessed May 1, 2016).

Shinder, D. 2003. Understanding the role of the PKI. http://www.windowsecurity.com/articles-tutorials/authentication_and_encryption/Understanding_the_Role_of_the_PKI.html (accessed April 30, 2016).

SSL Shopper. 2016. SSL certificate reviews. https://www.sslshopper.com/certificate-authority- reviews.html (accessed April 30, 2016).

StackOverflow. 2010. Linux equivalent for the windows certificate store. http://stackoverflow.com/questions/4267573/linux-equivalent-for-the-windows-certificate-store (accessed April 30, 2016).

Symantec. 2014. How does SSL work? What is an SSL handshake? http://www.symantec.com/connect/blogs/how-does-ssl-work-what-ssl-handshake (accessed May 7, 2016).

Szmanski, P. 2007. How TLS protocol works. *Network World.* http://www.networkworld.com/article/2303078/lan-wan/how-tls-protocol-works.html (accessed May 7, 2016).

Techopedia. 2016. Digital envelope. https://www.techopedia.com/definition/18859/digital-envelope (accessed May 1, 2016).

TechTarget. 2016. Digital signature. http://searchsecurity.techtarget.com/definition/digital-signature (accessed May 1, 2016).

Tolkien, J.R.R. 1956. *The Lord of the Rings.* George Allen and Unwin, London, UK.

TutorialsPoint. 2016. Cryptography digital signatures. http://www.tutorialspoint.com/cryptography/cryptography_digital_signatures.htm (accessed May 1, 2016).

6 Microsoft Technologies Basics

6.1 MICROSOFT "WORLD" VERSUS THE REST OF THE WORLD

Over the years, Microsoft has had a number of business reasons to have their technologies be just a little different from other companies. For one thing, for many years they owned the desktop operating system market. So there was a big incentive to make technologies that mapped into the Windows operating system, and not nearly as many incentives to make sure that all those technologies also mapped into Linux, or Solaris, or OS/2 (which hasn't been supported for several years now, although I believe it still has some legacy places where it's being used). Remember that Microsoft has been a very important driver of the PC industry for three decades; other operating systems have come and gone in that same time period.

The world of Middleware has seen several different Microsoft offerings. Back in the 1990s, Distributed Component Object Model (DCOM) was a major competitor to CORBA (Common Object Request Broker Architecture). Starting in 2002, .NET Remoting became a widely used Microsoft middleware. Then in 2006, Microsoft released Windows Communication Foundation, which has been a competitor to JAX-WS, JAX-RS, and AJAX, while .NET Remoting has been a Microsoft competitor to CORBA and to Enterprise Java Beans.

We're going to look at .NET Remoting in Chapter 8, then at Windows Communication Foundation in Chapters 10 and 12. Here in this chapter, however, we're going to do an overview of some Windows technologies that will provide you with some background later on for understanding these Microsoft middleware technologies. And what's more important, it will give you some essential background you may need later on when you actually *use* these Microsoft middleware technologies.

6.2 DYNAMIC LINK LIBRARY FILES AND WINDOWS SIDE BY SIDE

Dynamic Link Library (DLL) files are what Microsoft used to implement a *shared library*. A shared library contains library routines that are stored separately from the calling program executable (.exe in Microsoft Windows) files. The library routines called by the calling program .exe file are not loaded into memory until runtime. The library routines are stored separately from the .exe file. That way the same library files can be shared by different .exe files.

The alternative to a shared library is a static library. With a static library, the library routines are compiled, and the calling program is compiled; then the calling program is linked together with the library routines by the linker, and included together in a single .exe file. A separate .exe file that also needed the same library routines as the first .exe file would have to link them together into its own .exe file. This means that there can be multiple copies of the same library routines on the same hard drive (or flash memory), one copy of the library routines for the first .exe file, and another copy of the library routines for the second .exe file. Having multiple copies of the same thing at the same time is a waste of memory, both hard disk (flash) and RAM (after the .exe file is loaded into RAM in order to run). So the .dll files (shared libraries) were intended to save the 'multiple copies of library routines' problem.

However, the use of .dll files by Microsoft led to a strange situation known as "DLL Hell." One example of this is a situation called "DLL Stomping": When installing Application B sometime after Application A was installed, the .dll file associated with Application B (which has the same name as the .dll file associated with Application A) overwrote the Application A .dll file. Unfortunately, Application B's .dll file is an older version of the .dll file that is used by Application A. So Application A no longer works.

The main fix for this is the Windows Side by Side directory (WinSxS). Go to \Windows\WinSxS to see this directory in either Windows 7 or Windows 8. Here is an example from the computer where I'm typing this—as I write this I'm using Windows 8.1:

\Windows\WinSxS\
x86_wpf-windowsbase_31bf3856ad364e35_6.3.9600.16384_none_ec0cd16b635fb4bd

contains the file:

WindowsBase.dll   Date modified: 7/6/2015 at 8:07am

It also contains the directory:

\Windows\WinSxS\
x86_wpf-windowsbase_31bf3856ad364e35_6.3.9600.17810_none_ec54726d632a972e

which contains the file:

WindowsBase.dll   Date modified: 4/30/2015 at 3:35pm

So we have two different .dll files, with the same name, each with a different date and inside a directory with a really long horrible name. These names are "strong names" and are generated by using the private key that comes with the public key distributed with the assembly.

The Windows Side by Side allows an application to keep its older version of the .dll file, and continue to use it, when an updated .dll file of the same name has been installed.

By the way, here is a helpful trick you can use to find out which version of Windows you've got: Google (or Bing) the following string, "Which Windows operating system am I running" and the first result will (probably) be the following web page:

http://windows.microsoft.com/en-us/windows/which-operating-system

which will tell you which version of Windows you have.

Of course you could always just go directly to this web page, but who remembers that URL. ☺ And of course there are other ways to do this, too.

6.3 COMMON LANGUAGE RUNTIME (CLR)

The Microsoft Common Language Runtime (CLR) is the virtual machine used by all .NET routines. CLR implements a program code execution environment which is defined by the Common Language Infrastructure (CLI). The lowest level human readable language in the CLI is called the Common Intermediate Language, Microsoft's implementation (the Microsoft bytecode) is called the Microsoft Intermediate Language (MSIL).

The CLR does many of the same things that the Java Virtual Machine (JVM) does; however, the CLR is Microsoft and .NET based, whereas Java implements its own separate technologies. The JVM predated the CLR: the CLR dates from .NET version 1, in 2002, whereas the JVM dates from the late 1990s. However, the concept of virtual machines in general can be dated from the late 1960s—see Everything VM (2010).

The CLR does garbage collection. That is, any memory that is no longer used is returned automatically to the list of free memory that can be reused (heap) by the CLR. This kind of data is called "managed" data because its lifetime is managed by some software entity (in this case the CLR). The primary reason for managed data is to prevent memory leaks. We'll discuss memory leaks in depth later on in Section 8.2, when we talk about how CORBA handles memory leaks. However, briefly, what happens in a memory leak is, somehow or other when you're done with using dynamically allocated memory, you forgot to return that memory to the heap. Even if this is an infrequent bug, eventually all the free memory on your system will be used up, and your system will crash! But the memory leak bug that caused the issue may have actually happened a long time before—hours or perhaps days. All you will be able to see when you look at the immediate cause of the bug is that your code tried to allocate new memory, but there was no free memory available, so the system crashed.

The CLR also supports a Common Type System that defines how types are declared, used, and managed in the CLR. The Common Type System is used to integrate different programming languages by specifying rules for languages to follow, which enables different languages to interact.

The Common Type Systems supports two different kinds of data types:

1. Value types—directly contain their own data. Allocated on the stack or inline in a structure. Can be user-defined or built in.
2. Reference types—store a reference to the memory address of a value. Allocated on the heap. They can be self-describing (arrays or class types), pointer types, or interface types.

The CLR also performs thread management.

6.4 GLOBAL ASSEMBLIES CACHE

Windows computers running the Common Language Runtime have a collection of assemblies located in the Global Assembly Cache, otherwise known as the "GAC." The GAC stores assemblies that are meant to be shared by multiple applications on the same computer.

The GAC is located at either the directory:

\Windows\Microsoft .NET\assembly

or

\Windows\assembly

depending on which version of .NET you are using. According to MSDN, \Windows\Microsoft .NET \assembly is for .NET Framework 4 and later.

As I write this, I'm using Windows 10 (yes, I upgraded from when I wrote the earlier parts of this chapter). When I look at the first directory, I see the information in Figure 6.1.

When I look at the second directory, I see the information in Figure 6.2.

So clearly there's some backward compatibility going on. ☺

Assemblies in the GAC_MSIL directory can run in either 32-bit or 64-bit mode, they're stored in MSIL format and converted to the correct word size on the fly (JIT compiled/interpreted). The 32-bit directory runs 32-bit code, and the 64-bit directory runs 64-bit code.

If you want to install an assembly yourself into the GAC to make the assembly global to your computer, one way to do it is to use the Global Assembly Cache Tool, gacutil.exe. This is part of the Microsoft Windows SDK. You have to have administrator privileges to use gacutil.exe.

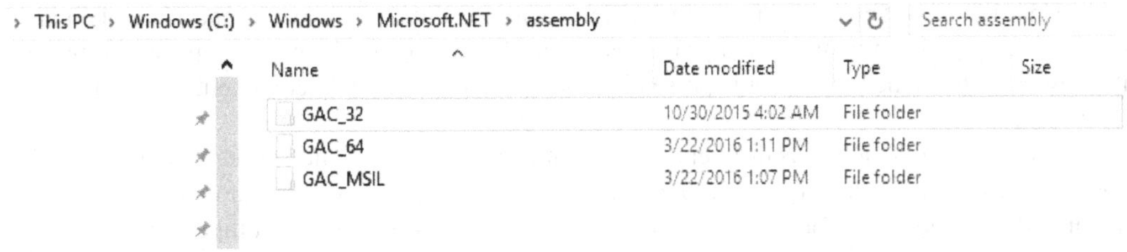

› This PC › Windows (C:) › Windows › Microsoft.NET › assembly			∨ ひ	Search assembly
Name	Date modified	Type	Size	
GAC_32	10/30/2015 4:02 AM	File folder		
GAC_64	3/22/2016 1:11 PM	File folder		
GAC_MSIL	3/22/2016 1:07 PM	File folder		

FIGURE 6.1 GAC at \Windows\Microsoft.NET\assembly.

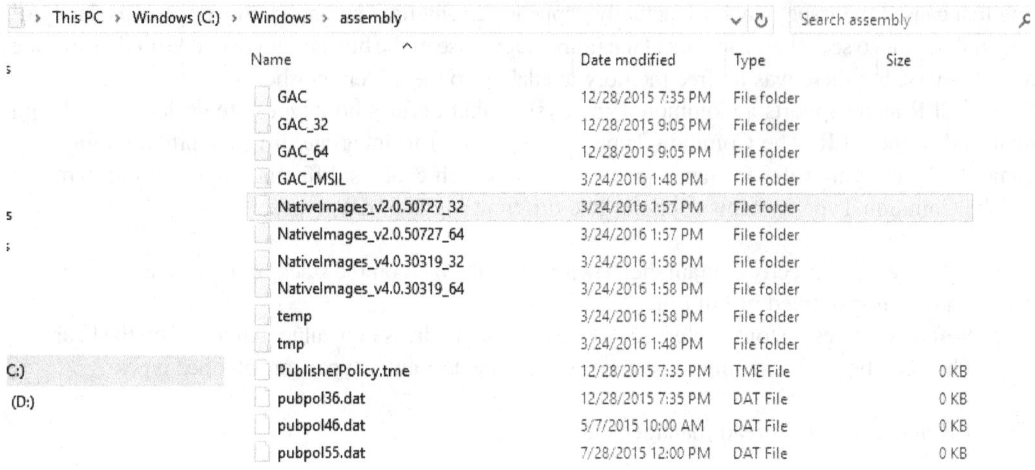

FIGURE 6.2 GAC at \Windows\assembly.

I don't want to go through the details of how to install an assembly in the GAC (there are some references in the bibliography that will help if you find you need to do this). Briefly:

- gacutil /i installs an assembly in the GAC
- gacutil /u uninstalls an assembly in the GAC

Note that you need to know more to do this; this isn't sufficient. ☺ Read through more details from the references before you try.

However, just to show a brief example of gacutil.exe, we will look at Figure 6.3, where I used gacutil.exe to simply look at the contents of my GAC (I ran this one on a Windows 7 machine— yes, we're seeing lots of different versions of Windows in this chapter).

6.5 NAMED PIPES IN WINDOWS

Dating back to the early days of UNIX back in the 1970s, a "pipeline" of processes is when the standard output stream of one process maps to the standard input stream of the next process. Each individual instance of mapping one process' output stream to the next process' input stream is called a "pipe." For example:

    process1 | process2 | process3

means that the output of process1 is the input to process2, etc. Here the individual pipes exist only inside the Linux kernel and are not accessible outside it.

On Unix/Linux systems, a "named pipe" is an extension of the pipeline concept where the name of the named pipe is a file name, and processes can read and write to the named pipe as if it were a file; however, the named pipe data is passed internally by the Linux kernel without storing it in the file system.

A named pipe in Windows is different from a named pipe in Unix/Linux systems in that it works more like a socket, providing a conduit for communication between a client and a server. In Windows (and in .NET Remoting), a named pipe is used for communication between a pipe server and pipe client(s) and can provide communication between processes on the same computer or processes on a network.

FIGURE 6.3 GAC contents shown using gacutil.exe.

EXERCISES

1. Think about garbage collection in terms of its use in middleware. What are its advantages? What are its disadvantages? Are there any middleware-related situations where someone would be better off *not* using garbage collection?
2. In middleware, especially in special-purpose small embedded systems (hint, hint), are there any situations in which shared runtime libraries such as .dlls would be useful? When would the positives outweigh the negatives?
3. Why did Microsoft bother implementing named pipes in Windows?

CONCEPTUAL QUESTIONS

1. Distributed Computing Object Model (DCOM) is still supported by several Windows systems. Do a web search to find this out: is DCOM still used for new development today? Also, did CORBA "win" versus DCOM in the middleware wars of the late 1990s and early 2000s?
2. Compare the Java Virtual Machine to the Common Language Runtime. How are they alike? How are they different? In terms of features, usability, and performance, is one better than the other?
3. Do you think shared libraries are a good idea? Why or why not? If you're interested in performance, especially in saving space in compiled applications, do you have any other options, other than shared libraries or statically-linked libraries?
4. Compare Microsoft middleware technologies in general to their major non-Microsoft competitors. What are the advantages? What are the disadvantages? Do a web search and a formal literature review.
5. Why do you think Value types are allocated on the stack, whereas Reference types are allocated on the heap?

BIBLIOGRAPHY

AskUbuntu. 2014. Why Use a Named Pipe Instead of a File? http://askubuntu.com/questions/449132/why-use-a-named-pipe-instead-of-a-file (accessed March 25, 2016).

Everything VM. 2010. History of Virtualization. http://www.everythingvm.com/content/history-virtualization (accessed May 22, 2016).

JoelOnSoftware. 2006. GAC_32, GAC_MSIL, GAC_64 – Why? 2006. http://discuss.joelonsoftware.com/default.asp?dotnet.12.383883.5 (accessed March 24, 2016).

Khanse, A. 2015. WinSxS Folder in Windows 7/8/10 Explained. The Windows Club. http://www.thewindowsclub.com/winsxs-folder-windows-7-8 (accessed March 24, 2016).

Miller, G. 2013. Installing a DLL into the Global Assembly Cache. CodeProject. http://www.codeproject.com/Tips/585817/Installing-a-DLL-into-the-Global-Assembly-Cache-GA (accessed March 24, 2016).

MSDN. 2015. About Side-by-Side Assemblies. https://msdn.microsoft.com/en-us/library/windows/desktop/ff951640(v=vs.85).aspx (accessed July 7, 2015).

MSDN. 2015. Strong-Named Assemblies. https://msdn.microsoft.com/en-us/library/wd40t7ad(v=vs.110).aspx (accessed March 24, 2016).

MSDN. 2016. Common Language Runtime. https://msdn.microsoft.com/en-us/library/cc265151(v=vs.95).aspx (accessed May 22, 2016).

MSDN. 2016. Gacutil.exe (Global Assembly Cache Tool). https://msdn.microsoft.com/en-us/library/ex0ss12c(v=vs.110).aspx (accessed March 24, 2016).

MSDN. 2016. Global Assembly Cache. https://msdn.microsoft.com/en-us/library/yf1d93sz(v=vs.110).aspx (accessed March 24, 2016).

MSDN. 2016. Working with Assemblies and the Global Assembly Cache. https://msdn.microsoft.com/en-us/library/6axd4fx6(v=vs.110).aspx (accessed May 22, 2016).

Vaught, A. 1997. Introduction to Named Pipes. http://www.linuxjournal.com/article/2156 (accessed March 25, 2016).

Wikipedia. 2015. DLL Hell. https://en.wikipedia.org/wiki/DLL_Hell (accessed July 7, 2015).

7 Cloud Technologies Basics

7.1 WHAT YOU NEED TO KNOW FOR THE CLOUD

In this chapter, we're going to examine various technologies that you must know in order to understand the later chapters on cloud computing. This includes the basics for operating system images that will be used in virtual machines; it includes how the virtual machines run on hypervisors. It also includes software-defined networking (SDN) because that includes virtual networks, which is how virtual machines talk to each other. Finally, we're going to look at some aspects of security that are particularly related to the cloud: what kinds of additional security problems arise when one is using a virtual machine? When one is using a type-1 hypervisor? What additional aspects of a working cloud might cause additional security holes? And lastly, since clouds consist of big server farms, how do you ensure that someone just doesn't walk up and haul your important data away in a pickup truck?

7.2 JUST WHAT ARE DISK IMAGES AND VIRTUAL MACHINE IMAGES, ANYWAY?

A disk image is a copy of the entire contents of a storage device, for example, a hard drive or DVD.

A virtual machine image is a single file which contains a virtual disk. The virtual disk has a bootable operating system installed on it.

7.2.1 VARIOUS KINDS OF DISK IMAGES AND VIRTUAL MACHINE IMAGES

Raw—a bit-for-bit copy of the data of either a disk or volume, with no additions or deletions

- The "dd" command in Linux will create this
- (similar tools have been created for Windows)
- This is an unstructured disk image format

Virtual Hard Disk (vhd)—originally used by Virtual PC and Windows Virtual Server, see MSDN (2016), now an open format

- Minimum size is 3 MB
- Versions are:
  - Fixed
    - Maximum size is pre-allocated
  - Expandable/Dynamic/Dynamically Expandable/Sparse
    - Uses only the space needed to store the actual data
    - The VHD API doesn't check to make sure the physical disk is big enough so it's possible to create an expandable disk that's too big for the physical disk
    - Maximum size is 2,040 GB
  - Differencing
    - A parent virtual disk is unchanged, changes to the parent are stored in a separate child image
    - Maximum size of a differencing virtual disk is 2,040 GB.

Virtual Machine Disk (vmdk)—originally developed by VMware

- Maximum VMDK file size is 2 TB
  - In Virtual Disk Format version 5, disk volume extent is approx. 60 TB.
- Supports more than 100,000 files per volume
- All disk space needed for a virtual disk's files may be allocated at the time it is created, or it can grow as needed to accommodate new data

VirtualBox Disk Image (vdi)—originally developed by VirtualBox

- Fixed size
  - Size allocated up front
  - Better performance than with dynamically expanding
- Dynamically expanding
  - Created at minimal size, but grows automatically
  - Can have slower performance (if disk is frequently enlarged)

iso image—represents the contents of an optical disc (CDs, DVD, etc.).

- Data formats supported are specified by:
  - CDs—originally from ISO 9660
  - DVD and BluRay—UDF format, specified in ISO/IEC 13346 and ECMA-167

QEMU Copy on Write (qcow2, qcow)—originally used by QEMU hypervisor

- qcow2 replaces the original qcow
  - qcow2 supports multiple snapshots
- Can grow dynamically as data is added
- Benefits over using raw image include:
  - Smaller file size (raw disk images allocate entire space to a file even if parts of the space are empty)
  - Copy-on-write support
    - Copy-on-Write (COW) means:
      - If there are two or more users that need very similar resources, then initially they are given pointers to the same resource. When a user tries to modify its own resource, only then is a private copy created. If no modifications are made, then no copies need be created.
  - Snapshot support, where the image can contain multiple snapshots of the image's history
  - Optional zlib compression
  - Optional AES encryption

Machine Images on Amazon

- These consist of:
  - Amazon Machine Image (AMI)
  - Amazon Kernel Image (AKI)
  - Amazon Ramdisk Image (ARI)
- According to Amazon Discussion Forum (2011):

  The AKI represents the vmlinuz portion of the kernel. It is basically the compiled kernel that gets loaded on boot.

The ARI represents the initrd/initramfs. This is the ramdisk that gets loaded with the kernel and has the initial driver modules for the kernel to find the root filesystem.

With traditional AKIs/ARIs (you need to match those) you will also need the corresponding kernel modules installed on the file system. Without these the system will normally not be able to boot. You can run a newer AKI on an older system if you have the right kernel modules installed. The NEW way:

We launched a set of AKIs called PV-Grub. These simulate grub as the kernel and allow you to install your kernel on the AMI and have it perform similar to [a] bare-metal system where it reads the kernel and ramdisk from the filesystem. These PV-Grub AKIs do not use ARIs. In fact, there are some edge case[s] where using an ARI will prevent PV-Grub AKIs from working, but they are rare.

- According to Debian (2016):

  An AKI (Amazon Kernel Image) is a preconfigured bootable kernel mini image that is prebuilt and provided by Amazon to boot instances. Typically one will use an AKI that contains pv-grub so that one can instantiate an instance from an AMI that contains its own Xen DomU kernel that is managed by the user.

  - PV-Grub is a ParaVirtual boot loader
    - A boot loader is the first software program that runs when a computer starts. It loads the operating system kernel and then transfers control to it.

Open Virtualization Format (OVF)—packages one or more image files and an XML metadata file (.ovf) containing information about the virtual machine, as well as possibly other files.

Note that OpenStack Glance (2016) supports the following disk image formats:

- raw
- vhd
- vmdk
- vdi
- iso
- qcow2
- aki
- ari
- ami

7.3   JUST WHAT ARE HYPERVISORS AND VIRTUAL MACHINES, ANYWAY?

A Virtual Machine is an emulator of a particular computer system. There are two main divisions of Virtual Machines:

1. System virtual machine
2. Process virtual machine

A System virtual machine (full virtualization) allows execution of a complete operating system and can provide a full up emulator of a particular computer architecture/hardware system. A Process virtual machine (application virtual machine or Managed Runtime Environment, MRE) allows a single application (program) to run, provides a platform independent execution environment. Example of a process virtual machine include the Java Virtual Machine (JVM) and the .NET Common Language Runtime (CLR).

A Hypervisor creates and runs virtual machines. TechTarget (2016) defines a hypervisor as follows:

A hypervisor, also called a virtual machine manager, is a program that allows multiple operating systems to share a single hardware host. Each operating system appears to have the host's processor, memory, and other resources all to itself. However, the hypervisor is actually controlling the host processor and resources, allocating what is needed to each operating system in turn and making sure that the guest operating systems (called virtual machines) cannot disrupt each other.

Hypervisors come in two main types:

1. Type 1 (native, bare metal)
   * Runs directly on host hardware
   * Controls the hardware and manages the guest OS
2. Type 2 (hosted)
   * Runs within a conventional OS environment

A "Host machine" is the physical host, and a "Guest machine" or "guest VM" is the VM (virtual machine) installed on top of the hypervisor.

Hypervisors can also be categorized based on the kind of virtualization they provide as follows:

* Full virtualization
* Paravirtualization

With full virtualization, the guest operating system *thinks* it is running directly on the hardware. That is, the hypervisor provides hardware emulation that is a complete simulation of the hardware that the guest operating system expects. Any calls to the underlying hardware must be trapped and emulated. With full virtualization, therefore, the guest operating system does not have to be modified in any way.

With paravirtualization, the kernel of the guest operating system has been modified so that instead of handling calls to the hardware itself using a privileged instruction (a privileged instruction is a special assembly language instruction that can only be used when the processor is in a special supervisory mode (generally called ring 0) that is generally only available to the operating system), it calls the hypervisor instead to do this work. These calls to the hypervisor are called *hypercalls.*

There is now a type of full virtualization called Hardware Assisted Virtualization. Processor manufacturers (such as Intel and AMD) implemented an extra-super supervisory mode (called ring −1). This allows hypervisors to run at ring −1, and thus privileged instructions in the operating system now trap automatically to the hypervisor.

Hybrid Virtualization combines paravirtualization with hardware assisted virtualization. Here parts of the guest operating system use paravirtualization for certain hardware drivers, but hardware assisted virtualization (or full virtualization if hardware assisted is not available).

7.3.1 SOME EXAMPLES OF TYPE 2 HYPERVISORS

Oracle VirtualBox and QEMU (Quick Emulator) are examples of type 2 hypervisors.

Oracle VirtualBox is an open source hypervisor. It can use hardware-assisted virtualization, when the hardware supports it. It supports paravirtualization for some Linux and Windows guests, which can improve performance.

QEMU has two basic operating modes:

1. Full system emulation
2. User mode emulation

With full system emulation, QEMU emulates hardware and peripherals. QEMU supports the emulation of numerous different kinds of hardware, these include (among others), together with associated peripheral devices:

* PC
* MIPS

- ARM
- Sparc32
- Sparc64

Full system emulation. In this mode, QEMU emulates a full system (for example a PC), including one or several processors and various peripherals. It can be used to launch different Operating Systems without rebooting the PC.

With User mode emulation, QEMU can launch one process that was compiled for one CPU on another CPU, but it only provides a subset of full system emulation, it assumes that the host system is doing some of the work. In this mode, the QEMU emulation libraries are used with individual binaries, which then think the host computer is their original computer, and see directories, etc., that they would have expected if running on the original computer.

QEMU also has two hosted modes, one with Kernel-based Virtual Machine (KVM) and one with Xen, we'll look more at those when we look at type-1 hypervisors.

Some other type 2 hypervisors include Microsoft Virtual PC and VMware Fusion.

7.3.1.1 Some VirtualBox Installation Hints

Installing VirtualBox and getting Ubuntu running inside it in a basic way is pretty easy. However, creating a shared folder (shared with Windows so you can copy files back and forth from Windows to Ubuntu) is a little trickier—you have to remember a few extra things to do.

First you have to add guest additions. Goto Devices on the window that's running Ubuntu and there will be an item to select that adds guest additions.

Reboot after this.

Then follow the normal directions to add a shared folder. Let's call it "VBOX_shared."

Then open a terminal window, and type:

```
sudo mkdir /mnt/myVBOX_shared
sudo mount –t vboxsf –o uid=1000, gid=1000 VBOX_shared /mnt/myVBOX_shared
```

If you get a mounting failed error, try:

```
cd /opt/VBoxGuestAdditions-*/init
sudo ./vboxadd setup
```

At this point you will have a shared folder, but it will belong to the super user, and only the super user will have access.

To give you access with your username, type:

```
sudo usermod -a –G vboxsf your-user-id
```

Then REBOOT.

7.3.2 Some Examples of Type 1 Hypervisors

The Kernel-based Virtual Machine (KVM) ships as part of the Linux kernel. However, it truly is a type-1 hypervisor (runs on bare metal) because when KVM is launched, it takes over the hardware, but still works with the Linux kernel for processing.

When running on x86 hardware, KVM employs the additional instructions that are provided by the processor for hardware-assisted virtualization (the ring −1 instructions).

KVM began on x86 processors but has been ported to ARM, MIPS, and PowerPC, among others.

KVM by itself does not perform hardware emulation. A common operating mode for KVM is to combine it with QEMU. According to Ahmed (2013), QEMU:

allocates RAM, loads the code, and instead of recompiling it, or calling KQemu, it spawns a thread (this is important); the thread calls the KVM kernel module to switch to guest mode and proceeds to execute the VM code. On a privilege instruction, it switches back to the KVM kernel module, which, if necessary, signals the Qemu thread to handle most of the hardware emulation.

(Note that KQemu was a Linux kernel module that was intended to run user mode code directly on the host CPU. KQemu has been replaced, as you can see, by KVM.)

RedHat provides a commercial virtualization product called Red Hat Enterprise Virtualization (RHEV) that is based on KVM.

Xen is a hypervisor that was originally developed at the University of Cambridge and released in 2003.

Xen's original mode was paravirtualization. Actually, the concept of paravirtualization was originally introduced in Xen.

However, it has since added hardware-assisted virtualization, which in Xen is known as a Hardware Virtual Machine.

Xen supports the following operating modes, see Xen Project Wiki (2016):

- Paravirtualization (PV)
- Hardware Virtual Machine (HVM)
- PVHVM—HVM guests using special paravirtual device drivers. These optimized driver bypass emulated disk and network I/O and thus improve performance
- PVH—a PV guest that uses PV drivers to boot and for I/O. Otherwise it uses HW virtualization extensions, without the need for emulation

When running on Xen, QEMU is used only for hardware emulation.

The Xen hypervisor runs on top of the hardware, and creates domains, which are divided into a privileged domain, called dom0, and unprivileged domains, called domUs. Dom0 includes a trusted kernel and hardware drivers. The idea is that the hypervisor is small and therefore maintainable. From within dom0, the other domains are controlled, this includes creating them, destroying them, saving them, etc. Also from within dom0, network and peripherals are controlled and assigned to kernel or to domUs.

When using paravirtualization, dom0 must include a paravirtualized-ready kernel. Several Linux kernels now support being used as a Xen dom0 kernel.

7.3.2.1 libvirt

libvirt is a management tool and API that can be used to manage various hypervisors:

- A C library but with bindings to other languages
- Supports several hypervisors, including KVM/QEMU, Xen, VMware ESX and VMWare Server/GSX, among several others
- Several GUIs that interact with libvirt are provided by different software manufacturers, one such is virt-manager (Virtual Machine Manager)

7.4   SOFTWARE-DEFINED NETWORKING AND NETWORK VIRTUALIZATION

There is some argument about whether or not there is a difference between a *Software-Defined Network* and *Network Virtualization*. There's also another term, *Network Functions Virtualization (NFV)* that is thrown around.

Garrison (2014) discusses *network virtualization* as follows:

Network virtualization literally tries to create logical segments in an existing network by dividing the network logically at the flow level (it is similar to partitioning a hard drive).

NV is an overlay; it's a tunnel. Rather than physically connecting two domains in a network, NV creates a tunnel through the existing network to connect two domains. NV is valuable because it saves administrators from having to physically wire up each new domain connection, especially for virtual machines that get created.

Garrison discusses *network functions virtualization* as follows:

If NV offers the capability to create tunnels through a network and use per-flow service thinking, the next step is to put a service on a tunnel. NFV is virtualizing Layer 4–7 functions such as firewall or IDPS, or even load balancing (application delivery controllers).

And further:

If you have a specific tunnel you're punching through the infrastructure, you can add a firewall or IDS/IPS to just that tunnel.

Garrison discusses *software-defined networks* as follows:

While NV and NFV add virtual tunnels and functions to the physical network, SDN changes the physical network, and therefore is really a new externally driven means to provision and manage the network.

However, Baldwin (2014) says:

So there's really no reason to introduce fear, uncertainty, and doubt about a supposed difference between SDN, NFV, and network virtualization. Because there isn't one.

McCouch (2014) says that *Software Defined Networking* means separating a data network's control functions from its packet forwarding functions. With this, independently developed products can easily work together, and the user can mix and match vendors. Also, separating the control functions (the control plane) allows an easy way to configure, monitor, etc., a large heterogeneous network. But finally it allows network programmability, and allows APIs to control the network.

He says that *Network Virtualization* refers to isolation of applications or tenants through creating virtual instances of a physical device. He says that virtual routers and switches can be created, and can be used to create logical networks (for example, VLANs).

He says that *Network Functions Virtualization* consists of running a function such as a firewall or load balancer in virtual machines on the virtual server infrastructure.

The Open Networking Foundation (2016) defines *Software-Defined Networking* as follows:

SDN is a new approach to networking in which network control is decoupled from the data forwarding function and is directly programmable.

The Open Networking Foundation (2016) says further that the SDN architecture decouples the network control and forwarding functions. This enables the network control to become directly programmable and the underlying infrastructure to be abstracted. The SDN architecture is therefore:

- Directly programmable
- Agile
- Centrally managed

- Programmatically configured
- Open standards-based and vendor-neutral

So let's try to develop our own definition to go forward with. I'm going to sort of combine the three terms and use the term *Software-Defined Network* loosely to refer to a virtual network that includes both physical connections and switches and logical connections and switches. The data plane (packet forwarding) will be separated from the control plane (decisions on where packets will be forwarded), and the control plane is controlled programmatically through an API, so the behavior of the network can change dynamically. We will have VLANs that will include both physical and logical (virtual) connections. Additional services can be applied to switches or connections, including load balancing and firewall support. Note that this definition is a peek ahead to how the OpenStack Neutron network manager works.

7.4.1 Open vSwitch/OpenFlow and Linux Bridge

As we previously discussed, for a Virtual Machine (VM) to do useful work, typically it must be connected to a physical network, and also to other VMs. This must be done through the hypervisor. For Linux-based hypervisors, in the past the Linux bridge was typically used—the Linux bridge is a virtual switch that is included in the Linux kernel.

More recently, Open vSwitch has come to be often used instead of a Linux bridge. Open vSwitch is targeted at networks that include multiple servers and run virtual machines in a highly dynamic environment—a cloud environment is a typical example of the networking characteristics that Open vSwitch was intended to address. For example, Open vSwitch allows migration of a live network state between different hosts. Open vSwitch also supports monitoring of network events, largely through the use of the Open vSwitch Database (OVSDB) which stores network state and supports remote triggers. This allows Open vSwitch to react to and track network events such as VM migrations. Open vSwitch also includes support for offloading packet processing to hardware chipsets.

Open vSwitch supports various kinds of monitoring:

- NetFlow
  - Cisco NetFlow examines IP packets at an interface, for IP traffic flow analysis including network usage, traffic routing, security, etc. This works by aggregating multiple packets into a flow (packet sequence) then analyzing the flow; however, most of the data field is lost in this aggregation, which mainly contains source and destination IP addresses, protocols, type, Quality of Service (QoS), etc. (Later versions can also examine layer 2.)
- sFlow
  - sFlow is a packet sampling technology. It provides continuous statistics on any protocol (L2, L3, L4, and up to L7). sFlow can either (a) monitor interface counters and CPU usage, or (b) capture the first 256 bytes (quantity of bytes configurable) of each frame from 1 in N (with N configurable) frames. Its information is sent in a UDP datagram to a collector to be analyzed
- SPAN, and RSPAN
  - Mirror traffic from one interface on a switch to another interface on the same switch (layer 2). Remote SPAN (RSPAN) mirrors traffic from an interface over a dedicated VLAN to an interface on a different switch

It supports QoS in terms of traffic queueing and shaping, and security in terms of traffic filtering and VLAN isolation.

Open vSwitch works with most hypervisors (including Xen and KVM) and container systems (Docker).

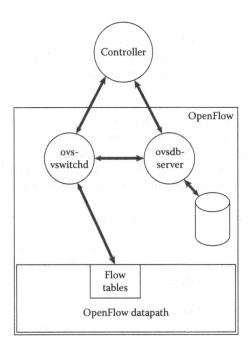

FIGURE 7.1   Open vSwitch internals.

Let's look more in depth at how Open vSwitch works. This isn't meant to make you an expert, just give you a good idea about what's going on.

An overview of Open vSwitch internals, including OpenFlow, is shown in Figure 7.1.

7.4.1.1   OpenFlow

Open vSwitch employs OpenFlow, a switching technology for SDNs, see Open Networking Foundation (2016).

OpenFlow breaks a network connection into a separate data plane and control plane. In traditional network equipment, both these activities were in the same device. The control plane determines where a packet is routed and stores the routing information in the flow table, and then the data plane routes packets according to the flow table.

An OpenFlow flow table contains a set of headers, and actions that are taken when a packet with the specified headers arrived. Headers plus their associated actions (plus some additional information, such as priority) are called "flows" or "flow rules" or "flow entries."

Headers—some examples are (among others):

- Port where the packet arrived
- Ethernet—Media Access Control (MAC)—source address
- Ethernet (MAC) destination address
- IP source address
- IP destination address
- VLAN identifier

Actions—some examples are (among others):

- Can send a packet to an outgoing port
- Can modify an IP address in a packet and send that packet to an outgoing port (this is an example of Network Address Translation)

- Can send a packet to the controller. This is a "packet in" event, it would happen in situations where there is not a flow to handle this packet:
  - If there is a packet for which no flow is defined, that packet will be sent to the controller, and the controller will create a new flow to handle the packet
- Drop packet

Each flow rule has a priority associated with it. In the case where a packet matches multiple flow rules, the flow rule with the highest priority is the rule that is applied.

Flow rules can have timeouts associated with them. In the case of an idle timeout, if a flow has not received a packet in a certain amount of time, the flow is removed from the flow table. In the case of a hard timeout, after a certain amount of time, the flow is removed from the table (regardless of whether it is still receiving packets).

There are per-table counters, per-flow counters, per-port counters, and per-queue counters, that can count the packets that have come through.

OpenFlow itself is focused on flow-based control of a switch. All configuration information related to creating or destroying OpenFlow switchings, adding or removing ports or queues, etc., is handled through the configuration database.

7.4.1.2   How Open vSwitch Works

Referring back to Figure 7.1, ovs-vswitchd is a daemon that manages the Open vSwitch switches on one computer.

The ovsdb-server controls a database that stores switch configuration, including definitions of bridges (a logical datapath is referred to as a bridge), interfaces, and tunnels.

Refer to Figure 7.1 to see the relationship between ovs-vswitchd, ovsdb-server, the OpenFlow datapath, and the controller. Note that there is also a separate manager that configures the Open vSwitch instance, the manager is not shown in Figure 7.1.

Management and configuration on the Open vSwitch instance is performed using the OVSDB management interface (IETF 2013). The operations on this interface include:

- Creation, modification, and deletion of OpenFlow datapaths (bridges)
- Configuration of the set of controllers to which an OpenFlow datapath connects
- Configuration of the set of managers to which the OVSDB server connects
- Creation, modification, and deletion of ports on OpenFlow datapaths

The ovsdb-server uses the OVSDB protocol to talk to the ovs-vswitchd daemon and to the controller.

At startup, ovs-vswitchd contacts the ovsdb-server to retrieve configuration information. Based on this information, it sets up the datapaths (bridges) and sets up the switching in the flow tables. When the database changes, ovs-switchd will automatically update its datapaths and flow tables.

7.5   VIRTUALIZATION SECURITY

In 2011, the NIST released guidelines, see Scarfone et al. (2011), for using and configuring virtualization technologies.

First they addressed issues with guest operating system isolation. The hypervisor is responsible for partitioning resources so that each guest operating system can see only its own resources. Resources may be partitioned physically, by assigning guest operating systems to separate physical devices, or may be partitioned logically, by the hypervisor securely allocating resources. Logical isolation is also known as the guest operating system being in a "sandbox."

Isolation of guest operating systems is important because (among other things) it prevents *side channel attacks* that monitor usage patterns of hardware resources. Another attack vector is for an attacker to *escape* from the guest operating system in the virtual machine, in order to attack another virtual machine or the hypervisor itself. The hypervisor is a single point of failure, if the attacker can gain control over the hypervisor then the attacker can gain control over all other guest operating systems in their virtual machines.

Sharing resources between different guest operating systems can present additional attack vectors.

The hypervisor should monitor all guest operating systems as they run, including memory usage, network traffic, processes, etc. This is called *introspection*. Monitoring network traffic can be more difficult since traffic between virtual machines often does not pass over a physical network.

Images and snapshots of guest operating systems can be security risks, since they contain passwords and personal data. Snapshots in particular are risky because they can contain the contents of RAM at the time the snapshot was taken, so additional sensitive information may be included in the snapshot. When images and snapshots are moved around and stored, maintaining good security procedures to prevent unauthorized access is very important. It is easy to create images, so unnecessary images may be created—each of these images is a possible security breach.

Stored images will likely not receive ongoing operating system security patches, so if those images are retrieved and run, security holes that are well known to potential attackers may very well be present. The longer an image is stored, the more vulnerabilities it will possess.

If a virtual machine contains malware, and an image or snapshot is taken of that virtual machine, and then migrated elsewhere, then that malware will be spread. Images should be periodically monitored using cryptographic hashes to make sure that no malware has been added while the image is stored.

Organizations should implement formal image management that takes these problems into account.

In general, migration of a virtual machine from one host to another represents a possible security threat, since if the virtual machine had malware it then spreads that to a new host.

Hypervisor management communications should be protected. One good way is to have a separate management network that is separate from all user networks and can be accessed only by system administrators. Limiting access to the hypervisor is critical to the whole system's security. The hypervisor itself should be carefully monitored for signs that it could be compromised.

Disconnect any physical hardware when it is not being used, particularly Network Interface Cards (NICs). Similarly, for virtual machines disconnect any unused virtual hardware (virtual CDs, etc.).

If a guest operating system has been compromised, assume that all other guest operating systems on the same hardware have been compromised.

7.5.1 Hypervisor Security

In 2014, the NIST released a draft standard for hypervisor security, see Chandramouli (2014). According to Mimoso (2014):

> The 22 security recommendations in the draft are mapped to each of the five primary hypervisor functions, and run the gamut from suggestions for reducing a hypervisor's attack surface to determining which drivers are allowed to run emulation code, memory rules, monitoring recommendations, access control and permissions, patch and vulnerability management, and logging of security events among others.

According to Chandramouli (2014), the five primary hypervisor functions are:

HY-BF1: Execution Isolation for Virtual Machines (VMs)
- Scheduling VMs
- Managing CPU and memory related to processes running in VMs
- Processor context switching during running of applications inside VMs

HY-BF2: Devices Emulation & Access Control
- Emulating network devices as expected by native drivers in the VMs
- Emulating storage devices as expected by the native drivers in the VMs
- Controlling how different VMs access physical devices

HY-BF3: Execution of Privileged Operations for Guest VMs
- Execute privileged operations in hypervisor instead of on host hardware

HY-BF4: Management of VMs
- Configure VM images
- Configure VM states (start, stop, pause, etc.)

HY-BF5: Administration of Hypervisor Platform and Hypervisor Software
- Configure parameters for user interaction with hypervisor host

The security recommendations are:

HY-SR-1: A Type 1 hypervisor has fewer security vulnerabilities than a Type 2 hypervisor since there is no host operating system that can be attacked.

HY-SR-2: A hypervisor with hardware assisted virtualization (instruction set and memory management) has fewer security vulnerabilities than a hypervisor with only software assisted virtualization because:
- Buffer overflow and similar attacks are prevented through good control over memory management
- Hardware-based memory protection and privilege isolation helps better control shared devices
- Guest operating systems can be easily updated, since they need not be modified to run on paravirtualized platforms
- Support of virtualization in hardware results in smaller hypervisor code, which is easier to examine for vulnerabilities

HY-SR-3 (optional): The hypervisor that is launched should be part of a platform and an overall infrastructure that contains a Measured Launch Environment (MLE) and a Trusted Platform Module (TPM) in order to ensure boot integrity:
- An MLE is a hardware boot sequence that compares the hashes of the components being booted (firmware, BIOS, and hypervisor modules) to make sure the components are correct and unmodified. This also includes a TPM that stores the results of the measurements and allows reporting of discrepancies.

HY-SR-4: The hypervisor management console should be kept small with few exposed interfaces so as to provide fewer vulnerabilities and to be easier to examine for vulnerabilities.

HY-SR-5: The hypervisor boot configuration should be settable so that non-certified drivers are not allowed. Also, when possible, the hardware emulation (QEMU) should be run in an unprivileged VM so that the application VM is not impacted by a faulty device driver.

HY-SR-6: A hypervisor normally meets memory requirements through a combination of physical RAM and swap files. Also, a VM normally would not require all its configured memory all the time. Therefore, it's reasonable to have the total memory configured to belong to all VMs on a host to exceed the total physical RAM available on the host. However, if the amount of VM-configured memory is too large compared to the physical RAM then performance may degrade and the host may not be available for certain VM workloads. Therefore the ratio of combined configured VM memory to RAM memory should typically be around 1.5 to 1, but in any case not very high.

HY-SR-7: Similarly, there should be a way for the hypervisor to configure a guaranteed quantity of physical RAM and also a limit on the quantity of physical RAM for every VM. The hypervisor should also be able to prioritize RAM resources among multiple VMs.

HY-SR-8: Each VM should have a way to guarantee that it will eventually run. For example, a VM may need two cores in order to run and have to wait until those cores are available at the same time. Therefore, a hypervisor should have a way to reserve a minimum CPU allotment.

Also, a VM should have an upper bound on its CPU allotment in order to prevent a (possibly compromised) VM from taking up all CPU resources and not allowing other VMs to run. To achieve this, the number of virtual CPUs allocated to any VM must be less than the total number of cores in the host machine.

HY-SR-9: Similarly, every VM must have a lower bound and a lower bound on CPU clock cycles, and each VM must have a priority. This will enable scheduling VMs when they compete for CPU resources.

HY-SR-10: VM images can be a big security threat. Thus, the VM image library should be located elsewhere outside the host machine running the hypervisor, and each image should be digitally signed to ensure it is authentic and that it has not been compromised.

HY-SR-11: Running VMs should be monitored (introspection by the hypervisor) to search for malware inside VMs and malicious network traffic to or from VMs. (Would employ anti-virus and intrusion detection and prevention.)

HY-SR-12: Security monitoring and security enforcement should use introspection (monitoring of the VMs by the hypervisor). One typical way to do this would be to run a security tool (Security Virtual Appliance) in a trusted VM.

HY-SR-13: Access control security permissions should be able to be granted to a single VM, to a physical group of VMs, or to a logical group of VMs. It should be possible to selectively deny access of group members to individual VMs within a group, if those VMs have sensitive data (perhaps on a temporary basis).

HY-SR-14: The number of user or system administrator accounts accessing the hypervisor should be kept very low, perhaps two or three system administrators should be allowed access.

HY-SR-15: All accounts that access a hypervisor should be heavily authenticated through the company's user directory, with addition and deletion of accounts immediately updated. All password, etc., policies should be enforced.

HY-SR-16: It should be possible to prevent remote access to the hypervisor administrative console, to deny root account access, or to restrict remote access to a small list of administrative accounts.

HY-SR-17: It should be possible to define a complete set of known good configuration settings, to automatically apply these known good settings to a new hypervisor installation or to an existing hypervisor installation, or to check an existing hypervisor installation to make sure it matches those known good settings.

HY-SR-18: All hypervisor patches should be applied immediately or very soon.

HY-SR-19: The hypervisor's firewall should only allow ports and network traffic that are actually needed for services that are enabled in the hypervisor.

HY-SR-20: Hypervisor logs should be kept in a standard format so they can be easily analyzed. Logs should be located on an external machine in case the machine the hypervisor is running on crashes or its security is compromised.

HY-SR-21: The hypervisor management interface should be accessed by an isolated virtual network. Incoming traffic into the management interface should be controlled by a firewall, for example, only traffic into the management interface from certain subnets should be allowed.

HY-SR-22: To prevent bottlenecks in network communication, multiple communication channels from a given VM to the outside network should be created. Usually this is done by providing multiple physical network interface cards (NICs) that traffic from a given VM can flow through.

Chandramouli (2014) provided a table in an appendix that mapped the security recommendations to the baseline functionalities. One thing to learn easily from the way Chandramouli's table is drawn is that HY-SR-1 and HY-SR-3 don't map to any of the hypervisor baseline

TABLE 7.1

Baseline Functionalities Supported by Which Security Recommendations

HY-BF1	HY-BF2	HY-BF3	HY-BF4	HY-BF5
HY-SR-2	HY-SR-5		HY-SR-4	HY-SR-4
			HY-SR-6	HY-SR-14
			HY-SR-7	HY-SR-15
			HY-SR-8	HY-SR-16
			HY-SR-9	HY-SR-17
			HY-SR-10	HY-SR-18
			HY-SR-11	HY-SR-19
			HY-SR-12	HY-SR-20
			HY-SR-13	HY-SR-21
				HY-SR-22

functionalities. Makes sense, HY-SR-1 is just saying that if you have less code there's less to attack. HY-SR-3 says it's good to make sure the right code always is loaded in when you boot. Those are more general security recommendations than particularly related to hypervisors.

I turned Chandramouli's table backwards in Table 7.1 in that I've mapped the baseline functionalities to the security recommendations. This is instructive in a couple of ways. First of all, we can see that none of the security recommendations map to HY-BF3. Presumably this is just because HY-BF3 says your hypervisor should replace operating system calls to the hardware with hypercalls to the hypervisor. This is a pretty standard hypervisor operation. However, as Chandramouli says earlier, when you have problems here it's because the hypervisor has faulty code. Since this is buried inside the hypervisor, he cannot make security recommendations related to configuration, deployment, or procedure.

Also, we see that most of the security recommendations are related to management of VMs (HY-BF4) and administration and configuration of the hypervisor itself (HY-BF5).

7.6   CLOUD SECURITY

We will look now at what is generally termed "cloud" security. There is considerable overlap between "virtualization" security and "cloud" security, in that clouds employ virtualization. However, there are some aspects of cloud security that go beyond virtualization. For example, control of user accounts can be considered a more general security problem than a virtualization problem. Also, a denial of service attack is a cloud problem but is not necessarily directly related to virtualization.

The Cloud Security Alliance (CSA) is a non-profit organization, formed in 2008, that defines best practices for cloud security. Numerous corporations participate in this organization, including (as of 2016): Microsoft, Rackspace, VMware, HP Enterprise, Cisco, Citrix, RedHat, Symantec, among numerous others. It has chapters all over the world. It has numerous working groups that work in cloud standards, certification, and education, among several other areas.

It provides a third-party assessment of a cloud service provider's security through the CSA Star Certification and assessment process. The associated CSA Star registry indexes the security features supported by cloud providers. Numerous cloud providers are listed on this registry, including (as of 2016): Microsoft Azure, RedHat OpenShift, VMware, Citrix Sharefile, among several others.

It sponsors cloud symposiums, including the Cloud Security Summit, and the CSA Federal Summit.

For individuals working in cloud computing, CSA provides cloud computing certifications, including the Certificate of Cloud Security Knowledge, and the Certified Cloud Security Professional.

The Cloud Security Alliance Top Threats Working Group performs ongoing analyses of the top threats to cloud security. From CSA Top Threats Working Group (2016), the top threats from 2016 are:

1. Data Breaches
   * A data breach is when an unauthorized individual can see and use data
2. Insufficient Identity, Credential, and Access Management
   * Identity access management systems cannot scale to the size needed
   * Authentication should be performed using multiple kinds of identifying information
   * Weak passwords are used
   * Cryptographic keys, passwords, and certificates are not rotated automatically
   * Credentials and cryptographic keys are embedded in source code
   * Public Key Infrastructure systems are needed to ensure key management is appropriately performed
3. Insecure Interfaces and APIs
   * All APIs must be well designed because overall cloud security depends on the basic interfaces. These APIs are heavy attack targets.
4. System vulnerabilities
   * Bugs in programs are a big problem
   * Since systems from different organizations share resources, this leads to a new attack vector
5. Account Hijacking
   * Phishing and fraud are ongoing problems
   * Credential sharing among users should be prohibited
   * Two or more factor authentication should be used where possible
   * All accounts should be monitored and traceable to a human
6. Malicious Insiders
   * A malicious system administrator is a big problem
   * System administrator duties should be separated, access controlled by role
   * Users should control encryption and keys themselves
   * Administrator activities should be logged, monitored, and audited
7. Advanced Persistent Threats
   * Attackers infiltrate systems to smuggle data and intellectual property
8. Data Loss
   * Permanent loss of a user's data
   * Cloud provider must take care to follow best practices for data backup and recovery, including off-site storage
   * Users must take care not to lose their encryption keys
9. Insufficient Due Diligence
   * When companies move to the cloud they must carefully analyze commercial, technical, and legal issues (data privacy, etc.) involved
10. Abuse and Nefarious Use of Cloud Services
    * Cloud service deployments without sufficient attention to security, free cloud service trials and fraudulent accounts can lead to misuse of cloud computing resources, including:
      * Denial of service attacks
      * Phishing and email scams
      * Bitcoin mining
      * Brute force computing attacks
      * Hosting pirated content
11. Denial of Service
    * Denial of service attacks can be performed against the cloud provider itself, or specifically against a user of the cloud provider

- According to Rashid (2016), in regard to the CSA "dirty dozen" security threats: "DoS attacks consume large amounts of processing power, a bill the customer may ultimately have to pay."
12. Shared Technology Issues
    - Underlying hardware and software may not have been designed to provide the isolation required when shared by multiple users
    - An in-depth strategy to enforce user isolation at all levels is necessary

7.6.1 PHYSICAL DATA CENTER SECURITY

When you think about security in the cloud, typically you're thinking about hacking. But now let's think about a few other scenarios of alternate methods to steal data:

- A team armed with machine guns breaks into your data center, loads up a truck with several storage devices, and drives off
- One person sneaks a gun into the data center and holds it to a system administrator's head to make him upload a lot of data
- A person breaks into your data center at night, and collects a lot of data on a few USB drives
- A person goes to the garbage dump where your company has been throwing away its old hard drives and collects a few

Remember, this is valuable data, possibly worth millions of dollars. So physical security of your data center is very important.

Let's think about a few other physical issues that might be related to data loss (as opposed to data being stolen) or temporary, short or long term, data unavailability:

- Your data center is in an earthquake zone, an earthquake takes it out
- Your data center is taken out by a tornado
- The power lines leading to your data center are taken out by a tornado
- Someone physically cuts the power lines or phone lines leading into your data center
- Someone with a backhoe digs up the fiber line leading into your data center (this can be done either by accident or on purpose)—see Lawler (2011) for several things that can happen to your fiber lines
- An arsonist breaks in and sets fire to your data center
- Someone sends you a bomb in a package, the bomb blows up your data center

Lawton (2014) and Scalet (2015) discuss some ways to ensure physical security:

- First of all, pay attention to earthquake zones and flood or hurricane areas, don't build your data center there.
- Put the data center in a boring looking building without your company logo, that is, don't advertise what it is—make it hard to find and don't invite casual security breaches.
- It shouldn't be easily seen from the street—again, make it hard to find and don't invite casual security breaches.
- All computer rooms should be in the interior of the building, not at outside walls.
- Don't put it near a road, particularly not near a main road. Also, put in crash-proof barriers. This helps make it hard to find, and also helps prevent someone breaking through the wall with a truck.
- Have a 100-foot buffer zone around the building. This prevents someone parking a truck containing a bomb right next to the door.
- Surround the building with a 20-foot fence. Have limited entry points, with guards.

- Plan for bomb detection at all entry points.
- Have surveillance cameras all around the building.
- All power systems including generators, should be off limits to all but authorized personnel. Should be surrounded by heavy walls.
- Have redundant utilities. Two sources for electricity, voice, data, and water. All lines should be underground, the two sources should enter two different parts of the building.
- Ensure nothing can hide in the walls or the ceiling. No drop-down ceilings.
- Do not allow employees to bring weapons into the building.
- Do not allow employees to bring USB drives into the building.
- Background checks for all employees.

Oh, and invest in a hard drive shredder or something similar. Have good procedures that make sure all hard drives are completely destroyed before the remains are taken to the dump.

It's all kind of scary, isn't it? ☺

EXERCISES

1. Can a hard disk image be converted to be run on a virtual machine?
2. Virtual machine images can be created as fixed size or as expanding. What are the pros and cons of each?
3. Are there any possible problems or advantages with a raw disk image?
4. When would a type-1 hypervisor be appropriate to use? When would a type-2 hypervisor be appropriate to use?
5. Why might hardware emulation be important to be used within a Virtual Machine?
6. Why is it important for flow rules in OpenFlow to have priorities?
7. If your application is running on a virtualized system, is it more dangerous to have an attacker break into your own virtual machine, or into the underlying hardware.
8. Why might a type-1 hypervisor be more secure than a type-2 hypervisor?
9. Providing paravirtualized versions of operating systems is a good thing from an efficiency standpoint because they have higher performance on virtual machines. Are there any reasons why a paravirtualized operating system might not be the best choice from a security standpoint?
10. Why is it a bad idea for Operating System images to be stored on the same machine where the Virtual Machines are running?
11. The Cloud Security Alliance lists a malicious insider as one of the top cloud security threats. How bad a threat is this? Do you think it's likely that a malicious system administrator could sneak through a cloud's ongoing security checks?
12. Do you really think physical security of servers is necessary?

CONCEPTUAL QUESTIONS

1. Are type-2 hypervisors really needed? Or could you make use of a type-1 hypervisor for everything?
2. Think about putting OpenFlow and open vSwitch in a hardware switch. How would this work?
3. Think about hypervisor introspection in regards to network traffic between virtual machines on the same computer. What are the difficulties? How might this work?
4. Hypervisor security is very important, as we saw above. How might you go about monitoring the security of a hypervisor itself?
5. Do you have a server-like setup in your home, with perhaps centralized data storage (perhaps with Wi-Fi access)? (If you don't, then imagine that you do.) How do you handle physical security of your servers in your home?

BIBLIOGRAPHY

Ahmed, S. 2013. *Virtualization: What is the difference between KVM and QEMU?* Quora. https://www.quora.com/Virtualization-What-is-the-difference-between-KVM-and-QEMU (accessed May 25, 2016).

Allegheny Shredders. 2016. Hard drive shredders. http://alleghenyshredders.com/equipment-page/hard-drive-shredders/ (accessed May 9, 2016).

Amazon Web Services Discussion Forum. 2011. Relationship between EC2 AMI, AKI, and ARI. https://forums. aws.amazon.com/message.jspa?messageID=256534 (accessed February 20, 2017).

Baldwin, H. 2014. *Network virtualization vs. software-defined networks: What the heck is the difference?* http:// www.infoworld.com/article/2841882/networking/network-virtualization-vs-software-defined-networks-what-the-heck-is-the-difference.html (accessed May 9, 2016).

Chandramouli, R. 2014. *Security recommendations for hypervisor deployment, Draft 800-125-A.* National Institute of Standards and Technology. http://csrc.nist.gov/publications/drafts/800-125a/sp800-125a_draft.pdf (accessed May 7, 2016).

Cisco Learning Network. 2014. What's the difference between SPAN and NetFlow? https://learningnetwork. cisco.com/thread/71977 (accessed May 9, 2016).

Cisco Support Community. 2016. Understanding SPAN, RSPAN, and ERSPAN. https://supportforums.cisco. com/document/139236/understanding-spanrspanand-erspan (accessed May 9, 2016).

Cloud Security Alliance. 2016. Home page. https://cloudsecurityalliance.org/ (accessed May 7, 2016).

Cloud Security Alliance Top Threats Working Group. 2016. The Treacherous 12. CSA's Cloud Computing Top Threats in 2016. https://cloudsecurityalliance.org/download/the-treacherous-twelvecloud-computing-top-threats-in-2016/ (accessed May 7, 2016).

Debian. 2016. Amazon EC2 FAQs. https://wiki.debian.org/Amazon/EC2/FAQ#Q:_What_is_an_AKI.3F (accessed May 25, 2016).

Digital Preservation. ISO Disk Image File Format. Sustainability of Digital Formats, Planning for Library of Congress Collections. http://www.digitalpreservation.gov/formats/fdd/fdd000348.shtml (accessed May 25, 2016).

Dix, J. 2012. *Push your cloud supplier to participate in CSA STAR.* Network World. http://www.networkworld. com/article/2187089/cloud-computing/push-your-cloud-supplier-to-participate-in-csa-star.html (accessed May 7, 2016).

Fischer, T. 2016. *What is an ISO File? aboutTech.* http://pcsupport.about.com/od/termsi/g/isofile.htm (accessed May 25, 2016).

Garrison, S. 2014. *Understanding the differences between software defined networking, network virtualization and network functions virtualization.* Network World. http://www.networkworld.com/article/2174268/ tech-primers/understanding-the-differences-between-software-defined-networking-network-virtualizati. html (accessed May 9, 2016).

Github. 2014. Why Open vSwitch. https://github.com/openvswitch/ovs/blob/master/WHY-OVS.md (accessed May 6, 2016).

Gnome. 2008. The QCOW2 image format. https://people.gnome.org/~markmc/qcow-image-format.html (accessed May 25, 2016).

htpcBeginner. 2016. Mount VirtualBox shared folder on ubuntu or linux guest. http://www.htpcbeginner.com/ mount-virtualbox-shared-folder-on-ubuntu-linux/ (accessed September 18, 2016).

IETF (Internet Engineering Task Force). 2013. The Open vSwitch database management protocol. https://tools. ietf.org/html/rfc7047 (accessed May 9, 2016).

Jacobs, D. 2012. *OpenFlow protocol primer: Looking under the hood.* TechTarget. http://searchsdn.techtarget. com/feature/OpenFlow-protocol-primer-Looking-under-the-hood (accessed May 9, 2016).

Lawler, F. 2011. *The 10 most bizarre and annoying causes of fiber cuts.* Beyond Bandwidth. http://blog.level3. com/level-3-network/the-10-most-bizarre-and-annoying-causes-of-fiber-cuts/ (accessed May 9, 2016).

Lawton, S. 2014. *A guide to physical data center security solutions.* Tom's IT Pro. http://www.tomsitpro.com/ articles/physical-data-center-security,2-831.html (accessed May 9, 2016).

Libvirt. 2016. *Libvirt Virtualization API.* Home page. https://libvirt.org/ (accessed May 25, 2016).

McCouch, B. 2014. *SDN, network virtualization, and NFV in a nutshell.* http://www.networkcomputing.com/ networking/sdn-network-virtualization-and-nfv-nutshell/1655674152 (accessed May 9, 2016).

Mimoso, M. 2014. *NIST publishes draft hypervisor security guide.* ThreatPost. https://threatpost.com/nist-publishes-draft-hypervisor-security-guide/108966/ (accessed May 7, 2016).

MSDN. 2016. About VHD. https://msdn.microsoft.com/en-us/library/windows/desktop/dd323654(v=vs.85). aspx (accessed May 25, 2016).

Open Networking Foundation. 2016. ONF overview. https://www.opennetworking.org/about/onf-overview (accessed May 9, 2016).

OpenFlow. 2009. OpenFlow Switch Specification, v.1.0.0. http://archive.openflow.org/documents/openflow-spec-v1.0.0.pdf (accessed May 9, 2016).

OpenStack Glance. 2016. Disk and container formats. http://docs.openstack.org/developer/glance/formats.html (accessed May 25, 2016).

OpenStack Image Guide. 2016. Introduction. http://docs.openstack.org/image-guide/introduction.html (accessed May 25, 2016).

Pettit, J. 2013. *OpenStack: OVS deep dive*. VMware. http://openvswitch.org/slides/OpenStack-131107.pdf (accessed May 9, 2016).

Pfaff, B., Pettit, J., Koponen, T., Jackson, E.J., Zhou, A., Rajahalme, J., Gross, J., Wang, A., Stringer, J., Shelar, P., et al. 2015. The design and implementation of Open vSwitch. *Proceedings of the 12th USENIX Symposium on Networked Systems Design and Implementation (NSDI '15)*. https://www.usenix.org/system/files/conference/nsdi15/nsdi15-paper-pfaff.pdf (accessed May 9, 2016).

QEMU. 2016. QEMU Emulator user documentation. http://wiki.qemu.org/download/qemu-doc.html (accessed March 24, 2017).

Rashid, F. 2016. Introducing the "Treacherous 12," the top security threats organizations face when using cloud services. *InfoWorld*. http://www.infoworld.com/article/3041078/security/the-dirty-dozen-12-cloud-security-threats.html (accessed March 24, 2017).

Reese, B. 2008. NetFlow or sFlow: Which is the open standard? Network World. http://www.networkworld.com/article/2350352/cisco-subnet/netflow-or-sflow--which-is-the-open-standard-.html (accessed May 9, 2016).

Scalet, S.D. 2015. How to build physical security into a data center. http://www.csoonline.com/article/2112402/physical-security/physical-security-19-ways-to-build-physical-security-into-a-data-center.html?page=3 (accessed May 9, 2016).

Scarfone, K., Souppaya, M., and Hoffman, P. 2011. Guide to security for full virtualization technologies, NIST 800-125, National Institute of Standards and Technology. http://www.nist.gov/itl/csd/virtual-020111.cfm (accessed May 7, 2016).

sdxCentral. 2016. What is Open vSwitch (OVS)? https://www.sdxcentral.com/resources/open-source/what-is-open-vswitch/ (accessed May 9, 2016).

Smith, R. 2010. Using QEMU for cross-platform development, developerWorks. https://www.ibm.com/developerworks/library/l-qemu-development/ (accessed May 25, 2016).

StackExchange. 2013. What is the difference between NetFlow and sFlow? http://networkengineering.stackexchange.com/questions/1160/what-is-the-difference-between-netflow-and-sflow (accessed May 9, 2016).

StackOverflow. 2009. What is Copy-on-Write? http://stackoverflow.com/questions/628938/what-is-copy-on-write (accessed May 25, 2016).

StackOverflow. 2015. VirtualBox: mount.vboxsf: Mounting failed with the error: No such device. http://stackoverflow.com/questions/28328775/virtualbox-mount-vboxsf-mounting-failed-with-the-error-no-such-device (accessed September 18, 2016).

TechTarget. 2016. Hypervisor. http://searchservervirtualization.techtarget.com/definition/hypervisor (accessed May 25, 2016).

Virt-manager. Home page. 2016. https://virt-manager.org/ (accessed May 25, 2016).

virtualization@IBM. 2012. KVM myths—Uncovering the truth about the Open Source hypervisor. https://www.ibm.com/developerworks/community/blogs/ibmvirtualization/entry/kvm_myths_uncovering_the_truth_about_the_open_source_hypervisor?lang=en (accessed May 25, 2016).

Virtuatopia. 2016a. Building a Xen virtual guest filesystem on a disk image (Cloning Host System). http://www.virtuatopia.com/index.php/Building_a_Xen_Virtual_Guest_Filesystem_on_a_Disk_Image_(Cloning_Host_System) (accessed May 25, 2016).

Virtuatopia. 2016b. Understanding and configuring VirtualBox virtual hard disks. http://www.virtuatopia.com/index.php/Understanding_and_Configuring_VirtualBox_Virtual_Hard_Disks (accessed May 25, 2016).

VMWare. 2007 .Understanding full virtualization, paravirtualization, and hardware assist, whitepaper. https://www.vmware.com/files/pdf/VMware_paravirtualization.pdf (accessed May 25, 2016).

VMware. 2016. Virtual disk format 5.0, technical note. https://www.vmware.com/support/developer/vddk/vmdk_50_technote.pdf (accessed May 25, 2016).

Xen Project. 2016. Home page. http://www.xenproject.org/ (accessed May 25, 2016).

Xen Project Wiki. 2016. Xen project software overview. http://wiki.xen.org/wiki/Xen_Project_Software_Overview#PVHVM (accessed May 25, 2016).

Section III

Middleware Using Distributed Object-Oriented Components

8 Distributed Object-Oriented Components

8.1 JUST WHAT DO WE MEAN BY "OBJECT-ORIENTED MIDDLEWARE" AND "COMPONENT MIDDLEWARE," ANYWAY?

We previously defined Middleware back in Chapter 1. As you recall also from Chapter 1, the first attempts at middleware were things like sockets and Sun's Remote Procedure Calls. Those were functionally oriented because they came along before the object-oriented paradigm was widely used in industry. Functionally oriented means they focused on procedure calls—data was separate. In the object-oriented paradigm, of course, data and procedure calls are encapsulated inside an object.

So as industry moved toward using the object-oriented paradigm in the late 1980s and early 1990s, a need to have distributed objects talk to one another arose. One of the best known early technologies was Common Object Request Broker Architecture (CORBA) which dates back to 1991. Surprisingly, CORBA is still very much with us, although in terms of new development it has become more of a niche product today, targeted toward embedded systems. We will look in depth at CORBA in Section 8.2.

As the 1990s progressed, other object-oriented middlewares arose. Another well-known middleware was, or still is (because to my understanding it is still supported) Microsoft's Distributed Component Object Model (DCOM). Both CORBA and DCOM were originally expected to be major players in the internet. However, when firewalls became necessary, these technologies fell behind, largely because they didn't work well through firewalls.

In the early 2000s, when Microsoft brought out their .NET framework, they also brought out .NET Remoting, which was intended to solve some of the problems originally experienced by DCOM. We will discuss .NET Remoting in depth in Section 8.3. More recently, however, although .NET Remoting is still supported in Windows, Microsoft has deprecated new development .NET Remoting in favor of Windows Communication Foundation (WCF). We will look at WCF in future chapters (Chapters 10 and 12).

Both CORBA and .NET Remoting are intended to handle client-side issues as well as server-side issues such as persistence, object lifetime, etc.

In the late 1990s, Enterprise Java Beans (EJBs) was developed, primarily by Sun Microsystems. EJBs are primarily targeted toward server-side issues such as persistence and object lifetime, although considerable client-side processing (such as asynchronous client support) is also included. We will look at EJBs in Section 8.4.

All three of these technologies can be considered "component-based" technologies, speaking in general terms. Generally speaking, component-based software engineering consists of combining loosely coupled components into systems. There have been arguments about whether there is, in fact, a difference between component-based systems and object-oriented systems. The general argument is that objects in an object-oriented system focus modeling real world situations, whereas instead components in a component-based system are focused solely on combining existing components into systems. (But where do the existing components come from in the first place goes the other argument.)

However, there is a bigger distinction between a component and an object, for EJBs. EJBs on the server side do not run independently, but rather exist inside a container inside an application server. These server-side EJBs would receive all communication through the container. In some EJB terminology, this makes a server-side EJB a component, while an object that does not run inside a container is not a component.

In the following sections, we will look at CORBA (languages used are C++ and Java), at .NET Remoting (in the C# language), and EJBs (in Java). So you'll see how to do middlewares for a wide swath of object-oriented languages. Note that I've tried to write each of the sections so you can read them independently. For the main purpose of this textbook, you will want to read all these sections so you can compare. But for programming purposes, you want to have what you need in the appropriate section. ☺

As you read these sections, think about the capabilities and limitations of each of these middlewares versus the others.

For each of these technologies, there is an associated larger practical example provided in Chapter 17 (CORBA, .Net Remoting) or Chapter 18 (EJB). Chapters 17 and 18 are available in online resources.

8.2 TECHNOLOGY REVIEW: COMMON OBJECT REQUEST BROKER ARCHITECTURE (CORBA)

Common Object Request Broker Architecture (CORBA) is a mature technology, having originally been developed in the early 1990s: the first version of the CORBA specification came out in October, 1991. So at this writing, CORBA has been around for a quarter century! This timeframe doesn't compare to the C language or the TCP/IP protocols, which date from the early 1970s, but as most technologies go, this is a very respectable lifetime—and it's not over yet. ☺ CORBA is still a major force in the embedded systems world, considerable new development is being done there (Schuster 2012). Also, a large base of installed CORBA exists.

However, CORBA is much reduced from how it was seen in the 1990s. Throughout the 1990s, the assumption was that CORBA was going to be the primary Middleware of the internet. There were two major reasons that CORBA lost its title as the primary Middleware of the internet. The main one was the fact that it came along early, and did not foresee the growth of the World Wide Web, and the corresponding growth of hacking, and the firewalls that grew up to address the hacking problem. CORBA traditionally does not work well through firewalls, as firewalls tend to focus on port 80 (and HTTP), and CORBA was designed to run directly on top of TCP/IP. The other reason CORBA lost market share was the complexity of its Application Programming Interface (API) and the fact it tried to do everything for everybody (Henning 2006), companies were unable to find sufficient well-trained CORBA programmers to meet their needs.

Let's discuss further the idea that CORBA tried to do everything for everybody: One of CORBA's main concepts was that connections between just about all combinations of programming language/ operating system/computer hardware should be possible. There are "bindings" from CORBA to many programming languages—C/C++, Java, COBOL, Fortran—the list is very long. As an example, it's completely reasonable to use CORBA to connect between a program written in Java using the omniORB CORBA ORB (that is, the omniORB implementation of CORBA libraries (see more below) running on Linux) to a program written in C++ using the TAO ORB running on Windows. Back in the early 2000s when CORBA popularity in the industry was enormously high, I used to have students in my Client/Server course do connections between three different ORBs on two different operating systems.

Remember also that CORBA was intended to connect between all different kinds of computer systems hardware: PCs, embedded systems, mainframes. So some decisions in CORBA were made to enable the use of any kind of underlying computer hardware. We will see this from time to time as we examine CORBA, most notably when we discuss the use of "integer" and "octet" in the Interface Description Language (IDL).

Why did CORBA end up trying to do everything for everybody? Probably because so many different entities with different needs were involved in its creation and evolution. The CORBA specification was produced by the Object Management Group (OMG), whose membership has included/currently includes many different companies and organizations (Henning 2006). The OMG is also notable for being the organization in charge of the Unified Modeling Language (UML) specification and the Data Distribution Service (DDS) among many others.

CORBA also has another concept that was intended to reduce complexity but in some cases may have actually increased complexity: this is called *location transparency* or the idea that the actual location of an object being called doesn't matter. That is, objects that are local are treated the same as remote objects, with the result that the most complex case always occurs, that is, that local objects do not have optimized calls relative to calls to remote objects running on different hardware.

One major development in the CORBA world was the advent of the real-time CORBA specification. This allowed end-to-end predictability of how long CORBA invocations would require, an extremely important concept in a real-time/embedded systems world. To handle this, the real-time CORBA standard specified the use of object and thread priorities and predictable scheduling via threadpools, among other benefits.

Note that the word "ORB" in CORBA stands for Object Request Broker. It is used inside CORBA to refer to the CORBA libraries. It is also used colloquially to refer to different CORBA implementations by different CORBA "manufacturers" or producers, which is how I was using the term earlier when I referred to omniORB and the TAO ORB. In this textbook, we will examine implementations of the same examples in three different ORBs, the ones I've chosen are the MICO orb, omniORB, and the CORBA ORB that is included as part of the Java Development Kit (JDK)—I will call this the JDK ORB. With MICO and omniORB, we will be looking at the C++ CORBA bindings, whereas with the JDK ORB we will look at the Java CORBA bindings.

For the code provided for the instructor with this textbook, the MICO and omniORB C++ examples were developed on Linux, while the JDK Java examples were developed on Windows. I didn't provide C++ CORBA examples for Windows because the way I've always done that in the past was through Microsoft Visual Studio, and I find every new version of Visual Studio has changed around some of the ways required to configure it to make these different ORBS compile and run. So just sticking with Linux for these wasn't so much of a moving target. In the past, I've had many CORBA ORBs running on Windows as well as Linux, however.

8.2.1 Basic CORBA Concepts

CORBA is primarily Client/Server oriented (as opposed to, say, peer-to-peer, or publish-and-subscribe) and is based on remote procedure calls to methods on remotely located objects. The client-side code contains a proxy object, this object represents the remote object in the local client space. When the Client calls a method on the proxy object, the proxy object performs all actions necessary to serialize and encode the data parameters of the method, and passes those over the underlying network (usually TCP/IP on the internet), using a special protocol called General Inter-Orb Protocol (GIOP) (which runs on top of TCP/IP) to the remote server. The remote server does the necessary processing to determine the appropriate servant code to handle the remote procedure call, and passes the data parameters to that servant. After the servant has performed appropriate processing, the response data (if any) is serialized and encoded appropriately and returned (again using GIOP, usually running on top of TCP/IP) to the Client. As you may surmise, the phrases "all actions necessary," "necessary processing," "serialized and encoded appropriately" involve considerable work that is performed by various calls to the CORBA libraries. We will discuss these issues in the following sections.

First of all, there are two major interfaces in CORBA, the static interface and the dynamic interface. The static interface is defined at compile time, whereas the dynamic interface operates primarily at runtime. We are going to focus primarily on the static interface; however, we will also be going

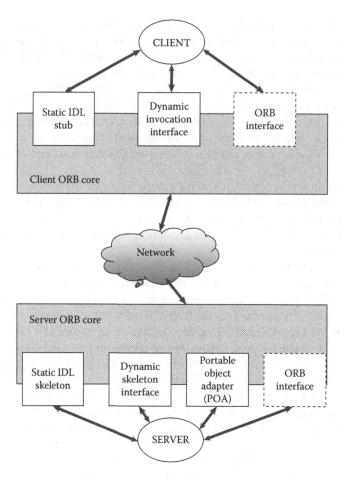

FIGURE 8.1 Client and server CORBA interconnections.

over the "any" data type, which although it can be used in a static interface is an important component in the dynamic interface.

Figure 8.1 shows a fairly common view of the connection between Client and Server using CORBA.

The interface between the Client and Server is specified using the IDL. Each implementation of CORBA (CORBA "ORB" such as omniORB or MICO) includes an IDL compiler that is used to create the static interface. The IDL compiler translates the interface that was described using the IDL into the appropriate calls to the particular implementation of the CORBA library (to CORBA libraries implemented in omniORB, MICO, or etc.) in a particular programming language (such as C++ or Java).

If you look at the client side you will see the IDL stub, whereas on the server-side is the IDL skeleton. The IDL stub is client-side code (in the appropriate programming language) that calls the CORBA library API related to Client operation. The IDL skeleton is server-side code (in the appropriate programming language) that calls the CORBA library API related to server operation. At compile time, the IDL compiler runs and creates the IDL stubs and skeletons. After the stubs and skeletons are created, the IDL stubs and the client code itself are compiled and linked together into an executable, and the IDL skeletons and the server code itself are compiled and linked together into an executable. The servant code may be linked in with the server code, or may be separately compiled and separately called by the server.

On the server-side you will also see the Object Adapter. Since CORBA 2.2, which dates from the 1998 timeframe, the Object Adapter that is used is called the Portable Object Adapter, or POA (which is pronounced POH-ah). Prior to 1998, there was a different object adapter, called the Basic Object Adapter, or BOA (pronounced BOH-ah). Unfortunately, client code written to connect to a BOA will not connect to a POA, and vice versa. Many ORBs in the past have provided separate POA and BOA implementations. However, we will focus only on the POA, since now the BOA is largely obsolete (except possibly for some remaining legacy code).

The POA is very powerful and does many server-side functions that in many other technologies would be performed by a container (as in EJBs) or perhaps by a non-standardized application server (sometimes a web server, in the case of web technologies). In CORBA, much of what a POA does, including its interfaces and the policies that control its internal behavior, are part of the CORBA standard, although some ORB manufacturers have added additional functionality. We'll discuss the POA more below, when we get to some of the code that uses it.

8.2.1.1   First Look at CORBA: Overview of Simple Echo Example

We will look very briefly at a very simple example of an echo client that sends a string to the echo server (with associated echo servant) and the servant sends that same string back to the Client. I'm using Java and the JDK ORB for this example, because for simple things CORBA code written in Java is usually easier to understand (we'll see why later on in this textbook).

To begin with, we will see the actual interface definition in a language called Interface Description Language (IDL) in Listing 8.1. Then we will see the actual Java Servant code that implements this interface on the Server, this is shown in Listing 8.2. Then we will see pseudo-code for the Server in Listing 8.3, and pseudo-code for the Client in Listing 8.4.

Finally we will see the real code for the Server in Listing 8.5 and the real code for the Client in Listing 8.6.

Here, I'm leading into the actual server and client code bit by bit, because at this point you just simply won't understand what's going on in Listing 8.5 and Listing 8.6—there's a lot of CORBA you will have to learn first. But this will give you a feel for what is to come.

In Listing 8.1 we define a very simple remote procedure call, that passes some string in from the Client to the Server, and the Server is expected to return a copy of the string that was passed in back to the Client. The remote procedure is named "echostring."

LISTING 8.1   Simplest Echo Interface—Actual Code

```
interface echo {
    string echostring (in string the_echostring);
};
```

In Listing 8.2, we see the actual Servant code in Java that will implement the interface in Listing 8.1. It may bother you that instead of implementing the interface echo, such as you would do in vanilla Java code (that is, in Java code that does not include CORBA), here the class myecho extends a class called echoPOA. For now at least, try not to worry about it—somewhere under the hood of CORBA implementing the interface echo has been taken care of. The echoPOA class is something that was generated by CORBA based on the interface from Listing 8.1.

We can see what the remote procedure call echostring on the Servant is doing. It prints out the string that was passed in, and then it returns that same string back to the Client.

LISTING 8.2   Pseudo-Code for Servant—Actual Code

```
class myecho extends echoPOA {
        public String echostring(String the_echostring) {

                System.out.println(the_echostring);
                return the_echostring;
        }
}
```

Now, let's look at the general flow of execution on Server and Client, and the interaction between Server and Client, as shown in the pseudo-code in Listings 8.3 and 8.4.

For this implementation to work, you have to start the Server first. It has to be up and running and waiting for the Client before the Client can do anything.

First, on the Server, the ORB has to be initialized. There is usually some configuration information that must be read into the ORB for execution, and also various configuration choices can be made at this step.

Next, on the Server, a reference to the POA is obtained. The POA on the Server is responsible for many server-side functions. One of the most important is that the POA maps the CORBA object to a Servant that implements it.

On the Server side, a CORBA object is a representation of the interface. As the Server receives remote procedure calls from the Client, these are routed to the appropriate CORBA object for that interface.

The POA "activates" a CORBA object by creating an appropriate Servant and mapping that Servant to the CORBA object such that when the CORBA object receives remote procedure calls from the Client, those are routed on to the Servant.

After the Server has created a CORBA object and activated it with an appropriate Servant, the Server writes the reference to (address of) the CORBA object to a file in a string format. This is so the Client can later retrieve the address of the CORBA object so it can call remote procedures associated with that CORBA object.

Finally, the Server starts listening for remote procedure calls from the Client.

Next, on the Client, the ORB has to be initialized. Again, there is usually some configuration information that must be read into the ORB for execution, and also various configuration choices can be made at this step.

The Client retrieves the reference (in string format) to the CORBA object on the Server side from the file where the Server previously wrote it. The Client uses this reference to create a Proxy Object. The Proxy Object represents the interface on the client side.

Finally, the Client calls a procedure (method) on the Proxy Object. This results in a remote procedure call to the CORBA object on the Server side.

The Server receives the remote procedure call from the Client, and routes this to the appropriate CORBA object. From the CORBA object, the remote procedure call is routed on to the associated Servant.

The Servant performs the appropriate processing and returns the appropriate response. This goes to the CORBA object, and from there back across the communication link to the Proxy Object on the Client.

LISTING 8.3   Pseudo-Code for Server

1. Initialize the ORB
2. Get a reference to the POA
3. Create a servant object that implements the interface
4. Create a CORBA object and associate the servant object with that CORBA object
5. Get the reference to (address of) that CORBA object

6. Save the reference to (address of) that CORBA object in a file
7. Start the Server listening for calls from the Client

LISTING 8.4 Pseudo-Code for Client

1. Initialize the ORB
2. Retrieve the reference to (address of) the CORBA object from a file (the CORBA object represents the interface on the server-side).
3. Using the reference to the CORBA object, create a Proxy Object that represents the interface on the client side.
4. Using the Proxy Object, call the Remote Procedure.

Now, compare the pseudo-code for the Server in Listing 8.3 to the actual Server code shown in Listing 8.5. Compare the pseudo-code for the Client in Listing 8.4 to the actual Client code shown in Listing 8.6. Although there's a lot you won't understand until you've read a lot more about CORBA, now that you know the overall flow from the pseudo-code you should be able to kind of see what's going on.

Actually, at this point, if you keep things really simple and do cut/paste, monkey see/monkey do, you should be able to run this code and even modify it a little and play with it. This echo example, using the interface in Listing 8.1, is included in the code provided for the instructor with this textbook. I've provided this Java example that runs on the JDK ORB, but also C++ examples for the MICO ORB and for omniORB, along with instructions for how to execute them.

Since you don't really know yet what you're doing, though, if you try to do too much you *will* get yourself into a problem. CORBA is pretty complicated. Read more of the book and learn a little first before you get too deep into it.

LISTING 8.5 Simplest Echo Server

```
import org.omg.CORBA.*;
import org.omg.PortableServer.*;
import org.omg.PortableServer.POA;

import java.util.Properties;
import java.io.*;

...echo servant code from Listing 8.2. would be located here...

Start the Server listening for calls from the Client

//This is the echo Server
public class server {
  public static void main(String args[]) {
    try {
      // Initialize the ORB
      ORB orb = ORB.init(args, null);
```

```
        // Get a reference to the POA (and POA Manager)
        org.omg.CORBA.Object the_rootPOA=orb.resolve_initial_references("RootPOA");
        POA mypoa = POAHelper.narrow(the_rootPOA);
        mypoa.the_POAManager().activate();;                     //activate the POA manager

        // Create a servant object that implements the interface
        myecho the_echo=new myecho();

        // Create a CORBA object and associate the servant object with that CORBA object
        // Get the reference to (address of) that CORBA object
        byte [] servant_id = mypoa.activate_object(the_echo);

        // Save the reference to (address of) that CORBA object in a file
        String line=null;
        FileWriter thefile = new FileWriter("echo.ior");
        BufferedWriter bufferedWriter = new BufferedWriter(thefile);
        org.omg.CORBA.Object theref = mypoa.id_to_reference(servant_id);
                // convert the servant ID to a CORBA object reference
        String mystr = orb.object_to_string(theref);
                // Convert the CORBA object reference to a string

        bufferedWriter.write(mystr);
        bufferedWriter.close();

        // Start the server listening for calls from the Client
        orb.run();
    }
    catch (Exception the_exception)
    {
        System.err.println("Exception happened, exception is "+the_exception);
    }
    }
}
```

LISTING 8.6   Simplest Echo Client

```
import org.omg.CORBA.*;
import java.io.*;

public class client
{
  public static void main(String args[])
    {
      try
        {
          // Initialize the ORB
          ORB orb = ORB.init(args, null);
```

```
        // Retrieve the reference to (address of) the CORBA object from a file (the CORBA
                object represents
        // the interface on the server-side).
        String line=null;
        FileReader thefile = new FileReader("echo.ior");
        BufferedReader bufferedReader = new BufferedReader(thefile);
                // since only reading one value probably not necessary but I'm used to
                // using bufferedReader around all FileReaders
        line=bufferedReader.readLine();

        if (line==null)
            System.out.println("no IOR found in IOR file");

        bufferedReader.close();

        // Using the reference to the CORBA object, create a Proxy Object that represents
                the interface on /
        // the client side
        org.omg.CORBA.Object obj = orb.string_to_object(line);
        echo myecho = echoHelper.narrow(obj);

        // Using the Proxy Object, call the Remote Procedure
        System.out.println(myecho.echostring("hi there"));
    }
    catch (Exception the_exception)
    {
        System.err.println("Exception happened, exception is "+the_exception);
    }
    }
}
```

8.2.2 INTERFACE DESCRIPTION LANGUAGE

In this section, we examine the IDL and learn how to define interfaces to be used between CORBA clients and CORBA servers.

The "interface" keyword in these examples is used very much like the "interface" keyword is in Java: it defines a set of methods that can be called, and that must be implemented (in the case of CORBA, on the server-side), usually by a class definition. Remember that CORBA maps to many different languages, and not all those languages have built in the concept of a "class." In C++ and Java, however, which we focus on here, these will be implemented on the server-side by a user-defined class that inherits from and extends a CORBA library class. (The CORBA library class will be located in the stubs or skeletons that are generated by an IDL compiler.)

First, look again at Listing 8.1. In Listing 8.1, we have a very simple remote procedure call, that passes some string in from the Client to the Server, and the Server is expected to return a copy of the string that was passed in back to the Client. (Note that in practice, the fact that the name of the remote procedure is "echostring" does not in fact constrain the Server to return or echo the same string; what string is returned is totally up to the Server. However, the server code provided for the instructor with this textbook that works with this particular echo interface does, in fact, echo back the passed in string to the Client.)

Here, the data type of the parameter being passed from the Client to the Server is "string." This could be many different data types, however. If you look at Listing 8.7 you will see the data type of the parameter is "short."

The IDL uses "short" to mean a 16-bit integer, and "long" to mean a 32-bit integer. In the CORBA IDL, we also have "unsigned short" and "unsigned long." So a "short" is a signed 16-bit integer, and a "long" is a signed 32-bit integer. This means that you could send, say, a −1 in a "short" but not in an "unsigned short," which would only allow you to send a +1. (It also means that since you're not using it to store negative numbers, an "unsigned short" can contain (almost) twice as many positive numbers as a "short." I use the word "almost" here since zero is considered a positive number. Think about it in hexadecimal and binary and work it out. Nice little exercise for the student. You can do it!). The IDL also supports "long long" and "unsigned long long" for 64 bit numbers.

The CORBA standard did not use the keyword "integer" in the IDL because the word "integer" has meant different things to different computer hardware/operating systems in the history of computers. Traditionally, "integer" has been a data type associated with a non-signed value that is stored in one word of the computer hardware. And in the history of computing, the size of a "word" has varied quite a bit. Some old microprocessors had words that were 8 bits wide. Other microprocessors have had word sizes that were 16 bits, 32 bits, 64 bits. Some old mainframe computers, the Control Data Cyber computers, had 60-bit wide words. (Note that the number 60, although an even number is not a power of 2. In the old days, that obviously wasn't considered a necessary requirement for word size). As an interesting tidbit of information for you, the first computer I ever programmed on was a CDC Cyber computer.

The IDL uses the word "octet" to refer to 8 bits. Why didn't the CDC use the word "byte" for 8 bits? Well, in the old days, like on the CDC Cyber computers, a byte was not 8 bits. According to Wikipedia, the CDC 6600 used a 12-bit byte and a 6-bit character. My own memory is that the CDC Cyber computer I programmed on back in undergraduate school at Georgia Tech used 6-bit bytes, which is what I've been telling students for years. Maybe the Wikipedia article is correct, however, it's been a while. In any case, we see here that the word "integer" and the word "byte" could not be used by any IDL that intended to target old mainframe computers and such. So we can see some of the choices made in the CORBA standard.

Perhaps oddly, CORBA didn't make some restrictions in the IDL that you might have expected: for example, it's perfectly acceptable to use the word "if" and "while" and "switch" and "for" as names. It would be legal to have the following:

```
interface if {
  while switch (in for the_data);
}
```

Of course, this wouldn't compile when the IDL compiler tries to convert it to C++ or Java, but in other languages, perhaps. ☺ Yet another way in which CORBA was trying to be everything to everybody.

Consider Listing 8.1 again. The word "in" here means that the data is going *from* Client to Server, but not back from Server to Client. That is, the Server cannot change the data in the_echostring.

In CORBA, the direction from Client to Server is *in*, and from Server to Client is *out*. So if we wanted to send another data item back (in addition to the string that is the return type of the function), we could make it an *out* data type. The IDL also supports *inout* data types, an example is shown in Listing 8.7. With an *inout* data type, the Client can send a value to the Server in the data item of type *inout*, and the Server can also send a value back to the Client.

Note that CORBA assumes IDL strings are null terminated. See Section 8.2.7.1 for a discussion of how IDL strings are stored as they are being transmitted to/from Client and server.

LISTING 8.7   Echo Interface Using Data Type Short

```
interface echo {
  string echoshort (inout short the_echoshort);
};
```

LISTING 8.8   Echo Interface with inout

```
interface echo {
  string echostring (inout string the_echostring);
};
```

In the IDL, you can also group different interfaces into namespaces (called "modules"). If you have a complex set of interfaces, that allows you to organize the interfaces for better understanding. It also allows you to reuse interface names in different modules. If you want to access these interfaces inside the modules, however, you now have to use the whole name for an interface, for example, the one in Listing 8.9 would be referred to as: echomodule.echo. Or alternately, for example, in C++, you could say "using namespace echomodule" at the beginning of your code.

LISTING 8.9   Echo Interface with Namespace

```
module echomodule {
  interface echo {
    string echostring (in string the_echostring);
  };
};
```

CORBA also provides numerous built-in system exceptions, or you can define user exceptions of your own. Listing 8.10 shows a user-defined exception named "Bad_Message."

There is a fairly long list of CORBA-provided system exceptions. Some of the more commonly seen of these are COMM_FAILURE (this usually means the ORB could not set up basic communication over the network to the other side or else loses it), MARSHAL (this means the request or response is not correct; in my own experience this often means that one of the ORBs is not working correctly, perhaps it was not compiled correctly), BAD_PARAM (data parameter out of range), OBJECT_NOT_EXIST (the CORBA object on the server-side is not there), or the very common (in my own experience) TRANSIENT exception. TRANSIENT means the ORB could not find the object but doesn't know why, and for all it knows it might be a temporary condition. TRANSIENT is often thrown when the client side does a *narrow* and the Server is not running. But we'll see this again later.

Unfortunately, the UNKNOWN system exception is also common. This means it was some exception that the CORBA implementation you're using doesn't understand. Usually it's a non-CORBA exception.

LISTING 8.10   Echo Interface with Exceptions

```
interface echo {
  exception Bad_Message{};
  string echostring (in string the_echostring) raises (Bad_Message);
};
```

Now we're going to expand beyond the echo example, and look at various interface examples that are transferring slightly more complicated data—that therefore we don't really want to echo back. ☺

In Listing 8.11, we see a user-defined struct being passed in the interface, as a parameter in a remote procedure call. Here the struct is named "theData" and we define a new data type called StructType. Then we define a parameter in the remote procedure call as a struct of type StructType.

LISTING 8.11   Interface Sending a Struct

```
struct theData {
  long firstvalue;
  string secondvalue;
};

typedef theData StructType;

interface sending_stuff {
  string sendvalue (in StructType mystruct);
};
```

In Listing 8.12, we see an interface that is returning a struct as the return value of a remote procedure call. Here the struct and the data type StructType are the same as in Listing 8.11.

LISTING 8.12   Interface Returning a Struct

```
struct theData {
  long firstvalue;
  string secondvalue;
};
typedef theData StructType;

interface sending_stuff {
  StructType  sendvalue (in string mystring);
};
```

In Listing 8.13, we see a user defined array being passed as a parameter in a remote procedure call. In CORBA, the whole array will be sent. That is, if you have an array on the Client of length 20, but you only have set 3 data values in that whole array, it's going to send those 3 values but it's also going to send 17 other empty values (maybe zero, maybe who knows what, depends on whether you've initialized the array or not).

One of the *gotcha* aspects of CORBA is, you have to remember that when CORBA sends an array, it doesn't say anything about whether the array index begins at 0 or at 1 (or for that matter at any other number). Remember that CORBA is intended to connect practically any arbitrary language to any other arbitrary language. So you can never make any assumptions about how the array indices will be used at the other end.

LISTING 8.13   Interface Sending an *in* Array

```
typedef short ArrayType[20];
const short MAX=20;

interface sending_stuff {
  string sendvalue (in ArrayType myarray, in short size);
};
```

In Listing 8.14, we see a sequence being sent as a parameter in a remote procedure call. Sequences in CORBA transmit only the data that was actually set in the sequence. That is, a sequence can be up to a certain size (perhaps 20 as in the earlier array example), but if you have only 3 elements set in the sequence, only 3 will actually be sent. This is very useful in the case of sparse data (that is, data with lots of holes in a data structure and only a few data items).

Here we are sending a sequence of long (that is, 32-bit integer) values. If we wanted to send a sequence of, say, floats (that is, IEEE single-precision floating point, 32 bits), we would do instead:

```
typedef sequence<float> SequenceType;
```

whereas if we wanted to send doubles (that is, IEEE double-precision floating point, 64 bits), we would do:

```
typedef sequence<double> SequenceType;
```

For whatever IDL mapping you're using, there will be a length() function attached to a sequence that will allow you to find out how long the sequence is. We'll look at this later in the C++/C mapping.

LISTING 8.14   Interface Sending a Sequence

```
typedef sequence<long> SequenceType;
interface sending_stuff {
  string sendvalue (in SequenceType mysequence);
};
```

LISTING 8.15   Interface Using an Attribute

```
interface sending_stuff {
  attribute short the_value;
};
```

Next, we will discuss the "attribute" keyword in IDL. We see an example of this in Listing 8.15. I thought about *not* discussing the "attribute" keyword because there are always a few students who don't listen and therefore don't understand the "attribute" keyword but try to use it incorrectly and cause themselves a lot of grief. But lots of CORBA code out there in the wild uses it, from what I've seen, so I finally decided I better discuss it.

Before I do, though, let's review what CORBA *is* and what CORBA *is not*. CORBA *is* a way to send data from one computer to another computer across a network. When you use CORBA, you're generally pretending that the Client is connecting direct to the Server, that is, since you're ignoring the lower networking layers (as in most middlewares), and that therefore you don't have to know how that data is being routed between any intermediate computers on the network. That is, most of the time you're only worried about the end-to-end connection.

Think about what a network is. The simplest network would be a wire stretching from one computer to another. Well, obviously our networks that we're going to use are a lot more complicated than that. But when we're doing CORBA, for the most part we can think about our network as being as simple as that wire. Because the main purpose of middleware is to let us ignore the network layers below the middleware. And because CORBA is usually considering only the endpoints (Client and Server).

So it's reasonable in a large sense to *pretend* for the sake of an example that CORBA is working from one computer to another computer across one wire.

Now let's look at that wire. It's just a wire, right? I can send bits of data moving across that wire, from one end to another, by changing the voltage on the wire. That is, at one end I raise the voltage levels and lower the voltage levels. A high-voltage level might be a logic 1 and a low voltage level might be a logic 0. At the other end, I look at what voltage levels are there to determine which bits have been sent. But the voltage levels are only temporary, so I have to look quick because *they will go away*.

Whew, this is an oversimplification. ☺ But I'm going to make an important point using this super simple example. Here comes the point:

- I don't see *anywhere* on that wire that I can actually *store* any data, do you?
- I mean, I didn't put any flip flops on the wire. I didn't put any registers of any kind on the wire. For those of you who might have an electrical background, I didn't put any capacitors on the wire.
- SO THERE IS NO WAY TO STORE ANY DATA AT ALL ON THIS WIRE.

Let me say that again: There is no way to store any data on the wire.

Reasoning toward the larger world: You don't store data on network connections! You might store data at one end of a network, or possibly at an intermediate point in a network. But on the network connections themselves, no, it's just a collection of wires, or maybe radio or laser signals, sending data from one point to another point.

But in CORBA we're pretending we have an end-to-end, Client to Server, connection, and we're ignoring any intermediate points on the network. So there is NO DATA STORAGE in the network interface.

So the "attribute" keyword in the IDL *cannot possibly* be used to mean any data is stored, or that any kind of data variable is being defined.

What the "attribute" keyword *is*, it's a shorthand notation to signify getting and setting a particular variable at the servant. That is, it defines a *set* routine that allows the Client to send a value to be written to a particular variable on the Servant, and it defines a *get* routine that allows the Client to request that the Servant send it back the value of a particular value.

For example, the attribute the_value in the interface in Listing 8.15 would result in two remote procedure definitions:

1. A remote procedure named the_value with no parameters passed, that returns a Short value
2. A remote procedure named the_value with a Short value passed as a parameter, that does not return any values (has a void value as the return value)

If we look at the C++ code using either omniORB or the MICO ORB that would implement these remote procedure calls, they look like this:

- virtual CORBA::Short the_value();
- virtual void the_value(CORBA::Short the_new_value);

So now you know what an attribute is. *Please* don't try to store any data in your IDL !!!

Now let's look at the "any" data type. Listing 8.16 shows an "any" data type. The "any" data type is just what it says, using this data type you can send any kind of data. You could write a float value into an "any" on the Client and send it as the mydata parameter to the sendvalue method in Listing 8.16. You could write a string value into an "any" on the Client and send it as the mydata parameter to the sendvalue method in Listing 8.16.

The way this works, an "any" data value contains a TypeCode value that specifies what kind of data is stored in the "any." Let's say that a Client is sending an "any" to the Server. The Server can extract the TypeCode from the "any" and then the Server will know what kind of data has been sent and can handle it appropriately.

Note, however, if the Client and Server have previously agreed on the type of data that will be sent (perhaps for a period of time?) then the Server has easier ways to extract the data type from the "any" in which the Server does not have to check the TypeCode. We will see an example of this later on.

However, we're not going to get into handling "any" with any depth. That's because probably the most common use of an "any" data type is in the dynamic interfaces, which we're only going to look at briefly.

There is one thing to note about TypeCodes. CORBA exceptions have an associated TypeCode, that you can check if you need to, to determine what kind of exception has occurred.

LISTING 8.16   Interface Sending an Any

```
interface sending_stuff {
  string sendvalue (in any mydata);
};
```

A few other leftover IDL items:

First the CORBA IDL enumerated type called "enum" looks like this:

```
enum Money {euro, dollar, pound, yen};
```

which of course should remind you of C++/C enums.

One thing to remember about IDL enums: You don't know which actual numbers will be mapped to the values—for example, "euro" above might be mapped to the number 0 or it might be mapped to the number 99. You can't control it and you shouldn't make any assumptions about the numerical values.

There's a thing in IDL called "discriminated unions." It allows you to swap at runtime from sending one kind of data to sending another kind of data, based on a discriminator value that allows you to swap from sending one kind of data to sending a different kind of data. It's supposed to be more efficient than sending all the different kinds of data you need to send every time, when you only need to send one kind of data at any one time. It's supposed to be easier and cleaner to understand than using an "any" data type. Well, I believe it is more efficient but as far as being easier to understand than an "any," that has not been my experience with students trying to learn this in the past. I'm not giving an example here because I think you should avoid it, ☺ at least while you're a CORBA beginner. Later on, once you know what you're doing, you can look it up, and use it if you really feel you need it.

8.2.3   CORBA IDL TO C++/C AND CORBA IDL TO JAVA BINDINGS

When the IDL compiler creates stubs and skeletons, what it is really doing is automated code generation. The stubs and the skeletons are code in whatever language you're using—C, C++, Java, Python, could be many different languages—that implement various calls to the CORBA libraries (the CORBA libraries themselves have been compiled as part of the ORB when it compiled, and are located in a directory somewhere; you'll have to link to that directory).

The stubs and skeletons implement various definitions that you use in your own code. For example, in the MICO ORB in the echo.h that defines the skeleton (that is, server-side) file that was created using the IDL compiler on the echo example, you would have the following definition that is part of the interface implementation between your code and the MICO ORB:

```
class POA_echo : virtual public PortableServer::StaticImplementation
        ...
```

whereas in omniORB in the echo.hh file that was created using its IDL compiler, you would have:

```
class POA_echo :
        public virtual _impl_echo,
        public virtual ::PortableServer::ServantBase
            ...
```

So as you see, somewhat different implementations but leading to the same CORBA class to be used to implement an interface.

The servant class you use that actually implements the interface, would begin like this:

```
class myecho : public virtual POA_echo
        ...
```

for both the MICO ORB and omniORB.

In Java this of course looks a little different. Using the JDK ORB on a similar echo example, you have a file named echoPOA.java that is part of the skeleton (server-side) code. The part of the implementation of the echo interface in this skeleton looks like this:

```
public abstract class echoPOA extends org.omg.PortableServer.Servant
        implements echoOperations, org.omg.CORBA.portable.InvokeHandler
        ...
```

and your servant class that actually implements the interface would look like this:

```
class myecho extends echoPOA
        ...
```

But again, you're using a very similar CORBA class to implement the interface to what you did in the C++ ORBs.

In all these cases, very similar stuff, obeying the same rules. It's just a little different because in these cases, different people implemented it in a different way, and in two different languages.

So these are some of the things that can be seen when talking about different ORB implementations. And now we're also beginning to look at different bindings to different languages.

When we consider the different language bindings, there are some major differences between different languages. They all generally have to do the same calling-CORBA-libraries kinds of things, but each language has its own peculiarities that you have to learn.

When the CORBA standard was originally created in 1991, the very first language mapped to was C. Yes, C, not C++, the mapping to C++ didn't occur until 1996. The Java language mapping didn't happen until 1998. (Java itself was released in the 1995 timeframe.)

When we compare the C++/C binding to the Java binding, the biggest difference between them is that Java does garbage collection and C++/C does not. So the CORBA standard tried to help with C++/C memory management, and the C++/C binding acquired a lot of— useful, interesting, annoying (depending on your viewpoint)—features related to memory management.

Have you ever heard of a bug called a memory leak? In my experience it is the most aggravating and difficult kind of bug to catch of all bugs. Fixing it, however, is usually a breeze—if you're using C++ usually you just have to add one more "delete" or "free" statement, somewhere in your code. It's finding the appropriate "somewhere" that is the difficult part.

What happens in a memory leak is, somehow or other when you're done with using dynamically allocated memory, you forgot to return that memory to the list of free memory that can be reused (heap). Even if this is an infrequent bug, eventually all the free memory on your system will be used up, and your system will crash! But the memory leak bug that caused the issue may have actually happened a very long time before—perhaps hours or days. All you will be able to see when you look at the immediate cause of the bug is that your code tried to allocate new memory, but there was no free memory available, so the system crashed.

Back in the 1980s, I used to work at a modem company. We had a major customer who bought thousands of our modems and mounted them in racks. What the customer found was, if they didn't reboot all those thousands of modems at least once every week, then they would crash in different ways at different times. I and one other software engineer tracked that bug for weeks, all the time with a major customer breathing down our necks and being checked on repeatedly by important managers. We finally set up test modems to trap various bug possibilities, and any time a combination of circumstances happened, we started a modem light blinking (so the customer could tell this situation had happened), and we wrote the contents of the modem memory, in hexadecimal, out an I/O port. The customer captured this data and sent it back to us as very long printouts. Then we spent weeks examining this hexadecimal data. When we finally found the bug, it was a one-line fix.

Java has a wonderful thing called garbage collection that fixes this kind of thing. Every so often, Java runs through and returns all unused memory to the heap (free memory list). There can be some performance negatives versus C++/C involved, the arguments pro and con are lengthy.

The CORBA C++ bindings attempted to make memory management harder to forget and largely required. In my opinion, they achieved this, but at the cost of making the code much harder to understand, that is, it kind of looks like a new language and not C++ at all. Sometimes (especially in the past when CORBA was the hottest technology around) I've had my students do a CORBA program in C++ and get it working there, then re-do the same CORBA program in Java. Invariably the students thought the Java program was easier. That's because CORBA in Java didn't have to add a lot to the Java language to do memory management.

We will look at the CORBA C++ binding next, after that at the CORBA Java binding, so we can compare the two.

8.2.3.1   CORBA IDL to C++ Binding

The CORBA C++ binding maps IDL basic types to C++ using a CORBA namespace. That is, the type "float" in IDL would show up as "CORBA::float" in C++. The type "boolean" in IDL would show up as "CORBA::Boolean" in C++, while an unsigned short in IDL would show up in C++ as "CORBA::UShort" and an unsigned long long in IDL (64 bits) would be "CORBA::ULongLong."

You get the idea: for the basic types add "CORBA::" in front of the IDL name, then capitalize the first letter of each instance of the data type. The IDL "unsigned" becomes "U" in front of the data type.

Arrays in IDL are mapped to C++ arrays and have the same name as in the IDL (they're user-defined types so you don't add "CORBA::" in front). For example, the servant code in Listing 8.17 implements the IDL interface previously shown in Listing 8.13. (By the way, ignore the string versus char * stuff for now, we'll talk about this later.)

LISTING 8.17   CORBA IDL *in* Array Servant in C++ Example

```
class myreceiver : public virtual POA_sending_stuff
{
  public:
      virtual char * sendvalue (const ArrayType myarray, const short size);
};

char * myreceiver::sendvalue (const ArrayType myarray, const short size)
{
      int the_real_size;

      the_real_size=size;
      if (the_real_size > MAX)
          the_real_size=MAX;

      for(int i=0;i<the_real_size;++i)
      {
          cout << "myarray[" << i << "] is " << myarray[i] << endl;
      }

      char *smsg= CORBA::string_dup("got here");
      return smsg;
}
```

The array is defined in the parameter "ArrayType myarray" and myarray is accessed similarly to any other C++ array:

```
myarray[i]
```

The IDL sequence from Listing 8.14 would map to servant code such as that shown in Listing 8.18.

LISTING 8.18   CORBA Sequence in C++ Example

```
class myreceiver : public virtual POA_sending_stuff
{
  public:
      virtual char * sendvalue (const SequenceType &mysequence);
};

char * myreceiver::sendvalue (const SequenceType &mysequence)
{
      for(CORBA::ULong i=0;i<mysequence.length();++i)
      {
              cout << "mysequence[" << i << "] is " << mysequence[i] << endl;
      }
      char *smsg= CORBA::string_dup("got here");
      return smsg;
}
```

As you can see, the sequence is accessed the same way any other C++ sequence is accessed: mysequence[i].

If you want to find out how long the sequence currently is, you can do:

    CORBA::Ulong the_length=mysequence.length();

You can set the length of a sequence forcibly by doing:

    mysequence.length(15);

or:

    mysequence.length(2);

That is, you can extend the length or truncate the length (and thereby drop off the last few characters).

You can find the current maximum length of a sequence by doing something like:

    CORBA::ULong the_max=mysequence.maximum();

One tricky thing in the CORBA C++ binding is that an IDL string maps to: char *. When you allocate a new string, you don't use new or delete. There are special functions in the namespace CORBA that allow string manipulation: CORBA::string_dup duplicates a string, CORBA::string_alloc (ULong length) allocates a string of the given length, and CORBA::string_free (char *) deallocates the specified string.

This was done, according to Schmidt and Vinoski (2000) partly because when the IDL to C++ mapping was created back in 1994, C++ did not contain a string data type. Also, the CORBA IDL to C binding mapped "string" to "char *." Additionally, there were some inter-language call issues, and one particular company (IBM) required the IDL string to "char *" mapping.

The easiest way to allocate a string and initialize it at the same time is:

```
char * mystring = new CORBA::string_dup("ThisIsTheBeginning");
```

Then you can explicitly free it, if you want to, using:

```
CORBA::string_free(mystring);
```

However, there's another way to handle a string that does automatic memory management of the string. That is to use an "_var" type. When you use "_var" attached to a particular data type, you're telling CORBA to do some memory management. Here's a very short example, in Listing 8.19.

LISTING 8.19   CORBA _var Example

```
int i;
(…i is read in from somewhere…)
if (i==4)
{  // this is the beginning curly bracket
     CORBA::String_var mystring= new CORBA::string_dup("ThisIsTheBeginning");
     …do some other stuff…
}  // this is the ending curly bracket
```

Note that we have turned our original char * string into a string of type CORBA::String_var. Do you see the curly brackets? See that we have defined mystring *inside* these curly brackets. That means that the *scope* or lifetime of mystring is the lifetime of the curly brackets. Because we used an _var type here, when the code exits the curly brackets, the memory containing the "ThisIsTheBeginning" is returned to the heap (list of free memory) for use by other programs. (We're assuming in this case that "…do some other stuff…" didn't change the contents of mystring.)

The String_var is a class that is defined in the CORBA namespace. It is a *wrapper* around "char *." So the "ThisIsTheBeginning" is pointed to by a pointer of type char * that is defined *inside* the String_var class.

You can also wrap an IDL "any" data type with a _var (CORBA::Any_var), and you can similarly wrap the user defined C++ types: struct, class, or union. Additionally, you can wrap an array or a sequence with a _var type. For example, let's look at the following IDL for a struct:

```
struct thestruct {
     short value;
};
```

In the associated C++ mapping, you could use:

```
thestruct_var mystruct;
mystruct->value = 10;
```

Note that you *don't* do "CORBA::thestruct_var." You just do "thestruct_var." That's because it's a user defined type, and not one of the CORBA basic types that's built in to CORBA. Your wrapper class that creates the _var type based on the struct is generated by your ORB's IDL compiler, and it's defined in your stub/skeleton.

Note that you *must* access the items in the struct like this:

mystruct->value=10;

You *cannot* use:

mystruct.value=10; //WRONG

That's because the automatically generated wrapper class just works that way.

There are methods defined in all _var wrapper classes that access the wrapped data type directly. Three of these (in(), inout(), and out()) can be used to help you in passing _var data types as parameters to a function. In one case, the method _retn() can be used to return the wrapped data type as a return value from a function.

For example, in a CORBA::String_var class, to get at the char * string inside the String_var class for the purpose of using the char * string as a parameter in a function call, you could do one of three different things, depending on your needs:

Consider the following String_var variable:

CORBA::String_var mystring=CORBA::string_dup("Hello World");

- To pass mystring into a function that will not change mystring, that looks like this:

    void myfunc(const char * thestring)

  you could call it as follows:

    myfunc(mystring.in());

- To pass mystring to a function that could change mystring and return it to the calling program, in that case the function to call looks like this:

    myfunc(char * & thestring)

  and you could call it as follows:

    myfunc(mystring.inout());

- To pass mystring to a function that could use mystring, but then will deallocate its memory and *not* return the mystring value to the calling program, in that case the function to call looks like this:

    myfunc(char * & thestring)

  and you could call it as follows:

    myfunc(mystring.out());

Now let's assume that we have a function defined as follows:

```
char * myfunc()
{
...
```

```
CORBA::String_var mystring=CORBA::string_dup("Hello World");
...
}
```

to return the string wrapped by the String_var mystring, we would do:

```
return mystring.retn();
```

so the function now would look like this:

```
char * myfunc()
{
...
CORBA::String_var mystring=CORBA::string_dup("Hello World");
return mystring.retn();
}
```

I should note that you could also pass a parameter such as CORBA::String_var in mystring by defining your array parameter as a String_var, such as this:

```
void myfunc(String_var the string)
```

However, this is *not* a good idea as it is very inefficient: a new String_var object is created every time this function is called. Just how inefficient this would be depends on the ORB implementation, but remember that when you're using String_var you're telling CORBA to do your memory management for you: Think about it. ☺

Another *gotcha* in CORBA: It's generally a bad idea to mix C++/C style pointers and _var variables pointing to each other/storing the same data because every time your code exits a pair of curly brackets (exits scope), your _var variable will have its memory returned. If you've got any other C++ pointers pointing to that same _var variable, or to the contents (the wrapped data) inside that _var variable, after the _var variable exits the pair of curly brackets your pointers will be pointing to garbage. That is, your C++/C pointers will be pointing to memory on the heap, that some other program could have used for something. Basic way to fix this: Don't have C++/C style pointers point to _var variables.

Also, when I first started doing CORBA stuff, I was working for a U.S. Army contract where the army wanted me to determine the degree to which CORBA was interoperable. That is, their primary concern was, if they were going to use CORBA, then they wanted to be able to swap ORB vendors at any time; they didn't want to be stuck with one vendor. There are two aspects of this: One, the CORBA code needs to be able to *connect* with any given CORBA ORB, and two, it should be possible to transfer your CORBA code from any ORB to another (at least in the same programming language).

When I started working on this contract, it seemed to me originally that the best way to do this was to use as little CORBA style code (such as _var constructs and _ptr constructs—we haven't talked about _ptr yet, we'll see that later) as possible, and use vanilla C++/C wherever I could. This turned out to be largely a bad idea. A lot of C++/C CORBA ORBS just plain refused to work (in certain places) unless I was using the CORBA constructs when I was accessing the ORB. So this was just a bad idea and I shouldn't have gone down that path in the first place—if you're using a standard CORBA library, for goodness' sake, use the standard CORBA library.

I mention this here because this is the very thing that I've found a lot of my students have tried to do over the years. Believe me, I understand the reasoning: you the student already know C++/C and this CORBA C++/C language mapping is tough to understand so you think maybe you can bypass it. Take it from me, it can be done to a degree but not completely, and the effort is much worse doing it this way. And your code looks weird and is hard to debug. So *don't* do that. (On the positive side, the main place you end up using _var variables is with return values and out parameters, where you are looking at possible memory leaks. So you don't necessarily have to use these everywhere in your code. Be careful and try to keep your true C++/C code separate from your CORBA C++/C binding code.)

The TAO ORB (TAO stands for The ACE ORB, so saying "TAO ORB" is like saying "The ACE ORB ORB," but you understand what I'm saying so who cares if it's a bit silly) especially gave me grief when I was trying to do this. The TAO ORB is based on The Adaptive Communication Environment (ACE) which is an object-oriented framework that implements various communication patterns and is quite powerful. Back when I was using TAO in the early 2000s, ACE was implemented in a macro language (I assume it still is, I haven't looked recently). I spent a lot of time converting ACE macros to standard C++/C just to prove TAO would work without those macros themselves actually being used. There were a few places where this just wasn't possible, the ORB wouldn't compile without the appropriate macro. Bottom line: If you're using TAO then I recommend using ACE like you are supposed to.

As part of this _var discussion, we've seen parameter passing now using CORBA::String_var as an example. Passing other data types as parameters to functions is similar: for "in" data types this maps to "const" parameters, for "inout" and "out" parameters to functions, you would use "datatypename &." For example, to do a struct as either an "in" or an "inout" parameter you would use "struct &" and to do an enum as either an "in" or an "inout" parameter you would use an "enum &."

Note that the array data type is different. When you use an array data type as an "in" parameter, it would be "const arraytype," similar to what you did with any other "in" parameter. However, for "inout" or "out" you would say "array_slice *." For return type you would also use "array_slice *."

For return types for sequence, union, and struct, you would use "sequence *," "union *," and "struct *," respectively.

There's another CORBA C++ binding item that is important to talk about: _ptr. The "_ptr" type acts a lot like a pointer to a C++ class. It's normally used on the client side to point to a proxy object (the proxy object represents the servant in the address space of the Client, we'll talk about this more later on). You can also use a _var type to point to the proxy; it works similarly to the _ptr but it also does memory management of the proxy (deletes the proxy object when the code leaves the immediate curly bracket scope).

The way the _ptr operates is as follows, let's assume we're calling an echostring type method on the remote servant. This is part of the client code we'd use to call the servant, when we're using the interface previously shown in Listing 8.1 (here the class "echo" is the proxy class):

```
echo_ptr myecho = do a lot of stuff to create a proxy that is connected to the remote
if (CORBA::is_nil (myecho)) {
    cout << "the server is missing" << endl;
    exit (1);
}
```

Sometime in the future you would have to do:

```
CORBA::release(myecho);
```

to return the memory used by that echo object to the heap (list of unused memory).

Or you could use echo_var instead of echo_ptr:

```
echo_var myecho = do a lot of stuff to create a proxy that is connected to the remote.
```

The "is_nil()" method that is automatically generated by the IDL compiler to check the _ptr (or _var) that points to the proxy can be used to see if the echo_ptr (or echo_var) has been initialized or not.

When you're using _ptr, it keeps a reference count of the number of instances of "echo" being pointed to by the echo_ptr. For example, there's a method called _duplicate that could be used to make a copy of the original echo_ptr. In that case, there would be two (or more, depending on the number of calls to _duplicate) that point to the same proxy object. So in this case, CORBA::release would have to be called for the original proxy object, plus once for every time _duplicate had been previously called, before the echo object itself is returned to the heap.

Let's take a brief look at the Any data type and how it can be handled in the CORBA to C++ binding. We originally saw an IDL that used Any back in Listing 8.16. Let's say, for example, that we want to send data of type "long", then on the Client we could do:

```
long the_real_value;
    the_real_value=1934;

CORBA::Any myvalue;
myvalue<<=(CORBA::Long) the_real_value;
```

Then on the servant if we *knew* the data we were getting was of type "long", then we could do:

```
CORBA::Long myvalue=0;

mydata >>= myvalue;
```

I'm ignoring the situation where we *don't* know what the data type is, and have to extract it from the TypeCode in the Any. That's getting away from the static interfaces and more into the dynamic interfaces, and I'm largely ignoring those for this (introductory) textbook.

8.2.3.2 CORBA IDL to Java Binding

The CORBA IDL to Java language binding is in many ways easier to understand than the CORBA IDL to C++/C binding: Since Java does garbage collection, there was no need to memory management to the language. This simplified basic CORBA interactions—there are no _var types and there are no _ptr types in the Java binding. For the most part, CORBA IDL types map directly to Java types.

For example, a module in CORBA IDL maps to a Java package. A boolean maps to a Boolean, an octet maps to a byte. The IDL types *short* and *unsigned short* map to a Java short. An octet maps to a Java byte. A *long* and *unsigned long* map to a Java int. A *long long* and an *unsigned long long* map to a Java long. *Float* maps to *float* and *double* maps to *double*.

Very conveniently, a *string* maps to java.lang.String. IDL *sequences* and *arrays* both map to Java arrays. IDL *enums*, *structs*, *unions*, and *exceptions* map to Java classes.

The IDL *Any data type* maps to org.omg.CORBA.Any.

Probably, the most complicated-looking part of the CORBA IDL to Java mapping are the *Helper* and *Holder* classes. There are Helper and Holder classes for the basic data types defined in the CORBA libraries. For any user-defined types, the IDL compiler generates a Helper class and a Holder class for each one.

The Helper classes allow reads and writes to CORBA I/O streams (org.omg.CORBA.portable. InputStream and org.omg.CORBA.portable.OutputStream) and inserting/extracting values from type Any data. (The org.omg.CORBA.portable.InputStream and org.omg.CORBA.portable.

OutputStream are the Java mapping classes for marshaling data to and from the format (Common Data Representation [CDR]) that CORBA converts data into for transmission between computers. We'll see more about this later on.)

The Helper class also implements the *narrow* routine, among other utility routines. We'll look at the narrow routine later on, but among other things it does a type downcast of a general CORBA object to a particular interface type.

For both the interface shown in Listing 8.13, and the interface shown in Listing 8.20, the Client would call the remote as follows):

```
sending_stuff proxy = sending_stuffHelper.narrow(obj);
```

This is one example of a Helper class, in this case calling a narrow (after creating a proxy object, we'll discuss that later).

The Holder classes are used when there is an *inout* or an *out* parameter to an operation in the IDL. Method parameters in Java are implemented as pass-by-value; that means a copy of the variable is passed in the parameter rather than the parameter itself. So if you need a pass-by-reference (as when you're using an in or inout parameter), that is, when you want the routine you're calling to be able to change the value—in the calling program—of that variable you're passing, you have to do something else. What a Holder class does is, it's a wrapper around the data type you're wanting to pass-by-reference. Then you change the contents of the Holder class. Holder classes pass data to the Helper classes to be read or written.

An IDL interface maps to: Operations, Helper, and Holder classes. The *operations* class simply provides the definitions of the remote procedure calls that are part of the IDL interface.

In Listing 8.20, we have the Java code for the servant that implements the interface previously shown in Listing 8.13. (Compare this to the C++ servant shown in Listing 8.17 that implements the same interface.) This illustrates an array passed as an *in* parameter. It also shows how the IDL to Java binding handles IDL constants and typedefs.

LISTING 8.20   CORBA IDL *in* Array in Java Example

```
public class myreceiver extends sending_stuffPOA
{
    public String sendvalue (short[] myarray, short size)
    {
        int the_real_size;
        the_real_size=size;
        if (the_real_size > MAX.value)
            the_real_size=MAX.value;
        for(int i=0;i<the_real_size;i++)
        {
            System.out.println("myarray["+i+"] is "+myarray[i]);
        }
        String mymsg="got here";
        return mymsg;
    }
}
```

Here we are passing an array as an *in* parameter, so no Holder classes are used. Note we use the underlying element type rather than the type name (in this case, ArrayType) from the typedef used in the IDL. This is because Java as a language does not contain a "typedef" language construct. (A typedef could also be implemented by a Helper class.)

Note that the array is accessed just like all Java arrays:

    myarray[i]

Also, in Java, to access an IDL const, we use (the constant's name).value. This is because Java as a language does not contain a "constant" language construct. So what the IDL mapping to Java does, it creates an interface with the name of the constant (in the code included with this textbook, this is contained in the file Max.java):

```
public interface MAX
{
  public static final short value = (short)(20);
}
```

which has a public static value that contains the constant value. You get at this value by using (the interface's name).value.

Now in Listing 8.21, we modify the previous IDL array example from Listing 8.13 to now send an array as an *inout* parameter.

LISTING 8.21   Interface Sending an *inout* Array

```
typedef long ArrayType[20];
const long MAX=20;

interface sending_stuff {
      string sendvalue (inout ArrayType myarray, in long size);
};
```

In Listing 8.22, we have the Java code for the servant that implements the interface in Listing 8.21. Here, since we have sent an array as an *inout* parameter, we must use a Holder class, in this case "ArrayTypeHolder" is the name of the class.

Because we are sending the array as an *inout* parameter, that says we are supposed to modify the array inside the servant. So this servant multiplies each array value by 10. Just for something to do. ☺

LISTING 8.22   CORBA IDL *inout* Array in Java Example

```
public class myreceiver extends sending_stuffPOA
{
   public String sendvalue (ArrayTypeHolder myarray, int size)
   {
     int the_real_size;
     the_real_size=size;
     if (the_real_size > MAX.value)
        the_real_size=MAX.value;
     for(int i=0;i<the_real_size;i++)
     {
```

```
        System.out.println("Original value of myarray["+i+"] is "+myarray.value[i]);
        myarray.value[i]=myarray.value[i]*10; // Multiply each myarray value times 10
        System.out.println("Value to pass back to client of myarray["+i+"] is "+myarray.value[i]);
      }
      String mymsg="Hello there from servant to client";
      return mymsg;
    }
}
```

To access an item in an Object of type Holder class, you use ".value" to talk direct to the item, then you access it as usual. In this case, we're talking to an array, so we access it by using square brackets:

    myarray.value[i]

As we previously did with the CORBA IDL to C++ binding, let's take a brief look at the Any data type and how it can be handled in the CORBA IDL to Java binding. We originally saw an IDL that used Any back in Listing 8.16. Let's say, for example, that we want to send data of type "string", then on the Client we could do:

    Any mymsg=orb.create_any();
    mymsg.insert_string("hi there");

whereas if we wanted to send data of type "double", then on the Client we would do:

    Any othermsg=orb.create_any();
    othermsg.insert_double(3.1415);

Then on the servant if we *knew* the data we were getting was of type "string", then we could do:

    String themsg=mymsg.extract_string();

Whereas if we *knew* the data we were getting was of type "double", then we could do:

    double thefloat=othermsg.extract_double();

As before, I'm ignoring the situation where we *don't* know what the data type is, and have to extract it from the TypeCode in the Any. That's getting away from the static interfaces and more into the dynamic interfaces, and I'm largely ignoring those for this (introductory) textbook.

8.2.4 CORBA ADDRESSING—HOW DOES THE CLIENT FIND THE SERVER AND ASSOCIATED SERVANT?

The major address formats that a Client can use to find (address) a server/servant in CORBA are:

- Interoperable Object Reference (IOR) format:
  - Used with or without the original CORBA Naming Service
- Uniform Resource Identifier (URI) formats from the CORBA Interoperable Naming Service:
  - Corbaloc
  - Corbaname

The way an IOR, a corbaloc URI, or a corbaname URI are accessed on the Client is by using a CORBA function called string_to_object. That is, the appropriate address information is stored in a string, usually in one of the three formats above, then on the Client the string is converted into an object reference. Then this object reference is narrowed to a proxy object that points to the correct interface.

In Java, this looks like (here the variable "line" is of type String—also note the use of the Helper class to reference the interface):

```
org.omg.CORBA.Object obj = orb.string_to_object(line);
echo myecho = echoHelper.narrow(obj);
```

and in C++ this looks like:

```
CORBA::Object_var obj = orb->string_to_object (line.c_str());
echo_var myecho = echo::_narrow (obj);
```

In the C++ example, the variable "line" is a C++ string, and is converted to a C style string by the use of the ".c_str()" function applied to the C++ string.

We will see the IOR, corbaloc, and corbaname formats and how they are handled below.

Other format options that can be used instead of IOR, corbaloc, or corbaname to be read by string_to_object are (these are optional and may be implemented by a vendor):

- file://filename
  - Name of a file that contains a stringified IOR or a URL of a CORBA object
- http://url
  - A URL that allows retrieval of a stringified IOR or a URL of a CORBA object
- ftp://filename
  - Can use ftp to retrieve a file that contains stringified IOR or a URL of a CORBA object

8.2.4.1   Interoperable Object Reference and the CORBA Naming Service

The Interoperable Object Reference (IOR) format is the only way that CORBA had to begin with to pass address information around, starting back in 1991. For getting started, you can think simply of an IOR as containing the IP address and port number of the Server, together with an object reference that gives you a way, after you've connected to the IP address and port number, to find the correct servant object that implements the interface.

8.2.4.1.1   The IOR Format

Typically, the IOR is created on the Server, then "stringified" (that is, turned into a string of hex digits that begins with the characters "IOR:") and then sent to the Client some way (via email for example, or via putting the stringified IOR in a file and transferring it with sftp).

An example of how to do this in C++ is:

```
ofstream thefile ("echo.ior");
        CORBA::Object_var theref = mypoa->id_to_reference (object_identifier.in());
        CORBA::String_var mystr = orb->object_to_string (theref.in());
        thefile << mystr.in() << endl;
thefile.close ();
```

and how to do it in Java is:

```
FileWriter thefile = new FileWriter("echo.ior");
BufferedWriter bufferedWriter = new BufferedWriter(thefile);
    org.omg.CORBA.Object theref = mypoa.id_to_reference(servant_id);
    String mystr = orb.object_to_string(theref);
bufferedWriter.write(mystr);
bufferedWriter.close();
```

In both cases, a file named "echo.ior" is created that contains the stringified IOR.

Also in both cases, we begin with an object_identifier that refers to the servant: it's called "object_identifier" in the C++ code and "servant_id" in the Java code.

In both cases, we see that a CORBA routine called "id_to_reference" is used to translate the Object Identifier to an Object Reference (a pointer to a CORBA object, that is, something in CORBA that can contain pointers to a particular interface).

Finally, the object reference is "stringified," or converted to a string, using the CORBA routine called "object_to_string" and written to the echo.ior file.

The echo.ior file is passed to the Client in some way, then the Client reads the file and reverses the process. We saw earlier in this section how a CORBA string_to_object routine is used in the Client to translate a string read from the echo.ior file into a proxy reference.

We have seen the most basic way in which an IOR is used. However, the IOR does more than just specify IP address port number, and object reference. For example, embedded inside the IOR are the repository_id/type_id that contains a unique identifier for the interface, and the version of the Internet Inter-Orb Protocol (IIOP) that is being used (I'll talk about repository_ids, which are related to Interface Repositories, and the IIOP later on in Section 8.2.7.1—note also that other transport protocols than IIOP could also be used), as well as the host address, port number, and object key (object identifier).

IORs are meant to be opaque, that is, the user isn't supposed to have to look at the internals of an IOR. However, there are utilities provided with various ORBs that allow you to view and interpret the contents of a "stringified" IOR. Some utilities include:

- catior—omniORB and the TAO ORB
- iordump—MICO and ORBacus
- There's an online web tool that will do it for you:
  - http://www2.parc.com/istl/projects/ILU/parseIOR/

(NOTE: omniORB also contains a utility called geniorb that will generate a stringified IOR if you give it a type_id, IP address, port number, and Object key. But you have to know what you're doing if you do that, plus the need to do that should seldom arise.)

One major additional capability of an IOR is that of "tagged profiles." An IOR can contain several different sets of information on how to contact it, each stored in a tagged profile. For example, one tagged profile could use IIOP and a different tagged profile could specify the use of some other transport protocol. Or an IOR could contain two tagged profiles that use IIOP, but one of the profiles specifies some vendor-specific operation while the other tagged profile is a vanilla profile meant to connect with ORBs from other vendors. Probably, the most common use of tagged profiles would be for vendors to provide added features for customers who use their ORB on both Client and Server. I'm not telling you how to do that because you're a student and it's a little more than you need in an introductory class. One of those nasty little exercises for the reader things.

8.2.4.1.2 The Original CORBA Naming Service

Now, we will look at the CORBA Naming Service. The CORBA Naming Service works a lot like the Domain Name Service used in the World Wide Web: the Domain Name Service translates URLs (such as www.uah.edu) to their associated IP addresses, whereas the CORBA Naming Service is used to translate to/from names to object references. It's useful to use names rather than object references, because transferring IORs around can be a pain.

Note that I just snuck in a plug for my home university, UAH. Feel free to look up the Computer Science department here. ☺

If you're older folks like me, you remember the old White Pages and the Yellow Pages, provided by the telephone company. The old White Pages were the equivalent of the CORBA Naming Service; they map a person to address and phone number. If you don't remember what a White Pages was, don't worry about it. It's swiftly going over the event horizon.

(The old Yellow Pages had advertisements for products and services; they mapped service/product offerings to names/addresses/phone numbers. The CORBA Trading Service is an equivalent to the Yellow Pages. Although this is largely historical information, we will look at the Trading Service later on because it led to several spin-off technologies that are still in use in other places.)

The Naming Service runs as a separate executable. Each ORB vendor provides its own version of a CORBA compatible naming service.

Note that some ORB vendors may also provide proprietary (extra non-CORBA compliant) extensions to the Naming Service, and some ORB vendors may also provide their own proprietary naming service as a separate executable. Back in 2001, during a contract I had with the U.S. Army to determine CORBA interoperability, I was trying to connect the Visibroker ORB to the TAO ORB. As I recall, all worked well as long as I was using the TAO Naming Service. I could use a Visibroker server to bind a Visibroker CORBA object (with associated servant) to a name on the TAO Naming Service, and alternately I could use a TAO server to bind a TAO CORBA object (with associated servant) to a name on the TAO Naming Service. However, when I swapped and tried to connect a TAO server to the Visibroker Naming Service, it just plain didn't work. After numerous hours, I finally found a footnote on about page 300 of the Visibroker manual that said I had to use a different executable program for the naming service if I wanted something CORBA compliant. Sigh.

When using the Naming Service, the Server provides a name and reference to a CORBA object to the Naming Service, such that later on, when a client calls the Naming Service and passes it that name, the Naming Service will return the associated object reference to the Client. When the Server does this, it is called *binding* the name to the object reference.

There is a call in the CORBA Naming Service interface called "bind" that will do this. However, if you call it again with the same name, it will return an AlreadyBound exception. Although I can see the utility of this in a production setting, this is a pain for a student who is developing code, because you may kill your server and start it again but not remember to kill the Naming Service. It's easiest to use the *other* Naming Service interface call, "rebind," because rebind won't fail on a second call using the same name, it just writes over the old reference. I highly recommend that students use "rebind" because I've seen students spend hours trying to figure out what's wrong when all they did was forget to restart the Naming Service.

However, although you can just bind a name to an object reference, it's not quite as simple as that overall. You can also create graphs of names in a hierarchy. This works sort of like a directory hierarchy. For example, in a directory hierarchy you could have:

    dirA/subdirA/myfile

and

    dirA/subdirB/myfile

That is, since subdirA is different from subdirB, you can have a file named myfile under subdirA that is different from the myfile under subdirB.

The CORBA Naming Service works similarly in regard to hierarchy compared to how a directory structure works. Unfortunately, in CORBA we can't quite do it this way, since in the CORBA Naming Service they didn't reserve the slash marks "/" or "\" or for that matter any other character to serve as a separator between name components. So in CORBA, if your name has more than one component, you can't represent it in a single string. This is yet another thing CORBA did to try to be everything to everybody—the argument here was that you didn't know all the languages you were binding to, so you couldn't reserve a slash mark to mean anything special to CORBA. That is, a slash mark could be part of a valid name. For that matter, any kind of non-printing character can be part of a valid name in the CORBA naming service. Sigh.

The collection of names in a hierarchy is called a *naming graph*. A leaf node on this naming graph is a Name, whereas the base nodes and any intermediate nodes are called naming contexts. Using the similarity to a directory structure again, a naming context contains names (together with their associated bindings) and other sub-naming contexts like a directory would contain files and other subdirectories.

```
Base name contextA    → NameA
                      → sub name contextA   → NameB
                                            → NameC
Base name contextB    → sub name contextB   → NameB
```

Here, Base name context, Base name context, sub name context, sub name context are all name contexts that serve as starting points for reading a complete name (including the hierarchy).

NameA, NameB, NameC, and NameD are names that are normally associated with object references, that have been bound to object references using either "bind" or "rebind."'

Sub name contextA contains two names, NameB and NameC.

Note that the sub-graph beginning with Base name contextB is not connected at all to the sub-graph beginning with Base name contextA. This is allowed. It's reasonable since you might be running several servers that are only loosely related, or potentially not related at all, so that their names don't overlap.

A naming graph is allowed to have loops. Sigh.

The Naming Service interface is represented in an IDL. You can generally find this IDL file in your ORB source code. For example, the version of omniORB I'm currently using has a file called Naming.idl in the directory: /omniorb-4.2.1/idl. In the version of MICO I'm using, there is a file called CosNaming.idl in the directory /mico/include/coss.

The module name is CosNaming. A name in the CORBA Naming Service is stored in a struct called NameComponent:

```
typedef String Istring;
struct NameComponent {
    Istring id;
    Istring kind;
};
```

Then a complete Name (including the name hierarchy) is a sequence of NameComponents. The name of each separate NameComponent is stored in the "id" field.

The "kind" field is an annoying thing that apparently originally the authors of the CORBA speci-fication meant to use to provide some description of what the "id" field was. I guess, for example, you could have an "id" field such as "Images" and a kind field that said "FileServer." To the best of my knowledge, the "kind" field is not often used. It's safest to always explicitly set it to the empty string.

LISTING 8.23   Bind an Object Reference to Simple Name

```
//Create a name for the CORBA object (and its servant) to be associated with on the
        Naming Service
CosNaming::Name name;
name.length (1);
name[0].id = CORBA::string_dup ("echoservant");
name[0].kind = CORBA::string_dup (""); // make sure the "kind" field is empty

// Rebind the name to its reference on the Naming Service.
// We do a "rebind" in case you did this before and didn't restart the Naming Service ☺
namingcontext->rebind (name, echo_ref);
```

In Listing 8.23, we see server code (using omniORB in C++) where an echo servant is bound to a simple name on the CORBA Naming Service. I'm calling it a "simple name" because it's only using one base naming context (or initial naming context), and that doesn't have a name (it's an "orphaned" context) and one name. Because there's only one name, we do:

```
name.length(1);
```

We're assuming in Listing 8.23 that the variable "namingcontext" was determined before this code executes. We'll look at how that works a little later. We're also assuming that "echo_ref" is a CORBA object that was previously determined.

Note that I've explicitly set the "kind" field to empty string. A string such as the "kind" field is supposed to default to empty string (in CORBA 2.3 and later) but I always figure why take chances.

I used "rebind" here. We talked about "bind" and "rebind" earlier, but those only bind the names (the leaf nodes on the naming graph) to the object references. For the name contexts, you use bind_new_context. Let's suppose that I wanted the whole name to look like this:

```
allechos → echoservant
```

Then I would have done the code in Listing 8.24.

LISTING 8.24   Bind an Object Reference to Simple Name

```
// Create a name for the CORBA object (and its servant) to be associated with on the
        Naming Service
CosNaming::Name name;
name.length (1);
name[0].id = CORBA::string_dup ("allechos");
name[0].kind = CORBA::string_dup (""); // make sure the "kind" field is empty

namingcontext->bind_new_context(name);
```

```
name.length (2);
name[1].id = CORBA::string_dup ("echoservant");
name[1].kind = CORBA::string_dup (""); // make sure the "kind" field is empty

namingcontext->bind (name, echo_ref);
```

Note in Listing 8.24, I used "bind" instead of "rebind." This is because I'm using bind_new_context. Since bind_new_context will return an AlreadyBound exception if the context name is already being used, I'll already have that exception before I would get to the rebind, so no point in using a rebind.

Note that there are also separate routines to create a context (new_context()) and bind to an already existing context (bind_context()) if you wanted to do it that way instead.

Now, I said earlier that in Listing 8.23 the variable "namingcontext" was determined before the code executed. This can be done in a couple of different ways. The usually recommended one is to use a CORBA routine called "resolve_initial_references." We see how this is done in Listing 8.24, this code was used on the C++ omniORB.

LISTING 8.25   Using Resolve Initial References to Find an Initial Naming Context

```
// Find the Naming Service itself
    naming_service_ref =
        orb->resolve_initial_references ("NameService");

CosNaming::NamingContext_var namingcontext=
        CosNaming::NamingContext::_narrow (naming_service_ref);

if (CORBA::is_nil (namingcontext)) {
    cerr << "Couldn't find the Naming Service" << endl;
    exit (1);
}
```

In Listing 8.25, the call to resolve_initial_references is asking for the Naming Service.

(The resolve_initial_references call can also be used for other major CORBA functions such as "RootPOA." We'll discuss this later when we talk about CORBA server-side processing.) However, for resolve_initial_references to find the Naming Service, the Naming Service has to be configured somehow prior to this call. For example, one way the omniORB Naming Service, omniNames, works is that it reads a file called omniORB.cfg at startup. Inside this file an object reference to the root context of the Naming Service is available.

Sometimes there are ways that individual ORB vendors created to find the IOR of their Naming Service. For example, you will see in the code included with this textbook that omniNames can write out its initial object reference IOR when it is started, this can be saved to a file, and passed to Server and Client. Then the Server and Client can each be started using the command-line parameter:

    -ORBInitRef NameService= ...object reference...

which will allow calls to resolve_initial_references("NameService").

We'll see more how -ORBInitRef works in the next section, when we talk about the CORBA Interoperable Naming Service.

Similarly, the MICO Naming Service has a proprietary command-line parameter that can be used when calling the MICO Naming Service, that allows the initial object reference IOR to be written to a file:

    nsd --ior Naming_Service.ref

where nsd is the MICO Naming Service, "-ior" is the proprietary command-line parameter, and Naming_Service.ref is the file name written to.

On the JDK Java ORB, the Naming Service (orbd) is started on a particular port number, using the following command-line parameter when the Naming Service is started, and again when the Client is started and when the Server is started:

    -ORBInitialPort 1163

then as usual, the Client and Server each calls: resolve_initial_references("NameService").

You can also use other methods specified in the Interoperable Naming Service to find the Naming Service, we'll talk about these in the next section when we talk about the Interoperable Naming Service.

The TAO ORB also supports another, different method for having a server or client find the TAO Naming Service, it uses an IP multicast. Basically, when a client or server calls resolve_initial_references, the TAO ORB sends out an IP multicast looking for any TAO Naming Service on the Local Area Network (LAN). (IP multicasting is a way to have one entity send IP packets addressed to several different recipients at the same time.) A running TAO Naming Service recognizes this IP multicast, and responds, with the result that the resolve_initial_reference ("NameService") that is called from the Server or Client connects automatically to the TAO Naming Service, without the need for other command-line parameters or passing any kinds of files around.

Back in the 2000 through 2004 or so timeframe, I often taught two classes at a time of 30+ students, who all used the TAO ORB at the same time, and who all started their own copies of the TAO Naming Service at similar times. It often occurred that one student's code would connect to a second student's instance of the TAO Naming Service, and the first student's code would suddenly and (incomprehensibly to the student) stop working when the second student decided to shut things down and go to lunch. The TAO ORB allows an environment variable (called NameServicePort) to be set, to put the Naming Service on its own port and to allow Server and Client to look for the Naming Service on that port, but students almost never remembered to use this, no matter how often I reminded them. ☺ Of course there are numerous other ways for a student's code to find that student's Naming Service, but using the built in IP multicast always seemed so convenient to them. Until it suddenly wasn't.

But let's look back again now at Listing 8.24, at the call to CosNaming::NamingContext::_narrow() in the second statement. The narrow() routine does a type downcast from a general CORBA object to a derived object. In this case, the derived object is the NamingContext.

However, the narrow() routine does a whole lot more than a type downcast, at least when CORBA is using its more common synchronous communications (that is, a client calls a server and expects an immediate response) as opposed to asynchronous (the Client calls a Server but doesn't expect an immediate response, and the Client goes on about its business). When using synchronous communications, the narrow results in data communications across the network (!).

The reason it does, the creators of CORBA decided that CORBA had to check to make sure it was appropriate to do a type downcast before the type downcast occurred. Therefore, the narrow calls across the communications link to make sure the object being called is actually there at the appropriate address, and that it has the appropriate type. So for the narrow to work, there has to be a server of some kind there running, and it has to be running something of the correct type!

The CORBA Specification, Version 3.3 Part 1: CORBA Interfaces says:

> To do such down-casting in a type safe way, knowledge of the full inheritance hierarchy of the target interface may be required. The implementation of down-cast must either contact an interface repository or the target itself, to determine whether or not it is safe to down-cast the Client's object reference.

(If there's an asynchronous communication going on, the narrow() would return an un-type-checked stub.)

This confuses students terribly. I've had so many students tell me, I've traced my code to a narrow, which is supposed to do a type downcast, and the narrow is failing! How can a type downcast fail! The ORB itself must be broken, maybe you didn't compile it right.

The ones who delve a little further tell me, it's throwing a TRANSIENT exception (or sometimes depending on what they're trying to narrow, it's throwing an OBJECT_NOT_EXIST exception). Why does a type downcast throw a TRANSIENT (or OBJECT_NOT_EXIST) exception. The ORB must be broken!

What has happened in this particular case is that your Naming Service wasn't running (a TRANSIENT exception is thrown when the ORB tried to reach the Server and failed).

I already talked about narrow() briefly back in Section 8.2.2. We'll see this same discussion again later on, when we discuss how a client tries to narrow to find the reference for a servant: I'm going to repeat all this stuff about narrow there. In my experience, it's one of the more aggravating things that students learning CORBA go through.

We've been talking so far about using individual Naming Services. That is, each Naming Service is a separate executable file, running independently of the Server and of the Client, but so far we've only been using one executing Naming Service. However, there are often reasons to use groups of Naming Services, with interconnected Naming Graphs: these are called *federated Naming Services*. Maybe you have a bunch of different departments in your company, and each runs and maintains its own Naming Service. So these may be interconnected to create a company-wide Naming Service. All you have to do is link the IORs of individual CORBA objects. CORBA doesn't care where your objects are located as long as the correct IORs are passed around (location transparency, again).

8.2.4.2   CORBA Interoperable Naming Service (corbaloc and corbaname)

The addressing formats corbaloc and corbaname are parts of the Interoperable Naming Service, which was added in the CORBA 2.4 specification back in 2000.

The corbaloc format looks generally either like this:

    corbaloc:iiop: < host IP address>:< port number>/object_key
        (without a port number specified, the port number defaults to port 2809)
    Or like this:
    corbaloc:rir: < host IP address>:< port number>/object_key

whereas the corbaname format looks generally like this:

    corbaname: <corbaloc format including object key as before> #name string

Some corbaloc examples using iiop are:

> corbaloc:iiop:localhost:4321/theObjectKey
> corbaloc::localhost:4321/theObjectKey
>   (if you leave off the iiop and do "::" instead it assumes iiop)
> corbaloc:iiop:localhost/theObjectKey
>   (remember without a port number specified, the port number defaults to port 2809)
> corbaloc:1.2@theserver.com:4321/theObjectKey
>   (this selects IIOP version 1.2. The default version of IIOP is version 1.0. We will discuss the Internet
>   Inter-Orb Protocol (IIOP) later on in Section 8.2.7.1.)

You can also use corbaloc to specify an IPv6 address:

> corbaloc:iiop:1.2@[ipv6 address]:port number/theObjectKey

As we discussed earlier, these can be accessed using the CORBA string_to_object routine. The string_to_object routine is smart enough to determine whether the string being passed to it is an IOR, a corbaloc, or a corbaname, and it handles the string differently, depending on which it is.

Let's look further at the corbaloc:rir format. Here, "rir" stands for "resolve initial references." There is another CORBA routine called "resolve_initial_references", we saw this back when we talked about the original CORBA naming service. If you have a corbaloc URL that uses "rir," and you pass this corbaloc URL to the CORBA string_to_object routine, then the string_to_object routine will first pass the corbaloc URL to resolve_initial_references, and create the object reference using the returned value. For example, it would be reasonable to do: corbaloc:rir:/NameService to find the CORBA Naming Service.

However, normally you would use corbaname to find a name on the CORBA Naming Service. Here are two examples:

> corbaname::theServer.edu:1234#echo
> Here, "echo" is the name of the CORBA object you're looking for on the Naming Service, whereas "theServer.edu:1234" is the URL including port number of the Naming Service itself. Note that we're doing a "::" here so it's defaulting to "iiop". It's also defaulting to port number 2809.
> corbaname::localhost:1234#echo
> Says that your naming service is running on localhost at port 1234 and you're looking for the server/servant named "echo".

You could also do:

> corbaname:rir: /NameService#echo

If you use the corbaname "rir" format, then what it means is the Naming Service is found using: resolve_initial_reference("NameService") prior to passing "echo" to the Naming Service. (So you can actually leave off the "/NameService" here, it's the default.)

The Interoperable Naming Service specification also allows the location of particular services to be set using command-line parameters to the ORB. For example, you can do the following:

- -ORBInitRef NameService=IOR:...
  or
- -ORBInitRef NameService=corbaloc::myserver.edu/NamingService

After you've done this, however, then resolve_initial_references("NameService") will return the NamingService previously specified using -ORBInitRef

This can be done for any CORBA service, not just the Naming Service.

LISTING 8.26   Using corbaloc to Find an Initial Naming Context

```
org.omg.CORBA.Object naming_service_ref =
    orb.string_to_object("corbaloc:iiop:1.2@localhost:1163/NameService");

NamingContextExt namingcontext= NamingContextExtHelper.narrow
    (naming_service_ref);
```

In Listing 8.26, we see how corbaloc can be used with the JDK Java ORB to find the orbd Naming Service. This assumes that orbd is running at port 1163, and that JDK is using IIOP version 1.2 to find the Naming Service. (Actually it's sending a locateRequest with parameter = NameService, we'll look at locateRequest later on when we look at GIOP in Section 8.2.7.1.)

This assumes you previously started orbd on port 1163 as follows:

```
orbd -ORBInitialPort 1163
```

The narrow() works as before in Listing 8.24, see Section 8.2.4.1.2.

LISTING 8.27   Using corbaname to Find an Initial Naming Context

```
org.omg.CORBA.Object proxy = orb.string_to_object("corbaname::localhost:1163#echo");
echo myecho = echoHelper.narrow(proxy);
```

In Listing 8.27, we see how corbaname can be used with the JDK Java ORB to find the orbd Naming Service. The portion "corbaname::localhost:1163" says that the naming service is located at localhost on port 1163. The text "echo" after the "#" specifies the name of the CORBA object (with associated servant) that was previously attached to the naming service by the server.

Again, the narrow() works as before in Listing 8.26 and Listing 8.24.

8.2.5   SIMPLEST ECHO EXAMPLE

We're now going to look again at the Client, Server, and servant code that goes with the simplest echo interface previously shown in Listing 8.1. Since you've read everything between when the simplest echo interface originally showed up back in Section 8.2.1.1, you now know enough to understand this. ☺ We're going to look at both the C++ and Java versions, in two C++ ORBS (MICO and omniORB) and one Java ORB (JDK ORB).

8.2.5.1   Echo Example—Server Side

We're going to start with the Server/Servant code. In Listing 8.28, we see the Server/Servant code for the C++ MICO ORB. In Listing 8.29, we see the Server/Servant code for the C++ omniORB. I previously showed you the Java Server and Servant code for the JDK ORB back in Listing 8.2 and Listing 8.5 in Section 8.2.1.1, but I'm going to show it in a listing again here, so you can easily compare it to the C++ versions (plus the way the code is written, it really belongs in a single listing instead of two).

In the Server, the first thing that happens is initializing the ORB. This is done in C++ by a call to:

```
CORBA::ORB_var orb CORBA::ORB_init (argc, argv);
```

And in Java by a call to:

```
ORB orb = ORB.init(args, null);
```

Both these examples allow command-line parameters to be used to initialize the ORB. For example, on the JDK Java ORB, assuming the Naming Service (orbd) is started on a particular port number (1163), when you pass in the following command-line parameter as an argument, this initial port information will be provided to the ORB initialization routine in the "args" parameter:

```
-ORBInitialPort 1163
```

Note that we could alternately have done something like (in this case, in Java, to do this you would also have to import java.util.Properties):

```
Properties props = new Properties();
props.put("org.omg.CORBA.ORBInitialPort", "1163");
ORB orb = ORB.init(args, props);
```

Here the initial port information is provided to the ORB initialization routine in the "props" parameter.

Note that in both C++ and Java, the ORB is just another object, it contains data and has associated routines.

The next thing to do on the Server is to get a pointer to the Root POA and to the POA Manager. In C++ this looks like:

```
CORBA::Object_var the_rootPOA = orb->resolve_initial_references ("RootPOA");
PortableServer::POA_var mypoa = PortableServer::POA::_narrow (the_rootPOA);
PortableServer::POAManager_var mgr = mypoa->the_POAManager();
```

and in Java this looks like:

```
org.omg.CORBA.Object the_rootPOA=orb.resolve_initial_references("RootPOA");
POA mypoa = POAHelper.narrow(the_rootPOA);
mypoa.the_POAManager().activate();
```

We talked earlier about how the POA does a lot of server-side functions, the most basic of which is mapping the interface to a CORBA object and from there to a Servant. It does a lot more than that, we'll discuss it in much more depth in Section 8.2.8. But before you can do anything at all involving a POA, you have to create a Root POA object and activate it. You can have other POA objects that are children of the Root POA, but the Root POA is the most basic POA and must be defined first.

The way to find a root POA is through resolve_initial_references("RootPOA"). Note that resolve_initial_references("RootPOA") works differently from how resolve_initial_references ("NameService") works, in that with the RootPOA, everything is built into the ORB, whereas the

Naming Service runs as a separate executable. So you *don't* have to start a root POA running before you call resolve_initial_reference("RootPOA")—just go ahead and do the call.

The narrow routine does a type downcast as before. However, since the RootPOA (and for that matter all POAs) are built into CORBA, in this case the narrow doesn't have to do any across the communication link checks—so you don't have to worry about this call to narrow throwing a TRANSIENT exception. ☺

In the last step, the POA Manager is created and activated, and the POA Manager activates the RootPOA (makes the RootPOA start working). The POA Manager controls one or more POA objects. The POA Manager controls whether requests to a POA are queued for the POA or discarded. The POA Manager activates the POA and deactivates the POA.

As we said before, you can have other POAs that are children of the Root POA. The reason you might want to have multiple POAs is that you may want different groups of servants to be treated in a different way, to have different behaviors as to how they start up, what their lifetime is, etc. These different behaviors would be set as policies on the POA that controlled the groups of servants. (We will examine how these policies work in Section 8.2.8.) The idea is that one POA would be created with a set of policies, and the servants that obey those policies are controlled by that POA. A different POA would be created with a different set of policies, and the servants that obey those policies are controlled by this POA.

POAs are set with certain policies by default, when they are created. For example, one default policy of a POA would be SYSTEM_ID for the Id Assignment policy. This allows CORBA to automatically define a name for a CORBA object rather than requiring the programmer to do so. This is useful for transient objects that only last the lifetime of the Server. We're doing that in this case: the default value of the LifeSpan policy is TRANSIENT, so since we didn't tell the POA otherwise, we're using a Lifespan Policy of transient, and so our object will last only as long as the Server lasts.

The child POAs do *not* inherit the policies of the parent POAs. Instead, they are initialized with the default POA policies, unless certain policies are explicitly set when the child POA is created.

In this example, after we activate the POA, we define the servant (the_echo), and activate it using explicit activation:

```
PortableServer::ObjectId_var object_identifier = mypoa->activate_object (the_echo);
```

This tells the POA that when a request comes in for a CORBA object, it's going to be forwarded on to the servant the_echo.

Then we save the IOR of the activated CORBA object to a file so the Client can eventually find it.

Finally, we set the POA looking for input requests from a Client.

LISTING 8.28   Echo Example, Server and Servant, MICO ORB, in C++/C

```cpp
#include "echo.h"
#include <fstream>
using namespace std;

// This is the Servant
class myecho : public virtual POA_echo
{
    public:
        virtual char * echostring (const char *the_echostring);
};
```

```cpp
char * myecho::echostring (const char *the_echostring)
{
    cout << "string received is " << the_echostring << endl;
    char *smsg= CORBA::string_dup(the_echostring);
    return smsg;
}
// This is the Server
int main (int argc, char *argv[])
{
  // Begin by initializing the ORB
    CORBA::ORB_var orb = CORBA::ORB_init (argc, argv);

  // Get POA and the POA Manager
    CORBA::Object_var the_rootPOA = orb->resolve_initial_references ("RootPOA");
    PortableServer::POA_var mypoa = PortableServer::POA::_narrow (the_rootPOA);
    PortableServer::POAManager_var mgr = mypoa->the_POAManager();

  // Create a servant
    myecho * the_echo = new myecho;
  // use explicit activation to map the CORBA object to the servant
    PortableServer::ObjectId_var object_identifier = mypoa->activate_object (the_echo);

  // Save the IOR in a file
    ofstream thefile ("echo.ior");
    CORBA::Object_var theref = mypoa->id_to_reference (object_identifier.in());
    CORBA::String_var mystr = orb->object_to_string (theref.in());
    thefile << mystr.in() << endl;
    thefile.close ();

  // Start the POA, start looking for input requests
    mgr->activate ();
    orb->run();

    mypoa->destroy (TRUE, TRUE);
    delete the_echo;

    return 0;
}
```

LISTING 8.29   Echo Example, Server and Servant, omniORB, in C++/C

```cpp
#include "echo.hh"
#include <iostream>
#include <fstream>
using namespace std;

#define TRUE 1
#define FALSE 0
// This is the Servant

class myecho : public virtual POA_echo
{
    public:
            virtual char * echostring (const char *the_echostring);
};
char * myecho::echostring (const char *the_echostring)
{
    cout << "string received is" << the_echostring << endl;
    char *smsg= CORBA::string_dup(the_echostring);
    return smsg;
}
// This is the Server
int main (int argc, char *argv[])
{
  // Begin by initializing the ORB
    CORBA::ORB_var orb = CORBA::ORB_init (argc, argv);

  // Get POA and the POA Manager
    CORBA::Object_var the_rootPOA = orb->resolve_initial_references ("RootPOA");
    PortableServer::POA_var mypoa = PortableServer::POA::_narrow (the_rootPOA);
    PortableServer::POAManager_var mgr = mypoa->the_POAManager();
  // Create a servant
    myecho * the_echo = new myecho;

  // use explicit activation to map the CORBA object to the servant
    PortableServer::ObjectId_var object_identifier = mypoa->activate_object (the_echo);

  // Save the IOR in a file
    ofstream thefile ("echo.ior");
    CORBA::Object_var theref = mypoa->id_to_reference (object_identifier.in());
    CORBA::String_var mystr = orb->object_to_string (theref.in());
    thefile << mystr.in() << endl;
    thefile.close ();

  // Start the POA, start looking for input requests
    mgr->activate ();
    orb->run();

    mypoa->destroy (TRUE, TRUE);
    delete the_echo;

    return 0;
}
```

LISTING 8.30   Echo Example, Server and Servant, JDK ORB, in Java

```java
import org.omg.CORBA.*;
import org.omg.PortableServer.*;
import org.omg.PortableServer.POA;

import java.util.Properties;
import java.io.*;

// This is the Servant
class myecho extends echoPOA {

    public String echostring(String the_echostring) {

        System.out.println(the_echostring);
        return the_echostring;
    }
}

// This is the Server
    public class server {
    public static void main(String args[]) {

      try {

    // Begin by initializing the ORB
    ORB orb = ORB.init(args, null);

    // Get POA and the POA Manager
            org.omg.CORBA.Object the_rootPOA=orb.resolve_initial_references
                ("RootPOA");
            POA mypoa = POAHelper.narrow(the_rootPOA);
            mypoa.the_POAManager().activate();              //activate the POA manager
    // create servant and register it with the ORB
            myecho the_echo=new myecho();

    // get object reference from the servant
            byte [] servant_id = mypoa.activate_object(the_echo);

    // Write the IOR to a file
            String line=null;
            FileWriter thefile = new FileWriter("echo.ior");
            BufferedWriter bufferedWriter = new BufferedWriter(thefile);
                // since only writing one value probably not necessary but I'm used to
                // using bufferedWriter around all FileWriters

            org.omg.CORBA.Object theref = mypoa.id_to_reference(servant_id);
            // convert the servant ID to a CORBA object reference
            String mystr = orb.object_to_string(theref);
            // Convert the CORBA object reference to a string

            bufferedWriter.write(mystr);

            bufferedWriter.close();

            System.out.println("Server is waiting for input");
```

```
                    orb.run();

               }
              catch (Exception the_exception)
              {
                   System.err.println("Exception happened, exception is"+the_exception);
              }
         }
}
```

8.2.5.2   Echo Example—Client Side

Here we see the Clients that go with the Server/Servant for each of the three ORBS: MICO ORB, omniORB, and JDK ORB. Refer to Listing 8.31 for the MICO ORB, Listing 8.32 for omniORB, and Listing 8.33 for the JDK ORB.

If you want to run these, you *DON'T* have to use the same language and ORB for both Client and Server. For example, try connecting the JDK ORB to omniORB. It will work. ☺ Remember that you have to move the IOR file from the directory where the Server created it, to the directory where the Client will read it.

In all three examples, we do the following steps:

- Initialize the ORB
- Retrieve the stringified IOR from the file where the server originally wrote it
- Convert the IOR into an object reference
- Using narrow(), type downcast the object reference to be an object of the type of the echo inter-
  face. (Remember that the narrow() routine will do a call across the communications link to
  check the type, and if the server isn't running this call to narrow() will throw an exception.)
- Do a remote procedure call to the echostring routine on the Servant

Note that there's not a lot of difference between the C++ versions and the Java version. Do note that you have to use echoHelper to call the narrow() routine when you're using Java and the JDK ORB.

LISTING 8.31   Echo Example, Client, MICO ORB, in C++/C

```cpp
#include "echo.h"
#include <unistd.h>
#include <fstream>
using namespace std;

int main (int argc, char *argv[])
{
     CORBA::ORB_var orb = CORBA::ORB_init (argc, argv);

  // Get the IOR from a file
     string line;
     ifstream thefile("echo.ior");
     getline(thefile,line);
     thefile.close();

  // Find the server
     CORBA::Object_var obj = orb->string_to_object (line.c_str());
     echo_var myecho = echo::_narrow (obj);
```

```
if (CORBA::is_nil (myecho)) {

        cout << "the server is misssing" << endl;
        exit (1);
}
CORBA::String_var the_echostring = myecho->echostring("hi over there");
cout << "string returned is " << the_echostring << "\n";
return 0;
}
```

LISTING 8.32   Echo Example, Client, omniORB, in C++/C

```cpp
#include "echo.hh"
#include <stdio.h>
#include <stdlib.h>
#include <iostream>
#include <unistd.h>
#include <fstream>
using namespace std;

int main (int argc, char *argv[])
{
    CORBA::ORB_var orb = CORBA::ORB_init (argc, argv);

// Get the IOR from a file

    string line;
    ifstream thefile("echo.ior");
    getline(thefile,line);
    thefile.close();

// Find the server
    CORBA::Object_var obj = orb->string_to_object (line.c_str());
    echo_var myecho = echo::_narrow (obj);

    if (CORBA::is_nil (myecho)) {
        cout << "the server is misssing" << endl;
        exit (1);
    }

    CORBA::String_var the_echostring = myecho->echostring("hi over there");
    cout << "string returned is" << the_echostring << "\n";
    return 0;
}
```

Let's revisit the narrow() routine again. I'm going to repeat (with a few small changes and expansions) a little discussion that I previously gave when I described narrow()-ing to a Naming Service. The reason I'm going to repeat it here is, using a narrow() on the Naming Service, and using a narrow() trying to call the Server direct (with an IOR from a file) are two instances of this issue where I've seen students become very confused. I want to make sure you've read it.

LISTING 8.33   Echo Example, Server and Servant, JDK ORB, in Java

```java
import org.omg.CORBA.*;
import java.io.*;

public class client

{
    public static void main(String args[])
    {
        try
        {
        // create and initialize the ORB
            ORB orb = ORB.init(args, null);

        // Get the IOR from a file
            String line=null;
            FileReader thefile = new FileReader("echo.ior");
            BufferedReader bufferedReader = new BufferedReader(thefile);

            line=bufferedReader.readLine();
            if (line==null)
                System.out.println("no IOR found in IOR file");

            bufferedReader.close();

        // Find the server
            org.omg.CORBA.Object obj = orb.string_to_object(line);

            echo myecho = echoHelper.narrow(obj);

            System.out.println(myecho.echostring("hi there"));
        }
        catch (Exception the_exception)
        {
            System.err.println("Exception happened, exception is "+the_exception);
        }
    }
}
```

As you recall if you've previously read the section on the Naming Service ☺, the narrow() routine does a whole lot more than a type downcast, at least when CORBA is using its more common synchronous communications (that is, a client calls a server and expects an immediate response) as opposed to asynchronous (the Client calls a server but doesn't expect an immediate response, and the Client goes on about its business). (When you're doing asynchronous communication, you can use the unchecked narrow(), which simply does a type downcast. The actual type check then wouldn't occur until the remote procedure is actually called on the object.) When using synchronous communications, the narrow results in data communications across the network (!).

The reason it does, the creators of CORBA decided that CORBA had to check to make sure it was appropriate to do a type downcast before the type downcast occurred. Therefore, the narrow calls across the communications link to make sure the object being called is actually there at the appropriate address, and that it has the appropriate type. So for the narrow to work, there has to be a server of some kind there running, and it has to be running something of the correct type!

The CORBA Specification, Version 3.3 Part 1: CORBA Interfaces says:

> To do such down-casting in a type safe way, knowledge of the full inheritance hierarchy of the target interface may be required. The implementation of down-cast must either contact an interface repository or the target itself, to determine whether or not it is safe to down-cast the client's object reference.

This confuses students terribly. I've had so many students tell me, "I've traced my code to a narrow, which is supposed to do a type downcast, and the narrow is failing! How can a type downcast fail!" The ORB itself must be broken, maybe you didn't compile it right.

The ones who delve a little further tell me, it's throwing a TRANSIENT exception (or sometimes depending on what they're trying to narrow, it's throwing an OBJECT_NOT_EXIST exception). Why does a type downcast throw a TRANSIENT (or OBJECT_NOT_EXIST) exception. The ORB must be broken!

What has happened in this particular case is that your Server wasn't running (a TRANSIENT exception is thrown when the ORB tried to reach the Server and failed).

8.2.6 ECHO EXAMPLE USING NAMING SERVICE

In this section, we will see a variation on the echo example, but this time instead of passing around an IOR, we're going to use a Naming Service. We're only going to look at the version in Java using the JDK ORB here. Back in Section 8.2.4.1.2 when we originally discussed the Naming Service, all the examples were in C++. Also, this is a complete example of Server/Servant and Client using the Naming Service, whereas in Section 8.2.4.1.2 we were looking at code fragments only. Be sure to compare how the Naming Service is accessed and used in Java to how the Naming Service is accessed and used in C++.

Here in the Server/Servant code shown in Listing 8.34, the Servant is called "myecho" and extends echoPOA. The echoPOA was automatically generated by the IDL compiler.

The Server itself does the following steps:

- Initializes the ORB
- Sets properties for the POA so that it knows where to find the Naming Service (IP address and port number)
  - If it's done this way, then the Server can be started without using the command-line parameters: -ORBInitialPort 1163 -ORBInitialHost localhost (compare this example to the example given in the code provided for the instructor with this textbook).
- Gets pointers to the Root POA and the POA Manager, and starts the POA Manager (this is the same as in Section 8.2.5.1, simplest echo example). We'll see much more about the POA later in Section 8.2.8.
- Creates a servant object (the_echo)
- Registers the CORBA object associated with the servant on the POA (set it ready to receive input from the client)
- Uses resolve_initial_references to find the Naming Service, create an object_reference pointing to it
- Creates a "name" (NameComponent) with id = "echo" and kind = empty string
- Uses a "rebind" to map the NameComponent to the Servant CORBA object, on the Naming Service
- Starts the Server listing for requests from the Client

LISTING 8.34   Echo Example, Server and Servant, JDK ORB, in Java

```java
import org.omg.CosNaming.*;
import org.omg.CosNaming.NamingContextPackage.*;
import org.omg.CORBA.*;
import org.omg.PortableServer.*;
import org.omg.PortableServer.POA;

import java.util.Properties;
import java.io.*;

class myecho extends echoPOA {
    public String echostring(String the_echostring) {

        System.out.println(the_echostring);
        return the_echostring;
    }
}
public class server {

    public static void main(String args[]) {
        try {
// Begin by initializing the ORB

// These properties let the server find the orbd naming service
// (later on in the code) using resolve_initial_references
        Properties props = System.getProperties();
        props.put("org.omg.CORBA.ORBInitialPort", "1163");
        props.put("org.omg.CORBA.ORBInitialHost", "localhost");
        ORB orb = ORB.init(args, props);

// Get POA and the POA Manager
        org.omg.CORBA.Object the_rootPOA=orb.resolve_initial_references
            ("RootPOA");
        POA mypoa = POAHelper.narrow(the_rootPOA);
        mypoa.the_POAManager().activate();;            //activate the POA manager

// create servant
        myecho the_echo=new myecho();

// get object reference from the servant and register it on the POA
        byte [] servant_id = mypoa.activate_object(the_echo);

        org.omg.CORBA.Object theref = mypoa.id_to_reference(servant_id);
                // convert the servant ID to a CORBA object reference
        echo echo_ref = echoHelper.narrow(theref);
```

```
// Find the Naming Service, it's part of orbd
        org.omg.CORBA.Object naming_service_ref = orb.resolve_initial_references
            ("NameService");

        NamingContextExt namingcontext= NamingContextExtHelper.narrow
            (naming_service_ref);

// bind the object reference to the naming service
        NameComponent name = new NameComponent("echo","");
                        // set name field to "echo" and kind field to empty string
        NameComponent path[] = {name};
                        // Put name in an array of names, needed to call the rebind
        namingcontext.rebind(path, echo_ref);

        System.out.println("Server is waiting for input");

        orb.run();

    }
    catch (Exception the_exception)
    {
        System.err.println("Exception happened, exception is"+the_exception);
    }
  }
}
```

Here in the client code shown in Listing 8.35, the Client does the following steps:

- Initialize the ORB
- Use resolve_initial_references to find the Naming Service, create an object_reference pointing to it
- Create a "name" (NameComponent) with id = "echo" and kind = empty string
- Resolve the echo name on the Naming Service (use an echoHelper to do this) to create a proxy object called myecho
- Call the remote procedure echostring, using the proxy object myecho

LISTING 8.35   Echo Example, Client JDK ORB, in Java

```
import org.omg.CosNaming.*;
import org.omg.CosNaming.NamingContextPackage.*;
import org.omg.CORBA.*;

import java.io.*;
public class client
{
    public static void main(String args[])
    {
```

```
        try
        {

    // create and initialize the ORB
            ORB orb = ORB.init(args, null);

    // Find the Naming Service, it's part of orbd
            org.omg.CORBA.Object naming_service_ref =
                orb.resolve_initial_references("NameService");

            NamingContextExt namingcontext= NamingContextExtHelper.narrow
                (naming_service_ref);
    // Create a name to be used for searching the Naming Service
            NameComponent name = new NameComponent("echo","");
                        // set name field to "echo" and kind field to empty string
            NameComponent path[] = {name};
                            // Put name in an array of names
    // Find the server
            org.omg.CORBA.Object proxy = namingcontext.resolve(path);
            echo myecho = echoHelper.narrow(proxy);

            System.out.println(myecho.echostring("hi there"));
        }
        catch (Exception the_exception)
        {
            System.err.println("Exception happened, exception is "+the_exception);
        }
    }
}
```

8.2.7 CORBA Under the Hood and Some Leftover CORBA Stuff

We're going to look briefly here at the underpinnings of CORBA, it's a lot for beginners but it's important to know this because later on we'll have to use it to compare different middlewares. Then we'll look at a few kind of leftover topics that I couldn't figure out a good place to put otherwise. ☺

8.2.7.1 CORBA Under the Hood

General Inter-ORB Protocol (GIOP) is what CORBA uses instead of HTTP. It's got some in common with HTTP, in that it runs on top of TCP/IP (by default, anyway) and sends messages between a client to a server. However, the messages are fairly different from HTTP messages, and GIOP is not associated with web pages.

GIOP consists of eight GIOP messages to manage communication between Client and Server and a CDR (a data representation for data being sent over a communications link).

The GIOP messages are the following:

1. Request—from Client to Server, used to call a remote procedure on an object on the Server
   a. Includes a request_id, this is used to associate a later Reply with this Request
   b. NOTE: later versions of GIOP allow a servant to send a Request on a connection that a client previously opened.

2. Reply—from Server to Client, contains the response to the remote procedure call:
    a. Return value
    b. Out parameters
    c. Inout parameters
    d. Exceptions if they occur
    e. Includes a request_id, this is used to associate the Reply with a previous Request
3. CancelRequest—from Client to Server, tells the Server that the Client no longer expects to receive a Reply to a previous Request or LocateRequest
    a. Includes a request_id, this is used to associate the CancelRequest with a previous Request
4. LocateRequest—from a client to a server, to ask the Server whether it could handle a Request to a particular object reference. The Server replies with a LocateReply.
    a. Includes a request_id, this is used to associate a later Reply with this Request
5. LocateReply—from a server to a client, in response to a LocateRequest. The Server replies with one of:
    a. UNKNOWN_OBJECT—the Server doesn't recognize that object reference
    b. OBJECT_HERE—the Server is able to receive requests for that object reference
    c. OBJECT_FORWARD—includes the IOR of a server where that object reference is located
    d. Includes a request_id, this is used to associate the LocateReply with a previous LocateRequest
6. CloseConnection—from Server to Client, tells the Client that the Server is no longer processing requests, and no more replies will be forthcoming
7. MessageError—bad GIOP message
8. Fragment—follows a previous Request or Reply message, allows the Request or Reply to be broken into multiple chunks called Fragments. This fixes a problem where the Request or Reply had to know up front at the time the message header is being created, how many bytes (octets) would be in the message.

There is a general GIOP message header that is sent at the beginning of each of these messages. Among other items, the message header includes a field called (in later versions of GIOP) "flags." The next to least significant bit in this field says whether any more fragment messages follow (0=no more fragments, 1=more fragments). The least significant bit of this field specifies whether the data in the message is in big-endian format or little-endian format.

Common Data Representation (CDR) is a format that is used to store IDL data when the data is in transmission over the communication link between the Client and the Server and vice versa. Since the GIOP message header "flags" field tells the receiver whether or not the data in the message is being sent is big-endian or little-endian (see Sidebar on Big-endian and Little-endian in Chapter 1). Then if both sides are little-endian, no conversion of data is necessary, and if both sides are big-endian, no conversion of data is necessary. If one side is big-endian and the other side is little-endian, then the receiver is responsible for converting the data in the message to the appropriate endianness, according to the local format.

CDR specifies the number of bytes (octets) in the data stream allocated to each primitive IDL type. If the data isn't long enough for its specified data type, the data in the data stream is padded, so that the primitive data types are always on the appropriate boundaries. For example, an IDL short is 2 bytes, a long is 4 bytes, a float is 4 bytes, and a double is 8 bytes.

The elements of a Struct are sent in CDR in the order in which they are defined within the Struct. Each individual element within the Struct is sent in the appropriate order according to its own type.

Array elements are sent in sequence, with each individual element sent in the appropriate order according to its own type. The rightmost index varies the quickest, the leftmost index varies the slowest.

Sequences are sent as followed:

- Unsigned long, 4-byte length field, specifies number of elements in the sequence
- Elements of the sequence, with each individual element sent in the appropriate order according to its own type

IDL strings are sent in CDR as follows:

- Unsigned long, 4-byte length field, specifies length of the string
- Bytes of the string
- Null byte (note that the string length field counts this byte)

Internet Inter-ORB Protocol (IIOP) maps GIOP onto TCP/IP (specifies how TCP/IP connections are used to transmit GIOP messages). This defines the format of IORs for use in GIOP over TCP/IP. We previously discussed IORs in Section 8.2.4.1.

8.2.7.2   Some Leftover CORBA Stuff

The *Interface Repository* is used to contain all IDL type definitions so it can be queried for which interfaces are available and what they look like. The Interface Repository is itself a CORBA server and obeys the CORBA Interface Repository Interfaces.

When an IDL file is compiled using the IDL compiler, its type definitions can be stored in an Interface Repository to be retrieved by other Clients or Servers. The IDL compilers create unique identifiers for each IDL type. For example, each interface in an IDL file would have its own repository id: the omniORB IDL compiler for the interface shown in Listing 8.1 generates the following repository id (in the echoSK.cc file) and the JDK ORB IDL compiler also generates the same repository id (in the echoPOA.java file):

    IDL:echo:1.0

The *Dynamic Invocation Interface* (DII) is the client-side interface for dynamic applications that discover interfaces at runtime. That is, using DII, the Client doesn't have to know what the interface looks like at compile time, but can read the interface description sometime later on.

The base CORBA::Object implements the DII, so the calls to create a request object, and look at the return type of the request object, are invoked on an instance of CORBA::Object.

Let's look at Listing 8.36, which represents a client-side call using the interface defined in Listing 8.1. The DII calls on the CORBA::Object here are:

- _request(name of interface to call)—creates an empty request object
- add_in_arg()—adds an *in* argument to the request (creates an empty argument, returns its data type as "Any&", then the Any insertion operators write a string value into this argument)
  - Arguments must be added in the order they appear in the IDL interface
  - Other options would be:
    - add_out_arg()
    - add_inout_arg()
- set_return_type(CORBA::TypeCode)—initialize the return type on the request object
- invoke()—perform the remote procedure call
- return_value()—once you're sure there was a normal return (no exceptions), extract the return value from the Any

There are also calls to the return environment to check for exceptions:

- CORBA::Environment_ptr the_env = myrequest->env ();

CORBA::Object_var myobj=…find object reference, perhaps using Naming Service as before

---

LISTING 8.36   Dynamic Invocation Interface Example, in C++

```
// Create the Request
CORBA::Request_var myrequest=myobj->_request("echostring");
myrequest->add_in_arg() <<= "hi there";
myreques->set_return_type(CORBA::_tc_string);

// Perform the remote procedure call
myrequest->invoke();

// Check for exceptions
CORBA::Environment_ptr the_env = myrequest->env ();
                                        // check the returned environment
if (the_env->exception())
{
     Cout << "exception occurred\n";
}
else
{
   // extract the return value
     String the_return_value;
     myrequest->return_value() >>=the_return_value;
     cout << "The value returned is " << the_return_value << endl;
}
```

The *Dynamic Skeleton Interface* (DSI) is the server-side interface for dynamic applications that implement interfaces which they discover at runtime. We will not look in depth at this interface, this is getting fairly advanced for a beginner textbook. However, just a short overview to get you started if you ever need to work on this (code snippets here are in C++).

The DSI servant must inherit from PortableServer::DynamicImplementations.

The CORBA::ServerRequest class is what is used to define a Request object once the request has reached the server-side. When the POA receives a request, it will pass an instance of ServerRequest to the servant, using:

- invoke (ServerRequest_ptr server_request);

After the servant has figured out which operation it must implement, it has to retrieve the arguments for that operation. So the servant tells the ORB the number of arguments, their type, whether they're in, inout, or out using ServerRequest::arguments.

Inside the invoke routine which is implemented in the servant, to create the description of the arguments in order to query the ORB, do:

- CORBA::NVList_ptr args;
- orb->create_list(0, args);

The purpose of the CORBA::NVList object is to describe arguments in the DSI and DII.

Then create an Any data value, and do something like (this code assumes we're doing an echostring as in Listing 8.1):

- the_any.replace(CORBA::_tc_string,0);
- args->add_value("", the_any, CORBA::ARG_IN);

and finally call, to extract the argument values from the ORB:

- server_request->arguments(args);

Then to extract the values from the arguments, do something like:

- args->item(0)->value()

Then do the required processing to implement the request.

After the required processing is complete, create a pointer to another Any data type:

- CORBA::Any *the_result_any;

Put the return data in the_result_any, and then call:

- server_request->set_result(*the_result_any);

8.2.8 PORTABLE OBJECT ADAPTER

As we discussed earlier, the Portable Object Adapter (POA) is concerned with how Servers and Servants handle the requests from the Clients. At least one POA per Server (the Root POA) is required.

The policies of the POA are concerned:

- With how servants are mapped to the CORBA objects that represent the interface (Implicit Activation Policy, Servant Retention Policy, Request Processing Policy)
- With the lifespan of the CORBA object that represents the interface, and the associated servant (Lifespan policy)
- With whether a CORBA object and servant can share the same identifier or must have unique identifiers (Id Uniqueness policy), and whether the system or the user assigns the identifiers (Id Assignment policy)
- With whether the server-side CORBA ORB can handle multiple requests at the same time, or whether all requests must be queued (Thread Policy)

Note that several of these policies are interacting. For example, which values you chose for the Id Uniqueness and Id Assignment policies are heavily related to which values you chose for the Lifespan policy. We'll discuss these in the following sections.

Also in the following sections, we'll be looking at *why* and *how* the POA does certain things certain ways. That is, we'll be learning how the POA in CORBA operates. It's convenient to do that as part of a discussion about the POA policies, because the policies control the behavior of the POA.

8.2.8.1   Introduction to POA Policies

All POAs, by default, are set to the following policies: TRANSIENT, USE_ACTIVE_OBJECT_MAP_ONLY, SYSTEM_ID, UNIQUE_ID, RETAIN, and ORB_CTRL_MODEL.

The Root POA, by default, is set to the IMPLICIT_ACTIVATION policy, whereas all other POAs are set to NO_IMPLICIT_ACTIVATION by default.

8.2.8.1.1   Servant Retention Policy

Possible values are RETAIN and NON_RETAIN. The default value is RETAIN.

With RETAIN, the POA maintains an Active Object Map. With NON_RETAIN, no Active Object Map is used.

In CORBA, "activation" means that a servant is associated with (maps to) a CORBA object that represents the interface. The CORBA terminology is that the servant *incarnates* the CORBA object. We'll talk more about how this works later on.

An Active Object Map is stored inside the POA, and maps CORBA objects that represent interfaces to the servants that incarnate them. When an incoming request related to a particular interface is received from the Client, the Active Object Map is used to map this request to the appropriate servant. If the servant is not found, an exception is thrown.

8.2.8.1.2   Request Processing Policy

Possible values are USE_ACTIVE_OBJECT_MAP_ONLY, USE_DEFAULT_SERVANT, and USE_SERVANT_MANAGER.

The default is USE_ACTIVE_OBJECT_MAP_ONLY.

If USE_ACTIVE_OBJECT_MAP_ONLY is selected then the Servant Retention Policy must be set to RETAIN. Normally the id uniqueness policy will be set to UNIQUE_ID.

If USE_DEFAULT SERVANT is selected, then:

- If the Servant Retention policy is set to RETAIN, then a request from the Client related to a particular interface is looked up first in the Active Object Map. If the CORBA object that implements that interface is not found in the Active Object Map, or if the CORBA object is in the Active Object Map but has not been incarnated by a servant, then the request is sent to the specified default servant.
- If the Servant Retention policy is set to NON_RETAIN, then a request from any client is sent to the specified default servant.

If USE_SERVANT_MANAGER is selected, then:

- If the Servant Retention policy is set to RETAIN, then a request from the Client related to a particular interface is looked up first in the Active Object Map. If the CORBA object that implements that interface is not found in the Active Object Map, then the servant manager is called. In this case, the servant manager supports the Servant Activator interface.
- If the Servant Retention policy is set to NON_RETAIN, then a request from any client is sent to the servant manager. In this case, the servant manager supports the Servant Locator interface.

A Servant Manager that is behaving as a Servant Activator is responsible for creating an appropriate servant to handle the request. In this way, the servant is created on demand, rather than pre-existing prior to being needed. After the servant is created, it is added to the Active Object

Map to be ready for future requests from the Client. McHale refers to a POA that works this way as a "lazy loader" POA.

A Servant Manager that is behaving as a Servant Locator first calls the CORBA function preinvoke on the POA. The preinvoke function is responsible for creating the servant. Then the servant manager calls the request on the servant. After the servant call returns, the servant manager calls postinvoke.

McHale says that a POA using Servant Manager that is behaving as a Servant Locator can store some, but not all, of the needed servants. McHale says this should be referred to as a "cache" POA since typical use of this would be to have some pre-existing servants to store cached information for a read only database.

Note that the routines create_reference and create_reference_with_id can create a CORBA object to instantiate an interface without incarnating a servant. The servant could later be incarnated with a servant manager. These two routines require an Interface Repository Identifier as a parameter. The IDL compilers generate these for every item in the IDL file, all type definitions in an IDL file have these identifiers. See Section 8.2.7.2 for a discussion of Interface Repository identifiers.

8.2.8.1.3   Id Uniqueness Policy

Possible values are UNIQUE_ID and MULTIPLE_ID.

The default is UNIQUE_ID.

The Id Uniqueness policy says whether or not a servant can incarnate more than one CORBA object that represent interfaces. That is, can a servant serve to implement more than one interface or not?

If UNIQUE_ID is set, then a servant can incarnate exactly one interface.

If MULTIPLE_ID is set, then a servant can incarnate multiple interfaces (an interface would be associated with a CORBA object).

8.2.8.1.4   Id Assignment Policy

Possible values are SYSTEM_ID and USER_ID.

The default is SYSTEM_ID.

If SYSTEM_ID is set, then the POA assigns an Object Identifier to a CORBA object that represents an interface, when the CORBA object has been activated.

If USER_ID is set, then the user gives the CORBA object an Object Identifier.

Normally, a USER_ID would only be used when the Lifespan policy is set to PERSISTENT. This would typically occur when a persistent object is being used to reference something like a database or a file system.

8.2.8.1.5   Lifespan Policy

Possible values are TRANSIENT and PERSISTENT.

The default is TRANSIENT.

If TRANSIENT is selected, then the lifetime of a CORBA object in this POA is the lifetime of the Server. That is, when the Server is terminated, the CORBA object is terminated.

If PERSISTENT is selected, then the lifetime of a CORBA object is not associated with the lifetime of the Server. If the Server is terminated and restarted, then the CORBA object is still valid. (This would typically occur when a persistent object is being used to reference something like a database or a file system.)

8.2.8.1.6   Thread Policy

Possible values are ORB_CTRL_MODEL, SINGLE_THREAD_MODEL, and MAIN_THREAD_MODEL.

The default is ORB_CTRL_MODEL.

If ORB_CTRL_MODEL is specified, then how the thread model is implemented is up to the ORB vendor, but typically a multithreaded model of some kind is implemented. However, this depends on the ORB. Some possibilities for implementations include: a pool of threads assigned to requests as they come in, a thread per request, etc. The original MICO implementation used a single-thread model, but has been updated with a multithread model. (The single-thread model was also CORBA compliant.)

If SINGLE_THREAD_MODEL is used, then requests within a single POA are handled in sequence, but multiple POAs on the Servant obeying the SINGLE_THREAD_MODEL are treated concurrently.

If MAIN_THREAD_MODEL is used, then requests are handled in sequence across all the POAs on the Servant that obey the MAIN_THREAD_MODEL (the main thread of the process handles all requests sequentially across all POAs that obey the MAIN_THREAD_MODEL).

8.2.8.1.7   The Implicit Activation Policy: Implicit Activation versus Explicit Activation

Before you can understand the Implicit Activation policy you will have to understand more about what CORBA means by activation, and then we can discuss the pros and cons of *implicit* activation versus *explicit* activation.

Activation means that a servant is associated with (maps to) a CORBA object that represents the interface. The CORBA terminology is that the servant *incarnates* the CORBA object.

The POA is in charge of doing this. Part of the issue here is understanding the different activation mechanisms the POA provides, and why those are important. One method is called *implicit activation*, this is a shorthand that allows the programmer to assume a few defaults. An implicit activation example is shown in Listing 8.37.

In this example, a servant called "myecho" is created first, then the "_this()" routine is used to perform the implicit activation that maps the "echo_obj" CORBA object representing the interface to the "myecho" servant. The "_this()" routine creates a CORBA object, registers the CORBA object under the POA, and then returns a reference to this CORBA object.

Next the "object_to_string" routine is used to convert the "echo_obj" to a string (stringify the echo_obj reference) that can be written to the "echo.ior" file.

Note that in order for implicit activation to be used, the implicit activation policy on the POA must have previously been set to IMPLICIT_ACTIVATION, that is, to allow implicit activation. The Root POA allows implicit activation by default, but the other POAs default to NO_IMPLICIT_ACTIVATION.

Note that if you're using implicit activation, the id assignment policy and the id uniqueness policy should normally be set to default values. That is, id assignment is set to SYSTEM_ID, which means that the POA is going to automatically assign an object identifier to the CORBA object when it has been activated. Also, id uniqueness is set to UNIQUE_ID, which means that the servant will map *only* to the current CORBA object (that it was just mapped to, that is, that it just *incarnated*) and not to any other CORBA objects.

The alternative (non-default) setting for the id assignment policy would be USER_ID, which means the user chooses a name (or identifier) for the CORBA objects that are created by the POA. Also, the alternative (non-default) setting for the id uniqueness policy would be MULTIPLE_ID.

One would normally use USER_ID for persistent objects (lifespan policy is set to PERSISTENT) that are meant to live beyond the lifetime of the Client, and one would normally use MULTIPLE_ID for a servant that is meant to map to multiple interfaces (the interface would be associated with a CORBA object). By using implicit activation, we are normally assuming that these are not the case. For implicit activation, we assume that we are using a TRANSIENT object (lifespan policy is set to TRANSIENT), which means the CORBA object does not live longer than the server object.

LISTING 8.37   Implicit Activation, MICO ORB, in C++

```
// Create a servant
myecho * the_echo = new myecho;

// use implicit activation to map the CORBA object to the servant
echo_var echo_obj = myecho._this();

// create a stringified object reference, and write this to a file.
ofstream thefile ("echo.ior");
CORBA::String_var mystr = orb->object_to_string (echo_obj.in());
thefile << mystr.in() << endl;
thefile.close ();
```

The alternative to implicit activation is *explicit activation*. There are two routines to do explicit activation: activate_object(servant name) and activate_object_with_id(object identifier, servant name).

We've been using explicit activation all along, in all our other CORBA server examples. For example, in the Java Server for the JDK ORB shown in Listing 8.30, we saw:

```
// create servant
myecho the_echo=new myecho();

// get object reference and register it with the ORB
byte [] servant_id = mypoa.activate_object(the_echo);
```

and in the C++ Server using omniORB from Listing 8.29, we saw:

```
// Create a servant
myecho * the_echo = new myecho;

// use explicit activation to map the CORBA object to the servant
PortableServer::ObjectId_var object_identifier = mypoa->activate_object (the_echo);
```

In both cases, the *explicit activation* is performed using:

```
activate_object(the_echo);
```

The other method for explicit activation, if it were used instead, would look like, in a Java Server using the JDK ORB:

```
// create servant
myecho the_echo=new myecho();

// get object reference and register it with the ORB
byte[] oid = "echo".getBytes();
byte [] servant_id = mypoa.activate_object_with_id(oid.in(), the_echo);
```

In this case, the *explicit activation* is performed using:

```
activate_object_with_id(oid.in(), the_echo);
```

The explicit activation routines, activate_object and activate_object_with_id, will both work even if you're using the Root POA, with the implicit activation policy set to IMPLICIT_ACTIVATION. This is what we saw in Listings 8.28 and 8.29. So for these routines, the implicit activation policy doesn't really matter. What *does* matter are the id assignment policy, the id uniqueness policy, and the servant retention policy.

Both activate_object and activate_object_with_id require that the servant retention policy be set to RETAIN, or an exception will be thrown. This means that for both these, we must use an Active Object Map in some way. (Note that even if we're using the Active Object Map, depending on what the Request Processing Policy is set to, we could still be using either a default servant or a servant manager.)

The activate_object routine requires that the Id Assignment policy be set to SYSTEM_ID or an exception will be thrown. The activate_object_with_id requires that the Id Assignment policy be set to USER_ID.

There is an alternative to _this, activate_object, and activate_object_with_id: the routines create_ reference and create_reference_with_id can create a CORBA object to instantiate an interface without incarnating a servant. This servant could later be incarnated with a servant manager. These two routines require an Interface Repository Identifier as a parameter. The IDL compilers generate these for every item in the IDL file: all type definitions in an IDL file have these identifiers. See Section 8.2.7.2 for a discussion of Interface Repository identifiers for interfaces.

In the CORBA examples so far, we've seen only the most basic use of POA policies. In the next two sections, we will see somewhat more advanced examples using some POA policies.

8.2.9   Echo Example—Default Servant

An echo example with the JDK ORB in Java that uses a default servant is shown in Listing 8.37. The first part of this code to note is the following, which sets the POA Request Processing policy to use a default servant:

```
// Create policies for a child POA that uses a default servant

    Policy[] thePolicy = new Policy[1];

    thePolicy[0] = root_poa.create_request_processing_policy(
                RequestProcessingPolicyValue.USE_DEFAULT_SERVANT
                );
```

The next code segment to note is the creation of a child POA that is set with the default servant policy:

```
    POA myPOA = root_poa.create_POA("childPOA", null, thePolicy);
```

Next, a name has to be presented to the Naming Service, but this name has to be associated with a CORBA object. Previously, in Section 8.2.6, we had code that created a servant object, and then registered the CORBA object that was associated with that servant on POA, then bound that CORBA object with the name "echo" on the Naming Service.

Now, we don't want to activate a CORBA object with a servant. We want to create a CORBA object on the child POA, and then bind it to the Naming Service with the name "echo." However, we don't want a servant bound to it immediately. What we do instead is the following:

```
    org.omg.CORBA.Object echo_ref=
        myPOA.create_reference("IDL:DefaultServantExample:1.0");
```

we previously discussed the create_reference routine and the create_reference_with_id routine in Section 8.2.8. These two routines require an Interface Repository Identifier as a parameter. The IDL compilers generate these for every item in the IDL file: all type definitions in an IDL file have these identifiers. See Section 8.2.7.2 for a discussion of Interface Repository identifiers for interfaces.

What this routine does, it registers a CORBA object with the child POA. But there is no servant associated with that object. So in the future, when a request comes in from the Client, it will be routed to the default servant.

LISTING 8.38   Echo Example, Default Servant on Server, JDK ORB, in Java

```java
import java.util.Properties;
import org.omg.CORBA.Object;
import org.omg.CORBA.ORB;
import org.omg.CosNaming.NameComponent;
import org.omg.CosNaming.NamingContextExt;
import org.omg.CosNaming.NamingContextExtHelper;
import org.omg.CORBA.Policy;
import org.omg.PortableServer.POA;
import org.omg.PortableServer.*;
import org.omg.PortableServer.Servant;

public class server {

    public static void main( String args[] ) {

        try {

            Properties properties = System.getProperties();

            ORB orb = ORB.init(args, null);

            // Get POA and the POA Manager
            org.omg.CORBA.Object the_rootPOA=orb.resolve_initial_references
                ("RootPOA");
            POA root_poa = POAHelper.narrow(the_rootPOA);

            // Create policies for a child POA that uses a default servant

            Policy[] thePolicy = new Policy[1];

            thePolicy[0] = root_poa.create_request_processing_policy(
                    RequestProcessingPolicyValue.USE_DEFAULT_SERVANT
                    );
            POA myPOA = root_poa.create_POA("childPOA", null, thePolicy );

            // Create a servant to use as the default servant
            myecho servant = new myecho();

            // set the default servant
            myPOA.set_servant(servant);

            // Activate the root POA and the child POA
            root_poa.the_POAManager().activate();
```

```
            myPOA.the_POAManager().activate( );

    // Create a CORBA Object (but don't activate it!!! the default servant will be used instead)
    // This code can use EITHER create_reference_with_id, in which case you have to give an ID
    // name or just create_reference, in which the name is system generated.

    // Note that you MUST use the IDL name format, or this won't run (it will compile but not run).
    // (Note that you MUST have the interface number, but you could potentially skip the "IDL:",
    but
            //  I don't see any reason why you should do that.)
    // The calls create_reference and create_reference_with_id must pass in an interface
    repository ID.

    org.omg.CORBA.Object echo_ref=myPOA.create_reference("IDL:DefaultServant
    Example:1.0");

    // Find the Naming Service, it's part of orbd
    org.omg.CORBA.Object naming_service_ref = orb.resolve_initial_references
    ("NameService");

    NamingContextExt namingcontext= NamingContextExtHelper.narrow
    (naming_service_ref);

    // bind the object reference to the naming service
    NameComponent name = new NameComponent("echo","");
    // set name field to "echo" and kind field to empty string
    NameComponent path[] = {name};
    // Put name in an array of names, needed to call the rebind
    namingcontext.rebind(path, echo_ref);

    System.out.println("Server is waiting for input");

    // Listen for incoming requests
    orb.run();
    }

    catch (Exception the_exception)

    {
        System.err.println("Exception happened, exception is "+the_exception);
    }
  }
}
```

LISTING 8.39   Echo Example, Client, JDK ORB, in Java

```
import org.omg.CORBA.ORB;
import org.omg.CosNaming.NameComponent;
import org.omg.CosNaming.NamingContextExt;
import org.omg.CosNaming.NamingContextExtHelper;
```

```java
import echo_namespace.echoHelper;
import echo_namespace.echo;

public class client {
    public static void main(String args[]) {

        try {
        // create and initialize the ORB
                ORB orb = ORB.init(args, null);

        // Find the Naming Service, it's part of orbd
                org.omg.CORBA.Object naming_service_ref = orb.resolve_initial_references
                    ("NameService");

            NamingContextExt namingcontext= NamingContextExtHelper.narrow
                (naming_service_ref);

        // Create a name to be used for searching the Naming Service
            NameComponent name = new NameComponent("echo","");
                                        // set name field to "echo" and kind field to empty string
            NameComponent path[] = {name};  // Put name in an array of names

        // Find the servant

                org.omg.CORBA.Object proxy = namingcontext.resolve(path);
                echo myecho = echoHelper.narrow( proxy );

        // Call the operation on the remote servant
                String return_string=myecho.echostring("hi there");

            System.out.println("");             // print a blank line, just for clarity in the output
            System.out.println("The remote servant returned: "+return_string);
                                        // print the value returned from the remote servant
            System.out.println("");             // print a blank line, just for clarity in the output
        }
        catch (Exception the_exception)
        {
            System.err.println("Exception happened, exception is "+the_exception);
        }
    }
}
```

For completeness, I've included a Client that can call the Server with the Default Servant. However, it's the same as previous clients that use the Naming Service: compare this to Listing 8.35.

8.2.10 Echo Example—Persistent POA and Default Servant
In this section, we see an example that uses a Persistent POA (and also still uses a default servant).

To set the POA to persistent, we set the Lifespan Policy to PERSISTENT. If PERSISTENT is selected, then the lifetime of a CORBA object is not associated with the lifetime of the Server.

If the Server is terminated and restarted, then the CORBA object is still valid. This would typically occur when a persistent object is being used to reference something like a database or a file system.

When we are using a default servant, it is appropriate to also set ID Uniqueness to MULTIPLE_ID. Remember that MULTIPLE_ID means that a servant can implement more than one interface (the interface would be associated with a CORBA object). Thus, different interfaces are supported if necessary by this one default servant.

These policies are set using the following code:

```
// Create policies for a child POA that is persistent, maps multiple IDs to the same servant,
// uses a default servant
Policy[] thePolicy = new Policy[3];

thePolicy[0] = root_poa.create_lifespan_policy(LifespanPolicyValue.PERSISTENT);
thePolicy[1] =
    root_poa.create_request_processing_policy(
        RequestProcessingPolicyValue.USE_DEFAULT_SERVANT);
thePolicy[2] =
    root_poa.create_id_uniqueness_policy(IdUniquenessPolicyValue.MULTIPLE_ID);
POA myPOA = root_poa.create_POA("childPOA", null, thePolicy );
```

Otherwise, the example Server in Listing 8.39 is very similar to the example Server in Listing 8.37.

LISTING 8.40   Echo Example, Server with Persistent POA and Default Servant, JDK ORB, in Java

```java
import java.util.Properties;
import org.omg.CORBA.Object;
import org.omg.CORBA.ORB;
import org.omg.CosNaming.NameComponent;
import org.omg.CosNaming.NamingContextExt;
import org.omg.CosNaming.NamingContextExtHelper;
import org.omg.CORBA.Policy;
import org.omg.PortableServer.POA;
import org.omg.PortableServer.*;
import org.omg.PortableServer.Servant;

public class server {
    public static void main( String args[] ) {
        try {

            Properties properties = System.getProperties();

            // Begin by initializing the ORB
            ORB orb = ORB.init(args, null);

            // Get POA and the POA Manager
            org.omg.CORBA.Object the_rootPOA=orb.resolve_initial_references
            ("RootPOA");
            POA root_poa = POAHelper.narrow(the_rootPOA);
```

```
// Create policies for a child POA that is persistent, maps multiple IDs to the
        same servant,
// uses a default servant

Policy[] thePolicy = new Policy[3];

thePolicy[0] = root_poa.create_lifespan_policy(LifespanPolicyValue.
    PERSISTENT);

thePolicy[1] =
            root_poa.create_request_processing_policy(
            RequestProcessingPolicyValue.USE_DEFAULT_SERVANT);

thePolicy[2] =
            root_poa.create_id_uniqueness_policy(IdUniquenessPolicyValue.
                MULTIPLE_ID);
POA myPOA = root_poa.create_POA("childPOA", null, thePolicy);
// Create a servant to use as the default servant
myecho servant = new myecho();

// set the default servant
myPOA.set_servant(servant);s

// Activate the root POA and the child POA
root_poa.the_POAManager().activate();
myPOA.the_POAManager().activate( );

// Create a CORBA Object (but don't activate it!!! the default servant will be used
instead)

// This code can use EITHER create_reference_with_id, in which case
        //you have to give an ID name,
// or just create_reference, in which the name is system generated.
// Note that you MUST use the IDL name format, or this won't run (it will compile
        but not run).
// (Note that you MUST have the interface number, but you could potentially skip
    the "IDL:", but
// I don't see any reason why you should do that.)
// The calls create_reference and create_reference_with_id must pass in an
        interface repository ID.
org.omg.CORBA.Object
            echo_ref=myPOA.create_reference("IDL:DefaultServantExample:
            1.0");

// Find the Naming Service, it's part of orbd
org.omg.CORBA.Object naming_service_ref = orb.resolve_initial_references
    ("NameService");
```

```
        NamingContextExt namingcontext= NamingContextExtHelper.narrow
                (naming_service_ref);


        // bind the object reference to the naming service
        NameComponent name = new NameComponent("echo","");
                                // set name field to "echo" and kind field to empty string
        NameComponent path[] = {name}; // Put name in an array of names, needed to call
        rebind namingcontext.rebind(path, echo_ref);


        System.out.println("Server is waiting for input");
        // Listen for incoming requests
        orb.run();
        }
        catch (Exception the_exception)
        {
            System.err.println("Exception happened, exception is "+the_exception);
        }
    }
}
```

8.3   TECHNOLOGY REVIEW: .NET REMOTING

Microsoft's .NET Remoting allows communication between different processes, whether or not the processes are located on the same computer or different computers across a network. .NET Remoting has been deprecated and is retained for legacy applications. .NET Remoting has been in existence since the .NET Framework release 1.0, back in 2002.

Microsoft currently recommends that new distributed application development should be done using Windows Communication Foundation (WCF) (we will look at WCF in the next section).

One major advantage of WCF compared to .NET Remoting is performance. A study by Gupta at MSDN found that WCF is approximately 50% faster than .NET Remoting when comparing the server throughput in terms of number of "operations" per second, across processes on the same machine. Here an "operation" was defined as request/reply messages with little processing done by the service, while payloads of the messages were 128 bytes, 4 Kbytes, and 256 Kbytes.

Abdul Sami at CodeProject back in 2009 compared the features of .NET Remoting with WCF. He found that in terms of interoperability, .NET Remoting was restricted to a homogeneous environment with both sides in .NET, whereas a WCF hosted server can be accessed by clients written in different languages, and running on many different platforms. He found that .NET supported multiple lower level protocols (HTTP, TCP, and Simple Mail Transfer Protocol [SMTP]), but WCF also supported named pipes and Microsoft Message Queueing (MSMQ) (note that .NET Remoting currently also supports named pipes; we will see an example later on).

8.3.1   .NET REMOTING BASICS

.NET remoting takes place inside the Microsoft Common Language Runtime (CLR), which is the virtual machine used by all .NET routines. CLR implements a program code execution environment which is defined by the Common Language Infrastructure (CLI). The lowest level human readable language in the CLI is called the Common Intermediate Language, Microsoft's implementation (the Microsoft bytecode) is called the Microsoft Intermediate Langauge (MSIL). We previously discussed the CLR in Section 6.3.

The .NET framework supports several languages, two of the most common are C# and Visual Basic. The code examples in this textbook will be given in C#.

You might say to yourself, why do I have to learn a whole new language? Doesn't Visual Studio support C++? Note that when you're using C++ in Visual Studio but your code running on top of the CLR, the language you're using is not really C++, it's a different language called C++/CLI that has some similar syntax to C++, but is different in many ways (including garbage collection!). The C++ that was running on the CLR has varied a good bit over the years—originally it was called "managed C++" and was replaced by C++/CLI. Visual Studio does support native C++ but that doesn't run on top of the CLR.

Back in the 2007 timeframe, I wanted to call C# code from native C++. This was so students in our data structures courses, which are taught in C++, could access a robot whose control libraries were written in C# (and which we had need to modify). Over several somewhat painful but interesting days, I was able to make C++ call C++/CLI, and from C++/CLI I could call C#. Later on, in the 2009–2010 timeframe, one of my PhD students wanted to call the same robot code from Java—he was using a well-known mobile agent framework that was written in Java. We tried all kinds of ways and couldn't get it to work. He got on the Microsoft chat room and asked for help, they told him when we figured it out to please let them know ☺ because they didn't know how. We ended up using sockets to connect from Java to the C# robot code. So the moral of the story is, try to use the languages that the tools expect, whenever possible. It's just easier.

8.3.1.1 Application Domains (Appdomains)

In the .NET paradigm, an application runs inside an "application domain" ("appdomain"). These appdomains allow each application to be isolated from other applications so that a bug in one application can't affect another application, and similarly, from a security standpoint, malicious code in one appdomain cannot access another appdomain. For this reason, code in one appdomain cannot directly call code in another appdomain.

Note that the same .NET remote call mechanism can be used for a call between two appdomains in the same process, a call between two appdomains on two different processes but on the same computer, or a call between two appdomains on two different computers.

If a client is in the same appdomain as the Server, then it uses a direct reference to the Server. However, if the Client is in a different appdomain from the Server, then it uses a proxy object that represents the remote server object within the Client's appdomain. The proxy object is generated by .NET using the metadata associated with the remote server (we'll look at metadata in Section 8.3.1.2). Marshaling of the data is done through this proxy object.

All .NET components and applications run in the CLR. Therefore, windows processes which do not themselves run in the CLR, don't understand .NET.

However, appdomains run on top of an unmanaged windows process, and are the mechanism through which an unmanaged windows process can access the .NET framework. There may be multiple appdomains on a single unmanaged process.

An appdomain can start up and shut down separately from unmanaged windows process that it runs on. There can be one or more assemblies in a single appdomain. The assemblies inside an appdomain access the .NET services.

If two different appdomains make use of the same class library, that class library is loaded twice.

.NET managed threads are independent of appdomains. If one appdomain creates a thread, that thread can access threads in any other appdomain in the same unmanaged windows process. However, if an appdomain shuts down, any threads inside that appdomain also shut down.

When a .exe file containing a "main" function begins running, a default appdomain is created. The default appdomain has to stick around, you can't unload it. However, you can create new appdomains on the fly, and you can print out your appdomain's "friendly name" so you can see which appdomain you're in. Some code to do this, and the results from running this code are shown in Listing 8.41.

LISTING 8.41   Create AppDomain and Show Which Appdomain You're In

```
AppDomain currentAppDomain;
currentAppDomain = AppDomain.CurrentDomain;
Console.WriteLine("current appdomain is : " + currentAppDomain.FriendlyName);
AppDomain newAppDomain = AppDomain.CreateDomain("thenewdomain");
Console.WriteLine("child appdomain is : " + newAppDomain.FriendlyName);
```

Results from Running this code:

```
current appdomain is : Server.exe
child appdomain is : thenewdomain
```

8.3.1.2   Assemblies and Metadata

An assembly groups physical files into a single logical unit. A .dll assembly is a "library assembly" and a .exe assembly is an "application assembly." Usually (and by default in Visual Studio) an assembly has one exe or, alternately, one dll file, but more than one are possible.

When you "add a reference" in Visual Studio, what you are doing is accessing identifier(s) that are defined in a different assembly. In .NET assemblies, there are public components and private components. Only public components may be accessed outside the assembly in which they are defined.

The types in an assembly are defined in the metadata associated with that assembly. This metadata is embedded in the physical file itself (.dll file or .exe file). This metadata is used for "marshaling" in .NET remoting. That is, .NET remoting reads this metadata to determine the kinds of data being transmitted and how to format it for transmission and data receipt. When .NET remoting reads this metadata, it is called "reflection."

There is a tool called ILDASM provided with the Microsoft SDK that allows you to view the metadata in an assembly. Figure 8.2 shows the metadata associated with the class shown (later) in Listing 8.45. You can see that the metadata here shows that this class, named HelloWorld.HelloWorld (that is, the class is in a namespace called HelloWorld, and the class itself is named HelloWorld) extends MarshalByRefObject, and that the class contains a method named myHelloWorld which accepts a string parameter and returns a string.

Marshaling in .NET Remoting uses a proxy for an object. The proxy uses the metadata's exact description of the types and methods in an object to forward the data.

8.3.1.3   Manifest Files

Here we're going to look at the manifest files that are used in Windows. One reason for telling you what manifest files are is so you don't confuse them with the metadata. Also, however, the manifest information in an assembly is used to verify version compatibility, and to verify whether or not an assembly is to be trusted. At runtime, .NET verifies that only the referenced assemblies are used, and that only assemblies that employ compatible versions are loaded.

To clarify further, the purpose of the assembly metadata (in terms of .NET remoting) that we saw in Section 8.3.1.1 is to provide a view of the public calls and data in the assembly, so this information

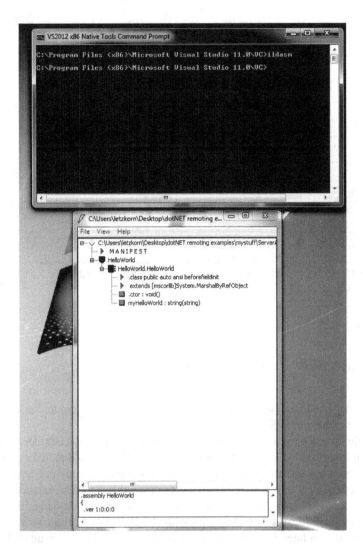

FIGURE 8.2   Using ILDASM to view assembly metadata.

can be used for marshaling (it replaces IDL in the CORBA world, for example). The purpose of manifest files is versioning (prevents .dll hell) and security (makes hacking harder).

There are two different kinds of manifest files in Windows: an "assembly manifest" and an "application manifest." An assembly manifest tells which files are part of the assembly, how the elements in the assembly relate to each other, all information required to specify version and security and to resolve references to external entities. An application manifest gives instructions to the operating system when the operating system is loading the application's executable to run it, including which Side-by-Side assembly dependencies the application must bind to a run time, operating system version compatibility, etc. (What is meant by Windows Side by Side was previously discussed in Section 6.2. How applications are stored in a Windows computer was previously discussed in Sections 6.2 and 6.4.)

An example assembly manifest that goes with the HelloWorld.HelloWorld library project from Listing 8.45 (shown later on) is shown here in Figure 8.3. This manifest was read using ILDASM. It tells you the assembly name is HelloWorld and the module name is Hello-World.dll.

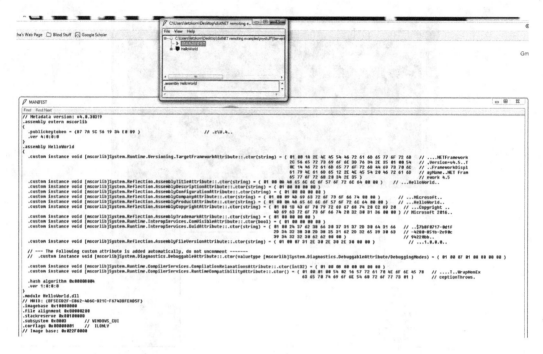

FIGURE 8.3   Using ILDASM to view assembly manifest.

You can potentially add to the assembly manifest yourself, for example, "assembly attributes" from System.Runtime.CompilerServices or System.Reflection.

The System.Runtime.CompilerServices namespace is mostly used by compiler writers. However, a class in this namespace called InternalsInvisibleToAttribute can be used to make an internal type or internal member from an assembly visible to a specific different assembly (a friend assembly).

The System.Reflection class can be used to read your assembly's own metadata to get information about assemblies, modules, parameters, etc., so this information can be used at runtime.

An example application manifest (that goes with the HelloWorld.HelloWorld library project from Listing 8.44, shown later on) is shown in Listing 8.42. I used Visual Studio 2012 to generate this manifest file: in Visual Studio 2012, you do Add New Item, and select Application Manifest File. If you wanted to do this in Visual Studio 2015, then manifest file generation is enabled by default. However, to enable it, select Project Pages, Configuration Properties, Linker, Manifest File, Generate Manifest.

In this file, you can see that to work with different versions of Windows you modify the code appropriately (for example, "If your application is designed to work with Windows 8, uncomment the following…").

To select who can run the application, the statement:

    <requestedExecutionLevel level="asInvoker" uiAccess="false" />

says that the application will run with the user's default security levels (actually it really means that it will run using the calling process' default security levels, but in this case this would be you, because you're presumably running Visual Studio direct on your account).

To instead force the user to run this application as an administrator, you would change that line to the following line:

    <requestedExecutionLevel level="requireAdministrator" uiAccess="false" />

LISTING 8.42   Example Application Manifest for Code from Listing 8.45

```
<?xml version="1.0" encoding="utf-8"?>
<asmv1:assembly manifestVersion="1.0" xmlns="urn:schemas-microsoft-com:asm.v1"
xmlns:asmv1="urn:schemas-microsoft-com:asm.v1" xmlns:asmv2="urn:schemas-microsoft-
com:asm.v2" xmlns:xsi="http://www.w3.org/2001/XMLSchema-instance">
  <assemblyIdentity version="1.0.0.0" name="MyApplication.app"/>
  <trustInfo xmlns="urn:schemas-microsoft-com:asm.v2">
    <security>

      <requestedPrivileges xmlns="urn:schemas-microsoft-com:asm.v3">
      <!-- UAC Manifest Options
      If you want to change the Windows User Account Control level replace the
      requestedExecutionLevel node with one of the following.

      <requestedExecutionLevel  level="asInvoker" uiAccess="false" />
      <requestedExecutionLevel  level="requireAdministrator" uiAccess="false" />
      <requestedExecutionLevel  level="highestAvailable" uiAccess="false" />

      Specifying requestedExecutionLevel node will disable file and registry virtualization.
      If you want to utilize File and Registry Virtualization for backward

      compatibility then delete the requestedExecutionLevel node.
      -->
         <requestedExecutionLevel level="asInvoker" uiAccess="false" />
      </requestedPrivileges>
    </security>

  </trustInfo>

  <compatibility xmlns="urn:schemas-microsoft-com:compatibility.v1">
    <application>
        <!-- A list of all Windows versions that this application is designed to work with.
Windows will automatically select the most compatible environment.-->

        <!-- If your application is designed to work with Windows Vista, uncomment the
following supportedOS node-->

        <!--<supportedOS Id="{e2011457-1546-43c5-a5fe-008deee3d3f0}"></supporte-
dOS>-->

        <!-- If your application is designed to work with Windows 7, uncomment the following
supportedOS node-->

        <!--<supportedOS Id="{35138b9a-5d96-4fbd-8e2d-a2440225f93a}"/>-->

        <!-- If your application is designed to work with Windows 8, uncomment the following
supportedOS node-->
```

```
<!--<supportedOS Id="{4a2f28e3-53b9-4441-ba9c-d69d4a4a6e38}"></supportedOS>-->

    </application>
</compatibility>

<!-- Enable themes for Windows common controls and dialogs (Windows XP and later) -->

<!-- <dependency>

    <dependentAssembly>

    <assemblyIdentity
        type="win32"
        name="Microsoft.Windows.Common-Controls"
        version="6.0.0.0"
        processorArchitecture="*"
        publicKeyToken="6595b64144ccf1df"
        language="*"
    />

    </dependentAssembly>
    </dependency>-->
</asmv1:assembly>
```

8.3.1.4 .NET Library Files

You should remember our previous discussion from Sections 6.2 and 6.4 about how DLL files are stored, and how the Global Assembly Cache (GAC) works. The .NET Remoting library files (.dll files) are stored in the GAC. I looked at these on my Windows 10 computer, for example, you can see the .dll file for System.Runtime.Remoting in Figure 8.4.

As you can see, these are installed using a strong name for the directory, under the GAC_MSIL directory. See Section 6.4 for a further discussion of how this works.

8.3.2 CALL C# FROM C#, NOT USING REMOTING

Before we get into what .NET Remoting looks like, let's first briefly look at what C# would look like calling a function when it's *not* using Remoting—just so we can compare ☺ in case you're not all that familiar with C#. In Listing 8.43 we see a class library, and in Listing 8.44 we see the client code to call this class library.

FIGURE 8.4   Windows 10 .NET Remoting files in the GAC.

LISTING 8.43   Basic Class Library, Doesn't Do Much. Should Be Stored in .dll File

```
using System;
using System.Collections.Generic;
using System.Text;
namespace ClassLibrary


{
    public class CalledClass
    {
        public string CallTheCalledClassObj()
        {
            Console.WriteLine("Got to called class");
            string stuff = "whew!";
            return stuff;
        }
    }
}
```

LISTING 8.44   Really Basic Client Code, Calls Class Library in Listing 8.43

```
using System;
using System.Collections.Generic;
using System.Text;
using ClassLibrary;
namespace ConsoleApplication1

{
    class Program
    {
        static void Main(string[] args)
        {
            CalledClass myobj = new CalledClass();
            Console.WriteLine("Just about to call other assembly");

            String s = myobj.CallTheCalledClassObj();
            Console.WriteLine("Just called other assembly, s is {0} ",s);
        }
    }
}
```

Not much to it, right? We create an object of the type of the class in the .dll file, and we call the method on that object. Pretty basic.

Now let's start adding some .NET Remoting.

8.3.3   .NET Remoting Using Marshaling by Value

There are two kinds of Remotable objects in .NET: Marshal by value objects, which are themselves copied and pass from the remote appdomain to the local appdomain, and Marshal by reference objects, in which a proxy object is created in the Client, and the Client accesses the remote object with the proxy object as an intermediary (note that if the Client is in the same appdomain as the marshal by reference object, the Client receives a direct reference to the object rather than marshaling through the proxy).

When you use Marshaling by Value in .NET Remoting, what you mean is that when a client calls a remote object, .NET serializes the object to a stream in the server appdomain, and then deserializes the object in the Client appdomain. Thus, it should be clear that the object must be serializable. The most common reason for marshal by value is to pass a struct (or a class) as a remote parameter.

.NET uses reflection to implement serialization. Note that .NET can also serialize an object to a file. However, when using .NET Remoting the object would be serialized to memory or to a network connection.

An example of a serializable class would be as follows:

```
[Serializable]
public class thisClass
{
    public string myname;
    public int mypublicintegervalue;
    private int myprivateintegervalue;
}
```

Note that when .NET serializes an object, it must serialize the internal structures within the object. .NET can also serialize more complicated data structures (doubly linked list, for example).

If a serialized class has some member that is nonserializable then .NET would throw an exception, and you the programmer can write special code to handle the data.

You can use one of the .NET formatters to serialize data. You can do this as part of object serialization for Marshal by Value, or you can do this to write your data in a selected format to a file. You can also do it as part of Marshal by Reference, which we will look at later.

.NET has two default formatters:

1. Binary formatter
2. Simple Object Access Protocol (SOAP) formatter

or you can write your own.

The advantages of a binary formatter are that the data representation is compact and therefore very fast to transmit. The advantages of the SOAP formatter are that it is human readable, platform independent, good for going through a firewall (when using HTTP as the transport protocol). However, it is less compact than the binary representation and therefore slower to transmit. For these reasons, if you're sure you're always going to be using the same platform, and you're not going through a firewall, it would be better to use the binary formatter. By the way, there's an in-depth discussion of SOAP in Section 10.2, as SOAP is also heavily used in non-RESTful web services.

We'll look at these again next when we discuss Marshal by Reference.

8.3.4   Marshal by Reference: The Heart of .NET Remoting

Okay, we've finally arrived at the important .NET Remoting stuff. ☺

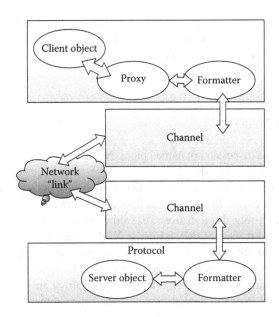

FIGURE 8.5   .NET Remoting architecture diagram.

When we say Marshaling by Reference, we mean that the Client has a proxy object that (together with the formatter and the channel) does the work of marshaling the data to and from the Client. Figure 8.5 shows a diagram of .NET Remoting when Marshal by Reference is being used.

As you can see from this diagram, the channel is responsible for transporting messages between client and server, that is, for actually transmitting the object, while the formatter is responsible for converting the data into the correct format for transmission (serializing the data).

Following the diagram in Figure 8.5, the Client interacts with the remote object through a proxy object. The proxy object is bound to only one remote object, but a client can have multiple proxy objects, each of which accesses the same remote object.

There are two parts to a proxy object: the transparent proxy, which provides the interface of the remote object to the Client (the Client thinks the transparent proxy really is the remote object), and the real proxy which does the data transmission work.

Still following the diagram in Figure 8.5, when a client makes a call on the proxy, the proxy creates the message object, sends the message object to the formatter, and then blocks, waiting for the call return. The formatter serializes the message object and sends it along to the channel object, which transmits it.

When the message object is received by the channel on the server-side, it forwards the message to a formatter. The formatter deserializes the message and gives it to a server-side entity that is responsible for mapping messages to objects (compare this "server-side entity" to a CORBA POA). The server-side entity constructs a method call that corresponds to the interface of the remote object, then it calls the remote object.

When the remote object finishes handling the method call, it sends the reply back to the same server-side entity that handles objects. The server-side entity creates a returned message object, which is sent to the formatter. The formatter serializes the returned message object and sends it to the server-side channel, which transmits it.

Finally, when the call returns from the channel object, the formatter deserializes the returned message object, and sends the returned message object to the proxy, which was blocked waiting. The proxy returns the returned value and output parameters (that it extracts from the returned message object) to the Client.

Note that if an exception is thrown on the Server, this is serialized and passed back to the client proxy. When the client proxy receives this exception, it re-throws the exception.

You can plug in your protocol to a channel. By default, however, .NET Remoting supports:

- HttpChannel
- TcpChannel
- IpcChannel (named pipes)

Refer to Section 6.5 for a discussion of named pipes. Named pipes were not present in the original .NET Remoting but were added in .NET 2.

An IpcChannel (named pipes) is your best choice for interprocess communication on the same computer (that's why it's called IPC—for Inter Process Communication). An HTTP channel is what you need if you're going through firewalls, although it's somewhat slower than the TCP channel since (by default) it uses SOAP, which is XML based, as its data format—the data is not very compact. As you recall from the previous section, the binary format (which the TCP Channel uses by default) is compact and fast to transmit. Note when there is a call between two appdomains in the same process, .NET Remoting employs an internal channel called the CrossAppDomainChannel instead of what channels the programmer selected. This is done for performance reasons.

You can change the formatter that you use with a particular channel. For example, the TCP channel uses binary by default, but you can change it to SOAP, and the HTTP channel uses SOAP by default but you can change it to binary. We'll see an example of this later on.

There are three kinds of .NET Marshal by Reference remote objects. (It's a "remote" object because it's "remote" to the Client. It will be running on the Server.):

- Client-Activated
- Server-Activated Single Call
- Server-Activated Singleton

For Client-Activated mode, the remote object on the Server is created when the Client requests it. For the two Server-Activated modes, the Server creates the remote object. When Server-Activated mode is used, the remote objects are also called "well-known" objects (possibly because they can be known by more than one client). Using a client-activated object doesn't scale well when a large number of clients are accessing the service, since each new client gets a new instance of the remote object, a lot of memory can be used, and each client can potentially hold on to that memory for a long time. If the Client is poorly written, the Client can hold on to the object even when the Client is no longer using it.

For Server-activated mode, you have two options: SingleCall and Singleton. The SingleCall remote object handles only one request at a time. It is instantiated at the beginning of the request and uninstantiated at the end of the request. It does not store any state between method calls (compare this to a stateless session EJB, see Section 8.4.3). This can be a good choice for scalability, since the server-side remote object uses up resources only when it absolutely needs them.

The Singleton remote object is instantiated one time, when it is called by the first client that accesses it, and after that the same instance handles requests from several clients. (Compare this to a singleton session EJB, see Section 8.4.4.) A Singleton object doesn't take up much space, but it may not be good for scalability because if you have a suddenly large number of client requests to handle then that one object could be a bottleneck.

For Client-Activated remote objects, each object is dedicated to the Client that requests it, and different clients get different objects. The lifetime of the object usually is the lifetime of the Client, although a client-activated object could be leased to another appdomain, in which case the lifetime of the object is extended (until a time specified by a timestamp). Note that the server process must register itself to accept client-activated calls prior to receiving them, and therefore the Server has to be running prior to receiving these requests. It makes sense, by the way, for a Client-Activated remote object to store a state, since the remote object is dedicated to a single client it can hold a running state (compare this to stateful session EJBs, see Section 8.4.5).

For Server-Activated Single Call remote objects, for each new method call a new remote object is created and at the end of the method call the object is uninstantiated. However, the client-side proxy object is not destroyed, so as far as the Client knows, the server-side remote object is there all the time. This means that in some cases the Single Call may have to pretend that it is there all the time—this means it may have to save state. If this is the case, then if, for example, it saves its state in a database, the connections to the database must be renewed every time.

Every remote object is associated with a URL as follows:

- tcp://localhost:8700
- http://localhost:8700
- When using an IpcChannel, you don't specify a port number, just the name of the named pipe:
  - ipc://servername

If you're using a Client-Activated object then all you need is the URL. If you're using a Server-Activated object, then you also must specify the name of the remote object:

- tcp://localhost:8700/remoteobjectname

Both the Client and the Server have to register their associated channels. If using one of the Server-Activated modes, then Server also has to register the servant object types. The Client has to create a proxy object of the correct type.

There are two registration methods: programmatic and administrative. Administrative is done through the use of config files. We are going to concentrate on programmatic registration here only because this compares best to the other middlewares we examine in this textbook.

Following are short examples for how to register channels, for each kind of channel:
For TcpChannel:

```
using System.Runtime.Remoting.Channels;
using System.Runtime.Remoting.Channels.Tcp;
IChannel mychannel = new TcpChannel(8700);
ChannelServices.RegisterChannel(mychannel, false);
            // false turns off lower level protocol security
```

For an HttpChannel:

```
using System.Runtime.Remoting.Channels;
using System.Runtime.Remoting.Channels.Http;
IChannel mychannel = new HttpChannel(8700);
ChannelServices.RegisterChannel(mychannel, false);
            // false turns off lower level protocol security
```

For an IpcChannel (named pipes):

```
using System.Runtime.Remoting.Channels;
using System.Runtime.Remoting.Channels.Ipc;
IChannel mychannel = new IpcChannel("MyChannelName"); // named pipe does not have port #
```

```
ChannelServices.RegisterChannel(mychannel, false);
        // false turns off lower level protocol security
```

When a server registers a channel, .NET starts listening for activation requests on a background thread, so your server can continue processing if desired.

It would be a good idea, however, to turn on lower-level protocol security when possible. If this ensured security parameter is true, then if the channel supports security properties then encryption and digital signatures are enabled.

You can only register one channel on a particular port number. Also, you can only register one channel type per appdomain, unless you change the channel name. For example, by default, a TcpChannel is named "tcp," so to use another TcpChannel you'd have to give it a different name. Similarly for HttpChannel and IpcChannel.

When the Server terminates, the ports and named pipes are automatically freed:

- However, it can be useful to explicitly return resources rather than wait for the garbage collector, so unregister each channel when it's through:
    - ChannelServices.UnregisterChannel(mychannel);

We will go through several examples in the next sections where we examine the various options of .NET Remoting. We will be using programmatic registration in all cases.

8.3.5 CLIENT-ACTIVATED OBJECT

In this example, we will examine Client-Activated Object mode.

In Listing 8.45 is shown a remote object, which receives a string, prints it's about to return a Hello-World message, and then returns the HelloWorld message. In the code provided for the instructor with this textbook, this is compiled into a .dll file (class library). The .dll file is then added as a reference to a separate Visual Studio Server project and to a separate Client project. The Server project and the Client project compile into separate .exe files (Server.exe and Client.exe).

LISTING 8.45 HelloWorld Remote Object in Class Library (.dll File)

```
using System;
using System.Collections.Generic;
using System.Linq;
using System.Text;
using System.Threading.Tasks;
namespace HelloWorld
{
    public class HelloWorld : MarshalByRefObject
    {
        public string myHelloWorld(string msg)
        {
            string mymsg;
            mymsg = "Hello, World, especially to: " + msg;
            Console.WriteLine("about to return the Hello World message");
            return mymsg;
        }
    }
}
```

Let's look now at the Server in Listing 8.46. Here, we first register the channel. After that, we register the remote object's name:

```
RemotingConfiguration.ApplicationName = "HelloWorld";
```

And finally we register that we are working in Client-Activated mode, and pass it the remote object we're working with:

```
RemotingConfiguration.RegisterActivatedServiceType( typeof(HelloWorld.HelloWorld) );
```

Then we create a local proxy object:

```
HelloWorld.HelloWorld myobj = new HelloWorld.HelloWorld();
```

LISTING 8.46   Server for Client-Activated Object

```
using System;
using System.Collections.Generic;
using System.Linq;
using System.Text;
using System.Threading.Tasks;
using System.Runtime.Remoting;
using System.Runtime.Remoting.Channels;
using System.Runtime.Remoting.Channels.Http;

using HelloWorld;

public class Server
{
    static void Main(string[] args)
    {

        // Set up the channel, let's use HTTP
        HttpChannel mychannel = new HttpChannel(32000);
        ChannelServices.RegisterChannel(mychannel, false /* turn off lower level
            protocol security */);

        RemotingConfiguration.ApplicationName = "HelloWorld";

        RemotingConfiguration.RegisterActivatedServiceType( typeof(HelloWorld.
            HelloWorld) );

        Console.WriteLine("Server is now waiting for calls from client");
        Console.ReadLine(); // wait for calls
    }

}
```

Now let's examine the Client in Listing 8.47. We first register the channel. Then we set the kind of remote object we plan to activate, and the URL where it is located:

```
RemotingConfiguration.RegisterActivatedClientType( typeof(HelloWorld.HelloWorld),
    "http://localhost:32000/HelloWorld");
```

And finally we call the proxy object, which will itself, through the magic of .NET Remoting, call the remote object:

```
string returnedvalue = myobj.myHelloWorld(myname);
```

LISTING 8.47   Client for Client-Activated Object

```
using System;
using System.Collections.Generic;
using System.Linq;
using System.Text;
using System.Threading.Tasks;
using System.Runtime.Remoting;
using System.Runtime.Remoting.Channels;
using System.Runtime.Remoting.Channels.Http;

using HelloWorld;
public class Client
{
    static void Main(string[] args)
    {
        // Set up the channel, let's use HTTP
        HttpChannel mychannel = new HttpChannel();  // Don't bind the Client to a
            particular port
        ChannelServices.RegisterChannel(mychannel, false /* turn off lower level
            protocol security */);

        RemotingConfiguration.RegisterActivatedClientType( typeof(HelloWorld.
            HelloWorld),
                "http://localhost:32000/HelloWorld");

        HelloWorld.HelloWorld myobj = new HelloWorld.HelloWorld();

        // Get the name to send to the remote
        Console.Write("Please enter your name: ");
        string myname=Console.ReadLine();

        // Call the remote object (call the proxy and the proxy will call the remote)
        string returnedvalue = myobj.myHelloWorld(myname);
        string mymsg = "value received from server is : "+returnedvalue;
        Console.WriteLine(mymsg);
    }
}
```

Since this is a Client-Activated object, the object will not actually be created on the Server until the Client calls the proxy object, and the proxy object passes its request message to the Server.

8.3.6   SERVER-ACTIVATED SINGLE CALL

Here we will examine the Server-Activated Single Call mode. In this example, we are again using the remote object from Listing 8.45. Listing 8.48 shows the Server that handles the Server-Activated Single Call mode, while Listing 8.49 shows the Client that goes with this mode.

In Listing 8.48, after the Server registers the channel, note that it registers the channel on port 32000, and it explicitly registers the remote object for access in single call mode:

```
RemotingConfiguration.RegisterWellKnownServiceType(
                typeof(HelloWorld.HelloWorld),
                "myHelloWorldObject",
                WellKnownObjectMode.SingleCall
            );
```

Note that this sets the name of the remote object to "myHelloWorldObject." After this, it waits for calls from the Client.

LISTING 8.48   Server for Server-Activated Single Call

```
using System;
using System.Collections.Generic;
using System.Linq;
using System.Text;
using System.Threading.Tasks;
using System.Runtime.Remoting;
using System.Runtime.Remoting.Channels;
using System.Runtime.Remoting.Channels.Http;

using HelloWorld;

public class Server
{
    static void Main(string[] args)
    {
        // Set up the channel, let's use HTTP
        HttpChannel mychannel = new HttpChannel(32000);
        ChannelServices.RegisterChannel(mychannel, false /* turn off lower level
            protocol security */);
        // Register the Single Call
        RemotingConfiguration.RegisterWellKnownServiceType(

                typeof(HelloWorld.HelloWorld),
                "myHelloWorldObject",
                WellKnownObjectMode.SingleCall
                );
```

```
            Console.WriteLine("Server is now waiting for calls from client");
            Console.ReadLine(); // wait for calls
    }

}
```

On the client side, after it registers the channel, the Client explicitly acquires a proxy object, and sets the URL of the proxy at this time, which includes channel 32000 (same port number set by the Server), and uses the same remote object name ("myHelloWorldObject") that the Server previously used:

```
// Now get a proxy object, this proxy object
// represents the remote object in this local space
        object myproxy = Activator.GetObject(
        typeof(HelloWorld.HelloWorld),
        "http://localhost:32000/myHelloWorldObject"
        );
```

Note that this is very different from what we did in the previous section with a Client-Activated object, where we simply used the "new" operator to create a proxy object (see Listing 8.47).

LISTING 8.49   Client for Server-Activated Single Call

```
using System;
using System.Collections.Generic;
using System.Linq;
using System.Text;
using System.Threading.Tasks;
using System.Runtime.Remoting;
using System.Runtime.Remoting.Channels;
using System.Runtime.Remoting.Channels.Http;

using HelloWorld;

public class Client
{
    static void Main(string[] args)
    {
        // Set up the channel, let's use HTTP
        HttpChannel mychannel = new HttpChannel();   //Don't bind the channel to a particular
            port
        ChannelServices.RegisterChannel(mychannel, false /* turn off lower level
            protocol security */);


        // Now get a proxy object, this proxy object
        // represents the remote object in this local space
        object myproxy = Activator.GetObject(
                        typeof(HelloWorld.HelloWorld),
                        "http://localhost:32000/myHelloWorldObject"
                        );
```

```
        // Get the name to send to the remote
        Console.Write("Please enter your name: ");
        string myname=Console.ReadLine();

        // Call the remote object (call the proxy and the proxy will call the remote)

        HelloWorld.HelloWorld myHello = (HelloWorld.HelloWorld)myproxy;
        string returnedvalue = myHello.myHelloWorld(myname);
        string mymsg = "value received from server is : "+returnedvalue;
        Console.WriteLine(mymsg);


    }
}
```

Finally, we call the remote object by calling it on the proxy object:

```
        HelloWorld.HelloWorld myHello = (HelloWorld.HelloWorld)myproxy;
            string returnedvalue = myHello.myHelloWorld(myname);
```

Note that you have to typecast the proxy for it to match the correct type of the HelloWorld remote object.

Every time this call occurs, the remote object on the Server is instantiated at the beginning of the call, then is executed, and is uninstantiated after it returns the results to the Server channel.

8.3.7 SERVER-ACTIVATED SINGLETON

Here we will examine the Server-Activated Singleton mode. In this example, we are again using the remote object from Listing 8.45. The Server for Server-Activated Singleton is shown in Listing 8.50, and the Client for Server-Activated Singleton is shown in Listing 8.51.

First of all, note that the Client used for Server-Activated Singleton (Listing 8.51) is exactly the same as the Client used for Server-Activated SingleCall (Listing 8.49). I included Listing 8.51 for comparison here (and also for completeness).

LISTING 8.50   Server for Server-Activated Singleton

```
using System;
using System.Collections.Generic;
using System.Linq;
using System.Text;
using System.Threading.Tasks;
using System.Runtime.Remoting;
using System.Runtime.Remoting.Channels;
using System.Runtime.Remoting.Channels.Http;

using HelloWorld;

public class Server
{
    static void Main(string[] args)
    {
        // Set up the channel, let's use HTTP
```

```
        HttpChannel mychannel = new HttpChannel(32000);
        ChannelServices.RegisterChannel(mychannel, false /* turn off lower level protocol
security */);

        // Register the Singleton object
        RemotingConfiguration.RegisterWellKnownServiceType(
                                typeof(HelloWorld.HelloWorld),
                                "myHelloWorldObject",
                                WellKnownObjectMode.Singleton
                                );
        Console.WriteLine("Server is now waiting for calls from client");
        Console.ReadLine(); // wait for calls
    }
}
```

Now let's look at the Server. After we register the channel, we register the Singleton object as follows:

```
    // Register the Singleton object
    RemotingConfiguration.RegisterWellKnownServiceType(
                            typeof(HelloWorld.HelloWorld),
                            "myHelloWorldObject",
                            WellKnownObjectMode.Singleton
                            );
```

Note that this is almost the same as we did when we registered a SingleCall object in the Server in Listing 8.48. The only difference between that server and this server is that previously we used the parameter;

```
    WellKnownObjectMode.SingleCall
```

whereas now we are using the parameter:

```
    WellKnownObjectMode.Singleton
```

LISTING 8.51   Client for Server-Activated Singleton

```
using System;
using System.Collections.Generic;
using System.Linq;
using System.Text;
using System.Threading.Tasks;
using System.Runtime.Remoting;
using System.Runtime.Remoting.Channels;
using System.Runtime.Remoting.Channels.Http;

using HelloWorld;
```

```
public class Client
{
    static void Main(string[] args)
    {

        // Set up the channel, let's use HTTP
        HttpChannel mychannel = new HttpChannel();    // don't bind the client channel to a
particular port
        ChannelServices.RegisterChannel(mychannel, false );
                // "false" here is to turn off lower level protocol security

        // Now get a proxy object, this proxy object
        // represents the remote object in this local space
        object myproxy = Activator.GetObject(
                        typeof(HelloWorld.HelloWorld),
                        "http://localhost:32000/myHelloWorldObject"
                        );

        // Get the name to send to the remote
        Console.Write("Please enter your name: ");
        string myname=Console.ReadLine();

        // Call the remote object (call the proxy and the proxy will call the remote)

        HelloWorld.HelloWorld myHello = (HelloWorld.HelloWorld)myproxy;
        string returnedvalue = myHello.myHelloWorld(myname);
        string mymsg = "value received from server is : "+returnedvalue;
        Console.WriteLine(mymsg);

    }
}
```

With this mode, only one single remote object is used for all clients.

8.3.8   HOW TO HANDLE DIFFERENT KINDS OF CHANNELS

So far we've been using only HTTP channels. Now we will look at TCP channels and Named Pipes. The code examples provided with the book do these channels as variations on a Server-Activated Singleton example. Here, however, we're only going to examine the code that is specifically associated with the particular channels.

In Listing 8.52, we see the server-side registration for a TCP channel, and in Listing 8.53, we see the client side registration for a TCP Channel. The only difference between the two is that you can't set the client-side channel on the same port as the server-side channel. I set a separate port number explicitly here, but it would probably be better not to set a particular port number on the client side, because that's more like what we did with the previous HTTP examples.

The code in Listing 8.52 is the only difference required in the server code, compared to an HTTP channel.

LISTING 8.52   Server-Side TCP Channel Registration

```
// Set up the channel, let's use TCP
TcpChannel mychannel = new TcpChannel(32000);
ChannelServices.RegisterChannel(mychannel, false /* turn off lower level protocol security */);
```

LISTING 8.53   Client-Side TCP Channel Registration

```
// Set up the channel, let's use TCP
TcpChannel mychannel = new TcpChannel(8700);
ChannelServices.RegisterChannel(mychannel, false /* turn off lower level protocol security */);
```

Now in Listing 8.54, we see the proxy creation used with a TCP Channel. The only difference between this and the previous Client proxy creation that we saw in Listings 8.49 and 8.51 is the URL parameter. Here we use the URL:

"**tcp:**//localhost:32000/myHelloWorldObject"

whereas in the previous Client HTTP examples (Listings 8.49 and 8.51), the URL was:

"**http:**//localhost:32000/myHelloWorldObject"

LISTING 8.54   Client-Side Proxy Creation Using TCP Channel

```
// Now get a proxy object, this proxy object
// represents the remote object in this local space
object myproxy = Activator.GetObject(
                    typeof(HelloWorld.HelloWorld),
                    "tcp://localhost:32000/myHelloWorldObject"
                );
```

Now let's look at named Pipes. In Listing 8.55, we see the server-side registration for an IPC Channel, and in Listing 8.56, we see the client-side registration for an IPC channel. Note that the channel doesn't have a port number here, it has a name. The Client channel has a different name from the Server channel.

LISTING 8.55   Server-Side Ipc Channel Registration

```
// Set up the channel, let's use IPC
IpcChannel mychannel = new IpcChannel("thechannel");
            // named pipe uses a channel name instead of a port number
ChannelServices.RegisterChannel(mychannel, false /* turn off lower level protocol security */);
```

LISTING 8.56   Client-Side Ipc Channel Registration

```
// Set up the channel, let's use IPC (Named Pipes)
IpcChannel mychannel = new IpcChannel("theClient");
                  // named pipe uses a channel name instead of a port number
ChannelServices.RegisterChannel(mychannel, false /* turn off lower level protocol security */);
```

In Listing 8.57, we see that the Client creates a proxy object similarly to the way it did it in our previous HTTP and TCP examples, only the URL is different. Here, the URL is:

ipc://thechannel/myHelloWorldObject");

whereas previously the URLs for TCP and HTTP were:

"**tcp:**//localhost:**32000**/myHelloWorldObject"

and:

"**http:**//localhost:**32000**/myHelloWorldObject"

Note that these differ in "ipc://" versus "tcp://" versus http:// but that also named pipes (IpcChannel) does not use port numbers.

LISTING 8.57   Client-Side Proxy Creation using Ipc Channel

```
// Now get a proxy object, this proxy object
// represents the remote object in this local space
object myproxy = Activator.GetObject(
                  typeof(HelloWorld.HelloWorld),
                  ipc://thechannel/myHelloWorldObject");
```

8.3.9   How to Handle Different Kinds of Formatters

Now we will look at how to use a different formatter than the default formatter. We will look at an example that uses a binary formatter along with an HTTP channel. As you recall, an HTTP channel defaults to using the SOAP formatter, so we are replacing the SOAP formatter with the binary formatter. This means that the data will be sent in binary format rather than SOAP format, which as you recall from Sections 8.3.3 and 8.3.4 has advantages in terms of compactness and transmission speed, although of course you give up the SOAP advantage of human readability. You normally wouldn't want to use a binary format if you were going through a firewall, but it can make for very efficient communications inside a company network, or in an embedded system, although more commonly you would choose TCP with its default binary formatter rather than using HTTP and changing its formatter to binary. However, perhaps there are situations where one instance of your code will be going through a firewall while a different instance is totally inside the firewall, such a situation would benefit from this approach because you could use binary format for inside the firewall and SOAP format for through the firewall, but keep the same kind of URL in both cases that employs http:// as follows:

http://localhost:32000/myHelloWorldObject

whereas if you used TCP internal you'd have to use "tcp://" for internal but still use http:// for external firewall use, which could perhaps be confusing.

Note, however, that .NET Remoting has been shown to have some issues with firewalls in regard to Network Address Translation (NAT). This is getting a bit advanced for an introductory textbook, so we won't go into that here. However, this is one reason that .NET Remoting has been deprecated in favor of Windows Communication Foundation (or perhaps you could choose a totally different middleware! We're looking at a bunch of them in this textbook.).

LISTING 8.58   Server Side HTTP Channel Registration with Binary Formatter

```
Hashtable settings = new Hashtable();
settings.Add("name", "httpbinary");
settings.Add("port", "32000");

HttpChannel httpbinary = new HttpChannel(settings, new BinaryClientFormatterSinkProvider(),
                                         new BinaryServerFormatterSinkProvider());
ChannelServices.RegisterChannel(httpbinary, false);
```

This is done using channel registration. How to do this is shown for the Server side in Listing 8.58, and for the Client side in Listing 8.59.

LISTING 8.59   Client-Side HTTP Channel Registration with Binary Formatter

```
Hashtable settings = new Hashtable();
settings.Add("name", "httpbinary");
settings.Add("port", "31000");

HttpChannel httpbinary= new HttpChannel(settings, new BinaryClientFormatterSinkProvider(),
                                        new BinaryServerFormatterSinkProvider());
ChannelServices.RegisterChannel(httpbinary, false);
```

Basically you specify that a BinaryClientFormatterSinkProvider and a BinaryServerSinkProvider will be used (instead of the default SOAP providers). Note again that the Server and Client have different port numbers.

8.3.10   REMOTE OBJECT LIFETIMES—LEASES ON OBJECTS

We previously talked about remote object lifetimes in Section 8.3.4 when we talked about Client-Activated Objects, Server-Activated Single Call, and Server-Activated Singleton. Remote object lifetimes is really the whole point when we're talking about these modes. With the Client-Activated remote object, the lifetime of the remote object is determined by the Client, while with the Server-activated modes (SingleCall and Singleton), the lifetime of the remote object is determined by the Server.

However, as we will see next, there are some problems with these basic ideas of remote object lifetimes that are handled by the .NET Remoting lifetime lease system. The basic idea behind a lifetime lease is that each remote object is associated with a separate lease object that stores the allowed lifetime of the object. When the lifetime in the lease expires, the remote object is destroyed.

First of all, the lifetime of a Server-Activated SingleCall doesn't participate in the .NET Remoting lifetime lease system because the object is recreated for every separate method call and terminated at the end of the method call. Since the lifetime is so well defined, further lifetime management is not necessary.

As you recall, the lifetime of a Client-Activated remote object is the lifetime of the Client: The remote object is created when the Client creates it, and it is destroyed when the Client terminates. But now we ask the question, how does the Server know that the Client has terminated? This is one application of the .NET Remoting lifetime lease system. The lease object associated with the remote object specifies a lifetime, when that lifetime expires the remote object is destroyed.

Also, as we previously discussed, the lifetime of a Server-Activated Singleton remote object is meant to be able to handle all client calls. But suppose there is a very long pause between calls from a client? Should the Server have to have the resources needed for the Singleton remote object tied up for this long period of time? This is another application of the .NET Remoting lifetime lease system: because there may be a pause between client calls, the Singleton objects will have an associated lease object that specifies an object lifetime. After that lifetime expires, the Singleton object is destroyed by the Server. If a client calls the Server-Activated Singleton remote object after that, then a new Singleton object is created (together with a new lifetime lease), and the Client won't know the difference between this new Singleton remote object and the previous Singleton remote object.

Now let's examine how the lifetime lease system works. The default initial lease time for a remote object is five minutes (it's stored in a value called "InitialLeaseTime"). It is possible to renew leases. The way this works is as follows:

- *Implicit renewal of lease.* The lease renewal is done automatically when the Client calls the remote object. There is a value called "RenewOnCallTime" that can be used to specify how long a time period that the lease will be renewed, it defaults to two minutes.
- *Explicit renewal of lease.* This is done with the Renew method on the System.Runtime. Remoting.Lifetime.ILease interface (we will see an example of the code to do this later on).
- *Sponsorship.* The client registers a separate object called a "sponsor" (implements the ISponsor interface) using the ILease interface. Then when the remote object's lease expires, the Renewal() method on the sponsor is called, and the sponsor can renew the lease.

Now we will look at an example that illustrates use of the ILease interface, shown in Listing 8.60. I did this by modifying the HelloWorld object, originally shown in Listing 8.44, rather than doing it on the Client, I did this to show that it can be done that way, rather than always having it located in the Client or in the Sponsor. However, I did it as a method on the HelloWorld interface that is called by the Client (this is also shown in Listing 8.60). The activation mode that was used in this example was Server-Activated Singleton.

LISTING 8.60   HelloWorld Remote Object, Uses ILease Interface, and Associated Client Call

```
using System;
using System.Collections.Generic;
using System.Linq;
using System.Text;
using System.Threading.Tasks;
using System.Runtime.Remoting.Lifetime;
using System.Threading;
```

```csharp
namespace HelloWorld

{
   public class HelloWorld : MarshalByRefObject

   {
      public string myHelloWorld(string msg)
      {
         string mymsg;
         mymsg = "Hello, World, especially to: " + msg;
         Console.WriteLine("about to return the Hello World message");
         return mymsg;
      }

      public override object InitializeLifetimeService()
      {
         // Get a reference to the lease and determine if it has been initialized yet
         ILease CurrentLease = (ILease)base.InitializeLifetimeService();

         Console.WriteLine("A:  At top, current lease state is " + CurrentLease.CurrentState);

         if (CurrentLease.CurrentState == LeaseState.Initial)
         {
            CurrentLease.InitialLeaseTime = TimeSpan.FromSeconds(3);

            Console.WriteLine("B:  After setting initial, current lease state is " +
                              CurrentLease.CurrentState);

            CurrentLease.Renew(TimeSpan.FromMilliseconds(2000));

            Console.WriteLine("C:  After setting renew time, current lease state is " +
                              CurrentLease.CurrentState);

   //       Thread.Sleep(10000);
            Console.WriteLine("D:  After waiting long enough, current lease state is " +
                              CurrentLease.CurrentState);
         }

         return null;
      }
   }
}
```

Client Call to InitializeLifetimeService method:

```csharp
   HelloWorld.HelloWorld myHello = (HelloWorld.HelloWorld)myproxy;
            ... code as before to call the myHelloWorld method...
   myHello.InitializeLifetimeService();   // work with the lease
```

The important portion of the HelloWorld code in Listing 8.60 for the purposes of our current discussion is of course the InitializeLifetimeService method. It begins by getting a reference to the current lease, using the ILease interface (in System.Runtime.Remoting.Lifetime):

```
ILease CurrentLease = (ILease)base.InitializeLifetimeService();
```

Next it checks to see if the lease is in its initial state:

```
if (CurrentLease.CurrentState = LeaseState.Initial)
```

The possible states of a lease are as follows:

- Null—error state, not defined
- Initial—beginning state of the lease after the creation of the lease object (to begin with, upon creation of the remote object)
- Active—lease object currently specifies the lifetime of the remote object
- Renewing—the lease has expired, and is in the process of being renewed
- Expired—the lease has expired

Back to the InitializeLifetimeService method code: after it is determined that the lease is in initial state, we set the initial lease time to be different from the default—the default is five seconds, we set it to three just to show we can explicitly set the value:

```
CurrentLease.InitialLeaseTime = TimeSpan.FromSeconds(3);
```

Next we'll immediately renew the lease, not because it has expired but just to watch things happen, we're going to explicitly set this to two seconds—this time we're using milliseconds:

```
CurrentLease.Renew(TimeSpan.FromMilliseconds(2000));
```

Notice that we're looking at the state of the lease repeatedly as we go through this code, for example:

```
Console.WriteLine("B: After setting initial, current lease state is " +
                        CurrentLease.CurrentState);
```

We're going to use these print statements to watch the state of the lease as it changes. Note that the line:

```
Thread.Sleep(10000);
```

has been commented out in this version. What this line is for, is to wait 10 seconds (10000 milliseconds) to allow the lease to expire so we can see in our print statements that the lease has expired. In the case where we don't have this Thread.Sleep line, the lease won't have time to expire before the code stops executing.

Let's look first at the results from this code when the Thread.Sleep line is commented out (the lease won't have time to expire). This is shown in the window that was executing the server. See Figure 8.6.

From Figure 8.6, we can see that the lease is originally in Initial State, but moves to Active state after the lease has been renewed.

Now look at Figure 8.7. In Figure 8.7, we see the results from this code when the Thread.Sleep line has *not* been commented out, that is, we give the lease time to expire. Again, this is shown in the window that was executing the Server.

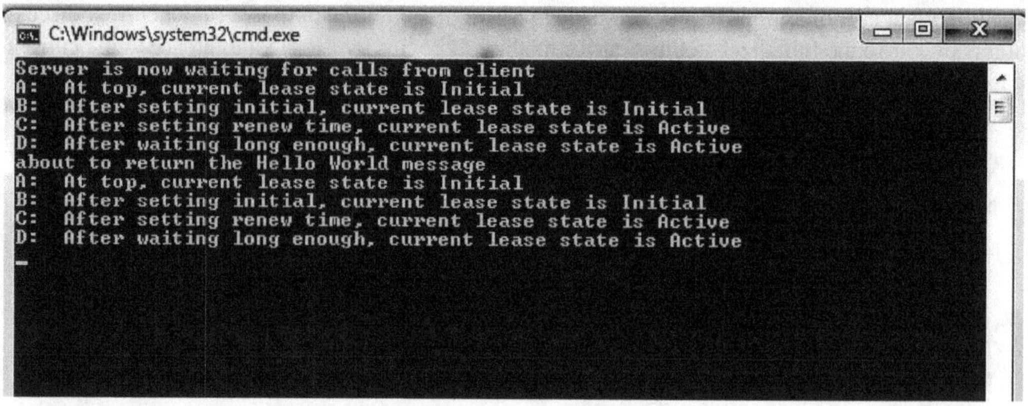

FIGURE 8.6 Lease without thread. Sleep doesn't have time to expire.

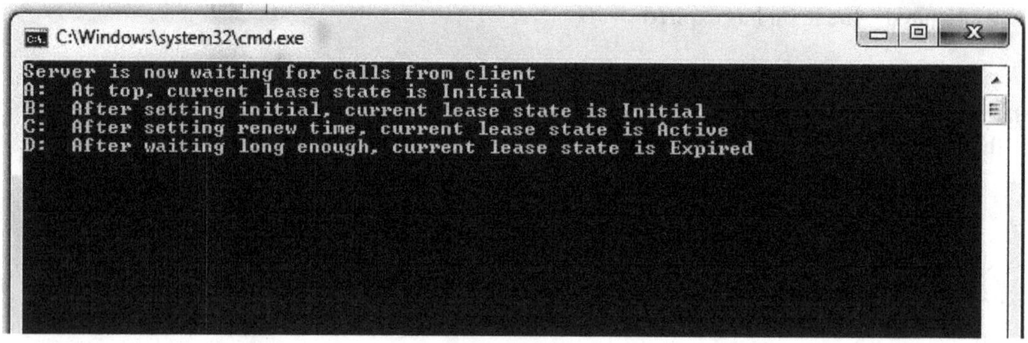

FIGURE 8.7 Lease with thread. Sleep had time to expire.

Here we see that we began with the Initial state, after the lease was renewed we moved to Active state. We gave the lease time to expire using the Thread.Sleep for 10 seconds, and we can see that the lease has moved to Expired state.

8.3.11 ASYNCHRONOUS .NET REMOTING

In all the examples we've seen so far, we have used synchronous mode. That is, the Client calls the Server and waits (blocks) until the response comes from the Server. However, in many cases it could be helpful for the Client to continue to do useful work while waiting for the Server's response, especially in cases where the Server might take a long time to come back. This is where asynchronous mode comes in. Asynchronous mode means in general that the Client and the Server execute independently—neither blocks while waiting on the other, they continue to do useful work.

There are two ways this is done in .NET Remoting:

1. *Polling*. The Client calls the Server and continues to do useful work but asks the Server every so often if the Server has completed the Client's response.
2. *Callback function*. The Client calls the Server and tells the Server the name and location of a function located on the Client that the Server can call when the Server completes the Client's response.

8.3.11.1   Asynchronous .NET Remoting—Polling

We will look at the polling example first. I modified the HelloWorld object as shown in Listing 8.61; it now contains a loop with a Thread.Sleep and an occasional print statement so that a fairly long time is passing, and so you can *see* that the time is passing. The idea here is that it's a good idea for the Client to use asynchronous operation so it can get some work done, because the Server is going to take a long time to finish, and it would be inefficient for the Client to wait for it. Note that the Server itself hasn't changed, it's the same server we saw back in the Singleton example in Listing 8.50.

LISTING 8.61   HelloWorld with a Delay Used to Illustrate Asynchronous Operation

```
using System;
using System.Collections.Generic;
using System.Linq;
using System.Text;
using System.Threading;
using System.Threading.Tasks;
namespace HelloWorld
{
    public class HelloWorld : MarshalByRefObject
    {
        public string myHelloWorld(string msg)
        {
            string mymsg;

            Console.WriteLine("Inside myHelloWorld, received string :"+msg);
            for (int i = 0; i < 20000;  i++)
            {
                if ((i % 4000)==0)
                {
                    Console.WriteLine("Unfortunately, it takes a long time to say hello");
                    Thread.Sleep(1000); // Sleep for one second

                }
            }
            mymsg = "Hello, World, especially to: " + msg;
            Console.WriteLine("about to return the Hello World message");
            return mymsg;
        }
    }
}
```

The asynchronous Client that polls the Server to see if it is done is shown in Listing 8.62. Here a function is defined to wrap the remote method call—this function is called "RemoteAsyncDelegate" and is a "delegate" function. The delegate function must be defined so that it has the same signature, that is, the same parameters and return value, as the method on the remote object that you wish to call.

A delegate function has a "BeginInvoke" method and an "EndInvoke" method associated with it. The BeginInvoke method starts the asynchronous call, but it returns immediately and does not block waiting for the call to complete. When the call has eventually completed, the Client will call EndInvoke to retrieve the results of the remote procedure call.

LISTING 8.62   Asynchronous Client—Uses Polling

```
using System;
using System.Collections.Generic;
using System.Linq;
using System.Text;
using System.Threading;
using System.Threading.Tasks;
using System.Runtime.Remoting;
using System.Runtime.Remoting.Channels;
using System.Runtime.Remoting.Channels.Http;
using System.Runtime.Remoting.Messaging;

using HelloWorld;

public delegate string RemoteAsyncDelegate(string msg);
   /* a function to wrap the remote method call, returns a string because the remote method
      returns a string */

public class Client
{
   void doWork()
   {
      // Set up the channel, let's use HTTP
      HttpChannel mychannel = new HttpChannel(8700);
      ChannelServices.RegisterChannel(mychannel, false /* turn off lower level protocol
            security */);

      // Now get a proxy object, this proxy object
      // represents the remote object in this local space
      object myproxy = Activator.GetObject(
                           typeof(HelloWorld.HelloWorld),
                           "http://localhost:32000/myHelloWorldObject"
                           );

      // Get the name to send to the remote
      Console.Write("Please enter your name: ");
      string myname = Console.ReadLine();

      HelloWorld.HelloWorld myHello = new HelloWorld.HelloWorld();

      RemoteAsyncDelegate thedelegate = new RemoteAsyncDelegate(myHello.myHello-
            World);

      IAsyncResult RemoteResult = thedelegate.BeginInvoke(myname, null, null);

      while(RemoteResult.IsCompleted==false)
      {
         Console.WriteLine("Doing useful work while waiting for results from server");
         Thread.Sleep(1000);  // wait one second
      }
```

```
        AsyncResult theResultObject = (AsyncResult)RemoteResult;

        string mymsg;

        RemoteAsyncDelegate theDelegate = (RemoteAsyncDelegate)theResultObject.Async-
            Delegate;

        mymsg = theDelegate.EndInvoke(theResultObject);

        Console.WriteLine("data received is :  " + mymsg);

    }
    static void Main(string[] args)
    {

        Client myClient = new Client();
        myClient.doWork();
    }
}
```

In the Client in Listing 8.62, we first create an instance of the remote object:

```
    HelloWorld.HelloWorld myHello = new HelloWorld.HelloWorld();
```

Then we wrap the remote object with our delegate object:

```
    RemoteAsyncDelegate thedelegate = new RemoteAsyncDelegate(myHello.myHelloWorld);
```

And then we call the remote object using BeginInvoke:

```
    IAsyncResult RemoteResult = thedelegate.BeginInvoke(myname, null, null);
```

Note that the BeginInvoke returns an IAsyncResult object that we called Remote Object. We use this to check to see if the Server has finished creating the result, as follows:

```
    while(RemoteResult.IsCompleted==false)
```

When the result eventually completes, we retrieve our end result using EndInvoke as follows;

```
    AsyncResult theResultObject = (AsyncResult)RemoteResult;

    string mymsg;

    RemoteAsyncDelegate theDelegate = (RemoteAsyncDelegate)theResultObject.AsyncDelegate;

    mymsg = theDelegate.EndInvoke(theResultObject);
```

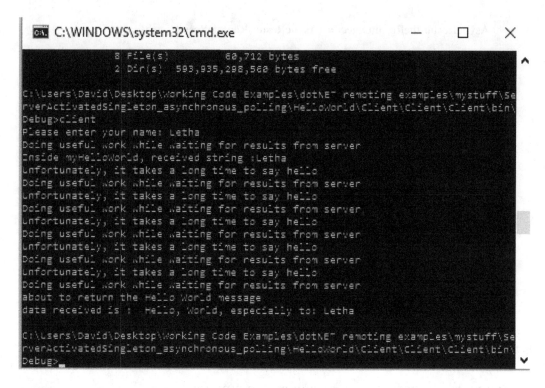

FIGURE 8.8   Client-side results from asynchronous polling example.

The results from running this asynchronous polling example are shown in Figure 8.8. You can see from this that the Server is doing its own work:

  Unfortunately, it takes a long time to say hello

At the same time, the Client is continuing independently to do its own useful work:

  Doing useful work while waiting for results from server

8.3.11.2 Asynchronous .NET Remoting—Callback Function

In this example, we're going to look at how .NET Remoting can use a callback function for asynchronous operation. As you recall from Section 8.3.11.2, with a callback function, the Client calls the Server, and tells the Server the name and location of a function located on the Client that the Server can call when the Server completes the Client's response. We will look at two different callback functions here, a simple one with no output parameters, just a return value, and another one that returns output parameters as well as a return value.

In this example, the HelloWorld remote object is the same as in Listing 8.61, it shows that a fairly long time is passing and you can see that time is passing. Again, the Server itself hasn't changed, it's the same server we saw back in the Singleton example in Listing 8.50.

The client code that uses a simple callback function is shown in Listing 8.63. Note that we are still using a Delegate function to wrap the remote procedure.

LISTING 8.63   Asynchronous Client with Simple Callback Function, No Output Parameters

```
using System;
using System.Collections.Generic;

using System.Linq;
using System.Text;
using System.Threading;
using System.Threading.Tasks;
using System.Runtime.Remoting;
using System.Runtime.Remoting.Channels;
using System.Runtime.Remoting.Channels.Http;
using System.Runtime.Remoting.Messaging;

using HelloWorld;

public delegate string RemoteAsyncDelegate(string msg);  /* a function to wrap the remote
method call, returns a string because the remote method returns a string */

public class Client
{
    [OneWayAttribute]
    public void myCallback (IAsyncResult theResult)
    {
        Console.WriteLine("Top of callback");

        AsyncResult theResultObject = (AsyncResult)theResult;

        string mymsg;

        RemoteAsyncDelegate theDelegate = (RemoteAsyncDelegate)theResultObject.Async-
            Delegate;

        mymsg = theDelegate.EndInvoke(theResult);

        Console.WriteLine("data received by callback is :  " + mymsg);

        Console.WriteLine("Bottom of callback");

    }
    void doWork()
    {
        // Set up the channel, let's use HTTP
        HttpChannel mychannel = new HttpChannel();  // don't put the Client on a particular port
        ChannelServices.RegisterChannel(mychannel, false /* turn off lower level protocol
            security */);
        // Now get a proxy object, this proxy object
        // represents the remote object in this local space
```

```
object myproxy = Activator.GetObject(
                    typeof(HelloWorld.HelloWorld),
                    "http://localhost:32000/myHelloWorldObject"
                    );


// Get the name to send to the remote
Console.Write("Please enter your name: ");
string myname = Console.ReadLine();

// Call the remote object (call the proxy and the proxy will call the remote)

//   HelloWorld.HelloWorld myHello = (HelloWorld.HelloWorld)myproxy;
//   string returnedvalue = myHello.myHelloWorld(myname);

HelloWorld.HelloWorld myHello = new HelloWorld.HelloWorld();

AsyncCallback theCallback = new AsyncCallback(this.myCallback);

RemoteAsyncDelegate thedelegate = new RemoteAsyncDelegate(myHello.myHello-
        World);

IAsyncResult RemoteResult = thedelegate.BeginInvoke(myname, theCallback, null);
for (int i = 0; i < 10; i++)
{
    Console.WriteLine("Doing useful work while waiting for results from server");
    Thread.Sleep(1000);  // wait one second
}

RemoteResult.AsyncWaitHandle.WaitOne();

//   string mymsg = "value received from server is : "+returnedvalue;
//   Console.WriteLine(mymsg);
}
static void Main(string[] args)
{
    Client myClient = new Client();
    myClient.doWork();

}
}
```

In this example, we do the BeginInvoke as follows:

```
HelloWorld.HelloWorld myHello = new HelloWorld.HelloWorld();

AsyncCallback theCallback = new AsyncCallback(this.myCallback);

RemoteAsyncDelegate thedelegate = new RemoteAsyncDelegate(myHello.myHelloWorld);

IAsyncResult RemoteResult = thedelegate.BeginInvoke(myname, theCallback, null);
```

As you can see, it's similar to before in the polling example, except that now you create an AsyncCallback function and pass this to BeginInvoke.

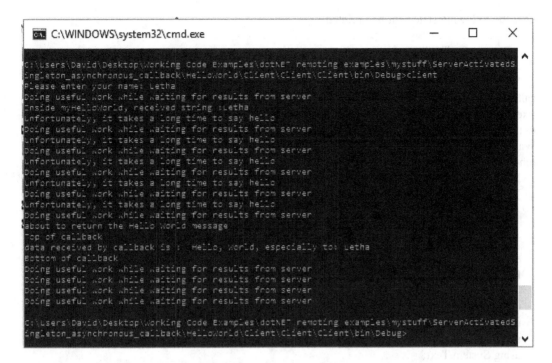

FIGURE 8.9   Client-side results from simple callback function example.

The call to EndInvoke is exactly the same as before in the polling example, except now it is done *inside* the callback function, after the callback is called when the Server has completed its processing:

AsyncResult theResultObject = (AsyncResult)theResult;

string mymsg;

RemoteAsyncDelegate theDelegate = (RemoteAsyncDelegate)theResultObject.AsyncDelegate;

mymsg = theDelegate.EndInvoke(theResult);

The client-side results are shown in Figure 8.9. As in the previous asynchronous polling example, you can see that the Server and the Client are executing independently, and that the Client continues to execute (doing useful work) while the Server is processing the client request. You can also see when the callback executes, and that the Client continues to work for a while after the callback executes before it completes.

There is one more item to mention:

RemoteResult.AsyncWaitHandle.WaitOne();

This statement would cause the Client to block until the remote call finished (the WaitOne() function would be called when the remote operation finished, at the same time the callback was called). It didn't actually do anything in this particular case because the callback had finished before the client code got to the WaitOne() call. How can I tell? Look at Figure 8.9, it shows the client code continuing to print the statement:

Doing useful work while waiting for results from server

after the following statement had printed:

   Bottom of callback

What happened here was that the useful work loop was still executing up until and after the callback ran. It just took long enough for the useful work loop to execute that this was the case. Exercise for the student, ☺ greatly shorten the time in the useful work loop and see when you get to the WaitOne call. Try removing the WaitOne call and see what happens (if you don't have the WaitOne call in that situation, your client will just exit when the loop finishes and you won't have time to do the callback before it quits).

Finally, let's look at the callback example with output parameters. This is shown in Listing 8.64. Your delegate function now has an output parameter, specified with the "out" keyword:

   public delegate string RemoteAsyncDelegate(string msg, out string extramsg);

LISTING 8.64   Asynchronous Client with Callback Function with Output Parameters

```
using System;
using System.Collections.Generic;
using System.Linq;
using System.Text;
using System.Threading;
using System.Threading.Tasks;
using System.Runtime.Remoting;
using System.Runtime.Remoting.Channels;
using System.Runtime.Remoting.Channels.Http;
using System.Runtime.Remoting.Messaging;

using HelloWorld;

public delegate string RemoteAsyncDelegate(string msg, out string extramsg);
    // a function to wrap the remote method call, returns a string because the remote method
returns a string

public class Client
{
    [OneWayAttribute]
            public void myCallback (IAsyncResult theResult)
    {
        Console.WriteLine("Top of callback");

        AsyncResult theResultObject = (AsyncResult)theResult;

        string mymsg, extramsg;

        RemoteAsyncDelegate theDelegate = (RemoteAsyncDelegate)theResultObject.
            AsyncDelegate;

        mymsg = theDelegate.EndInvoke(out extramsg, theResult);
```

```
            Console.WriteLine("the extra message was: " + extramsg);

            Console.WriteLine("data received by callback is :  " + mymsg);
            Console.WriteLine("Bottom of callback");

    }
    void doWork()
    {
        // Set up the channel, let's use HTTP
        HttpChannel mychannel = new HttpChannel(8700);
        ChannelServices.RegisterChannel(mychannel, false /* turn off lower level
            protocol security */);

        // Now get a proxy object, this proxy object
        // represents the remote object in this local space
        object myproxy = Activator.GetObject(
            typeof(HelloWorld.HelloWorld),
            "http://localhost:32000/myHelloWorldObject"
            );

        // Get the name to send to the remote
        Console.Write("Please enter your name: ");
        string myname = Console.ReadLine();

        HelloWorld.HelloWorld myHello = new HelloWorld.HelloWorld();

        AsyncCallback theCallback = new AsyncCallback(this.myCallback);

        RemoteAsyncDelegate thedelegate = new RemoteAsyncDelegate(myHello.
            myHelloWorld);

        string extramsg = "";
        IAsyncResult RemoteResult = thedelegate.BeginInvoke(myname,out extramsg,
            theCallback, null);

        for (int i = 0; i < 10; i++)
        {
            Console.WriteLine("Doing useful work while waiting for results from server");
            Thread.Sleep(1000);  // wait one second
        }
        RemoteResult.AsyncWaitHandle.WaitOne();

    }
    static void Main(string[] args)
    {

        Client myClient = new Client();
        myClient.doWork();
    }
}
```

When you call BeginInvoke you have to give it an extra parameter for the "out" parameter:

```
string extramsg = "";
IAsyncResult RemoteResult = thedelegate.BeginInvoke(myname,out extramsg, theCallback, null);
```

And now when you do the EndInvoke, you extract both the out parameter and the return parameter, as follows:

```
string mymsg, extramsg;
RemoteAsyncDelegate theDelegate = (RemoteAsyncDelegate)theResultObject.AsyncDelegate;
mymsg = theDelegate.EndInvoke(out extramsg, theResult);
```

And that's all there is to it. ☺

8.4   TECHNOLOGY REVIEW: ENTERPRISE JAVA BEANS

The Enterprise Java Bean (EJB) architecture is a Server-side component architecture, and is part of Java EE (Java Platform, Enterprise Edition). EJBs are intended to support several Server-side needs such as integrity of persistence, lifecycle, concurrency, deployment of components, a naming and directory service, asynchronous method invocation, and security, among others. The idea is that since EJBs do this kind of necessary Server-side work, the programmer can concentrate on writing the needed application code (the code for the *enterprise*).

This work is done in an EJB *container* that is implemented by an application server. The EJBs specify how applications (business software) interface to the application server. How the application server does the work is up to the application server.

For the work in this textbook, we are going to use the GlassFish application server.

The EJB specifications since version 3.0, which was released with Java EE in 2006, are fairly different from the earlier EJB specifications. For example, the Java Persistence API replaces *entity beans* from the earlier versions. We focus on the more recent versions of EJB here.

Note that *Enterprise Java Beans* are quite different from *Java Beans*. A "Java Bean" is a Plain Old Java Object (POJO) that conforms to certain conventions: a public default constructor that has no arguments, get/set accessor functions for data member (attribute) access, required to be serializable. ("Serializable" means to convert an object into a byte stream, so that it can be transmitted or stored, and later on be converted back into a copy of the same object.)

There are two major kinds of EJBs normally discussed:

1. Session Beans
2. Message Beans

Both qualify as EJBs because they both are Server-side components that run in an EJB container in an application server. However, Message Beans operate with a very different paradigm from Session Beans.

Message Beans employ a messaging paradigm. Unlike a Session Bean, a Message Bean does not have an interface that a client looks up in order to call a method on the interface. Rather, a Message Bean is not coupled directly to a client. A Session Bean would normally have an interface class and a bean class, whereas a Message Bean only has a Bean class.

In the case of a Message Bean, the Client sends messages to a queue. The Message Bean listens for messages on the queue. Message Beans can support any messaging protocol (queue-based as just described), but by default they support the Java Message Service (JMS). JMS is an example of Message-Oriented Middleware (MOM), and thus Message Beans also are MOM.

In MOM, one or more Producers creates messages and sends them to a queue. Then one or more Consumers retrieve messages from the queue. The queue, however, can actually be a message broker that does or can do value-added analyses on the messages, for example, can implement quality-of-service techniques based on priorities. The use of this intermediary message broker (queue) allows the Producers and Consumers to work asynchronously with respect to each other. Also, the use of this intermediary message broker allows loose coupling, which can help when it is necessary to have heterogeneous systems communicate.

Although Session Beans can operate asynchronously as well as synchronously, since the Client calls the interface of the Session Bean, the Session Bean is not an example of MOM.

In this chapter, we are looking at Object-Oriented and Component-Based Middleware, so we will save the Message Beans for Chapter 15, where we examine MOM. (Note, however, that in this textbook we don't focus heavily on MOM, that's just a bit more of an advanced concept, and this is an introductory textbook.)

8.4.1 A Brief Introduction to Session Bean Concepts

There are three kinds of Session Beans:

1. Stateless Session Beans
2. Stateful Session Beans
3. Singleton Session Beans

A Session Bean can handle a method call from one client at a time.

In this context, "state" means the values of all instance variables inside a Bean at any given time.

In a Stateless Session Bean, the state of the Bean is valid only while the method call from the Client is executing. When the method call from the Client is complete, the state (values of the instance variables) goes away. However, the container can maintain pools of Stateless Session Beans, and the container can assign a method call coming in from a client to an arbitrary Stateless Session Bean. In the case of pooled stateless beans, there can be a state across the pool that would apply to any client that is assigned a bean from the pool.

In a Stateful Session Bean, a client and a Stateful Session Bean are considered to be in a "session" (conversation). When the session (conversation) ends, the state (values of the instance variables) vanishes.

A Singleton Session Bean is shared by many clients. A Singleton Session Bean retains its state for a particular client in between different method calls from that client.

A Stateless Session Bean and a Singleton Session Bean can implement a web service endpoint, but a Stateful Session Bean cannot.

You would choose to use a Stateful Session Bean if you are interacting with a specific client. You would use a Stateless Session Bean to implement a generic task. You would use a Singleton Session Bean if there is a state that must be shared between multiple clients.

There are two ways a Client can acquire a reference to a Session Bean. If the Client is *outside* the Java EE server managed environment, such as Client implemented as a POJO, it must look up the interface by name using the Java directory service, which is accessed using the Java Naming and Directory Interface (JNDI).

If the Client is *inside* the Java EE server-managed environment (such as another EJB, a JAX-RS web service, a servlet, etc.) then the Client may use *dependency injection* (although it can still use JNDI lookup if desired).

A simple definition of *dependency injection* is that it is a way to stuff (inject) a reference to an interface associated with an EJB (right now we're only considering Session Beans but this can also be used with Message Beans) into an entity within a Java EE server-managed environment (such as another EJB, a JAX-RS web service, a servlet, etc.). This is done using an "@EJB" annotation. For example, a servlet could have injected into it (could contain) a reference to the interface of a Session Bean. A Session Bean could have injected into it (could contain) a reference to the interface of another Session Bean (we'll see an example of this later on).

If the Session Bean has a local interface (according to the annotation) then the local Client that calls that interface must run in the same application, that is, on the same Java Virtual Machine (JVM) as the Session Bean. Local Clients are more efficient than remote Clients, since they do not require marshaling and unmarshaling (serializing) of arguments or transmission of arguments across a network. Local clients employ pass-by-reference, that is, the Session Bean would be working on the same object that the local client is working on, instead of working on a copy of the object (pass-by value), which is what would happen in the case of a remote client accessing a remote interface. (Actual processing of this can depend on the implementation of the application server being used.)

Note that marshaling and unmarshaling in EJBs is less complicated than, say, in CORBA because EJBs are working Java to Java, and Java always stores integers (in the .class files, and inside the JVM) in big-endian order (note that the code actually implementing the JVM operation will store integers in the byte order of the underlying hardware, but this isn't normally seen by the Java programmer). So in case of more complicated data structures such as objects, it's primarily a question of serialization. Object serialization in Java consists of representing an object as a sequence of bytes that includes information about the data type of the object, and about the different data types that make up the object, as well as the data itself. Note that an object is only serializable if the class that defines the object inherits from java.io.Serializable.

A Session Bean can have both a remote interface and a local interface. We will see an example of this later on.

A local Client can only be used if the Client and the Session Bean are packaged in *either* the same jar file or in the same EAR file (or possibly inside a WAR file that is contained in an EAR file). A local Client cannot be used if it is in a web container, and the Session Bean is in a separate container.

A JAR (also sometimes called "jar" after its extension) file (Java Archive) is a type of archive file that is used to collect different Java class files and associated resources of an application (or library) into a single file so it can be deployed.

An EAR file (Enterprise Archive) is a type of archive file that Java EE uses to package multiple modules into a single archive for deployment. It also contains XML-based deployment files that describes how the modules inside the EAR file are to be deployed.

A WAR file (Web Application Archive) is a type of archive file that is used to package a web application. It may contain static web pages, XML files, Java classes, etc.

8.4.2 ENVIRONMENT AND PROCEDURES USED TO BUILD AND RUN EJB EXAMPLES

The examples in this textbook were developed using Java EE 7.

There are several different possibilities for how to build and run EJB examples. You can use an Integrated Development Environment (IDE) such as NetBeans or Eclipse. Each of these has its proponents. You can use the Maven or Apache Ant or Gradle build tools. Each of these has its own set of things you must do in order to get your code to build and run, and each set is different from the other.

In an attempt to be as generic as possible, for building these examples I have gone back to very vanilla, plain old Java stuff. I call javac directly from the command-line, and I don't use an IDE or a build tool at all.

And of course there are different application servers. I chose GlassFish because it's the Java EE reference implementation. To develop my examples, I downloaded the Java EE 7 and GlassFish bundle.

To compile an interface:

```
export GLASSFISH_HOME= ..put your stuff here…
export JAR_FILE_ONE=$GLASSFISH_HOME/glassfish/modules/javax.ejb-api.jar
javac -classpath ".:$JAR_FILE_ONE" -d . HelloWorld.java
```

To compile a bean:

```
export GLASSFISH_HOME=..put your stuff here…
export JAR_FILE_ONE=$GLASSFISH_HOME/glassfish/modules/javax.ejb-api.jar
javac -classpath ".:$JAR_FILE_ONE" -d . HelloBean.java
```

Then create a jar file containing HelloWorld.class (the interface) and HelloBean.class (the Stateless Session bean):

```
jar cvf helloworld.jar example
```

Here, "example" is the directory that was created when javac was run. This is because the package that HelloBean is in was defined as follows:

```
package example.helloworld;
```

To compile a POJO client:

```
javac -classpath . -d . HelloClient.java
```

HelloBean also has to run *inside* a container in an application server. We're using the GlassFish application server for these examples. To do this, start GlassFish. Then either use the GlassFish admin console or else the GlassFish command-line to deploy this jar file. How to start GlassFish and deploy applications such as EJBs or servlets on GlassFish is described in Section 4.11.2.1.

Note also that the code provided for the instructor with this textbook includes detailed instructions for how to compile all the EJB examples.

8.4.3 STATELESS SESSION BEANS

In this section, we examine Stateless Session Beans. Recall from our earlier discussion, that with a Stateless Session Bean, the state of the Bean is valid only while the method call from the Client is executing. When the method call from the Client is complete, the state (values of the instance variables) goes away. However, the container can maintain pools of Stateless Session Beans, and the container can assign a method call coming in from a client to an arbitrary Stateless Session Bean. In the case of pooled stateless beans, there can be a state across the pool that would apply to any client that is assigned a bean from the pool.

8.4.3.1 Very Simple Stateless Session Bean Example

First we will look at a very simple Stateless Session Bean example.

In Listing 8.65 we see a remote interface—it is called a *remote* interface because it is annotated with "@Remote." This means that any data that is sent to or received from this interface would be marshaled and unmarshaled (serializing) for transmission across a network (we are assuming distributed objects here).

In Listing 8.66 we see a very simple Stateless Session Bean. This defines a class called "HelloBean" that implements the HelloWorld Interface from Listing 8.65. This is pretty well just like any Java class implementing a Java interface. The difference in Listing 8.66 is that the HelloBean class is annotated with "@Stateless" (it has to import javax.ejb.Stateless to use this annotation) and that HelloBean implements an interface that was described as "@Remote."

Note that partly because of these annotations, HelloBean becomes a Stateless EJB and not just a POJO. Also, in order to be an EJB, HelloBean and the interface file also each have to be linked with the javax.ejb-api.jar file. And then the jar file containing the HelloBean has to be deployed and run in a container, such as the GlassFish container.

LISTING 8.65 HelloWorld Interface

```
package example.helloworld;
import javax.ejb.Remote;
@Remote
public interface HelloWorld {
        public String thehello();
}
```

LISTING 8.66 Simple Stateless Bean

```
package example.helloworld;
import javax.ejb.Stateless;
@Stateless
public class HelloBean implements HelloWorld {
        public String thehello() {
                        return "Hello to all the World!!!!!";
        }
}
```

In Listing 8.67, we see a Client call the simple Stateless Bean, this Client is implemented as a POJO. Since this Client is a POJO, the Client must use the JNDI to find the location of the Stateless EJB that it is calling.

The JNDI maps names to object locations. Typically, a name is simply a string.

JNDI names are organized into name hierarchies (similar to file directory systems). The base of this name hierarchy is called an *initial context*. When a Client passes a name to JNDI for lookup, JNDI starts at the initial context and looks down the name hierarchy to search for the matching name.

To find the initial context, we do:

```
Context ic= new InitialContext();
```

To look up a name (in this case, our HelloBean in the helloworld package) in this particular context, we do:

```
Object object_ref = ic.lookup("java:global/helloworld/HelloBean");
```

Note that we are using the *java:global* namespace here. Names in the java:global JNDI namespace are accessible to any application.

Finally, we must create an appropriate proxy object to represent the HelloWorld interface in the Client. We do this via a downcast from the object reference returned from JNDI:

```
HelloWorld proxy= (HelloWorld) PortableRemoteObject.narrow(object_ref,HelloWorld.class);
```

Finally, we call the remote procedure on the remote EJB using this proxy:

```
String returned_string = proxy.thehello();
```

Since the HelloWorld interface (see Listing 8.65) was annotated as "@Remote", when this call on the proxy is performed, parameters to the EJB (in this particular case there weren't any parameters in the "thehello()" call) and the returned function value from the EJB will be marshaled and unmarshaled (serialized) and also, in the case where the HelloBean is located on a different computer than the Client, transmitted across a network.

LISTING 8.67   POJO Client That Calls the Simple Stateless Bean

```java
package example.helloworld;
import javax.naming.InitialContext;
import javax.naming.Context;
import javax.naming.NamingException;
import javax.rmi.PortableRemoteObject;

public class HelloClient {
    public static void main (String[] args) {
        try {

            Context ic= new InitialContext();

            // Names in the  java:global JNDI namespace are accessible to any application.
            // (This is how EJB references may be accessed outside the application where
            //  they're defined.)
            Object object_ref = ic.lookup("java:global/helloworld/HelloBean");
            // This narrow downcasts the object_ref to type HelloWorld, this serves as the
                proxy
            HelloWorld proxy= (HelloWorld)
        PortableRemoteObject.narrow(object_ref,HelloWorld.class);

            // call the remote method on the local proxy
            String returned_string = proxy.thehello();

            System.out.println(returned_string);
        }
        catch (NamingException ex) {
                // You might get a naming exception if you forgot to deploy the jar file
                // You might get a naming exception if you forgot to start GlassFish
                System.out.println("Naming exception");
                System.out.println("cause is"+ex.getCause());
                System.out.println("stack trace is ");
                ex.printStackTrace();
        } catch (Exception ex) {
            System.out.println("general exception");
        }
    }
}
```

8.4.3.2 Very Simple Stateless Session Bean Example Passes an Array Parameter

In this section, we will look at how an array can be passed as a parameter to a Remote Stateless EJB. Remember that in EJB, all parameters passed to a remote interface are "passed by value" in that they are marshaled (serialized) for transmission and unmarshaled (deserialized) at the receiving end.

In this case, we are passing a byte array, see Listing 8.68. Note that unlike, say, CORBA, EJBs employ the word "byte" and not "octet." This is because with EJBs, you most commonly expect Java to be running on both ends, and Java uses the word "byte," so there is usually no confusion. (Note that EJBs since EJB 2.1 in 2003 can have their interfaces exposed as web services, so invocation of these interfaces using other programming languages is possible, but the traditional expectation using EJBs is that Java would be running on both sides.)

LISTING 8.68   HelloWorld Interface with Array Parameter

```
package example.helloworld;
import javax.ejb.Remote;
import java.io.*;


@Remote
public interface HelloWorld {
      public String thehello(byte[] myarray);
}
```

The Stateless HelloBean in Listing 8.69 that handles the interface from Listing 8.68 is annotated with "@Stateless" but after that there's nothing special about the Java code that handles the interface; it could be used for any interface that happens to pass an array, either local or remote. In this case, it extracts the bytes from the byte array and appends them to a "Hello, values received are " string, and then returns that string to the Client.

LISTING 8.69   Simple Stateless Bean with Array Parameter

```
package example.helloworld;
import javax.ejb.Stateless;

@Stateless
      public class HelloBean implements HelloWorld {
            public String thehello(byte[] myarray) {

                  int arrayLength=myarray.length;

                  String myreturnString="Hello, values received are:  ";

                  for (int i=0; i<arrayLength; i++)
                        {
                              myreturnString += myarray[i];
                              myreturnString += " ";
                        }
                  return myreturnString;
                  }

            }
```

In Listing 8.70, we see only the code required to set up a byte array and send it as a parameter to the proxy of the interface from Listing 8.68. Otherwise, this code is the same as the POJO Client earlier shown in Listing 8.67.

LISTING 8.70   Code Snippet from POJO Client That Calls Simple Stateless Bean with Array Parameter

```
// call the remote method on the local proxy

byte[] myarray={1,2,3};
String returned_string = proxy.thehello(myarray);
```

8.4.3.3   Very Simple Stateless Session Bean Example Passes an Object Parameter

In this section, we will look at how an object (of a particular class type) can be passed as a parameter to a Remote Stateless EJB. Remember that in EJB, all parameters passed to a remote interface must be marshaled and then unmarshaled.

The interface that sends an object is shown in Listing 8.71. Note that we have defined the class definition in this file as well. For an object of a class to be sent to a Remote interface, the class must be *serializable*. We previously discussed what that means back in Section 8.4.1. In terms of implementation, it means that the class must implement *java.io.Serializable*.

In this case, just for the object to have something to do, class A defines a private variable called j, and get and set accessor functions to manipulate j.

LISTING 8.71   HelloWorld Interface with Object Parameter

```
package example.helloworld;
import javax.ejb.Remote;
import java.io.*;

class A implements java.io.Serializable {
    int j;

    public void setj(int val) {
        j=val;
    }
    public int getj() {
        return j;
    }
}

@Remote
  public interface HelloWorld {
    public String thehello(A obj);
}
```

The Stateless HelloBean in Listing 8.72 that handles the interface from Listing 8.71 is annotated with "@Stateless" but after that there's nothing special about the Java code that handles the interface, it could be used for any interface that happens to pass an object that instantiates Class A, either local or remote. In this case, it uses an accessor function to get the value of i, and returns a message related to whether i is positive or negative.

LISTING 8.72   Simple Stateless Bean with Object Parameter

```
package example.helloworld;
import javax.ejb.Stateless;
@Stateless
  public class HelloBean implements HelloWorld {
      public String thehello(A myobj) {


          int myj=myobj.getj();

          if (myj <0)
                 return "Hello to all the World!! sadly j is negative";
          else
                 return "Hello to all the World!! happily j is positive";
      }
}
```

In Listing 8.73, we see only the code required to set up an object of type Class A and send it as a parameter to the proxy of the interface from Listing 8.71. In this case, it uses the set accessor function to set the value of i to a negative number. Otherwise, this code is the same as the POJO Client earlier shown in Listing 8.67.

LISTING 8.73   Code Snippet from POJO Client That Calls Simple Stateless Bean with Object Parameter

```
// call the remote method on the local proxy

A myobj = new A();
myobj.setj(-5);
String returned_string = proxy.thehello(myobj);
```

8.4.3.4 Very Simple Stateless Session Bean Example with Injection, and Local and Remote Interfaces

In this example, in addition to basic HelloWorld interface that is the same as the interface seen earlier in Listing 8.65, there is one interface that allows remote access (annotated by "@Remote"), shown in Listing 8.74, and another interface that allows local access (annotated by "@Local"), shown in Listing 8.75.

Note that the interface in Listing 8.74 is the same as the interface in Listing 8.65. Having a separate remote interface like this allows us to easily illustrate dependency injection from within the HelloBean that implements the interface in Listing 8.65. We'll talk more about this shortly.

LISTING 8.74   HelloWorld Remote Interface

```
package example.helloworld;
import javax.ejb.Remote;
@Remote
public interface HelloWorldRemote {
    public String thehello();
}
```

LISTING 8.75   HelloWorld Local Interface

```
package example.helloworld;
import javax.ejb.Local;
@Local
public interface HelloWorldLocal {
    public String thehello();
}
```

The Client used here to call the base interface (from Listing 8.65) is a POJO client that is the same as the Client seen earlier in Listing 8.67. This Client uses JNDI to call the basic Hello-World interface from Listing 8.65, which it must do because it is a POJO. We are going to look at *dependency injection* here, but as we discussed earlier in Section 8.4.1, injection can only be used if the Client is *inside* the Java EE server-managed environment (such as another EJB, a JAX-RS web service, a servlet, etc.), then the Client may use "dependency injection" (although it can still use JNDI lookup if desired). This is done using an "@EJB" annotation.

So in order to demonstrate dependency injection, we define a HelloBean that implements the basic HelloWorld interface class. Then from inside this HelloBean we employ dependency injection (instead of the alternative, using JNDI) to provide references to the remote interface, and separately to the local interface. Then from inside this HelloBean we perform a remote procedure call on the remote interface, and a local procedure call on the local interface. That is, although this HelloBean implements the basic interface as a session bean and is called by an external POJO client, this HelloBean also is serving as a EJB client to call other EJB session beans. This HelloBean is shown in Listing 8.76.

We will also see a HelloBean (HelloBeanRemote) that implements the remote interface, and a HelloBean (HelloBeanLocal) that implements the local interface. HelloBeanRemote is shown in Listing 8.77, and HelloBean Local is shown in Listing 8.78.

Let us first examine the dependency injection in Listing 8.76. There are two examples here, in both cases, this is performed using the "@EJB" annotation. First, an injection of the remote interface:

```
// Inject the Remote interface
@EJB
private HelloWorldRemote myremotebean;
```

And second, an injection of the local interface:

```
// Inject the Local interface
@EJB
private HelloWorldLocal mylocalbean;
```

What this does in each case is create a proxy object that contains the appropriate location (address) information. The procedure calls to these proxy objects are very similar. Here is a remote procedure call to the proxy object that represents the remote interface:

```
// Call the Remote interface
String returned_valueA;
returned_valueA = myremotebean.thehello();
```

And here is a local procedure call to the proxy object that represents the local interface:

```
// Call the Local interface
String returned_valueB;
returned_valueB = mylocalbean.thehello();
```

In Section 8.4.1, we previously discussed the difference between a local interface and a remote interface. Remember that if the Session Bean has a local interface (according to the annotation) then the local Client that calls that interface must run in the same application, that is, on the same JVM as the Session Bean. Local Clients are more efficient than remote Clients, since they do not require marshaling and unmarshaling (serializing) of arguments or transmission of arguments across a network. (Actual processing of this can depend on the implementation of the application server being used.)

However, although a Client calling local interface must be in the same application as the Session Bean called, it is possible for a Client to use a remote interface in the same application as the Session Bean that is called—that is what we have seen here.

LISTING 8.76   HelloBean Performs Dependency Injection

```
package example.helloworld;
import javax.ejb.EJB;
import javax.ejb.Stateless;
import example.helloworld.HelloBeanRemote;
@Stateless
    public class HelloBean implements HelloWorld {

    // Inject the Remote interface
    @EJB
    private HelloWorldRemote myremotebean;

    // Inject the Local interface
    @EJB
    private HelloWorldLocal mylocalbean;

    public String thehello() {

            // Call the Remote interface
            String returned_valueA;
```

```
                    returned_valueA = myremotebean.thehello();

                    // Call the Local interface
                    String returned_valueB;
                    returned_valueB = mylocalbean.thehello();

                    String value_to_return;
                    value_to_return=returned_valueA+" and "+returned_valueB;
                    return value_to_return;
            }
    }
```

Note that the HelloBean that implements the HelloWorldRemote interface is almost the same as the one previously shown in Listing 8.66. Again, the purpose of using this here is to allow the HelloBean in Listing 8.76 to illustrate dependency injection of a Remote Session Bean.

LISTING 8.77   HelloBeanRemote Implements Hello Bean Remote Interface

```
package example.helloworld;
import javax.ejb.Stateless;
@Stateless
  public class HelloBeanRemote implements HelloWorldRemote {
      public String thehello() {
      return "Hello from HelloBeanRemote";
      }
  }
```

In Listing 8.78, the notation "@LocalBean" is used. We really didn't need a separate interface such as the one we used in Listing 8.75 because this annotation can both define the interface and the bean that implements the interface (if we weren't using the separate interface we would leave off the "implements" clause). We could instead have annotated the class as "@Local" or alternately annotated the class as @Local(LocalHelloBean.class). Or if we hadn't been using a separate interface, and hadn't annotated this class at all, it would have defaulted to local. It's generally best to be explicit about whether an interface (or class) is local or remote. And defining separate interfaces is a good way to describe and clarify the code, so that should be what you normally do.

LISTING 8.78   HelloBeanLocal Implements Hello Bean Local Interface

```
package example.helloworld;
import javax.ejb.LocalBean;
import javax.ejb.Stateless;
@Stateless
@LocalBean
public class HelloBeanLocal implements HelloWorldLocal {
```

```
    public String thehello() {
    return "Hello from HelloBeanLocal";
    }
}
```

8.4.3.5 Simple Stateless Session Bean Example That Illustrates Stateless Characteristics

This is an example that illustrates that a Stateless Session Bean really is Stateless. To do this, we see a slightly more complicated interface than what we've been using so far; see the interface in Listing 8.79. This one implements getcount and setcount accessor functions, and an increment count function, in addition to the original thehello() function.

The HelloBean shown in Listing 8.80 implements this interface. It's more complicated than the original Stateless HelloBean from Listing 8.66 because it has to implement the additional functions. However, it is still very simple, as you can see.

LISTING 8.79   Slightly More Complicated HelloWorld Interface—getcount, setcount, incrementcount

```
package example.helloworld;
import javax.ejb.Remote;
@Remote
public interface StatelessHelloWorld {
        public String thehello();
        public int getcount();
        public String setcount(int value);
        public String incrcount();
}
```

LISTING 8.80   Stateless HelloBean Implements Slightly More Complicated HelloWorld Interface

```
package example.helloworld;
import javax.ejb.Stateless;
@Stateless
  public class StatelessHelloBean implements StatelessHelloWorld {
      private int count=0;
      public String thehello() {
          return "Hello to all the World!!!!!";
      }

      public int getcount() {
          return count;
      }
      public String setcount(int value) {
          count=value;
```

```
            return "set the stateless counter";
    }
    public String incrcount() {
            count++;
            return "incremented the stateless counter";
    }
}
```

The Client shown in Listing 8.81 is where most of the work is done to illustrate that the HelloBean from Listing 8.80 really is stateless. Remember that the application server retains a pool of Stateless Beans. What this Client will show is that the initial value returned will be the value from the most recent Stateless Bean used by *any* Client proxy object, rather than the value that was previously used by the *same* Client proxy object that is currently being used. That is to say, the Stateless HelloBean is not retaining a conversational state with each Client proxy object that is used to call it.

To clarify a little more: the Client in Listing 8.81 creates two proxy objects: Proxy A and Proxy B. Proxy A does a remote procedure call on the HelloBean, reads the initial value of count, sets its count to 3 and increments it to 4 (this is done in a subroutine on the Client named *calltheremote*). Then Proxy B does a remote procedure call on the HelloBean, reads the initial value of count, sets its count to 100 and increments it to 101. Finally, Proxy A does another remote procedure call on the HelloBean, reads the initial value of count, sets its count to 7 and increments it to 8. (Note that I could have left out the increment count and done this just with getcounts and setcounts, but I thought a little bit more EJB examples wouldn't hurt. ☺)

Finally, at the end Proxy A does a getcount (get the value) and Proxy B does a getcount (get the value) on the HelloBean, one after the other.

The output from a run of this Client is shown in Table 8.1.

Note that the initial value of Proxy B is 4, which is the final value from Proxy A. Also, note that the initial value for the second set of calls by Proxy A is 101. If a conversation were being maintained

TABLE 8.1

**Output from a Run Illustrating
Statelessness of the Stateless Bean**

	Count Value
Proxy A initial value	8*
Proxy A set value	3
Proxy A value incremented to	4
Proxy B initial value	4
Proxy B set value	100
Proxy B value incremented to	101
Proxy A initial value	101
Proxy A set value	7
Proxy A value incremented to	8
Final Proxy A value	8
Final Proxy B value	8

using the call from the Client on Proxy A, then when Proxy A was used a second time, the initial value would have been 4 and not 101.

If Proxy A and Proxy B had separate conversations going, and the state was maintained by the HelloBean for each proxy between separate sets of calls from each Proxy, then Proxy A would get the value that Proxy A set on the HelloBean, and the fact that Proxy B set another value on the HelloBean *after* Proxy A's first set of calls and before Proxy A's second set of calls wouldn't matter.

What is clearly happening here is that the container running on the application server is returning from the pool the most recent bean used, regardless of which Proxy object had just been used to access it, and it retains the value from the most recently completed call, until it is explicitly set on the current set of calls.

Note that the very first initial value for a Proxy A call contained an 8. This is marked with an asterisk, because what really happened here is that this was the second time I had run this code, so the most recent object available in the pool contained the 8 that was the value from the first run I did.

Conclusion: The Stateless Hello Bean is really stateless.

LISTING 8.81   Client That Illustrates Statelessness of Stateless Session Bean

```
package example.helloworld;
import javax.naming.InitialContext;
import javax.naming.Context;
import javax.naming.NamingException;
import javax.rmi.PortableRemoteObject;

public class StatelessHelloClient {
    public static void main (String[] args) {
        try {
            Context ic= new InitialContext();

            // Get one proxy object
            Object object_ref = ic.lookup("java:global/statelesshelloworld/Stateless
                HelloBean");
            // This narrow downcasts the object_ref to type StatelessHelloWorld, this
                serves as the proxy
            StatelessHelloWorld proxyA= (StatelessHelloWorld)
                PortableRemoteObject.narrow(object_ref,StatelessHelloWorld.class);

            call_the_remote(proxyA,3);  // call all the methods on the proxy

            // Get another different proxy object
            object_ref = ic.lookup("java:global/statelesshelloworld/
                StatelessHelloBean");
            // This narrow downcasts the object_ref to type StatelessHelloWorld, this
                serves as the proxy
            StatelessHelloWorld proxyB= (StatelessHelloWorld)
                PortableRemoteObject.narrow(object_ref,StatelessHelloWorld.
                class);

            call_the_remote(proxyB, 100);  // call all the methods on the proxy
```

```
                System.out.println("Now get the count from original proxy");
                int count_returned = proxyA.getcount();
                System.out.println("proxyA count is "+count_returned);

                System.out.println("Now get the count from the second proxy");
                count_returned = proxyB.getcount();
                System.out.println("proxyB count is "+count_returned);

                call_the_remote(proxyA, 7);  // call all the methods on the proxy

                System.out.println("Now get the count from original proxy");
                count_returned = proxyA.getcount();
                System.out.println("proxyA count is "+count_returned);

                System.out.println("Now get the count from the second proxy");
                count_returned = proxyB.getcount();
                System.out.println("proxyB count is "+count_returned);

                System.out.println("When I ran this, whatever the last value was");
                System.out.println("proxyA got it and proxyB also got it");
                System.out.println("The EJB is stateless so it's not really");
                System.out.println("retaining its state between method calls.");
                System.out.println("What happens is the container is repeatedly");
                System.out.println("giving back the same bean from the pool.");
                System.out.println("So it gets rewritten every time.");          }
        catch (NamingException ex) {
                // You might get a naming exception if you forgot to deploy the jar file
                // You might get a naming exception if you forgot to start GlassFish
                System.out.println("Naming exception");
                System.out.println("cause is"+ex.getCause());
                System.out.println("stack trace is ");
                ex.printStackTrace();
        } catch (Exception ex) {
                System.out.println("general exception");
        }
    } // end Main()
    public static void call_the_remote(StatelessHelloWorld proxy,int value) {
        // call the remote method on the local proxy
        String returned_string = proxy.thehello();
        System.out.println(returned_string);

        int count_returned = proxy.getcount();
        System.out.println("first value of count is "+count_returned);

        returned_string = proxy.setcount(value);
        System.out.println(returned_string);

        count_returned = proxy.getcount();
        System.out.println("count is now "+count_returned);
```

```
            returned_string = proxy.incrcount();
            System.out.println(returned_string);

            count_returned = proxy.getcount();
            System.out.println("count is now "+count_returned);

    } // end call_the_remote
} // end class
```

8.4.4 SINGLETON SESSION BEANS

In this section, we examine Singleton Session Beans. You should recall from Section 8.4.1 that a Singleton Session Bean is shared by many clients, and a Singleton Session Bean retains its state for a particular client in between different method calls from that client.

In Listing 8.82, we see a HelloWorld interface that also includes getvalue and setvalue accessor functions (they access an integer).

LISTING 8.82   HelloWorld Interface Including getvalue and setvalue Accessor Functions

```
package example.helloworld;
import javax.ejb.Remote;
@Remote
public interface HelloWorld {
    public void set_value(int i);
    public int get_value();
    public String thehello();
}
```

In Listing 8.83, we see a Singleton Bean, annotated with "@Singleton," that implements the interface in Listing 8.83. Note that this example is also annotated with "@Startup." What this means is that the container in GlassFish must immediately create the HelloBean when the application runs. If you don't specify "@Startup" then its up to the container when to create the HelloBean object.

LISTING 8.83   Simple Singleton Session Bean

```
package example.helloworld;
import javax.ejb.Startup;
import javax.ejb.Singleton;
@Startup
@Singleton
public class HelloBean implements HelloWorld {
    int value;
    public HelloBean() {
        value=999;
```

```
        }
    public void set_value(int i) {
        value=i;
    }

    public int get_value() {
        return value;
    }
    public String thehello() {
        return "Hello to all the World!!!!!";
    }
}
```

In Listing 8.84, we see a Client that accesses the interface from Listing 8.82. To illustrate that our HelloBean is truly a Singleton Session Bean, we need two clients with almost the same code, Client A is exactly as shown in Listing 8.84. Client B is the same as Client A except that only Client A calls setvalue, Client B does not call setvalue, that is, the following code appears in Client A but not in Client B:

```
proxy.set_value(77);
 System.out.println("Just set the value to 77");
```

Since Client B is actually a separate file, it uses a separate proxy object to contain the reference to the HelloBean. So it really is a totally separate client.

If we look at the HelloBean class (see Listing 8.83 again), we see its constructor sets its original value to 999. If a new HelloBean were ever created then its constructor would run again and reset its value to 999.

So now we run Client A first. Its initial value (prior to ClientA calling setvalue) returned is 999. This is the value that was set by the constructor when it was called. Then Client A calls set_value to set the value to 77.

So then we run Client B, which only gets the value (does *not* set the value). Client B returns the value 77. Then every time we run Client B again after that, even if we run Client B several times, the value returned is always 77.

That is, the HelloBean is *NOT* newly created, because the constructor is never called again. Therefore, all Clients are using the same Session Bean.

This illustrates that we are using a Singleton Session Bean.

LISTING 8.84   Client A—getsvalue Then setsvalue to 77

```
package example.helloworld;
import javax.naming.InitialContext;
import javax.naming.Context;
import javax.naming.NamingException;
import javax.rmi.PortableRemoteObject;

public class HelloClientA {
    public static void main (String[] args) {
```

```
        try {
                Context ic= new InitialContext();
                Object object_ref = ic.lookup("java:global/helloworld/HelloBean");
        // This narrow downcasts the object_ref to type HelloWorld, this serves as the proxy
                HelloWorld proxy= (HelloWorld)
                            PortableRemoteObject.narrow(object_ref,HelloWorld.class);

                // call the remote method on the local proxy
                String returned_string = proxy.thehello();
                System.out.println(returned_string);

                int value=proxy.get_value();
                System.out.println("Got original value, the value was "+value);

                // Included in Client A only, not in Client B
                proxy.set_value(77);
                System.out.println("Just set the value to 77");

        } catch (NamingException ex) {
                // You might get a naming exception if you forgot to deploy the jar file
                // You might get a naming exception if you forgot to start GlassFish
                System.out.println("Naming exception");
                System.out.println("cause is"+ex.getCause());
                System.out.println("stack trace is ");
                ex.printStackTrace();
        } catch (Exception ex) {
                System.out.println("general exception");
        }
    }
}
```

8.4.5 STATEFUL SESSION BEANS

In this section, we will look at Stateful Session Beans. As you recall from Section 8.4.1, in a Stateful Session Bean, a Client and a Stateful Session Bean are considered to be in a "session" (conversation). When the session (conversation) ends, the state (values of the instance variables) vanishes.

We will first look at a fairly simple Stateful Session Bean example that illustrates the Stateful session/connection oriented behavior. Next, we will look at an example that accesses a Stateful Session Bean asynchronously. Then, we will expand the server-side code (the Stateful Session Bean) to look at additional server-side processing that is implemented by the container but controlled through the Session Bean: a lifecycle example, and a lifecycle example that forces a passivate.

With a Stateful Session Bean, since its lifetime is the lifetime of the connection or session with the Client, the Stateful Session Bean may potentially need to be instantiated, active, and requiring resources for a considerable amount of time, although sometimes it is not actively being accessed by the Client the entire time.

Sometimes, so many requests come in that the container in the application server can become overcommitted. In this case, the container has to temporarily suspend any entities in the container that are not currently being actively used, including Stateful Session Beans. In the case of a Stateful Session Bean, this would mean saving all the information about the Stateful Session Bean (this is called *passivating* the Stateful Session Bean) so it can later be retrieved, when it has been accessed again by a remote Client (this is called *activating* the Stateful Session Bean). Note that this means the Stateful Session Bean must be serializable. (Note that only Stateful Session Beans can be activated or passivated, this does not apply to either Stateless Session Beans or Singleton Session Beans.)

8.4.5.1 Stateful Session Bean Example

For our simple Stateful Session Bean example, we will use the same interface previously seen in Listing 8.79 that we used before to illustrate the behavior of a Stateless Session Bean.

In Listing 8.85, we see the Stateful HelloBean that implements the interface in Listing 8.79. This HelloBean is very similar to the Stateless HelloBean we previously saw in Listing 8.78, the biggest difference is that here it is annotated with "@Stateful."

LISTING 8.85   Stateful HelloBean

```
package example.helloworld;
import javax.ejb.Stateful;

@Stateful
public class HelloBean implements HelloWorld {
    private int mycount=0;
    public String thehello() {
        return "Hello to all the World!!!!!";
    }
    public int getcount() {
        return mycount;
    }
    public String setcount(int value) {
        mycount=value;
        return "mycount has been set" ;
    }
    public String incrcount() {
        mycount++;
        return "mycount has been incremented" ;
    }
}
```

In Listing 8.86, we see a Client that is very similar to the Client previously shown in Listing 8.81. The difference is that in Listing 8.81, the Client called the "calltheremote" subroutine three times, once for Proxy A, then for Proxy B, then for Proxy C, whereas in this Client in Listing 8.86 calls the "calltheremote" subroutine only twice, once for Proxy A, then for Proxy B.

To clarify a little more: the Client in Listing 8.81 creates two proxy objects: Proxy A and Proxy B. Proxy A does a remote procedure call on the HelloBean, reads the initial value of count, sets its count to 10 and increments it to 11 (this is done in the subroutine on the Client named "calltheremote").

TABLE 8.2

Output from a Run Illustrating
Session/Connection of Stateful Bean

	Count Value
Proxy A initial value	0
Proxy A set value	10
Proxy A value incremented to	11
Proxy B initial value	0
Proxy B set value	100
Proxy B value incremented to	101
Final Proxy A value	11
Final Proxy B value	101

Then Proxy B does a remote procedure call on the HelloBean, reads the initial value of count, sets its count to 100 and increments it to 101.

Finally, at the end Proxy A does a getcount (get the value) and Proxy B does a getcount (get the value) on the HelloBean, one after the other.

The output from a run of this Client is shown in Table 8.2.

See how the final counts are different? That's because they are two different proxy objects each of which is handling its own separate session/connection.

Note that the initial value of Proxy A is 0, and the initial value of Proxy B is 0. This is because they are being initialized the first time the Stateful HelloBeans associated with those proxies are created.

If we call Proxy A 100 times or 1000, it will always return Proxy A's value and not Proxy B's value, and vice versa. This is because Proxy A has its own session/connection, and Proxy B has its own session/connection.

Conclusion: The Stateful HelloBeans are retaining the state across a session/connection.

LISTING 8.86   Client That Illustrates that Stateful Session Bean Retains Values
Throughout Session/Connection

```
package example.helloworld;
import javax.naming.InitialContext;
import javax.naming.Context;
import javax.naming.NamingException;
import javax.rmi.PortableRemoteObject;


public class HelloClient {
    public static void main (String[] args) {
        try {
            Context ic= new InitialContext();

            Object object_ref = ic.lookup("java:global/helloworld/HelloBean");

            // This narrow downcasts the object_ref to type HelloWorld, this serves as
                the proxy HelloWorld proxyA= (HelloWorld)
```

```
                    PortableRemoteObject.narrow(object_ref,HelloWorld.class);

                    call_the_remote(proxyA,10);  // call all the methods on the proxy

                    // Get another different proxy object
                    object_ref = ic.lookup("java:global/helloworld/HelloBean");

                    // This narrow downcasts the object_ref to type HelloWorld, this serves as the
                        proxy HelloWorld proxyB= (HelloWorld)
                    PortableRemoteObject.narrow(object_ref,HelloWorld.class);

                    call_the_remote(proxyB, 100);  // call all the methods on the proxy

                    System.out.println("Now get the count from original proxy");
                    int count_returned = proxyA.getcount();
                    System.out.println("proxyA count is "+count_returned);

                    System.out.println("Now get the count from the second proxy");
                    count_returned = proxyB.getcount();
                    System.out.println("proxyB count is "+count_returned);

                    System.out.println("See how the counts are different?");
                    System.out.println("That's because they are two different proxy objects");
                    System.out.println("each of which is handling its own separate session");
                    System.out.println("If I call proxyA 100 times it will always return");
                    System.out.println("proxyAs value and not proxyBs value. And vice versa.");
            }
        catch (NamingException ex) {
                System.out.println("Naming exception");
                System.out.println("cause is"+ex.getCause());
                System.out.println("stack trace is ");
                ex.printStackTrace();
        } catch (Exception ex) {
                System.out.println("general exception");
        }
    } // end Main()

    public static void call_the_remote(HelloWorld proxy,int value) {
            // call the remote method on the local proxy
            String returned_string = proxy.thehello();
            System.out.println(returned_string);

            int count_returned = proxy.getcount();
            System.out.println("first value of count is "+count_returned);

            returned_string = proxy.setcount(value);
            System.out.println(returned_string);

            count_returned = proxy.getcount();
```

```
            System.out.println("count is now "+count_returned);
            returned_string = proxy.incrcount();
            System.out.println(returned_string);

            count_returned = proxy.getcount();
            System.out.println("count is now "+count_returned);

    } // end call_the_remote
} // end class
```

8.4.5.2 Stateful Session Bean Asynchronous

First let's look at the difference between *synchronous* and *asynchronous*. In the context of EJBs, *synchronous* means that when a Client calls a Servant/Server, the Client waits until the Server responds before the Client continues operation. Here, *asynchronous* means that the Client calls the Servant/Server and then goes about its business, doing whatever it needs to do, and when the Servant/Server eventually finishes its work and returns the result to the Client, the Client can go ahead and finish up whatever it needed to do related to that call.

An asynchronous interface is shown in Listing 8.87, a Stateful HelloBean that implements this interface is shown in Listing 8.88, and a Client that calls the asynchronous interface is in Listing 8.89.

In EJBs, asynchronous operation is implemented with the Future<V> interface, the AsyncResult<V> return value, and the "@Asynchronous" annotation.

In the asynchronous interface in Listing 8.87, the asynchronous method has the return type:

Future<String>

LISTING 8.87   HelloWorld Interface—Asynchronous

```
package example.helloworld;
import java.util.concurrent.Future;
import javax.ejb.Remote;

@Remote
public interface HelloWorld {
    public Future<String> thehello();
    public int getcount();
    public String setcount(int value);
    public String incrcount();
}
```

In the Stateful HelloBean that implements the asynchronous interface, the asynchronous method is annotated with "@Asynchronous." It imports javax.ejb.AsyncResult and javax.ejb.Asynchronous. It defines the asynchronous method as follows:

```
@Asynchronous
    public Future<String> thehello()
```

and it asynchronously returns a value as follows:

```
return new AsyncResult<String>("Hello to all the World!!!!!");
```

In the asynchronous Client, the asynchronous method is called as follows:

```
Future<String> mystring = proxyA.thehello();
```

LISTING 8.88   Stateful Asynchronous HelloBean

```
package example.helloworld;
import javax.ejb.AsyncResult;
import javax.ejb.Asynchronous;
import java.util.concurrent.Future;

import javax.ejb.Stateful;
import java.lang.*;

@Stateful
  public class HelloBean implements HelloWorld {
      private int mycount=0;
      @Asynchronous
       public Future<String> thehello() {
          try {
               Thread.sleep (10000); // sleep for 10 seconds
          }
          catch (InterruptedException e) {
               e.printStackTrace();
          }
          return new AsyncResult<String>("Hello to all the World!!!!!");
      }
      public int getcount() {
          return mycount;
      }
      public String setcount(int value) {
          mycount=value;
          return "mycount has been set" ;
      }
      public String incrcount() {
          mycount++;
          return "mycount has been incremented" ;
      }
  }
```

To illustrate how an asynchronous call works, the HelloBean pauses in the middle of the call for a considerable period of time:

```
Thread.sleep (10000); // sleep for 10 seconds
```

During the time the HelloBean is taking to process the request, the Client continues to execute.

LISTING 8.89   Asynchronous Client

```
package example.helloworld;
import javax.naming.InitialContext;
import javax.naming.Context;

import javax.naming.NamingException;
import javax.rmi.PortableRemoteObject;

import javax.ejb.AsyncResult;
import javax.ejb.Asynchronous;
import java.util.concurrent.Future;

public class HelloClient {
    public static void main (String[] args) {
        try {
            Context ic= new InitialContext();

            Object object_ref = ic.lookup("java:global/helloworld/HelloBean");

            // This narrow downcasts the object_ref to type HelloWorld, this serves as the
                proxy HelloWorld proxyA= (HelloWorld)
                        PortableRemoteObject.narrow(object_ref,HelloWorld.class);

            System.out.println("Now get the count from original proxy");

            Future<String> mystring = proxyA.thehello();

            int i=0;
            while (!mystring.isDone() )
            {
                // We could actually be doing something useful now.
                // I'll just count to simulate the useful work ☺
                System.out.println("Doing useful counting, i = "+i);
                i++;
            }
            String myfinalstring = mystring.get();
            System.out.println("string returned was "+myfinalstring);
        }
        catch (NamingException ex) {
            // You might get a naming exception if you forgot to deploy the jar file
            // You might get a naming exception if you forgot to start GlassFish
            System.out.println("Naming exception");
            System.out.println("cause is"+ex.getCause());
            System.out.println("stack trace is ");
            ex.printStackTrace();
        } catch (Exception ex) {
            System.out.println("general exception");
        }
    } // end Main()
} // end class
```

So the results from running the Client look something like this:

Now get the count from original proxy
Doing useful counting, i = 0
Doing useful counting, i = 1
Doing useful counting, i = 2
Doing useful counting, i = 3
Doing useful counting, i = 4
Doing useful counting, i = 5

... etc. ...

Doing useful counting, i = 8930
Doing useful counting, i = 8931
Doing useful counting, i = 8932
Doing useful counting, i = 8933
Doing useful counting, i = 8934
string returned was Hello to all the World!!!!!

This illustrates that the Client was able to continue working while the Servant/Server processed the Client's asynchronous request.

8.4.5.3 Stateful Session Bean Lifecycle Callbacks

As previously discussed in Section 8.4.5, with a Stateful Session Bean, since its lifetime is the lifetime of the connection or session with the Client, the Stateful Session Bean may potentially need to be instantiated, active, and requiring resources for a considerable amount of time, although sometimes it is not actively being accessed by the Client the entire time.

Sometimes, so many requests come in for different EJBs (and other entities in the Java EE server managed environment) that the container in the application server can become overcommitted. In this case, the container has to temporarily suspend any entities in the container that are not currently being actively used, including Stateful Session Beans. In the case of a Stateful Session Bean, this would mean saving all the information about the Stateful Session Bean (this is called *passivating* the Stateful Session Bean) so it can later be retrieved, when it has been accessed again by a remote Client (this is called *activating* the Stateful Session Bean). Note that this means the Stateful Session Bean must be serializable. (Note that only Stateful Session Beans can be activated or passivated, this does not apply to either Stateless Session Beans or Singleton Session Beans.)

EJB permits methods to be defined that can be invoked at certain points in the lifecycle of an EJB.

These are referred to as *callbacks* because from the standpoint of the container in the application server that is what they are (in client/server lingo, a *callback* is when a server calls a routine on a client). That is, the EJBs start the container running (executing the EJB), so in that situation the EJBs are serving as a client. So when certain events happen on the Servant/Server, the Servant/Server can callback to the Client (call a callback routine) so the Client can handle these events.

A callback can be invoked on any kind of session beans. A Stateless Session Bean, a Singleton Session Bean, and a Stateful Session Bean can all three employ:

- @PostConstruct—invoked when the Session Bean is first created
- @PreDestroy—invoked just before a Session Bean is destroyed (or removed from the pool of beans)

However, only a Stateful Session Bean can employ:

- @PostActivate—invoked after a Stateful Session Bean is reloaded from storage into the container
- @PrePassivate—invoked just before a Stateful Session Bean is unloaded from the container and saved away to storage

There is also another annotation that is used to have an instance of a Stateful Bean removed from the container at the end of the call to the annotated method:

- @Remove

Routines that are annotated with @PostConstruct, @PreDestroy, @PostActivate, or @PrePassivate are invoked by the container in the application server, whereas the Client invokes the method that is annotated by @Remove. However, right after the method annotated with "@Remove" finishes, the container in the application server will remove the Stateful Session Bean.

In Listing 8.90, we have an interface that we're going to use to illustrate the lifecycle of a Stateful Session Bean. This interface is similar to interfaces we've seen before in Listing 8.79 and in Listing 8.87. However, this one has three new methods:

1. Initcount
2. Finishcounting
3. Remove

LISTING 8.90   Interface to Illustrate Stateful Session Bean Lifecycle

```
package example.helloworld;
import javax.ejb.Remote;
@Remote
public interface HelloWorld {
    public String thehello();
    public void initcount();
    public int getcount();
    public String setcount(int value);
    public String incrcount();
    public void finishcounting();
    public void remove();
}
```

The initcount routine is meant to be called right after the Session Bean is instantiated. Thus it is annotated with:

- @PostConstruct
- @PostActivate

We're really ignoring the PostActivate in this particular example, because the way we've got it set up, the container in the application server is not busy enough to need to do a Passivate. We'll see how that works later in Section 8.4.5.4.

The finishcounting routine is meant to be called just before the Stateful Session Bean is destroyed. So it is annotated with:

- @PrePassivate
- @PreDestroy

Again, we're really ignoring the PrePassivate in this particular example, because the container in the application server is not busy enough to need to do a Passivate.

The remove routine is meant to be called by the Client to remove the Stateful Session Bean from the container (the routine is called by the Client but the actual removal of the Stateful Session Bean is performed by the container). So it is annotated with:

- @Remove

Note that in this particular HelloBean example, we're using "@Override." @Override forces a compile time check of a method versus the interface. It prevents accidental overloading (instead of intended overriding), by generating a compile-time error when the method signature doesn't exactly match the method signature in the interface. We could have (and probably should have) been using this all along, but to save confusion and a necessary explanation I left it off until now.

LISTING 8.91   HelloBean to Illustrate Stateful Session Bean Lifecycle

```java
package example.helloworld;
import javax.ejb.Stateful;
import javax.annotation.PostConstruct;
import javax.annotation.PreDestroy;
import javax.ejb.Remove;
import javax.ejb.PostActivate;
import javax.ejb.PrePassivate;
@Stateful
public class HelloBean implements HelloWorld {
    private int mycount=0;

    @Override
    public String thehello() {
        return "Hello to all the World!!!!!";
    }
    @PostConstruct
    @PostActivate
    @Override
    public void initcount() {
        mycount=9999;
        System.out.println("Doing PostConstruct or PostActivate");
    }
    @Override
    public int getcount() {
        return mycount;
    }
    @Override
    public String setcount(int value) {
```

```
            mycount=value;
            return "mycount has been set" ;
    }
    @Override
    public String incrcount() {
            mycount++;
            return "mycount has been incremented" ;
    }
    @PrePassivate
    @PreDestroy
    @Override
    public void  finishcounting() {
            mycount=7777;
            System.out.println("Doing PreDestroy or PrePassivate");
    }
    @Remove
    @Override
    public void  remove() {
            System.out.println("About to Remove Bean from Container");
    }
}
```

We use the Client in Listing 8.92 to call the interface from Listing 8.90. We have two separate proxy objects, Proxy A and Proxy B. We find the interface using JNDI for each of these, then we call getcount() separately on each proxy object. Finally, we call remove() on each proxy object.

When we run the Client, the output looks like this:

```
Now get the count from Proxy A
proxyA count is 9999
Now get the count from Proxy B
proxyB count is 9999
```

However, for this example, the interesting results are shown in the Server log file. A screenshot of the server log file is available in Figure 8.10.

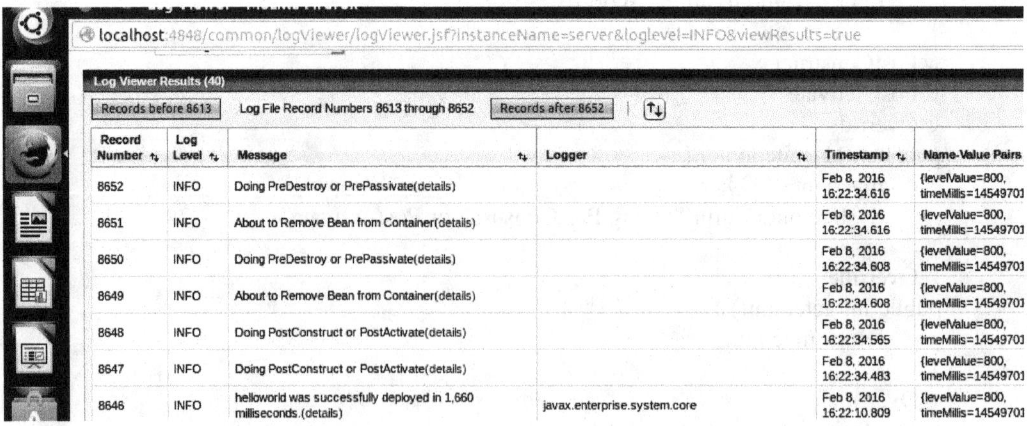

FIGURE 8.10   Screenshot of server log file from GlassFish—PostConstruct and PreDestroy.

LISTING 8.92   Client to Illustrate Stateful Session Bean Lifecycle

```java
package example.helloworld;
import javax.naming.InitialContext;
import javax.naming.Context;
import javax.naming.NamingException;
import javax.rmi.PortableRemoteObject;

public class HelloClient {
    public static void main (String[] args) {
        try {
            Context ic= new InitialContext();

            // Get a proxy object
            Object object_ref = ic.lookup("java:global/helloworld/HelloBean");
            HelloWorld proxyA= (HelloWorld)
                PortableRemoteObject.narrow(object_ref,HelloWorld.class);

            System.out.println("Now get the count from ProxyA");
            int count_returned = proxyA.getcount();
            System.out.println("proxyA count is "+count_returned);

            // Get another proxy object
            object_ref = ic.lookup("java:global/helloworld/HelloBean");
            HelloWorld proxyB= (HelloWorld)
                PortableRemoteObject.narrow(object_ref,HelloWorld.class);

            System.out.println("Now get the count from ProxyB");
            count_returned = proxyB.getcount();
            System.out.println("proxyB count is "+count_returned);

            // Explicitly remove the beans from the container
            proxyA.remove();
            proxyB.remove();

        }
        catch (NamingException ex) {
                System.out.println("Naming exception");
                System.out.println("cause is"+ex.getCause());
                System.out.println("stack trace is ");
                ex.printStackTrace();
        } catch (Exception ex) {
            System.out.println("general exception");
        }

    } // end Main()

} // end class
```

Figure 8.10, the server log, must be read from bottom to top. Thus, the first event that was logged was that HelloWorld was deployed. The next event logged was "Doing PostConstruct or PostActivate." If you look back at Listing 8.91, this was the initcount() routine running. It set the counter to 9999. This is called twice, once for Proxy A on the Client, and once for Proxy B.

Note that the calls to getcount() do not result in any messages being logged to the server log, there just weren't any put into this method (we would have had to do a System.out.println using some kind of interesting string, and we just didn't happen to do that.)

Next, we see from the logged messages ("About to Remove Bean from Container") that Remove is called for Proxy A, which then (when the remove() method completes) results in a call from the container to finishcounting(), resulting in the message "Doing PreDestroy or PrePassivate" in the log. This is followed immediately by the container removing the Stateful Session Bean from the container. Then this repeats for Proxy B.

8.4.5.4   Stateful Session Bean Lifecycle Callbacks Forces Passivate

This example is another example illustrating the lifecycle of a Stateful Session Bean. However, in this case we're going to force a Passivate so we can see what that looks like. We will use the interface in Listing 8.93 to do this. This interface is similar to the interface we previously saw in Listing 8.90. However, here we have split the initcount() routine into two separate routines, initcount_PostConstruct() and initcount_PostActivate() so we can distinguish between creation of the Stateful Session Bean and re-activation of an existing Stateful Session Bean that was previously Passivated. Similarly, we have split the finishcounting() routine into two separate routines, finishcounting_PrePassivate() and finishcounting_PreDestroy() so we can distinguish between a Stateful Session Bean that is about to be destroyed, and a Stateful Session Bean that is about to be Passivated.

You should remember from our previous discussions in Sections 8.4.5 and 8.4.5.3 that so many requests come in for different EJBs (and other entities in the Java EE server managed environment) that the container in the application server can become overcommitted. In this case, the container has to temporarily suspend any entities in the container that are not currently being actively used, including Stateful Session Beans. In the case of a Stateful Session Bean, this would mean saving all the information about the Stateful Session Bean (this is called *passivating* the Stateful Session Bean) so it can later be retrieved, when it has been accessed again by a remote Client (this is called *activating* the Stateful Session Bean). Note that this means the Stateful Session Bean must be serializable. (Note that only Stateful Session Beans can be activated or passivated, this does not apply to either Stateless Session Beans or Singleton Session Beans.)

LISTING 8.93   Interface to Illustrate Stateful Session Bean Lifecycle with Forced Passivate

```
package example.helloworld;
import javax.ejb.Remote;
@Remote
public interface HelloWorld {
     public String thehello();
     public void initcount_PostConstruct();
     public void initcount_PostActivate();
     public int getcount();
     public String setcount(int value);
```

```
    public String incrcount();
    public void finishcounting_PrePassivate();
    public void finishcounting_PreDestroy();
    public void remove();
}
```

If you look at the implementation of initcount_PostConstruct() and initcount_PostActivate() in Listing 8.94, you will see that initcount_PostConstruct() is annotated with "@PostConstruct" and initcount_PostActivate() is annotated with "@PostActivate." Similarly, the method

finishcounting_PrePassivate() is annotated with "@PrePassivate" and the method finishcounting_PreDestroy() is annotated with "@PreDestroy."

LISTING 8.94 HelloBean to Illustrate Stateful Session Bean Lifecycle with Forced Passivate

```
package example.helloworld;
import javax.ejb.Stateful;
import javax.annotation.PostConstruct;
import javax.annotation.PreDestroy;
import javax.ejb.Remove;
import javax.ejb.PostActivate;
import javax.ejb.PrePassivate;
@Stateful
public class HelloBean implements HelloWorld {
    private int mycount=0;

    @Override
    public String thehello() {
      return "Hello to all the World!!!!!";
    }
    @PostConstruct
    @Override
    public void  initcount_PostConstruct() {
      mycount=9999;
      System.out.println("Doing PostConstruct");
    }
    @PostActivate
    @Override
    public void  initcount_PostActivate() {
            mycount=1010;
            System.out.println("Doing PostActivate");
    }
    @Override
    public int getcount() {
            return mycount;
    }
```

```
    @Override
    public String setcount(int value) {
            mycount=value;
            return "mycount has been set" ;
    }
    @Override
    public String incrcount() {
            mycount++;
            return "mycount has been incremented" ;
    }
    @PrePassivate
    @Override
    public void  finishcounting_PrePassivate() {
            mycount=7777;
            System.out.println("Doing PrePassivate");
    }
    @PreDestroy
    @Override
    public void  finishcounting_PreDestroy() {
            mycount=8888;
            System.out.println("Doing PreDestroy");
    }
    @Remove
    @Override
    public void  remove() {
            System.out.println("About to Remove Bean from Container");
    }
}
```

Now deploy the Bean shown in Listing 8.94; your server log will look as shown in the screenshot in Figure 8.11.

Okay, this is fairly straightforward so far. Now comes the harder part of this project. We want to use up resources *inside* the container, so the container is forced to passivate a Stateful Session Bean.

To do this, I have chosen to use a servlet. I'm using this in advance of Chapter 11, where I describe servlets in much more detail. However, it's very convenient to use one for this particular example, as you will see. I'll try to explain everything you really need to know for this particular example here.

The big advantage to using a servlet is that the servlet itself is running *inside* the container in the application server. So if I use up resources in the servlet, I'm using up resources *inside* the container which is what I want when I'm trying to force the container to passivate some Stateful Session Beans.

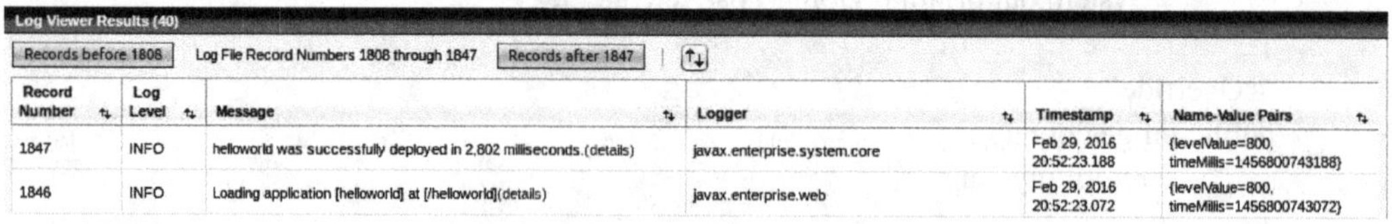
Log Viewer Results (40)

Records before 1808 | Log File Record Numbers 1808 through 1847 | Records after 1847

Record Number	Log Level	Message	Logger	Timestamp	Name-Value Pairs
1847	INFO	helloworld was successfully deployed in 2,802 milliseconds.(details)	javax.enterprise.system.core	Feb 29, 2016 20:52:23.188	{levelValue=800, timeMillis=1456800743188}
1846	INFO	Loading application [helloworld] at [/helloworld](details)	javax.enterprise.web	Feb 29, 2016 20:52:23.072	{levelValue=800, timeMillis=1456800743072}

FIGURE 8.11 Screenshot of server log file from GlassFish—Initial deployment.

A servlet runs in a container in an application server. Most servlets extend the HttpServlet class. Thus, inputs come to the servlet in the form of HTTP messages (from the HTTP protocol).

A servlet that extends the HttpServlet class can handle GET, POST, PUT, and DELETE messages. The HTTPServlet method doGet would handle GET messages, doPut handles PUT messages, doPost handles POST messages, and doDelete handles DELETE messages. These correspond to Create-Read-Update-and-Delete (CRUD) basic operations for managing persistent storage: PUT/doPut and POST/doPost correspond to Create, GET/doGet corresponds to Read, POST/doPost and PUT/doPut correspond to update, and DELETE/doDelete corresponds to Delete.

A servlet can be used to implement RESTful web services. Note that just using a servlet doesn't make a web service RESTful, it has to also be controlling a resource (we'll talk a lot more about this later in Chapter 11). But since a servlet implements the CRUD operations that would be used on persistent storage (an example of a resource), this is usually easy to do. However, servlets have often been considered to be the *assembly language* of RESTful middleware, that is, they're very low level compared to some other RESTful middleware options.

Yes, instead of using a servlet I could have done this by instantiating various EJBs using outside POJO clients (probably better off using Stateful Session Beans since they can hang around a while, Stateless Beans we'd just be using one of a pool and using Singletons would have required having a whole bunch of different Singletons—think about it, exercise for the student ☺). But using a servlet has a couple of advantages. First, using one here allows me to briefly introduce what a servlet is and does, which is yet another useful technology that you the student really want to learn. ☺ Also, the problem with using POJO Clients to call Stateful Session Beans is that even with Stateful Session Beans I would need to fix a way for the Stateful Session Beans to hang around and not finish—big wait loops/sleep, etc.

Also, a servlet has a convenient thing called an *attribute*, that makes it easy to store resources inside the servlet (and thus inside the container). (Attributes can also be used to pass information between servlets.) So I'm making use of this here. What I'm going to do in the servlet is I will create lots of Proxy objects that reference a Stateful Session Bean. Then I will store all those proxies in my servlet attribute, in session scope (we'll talk about that in a second), to use up container resources.

Attributes and parameters in a Java EE web application are related to the *servlet scope* that specifies where that attribute or parameter is available for use. The scope of the servlet is how the servlet maintains a state.

To use attribute information within a scope, these are the routines that one could call:

- SetAttribute(name, object) saves the object along with its name.
- GetAttribute(name) returns the object associated with the specified name
- RemoveAttribute(name) removes the object from the context
- GetAttributeNames() returns an enum containing the names of all attributes
  - Could do:
    - Enumeration the_names=request.getAttributeNames();

Servlets have three scopes:

1. Application (Context) scope—Lifetime of the Web Application. Available while a web application is in service, from start to finish (or reload). Valid during interaction of all users with a particular web application.
   - Javax.servlet.ServletContext interface—defines methods used by a servlet to communicate with the servlet container. There is one context for each web application in a JVM.
   - To access this, you can do:
     - ServletContext mycontext = getServletContext();
     - Or:
       - ServletConfig myconfig = getServletConfig();
         ServletContext mycontext=myconfig.getServletContext();

2. Request scope—Duration of the Request. From when an HTTP request is received by the servlet until an HTTP response is generated by the servlet. Valid during a single user's interaction with a web application during a single HTTP request.
   - Javax.servlet.http.HttpServletRequest interface—provides HTTP requests to HTTP servlets.
     - An HttpServletRequest object is created by the servlet container and passed to doGet, doPut, etc. in the servlet
       - To access this scope, you can call getAttribute(name), etc. on the request object passed into doGet (from inside doGet()), etc.
3. Session—Lifetime of the Client. From when a client establishes a connection with the application until the connection is closed. Valid across multiple HTTP requests from a single user.
   - Javax.servlet.http.HttpSession interface—used to create a session from an HTTP client (one user) to an HTTP server that persists for a specified period of time.
   - HttpSession session = request.getSession();
     - getSession()—gets the session, if there isn't already an HttpSession object, it creates one.
     - If cookies are enabled:
       - It generates a JSESSIONID cookie and value that is used to identify this session when further requests arrive from this client. This JSESSIONID cookie is sent to the Client in a response, the Client uses it in future requests.
       - The HTTP header, if displayed, would include:
         - Set-Cookie: JSESSIONID=..long messy hex value...; Path=/example; Expires= ..date.. ; Secure
         - (the secure attribute means that cookies should only be used in
     - If cookies are not enabled, it uses URL rewriting:
       - A JSESSIONID is added at the end of the URL, and the request is redirected to this URL
         - www.mstuff.com/hello becomes www.mystuff.com/hello/jsessionid=...long messy hex value…

URL rewriting consists of telling the Server to redirect a request from one URL to a different URL. Typically URL rewriting is done so a more readable URL can be the one the Client accesses first, then that URL is redirected to a less readable internal URL (the domain name is the same in both cases, but the rest of the URL would need to be redirected). In this particular case, however, URL rewriting is used to establish a session, so the more readable URL is rerouted to a less readable URL.

In this particular example in Listing 8.95 we are creating a number of proxy objects that reference our interface (from Listing 8.93). We do this by:

    ic.lookup("java:global/helloworld/HelloBean");

Similar to what we saw earlier in Section 8.4.3.1, we are using the *java:global* namespace here. Names in the java:global JNDI namespace are accessible to any application.

Then, again similar to what we saw earlier in Section 8.4.3.1, we must create an appropriate proxy object to represent the HelloWorld interface in the Client. We do this via a downcast from the object reference returned from JNDI:

    example.helloworld.HelloWorld proxyA=
    (example.helloworld.HelloWorld)
    PortableRemoteObject.narrow(object_ref,example.helloworld.HelloWorld.class);

We're storing these proxy objects in an attribute as follows:

```
request.getSession().setAttribute("current_bean"+i,proxyA);
```

This is storing the bean in Session scope. After we store a sufficient quantity of beans to use up the GlassFish resources allocated for the storage of session beans, we will force a passivate, and we will be able to see the passivate in a screenshot of the server log, similar to what we saw previously in Section 8.4.5.3 in regard to PostConstruct and PreDestroy.

LISTING 8.95   A Servlet to Force a Passivate

```
package example.helloworld;
import java.io.*;
import javax.servlet.annotation.WebServlet;
import javax.servlet.*;
import javax.servlet.http.*;

import javax.naming.InitialContext;
import javax.naming.Context;
import javax.naming.NamingException;

import javax.rmi.PortableRemoteObject;

        @WebServlet (
        urlPatterns="/myservlet"
        )
public class myservlet extends HttpServlet {

        public void doGet(HttpServletRequest request,
                HttpServletResponse response)
        throws ServletException, IOException

        {
                // put a text/html header in the HTTP response
                response.setContentType("text/html");

                // Following output will show up in GlassFish log file
                // because System.out is standard output it will show up
                // on the console
                System.out.println("Inside myservlet in doGet method–trying");

                // Write a small simple web page into the HTTP response
                PrintWriter myout = response.getWriter();
                myout.println("inside the servlet");

                example.helloworld.HelloBean mybean;

                String original_bean_counter;

                original_bean_counter = request.getParameter("thecount");

                int bean_counter;
```

```
                    System.out.println("o b c is "+original_bean_counter);
                    bean_counter=Integer.parseInt(original_bean_counter);

                    int i;

                    try {

                      i=0;
                      while (i < bean_counter)
                        {
                                Context ic= new InitialContext();
                                // Keep acquiring proxy objects to point to HelloBean
                                Object object_ref = ic.lookup("java:global/helloworld/HelloBean");
                                example.helloworld.HelloWorld proxyA= (example.helloworld.
                                   HelloWorld)
                                PortableRemoteObject.narrow(object_ref,example.helloworld.
                                   HelloWorld.class);

                                // An attribute in a servlet is an object that can be stored
                                // in request scope, session scope or application scope.
                                // Here the object is being stored in session scope.
                                // Attributes can be used to pass information between
                                // servlets.
                                // setAttribute(name, object) saves the object along with its name.
                                // getAttribute(name) returns the object associated with the
                                // specified name, while removeAttribute(name) removes the
                                // object from the context.
                                request.getSession().setAttribute("current_bean"+i,proxyA);
                                i++;
                        }
                    }

                catch (NamingException ex) {
                            System.out.println("Naming exception");
                            System.out.println("cause is"+ex.getCause());
                            System.out.println("stack trace is ");
                            ex.printStackTrace();
                } catch (Exception ex) {
                            System.out.println("general exception");
                }
        }
}
```

We read the number of proxy objects to store from a parameter on an HTTP GET that is sent to the servlet. This can be done through the browser as follows:

- http://localhost:8080/helloworld/helloworld?thecount=515

2390	INFO	Doing PrePassivate(details)	Feb 29, 2016 21:06:04.306	{levelValue=800, timeMillis=1456801564306}
2389	INFO	Doing PrePassivate(details)	Feb 29, 2016 21:06:04.300	{levelValue=800, timeMillis=1456801564300}
2388	INFO	Doing PrePassivate(details)	Feb 29, 2016 21:06:04.299	{levelValue=800, timeMillis=1456801564299}
2387	INFO	Doing PrePassivate(details)	Feb 29, 2016 21:06:04.293	{levelValue=800, timeMillis=1456801564293}
2386	INFO	Doing PrePassivate(details)	Feb 29, 2016 21:06:04.288	{levelValue=800, timeMillis=1456801564288}
2385	INFO	Doing PrePassivate(details)	Feb 29, 2016 21:06:04.284	{levelValue=800, timeMillis=1456801564284}
2384	INFO	Doing PrePassivate(details)	Feb 29, 2016 21:06:04.281	{levelValue=800, timeMillis=1456801564281}
2383	INFO	Doing PrePassivate(details)	Feb 29, 2016 21:06:04.273	{levelValue=800, timeMillis=1456801564273}
2382	INFO	Doing PrePassivate(details)	Feb 29, 2016 21:06:04.269	{levelValue=800, timeMillis=1456801564269}
2381	INFO	Doing PrePassivate(details)	Feb 29, 2016 21:06:04.267	{levelValue=800, timeMillis=1456801564267}
2380	INFO	Doing PrePassivate(details)	Feb 29, 2016 21:06:04.264	{levelValue=800, timeMillis=1456801564264}
2379	INFO	Doing PrePassivate(details)	Feb 29, 2016 21:06:04.260	{levelValue=800, timeMillis=1456801564260}
2378	INFO	Doing PrePassivate(details)	Feb 29, 2016 21:06:04.253	{levelValue=800, timeMillis=1456801564253}
2377	INFO	Doing PrePassivate(details)	Feb 29, 2016 21:06:04.249	{levelValue=800, timeMillis=1456801564249}
2376	INFO	Doing PrePassivate(details)	Feb 29, 2016 21:06:04.247	{levelValue=800, timeMillis=1456801564247}
2375	INFO	Doing PrePassivate(details)	Feb 29, 2016 21:06:04.187	{levelValue=800, timeMillis=1456801564187}
2374	INFO	Doing PostConstruct(details)	Feb 29, 2016 21:06:04.162	{levelValue=800, timeMillis=1456801564162}
2373	INFO	Doing PostConstruct(details)	Feb 29, 2016 21:06:04.161	{levelValue=800, timeMillis=1456801564161}

FIGURE 8.12   Screenshot of server log file from GlassFish—PrePassivate.

Or it can be sent with a cURL command as follows:

- curl --request GET "http://localhost:8080/helloworld/myservlet?thecount=515"

The variable "thecount" is read as follows:

```
original_bean_counter = request.getParameter("thecount");

int bean_counter;
bean_counter=Integer.parseInt(original_bean_counter);
```

where the getParameter("thecount") acquires the parameter from the GET request, and the parseInt converts it to an integer counter.

We picked 515 here because the GlassFish parameter max-cache-size defaults to 512. The max-cache-size parameter is a hint to GlassFish as to how many session beans GlassFish should support.

After we send the GET to the servlet, we can check the server log file to see that the passivate has occurred. (If for some reason you don't see a passivate in your server log file, just increase the size of the count.)

An example of what you're looking for is shown in the screenshot in Figure 8.12.

CORBA EXERCISES

1. In CORBA, define the IDL required to send an array of structs containing student data from the Client to the Server, where the struct contains a string called "name" and a float called "GPA." The array should be 100 items long.
2. In CORBA, you know that String_var is a wrapper around char *. How might you extract the char * contents out of a String_var wrapper?
3. In CORBA:
   Given:
   interface A {

      ...

   };
   interface B: A {

      ...

   };

```
A_ptr aptr = .... ; // Initialize
B_ptr bptr = B::_narrow(aptr);
```

What does the _narrow() routine do? (Give a short but complete explanation)

4. Does CORBA IDL support an integer data type? Why?
5. Does CORBA idl support multiple inheritance of interfaces?
6. Given:

```
myecho * the_echo = new myecho;
echo_var echo_obj = myecho._this();
```

What is the reason for the _this() routine in the above code?

7. Does an IDL attribute contain any data storage? Why or why not?
8. Create a variable of type "Any" and store "long" data in that variable, using C++ CORBA. Then do it again using Java CORBA.
9. In CORBA using Java, how do you access an IDL constant?
10. Why is it acceptable to use a "/" as part of a valid name in the CORBA Naming Service?
11. Is a naming graph in the CORBA Naming Service allowed to have loops?
12. How does the corbaloc:rir format work?
13. Does CORBA use HTTP?
14. If you want all incoming CORBA requests to be handled by the same servant, how would you set up the CORBA server?
15. You wish to write a function to update, or change your string. Your string is defined as follows in C++/CORBA on the client side:

```
        CORBA::String_var msg1= CORBA::string_dup("Hi there");
```

You will call myfunc as follows:
```
        myfunc(msg1);
```

What is the correct way to define the parameter definition in the servant myfunc?

.NET REMOTING EXERCISES

1. When doing Marshal by Value in .NET Remoting, what is the primary requirement for the remote object being called? How does the process of calling this remote object work?
2. If you're not going through a firewall, and you're always using the same platform, which .NET formatter should you use and why?
3. What happens in .NET Remoting, when using Marshal by Value, if a serialized class has some member that is not serializable?
4. What kind of .NET Remoting channel would you use if you're going through firewalls?
5. What .NET Remoting activation mode would you use if you want one servant to handle all clients?
6. What .NET Remoting activation mode would you use if you're concerned about scalability?
7. Is using one servant to handle all clients good when you're considering scalability?
8. How many channels can you register per port number?
9. How many channels can you register per appdomain?
10. When using asynchronous .NET Remoting with a callback function, are there any restrictions as to where the call to EndInvoke should be located?
11. If you wanted more than one result to be returned to a callback function, how would you do this?
12. What does the [OneWayAttribute] mean?
13. What happens when a lease expires?
14. What are the limitations with using client-activated objects?
15. When should you use a named pipe?

EJB EXERCISES

1. Can you simply say "Java Bean" to mean "EJB"?
2. Is it possible to have one EJB that handles many (maybe all) clients? If so, what kind?

3. What kind of EJB would you use if you are primarily worried about scalability?
4. When would you use a Stateful Session Bean?
5. What possible methods can a client use to access an EJB?
6. In what situation can a client be used to call a local interface?
7. What is meant by "passivating" an EJB?
8. Can a stateless session bean be passivated? Why?
9. Can a singleton session bean be passivated? Why?
10. What are the three contexts (scopes) of a Java servlet? Explain.
11. How does a Java servlet establish and maintain a session? And how is this different from how an EJB maintains a session?
12. How can you tell how many session beans GlassFish will support?
13. How does an asynchronous client retrieve its result when the asynchronous call has finished?
14. What is the purpose of the "@Startup" annotation?
15. Why do you have to do an explicit call to narrow() in the following code ?

```
Context ic= new InitialContext();
Object object_ref = ic.lookup("java:global/helloworld/HelloBean");
    // This narrow downcasts the object_ref to type HelloWorld, this serves as the proxy
HelloWorld proxy= (HelloWorld)
            PortableRemoteObject.narrow(object_ref,HelloWorld.class);
```

CONCEPTUAL QUESTIONS

1. Suppose you want your distributed transactions to be stateless? How would you do this in CORBA? How does this compare to how you would do the same with .NET Remoting or EJBs? What are the pros and cons? Now repeat for stateful transactions?
2. Which one of the technologies we examined is best suited to working on different operating systems? Why? Is this always a good thing? What about supporting different languages?
3. Think about persistent objects, such as objects that provide a front end to a database. What are the pros and cons for CORBA, .NET Remoting, and EJBs for handling persistent objects?
4. Which of these technologies is the hardest to learn? Justify your answer with examples. Which of these technologies is the hardest to use (assuming you have already spent the time to learn it). Justify your answer with examples.
5. Design your own object-oriented/component-based middleware. ☺ Which pieces would you pick from each of these three technologies: CORBA, .NET Remoting, EJBs? Which would you definitely throw out? Write a brief description of how your middleware would work, and justify why it's better than CORBA, .NET Remoting, or EJBs.

BIBLIOGRAPHY

CDC 6600, https://en.wikipedia.org/wiki/CDC_6600 (accessed January 9, 2016).
CDC Cyber Computers, https://en.wikipedia.org/wiki/CDC_Cyber (accessed January 9, 2016).
Erlang. Corba Assisted and User-defined Exceptions. 1997. http://www.erlang.org/doc/apps/orber/ch_exceptions.html (accessed January 9, 2016).
Esangbedo, I.S. Reflection in C# Tutorial. CodeProject. 2007. http://www.codeproject.com/Articles/17269/Reflection-in-C-Tutorial (accessed March 24, 2016).
Etzkorn, L., Sherrill, J., and O'Guin, R. The CORBA Notification Service: Applicability in a Real Time, Embedded Environment, *Embedded Systems Programming* (renamed Embedded Systems Design), 2002. http://www.embedded.com/print/4024457 (accessed March 24, 2017).
Giddings, V., and Beckwith, B. Real-Time CORBA Tutorial. OMG Workshop for Distributed Object Computing for Real Time and Embedded Systems. Arlington, VA, USA. 2003. http://www.omg.org/news/meetings/workshops/RT_2003_Manual/Tutorials/T1_RTCORBA_Giddings.pd (accessed January 31, 2016).
Gupta, S. A Performance Comparison of Windows Communication Foundation (WCF) with Existing Distributed Communication Technologies. MSDN. 2007. https://msdn.microsoft.com/en-us/library/bb310550.aspx (accessed March 18, 2016).

Heartin. Application, Request, Session, and Page Scopes in Servlets and JSPs. 2013. http://www.javajee.com/application-request-session-and-page-scopes-in-servlets-and-jsps (accessed February 10, 2016).

Henning, M. *The Rise and Fall of CORBA*. Vol. 4, Issue 5, 2006, https://queue.acm.org/detail.cfm?id=1142044 (accessed November 28, 2015).

Henning, M., and Vinoski, S. *Advanced CORBA Programming with C++*. 1999. Addison-Wesley, Reading, MA.

Ironside, E., Etzkorn, L., and Zajac, D., Examining CORBA Interoperability, *Dr. Dobbs' Journal*, June, 2001, 111–122.

Java Community Process. JSR 153: Enterprise JavaBeans 2.1. 2003. https://jcp.org/en/jsr/detail?id=153 (accessed February 7, 2016).

Java EE 6 Tutorial. Asynchronous Method Invocation. 2013. http://docs.oracle.com/javaee/6/tutorial/doc/gkkqg.html (accessed February 8, 2016).

Java EE 6 Tutorial. The Lifecycle of Enterprise Beans. 2013. http://docs.oracle.com/javaee/6/tutorial/doc/giplj.html (accessed February 9, 2016).

Java EE 6 Tutorial. Using Scopes. 2013. http://docs.oracle.com/javaee/6/tutorial/doc/gjbbk.html (accessed February 9, 2016).

JavaHowTo. Servlet without web.xml. 2009. http://javahowto.blogspot.com/2009/10/servlet-without-webxml.html (accessed February 7, 2016).

JavaTpoint. Attribute in Servlet. 2016. http://www.javatpoint.com/attribute (accessed February 7, 2016).

Johnson, M. A Beginner's Guide to EJBs. Java World. 1998. http://www.javaworld.com/article/2076777/learn-java/a-beginner-s-guide-to-enterprise-javabeans.html?page=2 (accessed March 26, 2016).

Kobashi Computing. How to Force a Windows Application to be Run with Administrator Privileges. 2013. http://www.kobashicomputing.com/how-to-force-a-windows-application-to-be-run-with-administrator-priviledges (accessed March 26, 2016).

Kozierok, C.M. IP Multicasting. TCPIP Guide. 2005. http://www.tcpipguide.com/free/t_IPMulticasting.htm (accessed January 22, 2016).

Maravitsas, N. EJB Passivation and Activation Example. 2013. www.javacodegeeks.com/2013/08/ejb-passivation-and-activation-example.html (accessed February 7, 2016).

McHale, C. Chapter 6 POA Policies. CORBA Explained Simply. www.ciaranmchale.com/corba-explained-simply/poa-policies.html (accessed January 24, 2016).

McHale, C. Chapter 10 Interoperable Object Reference. CORBA Explained Simply. http://www.ciaranmchale.com/corba-explained-simply/interoperable-object-reference.html (accessed January 19, 2016).

McHale, C. Chapter 12 The Corbaloc and Corbaname URLs. http://www.ciaranmchale.com/corba-explained-simply/the-corbaloc-and-corbaname-urls.html#toc63 (accessed January 19, 2016).

Mehra, P. Remote Object Lifetime in .NET. C#Corner. 2010. http://www.c-sharpcorner.com/UploadFile/puranindia/remote-object-lifetime-in-net/ (accessed March 26, 2016).

MSDN. Remotable Objects. 2003. https://msdn.microsoft.com/en-us/library/aa720494(v=vs.71).aspx (accessed March 24, 2016).

MSDN. Lifetime Leases. 2006. https://msdn.microsoft.com/en-us/library/23bk23zc(v=vs.85).aspx (accessed March 26, 2016).

MSDN. Remoting Example: Asynchronous Remoting. 2006. https://msdn.microsoft.com/en-us/library/0sa925ka(v=vs.85).aspx (accessed March 26, 2016).

MSDN. .NET Framework Remoting Overview. 2010. https://msdn.microsoft.com/en-us/library/kwdt6w2k(v=vs.100).aspx (accessed March 18, 2016).

MSDN. Application Manifests. 2014. https://msdn.microsoft.com/en-us/library/aa374191(v=vs.85).aspx (accessed March 24, 2016).

MSDN. 2.2.6 Lease State. [MS-NRLS]: .NET Remoting: Lifetime Services Extension. 2015. https://msdn.microsoft.com/en-us/library/cc236920.aspx (accessed March 26, 2016).

MSDN. Assembly Manifest. 2015. https://msdn.microsoft.com/en-us/library/1w45z383(v=vs.110).aspx (accessed March 24, 2016).

MSDN. Blocking Application Execution Using an AsyncWaitHandle. 2015. https://msdn.microsoft.com/en-us/library/ms228962(v=vs.110).aspx (accessed March 26, 2016).

MSDN. Calling Synchronous Methods Asynchronously. 2015. https://msdn.microsoft.com/en-us/library/2e08f6yc(v=vs.110).aspx (accessed March 26, 2016).

MSDN. Manifest Generation in Visual Studio 2015. 2015. https://msdn.microsoft.com/en-us/library/ms235229.aspx (accessed March 24, 2016).

MSDN. System Reflection Namespace. 2015. https://msdn.microsoft.com/en-us/library/system.reflection(v=vs.110).aspx (accessed March 24, 2016).

MSDN. Application Domains. 2016. https://msdn.microsoft.com/en-us/library/2bh4z9hs(v=vs.110).aspx (accessed March 18, 2016).

Object Management Group. CORBA. http://www.corba.org/ (accessed March 24, 2017).

Object Management Group. Common Object Request Broker Architecture (CORBA) Specification, Version 3.3 Part 1: CORBA Interfaces. 2012. http://www.omg.org/spec/CORBA/3.3/Interfaces/PDF/ (accessed January 22, 2016).

Object Management Group. History of CORBA. 2015. http://www.omg.org/gettingstarted/history_of_corba.htm (accessed November 28, 2015).

OmniORB. Chapter 12 The Dynamic Skeleton Interface. http://www.cl.cam.ac.uk/research/dtg/attarchive/omniORB/doc/3.0/omniORB/omniORB012.html (accessed January 31, 2016).

OmniORB3. Chapter 4 Interoperable Naming Service. http://www.cl.cam.ac.uk/research/dtg/attarchive/omniORB/doc/3.0/omniORB/omniORB004.html (accessed January 19, 2016).

OmniORB4. Chapter 6 Interoperable Naming Service. http://omniorb.sourceforge.net/omni40/omniORB/omniORB006.html (accessed January 19, 2016).

OmniORB4 The omniNames CORBA Naming Service. 2014. http://omniorb.sourceforge.net/omni42/omni-Names.html (accessed January 22, 2016).

Oracle. Chapter 22 Enterprise Beans. The Java EE 6 Tutorial. 2013. https://docs.oracle.com/javaee/6/tutorial/doc/gijsz.html (accessed February 7, 2016).

Oracle. CORBA Technology and the Java Platform Standard Edition. http://docs.oracle.com/javase/7/docs/technotes/guides/idl/corba.html (accessed November 28, 2015).

Oracle. max-cache-size. GlassFish Server 3.1 Application Deployment Guide. 2010. https://docs.oracle.com/cd/E18930_01/html/821-2417/beauo.html (accessed February 29, 2016).

Oracle. Oracle8i Enterprise JavaBeans and CORBA Developer's Guide, Chapter 3, https://docs.oracle.com/cd/A81042_01/DOC/java.816/a81356/corba.htm (accessed November 28, 2015).

Oracle. Serializable Objects. http://docs.oracle.com/javase/jndi/tutorial/objects/storing/serial.html (accessed January 31, 2016).

Oracle. Simple EJBs 3.0 Examples. 2016. https://docs.oracle.com/cd/E13222_01/wls/docs100/ejb30/examples.html (accessed February 7, 2016).

Oracle. Using the Dynamic Invocation Interface. https://docs.oracle.com/cd/E13203_01/tuxedo/tux91/creclient/dii.htm#1013394 (accessed January 31, 2016).

Oracle. The @Remove Method. The Java EE 6 Tutorial. 2010. https://docs.oracle.com/cd/E19798-01/821-1841/bnboi/index.html (accessed February 9, 2016).

Oracle. What Is a Session Bean. 2013. http://docs.oracle.com/javaee/6/tutorial/doc/gipjg.html (accessed February 2, 2016).

PCReview. .NET Remoting TCP or HTTP? 2005. http://www.pcreview.co.uk/threads/net-remoting-tcp-or-http.1234716/ (accessed March 25, 2016).

Programmers Stack Exchange. Why Do Languages Such as C and C++ Not Have Garbage Collection While Java Does? 2016. http://programmers.stackexchange.com/questions/113177/why-do-languages-such-as-c-and-c-not-have-garbage-collection-while-java-does (accessed January 11, 2016).

Puder, A., and Romer, K. *MICO: An Open Source CORBA Implementation*, Morgan-Kaufmann, San Francisco, CA, 2000.

Puder, A., Romer, K., and Pilhofer, F. *Distributed Systems Architecture: A Middleware Approach*, Morgan-Kauffman, San Francisco, CA, 2006.

Sami, A. WCF Comparison with Web Services and .NET Remoting. CodeProject. 2010. http://www.codeproject.com/Articles/45698/WCF-Comparison-with-Web-Services-and-NET-Remoting (accessed March 18, 2016).

Schmidt, D.C. Dynamic CORBA: Part 1: The Dynamic Invocation Interface. Dr. Dobb's. 2002. http://www.drdobbs.com/dynamic-corba-part-1-the-dynamic-invocat/184403833?pgno=2 (accessed January 31, 2016).

Schmidt, D.C. Overview of ACE. 2011. http://www.cs.wustl.edu/~schmidt/ACE-overview.html (accessed January 14, 2016).

Schmidt, D. TAO Interoperable Naming Service. http://www.dre.vanderbilt.edu/~schmidt/DOC_ROOT/TAO/docs/INS.html#oir (accessed January 19, 2016).

Schmidt, D.C., and Vinoski, S. The History of OMG C++ Mapping, C/C++ Users Journal C++ Experts Forum. 2000. https://www.dre.vanderbilt.edu/~schmidt/PDF/cuj-1.pdf (accessed January 12, 2016).

Schuster, W. Andrew Watson on the State of OMG, UML, CORBA, DDS. 2012. http://www.infoq.com/interviews/watson-omg (accessed November 28, 2015).

Siegel, J. *CORBA 3: Fundamentals and Programming*, Wiley, Hoboken, NJ, 2000.

Stack Overflow. Assigning a String of Characters to a Char Array. 2012. http://stackoverflow.com/questions/10088661/assigning-a-string-of-characters-to-a-char-array (accessed January 14, 2016).

Stack Overflow. Difference between Application Manifest and Assembly Manifest. 2010. http://stackoverflow.com/questions/3476089/difference-between-application-manifest-and-assembly-manifest (accessed March 24, 2016).

Stack Overflow. Difference between Java Bean and EJBs. 2010. http://stackoverflow.com/questions/2460048/difference-between-java-bean-and-enterprise-java-beans (accessed January 31, 2016).

Stack Overflow. Get the Client Orb Address and Port with Use of IIOP. 2014. http://stackoverflow.com/questions/14479816/corba-get-the-client-orb-address-and-port-with-use-of-iiop (accessed January 19, 2016).

Stack Overflow. IAsyncResult.AsyncWaitHandle.WaitOne() Completes Ahead of Callback. 2010. http://stackoverflow.com/questions/4099318/iasyncresult-asyncwaithandle-waitone-completes-ahead-of-callback (accessed March 26, 2016).

Stack Overflow. .Net Remoting, Issue with Firewall. 2010. http://stackoverflow.com/questions/2297663/net-remoting-issue-with-firewall (accessed March 26, 2016)

Stack Overflow. Servlet versus RESTful. 2011. http://stackoverflow.com/questions/7874695/servlet-vs-restful (accessed February 10, 2016).

Stack Overflow. What Is the Difference between Managed C++ and C++/CLI. 2010. http://stackoverflow.com/questions/2443811/what-is-the-difference-between-managed-c-and-c-cli (accessed March 18, 2016).

Tutorials Point. Callbacks—EJB. 2016. http://www.tutorialspoint.com/ejb/ejb_callbacks.htm (accessed February 8, 2016).

Tutorials Point. EJB Tutorial. 2006. http://www.tutorialspoint.com/ejb/ (accessed February 7, 2016).

ul Hassan, S.N. .NET Remoting with an Easy Example. CodeProject. 2006. http://www.codeproject.com/Articles/14791/NET-Remoting-with-an-easy-example (accessed March 26, 2016).

Vogel, A., and Duddy, K. *Java Programming with CORBA*, 2nd Edition, 1998.

Whiley, Java versus C++ Performance. 2012. http://whiley.org/2012/08/13/java-versus-c-performance/ (accessed January 11, 2016).

Wikipedia. Create, Read, Update, and Delete. 2016. https://en.wikipedia.org/wiki/Create,_read,_update_and_delete (accessed February 10, 2016).

Section IV

Middleware Using Web Services

9 Web Services Architectures

In this section, we examine various architectures that typically expect to make use of the World Wide Web to provide application services. This is done by providing web interfaces to application services. Applications with these web interfaces are typically called *web services*.

We look first at Service-Oriented Architectures (SOAs), a paradigm by which various web services are called by another application to provide sub-parts of that application's needed work.

Then we will do a high-level comparison of the two most popular technologies for web services: non-RESTful web services and RESTful web services. In order to do this comparison we will first examine what is meant by a RESTful architecture.

Later on in this chapter and in Chapter 10 we will do an in-depth look at several non-RESTful and RESTful web services technologies.

9.1 SERVICE-ORIENTED ARCHITECTURES

The first thing to do here is to define what a Service-Oriented Architecture is. I'm going to give you a brief high-level description just to get you started, then we'll delve down into the formal definitions. Here's my description, given as a sort of example:

- If application A does a particular task A, then application A can define an interface that allows access to the functionality provided by task A. This interface would be called "service A" and would be described by a *service description*. Typically, this service would be accessible through a particular web service technology (maybe WSDL/SOAP or perhaps JAX-RS).
- Then if application B does a particular task B, then application B can define an interface that allows access to the functionality provided by task B. This interface would be called "service B" and would be described by a "service description." Again, service B would be accessible by a particular web service technology.
- Now application C calls service A and service B (as well as potentially other services) using the appropriate web service technology in each case, to perform part of the work that application C needs in order to do its own task.
- We may also have application D that calls service A (as well as potentially other services) using the appropriate web service technology in each case, to perform part of the work that application D needs in order to do its own task.

Figure 9.1 shows a diagram of a service-oriented architecture.

The main advantage of SOA is reusability. Since each web service has a well-defined interface and is (typically) accessible using a well-known web service technology, any application can call that well-defined interface, and thus make use of that web service. The individual web service applications, therefore, are highly decoupled and can vary independently of other web service applications, as long as they support their defined interface. This promotes reusability but also aids in improving maintainability and reliability.

Another advantage is that since the interfaces (service A and service B in our example above) are defined using standard web-service technologies, internally the applications (application A and application B) can be written in different languages and can run on different operating systems.

New applications can easily access these web services, since they have well-defined interfaces. So integrating perhaps several of these web services together into newer, larger applications is relatively easy.

However, there are many different technologies used to create these web services. Some of these web service technologies are able to call other web service technologies and some are not. There are

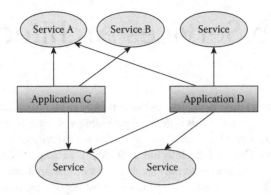

FIGURE 9.1   Service-oriented architecture.

two main categories of web services, one category is called "non-RESTful" and the other is "RESTful." Within a category, the web services can interact with each other, that is, for example, a RESTful technology can call another RESTful technology. But between categories they are not interoperable, that is, a non-RESTful technology cannot call a RESTful technology.

It can be difficult to determine which technology is the best for your particular application. Also, you have to learn these technologies before you use them, and there's quite a lot to learn. ☺

Before we get into more depth about SOAs, I do want to say that although typically SOAs are defined in terms of web services, and that's the common assumption, it's also possible to do the same thing with CORBA or EJBs or .NET Remoting. If you look at the SOA architectural style as described in the diagram in Figure 9.1, as long as you have well-defined interfaces, and your new applications calls these interfaces in order to chain them together, perhaps with glue code, and perhaps some additional code in order to do new work, you have a pretty good argument that you have an SOA. This kind of thing where you're using Distributed-Object Components would work well inside a company behind a firewall. Or perhaps you're working in some kind of large embedded system (for a small embedded system I think a full SOA implementation might be overkill).

9.1.1   IN-DEPTH LOOK AT SERVICE-ORIENTED ARCHITECTURE

According to the Open Group (2016) (a global consortium that develops open, vendor-neutral information technology [IT] standards), an SOA is an architectural style that supports service orientation. Service orientation is a way of thinking in terms of the outcomes of services, and how they can be developed and combined. In this definition, a *service* is a repeatable business activity that can be logically represented; the Open Group gives the examples: "check customer credit," and "provide weather data." Further, a service is self-contained, may be composed of other services, and consumers of the service treat the service as a black box.

According to the Open Group, when SOA was first defined, advocates of SOA claimed that SOA would replace all traditional IT architecture, while traditionalists claimed it was a rehash of ideas about loose coupling and encapsulation. The Open Group claims that neither position is correct. Rather, SOA is a distinct architectural style which is a major improvement over earlier ideas, although it includes some of the earlier ideas. Also, traditional architectural methods must be employed in order to obtain maximum benefit from using SOA.

Another definition of Service-Oriented Architecture comes from OASIS, Mackenzie et al. (2006):

> A paradigm for organizing and utilizing distributed capabilities that may be under the control of different ownership domains. It provides a uniform means to offer, discover, interact with and use capabilities to produce desired effects consistent with measurable preconditions and expectations.

According to Mackenzie et al. (2006), the focus of SOAs is to perform a task (business function). This is different from some other paradigms, such as object-oriented architectures, where the focus is more on structure of the solution—in the case of an object-oriented architecture, the focus is on how to package data inside an object. They say that with an SOA, although you can think of methods as providing access to services, the focus is not on the methods. They believe that SOAs map well into the normal ways that human activity behaves, because both humans and SOA work by delegation. Also, with both humans and SOA, ownership boundaries are an important consideration. SOAs address ownership boundaries through service descriptions and service interfaces. SOA provides reuse of externally developed frameworks by providing easy interoperability between systems.

Generally speaking, in order to perform a task, an SOA groups services on different systems, possibly running on different operating systems, possibly written using different programming languages. Most current SOA-based applications employ a synchronous client/server-type architectural style. A client issues requests to one or more servers, and the client blocks until the servers reply to these requests. However, Chou (2008) argues that this works well when the application is centrally managed, but even though the software components themselves are loosely coupled, at a business process level this kind of central management can cause tight coupling between different business processes. Apparently, the argument here is that a different business process would have to interact with the central manager of the current business process in order to get its own work done.

Chou (2008) also argues that an asynchronous event-driven architectural style is better for real time or proactive systems, since business processes are treated as a sequence of events, and therefore different business processes that have little relationship with each other, except for a few individual shared tasks, do not have to obey the same kind of centralized management.

In an asynchronous event-driven architecture, an event message carries a state change to an event server. The event server passes these events along to the servers, possibly with value added. Servers may then generate messages for other event servers. This is an example of a publish/subscribe architecture. We talked about variations of this and other message-oriented/group messaging paradigms back in Section 2.2; we'll look at them again later on in Chapter 15.

Note, however, that SOAs don't solve all your problems. According to Mulesoft (2015), in the early 2000s many companies thought SOAs were going to solve all their IT infrastructure problems, and they spent millions of dollars on top-down SOA initiatives.

In other words, Service-Oriented Architecture was the current fad that was going to make software development times predictable, and make software less complex and more secure. Just like all the other previous software paradigms that were going to solve all software problems: design patterns and object-oriented programming were going to do this back in the 1990s. Structured programming was going to do it back in the 1980s. ☺ Each new wonderful software thing gets overhyped, can't live up to overblown expectations, and people get disappointed.

By 2009, many of these top-down SOA initiatives had failed. Mulesoft (2015) says that some studies estimate only around 20% of these initiatives were fully completed. By 2009, this resulted in a backlash, for example, Maines (2009) stated:

> It's time to accept reality. SOA fatigue has turned into SOA disillusionment. Business people no longer believe that SOA will deliver spectacular benefits. "SOA" has become a bad word. It must be removed from our vocabulary.

Maine went on to say that instead of concentrating on services, which is what the SOA acronym stands for, people had gotten involved in technology debates, including non-RESTful (WS-*) versus RESTful.

Mulesoft (2015) claims that it wasn't SOA that was at fault, it was the top-down approach to SOA and that a bottom-up approach was needed instead. Reasons why the top-down approach didn't work:

- Companies gave the responsibility of SOA adoption to a single team
- This team was pressured to get SOA in place as quickly as possible

- This pressure led to adoption of a proprietary SOA governance product (Oracle, IBM, etc.)
  - Developers were seldom consulted about which proprietary product to choose
  - These proprietary products were very expensive
- Developers were tasked with moving to SOA in addition to their regular work
  - And now they had to employ a new mandated tool

The basic idea behind a top-down approach is that the group responsible for SOA identifies candidate services throughout the company, based on how the business itself works and interacts.

A bottom-up approach is where the process of moving to SOA starts with developers, and moving to SOA is done in a lightweight manner to begin with, primarily based on wrapping existing applications. This wrapping work is scheduled as part of developers' normal work tasks. One good way to work this is to begin by looking for problem areas; if you look into wrapping an existing application with a web service, it's perhaps also a good time to fix any problems in the application. Thus moving to an SOA becomes also a refactoring of your existing code, and can improve quality in other ways than just imposing the SOA architectural style.

However, Pomares (2010) quotes Rob Barry from SearchSOA as saying that a bottom-up approach has been criticized for requiring excessive updates and re-work later on. He also says, however, that the top-down approach has been faulted for taking excessive time to produce results due to the extensive planning required. Also, ServiceOrientation.com (2015) says that the top-down strategy requires a large initial investment because of the up-front analysis required, but that a bottom-up strategy results in services that have a shorter lifespan and require more maintenance and refactoring.

Before we stop looking at what an SOA really is, and what it gets you, we need to look at one more term that often shows up when SOAs are discussed: *mashup*. There are multiple definitions of mashup. One definition from Merrill (2009) says that:

> Mashups are an exciting genre of interactive Web applications that draw upon content retrieved from external data sources to create entirely new and innovative services.

According to Merrill, *mashup* was borrowed from popular music, where a mashup is a new song that is mixed from two different source songs.

Raj (2013) uses a more general definition:

> ...mashup is a smart blending of different resources from distributed sources.

According to Merrill, a mashup consists of the content providers, the mashup site, and a web browser. The work of combining the different sources can be done at the mashup site, or alternately in the web browser.

Chapman (2009) says that a mashup:

> ...implies easy, fast integration, frequently using Open APIs and data sources to produce results that were not the original reason for producing the raw source data.

So what is the difference between a mashup and an SOA?

McKendrick (2006) quotes Hendrick as saying that one difference is that a mashup must be web-based, whereas an SOA need not be web-based (note that this goes against the more common assumptions about SOA). McKendrick also says that mashups are developed in informal ways, whereas SOAs are developed in a formal manner. (I note myself that there may be some gray area in SOAs being developed formally when one is using bottom-up development, depending on the company.)

Perhaps, the clearest distinction between a mashup and an SOA that I've seen comes from Hiroshige (2010):

Service-Oriented Architecture (SOA) is one way of architecting a Mashup or any other composite solution. SOA makes it easy to combine the existing applications because they are already exposing their functionality or data via their Services. You could (not that you'd want to) also architect your combined solution in a non-Service-Oriented way—it would still be a composite application even without the SOA.

9.1.2 The Relationship between SOA and Cloud Computing

There is a question as to whether an SOA is necessary for an application to be moved to the cloud. There is some variation in opinion as to how heavily interrelated the two paradigms are. For example, Raines (2009) says:

Cloud computing and SOA can be pursued independently, or concurrently as complementary activities.

According to IBM (2009):

Some pundits have said that cloud is a flavor of SOA or a replacement for SOA. Neither of these statements positions the relationship between cloud and SOA accurately. They are actually complementary. Each supplies unique capability and functionality, and the two work together to provide an enterprise agility solution.

IBM (2009) also says:

SOA is an architectural approach that creates services that can be shared and reused

but further:

on the other hand, cloud computing is about providing ease of access to and usage of services.

And finally:

Together SOA and cloud can provide a complete services-based solution.

However, others find SOA and cloud computing more closely related. Krill (2009) quotes Cuomo, CTO of IBM WebSphere:

SOA is an architectural style for building applications, loosely coupled, allowing composition. Can we build a datacenter infrastructure on SOA principles? Yes, and that's the cloud, so it's a service-oriented infrastructure. It's taking that architectural principle of SOA and applying it to an infrastructure.

Mulholland et al. (2008) from HP said:

However, without Service-Oriented Architectures (SOA), organizations will find it almost impossible to reach the cloud.

Let's look in a little more in depth at these differences in opinion. Perhaps I should say first, none of these people are wrong, they're just looking at things from different perspectives.

First of all, what is a cloud? Generally this refers to a collection of computers (often organized into what is called a datacenter) that can be used to run applications and store data. A cloud can be a public cloud, that is, some organization allows customers to run their applications on the organization's computers, and store their data on the organization's computers. The organization provides system administrators (cloud administrators) to make sure the cloud runs correctly, and to ensure security. The customers pay a fee for using the public cloud. A cloud can be a private cloud, that is, an organization sets up some computers separately and allows others in the company to run their applications on these computers and to store data on these computers. Some system administrators who work for the company are tasked with making sure this separate group of computers run correctly and have good security. With either private cloud or public cloud, if one computer gets too busy, an application can be moved to another less busy computer.

So a cloud, loosely speaking, is a group of computers. An SOA is a distributed architecture where individual applications are loosely coupled together through access of well-defined interfaces, typically implemented as web services.

So it's easy to see that you can get a lot of bang for the buck if you run your SOA on a cloud. Each separate computer could potentially run a different web service application, and each web service application can potentially be moved to a different computer if the computer it's currently on gets too busy.

9.1.3 IMPLEMENTATIONS OF SERVICE-ORIENTED ARCHITECTURES

It is easy to argue that the implementation of the Sailboat Marina project from Section 1.5, using JAX-WS, as shown in Section 18.2 is an example of an SOA, at least when the graphical user interface (GUI) from Section 18.2.3 is used. From Listing 18.5, the Java self-publisher, we see that each of the services is located at a different URL. The GUI shown in Listing 18.16 accesses all these services at the different URLs in order to do its task of controlling the marina for its user, the marina manager. Note that Chapter 18 is provided in the online resources.

You can't actually see the URLs in Listing 18.16 because they're inside the wsimport-generated clients. See Listing 9.1 below, this is a portion of the wsimport-generated client to access the iddisplayitall service. You can see that it's grabbing the interface from the iddisplayitall URL:

```
url = new URL("http://localhost:8084/iddisplay?wsdl");
```

LISTING 9.1   Wsimport-Generated Support Code for JAX-WS

```
/**
 * This class was generated by the JAX-WS RI.
 * JAX-WS RI 2.2.4-b01
 * Generated source version: 2.2
 *
 */
@WebServiceClient(name = "iddisplayitallService", targetNamespace = "http://marina/",
      wsdlLocation = "http://localhost:8084/iddisplay?wsdl")
public class IddisplayitallService
  extends Service
{
  private final static URL IDDISPLAYITALLSERVICE_WSDL_LOCATION;
  private final static WebServiceException IDDISPLAYITALLSERVICE_EXCEPTION;
  private final static QName IDDISPLAYITALLSERVICE_QNAME = new
  QName("http://marina/", "iddisplayitallService");
  static {
    URL url = null;
    WebServiceException e = null;
    try {
      url = new URL("http://localhost:8084/iddisplay?wsdl");
    } catch (MalformedURLException ex) {
      e = new WebServiceException(ex);
    }
    IDDISPLAYITALLSERVICE_WSDL_LOCATION = url;
    IDDISPLAYITALLSERVICE_EXCEPTION = e;
  }
}
```

It's not possible really to argue that individual console clients accessing individual services represent an SOA, because they are using only one service. The basic idea behind an SOA is that you're making use of multiple services to perform a single task, which is what the JAX-WS GUI does.

Oddly enough, with our other java-based Sailboat Marina implementations, even though they have many similarities with the JAX-WS implementation, it's perhaps not as clear up front that they're examples of SOAs, even when using their GUIs, because they're loaded onto the same web server in the same war file, and use the same port number (port 8080). If you moved them to different port numbers or, better, to different base URLs then the argument they're an SOA becomes clearer. However, they do have slightly different URLs, for example:

- http://localhost:8080/marina/restful/create

versus

- http://localhost:8080/marina/restful/delete

Let's leave as an exercise for the reader whether our other Sailboat Marina examples or for that matter our Environmental Monitoring examples sufficiently meet the requirements to be considered an SOA.

9.2 RESTFUL ARCHITECTURAL STYLE AND NON-RESTFUL VERSUS RESTFUL WEB SERVICES

In this section, we will examine what is meant by the RESTful architectural style, and then we will examine RESTful and non-RESTful web services in this context.

9.2.1 RESTful Architectural Style

According to Fielding (2000), the RESTful architectural style focuses on:

> …the roles of components, the constraints upon their interaction with other components, and their interpretation of significant data elements…

The RESTful architectural style consists of constraints on data, constraints on the interpretation of data, constraints on components, and constraints on connectors between components.

Let us look first at the interpretation of information and data within the context of the RESTful architectural style. This view consists of *resources* and *representations*.

When using a RESTful architectural style, information is described as a *resource*, which is defined as the target of a hypertext reference. A resource can be empty, or it can be a collection of entities. A resource can be static, or it can change over time. One resource is distinguished from another resource by its mapping, that is, its hypertext reference. Fielding gives the example that a version of source code can have a hypertext reference that says it is the "latest revision." There can also be a separate hypertext reference that refers to "revision number 1.2.7." Note that when revision 1.2.7 is first released, the hypertext "latest revision" may refer to the same code that "revision number 1.2.7" refers to. However, this is a temporary condition since when revision 1.2.8 is released, the hypertext "latest revision" will no longer be referring to "revision number 1.2.7."

The "hypertext reference" used to specify the resource target is in the format of a URL or a URN.

A "representation" in the RESTful architectural style consists of the data and metadata that is used to describe the data (Fielding also mentions that sometimes additional metadata is used to describe the metadata in order to ensure message integrity). Typically, a "representation" would refer to an HTTP message plus its contents, or alternately a document or file (an HTTP message could of course include a document or file). There can be control data included in a representation (in this case an HTTP message) that specifies the purpose of the message. The format of the data in a representation is defined by an Internet Media type (MIME type). An example of a "representation" would be a JPEG image or an HTML document.

The simplest REST component is a "user agent"—an example would be a web browser that accesses some kind of server using a client connector. The server that is accessed would use a server connector to reply. (We'll look at connectors next.) Another kind of component is a proxy component that forwards requests and responses between client and server components.

The RESTful architectural style includes "connectors" that define how resources are accessed and how the representations of the resources are transferred. The concept of connectors is used to hide underlying networking issues, so a connector is a communication abstraction. Examples of RESTful connectors include: "client," "server," "cache," and "resolver." A "client" makes a request, while a "server" listens for connections and returns a response. A "cache" can be used by either client or server to save information so that it doesn't have to be regenerated again, or perhaps sent across the network again, in cases where the information has been unchanged since its previous generation or transmission. A "resolver" is an address translator that converts a name to a full address.

Thus, when considering an HTML web page, this is a resource (since it is located at a URL) and contains a representation (the HTML itself). The internet media type transferred in the HTTP response message along with this HTML data would be "text/html," this is an example of the representation metadata.

The RESTful architectural style possesses the following constraints:

- *Client/Server:* Separation of concerns, exemplified by a client–server architecture. The idea is that different components can evolve independently—the user interface in the client can evolve separately from the server, and the server is simpler.
- *Stateless:* The client–server interaction is stateless. There is no stored context on the server. Any session information must be kept by the client.
- *Cacheable:* Data in a response (a response to a previous request) is labeled as cacheable or non-cacheable. If it is cacheable, the client (or an intermediary) may reuse that for the same kind of request in the future.
- *Uniform Interface:* There is a uniform interface between components. In practice, there are four interface constraints:
  - Resource identification—requests identify the resources they are operating on (by a URI, for example)
  - Resource manipulation through the representation of the resource—when a client or server that has access to a resource, it has enough information based on understanding the representation of the resource to be able to modify that resource
  - Messages are self-descriptive—the message contains enough information to allow a client or server to handle the message, this is normally done through the use of Internet Media types (MIME types)
  - Use of hypermedia to change the state of the application—for example, the server provides hyperlinks that the client uses to make state transitions
- *Layered System:* Components are organized in hierarchical layers, the components are only aware of the layer within which the interaction is occurring. Thus, a client connecting to a server is not aware of any intermediate connections.
  - Intermediate filter components can change the message while it is in transit: because the message is self-descriptive and the semantics are visible, the filter components understand enough about the message to modify it
- *Code on Demand:* Code on demand is *optionally* supported, that is, clients can download scripts that extend their functionality.

So a RESTful web service is client/server-based, does not store state. The results of a request from client to server can be cached in the client. It has a uniform interface with self-descriptive messages, based on hypermedia. Oh, and the client and server aren't aware of intermediate connections between the two of them.

Note that these are the characteristics of the World Wide Web. It is client/server-based, consisting primarily of browsers and web servers. Each call to a web server is considered independent of another such call. Its uniform interface is provided by the HTTP protocol. The data format is specified by Internet Media types, which are included in the message, so the message is self-descriptive. And so forth.

Fielding et al. (1999) designed the HTTP 1.1 protocol according to the principles of the RESTful architectural style.

9.2.2   NON-RESTFUL VERSUS RESTFUL WEB SERVICES

Now that we have a handle on what a RESTful architecture is, let's ignore "RESTful" web services for now, and examine what a non-RESTful architecture is. Presumably a non-RESTful web service would be one that did not follow the RESTful architecture outlined in Section 9.2.1.

So let's look at the constraints from Section 9.2.1 and compare them to non-RESTful web services one by one. Let's take resources to begin with. Would a non-RESTful web service (such as JAX-WS) use a URL to access a resource? Hmmm. Well, it *might*. In fact, very likely it would. If you look at the JAX-WS code in Chapter 10 you will see numerous examples of this. Would a non-RESTful web service use Internet Media types (MIME types) to describe data? Er, ah, yes, very likely. If you look at Section 10.2.5 you will see that for SOAP (which is the data format used in JAX-WS), the kind of data format being used is shown using an Internet Media type. Also, the file data and etc. is described using Internet Media Types.

So do we have clients, servers, caches, and resolvers in non-RESTful web services? Clients and servers we certainly do have. Since a non-RESTful web service runs on top of the World Wide Web, and the World Wide Web is RESTful and possesses caches and resolvers, then you can't say those wouldn't be in use. Note however, that one important concept here is that the non-RESTful web service runs *on top of* the World Wide Web and the lower level protocols of the World Wide Web, such as HTTP are treated as a *transparent lower layer*. We'll come back to this concept in a bit, but it's one of the main differentiators between non-RESTful and RESTful web services.

Before we address the layering issue, however, let's look at the individual constraints. Client/server? Yes of course, we have those in non-RESTful web services. Stateless? Well, you *can* do non-RESTful web services without storing a state on the server, or you could store a state. Since you *can* do without a state, let's let that one go. Cacheable? Yes, it could be at a transparent lower layer. Or if you wanted, your non-RESTful web service could implement a cache (although it's not required).

Uniform interface. Well, this one is a bit arguable to my mind in regard to a RESTful interface (let's wait on non-RESTful for a moment) because it depends on what you mean by "interface." An interface to Fielding's way of thinking primarily consisted of the standard HTTP messages sent to a URL. Obviously, you can define any interface in terms of HTTP GETs and HTTP POSTs, etc. But this doesn't say anything about the kinds of data you'd be sending or receiving or for that matter the purpose of the interface. Fielding said that the *format* of the data would be specified using Internet Media types but not the purpose. So since everything is specified using HTTP GETs and POSTs, etc., and Internet Media Types, then the interfaces are all uniform in a RESTful architecture, even if they're sending wildly different kinds of data and have wildly different purposes.

You can *not* claim a uniform interface in a non-RESTful web service, since it treats the HTTP as a transparent lower layer. If you're using JAX-WS/WSDL (we'll see these in Chapter 10), then you use the WSDL to define your interfaces, which consists of a series of operations with parameters and return values. So each interface is different from all the other interfaces.

So we've managed to differentiate non-RESTful from RESTful, but for completeness let's look at the final two constraints. Layered system, well yes, non-RESTful is layered in the sense that it has transparent lower layers. In terms of transparent proxies in between client and server in a non-RESTful system, if it's happening at the web services layer above the HTTP layer, then it would have to be done with an intermediate proxy having a different URL than the final server, so in that sense the client would have to know (but the client might not know that you substituted a proxy and put the actual server at a different URL). Code on demand. Well, hmmm. This one's optional so let's ignore it. ☺ (You could say that any web page containing JavaScript inside <script> tags could be an example of code on demand.)

However, let's zoom in more on what is generally meant when people talk about non-RESTful web services. Let's look now at the common definition that a "non-RESTful web service" defines a remote procedure call using a specifically defined interface, where this remote procedure call treats the HTTP protocol as a transparent lower networking layer (it doesn't have to know anything about HTTP, it just assumes it's there and it works), and uses the SOAP messaging protocol (we will see SOAP in Section 10.1) that includes an XML-type data format. This definition is fairly widely accepted in the industry.

However, this is not a totally clear definition. For example, a web service that uses Web Services Description Language (WSDL) to define the interface (we will see WSDL in Section 10.2), which commonly employs SOAP, would be considered "non-RESTful" by this definition. However, it is possible to configure a WSDL interface that runs directly using HTTP (in which case it could be called RESTful). It's also possible to define a WSDL interface that runs on top of TCP and bypasses HTTP altogether—in this case the data would be sent in binary, and would normally not be considered either RESTful or non-RESTful.

Also, it's possible to have a remote procedure call and use SOAP, but have the data sent directly over TCP—we saw this earlier in .Net Remoting. But .Net Remoting is not a web service, but rather is object-oriented. So we're making some very small distinctions here.

However, since it's a common definition—even though there are problems with it—we will use it.

There are several advantages to requiring a well-defined remote procedure call-type interface similar to what you would get using WSDL. For one thing, the interface is documented to a certain degree, particularly if you're using WSDL. That is, you can read the name of the remote procedure, the names of the parameters to the remote procedure. You can read the types of the parameters and the return type. What you *don't* get, unfortunately, is any real description, at least in the interface description itself, about the purpose of any of these items. This can be very important, especially in a very large (perhaps enterprise-wide) application that is created with an SOA, in that at least a minimum level of documentation is required. (In an HTTP-only interface [an example of a RESTful interface], not even that much description is specifically required by the interface itself.)

The other big advantage of a well-defined remote procedure call-type interface is that clients can, in many situations, automatically read the interface and automatically configure themselves (or be configured automatically) to call that interface correctly.

Now let's think about RESTful web services in regard to the constraints from Section 9.2.1.

If you look at some of the RESTful technologies that we will examine later in Chapter 11: AJAX (XMLHttpRequest), Servlets, and JAX-RS, these all work by addressing URLs. They all use HTTP messages (GETs, POSTs, etc.) to send messages, and the data inside the messages is described using MIME types. Therefore, they obey the uniform interface constraint. They work as clients and servers. They *can* operate in a stateless manner (note that it is also possible for them to operate in a stateful manner), so at least when they choose to operate statelessly then they meet the stateless constraint.

They are knowledgeable about the HTTP layer, which is where their uniform interface is implemented, but they treat the lower internet layers transparently, so they do not know about any intermediate lower level nodes. Clients can cache data if desired. Code on demand is supported, for example, JavaScript inside <script> tags in an html web page can access RESTful interfaces (AJAX using XMLHttpRequest is a good example of this).

So it's pretty clear that the RESTful web services meet the constraints of the RESTful architecture.

Summarizing, a RESTful web service is client/server-based, does not store state. It accesses resources (web pages or data) located at a URL. The results of a request from client to server can be cached in the client. It has a uniform interface with self-descriptive messages, based on hypermedia. Oh, and the client and server aren't aware of intermediate connections between the two of them.

As we previously discussed in Section 9.2.1, these are the characteristics of the World Wide Web. It is client/server-based, consisting primarily of browsers and web servers. Each call to a web server is considered independent of another such call (unless you're using something like cookies or URL redirection, we'll talk about those later on in this chapter). Its uniform interface is provided by the HTTP protocol. The data format is specified by Internet Media Types, which are included in the message, so the message is self-descriptive. And so forth.

In short, RESTful web services make use of the basic functionality of the World Wide Web.

Speaking generally about RESTful web services, however, in terms of what is generally meant in practice in industry: a RESTful web service is anything that is defined using HTTP messages (GETs, POSTs, etc.) In industry, it is often the case that an interface that the developers call a RESTful interface does not always adhere to the "stateless" constraint, for example, they can make use of cookies which are inherently a stateful concept. In the OpenStack cloud examples we will see in Chapter 13, one could perhaps argue that using an authentication token is not a purely stateless transaction (since the tokens are included separately in each message, however, one could argue that individual messages are stateless, it's just that the authentication server is storing the fact that the user previously authenticated). Also, although Internet Media Types are commonly used, there are some RESTful interfaces that may have no need to send that kind of metadata information.

EXERCISES

1. What are the main characteristics of a Service-Oriented Architecture?
2. Why did SOA appear to fail at first, when implemented by companies?
3. So what really is the difference between a "mashup" and an SOA?
4. Must software on a cloud be organized as an SOA?
5. Let's say we have the following situation:

   A function named "storeData" is located on the web at address:

   > http://xxx.xxx.xxx.xx:8080/storeData

   This function accesses a database. There is another function named "readData" that is located on the web at address:

   > http://xxx.xxx.xxx.xx:8080/readData

   You send an HTTP POST to storeData and you send an HTTP GET to readData.
   Is this interface RESTful or not?

6. What is one main advantage of Web Services Description Language (WSDL)?
7. What are disadvantages of non-RESTful in regard to SOAP/WSDL?
8. Are HTTP methods really a standard interface according to the strict definition of RESTful?
9. Consider a cloud interface such as the OpenStack interface that OpenStack calls a RESTful interface. The basic way the OpenStack RESTful interface works is, a user sends a username and password to OpenStack, and OpenStack sends back a token to the user. Then the user includes this token in all future calls to OpenStack. Is the OpenStack interface truly RESTful? (*Hint:* consider the stateless concept.)
10. Are the use of Service-Oriented Architectures and Clouds going to greatly improve software development?

CONCEPTUAL QUESTIONS

1. Consider a real estate office, where you have pictures of homes for sale. Think about how you could design software to do a mashup that includes information from Google Maps as well as local school districts and local church and synagogue, etc. information. How would this map into a service-oriented architecture? Write up your design in detail. Show diagrams.

2. Google and also do a formal literature review using a library or library databases for non-RESTful versus RESTful web services comparisons. Using all these references, write a paper describing the differences. Include as part of this paper any new distinctions between non-RESTful and RESTful that were not covered in this textbook.

3. Google and also do a formal literature review using a library or library databases for implementing top-down SOA versus bottom-up SOA. Using all these references, write a paper describing the differences. Include as part of this paper any new advantages/disadvantages of non-RESTful and RESTful that were not covered in this textbook.

4. Go through Fielding's RESTful architecture constraints. Do you agree with all these constraints? Why or why not? Would you add any additional constraints? Repeat this exercise after you learn the non-RESTful and RESTful technologies in Chapters 10, Chapter 11, and Chapter 12.

5. What are the advantages and disadvantages of Distributed-Object Components versus either RESTful or non-RESTful web services? Also do a design for how Distributed-Object Components could be used to implement a Service-Oriented Architecture. Write your design up in detail and include diagrams. What are the limitations of an SOA implemented using Distributed-Object Components. Are there any advantages?

6. In this chapter, we discussed that the JAX-WS implementation of the Sailboat Marina project is an example of a Service-Oriented Architecture. For each of the Sailboat Marina and Environmental Monitoring examples in this textbook (or a subset), discuss whether they sufficiently meet the requirements to be considered a Service-Oriented Architecture. If not, then discuss what modifications would have to be made for them to be considered an SOA.

BIBLIOGRAPHY

Chapman, K. 2009. Mashups for SOA. WSO2. http://www.slideshare.net/wso2.org/mashups-for-soa (accessed April 9, 2016).

Chou, D. 2008. Using Events in Highly Distributed Architectures. *The Architecture Journal*. https://msdn.microsoft.com/en-us/library/dd129913.aspx (accessed April 9, 2016).

Fielding, R. 2000. Architectural Styles and the Design of Network-Based Software Architectures. Ph.D. Dissertation, University of California-Irvine. https://www.ics.uci.edu/~fielding/pubs/dissertation/top.htm (accessed April 2, 2016).

Fielding, R., Gettys, J., Mogul, J., Frystyk, H., Masinter, L., Leach, P., Berners-Lee, T. 1999. *Hypertext Transfer Protocol—HTTP/1.1*. IETF. RFC 2616. https://tools.ietf.org/html/rfc2616 (accessed April 9, 2016).

Hiroshige, S. 2010. Difference between SOA and Mashup Technology. Aris Community. http://www.ariscommunity.com/users/waltzba/2010-12-01-difference-between-soa-and-mashup-technology (accessed April 9, 2016).

IBM. 2009. How SOA Can Ease Your Move to Cloud Computing. http://www-01.ibm.com/software/solutions/soa/newsletter/nov09/article_soaandcloud.html (accessed April 9, 2016).

Krill, P. 2009. The Cloud-SOA Connection. *InfoWorld*. http://www.infoworld.com/article/2676125/cloud-computing/the-cloud-soa-connection.html (accessed April 9, 2016).

Mackenzie, C.M., Laskey, K., McCabe, F., Brown, P.F., Metz, R. 2006. OASIS Reference Model for Service Oriented Architecture 1.0. OASIS. https://www.oasis-open.org/committees/download.php/19679/soa-rm-cs.pdf (accessed April 9, 2016).

Maines, A.T. 2009. SOA Is Dead; Long Live Services. http://apsblog.burtongroup.com/2009/01/soa-is-dead-long-live-services.html (accessed April 9, 2016).

McKendrick, J. 2006. *Mashup vs. SOA App: What's the Difference*. ZDNet. http://www.zdnet.com/article/mashup-vs-soa-app-whats-the-difference/ (accessed April 9, 2016).

Merrill, D. 2009. *Mashups: The New Breed of Web App. IBM Developer Works*. http://www.ibm.com/developerworks/library/x-mashups/ (accessed April 9, 2016).

Mulesoft. 2015. SOA from the Bottom Up—The Best Approach to Service Oriented Architecture. http://www.mulesoft.com/resources/esb/bottom-up-soa (accessed April 9, 2016).

Mulholland, A., Daniels, R., Hall, T. 2008. *The Cloud and SOA*. HP. http://www.hp.com/hpinfo/analystrelations/wp_cloudcomputing_soa_capgemini_hp.pdf (accessed April 9, 2016).

Newcomer, E., Baker, S. 2005. Introduction to Web Services and Service-Oriented Architectures. MDA, SOA, and Web Services Workshop. Object Management Group. http://www.omg.org/news/meetings/workshops/MDA-SOA-WS_Manual/ (accessed April 9, 2016).

Open Group. 2016. Service Oriented Architecture: What is SOA? https://www.opengroup.org/soa/source-book/soa/soa.htm (accessed April 2, 2016).

Pomares, W.M. 2010. The Top-Down vs. Bottom-Up SOA Debate Revisited. *InfoQ*. http://www.infoq.com/news/2010/07/top-down-bottom-up-soa (accessed April 9, 2016).

Raines, G. 2009. Cloud Computing and SOA. https://www.mitre.org/sites/default/files/pdf/09_0743.pdf (accessed April 9, 2016).

Raj, P. 2013. *Cloud Enterprise Architecture*. CRC Press, Boca Raton, FL.

ServiceOrientation.com. 2015. Top Down vs. Bottom Up. Arcitura Education. http://serviceorientation.com/soamethodology/top_down_vs_bottom_up (accessed April 9, 2016).

10 Non-RESTful Web Services

10.1 JUST WHAT DO WE MEAN BY "NON-RESTFUL WEB SERVICES," ANYWAY?

As we saw earlier in Section 9.2, there are some differences of opinion as to what "RESTful" and "non-RESTful" mean. Ignoring "RESTful" for now, let's briefly re-examine what "non-RESTful" means.

Let's start with the common definition that a "non-RESTful web service" defines a remote procedure call using a specifically defined interface, where this remote procedure call treats the HTTP protocol as a transparent lower networking layer (it doesn't have to know anything about HTTP, it just assumes it's there and it works), and uses the SOAP messaging protocol (we will see SOAP in Section 10.2) that includes an XML-type data format. This definition is fairly widely accepted in the industry.

However, this is not a totally clear definition. For example, a web service that uses Web Services Description Language (WSDL) to define the interface (we will see WSDL in Section 10.3), which commonly employs SOAP, would be considered "non-RESTful" by this definition. However, it is possible to configure a WSDL interface that runs directly using HTTP (in which case it could be called RESTful). It's also possible to define a WSDL interface that runs on top of TCP and bypasses HTTP altogether—in this case the data would be sent in binary, and would normally not be considered either RESTful or non-RESTful.

Also, it's possible to have a remote procedure call and use SOAP, but have the data sent directly over TCP—we saw this earlier in .Net Remoting. But .Net Remoting is not a web service, but rather is object-oriented. So we're making some very small distinctions here.

However, since it's a common definition, even though there are problems with it, we will use this definition.

There are several advantages to requiring a well-defined remote procedure call-type interface. For one thing, the interface is documented to a certain degree, particularly if you're using WSDL. That is, you can read the name of the remote procedure, the names of the parameters to the remote procedure. You can read the types of the parameters and the return type. What you *don't* get, unfortunately, is any real description, at least in the interface description itself, about the purpose of any of these items. This can be very important, especially in a very large (perhaps enterprise-wide) application that is created with a service-oriented architecture, in that at least a minimum level of documentation is required. (In an HTTP-only interface [an example of a RESTful interface] not even that much description is specifically required by the interface itself.)

The other big advantage of a well-defined remote procedure call-type interface is that clients can, in many situations, automatically read the interface and automatically configure themselves (or be configured automatically) to call that interface correctly.

Okay, now we know generally what we're talking about. In the sections below, we're going to discuss multiple technologies related to non-RESTful web services. We're going to start with SOAP, which is an enabling technology. Then we will discuss WSDL, which is used one way or another in various implementations of non-RESTful web services. Then we will examine JAX-WS, originally created by Sun Microsystems and now supported by Oracle (Oracle purchased Sun Microsystems in 2010). Finally, we will look at Windows Communication Foundation (WCF), which provides Microsoft's implementation of non-RESTful web services.

For Windows Communication Framework, there is a larger practical example provided in Chapter 17, and for JAX-WS there is a larger practical example provided in Chapter 18. Chapters 17 and 18 are available in online resources.

10.2   SOAP MESSAGING PROTOCOL

SOAP is a protocol that sends and receives structured information in the form of XML documents, in a distributed environment.

The early SOAP standard, "Simple Object Access Protocol (SOAP) 1.1," referred to SOAP as the "Simple Object Access Protocol," but for the SOAP 1.2 standard, the original meaning of the acronym has been dropped ("SOAP Version 1.2 Part 1: Messaging Framework [Second Edition]") and only the term "SOAP" remains.

We will look first at SOAP message exchange. SOAP messages are created by a SOAP sender (for example, a client) and are received by a SOAP receiver (for example, a server). Between the SOAP sender and the SOAP receiver, the SOAP messages may be routed through other intermediary nodes. The intermediary nodes, the SOAP sender, and the SOAP receiver are all also referred to as "SOAP nodes":

> (SOAP node: SOAP Sender/Client)→
>> (SOAP node: SOAP Intermediary Node A)→
>>> (SOAP node: SOAP Intermediary Node B)→
>>>> (SOAP node: SOAP Receiver/Server)

In between SOAP sender and SOAP receiver (and through any intermediary nodes), a SOAP message is carried by an underlying protocol (it is "bound" to the underlying protocol). For example, consider a direct connection between a SOAP sender and a SOAP receiver (for the sake of this example, we will assume there are no intermediate nodes). Let us assume there is a World Wide Web connection between the SOAP sender and the SOAP receiver. If so, the HTTP protocol would be used to send data from the sender to the receiver. So, for example, the SOAP message could be enclosed in an HTTP POST message as the HTTP POST message's data.

Note that intermediary nodes can be involved in processing various SOAP headers (this is explained further later) and they can also do additional work on the data in the SOAP body, such as encrypting the data, even if this is not specified in a SOAP header. They can also add additional headers to the SOAP message. SOAP intermediary nodes are very important to scalability, they allow additional services to be added at runtime. Perhaps these could be related to security, such as authentication, or various Quality of Service issues. For those of you who are Design Pattern literate, this use of the Intermediary nodes is an example of the Chain of Responsibility from the Gang of Four design patterns book.

In distributed communications between computers, a "message exchange pattern" (MEP) refers to the pattern of messages required to exchange data between nodes. The basic SOAP message exchange patterns are:

* Request–response—Send a SOAP request, get a SOAP response.
* Response Only—Non-SOAP message serves as a request, SOAP response sent back.

SOAP itself only defines very basic message exchange patterns. However, there are other specifications, such as Web Services Description Language (WSDL), that make use of SOAP and that define additional message exchange patterns.

In SOAP 1.2, there is also the SOAP web method feature, which can be used to extend SOAP's ability to make use of HTTP (could also be used with other protocols if SOAP is bound to a different protocol). SOAP 1.1 (when using the HTTP binding) employed only the HTTP POST command. The web method feature in SOAP 1.2 allows a different HTTP command such as GET, POST, or DELETE in addition to POST to be used (this feature helps make SOAP more usable with RESTful architectures, we'll see this more later).

10.2.1 OVERALL SOAP MESSAGE FORMAT

A SOAP message is enclosed in a SOAP "envelope," that indicates that this XML document is a SOAP document.

Inside the SOAP envelope are a SOAP header and a SOAP body:

LISTING 10.1   SOAP Message Overall Format

```
<soap: Envelope>
        <soap:Header>
        ...header stuff included here...
        </soap:Header>
        <soap:Body>
        ...body stuff included here...
        </soap:Body>
</soap: Envelope>
```

The SOAP Header is optional, but the SOAP Body is required.

LISTING 10.2   Additional SOAP Envelope Information in SOAP Message

```
<soap: Envelope xmlns:soap="http://www.w3.org/2003/05/soap-envelope">
        ...SOAP headers and body here...
</soap: Envelope>
```

The SOAP Envelope is required to specify a namespace. This namespace tells you whether you're using SOAP 1.1 or SOAP 1.2. (The SOAP specification uses a namespace instead of version numbers to distinguish between SOAP versions.)

If you're using SOAP 1.1, then your envelope would specify the namespace:

$$xmlns:soap=http://schemas.xmlsoap.org/soap/envelope/$$

While if you're using SOAP 1.2, then your envelope would specify the namespace:

$$xmlns:soap=http://www.w3.org/2003/05/soap-envelope$$

An example showing a SOAP 1.2 namespace is given in Listing 10.2.

Since Headers are optional, I'm going to focus on the Body first and talk about how SOAP messages are sent, and then how SOAP faults are sent. We'll get back to the SOAP headers later on.

10.2.2 ENCODING OF SOAP MESSAGES

All SOAP messages are described in XML. We speak of *serializing* our data from our application, this means converting it into XML, while *deserializing* means converting the data from XML back into what is expected by our application.

What we mean by "encoding" is *how, in what way*, XML is used to describe the SOAP data. There are two ways to do this (these are called "encoding styles"): SOAP Encoding and what is called "Literal" encoding. With Literal encoding, an XML Schema is used to describe the data. If you are unfamiliar with XML Schema, see Section 4.4, XML Schema Basics. With SOAP Encoding, there is a method described by the SOAP standard that is used to describe the data.

Today, Literal Encoding is recommended, because storing the data in XML Schema format gives more control to the developer—you the developer can specify pretty well any data format to represent your data.

It may perhaps strike you as odd that the encoding style that is called SOAP Encoded is not generally recommended nowadays to use with SOAP. ☺ One reason is that the first version of SOAP, SOAP 1.1, predates the first full release of the XML Schema, so the creators of SOAP had to provide some mechanism for data encoding. However, XML Schema is more general than SOAP Encoding.

I don't want to focus a whole lot on SOAP Encoding since Literal Encoding is recommended nowadays, but it's likely you will see it, so there are some things we need to talk about, and you need to see at least a little of it.

I'm going to show a SOAP Encoding data example about horses, because I like horses and I own 3 horses (their names are Dolly, Foxy, and Misty), and also because I previously used horses in my XML Schema examples.

Dolly is a registered Shire horse, she weighs around 2000 pounds and is 17 hands tall (a hand is 4 inches) and her color is black. Foxy and Misty are registered Quarter horses. Foxy weighs around 1200 pounds and is 15 hands tall, and Misty is about 1000 pounds and 14.5 hands tall. Foxy's color is sorrel (light reddish brown) and Misty's color is palomino (light yellow with white mane and tail).

All three of my horses live on my mini-farm in North Alabama. See Listing 10.3 for a SOAP Encoding that describes my horses.

LISTING 10.3   SOAP Encoding Example

```
<soap: Envelope  xmlns:soap="http://www.w3.org/2003/05/soap-envelope"
                 xmlns:xsi="http://www.w3.org/2001/XMLSchema-Instance"
                 xmlns:xsd="http://www.w3.org/2001/XMLSchema">
      <soap:Body xmlns: myhorse="http://myhorse.com/myhorse"
      soap:encodingStyle="http://www.w3.org/2001/12/soap-encoding">
            <myhorse: Horse>
                  <myhorse: name>Dolly</name>
                  <myhorse: weight xsi:type="xsd:float"> 2000 </weight>
                  <myhorse: height xsi:type="xsd:float"> 17 </height>
                  <myhorse: color xsi:type="xsd:string"> black </color>
                  <myhorse: barnAddress id="theaddress">
                        <streetAddress xsi:type="xsd:string"> notgoingtotellyouthat
                              </streetAddress>
                        <state xsi:type="xsd:string"> North Alabama </state>
                        <country xsi:type="xsd:string"> USA </country>
                  </myhorse: endbarnAddress>
            </myhorse: Horse>
            <myhorse: Horse>
                  <myhorse: name>Foxy</name>
                  <myhorse: weight xsi:type="xsd:float"> 1100 </weight>
                  <myhorse: height xsi:type="xsd:float"> 15 </height>
                  <myhorse: color xsi:type="xsd:string"> sorrel </color>
                  <myhorse: barnAddress ref="theaddress">
            </myhorse: Horse>
            <myhorse: Horse>
                  <myhorse: name>Misty</name>
                  <myhorse: weight xsi:type="xsd:float"> 1000 </weight>
                  <myhorse: height xsi:type="xsd:float"> 14.2 </height>
                  <myhorse: color xsi:type="xsd:string"> palomino </color>
```

```
                    <myhorse: barnAddress ref="theaddress">
                    </myhorse: Horse>
              </soap:Body>
        </soap: Envelope>
```

I've put the encoding style attribute:

soap:encodingStyle=http://www.w3.org/2001/12/soap-encoding

at the beginning of the Body. This means it applies to all elements of the Body. I could instead have put it at the top of the envelope, or in the myHorse: Horse definition. If I had put it inside the myHorse:Horse definition, then I could have had other elements (Dog? Cat? Llama?) inside my SOAP envelope that had a Literal encoding. (But's that's getting complicated so we won't do that.)

If you look at the envelope, you'll see the following two lines:

xmlns:xsi="http://www.w3.org/2001/XMLSchema-Instance"
xmlns:xsd="http://www.w3.org/2001/XMLSchema"

Since you already read Section 4.4, XML Schema Basics, you know that these are related to XML Schemas. And I just told you that this is SOAP Encoding and that SOAP Encoding means I'm not using an XML schema to describe the data.

This isn't a trick or a bug, this is a feature. ☺ I'm using a predefined, public XML schema to define *some of* the data inside my SOAP message. SOAP Encoding allows this (the simple XML data types were already defined back when SOAP 1.1 was specified). I'm *not* using an XML schema to define the *whole* SOAP message, just part of it. And therefore I am really using SOAP Encoding. We'll see some more of this later when we go through the various SOAP message formats.

Note also that instead of repeating the address for each horse, I'm instead using the "ref" attribute to point back to the original address. This saves repetition. I can only use the term "ref" in SOAP 1.2. If I had instead been using SOAP 1.1, I would have had to call it "href" instead (and use a "#" sign in front of it if I were using a number, for example, I could have said: id="#1" and "href="#1").

Aw shucks, I forgot to put "breed" in as part of this example. This is left as an exercise for the reader. ☺

10.2.3   SOAP Message Formats

SOAP also has various "message styles." A "message style" (RPC or Document) together with an "encoding" (SOAP Encoding or Literal) together specify which message formats the data is converted to for transmitting or receiving.

The best known message formats are:

- Remote Procedure Call (RPC) with SOAP Encoding
- Remote Procedure Call (RPC) with Literal Encoding
- Document with Literal Encoding
- Document with Literal Encoding Wrapped

I'm going to go through these one after the other. In some cases I'm going to have to show a small amount of WSDL. We haven't studied that yet, but don't panic. I'm going to try to keep the WSDL portion very simple so you can understand the point of my discussion in each case. Then later, after you do read the WSDL portion of this textbook, you can come back and re-read this section and understand the WSDL parts better. It was a tradeoff here: Since WSDL and SOAP so often go together, you really needed SOAP to understand WSDL, but you also needed WSDL to understand SOAP. So I chose to talk about it this way.

10.2.3.1 RPC-SOAP Encoded Message Format

RPC message format is intended to map to procedure calls done by a standard programming language such as Java. It supports remote procedure calls by providing the name of the remote procedure and its parameters inside the SOAP message. Parameters in a SOAP request are called "in" parameters, whereas a SOAP response would include a response plus any "out" parameters, unless a fault is being returned instead.

In RPC message format, SOAP converts the remote procedure call (name of method) plus the parameter data into XML for transmission to the Server. Each parameter also has its type information along with it. For example, a value named "i" of integer type with the value 7 would be encoded as follows:

```
<i  xsi:type="xsd:int">7</i>
```

Note that a web interface in WSDL (we will discuss WSDL in more depth after we finish our discussion of SOAP) describes the name of the remote procedure plus the names and types of the parameters of the remote procedure, and the name and type of the return value from the remote procedure. So doing this in SOAP also is a bit wasteful, in that it results in extra data having to be sent (we will look at this again below).

See Listing 10.3. I'm providing *part of* a WSDL document along with the SOAP message here, so you can see the relationship between the SOAP message and the WSDL document. Note that the type of information as well as which procedure is being called is shown both in the SOAP message and in the WSDL document. The WSDL also describes the procedure being called plus the parameter "i" using "xsi:type" so having this information in the SOAP message as well is just extra data to send.

LISTING 10.4   SOAP Message Using RPC Message Format

SOAP Message Itself:

```
<soap: Envelope xmlns:soap="http://www.w3.org/2003/05/soap-envelope">
        <soap:Header>
        ...header stuff included here...
        </soap:Header>
        <soap:Body>
               <myHelloWorld>
                   <i xsi:type="xsd:int">7</i>
               </myHelloWorld>
        </soap:Body>
</soap: Envelope>
```

***Part of* a WSDL Document:**

```
<message name="myHelloWorldRequest">
        <part name="i" type="xsd:int" />
</message>
```

As a general rule, messages in XML Schema format are easy to validate (that is, to check whether the data being sent matches the type definition provided in the XML schema) because there are many good XML parsers that can be used to validate XML messages against XML schemas (XML schema is also supported in many implementations of SOAP). Note that an XML schema is different from plain XML. For a description of what is meant by an XML schema see Section 4.4.

However, here the type information in the SOAP message isn't easily used to validate the data, since any XML schema-type format validation related to the xsi schema is applicable only to the small sections that define the parameters. The SOAP message as a whole is not in XML schema format.

10.2.3.2 RPC-Literal Message Format

Next we look at RPC with literal message format. The primary difference from RPC with literal message format compared to simple RPC message format is that now the "xsi: type" stuff disappears. See Listing 10.4. The WSDL itself will still contain the type description of the data.

This is more efficient, since it's not sending extra unused type definition text, but again, this SOAP message is not easily validated against an XML schema since the whole SOAP message itself is still not in XML schema format. For example, it's still peskily including those method names.

(I note in passing that those method names being included in a SOAP message can help debugging. Some people like them for this reason. Also, they map fairly well into a mindset that is trained on remote procedure calls between objects, rather than between web service-type implementations.)

It would indeed be possible to define a schema (included as part of the WSDL) to compare the parameter "i" in this SOAP message against, although I didn't specifically do that here. But in any case, it would apply only to the "i" variable and not the whole SOAP message, so it's not very useful for validation.

LISTING 10.5   SOAP Example Using RPC with Literals Message Format

SOAP Message Itself:

```
<soap: Envelope  xmlns:soap="http://www.w3.org/2003/05/soap-envelope">
        <soap:Header
        …header stuff included here…
        </soap:Header>
        <soap:Body>
                <myHelloWorld>
                        <i>7</i>
                </myHelloWorld>
        </soap:Body>
</soap: Envelope>
```

***Part of* a WSDL Document:**

```
<message name="myHelloWorldRequest">
        <part name="i" type="xsd:int" />
</message>
```

10.2.3.3 Document-Literal Message Format

Next we will examine Document-literal message format. (There's also a Document-SOAP Encoded message format that has been seldom used and is pretty well obsolete and so we will just ignore it.) In Document-literal message format, an entire XML document is sent. That is, the SOAP message that is sent is entirely described within a well-formatted XML document.

In this method, you the developer will previously have created a schema that describes the XML document (this would typically be done as part of a WSDL document). In Listing 10.5, we see an example of a SOAP message, and the XML Schema that was previously created that the SOAP message can be validated against, using a standard XML parser.

I didn't show you the entire WSDL document here, because that would be confusing since you haven't learned much about WSDL yet. However, this XML schema would be included as part of the WSDL document.

LISTING 10.6   SOAP Example Using Document-Literal Message Format

SOAP Message Itself:

```
<soap: Envelope xmlns:soap="http://www.w3.org/2003/05/soap-envelope"
            xmlns:hw= "http://myhelloworld/myHelloWorldSchema">
    <soap:Header
            …header stuff included here…
    </soap:Header>
    <soap:Body>
            <hw: iElement>7</hw: iElement>
    </soap:Body>
</soap: Envelope>
```

Part of **a WSDL Document:**

```
<message name="myHelloWorldRequest">
    <part name="i"    element="hw:iElement" />
</message>
```

XML Schema the SOAP Message Is Validated Against:

```
<schema xmlns:xsd="http://www.w3.org/2001/XMLSchema"
    xmlns:hw="http://myhelloworld/myHelloWorldSchema"
    target_Namespace="http://myhelloworld/myHelloWorldSchema">
            <element  name=iElement type = "xsd:int"/>
</schema>
```

In Listing 10.6, we see that the schema is defined as an XML schema by specifying the namespace:

schema xmlns=http://www.w3.org/2001/XMLSchema

All this does is tell you that you are using an XML schema, that you are employing the standard XML schema "language."

The next two lines in the schema say that we are defining our own schema that specifies the format of any data that will be sent, and that our namespace where this schema is defined is called "hw":

xmlns:hw="http://myhelloworld/myHelloWorldSchema"
target_Namespace="http://myhelloworld/myHelloWorldSchema"

Now we can look back at the SOAP message. Wherever it refers to "hw" it is saying that the data types referred to there are defined in the previously defined "hw" schema.

This SOAP message can be fully validated against the XML schema (that is part of the WSDL) and is therefore easily supported by XML parsers that are included as part of SOAP implementations. For this reason, Document-Literal Message format is the recommended format for use nowadays.

10.2.3.4   Document-Literal Wrapped Message Format

An example of Document-Literal Wrapped format is shown in Listing 10.7. As you can see, the schema here is more complicated.

The idea of Document-Literal Wrapped format is that including the method names in the SOAP message is beneficial, but the need to be able to parse the entire SOAP message with an XML parser is also important. The idea is that this can be handled by providing an XML schema for the entire message content (as was done in Document-literal) but that this can be achieved by including the message name and the message parameter names as part of the XML schema that describes the message. The resulting SOAP message will look very much like the RPC-literal message. However, in the RPC-literal message, the name of the remote procedure (the method), in this case "myHelloWorld", was included in the SOAP message because that was the name of the operation in the associated WSDL (we'll see more about WSDL operations later on). However, in this case, "myHelloWorld" is the name, in the associated XML schema, of an element that "wraps" all the parameters of the remote procedure (method) call. In this case, only a single parameter (i) is shown. Note here that the element in the XML Schema must have the same name as the method (operation, remote procedure).

LISTING 10.7   SOAP Example Using Document-Literal Wrapped Message Format

SOAP Message Itself:

```
<soap: Envelope  xmlns:soap="http://www.w3.org/2003/05/soap-envelope">
        <soap:Header>
                …header stuff included here…
        </soap:Header>
        <soap:Body>
                <hw:myHelloWorld>
                        <hw:i >7</hw:i>
                </hw:myHelloWorld>
        </soap:Body>
</soap: Envelope>
```

***Part of* a WSDL Document:**

```
<message name="myHelloWorldRequest">
        <part name="parameters"  element="hw:myHelloWorld" />
</message>
```

XML Schema the SOAP Message Is Validated Against:

```
<schema xmlns:xsd="http://www.w3.org/2001/XMLSchema"
        xmlns:hw="http://myhelloworld/myHelloWorldSchema"
        target_Namespace="http://myhelloworld/myHelloWorldSchema">
                <element  name="myHelloWorld">
                        <complexType>
                                <sequence>
                                        <element name="i" type="xsd:int">
                                </sequence>
                        </complexType>

                </element>
</schema>
```

One thing that could potentially confuse you if you haven't seen it before, in the WSDL here, we had:

<part name="parameters"   element="hw:myHelloWorld" />

In XML, this goes with an element:

<element name="myHelloWorld">...
</element>

If instead you had:

<part name="parameters"   type="hw:myHelloWorld" />

Then in XML, this would go with a complexType:

<complexType name="hw:myHelloWorld">...
</complexType>

The wrapped style is the default if you select document-literal style in JAX-WS, as follows:

@SOAPBinding(style = Style.DOCUMENT)

However, if you want to use unwrapped style, you do the following:

@SOAPBinding(style = Style.DOCUMENT, parameterStyle=SOAPBinding.ParameterStyle.BARE)

The example code illustrating document/literal/wrapped versus document/literal/unwrapped provided with the textbook allows you to select either style and play with the output (the provided code assumes you'll be using tcpmon, so the Client is talking to a port number on tcpmon, whereas it is tcpmon that talks to the Server.) The particular example provided is not very in depth, but you should be able to see the difference. Play around with it more using different kinds of parameters and you will be able to understand it better. See Appendix B, provided in online resources, for a discussion of tcpmon.

10.2.3.5 Summary of Pros and Cons of the Different SOAP Message Formats

Here we will look at the pros and cons, positives and negatives, associated with choosing one SOAP message format versus another SOAP message format. In this section, among other things, I'll be talking about being "WS-I" compliant. You should read SideBar WS-I Compliant to understand more about this.

RPC-SOAP Encoded Message Format:

- Pros:
    - The operation name is included in the message, this makes it easy for the receiver to send it to the correct handler.
    - The associated WSDL is very simple.
- Cons:
    - It is not easily validated against an XML Schema, as only certain lines (the method parameters with xsi:type="xsd:int) could be compared to a schema.
    - The xsi:type-style encoding is just overhead—that is, extra data to be sent.
    - Not WS-I compliant.

RPC-Literal Message Format:

- Pros:
  - The operation name is included in the message, this makes it easy for the receiver to send it to the correct handler.
  - The associated WSDL is very simple.
  - No xsi:type-style encoding overhead in the SOAP message.
  - Is WS-I compliant.
- Cons:
  - It is not easily validated against an XML Schema, as only certain lines (the method parameters) could be compared to a schema.

Document-Literal Message Format:

- Pros:
  - It is easily validated against an XML Schema.
  - No xsi:type-style encoding overhead in the SOAP message.
  - Allows any kind of SOAP message to be sent, whatever you want just define it with a custom XML Schema.
- Both Pro and Con (has both advantages and disadvantages):
  - An associated XML Schema is required; however, since this is often included as part of the <type> section of WSDL, the associated WSDL is more complicated than with RPC-SOAP Encoded or RPC-literal.
- Cons:
  - The operation name is *NOT* included in the message, so it can be hard for the receiver to send it to the correct handler.
  - WS-I compliant, but has some limitations, such WS-I allows only one child of a Body. So any operation with more than one parameter would not be compliant (would require sending a single more complex type).

Document-Literal Wrapped Message Format:

- Pros:
  - It is easily validated against an XML Schema.
  - WS-I compliant.
  - The operation name is included in the message, this makes it easy for the receiver to send it to the correct handler.
  - No xsi:type-style encoding overhead in the SOAP message.
  - Allows any kind of SOAP message to be sent, whatever you want just define it with a custom XML Schema. (However, this must include the operation names so in that it is more restricted than Document-Literal.)
- Both Pro and Con (has both advantages and disadvantages):
  - An associated XML Schema is required; however, since this is often included as part of the <type> section of WSDL, the associated WSDL is more complicated than with RPC-SOAP Encoded or RPC-literal.
- Cons:
  - Document-Literal Wrapped does not support overloaded operations (even though WSDL does). This is because Document-Literal Wrapped requires the element to have the same name as the operation, but XML will not allow two elements with the same name.

SIDEBAR 10.1   WS-I COMPLIANT

Web Services Interoperability Organization (WS-I) is part of the Organization for the Advancement of Structured Information Standards (OASIS) standards body. Its task is to promote interoperability between different web service specifications.

WS-I has produced profiles that describe guidelines for interoperability for different web services. Its focus is primarily on the W* specifications, for example, WSDL and SOAP.

They have finalized a Basic Profile, a Simple SOAP Binding profile, and they are working on a Basic Security Profile. Test tools are provided, and a vendor must make use of a test tool before claiming to be compliant.

The two most recent versions of the Basic Profile are Basic Profile 1.2 and Basic Profile 2.0.

With the move of WS-I to OASIS in 2010, WS-I claimed "By publishing the final three profiles, WS-I marks the completion of its work." Some argue that this feeling by WS-I that they had completed their work resulted less from achieving full interoperability between web services than from the competition of the RESTful technologies that are primarily not covered by WS-I.

It is also interesting that WSDL 2.0 has not been specified in a WS-I basic profile. Some argue that a basic profile for WSDL 2.0 was not necessary because WSDL 2.0 is already interoperable, and was intended to fix interoperability problems with WSDL 1.1. Yet others believe that the reason is that WS-I develops profiles based on interoperability testing between different implementations of a specification, and not enough WSDL 2.0 implementations are available to make this possible/useful/necessary.

XML Schema Part 1: Structures Second Edition	XML Schema Part 1: Structures Second Edition
XML Schema Part 2: Datatypes Second Edition	XML Schema Part 2: Datatypes Second Edition
Attachments Profile Version 1.0 (profile for SOAP	Attachments Profile Version 1.0 (profile for SOAP
messages with Attachments using MIME)	messages with Attachments using MIME)

10.2.4   SOAP FAULTS

The SOAP basic fault format is shown in Listing 10.8.

LISTING 10.8   SOAP Message Basic Fault Format

```
<soap: Envelope  xmlns:soap="http://www.w3.org/2003/05/soap-envelope">
        <soap:Header
                …header stuff included here…
        </soap:Header>
        <soap:Body>
                <soap:Fault>
                        …fault stuff included here
                </soap:Fault>
        </soap:Body>
</soap: Envelope>
```

The SOAP Faults differ between SOAP 1.1 and SOAP 1.2. I have provided an overview of SOAP 1.2 faults in Table 10.1, and an overview of SOAP 1.1 faults in Table 10.2.

TABLE 10.1

Some Major Differences between Basic Profile 1.2 and Basic Profile 2.0

Basic Profile 1.2	Basic Profile 2.0
SOAP 1.1	SOAP 1.2
	WSDL 1.1 Binding Extension for SOAP 1.2
	RFC3023: XML Media Types

TABLE 10.2

Some Major Similarities between Basic Profile 1.2 and Basic Profile 2.0

Basic Profile 1.2	Basic Profile 2.0
WSDL 1.1	WSDL 1.1
HTTP/1.1	HTTP/1.1
RFC2246: TLS 1.0	RFC2246: TLS 1.0
RFC2818: HTTP over TLS	RFC2818: HTTP over TLS
RFC 2459: X.509	RFC 2459: X.509
XML 1.0 Fourth Edition	XML 1.0 Fourth Edition
Namespaces in XML 1.0 (Second Edition)	Namespaces in XML 1.0 (Third Edition)

Let's first consider SOAP 1.2 faults. The basic format of SOAP 1.2 faults is shown in Listing 10.9.

LISTING 10.9   SOAP 1.2 Message Fault Code Format

```
<soap: Fault>
      <soap: Code>
            <soap:Value>
                  … put the appropriate code here. See Table 10.3 for codes
            </soap:Value>
            <soap:Subcode>
                  <soap:Value>
                  …your application specific subcode.  Could be something like "Timeout"
                        or "InvalidRequest"
                  </soap:Value>
            </soap:Subcode>
      </soap:Code>
      <soap:Reason>
            <soap:Text xml:lang='en'>… a text sentence (in this case in English) saying
            more about the problem that occurred
            </soap:Text>
      </soap:Reason>
</soap: Fault>
```

In SOAP 1.2, there is one <soap:value> … </soap:value> following the <soap:Code> statement that gives the fault codes (predefined or custom application fault codes). If the <soap:Subcode> statement

TABLE 10.3
SOAP 1.2 Faults

Fault Name	Required or Not	Description
Code	Required	Tells what kind of Fault is present. Can be predefined or a custom application code.
		Predefined Codes — **Description**
		Version Mismatch: Received a SOAP 1.1 namespace (xmlns:soap=http://schemas.xmlsoap.org/soap/envelope/) (or other unexpected namespace) when it expected a SOAP 1.2 namespace (xmlns:soap=http://www.w3.org/2003/05/soap-envelope)
		MustUnderstand: A SOAP header element had a mustUnderstand attribute, but the SOAP receiver either couldn't understand it or couldn't process it
		DataEncodingUnknown: The SOAP receiver didn't support the encodingStyle attribute received. For example, it received soap:encodingStyle="http://www.w3.org/2001/12/soap-encoding but it was not expecting to use SOAP encoding.
		Sender: The SOAP message was badly formed, the SOAP sender (client) has to fix the format of the SOAP message before resending.
		Receiver: Something happened on the SOAP receiver (server side) so that the server was unable to process the message. This could be a temporary problem at the server (some needed resource is temporarily unavailable).
		Subcode: (optional) Provides an additional code that gives more information about the fault. This code is specified by the application developer. Could be defined within an XML Schema defined by the application developer. Provided inside <soap:Subcode>...</soap:Subcode>
Reason	Required	An explanation of the fault, must be readable by humans Text, provided inside <soap:Text xml:lang="en">...</soap:Text> (At least one is required if Reason is present. More than one is optional.). Provides a human readable explanation of the fault, in the specified language. xml:lang="en" means "English" xml:lang="es" is Spanish
Node	Optional	Which of the SOAP nodes is responsible for creating the Fault message Reason required. An explanation of the fault, must be readable by humans. Text, provided inside <soap:Text xml:lang="en">...</soap:Text> (At least one is required if Reason is present. More than one is optional.). Provides a human readable explanation of the fault, in the specified language. xml:lang="en" means "English" xml:lang="es" is Spanish? (SOAP Sender, SOAP receiver, or one of the intermediary nodes)
Role	Optional	This is related to the "role" attribute in a SOAP header. It specifies which Role a node was performing at the time a fault was generated (a single Node can perform multiple Roles). We'll see more about the "role" attribute later when we talk about headers.
Detail	Optional	Any additional information that the application cares to add about what caused the fault. There can be several different sub-items (children) of Detail. For example: <myschema: invalidformat>...</myschema: invalidformat> etc., where the sub-items are defined in an XML Schema called "myschema."

is present, then there is one <soap:value> ... </soap:value> following it, which contains the specific Subcode. Note that other options are possible, these are: <soap:Node.> ... </soap:Node> and <soap:Role> ... </soap:Role>. These are provided in Table 10.3 but not shown in Listing 10.9 to keep this example simple.

Now we will examine SOAP 1.1 faults. The format of SOAP 1.1 faults are given in Listing 10.10.

LISTING 10.10   SOAP 1.1 Message Fault Code Format

```
<soap: Fault>
    <faultcode>
        put the appropriate code here. See Table 10.2 for codes
    </faultcode>
    <faultstring
        xml:lang="en">... a text sentence (in this case in English) saying more about the
        problem that occurred
    </faultstring>
    <faultactor>
        URI of the SOAP node that caused the problem
    </faultactor>
    <detail>
        ..can put additional information such as a stack trace here
    </detail>
</soap: Fault>
```

In SOAP 1.1, the fault codes (predefined or custom application fault codes) are provided inside <faultcode> ... </faultcode>. Only one faultstring element is allowed. See Table 10.4.

TABLE 10.4
SOAP 1.1 Faults

Fault Name	Required or Not	Predefined Codes	Description
Faultcode	Required		Tells what kind of Fault is present. Can be a predefined or a custom application code.
		Version Mismatch	The namespace included in the envelope was not the required SOAP 1.1 namespace (http://schemas.xmlsoap.org/soap/envelope)
		MustUnderstand	A SOAP header element had a mustUnderstand attribute, but the SOAP receiver either couldn't understand it or couldn't process it.
		Client	The message was badly formed or lacked data (for example, Authentication information), the Client has to fix the format of the SOAP message before resending.
		Server	Something happened on the server side so that the server was unable to process the message. This could be a temporary problem at the server (some needed resource is temporarily unavailable).
faultstring	Required		A text description of the fault. Can use xml:lang="en" (for ex.) to describe the fault.
faultfactor	Optional		URI of the SOAP node that caused the problem. Could be something like /myhelloWorld/HelloWorld
detail	Optional		Any additional information that the application cares to add about what caused the fault. Could be something like a stack trace.

10.2.5   SOAP HEADERS

The format of a SOAP header with a mustUnderstand attribute and a Role attribute is shown in Listing 10.11.

LISTING 10.11   SOAP Header with mustUnderstand Attribute and Role Attribute

```
<soap:Header>
   <myschema:CurrentTransaction xmlns:myschema="http://myVeryOwnstuff/Transaction/"
       soap:role=predefined role URI (see Table 10.3) or custom, user defined Role
       soap:mustUnderstand="true"> ... insert current data for the current transaction here...
   </myschema:CurrentTransaction>
</soap:Header>
```

SOAP 1.2 uses the following attributes:

* mustUnderstand—must examine and process the header before forwarding on the SOAP message (default is false).
* Role—there are both predefined roles and custom roles possible. The predefined roles are shown in Table 10.3.
* Relay—whether or not to remove the header or include the header when forwarding on the SOAP message (default is false).

The attribute "Role" was called "actor" in SOAP 1.1.

All headers with a mustUnderstand are called *mandatory headers*. If an intermediary SOAP node or a SOAP receiver receives a mandatory header (mustUnderstand="true") and it is supposed to process it (for example, the role "next" was specified), but the SOAP node is unable to process the header, then the SOAP node must send a fault back to the SOAP sender. However, depending on the specified Role (the node may not be assigned the specified Role), a SOAP node may or may not examine the mandatory headers. If the SOAP node does not examine the header, then depending on the specified Relay, a SOAP node may or may not forward the SOAP header to the next SOAP node along the message path. We see pseudocode describing this in Listing 10.12.

LISTING 10.12   SOAP Message Path Header Processing

```
    if current SOAP node has the specified Role then
        if mustUnderstand="true" then
            examine the header
            if possible
                process the header
            else
                return fault to the SOAP Sender
        else
            if Relay = true then
                forward header on to next targeted node
            else
                remove header before forwarding
    else
        forward header without examining and processing
    In this algorithm, "current SOAP node" means SOAP intermediary or receiver.
```

TABLE 10.5
Predefined SOAP Roles

Role	Description	URI
None	Header blocks associated with this role must not be processed by the SOAP node. Perhaps there is some additional, supplemental information in this header block	http://www.w3.org/2003/05/soap-envelope/role/none
next	All SOAP intermediaries and the SOAP must process any mandatory headers that are targeted at this role if they can. These SOAP nodes may also process any optional headers.	http://www.w3.org/2003/05/soap-envelope/role/next
ultimateReceiver	This SOAP header is reserved for the ultimate receiver (SOAP Receiver/Server) of the message, and the Ultimate receiver must handle this header. This is the default role for headers which do not have a Role specified	http://www.w3.org/2003/05/soap-envelope/role/ultimateReceiver

There are three predefined SOAP roles, each is specified by a URI. These are shown in Table 10.5. Note that SOAP Roles can also appear in the Role field in SOAP Faults. There, they indicate which Role a SOAP Node was playing when the fault occurred (note that a SOAP Node can potentially play multiple Roles).

10.2.6 SOAP BINDING TO HTTP

Note that SOAP is very commonly "bound" to HTTP, that is, SOAP messages are embedded in HTTP packets.

An HTTP header containing a SOAP message must at a minimum include the HTTP Content-Type header, and the HTTP Content-Length header. The Content-Length specifies the number of bytes in the SOAP message.

A content-type is a header that uses internet media types to specify what kind of data (file-format) is being stored or transmitted (see Section 4.6). The content-type (Mime type) for SOAP 1.1 is text/xml but the content-type for SOAP 1.2 is application/soap+xml.

SOAP 1.1 (when using the HTTP binding) employed only the HTTP POST command. The web method feature in SOAP 1.2 allows a different HTTP command such as GET, POST, or DELETE in addition to POST to be used.

10.3 TECHNOLOGY REVIEW: WEB SERVICES DESCRIPTION LANGUAGE (WSDL)

Web Services Description Language is a language for describing interfaces to web services. WSDL specifies the message format and which protocol is to be used, and how it is to be used.

WSDL 1.1 was originally called "Web Services *Definition* Language" but "definition" was later changed to "description."

A WSDL document is in XML format.

WSDL can be bound to multiple messaging protocols, such as SOAP (versions 1.1 and 1.2) over HTTP (other bindings are also possible).

When WSDL talks about "binding," what it means is, which message and transmission protocol is going to be used to access the web service that is described by the WSDL document.

WSDL supports several different "styles" of SOAP formats. We looked at those before in Section 10.2.3. These include:

- Remote Procedure Call (RPC) with SOAP Encoding
- Remote Procedure Call (RPC) with Literal Encoding

- Document with Literal Encoding
- Document with Literal Encoding Wrapper

WSDL version 1.1 never officially became a World Wide Web Consortium (W3C) standard, whereas WSDL 2.0 did become a W3C standard. However, WSDL 1.1 is a defacto standard that is widely supported, including lots of new development occurring all the time, whereas it has been taking a long time for many different tools to support WSDL 2.0. This is possibly due to the concept of RESTful web services becoming very popular, including technologies such as AJAX, at about the same general time period that WSDL 2.0 came out.

In any case, for this reason we will look first and in more depth at WSDL 1.1. Note that there are various tools available to convert from WSDL 1.1 to WSDL 2.0, with greater or lesser degrees of success (do a google for "WSDL 1.1 to WSDL 2.0 converters").

10.3.1   WSDL 1.1 FORMAT

The overall format of WSDL 1.1 is shown in Listing 10.13. This is a generalized HelloWorld example. In this example, I have tried to show the overall outline of WSDL, including the major optional elements. However, it was convenient to focus on a particular implementation (HelloWorld) in order to show the connectivity between certain elements in a WSDL file. Obviously, this can be difficult to read, for any kind of complicated WSDL.

Note that "documentation" is used to include comments, or description, and can pretty well be inserted in any sub-element. I have shown this by putting "documentation" in most locations, in italics. I left it out of a couple really low-level places, though, just to save a little space on the page. It was getting really hard to read. ☺ By the way, in Listing 10.13, "tns" also means "targetNameSpace."

LISTING 10.13   Overall WSDL 1.1 Format

<definitions xmlns: soap=…(schema for SOAP 1.1 or SOAP 1.2)
        …other possible namespaces…
        xmlns:tns="http://myHelloWorld/"
        name="HelloWorldImplService" targetNamespace=http://myHelloWorld>
        <documentation …/>
        <import namespace="…" location="…">
        <types>
                <documentation…/>
                …various schemas could be defined here…
        </types>
        <message name="HelloWorld">
                <documentation…/>
                …
        </message<message >
        <message name="HelloWorldResponse">
                <documentation…/>
                …
        </message>
        <portType name="HelloWorld">
                <documentation…/>
                <operation name="HelloWorld">
                        <documentation…/>
                        <input name="…" message = "tns:HelloWorldRequest"/>
                        <output name="…" message="tns:HelloWorldResponse" />
                        <fault name="…" message="…" />
                </operation>

```
            </portType>
            <binding name="HelloWorldImplPortBinding" type="tns:HelloWorld">
                    <documentation>
                        <soap:binding transport="…soap 1.1 or soap 1.2 binding" style ="…rpc or
                        document  etc…" />
                        <operation name="HelloWorld">
                            <documentation… />
                            <input>
                            …
                            </input>
                            <output>
                            …
                            </output>
                        </operation>
            </binding>
            <service name="HelloWorldImplService">
                    <documentation…/>
                    <port name="HelloWorldImplPort" binding = "HelloWorldImplPortBinding">
                    …
                    </port>
            </service>
    </definitions>
```

Figure 10.1 shows the real WSDL file from my first JAX-WS HelloWorld example, included in the code provided for the instructor with this textbook. This example was simple enough to show in a textbook. ☺ It uses SOAP 1.1, which is the default in JAX-WS.

```
▼<!--
    Published by JAX-WS RI (http://jax-ws.java.net). RI's version is JAX-WS RI 2.2.9-b130926.1035 svn-revision#5f6196f2b90e9460065a4c2f4e30e065b245e51e.
  -->
▼<!--
    Generated by JAX-WS RI (http://jax-ws.java.net). RI's version is JAX-WS RI 2.2.9-b130926.1035 svn-revision#5f6196f2b90e9460065a4c2f4e30e065b245e51e.
  -->
▼<definitions xmlns:wsu="http://docs.oasis-open.org/wss/2004/01/oasis-200401-wss-wssecurity-utility-1.0.xsd" xmlns:wsp="http://www.w3.org/ns/ws-policy"
  xmlns:wsp1_2="http://schemas.xmlsoap.org/ws/2004/09/policy" xmlns:wsam="http://www.w3.org/2007/05/addressing/metadata"
  xmlns:soap="http://schemas.xmlsoap.org/wsdl/soap/" xmlns:tns="http://myHelloWorld/" xmlns:xsd="http://www.w3.org/2001/XMLSchema"
  xmlns="http://schemas.xmlsoap.org/wsdl/" targetNamespace="http://myHelloWorld/" name="HelloWorldImplService">
    <types/>
  ▼<message name="HelloWorld">
      <part name="arg0" type="xsd:string"/>
    </message>
  ▼<message name="HelloWorldResponse">
      <part name="return" type="xsd:string"/>
    </message>
  ▼<portType name="HelloWorld">
    ▼<operation name="HelloWorld">
        <input wsam:Action="http://myHelloWorld/HelloWorld/HelloWorldRequest" message="tns:HelloWorld"/>
        <output wsam:Action="http://myHelloWorld/HelloWorld/HelloWorldResponse" message="tns:HelloWorldResponse"/>
      </operation>
    </portType>
  ▼<binding name="HelloWorldImplPortBinding" type="tns:HelloWorld">
      <soap:binding transport="http://schemas.xmlsoap.org/soap/http" style="rpc"/>
    ▼<operation name="HelloWorld">
        <soap:operation soapAction=""/>
      ▼<input>
          <soap:body use="literal" namespace="http://myHelloWorld/"/>
        </input>
      ▼<output>
          <soap:body use="literal" namespace="http://myHelloWorld/"/>
        </output>
      </operation>
    </binding>
  ▼<service name="HelloWorldImplService">
    ▼<port name="HelloWorldImplPort" binding="tns:HelloWorldImplPortBinding">
        <soap:address location="http://localhost:8080/hello"/>
      </port>
    </service>
  </definitions>
```

FIGURE 10.1   Actual WSDL 1.1 file from myHelloWorld Example.

TABLE 10.6
WSDL 1.1 Elements

WSDL Element	Definition
Definitions	The root element of a WSDL document. Its attributes specify the targetNamespace, and other namespaces used in the WSDL document.
Import	This is used to import other WSDL documents.
Types	Provides schema definitions of the XML Schemas referenced in the WSDL document.
Message	The description of the messages that are passed from a client to a server (for example, when the Client calls an operation on the Server) or vice versa.
portType	Describes the web service itself by describing the interface of the service. It defines the operations (methods, remote procedure calls) that are available on the Server.
Operation	The description of the operation of the methods/remote procedure calls that are available to be called on the Server.
Binding	Specifies which data formats are associated with messages passed to or from operations, and specifies the lower-level protocol that is used to send data. When binding to soap, you specify "style" which could be, for example, RPC or Document, and "transport," which could be HTTP.
Service	A service is a collection of ports. Each supported protocol would have one port element.
Port	A port maps a network address (physical address) to a binding and gives it a name (specifies an endpoint). (An endpoint is a URL where, for example, a service can be accessed by a client). A web service can have multiple endpoints.

I'm going to describe the sub-parts of the WSDL document here. The elements are as shown in Table 10.6 (I already told you about the Documentation element).

As we will see later when we look at JAX-WS, one way to start building a web service is simply to type in the WSDL document. You can use Notepad on Windows to type this in if you want to, and you can use vi or nano or similar if you're a Linux person. However, as you should have been able to see from these very simple examples I've shown you, this can get messy pretty quickly.

There are several WSDL editors available that enable a programmer to correctly create a WSDL document. I did quick google search for "wsdl editors" and several came up.

10.3.2 WSDL 2.0 FORMAT

WSDL 2.0 replaces "definitions" from WSDL 1.1 with "description." It replaces "portType" with "interface". It replaces "port" with "endpoint." Also, "message" is defined inside "operation." In WSDL 2.0, fault messages can be declared inside an interface. It provides additional Message Exchange Patterns (see Section 10.3.3), and it allows interface inheritance.

LISTING 10.14   WSDL 2.0 Format

```
<wsdl:description
        xmlns:wsdl="http://www.w3.org/ns/wsdl"
        …other namespaces…>
        <wsdl:types>
                …define a schema here…
        </wsdl:types>
        <wsdl:interface>
                <wsdl:fault name="myfault" element=…refer to element in schema defined in
                    types… />
                <wsdl:operation name="myOwnOperation"
                        pattern="http://www.w3.org/ns/wsdl/in-out"
```

```
                              style="http://www.w3.org/ns/wsdl/style/iri"
                              wsdlx:safe="true">
                    <input messageLabel="In" element=...refer to element in schema
                                      defined in types...">
                    <output messageLabel="Out" element=...refer to element in schema
                                      defined in types...">
                    <outfault messageLabel="Out" element=refer to fault definition in
                                      schema defined in types>
            </wsdl:operation>
        </wsdl:interface>
        <wsdl:binding  name=...
            interface=..refer to interface above...>
                <fault ref=refer to fault definition in schema defined in types>
                <operation ref= refer to operation defined in interface>
        </wsdl:binding>
        <wsdl:service  name=...
            interface = refer to interface above>
        <wsdl:endpoint name=...
                binding=refer to binding defined above
                address="http://myservice/myOwn"
        </wsdl:service>
    </wsdl:description>
```

Note that I've left out some "tns" namespace references, when I say "refer to (some element) defined above" it is often requiring "tns" in front of the element name, because it is really referring to the targetNamespace. This clearly isn't a complete example of a WSDL 2.0 interface, but I'm not meaning it to be, it's here for discussion and comparison with WSDL 1.1.

The statement:

pattern=http://www.w3.org/ns/wsdl/in-out

refers to the WSDL 2.0 message patterns. We will see more of these in the following section.

The operation section in the WSDL 2.0 document can contain operation-style definitions that constrain how messages passed by the operations are formatted. The predefined operation styles in the WSDL 2.0 interface are:

- RPC, specified by: http://www.w3.org/ns/wsdl/style/rpc
- IRI, specified by: http://www.w3.org/ns/wsdl/style/iri
- Multipart, specified by: http://www.w3.org/ns/wsdl/style/multipart

The RPC style allows an interface to be easily mapped to a programming language construct in languages such as Java and C#. If RPC is used, then the message exchange pattern must be either in-only or in-out (see message patterns below).

The IRI style means that an XML Schema was defined (in the <types> section) that describes the messages sent as part of the operation definition. In Listing 10.14, where we see:

```
    input messageLabel="In" element=...refer to element in schema
                              defined in types...">
```

Here we could have defined the element as being named: tns:myInputElement, in that case the XML Schema in types would have had to also be named "myInputElement."

In IRI style, the content is a complex type containing a sequence, no attributes are allowed in the XML Schema definition of the element, and the element's children must be simple types.

By the way, the acronym "IRI" stands for Internationalized Resource Identifier, which is an extension to URIs that use the universal character set instead of ASCII. In WSDL 2.0, they call it "IRI" style because they're referring to how the message can be serialized (formatted for sending) in as an HTTP request (GET, etc.). For example, refer to URI encoding, which means characters are converted into a format that can be transmitted over the internet (ASCII), and replaces some characters with a "%" code, such as space being sent as %20.

Multipart style has similar restrictions to IRI style, but is intended to send messages with multiple sub-parts (multiple children elements). It has the additional restriction that the children elements must not have the same (local) name. It is different from IRI style in that the children elements are not restricted to simple types.

The wsdlx:safe attribute says that the client who calls the operation does not acquire any new obligation except that specified in the operation. For example, an unsafe (but not necessarily dangerous) interaction could change the state of some resource located on or accessed by the web server (such as modify a database through performing some kind of booking or order). This would normally mean that the HTTP binding was a "GET."

Note that WSDL 2.0 supports both SOAP 1.1 and SOAP 1.2 bindings.

10.3.3 WSDL Message Exchange Patterns

WSDL message exchange patterns are defined relative to the PortType. As mentioned earlier, the PortType defines operations. These operations are implemented on the Server, and the client remotely calls these operations on the Server. The WSDL message exchange patterns define, when these operations are invoked by the Client, whether messages are being sent *to* the Server, this is called the "In" direction, or the messages are being sent *from* the Server toward the client, this is called the "Out" direction, or both.

The WSDL message exchange patterns are as follows, from "Web Services Description Language (WSDL) version 2.0 Part 2: Adjuncts," that is, WSDL 2.0, in 2007:

- In-Only (One Way in WSDL 1.1)—The operation receives a request but does not send back a response (one way message, labeled "in", messageLabel="In" from the earlier WSDL 2.0 message), no faults returned.
- Robust In-Only—One way message, faults may be returned.
- In-Out (Request/Response in WSDL 1.1)—The operation receives a message and returns a response. The message received has direction in, labeled "in," followed by sending a message with direction "out" labeled "out" (messageLabel="Out", from the earlier WSDL 2.0 example). The second message can be a fault message.

The W3C further defined the following in "Web Services Description Language (WSDL) Version 2.0: Additional MEPS" in 2007:

- In-Optional-Out—A message with direction in, labeled "in," followed by an optional message with direction "out" labeled "out." The second message can be a fault message.
- Out-Only (Notification in WSDL 1.1)—The operation on the Server sends a request to some other node, but does not wait for a response. In this, a message with direction "out" labeled "out" is sent to some node. No faults are sent.
- Robust Out-Only—A message with direction "out" labeled "out" is sent to some node. This message can trigger a fault message in response.
- Out-In (Solicit Response in WSDL 1.1)—The operation on the Server sends a request to some other node, and waits for a response. Here, a message with direction "out" labeled "out" is sent to some node. That node sends back a message with direction in, labeled "in." The second message can be a fault message.

- Out-Optional-In—a message with direction "out" labeled "out" is sent to some node. That node optionally can send back a message with direction in, labeled "in." The second message can be a fault message.

With an In-Only message, the Client sends a message to the Server, but the Server is not expected to respond to this message. With an Out-Only message, the Server would send a message to the Client, and the Client may not have sent an earlier message. In–Out is a more standard request-response scenario.

10.3.4 RESTful Web Services through WADL and WSDL 2.0

Web Application Description Language (WADL) is a specification for describing RESTful web services (HTTP-based). WADL was submitted by Sun Microsystems to W3C, but did not become a standard. WSDL 2.0 also allows RESTful web services to be described, and WSDL 2.0 is a W3C standard. However, WSDL 2.0 is often considered to be more complex and generally harder to understand than WADL. Some argue that WSDL 2.0 is *service*-oriented whereas WADL is *resource*-oriented, so WADL is a better mapping to a RESTful architecture.

It has been also argued that neither WADL nor WSDL 2.0 is necessary, because a basic browser or RESTful client can create HTTP GET, POST, PUT, DELETE, and the web-based resource at the specified URI knows how to reply. However, some argue that a contract-first approach rather than a code-first approach is best, that in large systems it is useful to have a standard, published contract when performing interface activities, and that requiring WADL or WSDL 2.0 is a good way to impose this contract-first approach while still maintaining a RESTful architecture. One other benefit is that tools exist that can automatically generate client code based on a WADL description (or a WSDL 2.0 description, although WSDL 2.0 is still lacking in tool support compared to WSDL 1.1).

10.3.4.1 Web Application Description Language (WADL)

WADL provides a machine-processable interface description for a RESTful (HTTP-based) web service.

WADL allows a programmer to specify the resources (in URI format) being offered by the web service, links between these resources, all the HTTP methods (verbs) (GET, PUT, POST, DELETE) that can be used to access that resource, the inputs and outputs to those HTTP methods including their supported formats. It also lists supported data schemas and MIME types being used.

(Note that the Jersey reference implementation of JAX-RS supports WADL, so we will come back to this a bit sometime later when we talk about RESTful web services.)

LISTING 10.15 WADL Example

```
<application xmlns:xsd="http://wadl.dev.java.net/2009/02"
         xmlns:myAccount = "http://mywebaddress.com/AccountSchemas" >
  ...
    <resources base="http://mywebaddress.com/myinterface/">
      <resource path="myAccount">
        <method name="GET" id="viewAccount">
          <request>
            <param name="accountID" type="xsd:string"  style="query"
               required="true"/>
          </request>
          <response status="200">
             <representation mediaType="text/xml" element="myAccount:theResult" />
          </response>
```

```
          <response status="401">
              <representation mediaType="application/xml" element="myAccount:theError" />
          </response>
      </method>
   </resource>
 </resources>
</application>
```

This WADL defines a resource (mywebaddress.com/myinterface/myAccount)

In this example, the "style=query" indicates that we are using a URL query parameter (query string) which in this case is:

http://mywebaddress.edu/myinterface?name=accountID

(There's also a "style=header" command which you can use to put something into an HTTP header.)

A response showing the "GET" was successful is provided. The HTTP status code 200 in the response means that the request succeeded.

A response showing the "GET" was not successful is also provided. The HTTP status code 401 in the response means that the authentication using the accountID provided in the GET failed, probably there was no mechanism to send a password included, only an ID name. As a general thing, it's a bad idea to use HTTP GET to send any authentication information because it goes out-in cleartext in the HTTP command, as illustrated in the style=query example above.

Note that multiple resources can be defined on a resources base.

10.3.4.2 Web Services Description Language 2.0 RESTful Mapping

WSDL 2.0 provides an HTTP binding for HTTP 1.1 and HTTPS so these protocols can be used directly, instead of sending SOAP on top of HTTP or HTTPS.

The WSDL 2.0 HTTP binding allows selection of which HTTP operation is used (GET, PUT, POST, DELETE).

LISTING 10.16   WSDL 2.0 RESTful Format Using HTTP Binding

```
<wsdl:description
      xmlns:wsdl="http://www.w3.org/ns/wsdl"
      xmlns:thehttp="http://www.w3.org/ns/wsdl/http"="http://www.w3.org/ns/wsdl/http"
      xmlns:xsd="http://www.w3.org/2001/XMLSchema"
      ...other namespaces...>
      <wsdl:types>
          ...define a schema here...
      </wsdl:types>
      <wsdl:interface>
          <wsdl:operation name="myOwnOperation"
                          pattern="http://www.w3.org/ns/wsdl/in-out"
                          style="http://www.w3.org/ns/wsdl/style/iri"
                          wsdlx:safe="true">
                          <wsdl:input element="theParameters" />
                          <wsdl:output element="theResponse" />
          </wsdl:operation>
      </wsdl:interface>
      <wsdl:binding  name=...
          type="http://www.w3.org/ns/wsdl/http"
          interface=..refer to interface above...>
```

```
            <operation ref= refer to operation defined in interface
              thehttp:method="GET">:method="GET">
      </wsdl:binding>
      <wsdl:service  name=...
          interface = refer to interface above>
            <wsdl:endpoint name=...
                        binding=refer to binding defined above
                        address="http://myservice/myOwn"
      </wsdl:service>
  </wsdl:description>
```

The primary difference between non-RESTful WSDL 2.0 and the RESTful WSDL 2.0 shown here is that the binding here is set to HTTP binding, and the HTTP method is chosen to be "GET."

This version is, of course, not using SOAP since it is RESTful.

10.4 TECHNOLOGY REVIEW: JAVA API FOR XML WEB SERVICES (JAX-WS)

JAX-WS is an Application Programming Interface (API) for Java that is used to create web services. JAX-WS is part of the Java Platform, Enterprise Edition (Java EE). The Reference Implementation for JAX-WS is the GlassFish-Metro stack (a reference implementation is an implementation of a specification that is developed along with the specification, and serves as an initial implementation of the specification that clarifies what the specification is intended to do). The current version of JAX-WS as of this writing is version 2.2 which is specified by JSR224.

Although JAX-WS can be used to build both non-RESTful (SOAP-based) and RESTful web services, creating RESTful web services with JAX-WS is somewhat controversial. For example, Edureka! says "although JAX-WS can be used to write RESTful web services, it's not the best way to create REST-style services. In a production mode you should probably use JAX-RS." Also, Allamaraiu's opinion is that non-RESTful web services in general add too much complexity to the API through "hiding the protocol with layer upon layer" (RESTful web services normally do not try to hide their accesses to HTTP) and thus using JAX-WS in a RESTful way retains the added complexity of the protocol layering, so that using HTTP in JAX-WS is largely a wasted effort.

So most of the examples we will discuss here involve non-RESTful JAX-WS, using WSDL and SOAP. However, in the last section we will briefly discuss how a RESTful web service could be implemented using JAX-WS.

There are several cases of WSDL and SOAP constructs being used in this code. I will from time to time point these out. However, a complete explanation of the WSDL and SOAP constructs is given in Sections 10.2 and 10.3 above, which since they come before this in this textbook, you therefore should already have read. ☺ If you haven't read it first, then please do, or alternatively you can swap back and forth from that section to this section to understand how WSDL and SOAP is used in JAX-WS.

10.4.1 BRIEF INTRODUCTION TO JAX-WS CONCEPTS

We're going to start with a methodology that annotates Java code in order to create a web service. (You could instead start directly with a WSDL document; we'll look at that later on.)

I have chosen to use really basic Java code here—I'm not using Eclipse or any other Integrated Development Environment (IDE). My points for doing this are that not everybody knows the same IDE, and also that, in some cases, an IDE can help you out to the point that you don't learn basic concepts because the IDE did all the work for you.

First, let's start by looking at the Server side. The first concept to examine is the Service Endpoint Interface. This is a Java interface class that defines the methods by which the web service will be accessed. Listing 10.17 illustrates a Service Endpoint Interface.

LISTING 10.17   Service Endpoint Interface for HelloWorld Program

```
package myHelloWorld;
import javax.jws.WebMethod;
import javax.jws.WebService;
import javax.jws.soap.SOAPBinding;
import javax.jws.soap.SOAPBinding.Style;

//Service Endpoint Interface
@WebService
@SOAPBinding(style = Style.RPC)
public interface HelloWorld{

    @WebMethod String HelloWorld(String name);
}
```

In Listing 10.17, we see that the interface is named "HelloWorld." (Although the one method provided is also called "HelloWorld" this is not required to have the same name as the interface, it could instead have had another name such as "hiThere.")

Here, "@WebService" defines this interface as being a web service interface, while @WebMethod specifies the specific remote procedure calls that are part of the interface.

The @SOAPBinding annotation says which kind of lower-level protocol and format is going to handle the data transmission. In this case, it uses SOAP RPC with SOAP encoding (see Section 10.2).

Note that an explicit Service Endpoint Interface such as is shown in Listing 10.17 is not required. Instead, you can annotate a Java implementation class, and the Service Endpoint Interface will be implicit. We will look at this approach shortly. However, before we do this, let us finish our initial example by providing the implementation class that goes with the Service Endpoint Interface class from Listing 10.17. This implementation class is shown in Listing 10.18.

LISTING 10.18   Service Endpoint Implementation for Service Endpoint Interface
**   from Listing 10.17**

```
package myHelloWorld;
import javax.jws.WebService;

//Service Implementation
@WebService(endpointInterface = "myHelloWorld.HelloWorld")
public class HelloWorldImpl implements HelloWorld{

    @Override
    public String HelloWorld(String name) {
        System.out.println(name+" says hello");
        return "Hello World " + name;
    }

}
```

In Listing 10.18, we have two annotations, @WebService, and @Override. The @WebService annotation says that the interface associated with this implementation is the Service Endpoint Interface that was previously defined. Note that we also have "HelloWorldImpl implements HelloWorld." Perhaps unfortunately, except from a documentation standpoint, this is really optional, the important thing here in terms of web services, in order to map the interface to the implementation is the "@WebService" annotation. @Override simply says that this HelloWorld method is going to be used instead of the HelloWorld method in the interface (and that it is recognized as part of the web interface).

The Service Endpoint Interface together with the Service Endpoint Implementation together define the web service.

Now there are a couple of other things that have to happen before this web service can be used. First, one has to decide which URL and port number to make this web service available on, and second, one has to use some kind of web server, such as GlassFish or Apache Http Server or Tomcat. However, JAX-WS provides a class (called Endpoint) to publish your web service (Endpoint.publish) using a small HTTP server embedded in Java EE. This can be conveniently used to test your JAX-WS code (as long as you're not doing anything too fancy). A publisher for the web service we've just seen is provided in Listing 10.19.

LISTING 10.19   Web Service Publisher Using Endpoint.publish

```
package myHelloWorld;
import javax.xml.ws.Endpoint;
import myHelloWorld.HelloWorldImpl;

//Endpoint publisher
public class HelloWorldPublisher{

    public static void main(String[] args) {
        Endpoint.publish("http://localhost:8080/hello", new HelloWorldImpl());
    }

}
```

In Listing 10.19, the web service is being published at localhost. The term "localhost" means the current computer, and it corresponds to the IP (IPv4) address 127.0.0.1. It is a loopback address, which means that the underlying networking protocols, when sending packets to the localhost address, won't actually send them to the network but instead will copy output back to input.

What is happening here is that an instance of the Service Endpoint Implementation (HelloWorldImpl) is created, and is mapped to http://localhost:8080/hello. To start the web service running, type:

java -cp ../ myHelloWorld.HelloWorldPublisher

Here "-cp" sets the classpath to the directory above the current directory (the parent directory of the current directory). Note that in the code included with this textbook, I provided a convenient file called runpublisher.bat that will do the previous command (so you don't have to remember it) in a Windows command line. In Linux, just make runpublisher.bat executable by typing:

chmod +x runpublisher.bat

and you can use runpublisher.bat in Linux as well.

```
▼<definitions xmlns:wsu="http://docs.oasis-open.org/wss/2004/01/oasis-200401-wss-wssecurity-utility-1.0.xsd"
  xmlns:wsp="http://www.w3.org/ns/ws-policy" xmlns:wsp1_2="http://schemas.xmlsoap.org/ws/2004/09/policy"
  xmlns:wsam="http://www.w3.org/2007/05/addressing/metadata" xmlns:soap="http://schemas.xmlsoap.org/wsdl/soap/"
  xmlns:tns="http://myHelloWorld/" xmlns:xsd="http://www.w3.org/2001/XMLSchema" xmlns="http://schemas.xmlsoap.org/wsdl/"
  targetNamespace="http://myHelloWorld/" name="HelloWorldImplService">
  <types/>
▼<message name="HelloWorld">
    <part name="arg0" type="xsd:string"/>
  </message>
▼<message name="HelloWorldResponse">
    <part name="return" type="xsd:string"/>
  </message>
▼<portType name="HelloWorld">
  ▼<operation name="HelloWorld">
      <input wsam:Action="http://myHelloWorld/HelloWorld/HelloWorldRequest" message="tns:HelloWorld"/>
      <output wsam:Action="http://myHelloWorld/HelloWorld/HelloWorldResponse" message="tns:HelloWorldResponse"/>
    </operation>
  </portType>
▼<binding name="HelloWorldImplPortBinding" type="tns:HelloWorld">
    <soap:binding transport="http://schemas.xmlsoap.org/soap/http" style="rpc"/>
  ▼<operation name="HelloWorld">
      <soap:operation soapAction=""/>
    ▼<input>
        <soap:body use="literal" namespace="http://myHelloWorld/"/>
      </input>
    ▼<output>
        <soap:body use="literal" namespace="http://myHelloWorld/"/>
      </output>
    </operation>
  </binding>
▼<service name="HelloWorldImplService">
  ▼<port name="HelloWorldImplPort" binding="tns:HelloWorldImplPortBinding">
      <soap:address location="http://localhost:8080/hello"/>
    </port>
  </service>
</definitions>
```

FIGURE 10.2   WSDL created from the HelloWorld Web Service.

After the web service, if you want to see the WSDL that was automatically created by JAX-WS using the annotations on the Service Endpoint Interface, and the Service Endpoint Implementation, you can type:

http://localhost:8080/hello?wsdl

in your browser and you will see it. I did this myself, using Chrome. The WSDL I got is shown in Figure 10.2.

As you can see from this WSDL, it is using SOAP 1.1 (you can see this because http://schemas. xmlsoap.org/soap/http specifies that SOAP 1.1 is being used). It is using RPC type because it says "style='rpc'." You can also see that this is using WSDL 1.1, in part because it's using "<portType>" instead of "<interface>." From the <message> section, the SOAP input message (HelloWorld) is a string and the SOAP output message (HelloWorldResponse) is also a string.

Let's go back now and revisit the Service Endpoint Interface and the Service Endpoint Implementation. As mentioned earlier, an explicit Service Endpoint Interface such as is shown in Listing 10.17 is not required. Instead, you can annotate a Java implementation class, and the Service Endpoint Interface will be implicit. In Listing 10.20, I have done this for the same HelloWorld application.

LISTING 10.20   Annotated Service Endpoint Implementation, No Separate Service Endpoint Interface

```
package HelloWorld_class_only;
import javax.jws.WebMethod;
import javax.jws.WebService;
import javax.xml.ws.soap.Addressing;
```

```
@WebService
@Addressing(required = true)
public class HelloWorld {
  @WebMethod
  public String HelloWorld(String name) {
      System.out.println(name+" says hello");
      return "Hello World " + name;
  }
}
```

This is pretty simple; all you do is annotate it with @WebService and @WebMethod.

I've provided the @Addressing here mostly so I can briefly introduce the topic of WS-Addressing, which I've pretty well ignored before. (I didn't talk about it in the WSDL/SOAP Sections 10.2 and 10.3, for example.) WS-Addressing has several benefits. First of all, it allows message routing to be handled at the web service layer rather than only by lower-level protocols (such as TCP/IP). Second, it permits the use of many messaging patterns because it removes the connection between the SOAP messages and the underlying HTTP protocol's request/response message exchange format. For example, it allows a SOAP request to be performed on a different HTTP connection from the SOAP response. This enables the SOAP response to be done at a different time (not part of the original HTTP request/response) and thus allows asynchronous communication.

I don't want to go into this more than I have here; I believe it's above the level of an introductory text, but you the student need to know that it exists, and in a general way how it could be used.

10.4.2 Creating JAX-WS Clients

There are several ways to create JAX-WS clients. First of all, there are some tools to statically generate the Client, the one that is included with the JAX-WS reference implementation is called "wsimport." Other tools to do this are available (wsconsume from JBoss, ClientGen from WebLogic, for example). We will look at wsimport here next.

There are also other ways this can be done. A dynamic proxy client is one of these ways. A dynamic proxy client is given up front the URL where the web service resides, and a copy of the Service Endpoint Interface class (in a .class file and not in a .java file), then it reads the WSDL at runtime and automatically creates a proxy object which is used to access the web service. We will see an example of this later.

Yet another way is to use a Dispatch client. This can be used when you want a dynamic client, but you don't want to have to use JAX-WS artifacts (such as the Service Endpoint Interface Class), or it could be used when you want to focus on sending/receiving XML messages. I have provided two examples of a dispatch client; in these examples I have also focused on building my own SOAP messages using the Soap with Attachments API (SAAJ). One example uses SOAP 1.1, and the other example uses SOAP 1.2.

10.4.2.1 Client Created Using wsimport

For the first example, we will assume the web service we saw earlier has already been published, and that our wsimport command can grab the WSDL that has been published. Type:

wsimport -keep http://localhost:8080/hello?wsdl -d .

(Note the "." after the -d !!!)

This will create a client; it will keep all generated files (-keep option), that means it will keep the .java files it generates as well as their associated .class files, and put them in a directory under the current directory (-d .). (Here the name of the directory will be the package name.)

We need a stub client to call the files that were generated by the wsimport command. The stub client is shown in Listing 10.21.

LISTING 10.21   Stub Client Needed to Access Files Generated by wsimport

```
import myhelloworld.HelloWorld;
import myhelloworld.HelloWorldImplService;
public class HelloWorldClient {
    public static void main(String[] args) {
    HelloWorldImplService myHelloWorld = new HelloWorldImplService();
    HelloWorld myinterface = myHelloWorld.getHelloWorldImplPort();
    //Note the format of the operation call "helloWorld".
    //This matches the format in the wsimport-generated HelloWorld.java file.
    String response = myinterface.helloWorld(args[0]);


    System.out.println(response);
  }
}
```

Here the files HelloWorld and HelloWorldImplService that are accessed in Listing 10.21 were generated using the wsimport command. They are located in the subdirectory myHelloWorld.

The java file for the Service Endpoint Interface that was generated using wsimport is shown in Listing 10.22. You can see the other generated Java file, the one for the Service Endpoint Implementation, in the code that is included along with the textbook.

LISTING 10.22   HelloWorld Interface File Generated by wsimport

```
package myhelloworld;
import javax.jws.WebMethod;
import javax.jws.WebParam;
import javax.jws.WebResult;
import javax.jws.WebService;
import javax.jws.soap.SOAPBinding;
/**
 * This class was generated by the JAX-WS RI.
 * JAX-WS RI 2.1.6 in JDK 6
 * Generated source version: 2.1
 *
 */
@WebService(name = "HelloWorld", targetNamespace = "http://myHelloWorld/")
@SOAPBinding(style = SOAPBinding.Style.RPC)
public interface HelloWorld {
   /**
    *
    * @param arg0
    * @return
    *     returns java.lang.String
    */
```

```
@WebMethod(operationName = "HelloWorld")
@WebResult(partName = "return")
public String helloWorld(
    @WebParam(name = "arg0", partName = "arg0")
    String arg0);
}
```

Compare this to the original Service Endpoint Interface file we originally saw in Listing 10.17. This is wsimport's recreation of the original Service Endpoint Interface, from its associated WSDL.

In the next example, we will assume the web service we saw earlier is represented by a .wsdl file, but it may or may not have previously been published. (Remember that it is possible to begin building a JAX-WS type web service with either a WSDL or else with JAX-WS-annotated Java. So someone might have created the WSDL document first and still be working on the web service.)

Ways to cheat by automatically generating a WSDL document that you can use to play with wsimport using WSDL files:
- Start a web service running, go to its "?wsdl" page, and copy/paste the wsdl using Notepad (or vi or nano, etc.) to a text file with a .wsdl extension
- Use wsgen (we will look at this later)

Let's assume for now that we have created a WSDL document somehow and that it basically looks like the WSDL shown in Figure 10.2.

Now type:

wsimport -d . -keep -wsdllocation http://localhost:8080/hello mywsdl.wsdl

This will create the HelloWorld and HelloWorldImplService similarly to how we did it in the first wsimport example, and they will also be located in the myHelloWorld subdirectory of the current directory.

Note that before you can check this particular client out, that you must start the web service running first. For the first wsimport example that grabbed the WSDL direct from the URL, the web service already had to be running, but for this one maybe or maybe not.

10.4.2.2   Dynamic Proxy Client

LISTING 10.23   Dynamic Proxy Client

```
package myHelloWorld;

import java.net.URL;
import javax.xml.namespace.QName;
import javax.xml.ws.Service;
import myHelloWorld.HelloWorld;
/* This example does not use wsimport. Instead, it
creates a service instance manually. */

public class HelloWorldClient{
    public static void main(String[] args) throws Exception {
        URL location_of_wsdl = new URL("http://localhost:8080/hello?wsdl");
```

```
        QName name_of_service = new QName("http://myHelloWorld/", "Hello
            WorldImplService");
        Service service = Service.create(location_of_wsdl, name_of_service);
        HelloWorld hello = service.getPort(HelloWorld.class);
        String response = hello.HelloWorld(args[0]);
        System.out.println(response);
    }
}
```

As discussed earlier, a dynamic proxy client is given the URL where the web service resides, including the WSDL URL, which it reads at runtime. Then it is given a copy of the Service Endpoint Interface class (HelloWorld.class above), which tells the Client what the interface looks like. Using the URL, the WSDL, and the Service Endpoint Interface class, it generates a proxy object (the "hello" object of type HelloWorld in Listing 10.23). Using this proxy object, it can call the operations (methods/remote procedure call) from the Service Endpoint Interface.

This example is different from the wsimport example in that creating the proxy object happens at runtime, and does not require an extra command (such as wsimport). However, it does require that the Service Endpoint Interface be specified in Java and previously compiled to a .class file.

10.4.2.3   Dynamic Dispatch Client—SOAP 1.1

In Listing 10.24, we have a dynamic dispatch client.

The Dispatch client requires that XML-format messages be created in order to be sent. For example, the Oracle documentation for the Dispatch Interface says, "The client is responsible for ensuring that the msg object when marshaled is formed according to the requirements of the protocol binding in use." (The "msg" object is the message being sent.)

Note that the Dispatch client itself could handle other kinds of messages than SOAP (for example, JAXB objects, among others). In this case, however, we will focus on SOAP. To build the SOAP messages that are sent by this dispatch client, I use the SOAP with Attachments API (SAAJ).

LISTING 10.24   Dynamic Dispatch Client That Uses SAAJ to Send SOAP 1.1 Messages

```
public class HelloWorldClient {
    public static void main(String[] args) throws SOAPException {
        QName serviceName=new QName("http://localhost/","HelloWorldService");
        QName portName=new QName("http://localhost/","HelloWorldPortBinding");
        Service service = Service.create(serviceName);
        service.addPort(portName,
                        SOAPBinding.SOAP11HTTP_BINDING,"http://localhost:8082/
                            helloanother");
        Dispatch<SOAPMessage> dispatch =
                                service.createDispatch(portName,
                                SOAPMessage.class,
                                Service.Mode.MESSAGE,
                                new AddressingFeature());
        MessageFactory myMessageFactory =
                                MessageFactory.newInstance(
                                SOAPConstants.SOAP_1_1_PROTOCOL);
        SOAPMessage request = myMessageFactory.createMessage();
        SOAPPart part = request.getSOAPPart();
        SOAPEnvelope env = part.getEnvelope();
```

```
//        SOAPHeader header = env.getHeader();
          SOAPBody body = env.getBody();
          SOAPElement operation = body.addChildElement("HelloWorld", "ns",
                                   "http://HelloWorld_class_only_SOAP11_dispatch_client/");
          SOAPElement value0 = operation.addChildElement("arg0");

          value0.addTextNode(args[0]);
          request.saveChanges();
          dispatch.getRequestContext().put(BindingProvider.SOAPACTION_USE_PROPERTY,
             true);

          dispatch.getRequestContext().put(BindingProvider.SOAPACTION_URI_PROPERTY,
                   "http://HelloWorld_class_only_SOAP11_dispatch_client/HelloWorld/
                   Hello WorldRequest");
          SOAPMessage response=dispatch.invoke(request);

          // Get values from SOAP response
          String the_response =

          getSOAPBody().getElementsByTagName("return").item(0).getFirstChild().getNodeValue();

          System.out.println("The response is "+the_response);
    }
}
```

The basic structure of a (synchronous) Dispatch client itself is as follows:

```
Dispatch<SOAPMessage> dispatch = service.createDispatch (...);
SOAPMessage request = mymessageFactory.createRequest(...);
SOAPMessage response=dispatch.invoke(request);
```

Note that what makes this code synchronous is that we are calling "dispatch.invoke." If we had called "dispatch.invokeAsync" we would have been doing an asynchronous communication, and if we had called "dispatch.invokeOneWay" we would have been doing a one-way communication. Note however that according to the Oracle description of the Dispatch Interface, with SOAP over HTTP, the dispatch.invokeOneWay will block until an HTTP response is received.

There are two versions of invokeAsync, one provides a callback handler that the Server can call when it has completed the specified action. The other version of invokeAsync doesn't include that handler, so the Client would have to poll the Server to see when the specified action is complete.

One choice that must be made is whether or not you will be using MESSAGE mode or PAYLOAD mode (we're using Service.Mode.MESSAGE in Listing 10.24). If you choose MESSAGE mode then you will have to create the entire SOAP message, including the envelope (and any headers). If you choose PAYLOAD mode, then you are only responsible for creating the content of the SOAP Body (JAX-WS would do the envelope).

The SOAPMessage class is the root class for all SOAP messages.

With the following code, what we have done is to create an Endpoint and bind it to a port.

```
QName serviceName=new QName("http://localhost/","HelloWorldService");
QName portName=new QName("http://localhost/","HelloWorldPortBinding");
Service service = Service.create(serviceName);
service.addPort(portName,
          SOAPBinding.SOAP11HTTP_BINDING,"http://localhost:8082/helloanother");
```

As you can see, we have bound this particular implementation to SOAP 1.1.

Most of the rest of the example in Listing 10.24 is concerned with building a SOAP 1.1 request message using SAAJ. See Listing 10.25.

LISTING 10.25   Using SAAJ to Build a SOAP 1.1 Request Message

```
MessageFactory myMessageFactory =
                        MessageFactory.newInstance(
                        SOAPConstants.SOAP_1_1_PROTOCOL);
SOAPMessage request = myMessageFactory.createMessage();
SOAPPart part = request.getSOAPPart();
SOAPEnvelope env = part.getEnvelope();
//    SOAPHeader header = env.getHeader();
SOAPBody body = env.getBody();
SOAPElement operation = body.addChildElement("HelloWorld", "ns",
                    "http://HelloWorld_class_only_SOAP11_dispatch_client/");
SOAPElement value0 = operation.addChildElement("arg0");

value0.addTextNode(args[0]);
request.saveChanges();
```

We previously discussed SOAP format in Section 10.2. Listing 10.1 from Section 10.2.1 is replicated here as Listing 10.26.

LISTING 10.26   SOAP Message Overall Format

```
<soap: Envelope
      <soap:Header
           ...header stuff included here...
      </soap:Header>
      <soap:Body>
           ...body stuff included here...
      </soap:Body>
</soap: Envelope>
```

As you recall from Section 10.2.1, a SOAP message has an envelope, optional headers, and a body.

SOAP messages with Attachments include the original SOAP information in a SOAP Part but may also have an Attachment part. So a view of SOAP messages with Attachments is that there are two parts to it:

- A SOAP part, that contains the SOAP envelope (which itself contains headers (optional) and a body
- An Attachment part (optional), that contains the attachments

If a SOAP message has an attachment part, then the attachment part must contain a MIME header to describe the data in the attachment. See Section 4.6 for more information on how MIME types work.

I'm telling you this so you can understand about the SOAPPart object, but also where the "attachment" parts come in, relative to the name "SOAP with Attachments API" (SAAJ). However, we're going to ignore the attachment stuff, other than this, because I think it's a little confusing for an introductory text.

Now let's talk about how SAAJ builds a SOAP request message. First it creates a factory to create SOAP 1.1 messages (myMessageFactory in Listing 10.25). It uses this factory to create an empty SOAP 1.1 message:

SOAPMessage request = myMessageFactory.createMessage();

Then it uses:

```
SOAPPart part = request.getSOAPPart();
SOAPEnvelope env = part.getEnvelope();
```

to narrow in to the SOAP envelope inside the SOAP part. It uses the envelope to access the SOAP Body:

SOAPBody body = env.getBody();

(Note that you could also access a SOAP header here, I've included it in the code but I've commented it out because we're not using it.)

Then we set the needed items in the SOAP Body:

```
SOAPElement operation = body.addChildElement("HelloWorld", "ns",
                        "http://HelloWorld_class_only_SOAP11_dispatch_client/");
SOAPElement value0 = operation.addChildElement("arg0");

value0.addTextNode(args[0]);
```

Here we told it the name of the operation/request message (HelloWorld), and its namespace. And finally we make sure we have saved these changes back to the SOAP request object:

```
request.saveChanges();
```

At the end, in the long statement:

getSOAPBody().getElementsByTagName("return").item(0).getFirstChild().getNodeValue();

the call "getElementsByTagName" is a call to the Document Object Model, it will get all elements of the XML document named "return." (It is looking for "part name = 'return' " in the HelloWorldResponse if you look back at Figure 10.2).

Note that the two lines with SOAPACTION_USE_PROPERTY and SOAPACTION_URI_-PROPERTY are required in SOAP 1.1 but are not required in SOAP 1.2. In SOAP 1.1, the SOAP action is included in the SOAPAction HTTP header, but in SOAP 1.2 it is included in the Content-Type HTTP header.

A SOAP action specifies which URL will be used to call an operation, for example from the WSDL 1.1 specification we have the following example:

```
<operation name="GetLastTradePrice">
    <soap:operation soapAction="http://example.com/GetLastTradePrice"/>
    ...
```

10.4.2.4 Dynamic Dispatch Client—SOAP 1.2

For the SOAP 1.2 example, we're going to focus in on the differences from the SOAP 1.1 example in the previous section. A complete SOAP 1.2 dynamic dispatch client example is provided in the code that accompanies this textbook.

There are a couple of basic differences. For example, the addPort call in SOAP 1.2 now becomes, using SOAP1.2 binding:

service.addPort(portName, SOAPBinding.SOAP12HTTP_BINDING,"http://localhost:8080/hello");

and the SOAP message factory must now be instantiated to build empty SOAP 1.2 messages rather than empty SOAP 1.1 messages, as follows:

MessageFactory myMessageFactory =
        MessageFactory.newInstance(SOAPConstants.SOAP_1_2_PROTOCOL);

and as we previously discussed, you no longer need to specify a SOAP action. In the provided Dynamic Dispatch with SOAP 1.1 code, in one place I used an addBodyElement whereas in the SOAP 1.1 code I had only used addChildElements, but this is a fairly arbitrary coding choice.

However, the biggest difference is that you have to have a SOAP 1.2 server for a SOAP 1.2 client to connect to. We'll see this in the next section.

10.4.3 Service Endpoint Implementation Bindings

There really is no difference between a Service Endpoint Interface using SOAP 1.1 and a Service Endpoint Interface using SOAP 1.2. In the examples provided with this text, I've used an RPC binding on the SOAP 1.1 Service Endpoint Interface and a Document-Literal Binding on the Service Endpoint Interface using SOAP 1.2, but I could have used the same for each.

LISTING 10.27   Service Endpoint Implementation for SOAP 1.2

```
package myHelloWorld_SOAP12;

import javax.jws.WebService;
import javax.xml.ws.BindingType;
//Service Implementation
@WebService(endpointInterface = "myHelloWorld_SOAP12.HelloWorld", serviceName =
"HelloWorldService", targetNamespace = "http://myHelloWorld_SOAP12/")
@BindingType(value = "http://java.sun.com/xml/ns/jaxws/2003/05/soap/bindings/HTTP/")
public class HelloWorldImpl implements HelloWorld{
    @Override
    public String HelloWorld(String name) {
        System.out.println(name+" says hello");
        return "Hello World " + name;
    }
}
```

Where there is a difference is in the Service Endpoint Implementation (see Listing 10.27). In Listing 10.27, we bind to SOAP 1.2 using the following statement:

@BindingType(value = "http://java.sun.com/xml/ns/jaxws/2003/05/soap/bindings/HTTP/")

In the SOAP and WSDL discussion in Sections 10.2 and 10.3, I previously discussed that SOAP 1.2 bindings should be done to:

http://www.w3.org/2003/05/soap/bindings/HTTP/

However, the following link has also been used to generate SOAP 1.2 bindings, and this is what I've used in this example:

http://java.sun.com/xml/ns/jaxws/2003/05/soap/bindings/HTTP/

With this second binding, which is non-standard, JAX-WS was told to generate WSDL with SOAP 1.2 binding on the fly when requested by a client. (Nowadays this is done automatically.) In this case, the choice was totally arbitrary; I had used this URI for binding in previous examples and merely continued it here.

You can use wsimport to create clients, as before. Also, the dynamic proxy client is the same. Where there is a difference is between the dynamic dispatch clients for SOAP 1.1 versus SOAP 1.2, but we already saw that in the previous section.

10.4.4 A Few Other Comments

In the code provided for the instructor with this textbook, I've added a few additional examples. In one example, I simply showed how you could have web services listen on different port numbers. In other examples, I showed how to specify SOAP RPC binding versus SOAP document-literal binding in JAX-WS. (What this means is heavily discussed in the SOAP/WSDL Sections 10.2 and 10.3.)

I also provide a wsgen example. The wsgen tool takes a Service Endpoint Implementation class and generates the Java code required for JAX-WS to connect to this class. However, in the more recent versions of Metro (JAX-WS Reference Implementation) and core Java (Java 6 and above), these artifacts are automatically generated at runtime, so there is no need to run wsgen separately.

However, if you want to generate a wsdl file from a JAX-WS Service Implementation Interface, you can still do that (it still also generates the connecting Java code although that generation is done automatically). To generate a WSDL 1.1 file that employs SOAP 1.1, type the following:

wsgen -wsdl -cp ../ -verbose -keep -r WSDL_SOAP11 HelloWorld_wsgen.HelloWorldImpl

while to generate a WSDL 1.1 file that employs a SOAP 1.2 binding, type the following:

wsgen -wsdl:Xsoap1.2 -extension -cp ../ -verbose -keep -r WSDL_SOAP12 HelloWorld_wsgen.HelloWorldImpl

(or in either case you can just run an appropriate web service; go to http://...interfacename...?wsdl in your browser, and do a cut/paste to a wsdl file.)

10.4.5 Building RESTful Web Services with JAX-WS

I haven't created example code for a JAX-WS RESTful implementation because most people recommend using some technologies that are more directly targeted toward a RESTful architecture such as JAX-RS or perhaps AJAX instead. However, JAX-WS does provide RESTful support, and we will discuss it briefly.

In Sections 10.2 and 10.3 on WSDL/SOAP, we previously took a look at WADL and WSDL 2.0, both of which allow a mapping from a contract style interface to a RESTful HTTP-style mapping. As we discussed there, it has been argued that neither WADL nor WSDL 2.0 is necessary, because even a basic browser or RESTful client can create HTTP GET, POST, PUT, DELETE, and the web-based resource at the specified URI knows how to reply. However, some argue that a contract-first approach rather than a code-first approach is best, that in large systems it is useful to have a standard, published contract when performing interface activities, and that requiring WADL or WSDL 2.0 is a good way to impose this contract-first approach while still maintaining a RESTful architecture. One other benefit is that tools exist that can automatically generate client code based on a WADL description (or a WSDL 2.0 description, although WSDL 2.0 is still lacking in tool support compared to WSDL 1.1).

To use a RESTful implementation in JAX-WS, first do:

@WebServiceProvider

because this interface is able to send and receive raw XML data (XML message data).

Also, the Service Implementation Interface should be labeled with:

@ServiceMode(value = javax.xml.ws.Service.Mode.MESSAGE)

because you must craft your own XML message, you don't want any of it to be SOAP (if you had picked PAYLOAD it would be building a SOAP message, and SOAP is not used in RESTful web services) and you choose:

@BindingType(value = HTTPBinding.HTTP_BINDING)

to bind your web service directly to the HTTP protocol. In other words, instead of using SOAP messages, and treating the HTTP protocol as a transparent lower networking layer, you're now going to be using HTTP GET, PUT, POST, etc. directly.

You must specify:

    @Resource protected WebServiceContext mycontext;

This allows you to access the message context. The message context contains metadata associated with the message exchange, that is, it contains data that describes what's going on during the message exchange.

Then do the following (this will be inside the "invoke" method that is required when you use @WebServiceProvider):

```
MessageContext mycontext = myontext.getMessageContext();
String path= (String) mycontext.get(MessageContext.PATH_INFO);
String query= (String) mycontext.get(MessageContext.QUERY_STRING);
String myrequestMethod = (String)
        mycontext.get(MessageContext.HTTP_REQUEST_METHOD);
```

You can use various "if" statements to look for "GET" or "POST" or "PUT" etc. in the myrequestMethod string.

The Query string will contain the query string from a GET, for example, name?i=1&i=2.

The path will contain the information after the base URL but before the query string.

You can parse the strings that contain these, and thereby completely understand and process the HTTP command that you received.

10.4.6   JAX-WS Asynchronous Example

In this section, we examine how to make an asynchronous client using wsimport to connect to a JAX-WS server. We will use basically the same publisher from Listing 10.19 and basically the same service from Listing 10.20 (the package names are different, port number different, and name of service different; see code provided for the instructor with this textbook).

Our asynchronous client is shown in Listing 10.28. This client was generated by wsimport as shown in Listing 10.30, using the asynchronous binding shown in Listing 10.29. The asynchronous binding generates somewhat different function calls for the Client. The call to the asynchronous hello world method now looks as follows:

```
Response<thehello.HelloWorldResponse>
    response = myinterface.helloWorldAsync(args[0]);
```

See that the method name is different, it's now called "helloWorldAsync" instead of simply "hello-World" as it was in the synchronous client.

LISTING 10.28   Asynchronous Client Generated Using wsimport

```java
import java.util.concurrent.Future;
import javax.jws.WebMethod;
import javax.jws.WebParam;
import javax.jws.WebResult;
import javax.jws.WebService;
import javax.xml.bind.annotation.XmlSeeAlso;
import javax.xml.ws.Action;
import javax.xml.ws.AsyncHandler;
import javax.xml.ws.RequestWrapper;
import javax.xml.ws.Response;
import javax.xml.ws.ResponseWrapper;
import thehello.HelloWorld;
import thehello.HelloWorldService;
public class HelloWorldClient_Async {
    public static void main(String[] args) {
        // HelloWorldService_Service is a class
        HelloWorldService myHelloWorld = new HelloWorldService();
        // In this case, HelloWorld was generated by wsimport as an interface class
        HelloWorld myinterface = myHelloWorld.getHelloWorldPort();
        Response<thehello.HelloWorldResponse>
        response = myinterface.helloWorldAsync(args[0]);
        String theresponse="";
        try {
            while ( !response.isDone() ) {
                System.out.println("doing useful work");
            }
            // get the response itself
            thehello.HelloWorldResponse myresponse = response.get();
            // retrieve the string from within the response
            theresponse = myresponse.getReturn();
        }
        catch (InterruptedException e) {
            e.printStackTrace();
        }
        catch (Exception e) {
            e.printStackTrace();
        }
        System.out.println("Final response is "+theresponse );

    }
}
```

This asynchronous client employs poll waiting, as follows:

```
while ( !response.isDone() ) {
  System.out.println("doing useful work");
}
```

then when the response is ready, this client acquires the response as follows:

```
// get the response itself
thehello.HelloWorldResponse myresponse = response.get();
// retrieve the string from within the response
theresponse = myresponse.getReturn();
```

However, for this to work, wsimport had to create an asynchronous version of the client to begin with. To do this, we create a file called asyncbinding.xml. This file is shown in Listing 29. The most important portion of this file, to enable creation of a WSDL that allows asynchronous operation is the following statement:

<enableAsyncMapping>true</enableAsyncMapping>

Then we use this file as an input to wsimport as shown in Listing 10.30.

LISTING 10.29   Asynchronous Binding File

```
<bindings
  xmlns:xsd="http://www.w3.org/2001/XMLSchema"
  xmlns:wsdl="http://schemas.xmlsoap.org/wsdl/"
  wsdlLocation="http://localhost:8082/helloanother?WSDL"
  xmlns="http://java.sun.com/xml/ns/jaxws">
  <bindings node="wsdl:definitions">
    <package name="async.client"/>
    <enableAsyncMapping>true</enableAsyncMapping>
  </bindings>
</bindings>
```

LISTING 10.30   How to Add Asynchronous Binding to WSDL Using wsimport

```
wsimport -keep http://localhost:8082/helloanother?wsdl -b asyncbinding.xml -s.
```

The "-b" in the call to wsimport in Listing 10.30 is for binding.

10.5   TECHNOLOGY REVIEW: WINDOWS COMMUNICATION FOUNDATION (WCF)

Windows Communication Foundation (WCF) is a communication framework based on/integrated with Microsoft .NET, that is used to create service-oriented architecture-based systems. Systems created with WCF can be hosted on Microsoft IIS or they can be self-hosted in a separately running

.exe file. Note that it is very common to implement a system (that supplies one or more services) in a .DLL file. Then the code running in the hosting software must access the services in the .DLL file to perform the required actions.

10.5.1 Brief Introduction to WCF Concepts

Using WCF, a service is accessed through an "endpoint" which consists of:

- Address
- Binding
- Contract

Together these are known as the ABCs of WCF.

In WCF, a "channel" is a communication connection between the client and the Server. Messages sent/received over each channel are processed by a communication stack that Microsoft calls the "Channel Stack."

10.5.1.1 Address

An Address is the location where a service is hosted. This address is in URL format. The information in this URL format includes various choices that must be made in order to access the service. One possible address could be:

http://myownplace:5731/MyService

In this example, you could replace the "http" by other choices, associated with other protocols: for example, you could do:

https://myownplace:5731/MyService

(this one differs from the first address only in that we've replaced "http" with "https")
or

net.tcp://myownplace:5731/MyService

There are several other possible choices; we'll go through these in a little more depth below. Note that the port number (the example used here is ":5731") is optional.

10.5.1.2 Binding

The Binding specifies the chosen technologies to be used when connecting to the endpoint. Microsoft subdivides a "binding" into three sub-elements: transport, encoding, and protocol:

- Transport—HTTP versus HTTPS versus TCP, etc.
- Protocol—security settings, reliability settings, context flow settings
- Encoding—text/XML versus binary, etc.

In the Microsoft terminology the "Transport" element is associated with choosing the transport protocol that is to be used, rather than the "Protocol" element. Somewhat confusingly, the sub-element "Protocol" is used to select other items that are not really directly related to the protocols that form a network-protocol-stack: for example, it specifies such items as security settings rather than choosing, say, TCP/IP versus some other protocol such as X.25 (you, the reader, are too young to remember X.25). (Although "Protocol" is also used to select any user-defined protocols.)

I note that the items that Microsoft categorizes under "Transport" include TCP (which is a protocol), HTTP (which is another protocol), and HTTPS (which is yet another protocol), among others. These are Transport protocols so the term Transport makes sense, but the term Protocol would also have made sense in this context.

It is possible to define your very own binding that makes your own separate choices for the items that fall under the Transport, Protocol, and Encoding elements. However, for your convenience, Microsoft has defined several "system-provided," that is to say "canned" or "included along with WCF," bindings. Since this is an introductory book, we will talk about only a few of these: BasicHttp-Binding, WSHttpBinding, netTcpBinding, and WebHttpBinding.

BasicHttpBinding and WSHttpBinding are two commonly used bindings, whereas WebHttpBinding is the binding WCF uses to implement RESTful services. The other one, netTcpBinding, is included because it is a little different: the other three of these system-provided bindings employ HTTP in one way or another; however, netTcpBinding uses TCP for message delivery.

BasicHttpBinding is sort of a backward-compatibility binding, it works with old ASP.NET web services/ASMX clients, as well as new clients, using an old version of SOAP. Its primary advantage is that it is very interoperable. Its biggest disadvantage is that it is low on security. WSHttpBinding uses the WS* features (discussed elsewhere in this text), and is a much more full-up binding, but has more overhead than BasicHttpBinding. Both BasicHttpBinding and WSHttpBinding use SOAP.

Since netTcpBinding does not use HTTP, it is really only for use in intranets (one reason is that going through firewalls is much easier using HTTP; this is the same problem CORBA had when the World Wide Web came along) and is not for use with non-WCF clients. However, netTcpBinding is faster than the other three because the data it sends is in binary format instead of XML-type format, which saves quite a large number of bytes.

WebHttpBinding basically just sends HTTP GETs or POSTs to a web URL and receives back XML or JSON. In other words, it actually uses HTTP rather than using HTTP as a transport layer (that is to say, it uses HTTP messages themselves, rather than using other messages and considers HTTP to be a transparent lower layer). See the other discussions in this text on RESTful architectures and RESTful web services for further information.

We'll see some more detail about some of these bindings later.

10.5.1.3 Contract

There are three kinds of contracts in WCF: service, data, and message. The service contract specifies the interface, the data contract specifies in what order the data is sent "across the link" and how it is stored on the other side after it is received. (In this section, as in other sections in this text, we will use the phrase "across the link" to mean the data transmission path from client to server, across all physical and software network connections that is required to make the data transmission of a particular message happen.) The other contract (message) is a particular (and optional) form of data serialization.

10.5.1.3.1 Service Contract

The service contract is equivalent to an interface in older technologies: for example, to an interface in CORBA IDL, or to an interface in the IDL for Open Network Computing remote procedure calls (ONC RPC) (originally from Sun Microsystems). That is, it provides a set of procedure calls, where the procedures to be called can be located on a different computer (remote procedure calls). In WCF, .NET interfaces were used to implement the service contracts.

Look at Listing 10.31, which contains an example service contract for a WCF HelloWorld program. You have a Service Contract for the interface "ImyHelloWorldService" that contains an Operation Contract consisting of the HelloWorld remote procedure call.

LISTING 10.31   Example Service Contract

```
namespace SelfHost
{
    [ServiceContract]
    public interface ImyHelloWorldService
    {
        [OperationContract]
        string HelloWorld(string name);
    }
}
```

10.5.1.3.2   Data Contract

The data contract is a way to define what the data looks like that is going to be sent "across the link."

In the CORBA IDL and in WSDL, the data definitions were normally included as part of the same overall structure (in some formats used by WSDL, the data definitions can be in an XML schema that is either stored or referenced in a separate portion of the WSDL document) that defined the interfaces, whereas WCF splits the data definitions and the interface definitions into two separate contracts.

Look at Listing 10.32, which contains an example Data Contract. Here the Data Contract is a class that in this particular situation contains a very simple Data Member, the string WorldName. So here it is simply a class that contains one string that is going to be "sent across the link."

LISTING 10.32   Example Data Contract

```
[DataContract]
    public class worldview
    {
        private string the_world_name;
        [DataMember]
        public string WorldName
        {
            get { return the_world_name; }
            set { the_world_name = value; }
        }
        public worldview() // this is the constructor
        {
        }
    }
```

If you haven't seen the C# set and get accessor functions before, these may confuse you. What happens here, C# allows you to set and get a variable by doing something that looks like an assignment statement, rather than having to call functions to get the variable and set the variable. For example, the C# in the Client to do this might look like:

```
// Set the worldview in this client
worldview my_own_world_view = new worldview();
my_own_world_view.WorldName = "Earth";
```

10.5.1.3.3   Data Serialization

As discussed elsewhere in this text, when discussing middleware, the term *data serialization* refers to converting data from the format in which it is stored on a computer, into a separate series of bytes that are transmitted across the link. This series of bytes is in a particular pre-agreed-upon format. Then this series of bytes is converted into the appropriate format for the receiving computer.

In WCF, as in all middleware, the data (which in WCF is stored internally in the Client and the Server in .NET objects) must be converted to and from the appropriate selected format and messages (for example, SOAP messages) for transmission across the link. That is, WCF must serialize the data, or perform data serialization as part of the data transmission process.

In WCF, the default serialization method is called "DataContractSerializer." This converts data to XML format, and supports numerous types, including most simple types, DataContract types, data lists (arrays and collections of data), among others.

An alternative serialization method is XMLSerializer, which supports fewer types but allows the programmer to have more control over the XML format in which the data is transmitted. This is the same serialization method used by the ASP.NET web services.

Message Contracts (yes, we finally got to these) are an optional method to use for data serialization. They are used together with either the DataContractSerializer or the XMLSerializer. The DataContractSerializer or the XMLSerializer choose the XML format of the data, but the Message Contracts choose what parts of the SOAP messages will contain the data.

Message Contracts allow the programmer to exactly specify the SOAP messages (both SOAP header and SOAP body) employed in the data serialization. For example, the [MessageHeader] attribute, when applied to a data type in a Message Contract says that data of that particular type will be sent out across the link as part of a SOAP header. Similarly, the [MessageBodyMember] attribute will cause data of a particular data type to be sent out across the link as part of a SOAP body.

This being said, we're going to ignore both Message Contracts and XMLSerializer in our further examples in this textbook. Since we're an introductory text, and we have plenty of other stuff to learn, ☺ we're going to depend on the default DataContractSerializer.

10.5.1.4   Channels

In WCF, the Channel Stack consists of (what I will call) various "handlers." Each "handler" provides some important function associated with the binding.

I'm calling the libraries that implement each important function associated with the bindings "handlers." Microsoft apparently thinks of these as a series of separate channels at different layers, in other words it's a network protocol consisting of channel layers, and each channel layer is independent. Ergo the term "channel stack." As an old network-protocol-stack-coder I see what they mean, and they are using this terminology in a reasonable way. However, this could be confusing for you, the reader, because I didn't require you to have had a prior network course before reading this textbook. And anyway, the fact that they use the general word "channel" to specify the overall communication connection between client and server whereas they also use the word "channel" for separate layers that feed into the overall communications network might be confusing for even somewhat more experienced networking type people (I note that this terminology is consistent with how we usually call the TCP/IP network stack simply a "protocol" when we're connecting between computers, and we also call TCP taken by itself a "protocol," or IP taken by itself a "protocol." But I think this is probably confusing terminology too, and it's only because we've been doing it so long that we accept it. To clarify, we are using the same word to refer to a whole collection and to a sub-part of a collection.)

Refer to Figure 10.3. Let's go (briefly) through the different "handlers."

First of all let's examine the handlers associated with the transport: the Transport Handler and the Encoding handler (as I have called them):

The Encoding Handler is tasked with converting the data from the internal format into XML or XML +SOAP or binary or JSON (among other possible formats). For example, if you select the WebHttpBinding (which is intended for RESTful applications) you could select XML (plain old XML) or JSON, but you wouldn't be using SOAP because that is used in non-RESTful applications. Alternately, if you select the BasicHttpBinding, you will be encoding your data as SOAP/XML using an old version of SOAP.

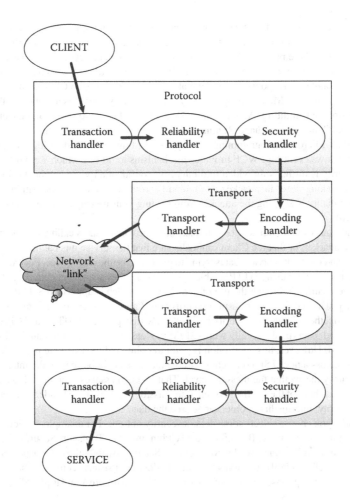

FIGURE 10.3   WCF channels.

If you select the WSHttpBinding, you will be encoding your data as SOAP/XML using a new version of SOAP. If you select netTcpBinding, then the Encoding Handler will encode your data in binary format. The Transport Handler employs which of the lower-level network protocols you're going to be making use of. If you select the WebHttpBinding, then you're going to be sending your data directly using HTTP, as HTTP GETs or PUTs, etc. (that is the RESTful method one uses for the World Wide Web). If you select the BasicHttpBinding or the WSHttpBinding then you will be using SOAP (either old or new), which will be running on top of HTTP (this is non-RESTful, so it won't be using the HTTP direct, it will treat the HTTP as a transparent lower network layer). If you select netTcpBinding, then you will be running on top of TCP, ignoring and not using HTTP, also not using SOAP. TCP will be your transparent lower network layer.

Next, let's examine the handlers associated with what Microsoft calls the protocol:

The Transaction handler is tasked with combining various tasks into a logical unit of work, that one can ensure either succeeds or fails, but that doesn't *partly* succeed or *partly* fail, and that in general the ACID (Atomicity, Consistency, Isolation, Durability) principles hold for all units of work (transactions) performed across the distributed systems that are connected using WCF. If you had a database course, you should be familiar with the ACID principles. In general, the idea behind the ACID principles when related to middleware is that problems such as failures in network communications or crashes of individual systems are prevented from causing an overall failure, or leaving the overall distributed system in an unrecoverable state. WCF supports multiple transaction models. One of the most common is WS-Atomic Transactions. Since this is an introductory textbook, however, we won't go further into this.

The Reliable messaging handler is tasked with making sure the message you send actually gets to the other side. How this works (or if it can be used at all) depends on the selected transport mechanisms being employed. For example, the primary reliable messaging technique employed is WS-Reliable Messaging (WS-RM), which works with SOAP. Since this is an introductory textbook, we won't go further into this.

The Security handler is responsible for several activities related to WCF security. WCF provides extensive security functions. Microsoft classifies the WCF security activities as follows: Transfer Security, Access Control, and Auditing. Access control says who is allowed to see what data, and is provided through the CLR (Common Language Runtime) which is the virtual machine that runs C# (and Visual Basic among other Microsoft programming languages). Auditing is related to logging security-related events to the Windows event log: WCF provides mechanisms to do this which we won't go into here.

Transfer Security is further subdivided into integrity, confidentiality, and authentication. Integrity is associated with making sure an attacker can't modify your message content without you knowing about it. Confidentiality is keeping the attacker from reading your messages (for example, the messages can be encrypted).

Authentication means that your service can make sure the Client that is calling your service is the real client and not an attacker, or that the Client can make sure that the service it is calling is really the service the Client wants, and not a fake service that is trying to pretend to be the real service. For example, WCF can achieve transport security by using HTTPS, which provides encryption and authentication. One way WCF achieves message security is through the use of WS-Security, which is applied to SOAP messages.

Note that we just used the terms "transport security" and "message security." (Note that it is often possible to use both together.) Transport security means that the transport level (HTTP or TCP, etc.) is authenticated and protected (encrypted), usually with TSL/SSL. Here, the complete communications sent out by WCF are encrypted. However, this encryption is point to point, and intermediate points have to forward the messages on across a new TSL connection. So the messages may be seen at the intermediate points.

Message security means that the message level. That is, the messages sent are authenticated, and the data in the messages (but not the overhead of the transmission, such as some headers) are encrypted. This is end-to-end security, intermediate points cannot see the data.

Which binding you choose selects some default security options. For example, by default, BasicHttpBinding does not use any security. By default, netTCPbinding uses Transport Security, in this case TLS (on top of TCP). WSHttpBinding uses SOAP Message Security by default (if Transport Security is also used it would be HTTPS). WebHttpBinding, by default, does not use any security. Note that it is possible to change these security options, for example, it's possible to configure WebHttpBinding to work with a Transport Security of HTTPS.

Since this is an introductory text covering a lot of different technologies, there's a big chance of getting too complicated too quick. Therefore, even though security is of course a very important topic for anyone who is doing communication, in all the WCF examples we will use the default security for the selected binding.

So, looking back at Figure 10.3, we now understand the various handler boxes. So as a message starts out from the Client, it goes first through the WCF Protocol handlers Transaction, Reliability, and Security (note that some of the security would be taking place in the Transport Handler), and then is encoded appropriately and sent out over the link by the WCF Transport handlers Encoding and Transport. On the other end, the service, this process is reversed. This process represents one particular "Channel" from Client to Server, with particular operations being performed by each handler as specified in the particular binding and its associated configuration.

There can be more than one channel between the same client and the same server. These channels can have different bindings, and be configured differently from each other.

Now let's look at Listing 10.33. This is an example of how to configure a WCF channel on the client side. Here we are using a Channel Factory. The WCF ChannelFactory allows the programmer to create a channel with a certain address and binding.

Here we have chosen to use the BasicHttpBinding. We have chosen an address (a real URL isn't shown here, you would have to insert your own). Together the binding and the address constitute the "A" and "B" of the WCF endpoint "ABC." The "C" of the endpoint, the contract, is ImyHelloWorld-Service, which is the interface of the service contract.

The code for the service contract that defines ImyHelloWorldService is shown in Listing 10.34. We can see that the interface is called ImyHelloWorldService, and the operation (the remote procedure call) is called HelloWorld.

In summary, the code in Listing 10.33 creates a channel called current_channel, that contains the A (the endpoint address your own URL), the B (the binding BasicHttpBinding), and the C (service contract, ImyHelloWorldService).

LISTING 10.33   Example of How to Explicitly Configure a Channel on the Client Side

```
BasicHttpBinding binding = new BasicHttpBinding();
EndpointAddress address = new EndpointAddress("http://your own url ");
ChannelFactory<SelfHost.ImyHelloWorldService> myChannelFactory = new
ChannelFactory<ImyHelloWorldService>(binding, address);
ImyHelloWorldService current_channel = myChannelFactory.CreateChannel();
```

LISTING 10.34   Service Contract Used by Channel in Listing 10.33

```
[ServiceContract]
public interface ImyHelloWorldService
{
    [OperationContract]
    string HelloWorld(string name);}
```

10.5.2   Examination of Specific WCF Examples

In this section, the aspects of WCF that are implemented in a non-RESTful way are illustrated. We will save the RESTful aspects for the chapter on RESTful architectures.

These are very simple programs of the HelloWorld variety. All the examples are in C#. The difference between the different examples are related to different things you can do with WCF.

As mentioned earlier, we're not going to look at all possible bindings. For illustration purposes here, I used BasicHttpBinding. BasicHttpBinding uses SOAP/WSDL. It's non-RESTful in that it's running on top of HTTP, and treats HTTP as a transparent lower layer, instead of directly controlling the HTTP itself (as would occur in a RESTful web service). However, to make full use of all the WSDL type services, one would likely use WSHttpBinding. For example, BasicHttpBinding by default has no security.

My argument for why I used BasicHttpBinding in these non-RESTful examples is that BasicHttp-Binding is the least likely binding to cause you, the reader, interoperability problems, and also while you're learning there's actually an advantage to having all your data sent in plain text—you can see more what's going on and see if it's correct. ☺ It should be pretty easy to convert to WSHttpBinding after you're confident with these examples.

I didn't use WebHttpBinding here because it's the RESTful binding, so we'll discuss it later in the RESTful chapter.

I didn't use netTcpBinding here because it's really special purpose, for intranets. Unless you really need it, you're better off sticking with WSHttpBinding. (I note, however, that Microsoft seems to think nowadays that ASP.NET MVC is more appropriate for web connections, whereas apparently they now believe the primary purpose for WCF is intranets.) Also, it doesn't map to either the non-RESTful web services or the RESTful web services (which are the subject of this chapter and the next chapter) because strictly speaking, it can be said that if it doesn't use a form of HTTP it's not part of the World Wide Web—it's part of a larger entity called the Internet (the general assumption is that web pages are accessed by HTTP, and web pages are the basis of the World Wide Web).

In all cases here, I've provided the programmatic way of handling WCF rather than the configuration way. I did this because the programmatic way provides a better comparison to the other, non-Microsoft technologies we examine in this textbook. It should be relatively easy to convert these to a configuration type programming

I've self-hosted the service(s) in an .exe file, rather than hosting them on IIS. I did this because I thought it was simpler for you, the reader. It avoids various IIS hosting problems. However, self-hosting is more often a debug sort of thing to do. Longer term it's likely you will want to use IIS.

The code, including projects, for all these examples are provided along with the text. I developed this code using Windows 7 and Visual Studio 2012. The code examples provided use the following kinds of URLs:

http://localhost:8731/ hello

It would be best if you run these examples on a computer where you have administrator privileges. There are ways around some issues, but that's the easiest way.

10.5.2.1   HelloWorld Service

```
LISTING 10.35   HelloWorld Service

Using System;
using System.Collections.Generic;
using System.Linq;
using System.Text;
using System.Threading.Tasks;
using System.ServiceModel;
using System.ServiceModel.Description;
namespace SelfHost
{
    [ServiceContract]
    public interface ImyHelloWorldService
    {
        [OperationContract]
        string HelloWorld(string name);
    }
    public class myHelloWorldService : ImyHelloWorldService
    {
        public string HelloWorld(string yourname)
        {
            string mymsg = "Hello, world, especially hello to " + yourname;
            return mymsg;
        }
    }
}
```

Listing 10.34, shown earlier, provided the Service Contract and an Operation Contract associated with the HelloWorld service. Those are shown here again in Listing 10.35, along with the class, called myHelloWorldService that implements them. In Visual Studio, I put this code into a Class Library project, which produces a .dll file.

10.5.2.2 Self-Host of the HelloWorld Service

LISTING 10.36 The Self-Host Itself

```
using System;
using System.Collections.Generic;
using System.Linq;
using System.Text;
using System.Threading.Tasks;
using System.ServiceModel;
using System.ServiceModel.Description;
using SelfHost;

   class Program
   {
      static void Main(string[] args)
      {

         Uri baseAddress = new Uri("http://localhost:8731/HelloWorldService");
         // Create the ServiceHost.

         ServiceHost host = new ServiceHost(typeof(myHelloWorldService), baseAddress);
         try
         {
            BasicHttpBinding current_binding = new BasicHttpBinding();
            host.AddServiceEndpoint(typeof(ImyHelloWorldService), current_binding,
               "helloService");
            host.Open();   // With host.Open there will be one endpoint per base address for each
               service
                      // in the contract by default, but we configured an endpoint instead
            Console.WriteLine("The service is running and is located at \n {0}. \n Call it and pass
               it your name: {1} \n", baseAddress, "someone's name");
            Console.WriteLine("To stop the service hit enter");
            Console.ReadLine(); // Keep the console window from disappearing so you can see
               it (by             //  making it wait for input)
            // Close the ServiceHost.
            host.Close();
         }
         catch (CommunicationException ce_exception)
         {
            Console.WriteLine("Exception {0} occurred.  Will abort\n", ce_exception.Message);
            host.Abort();
         }

      }

   }
```

In Listing 10.36, we created a ServiceHost. That means that this service is self-hosted in an .exe file, rather than being hosted in IIS. In Visual Studio, I put this in a Console Application, which produces an .exe file.

This is the listener side of the channel. I created a binding and put it in the variable current_binding:

```
BasicHttpBinding current_binding = new BasicHttpBinding();
```

Then I created an endpoint using current_binding, the contract name (ImyHelloWorldService) and the name of the service (helloService).

```
host.AddServiceEndpoint(typeof(ImyHelloWorldService), current_binding, "helloService");
```

Then I had the service start listening for input:

```
host.Open();
```

I only created one endpoint here. I didn't have to explicitly define the channel, like when I used ChannelFactory for a client in Listing 10.33, defining the endpoint did that for me. For example, I could have created several endpoints, perhaps each separate endpoint could have had a different binding. So each endpoint would correspond to a separate channel (would take a different path through the different handlers in the channel stack).

Now that we have a running, self-hosted service, let's look at different kinds of clients that we can use to call it.

10.5.2.3 Clients to Call the HelloWorld Service

There are two ways to create client code to call a service:

1. First, you can let Microsoft do the work of generating proxies: using:
   - Add-service reference inside Visual Studio
   - Call svcutil.exe from the command line
2. Second, you can use ChannelFactory like we saw earlier.

There are pros and cons with each approach. Which is better? There have been past and ongoing discussions on this subject (googling will find several of these).

Some aspects of these discussions include the following points, made by Bastante: Using the automatic generation tools is very easy. However, some proxy generation (such as using svcutil.exe) can result in a messy looking proxy (using ChannelFactory is cleaner than that). If during development, your interface contract changes a lot, you will have to regenerate the automatic proxies for every change, which can be time consuming. With ChannelFactory, on the other hand, clients and services share the assemblies (the .dll files, for example) and are immediately updated when changes are made. Also, with ChannelFactory you have more control with wrapper code for the proxies.

We will examine each approach for building a client in turn. They're presented in order of least complex to more complex, when considering the new programmer.

Code for a client that was connected to the HelloWorld service using an Add Service Reference in Visual Studio is provided in Listing 10.37. Note that we didn't have to do any difficult stuff here like defining endpoints or bindings or even addresses/URLs. To make this work, you have to START the SERVICE going first. (If you're working in Visual Studio, you have to go outside it and start the .exe file from the command line or this won't work.) Then you go to this client code, right click and select "Add Service Reference" and it will find the running URL. (If you don't see the URL then you didn't start the service correctly.) After that, you can compile the Client and run the Client.

See the Hello_Service_Reference in this code. If you don't do Add Service Reference, then that won't be defined.

LISTING 10.37   Client Using Add-Service Reference

```
using System;
using System.Collections.Generic;
using System.Linq;
using System.Text;
using System.Threading.Tasks;
using System.ServiceModel;
using System.ServiceModel.Description;
namespace Client_using_Add_Service_Reference
{
    class Program
    {
        static void Main(string[] args)
        {
            Hello_Service_Reference.ImyHelloWorldServiceClient myclient =
                    new Hello_Service_Reference.ImyHelloWorldServiceClient();
            Console.WriteLine("this is what I have = {0}", myclient.HelloWorld("John Doe"));
            Console.ReadLine(); // just to pause the console screen, don't really want to read
                anything
            myclient.Close(); // close it just because it's a good idea
        }
    }
}
```

Another way to create a proxy to use in a client is to use the svcutil.exe command-line tool. I'm not going to show the client code here (it's available in the code that the instructor is provided with the textbook). Instead, I'm going to show the proxy that was automatically generated by svcutil.exe; it's in Listing 10.38. Note that it provides several different ways to create the proxy: you can pass it the name alone, or the name and the address, or the binding and the address, etc.

LISTING 10.38   Automatic Code Generated by svcutil.exe (Run in Visual Studio 2012 Command Line)

```
//    This code was generated by a tool.
//    Runtime Version: 4.0.30319.18063
//
//    Changes to this file may cause incorrect behavior and will be lost if
//    the code is regenerated.
// </auto-generated>
//.............................................................................
[System.CodeDom.Compiler.GeneratedCodeAttribute("System.ServiceModel", "4.0.0.0")]
[System.ServiceModel.ServiceContractAttribute(ConfigurationName="ImyHelloWorld
    Service")]
public interface ImyHelloWorldService
{

    [System.ServiceModel.OperationContractAttribute(Action="http://tempuri.org/
        ImyHelloWorldService/
    HelloWorld", ReplyAction="http://tempuri.org/ImyHelloWorldService/HelloWorldResponse")]
        string HelloWorld(string name);
```

```
    [System.ServiceModel.OperationContractAttribute(Action="http://tempuri.org/
        ImyHelloWorldService/
    HelloWorld", ReplyAction="http://tempuri.org/ImyHelloWorldService/HelloWorldResponse")]
        System.Threading.Tasks.Task<string> HelloWorldAsync(string name);
}
[System.CodeDom.Compiler.GeneratedCodeAttribute("System.ServiceModel", "4.0.0.0")]
public interface ImyHelloWorldServiceChannel : ImyHelloWorldService,

System.ServiceModel.IClientChannel
{
}
[System.Diagnostics.DebuggerStepThroughAttribute()]
[System.CodeDom.Compiler.GeneratedCodeAttribute("System.ServiceModel", "4.0.0.0")]
public partial class ImyHelloWorldServiceClient : System.ServiceModel.ClientBase
        <ImyHelloWorldService>, ImyHelloWorldService
{

    public ImyHelloWorldServiceClient()
    {
    }

    public ImyHelloWorldServiceClient(string endpointConfigurationName) :
            base(endpointConfigurationName)
    {
    }
    public ImyHelloWorldServiceClient(string endpointConfigurationName, string
            remoteAddress) :
            base(endpointConfigurationName, remoteAddress)
    {
    }

    public ImyHelloWorldServiceClient(string endpointConfigurationName,
    System.ServiceModel.EndpointAddress remoteAddress) :
            base(endpointConfigurationName, remoteAddress)
    {
    }

    public ImyHelloWorldServiceClient(System.ServiceModel.Channels.Binding binding,
            System.ServiceModel.
    EndpointAddress remoteAddress) :
            base(binding, remoteAddress)
    {

    }
    public string HelloWorld(string name)
    {

        return base.Channel.HelloWorld(name);
    }
}
```

Listing 10.39 illustrates a client that uses ClientBase. ClientBase is used to create a WCF client object, for those thinking more in object-oriented terms than in service-oriented/interface terms. The ClientBase class is a wrapper for the System.ServiceModel.ChannelFactory<TChannel> class and is also a wrapper for the System.ServiceModel.IClient.Channel interface. So when ClientBase is used, this is what is really happening:

- Instantiate ClientBase object—create a channel factory (or find one in the Most Recently Used cache), use the channel factory to create a channel
- Call your function on ClientBase—call the function on the current channel
- Destruct ClientBase object—destruct current channel, return current channel factory to Most Recently Used cache (it goes away after it becomes less used)

Since ClientBase is really using ChannelFactory, you don't do an Add Service Reference. You don't have to do svcutil.exe, either (the Microsoft MSDN description of ClientBase has an example where you can use svcutil.exe to extend the ClientBase class). Without svcutil.exe, then, this needs only an Add Reference (NOT Add Service Reference) to the .dll file that contains the HelloWorld service contract.

LISTING 10.39   Client Created Using ClientBase

```
using System;
using System.Collections.Generic;
using System.Linq;
using System.Text;
using System.Threading.Tasks;
using System.ServiceModel;
using SelfHost;
namespace Client_using_ClientBase
{
    class ServiceClient : ClientBase<ImyHelloWorldService>, ImyHelloWorldService
    {
        public ServiceClient(BasicHttpBinding binding, EndpointAddress address
            )
            : base(binding, address)
            //calling base(binding,address) here means, call the appropriate constructor of the
            //parent ChannelFactory class
        {
        }
        public string HelloWorld(string value)
        {
            return base.Channel.HelloWorld(value);
            // calling the HelloWorld function as accessed by the current channel
            // that was previously defined by the ChannelFactory
        }
    }
    class Program
    {
        static void Main(string[] args)
        {
            BasicHttpBinding binding = new BasicHttpBinding();
            EndpointAddress address = new
```

```
    EndpointAddress("http://localhost:8731/ HelloWorldService/helloService");
        ServiceClient client = new ServiceClient(binding, address);
        Console.WriteLine(client.HelloWorld("Joe Blow"));
        Console.ReadLine();
    }
  }
}
```

Lastly, we will look at the client code that uses ChannelFactory. Similarly to when using ClientBase, we will do an Add Reference (NOT Add Service Reference) to the .dll file that contains the HelloWorld service. The code you originally saw in Listing 10.33, on how to establish a Channel, was drawn from this example.

LISTING 10.40   Client Created Using Channel Factory

```
using System;
using System.Collections.Generic;
using System.Linq;
using System.Text;
using System.Threading.Tasks;
using System.ServiceModel;
using System.ServiceModel.Description;
using SelfHost;
namespace client_using_ChannelFactory
{
  class Program
  {
    static void Main(string[] args)
    {
        BasicHttpBinding = new BasicHttpBinding();
        EndpointAddress address = new EndpointAddress("http://localhost:8731/
            HelloWorldService/helloService");
        ChannelFactory<SelfHost.ImyHelloWorldService> myChannelFactory = new
            ChannelFactory<ImyHelloWorldService>(binding, address);
        ImyHelloWorldService current_channel = myChannelFactory.CreateChannel();
        string msg;
        msg = "Hi to all, just received:   " + current_channel.HelloWorld("Jane Doe") + "\n";
        Console.WriteLine(msg);
        Console.ReadLine(); // Make console pause so we can read it
        myChannelFactory.Close();
    }
  }
}
```

10.5.2.4   Metadata

There are two standard ways to access the published metadata of a service:

1. HTTP/GET requests to access the WSDL (after the WSDL is published)
2. WS_MetadataExchange (also called MEX)

Similar to other service endpoints, endpoints that provide metadata have:

1. Address
2. Binding
3. Contract

WCF provides metadata publishing by using ServiceMetadataBehavior.
(Note, the below provides unsecure metadata publishing where anyone can access the metadata. There is a different method for secure metadata publishing.)
This is done by adding the service behavior called:

System.ServiceModel.Description.ServiceMetadataBehavior

To use HTTP/GET access of metadata, set the HttpGetEnabled property to true. This property is located on System.ServicModel.Description.ServiceMetadataBehavior
To use HTTPS access, set the HttpsGetEnabled property to true. This is also located on

System.ServiceModel.Description.ServiceMetadataBehavior

To use MEX, there is an IMetaDataExchange service contract. There are 4 different bindings associated with this in class MetadataExchangeBindings:

CreateMexHttpBinding, CreateMexHttpsBindings, CreateMexNamedPipeBinding, CreateMexTcpBinding

The web services policy specifications (such as WS-Policy 1.5) allows web services to show which policies they support (for example, security such as encryption supported, requirements for privacy, etc., and quality of service, etc.). When the service provider specifies a policy, and the service consumer specifies a policy, the assertions in the two separate policies are intersected and the resulting policy contains all policies specified that are not contradicted by the other side.
The example shown in Listing 10.42 is part of the code that is provided in the Self-Hosted service. This code publishes the WSDL description of the interface so that a client can read the metadata. Note that you can also get the metadata by using your web browser to access the URL, in the case of the provided examples, this would be:

http://localhost:8731/hello?wsdl

Better make sure the service is running first. ☺

LISTING 10.41   Service Code to Publish WSDL Metadata of the Service Contract

```
// Publish the metadata so it is accessible through http. This is not secure metadata, this allows the whole
// world to see it.
 ServiceMetadataBehavior smb = host.Description.Behaviors.Find<ServiceMetadata
    Behavior>();
```

```
    if (smb == null)
        smb = new ServiceMetadataBehavior();
    smb.HttpGetEnabled = true;        // This allows access of the metadata via http
    host.Description.Behaviors.Add(smb);
```

The code shown in Listing 10.42 is a client that can read the WSDL metadata previously published by the Self-Hosted Service. Note that I'm cheating just a bit here in this non-RESTful chapter. The Metadata was published so it was accessible using HTTP, so I'm using an HTTP-type request (WebRequest) to read it. This is a direct use of HTTP so it really qualifies as RESTful.

LISTING 10.42   Client to Read WSDL Metadata

```csharp
using System;
using System.Collections.Generic;
using System.IO;
using System.Linq;
using System.Net;
using System.Text;
using System.Threading.Tasks;
using System;
using System.Collections.Generic;
using System.IO;
using System.Linq;
using System.Net;
using System.Text;
using System.Threading.Tasks;
namespace Get_Metadata_client
{
    class Program
    {
        static void Main(string[] args)
        {
            string current_url;
            string CurrentLine = "";                    // Set the input line to empty to begin with
            Stream return_from_request_Stream;          // to hold the output of the request
            StreamReader return_from_request_Reader;    // to read the response from the request
            current_url = "http://localhost:8731/HelloWorldService?wsdl";
            WebRequest my_request = WebRequest.Create(current_url);
            return_from_request_Stream = my_request.GetResponse().GetResponseStream();
            return_from_request_Reader = new StreamReader(return_from_request_Stream);
            CurrentLine = return_from_request_Reader.ReadLine();  // All the metadata comes out
                at once, in
                                                          // one ReadLine
            Console.WriteLine(CurrentLine);
            Console.ReadLine(); // Pause so the console can be read (so the console won't disappear)
        }
    }
}
```

10.5.3   Message Exchange Patterns in WCF

WCF supports 3 basic message exchange patterns, if you count those with and without a session enabled, then that would be 6 total message exchange patterns. (A session combines messages between entities into a "conversation," the primary concept here is that messages are processed in the order in which they are received.)

The basic message exchange patterns supported are:v

- Request/response (this can also be called *half duplex*)—this is the most traditional message exchange pattern. Using this pattern, the Client sends a request to the service, and the service gives back a response to the Client.
- Datagram pattern (this can also be called "simplex")—the Client sends a message to the Server, but there is no guarantee that the service ever receives it. The Client doesn't worry whether or not the service, the Client just sends the message then goes on about its business.
- Duplex—either the Client or the Server can send messages, in any order, over the same WCF connection. A "callback" is normally implemented using this message pattern.

A typical "callback" situation would occur when the Client sends a message to the Server, but does not want to wait on a response. Instead the Client goes about its business. Then later, when the Server finishes its task, the Server would call a "callback" function on the Client. The Client would previously have established this callback function and given the Server permission to call it, in advance, for this particular purpose. Typically, a "callback" uses the same connection between client and server that the Client originally used, and the original client is the one the server calls.

A different arrangement (that would not normally be referred to as a "callback") could be to have a client and server on both computers. The Client on Computer A calls the Server on Computer B, then the Client on Computer B calls the Server on Computer A. Usually this would require two separate connections, one for each client/server pair.

Commonly, you would select duplex versus non-duplex by selecting a system-defined binding. Request/response is normally the default (the overall default when not specified differently by a particular binding). For example, BasicHttpBinding and WSHttpBinding do not support duplex, and neither does WebHttpBinding. However, netTcpBinding supports duplex by default. Note that there is a separate binding called WSDualHttpBinding that is basically the same as the WSHttpBinding except that it supports duplex.

To implement a datagram message exchange pattern, you would define a standard contract, set the return type of all operations to "void," and you would set the "IsOneWay" attribute in the operation definition = true), for example:

```
[OperationContract(IsOneWay=true)]
void HelloWorld(string name);
```

To implement the duplex pattern, you would do the same in that you would set the return type of all operations to "void." However, normally you would have a contract that specified separate interfaces, one for outgoing and one for callback. The outgoing interface would be specified as follows:

```
[ServiceContract(...put some stuff here...,CallbackContract=typeof(IMyHelloWorldCallback)]
public interface IMyHelloWorld {
    [OperationContract(IsOneWay=true)]
    void HelloWorld(string name);
}
public interface IMyHelloWorldCallback {
    [OperationContract(IsOneWay=true)]
    void DoneWithHello(string name);
}
```

These short code examples have been provided to give you the flavor of how these different message exchange patterns work. However, since this is an introductory textbook, we will not cover more of this here.

SOAP EXERCISES

1. What does the SOAP namespace tell you?
2. Which SOAP message style is preferred today, and why?
3. Given the following SOAP and WSDL code:
   SOAP Message Itself:
   ```
   <soap: Envelope  xmlns:soap="http://www.w3.org/2003/05/soap-envelope">
   <soap:Header
   ...header stuff included here...
   </soap:Header>
   <soap:Body>
       <myfunc>
           <myval>7</myval>
       </myfunc>
   </soap:Body>
   </soap: Envelope>
   ```

   Part of a WSDL Document:
   ```
   <message name="myfunc">
   <part name="myval"   type="xsd:string" />
   </message>
   ```

   What encoding is being used? How can you tell?
4. Given the following SOAP and WSDL code:
   SOAP Message Itself:
   ```
   <soap: Envelope  xmlns:soap="http://www.w3.org/2003/05/soap-envelope">
   <soap:Header
   ...header stuff included here...
   </soap:Header>
   <soap:Body>
       <hw:myfunc>
           <hw:myval>7</hw:myval>
       </hw:myfunc>
   </soap:Body>
   </soap: Envelope>
   ```

   Part of a WSDL Document:
   ```
   <message name="myfuncRequest">
       <part name="parameters"   element="hw:myfunc" />
   </message>
   ```
   XML Schema the SOAP Message Is Validated Against:
   ```
   <schema xmlns:xsd="http://www.w3.org/2001/XMLSchema"
           xmlns:hw="http://myfunc/myfuncSchema"
           target_Namespace="http://myfunc/myfuncSchema">
               <element  name="myfunc">
                   <complexType>
                       <sequence>
                       <element name="myval" type="xsd:int">
                       </sequence>
   ```

```
            </complexType>
        </element>
    </schema>
```

What encoding is being used? How can you tell?

5. What is the purpose of a "mustUnderstand" header?

WSDL AND WADL EXERCISES

1. What does WSDL mean by "binding"?
2. In what ways can a WSDL document be generated?
3. What is an Internationalized Resource Identifier in WSDL 2.0?
4. What does the wsdlx:safe attribute mean in WSDL 2.0?
5. What is the purpose of the WSDL 2.0 message exchange patterns?
6. What is WADL and how does it compare to WSDL, especially WSDL 2.0?
7. In terms of RESTful architectures and web services, what is an argument in favor of something like WSDL 2.0 and WADL?
8. How can you tell whether you're looking at a WSDL 1.1 document or a WSDL 2.0 document?

JAX-WS EXERCISES

1. What is a Service Endpoint Interface?
2. What are the pros and cons with defining a separate interface class compared to simply annotating a Java class?
3. In a Service Endpoint Implementation, why do you separately annotate methods with "@WebMethod"?
4. Why might you want to use SAAJ and a dispatch client?
5. What do you think a QName is? We used it but didn't explicitly define it.
6. If you specify "@BindingType(value = HTTPBinding.HTTP_BINDING)" then what's this for?

WCF EXERCISES

1. When should you use netTcpBinding?
2. When should you use WebHttpBinding?
3. What is the purpose of a Data Contract?
4. What is the purpose of a Message Contract?
5. What are the message exchange patterns supported by WCF? Compare these to the message exchange patterns used with WSDL 2.0?

CONCEPTUAL QUESTIONS

1. In regard to various SOAP formats:
   a. Why do you think JAX-WS uses document/literal/wrapped as the default SOAP format? What are the advantages of document/literal/wrapped compared to document/literal/unwrapped (bare). What are the advantages of document-literal (either wrapped or unwrapped/bare) compared to RPC/literal?
   b. Why do you think the later versions of JAX-WS ceased to support the RPC/encoded SOAP format?
2. We talked briefly about asynchronous communication in regard to SOAP over HTTP and WS-addressing and about the duplex message exchange pattern in Windows Communication Foundation. However, we didn't really discuss asynchronous communication in detail in Windows Communication Foundation.
   a. What are the advantages of asynchronous communication compared to synchronous communication?
   b. What are some situations where you might want to use asynchronous communication?
3. In what ways do JAX-WS or Windows Communication Foundation applications conform to the Service-Oriented Architectures paradigm (we discussed Service-Oriented Architectures in Chapter 9)? In what

way do JAX-WS and Windows Communication Foundation *not* conform to the Service-Oriented Architectures paradigm?

4. Windows Communication Foundation uses separate Data Contracts and Service Contracts. Compare this to how WSDL is used in JAX-WS. Consider all variations of WSDL/SOAP. Can any of these WSDL/SOAP variations be considered to have separate Data and Service descriptions?

5. What are the primary advantages of non-RESTful web services compared to object-oriented middlewares such as CORBA or EJB? What are the disadvantages?

BIBLIOGRAPHY

Allamaraiu, S. 2006. JAX-WS for RESTful Web Services? https://www..subbu.org/blog/2006/jax-ws-for-restful-web-services (accessed August 29, 2015).

Bitworking. 2007. Do We need WADL? http://bill.burkecentral.com/2009/05/21/to-wadl-or-not-to-wadl/ (accessed September 14, 2015).

Burke, B. 2009. To WADL or not to WADL. http://bill.burkecentral.com/2009/05/21/to-wadl-or-not-to-wadl/ (accessed September 14, 2015).

Bustamante, M. 2009. WCF and Client Proxies: Common Consideration for Proxy Generation. http://devproconnections.com/net-framework/wcf-and-client-proxies (accessed July 10, 2015).

Butek, R. 2005. Which Style of WSDL Should I Use? http://www.ibm.com/developerworks/library/ws-whichwsdl/ws-whichwsdl-pdf.pdf (accessed August 29, 2015).

Conway, A. 2012. Creating a WCF RESTful Service and Secure It Using HTTPS over SSL. http://www.allenconway.net/2012/05/creating-wcf-restful-service-and-secure.html (accessed July 10, 2015).

Edureka! 2015. How to Write RESTful Web Services with JAX-WS. http://www.edureka.co/blog/how-to-write-restful-web-services-with-jax-ws/ (accessed August 29, 2015).

Epartaud, S. 2009. What Every Web Developer Must Know About URL Encoding. http://blog.lunatech.com/2009/02/03/what-every-web-developer-must-know-about-url-encoding (accessed September 14, 2015).

Ewald, T. 2002. The Argument against SOAP Encoding. https://msdn.microsoft.com/en-us/library/ms995710.aspx#argsoape_topic4 (accessed September 7, 2015).

Gamma, E., Helm, R., Johnson, R., Vlissides, J., 1994. Design Patterns: Elements of Reusable Object-Oriented Software. Addison-Wesley, Reading, MA.

GlassFish Metro. 2015. JAX-WS. JAX-WS Reference Implementation Project. https://jax-ws.java.net/ (accessed August 29, 2015).

IANA (Internet Assigned Numbers Authority). 2015. Language Subtag Registry. http://www.iana.org/assignments/language-subtag-registry/language-subtag-registry (accessed September 10, 2015).

IBM. 2015. Working with RPC-Encoded SOAP Messages. https://www-01.ibm.com/support/knowledgecenter/SSMKHH_9.0.0/com.ibm.etools.mft.doc/bc19050_.htm (accessed September 7, 2015).

IBM. 2015. WSDL Binding Styles. http://www-01.ibm.com/support/knowledgecenter/SS7J6S_7.5.1/com.ibm.wbpm.wid.integ.doc/access/topics/rwsdlstyle.html (accessed September 7, 2015).

IBM Knowledge Center. 2015. Developing a Dynamic Client Using JAX-WS APIs. https://www-01.ibm.com/support/knowledgecenter/SSAW57_7.0.0/com.ibm.websphere.nd.doc/info/ae/ae/twbs_jaxwsdynclient.html (accessed September 20, 2015).

IBM Knowledge Center. 2015. Developing JAX-WS Web Services with Annotations. https://www-01.ibm.com/support/knowledgecenter/SSAW57_8.5.5/com.ibm.websphere.nd.doc/ae/twbs_devjaxwsendpt.html?cp=SSAW57_8.5.5%2F1-3-0-24-2-0 (accessed August 29, 2015).

IBM Knowledge Center. 2015. JAX-WS Client Programming Model. http://www-01.ibm.com/support/knowledgecenter/SSEQTP_7.0.0/com.ibm.websphere.base.doc/info/aes/ae/cwbs_jaxwsclients.html?lang=ko (accessed September 20, 2015).

IETF (Internet Engineering Task Force). 2015. Internationalized Resource Identifiers (IRIs). http://tools.ietf.org/html/rfc3987 (accessed September 14, 2015).

JAX-WS. 2015. A Little Bit about Message Context in JAX-WS. https://jax-ws.java.net/articles/MessageContext.html (accessed September 20, 2015).

JAX-WS. 2015. Java API for XML Web Services (JAX-WS) SOAP 1.2. https://jax-ws.java.net/jax-ws-21-ea1/docs/soap12.html (accessed September 20, 2015).

JAX-WS. 2015. JAX-WS User's Guide. https://jax-ws.java.net/nonav/2.2.6/docs/ch03.html (accessed September 20, 2015).

JCP (Java Community Process). 2015. Java Specification Request (JSR) 224. https://jcp.org/aboutJava/communityprocess/mrel/jsr224/index3.html (accessed August 29, 2015).

Kohlert, D. 2006. Publishing a RESTful Web Service with JAX-WS. https://weblogs.java.net/blog/2006/01/17/publishing-restful-web-service-jax-ws (accessed September 20, 2015).

Koirala, S. 2015. Difference between BasicHttpBinding and WSHttpBinding. http://www.codeproject.com/Articles/36396/Difference-between-BasicHttpBinding-and-WsHttpBind (accessed July 10, 2015).

Kumar, S. 2013. WSDL 2.0 vs. WSDL 1.1. http://javasolutionarchitect.blogspot.com/2013/11/wsdl-20-vs-wsdl-11.html (accessed September 12, 2015).

Linker, B. 2005 Introduction to WS-Addressing. Oracle. http://www.oracle.com/au/products/database/ws-addressing-intro-087619.html (accessed September 20, 2015).

Little, M. 2010. WS-I Closes Its Doors. What Does This Mean for WS-*, InfoQ. http://www.infoq.com/news/2010/11/wsi-closes (accessed September 15, 2015).

Manes, A.T. 2009. SearchSOA. WSDL 1.1 vs. WSDL 2.0. http://searchsoa.techtarget.com/answer/WSDL-11-vs-WSDL-20 (accessed September 15, 2015).

McKendrick, J. 2010. WS-I Calls It a "Wrap," Hands Work Over to OASIS. ZDNet. http://www.zdnet.com/article/ws-i-calls-it-a-wrap-turns-over-work-to-oasis/ (accessed September 15, 2015).

MSDN. 2015. Configuring System-Provided Bindings. Microsoft Corp. https://msdn.microsoft.com/en-us/library/ms731092(v=vs.110).aspx (accessed July 8, 2015).

MSDN. 2015. Duplex Services. Microsoft Corp. Microsoft Corp. https://msdn.microsoft.com/en-us/library/ms731064(v=vs.110).aspx (accessed July 13, 2015).

MSDN. 2015. Types Supported by the Data Contract Serializer. Microsoft Corp. https://msdn.microsoft.com/en-us/library/ms731923(v=vs.110).aspx (accessed July 9, 2015).

MSDN. 2015. Using Message Contracts. Microsoft Corp. https://msdn.microsoft.com/en-us/library/ms730255(v=vs.110).aspx (accessed July 9, 2015).

MSDN. 2015. WCF Security Fundamentals. Microsoft Corp. https://msdn.microsoft.com/en-us/library/ff650862.aspx (accessed July 10, 2015).

MSDN. 2015. Windows Communication Foundation Security. Microsoft Corp. https://msdn.microsoft.com/en-us/library/ms732362(v=vs.110).aspx (accessed July 10, 2015)

Oracle. 2015. Creating Dynamic Proxy Clients. http://docs.oracle.com/cd/E21764_01/web.1111/e13734/proxy.htm#WSADV454 (accessed September 20, 2015).

Oracle. 2015. Interface Dispatch<T>. https://docs.oracle.com/javaee/5/api/javax/xml/ws/Dispatch.html (accessed September 20, 2015).

Oracle. 2015. Java EE at a Glance. http://www.oracle.com/technetwork/java/javaee/overview/index.html (accessed August 29, 2015).

Oracle. 2015. The Java EE 5 Tutorial. Overview of SAAJ. https://docs.oracle.com/javaee/5/tutorial/doc/bnbhg.html (accessed September 20, 2015)

RFC2246. 1999. The TLS Protocol, Version 1.0. https://www.ietf.org/rfc/rfc22 6.txt (accessed September 15, 2015).

RFC2459. 1999. Internet X.509 Public Key Infrastructure Certificate and CRL Profile. https://www.rfc-editor.org/rfc/rfc2459.txt (accessed September 15, 2015).

RFC2818. 2000. Over TLS. http://tools.ietf.org/html/rfc2818 (accessed September 15, 2015)

RFC3023. 2001. XML Media Types. https://www.ietf.org/rfc/rfc3023.txt (accessed September 15, 2015).

Scribd. 2010. WS-I Basic Profile Comparison. http://www.scribd.com/doc/100832252/WS-I-Basic-Profile-Comparison#scribd (accessed September 15, 2015).

Spies, B. 2008. Web Services, Part 2: WSDL and WADL. http://www.ajaxonomy.com/2008/xml/web-services-part-2-wsdl-and-wadl (accessed September 14, 2015).

Stack Overflow. 2011. Why Does WS-I Basic Profile 2.0 Not Use WSDL 2.0. http://stackoverflow.com/questions/7647933/why-does-ws-i-basic-profile-2-0-not-use-wsdl-2-0 (accessed September 15, 2015).

Stack Overflow. 2015. WCF Channel Factory Caching. http://stackoverflow.com/questions/30718839/wcf-channel-factory-caching (accessed July 10, 2015).

TheSOATestingGeek. 2012. WSDL 1.1 vs. WSDL 2.0. https://thesoatestinggeek.wordpress.com/2012/03/12/wsdl-1-1-vs-wsdl-2-0/ (accessed September 12, 2015).

W3C. 2000. Simple Object Access Protocol (SOAP) 1.1. http://www.w3.org/TR/2000/NOTE-SOAP-20000508/ (accessed August 29, 2015).

W3C. 2001. Web Services Description Language (WSDL) 1.1. http://www.w3.org/TR/wsdl (accessed September 20, 2015).

W3C. 2004. XML Schema Part 1: Structures Second Edition. http://www.w3.org/TR/2004/REC-xmlschema-1-20041028/ (accessed September 15, 2015).

W3C. 2004. XML Schema Part 2: Datatypes Second Edition. http://www.w3.org/TR/2004/REC-xmlschema-2-20041028/ (accessed September 15, 2015).

W3C. 2006. Namespaces in XML 1.0 (Second Edition), (accessed September 15, 2015).

W3C. 2006. Web Services Addressing 1.0-Core. http://www.w3.org/TR/2006/REC-ws-addr-core-20060509/ (accessed September 20, 2015).

W3C. 2006. Web Services Addressing 1.0-SOAP Binding. http://www.w3.org/TR/2006/REC-ws-addr-soap-20060509/ (accessed September 20, 2015).

W3C. 2006. Web Services Addressing 1.0-Metadata. http://www.w3.org/TR/2007/REC-ws-addr-metadata-20070904/ (accessed September 20, 2015).

W3C. 2007. SOAP Version 1.2 Part 0: Primer (Second Edition). http://www.w3.org/TR/soap12-part0/ (accessed September 5, 2015).

W3C. 2007. SOAP Version 1.2 Part 1: Messaging Framework (Second Edition). http://www.w3.org/TR/soap12-part1/ (accessed September 5, 2015).

W3C. 2007. SOAP Version 1.2 Part 1: Messaging Framework (Second Edition). http://www.w3.org/TR/soap12/ (accessed September 5, 2015).

W3C. 2007. SOAP Version 1.2 Part 2: Adjuncts (Second Edition). http://www.w3.org/TR/soap12-part2/ (accessed September 5, 2015).

W3C. 2007. Web Services Description Language (WSDL) Version 2.0 Part 1: Core Language. http://www.w3.org/TR/wsdl20/ (accessed August 29, 2015).

W3C. 2007. Web Services Description Language (WSDL) Version 2.0: Additional MEPS. http://www.w3.org/TR/wsdl20-additional-meps/#meps (accessed September 12, 2015).

W3C. 2007. Web Services Description Language (WSDL) 2.0. http://www.w3.org/TR/wsdl20/ (accessed September 15, 2015).

W3C. 2007. Web Services Description Language (WSDL) Version 2.0: Primer. http://www.w3.org/TR/wsdl20-primer/ (accessed September 12, 2015).

W3C. 2008. Extensible Markup Language (XML) 1.0 (Fifth Edition). http://www.w3.org/TR/REC-xml/ (accessed September 15, 2015).

W3C. 2009. Web Application Description Language Member Submission. http://www.w3.org/Submission/wadl/ (accessed September 14, 2015).

W3C. 2011. Choosing a Language Tag. http://www.w3.org/International/questions/qa-choosing-language-tags (accessed September 10, 2015).

Wikipedia. 2015. ACID https://en.wikipedia.org/wiki/ACID (accessed July 10, 2015)

WS-I. 2006. Attachments Profile Version 1.0. http://www.ws-i.org/Profiles/AttachmentsProfile-1.0.html#introduction (accessed September 15, 2015).

WS-I. 2010. Basic Profile 1.2. http://ws-i.org/Profiles/BasicProfile-1.2-2010-11-09.html (accessed September 15, 2015).

WS-I. 2010. Basic Profile 2.0. http://ws-i.org/Profiles/BasicProfile-2.0-2010-11-09.html (accessed September 15, 2015).

11 RESTful Web Services

As we saw earlier in Section 9.2, there are some differences of opinion as to what "RESTful" and "non-RESTful" mean. We already looked at "non-RESTful" in Chapter 10, so let's briefly re-examine what "RESTful" means.

If you recall from Section 9.2, the primary ideas behind a RESTful architectural style are that it would possess the following constraints:

- *Client/server*: Separation of concerns, exemplified by a client/server architecture. The idea is that different components can evolve independently—the user interface in the client can evolve separately from the server, and the server is simpler.
- *Stateless*: The client–server interaction is stateless. There is no stored context on the server. Any session information must be kept by the client.
- *Cacheable*: Data in a response (a response to a previous request) is labeled as cacheable or non-cacheable. If it is cacheable, the client (or an intermediary) may reuse that for the same kind of request in the future.
- *Uniform interface*: There is a uniform interface between components. In practice, there are four interface constraints:
  - Resource identification—requests identify the resources they are operating on (by a URI, for example)
  - Resource manipulation through the representation of the resource—when a client or server has access to a resource, it has enough information based on understanding the representation of the resource to be able to modify that resource
  - Messages are self-descriptive—the message contains enough information to allow a client or server to handle the message, this is normally done through the use of Internet Media Types (MIME types)
  - Use of hypermedia to change the state of the application—for example, the server provides hyperlinks that the client uses to make state transitions
- *Layered system*: Components are organized in hierarchical layers, the components are only aware of the layer within which the interaction is occurring. Thus, a client connecting to a server is not aware of any intermediate connections.
  - Intermediate filter components can change the message while it is in transit: because the message is self-descriptive and the semantics are visible, the filter components understand enough about the message to modify it
- Code on demand: This is optionally supported, that is, clients can download scripts that extend their functionality.

So a RESTful web service is client/server-based, and does not store state. The results of a request from client to server can be cached in the client. It has a uniform interface with self-descriptive messages, based on hypermedia. Oh, and the client and server aren't aware of intermediate connections between the two of them.

As we previously discussed in Section 9.2, these are the characteristics of the World Wide Web. It is client/server-based, consisting primarily of browsers and web servers. Each call to a web server is considered independent of another such call (unless you're using something like cookies or URL redirection, we'll talk about those later on in this chapter). Its uniform interface is provided by the HTTP protocol. The data format is specified by Internet Media Types, which are included in the message, so the message is self-descriptive. And so forth.

We did a more in-depth look at this in Section 9.2. However, in short, RESTful web services make use of the basic functionality of the World Wide Web: They use the HTTP protocol, and they use Internet Media types. In general they are stateless.

Okay, now we know generally what we're talking about. In the sections below, we're going to discuss multiple technologies related to RESTful web services. We will start with Asynchronous JavaScript and XML (AJAX), which is fairly simple to understand and thus a good way to get started. Then we will discuss Java servlets, which can be used as an enabling technology for Java Application Programming Interface (API) for RESTful Web Services JAX-RS (JAX-RS can be deployed in servlets). (Java Servlets can also be used in a RESTful manner themselves.) Java Servlets date back to the late 1990s at Sun Microsystems. Then we will look at JAX-RS. We're going to save the .NET RESTful technologies for another chapter.

For JavaScript/PHP/AJAX, Java Servlets, and JAX-RS there are larger practical examples provided in Chapter 18. Chapter 18 is available in online resources.

11.1   TECHNOLOGY REVIEW: ASYNCHRONOUS JAVASCRIPT AND XML (AJAX)

Asynchronous JavaScript and XML (AJAX) is a name for a collection of technologies that are used together on the client so that a user's web page is updated a piece at a time (the overall web page does not change), in the background so the user can continue to do other work in the meantime.

When using "normal" HTTP connections as between a browser and a web server, the connection is synchronous, that is, the browser blocks until the web server provides its information, and the whole web page is rewritten at one time.

James Garrett originally used the term "AJAX" to refer to a collection of technologies. The various technologies that he considered to be part of AJAX were:

- Web page presentation technologies such as XHMTL and CSS
- Dynamic display using the Document Object Model
- Data interchange using XML (he included XSLT to use to convert one XML document into another XML document, or into other formats such as text)
- JavaScript running on the web client to handle background processing and all data transmissions (in Garrett's idea, JavaScript "bound everything together" meaning all the other technologies)
- Asynchronous data retrieval (to update part of a web page instead of the whole web page) using XMLHttpRequest

The idea behind AJAX is that, after the initial web page is loaded, the JavaScript code running on the client handles user input and web page updates as much as possible (for example, simple data validation or simple data editing can be handled locally to the client). When data is needed from the server, then that specific data alone is retrieved from the server, and is written only onto a portion of the web page. The web page as a whole remains the same.

In terms of web service communications, when data must be retrieved from the server, the primary technology employed in AJAX is XMLHttpRequest. After the data is retrieved from the server using XMLHttpRequest, then the JavaScript on the web client uses the Document Object Model (DOM) to update the appropriate portion(s) of the web page. Originally XML data would be sent from the web server back to the web client, but today AJAX more commonly employs JSON data (see Section 11.2).

XMLHttpRequest is an API (accessed from JavaScript running on a web client) that is used to build HTTP and HTTPS requests to be sent to the web server, and to hand the data (from the associated HTTP responses) returned by the web server back to the JavaScript code on the client.

AJAX using XMLHttpRequest is considered RESTful because all communication between the client and the server is doing using HTTP (or HTTPS) request/response.

The precursor to XMLHttpRequest was implemented by Microsoft back in 2000, and became a defacto standard in other browsers. Various draft versions have been provided by the World Wide Web Consortium (W3C) since 2006.

11.1.1 SIMPLE XMLHTTPREQUEST EXAMPLE

In Listing 11.1, we see a simple example using XMLHttpRequest. An extremely simple server to handle this, written in PHP, is shown in Listing 11.2: it will return XML data consisting of:

"Hi, (name you typed in)! This is new important data for your web page"

LISTING 11.1   Extremely Simple XMLHttpRequest Client

```
<html>
    <body>
        <h1 id="myHeader"> This is an AJAX example</h1>
        <p> This code describes how to do an AJAX example </p>
        <p id="thispart"> This is the part that is updated </p>
        <p> It cleverly updates only part of a web page </p>
        <form action = "simple_server.php"
            <p> Enter your name: <input type="text" name="myname" />
                <button type = "button"  onclick = "doAJAXstuff(this.form)">
                    Paint part of the web page
                </button>
            </p>
        </form>
        <script type = "text/javascript">
            function doAJAXstuff(theform)
            {
                request = new XMLHttpRequest();
                request.open("GET","simple_server.php?mydata="+theform.myname.value);
                request.onreadystatechange = function ()
                {
                    if (request.readyState == 4)
                        my_callback();
                }
                request.send();
            }
            function my_callback()
            {
                if (request.status == 200)
                {
                document.getElementById("thispart").innerHTML = request.responseText;
                document.getElementById("thispart").style.font = "italic bold 20px arial,serif";
                alert("There wasn't an error, just wanted to let you see how an alert works.
                        Received from the server:\n"+request.responseText);
                }
            }
```

```
                else if (request.status=404) {
                        alert("Server was not found: data returned is :\n"+request.responseText);
                }
        }
    </script>
  </body>
</html>
```

XMLHttpRequest is used to build an HTTP (or HTTPS) request. You start out by building a Java-Script object to hold the XMLHttpRequest:

```
request = new XMLHttpRequest();
```

Next, we call "open" on the XMLHttpRequest object. Open has the following format:
request.open(HTTP method type, url being called, asynchronous or not)

Normally the HTTP method type used would be "GET," "POST," or "PUT" but you could also use "HEAD," "PUT," or "DELETE."

There could also be additional username and password parameters.

When you specify asynchronous to be TRUE (this is supposed to be the default, although I have found some cases in browsers where this has not appeared to be the case, note that the default is used in Listing 11.1 because that parameter has not been specified), then the JavaScript code will not block and wait on the response from the server. Rather, it will continue execution. We will see another example later on that clearly illustrates an asynchronous example.

The request.send() sends an HTTP request to the server. Here, there is no additional data to send. The name that you would previously have entered in the HTML form is sent as the GET query string. If there were any additional data, it would be included as a parameter to the send() function.

There is another method on XMLHttpRequest, called setRequestHeader. This is not shown in this example, but could be used to put additional headers in the HTTP request.

After the send, the local web page (including JavaScript) can continue to execute until a reply comes back from the server. In the meantime, the onreadystatechange event listener is waiting for the response from the server.

LISTING 11.2   Extremely Simple PHP Server

```
<?php
 $mydata = $_REQUEST["mydata"];
 print "<p>Hi, $mydata! This is new important data for your web page.</p> ";
?>
```

When the response (eventually) arrives from the server, the function associated with the onreadysta-techange is called:

```
request.onreadystatechange = function ()
{
    if (request.readyState == 4)
        my_callback();
}
```

This checks to see if the request is finished (request.readyState is equal 4). If so, then it calls the my_callback function to handle the request.

The my_callback function checks the HTTP response code. If this was equal 200, then the request was successful, the data received from the server is good data, and it is written, using the DOM to a location in the middle of the overall web page, without having to rewrite the entire page.

Here it also does an "alert" just to show you how. ☺

If for some reason the web page was not available, the my_callback function would have received an HTTP response code of 404, and in this case an error alert would be generated. (NOTE: you can force this situation by renaming the .php file I gave you with this code.)

This example shows a web page where only a portion of the web page is updated. Figure 11.1 shows the web page immediately before pressing the button.

Figure 11.2 shows the web page immediately after pressing the button. Note that the one line was updated but that the rest of the web page is the same as in Figure 11.2.

11.1.2 RESPONSE CODES EXAMPLE

The XMLHttpRequest provides five different readyState response codes:

- 0: request was not initialized
- 1: the server connection has been established
- 2: the request was received by the server

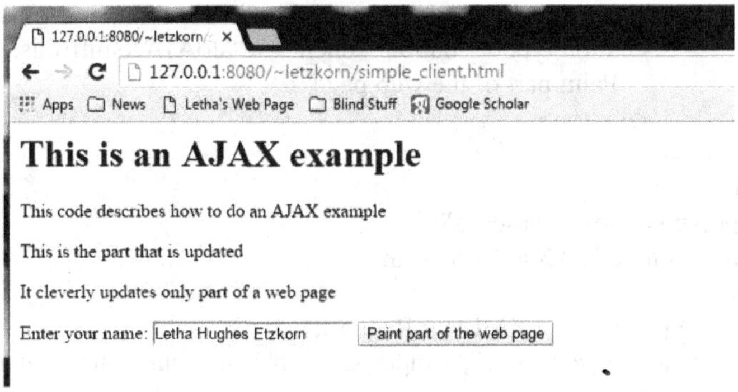

FIGURE 11.1   Immediately before running an extremely simple XMLHttpRequest example.

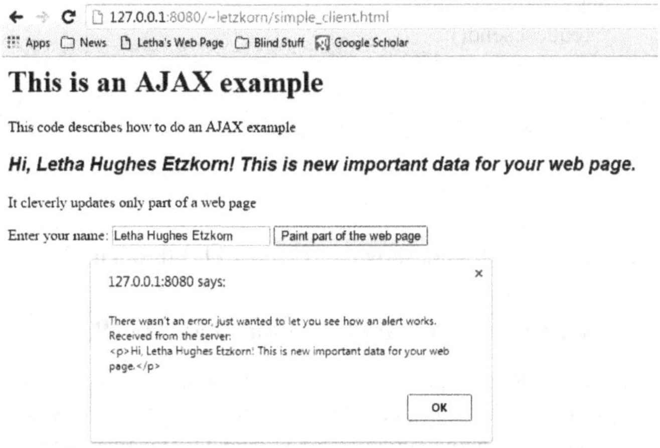

FIGURE 11.2   Immediately after running extremely simple XMLHttpRequest example.

- 3: the server is processing the request
- 4: the server has finished the request and the response is now ready

We saw the successful response code handled (request.readyState==4) in Listing 11.1.

The other response codes show intermediate conditions. The example Client in Listing 11.3 provides a way for you to see the various other response codes occur. I used an "alert" message here because the server is so fast that updating the DOM gives it time to finish so you never can see the intermediate codes. However, the "alert" pauses after it receives each code and waits for you to hit "OK" so it gives you a chance for each of the codes to come through so you can see them (and hit OK after you see each one). The Server here hasn't changed, it's the same as in Listing 11.2.

LISTING 11.3   Simple XMLHttpRequest Client Illustrates Response Codes

```
<html>
    <body>
        <h1 id="myHeader"> This is an AJAX example</h1>
            <p> This code describes how to do an AJAX example </p>
            <p id="thispart"> This is the part that is updated </p>
            <p> It cleverly updates only part of a web page </p>
        <form action = "simple_server.php"
            <p> Enter your name: <input type="text" name="myname" />
                <button type = "button"  onclick = "doAJAXstuff(this.form)">
                    Paint part of the web page
                </button>
            </p>
        </form>
        <script type = "text/javascript">
            function doAJAXstuff(theform)
            {
                request = new XMLHttpRequest();
                request.open("GET","simple_server.php?mydata="+theform.myname.value);
                request.onreadystatechange = function ()
                {
                        alert("testit data returned is :\n"+request.readyState);
                }
                request.send();
            }
        </script>
    </body>
</html>
```

The response codes at different states are shown in Figures 11.3 through 11.5.

11.1.3 EXAMPLE CLEARLY ILLUSTRATING ASYNCHRONOUS XMLHTTPREQUEST

In this section, we will look at an example that more clearly illustrates the asynchronous operation of XMLHttpRequest. The server used in this example is shown in Listing 11.4. Note that the only difference between this server and the previous server (from Listing 11.2) is that there is a 5-second sleep in the middle of processing—this is to give the Client enough time to show that it's doing processing while it waits for the server to get back, and not just sitting there blocked waiting for the server to finish.

FIGURE 11.3 Request received by server response code.

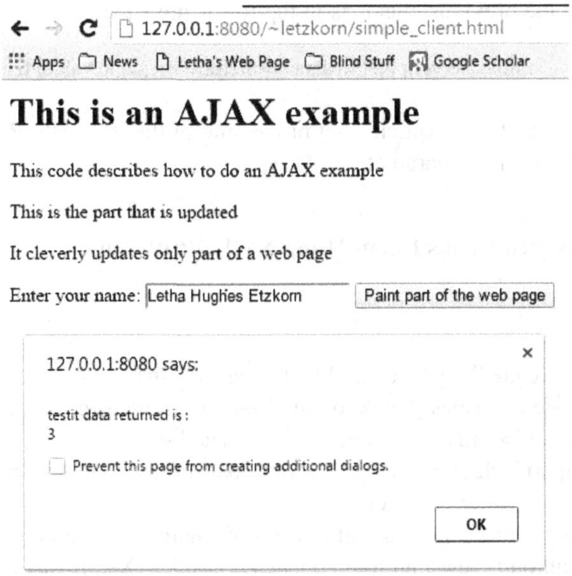

FIGURE 11.4 Server is processing request response code.

LISTING 11.4 PHP Server Used to Illustrate Asynchronous Operation

```php
<?php
    $mydata = $_REQUEST["mydata"];
    sleep(5);
    print "<p>Hi, $mydata! This is new important data for your web page.</p>";
?>
```

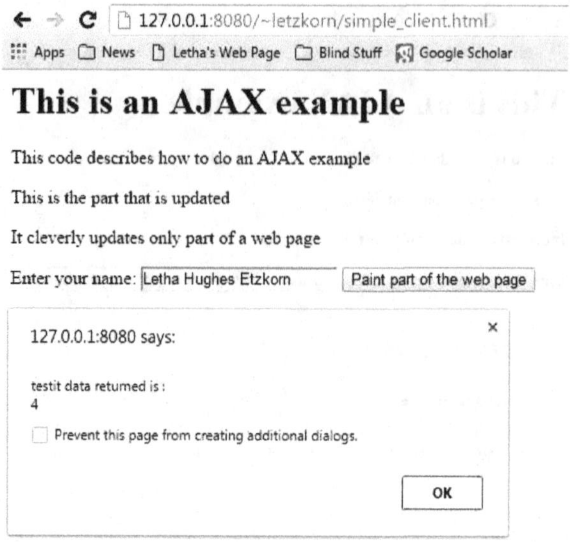

FIGURE 11.5   Server has finished request response code.

In Listing 11.5, we see the Asynchronous XMLHttpRequest Client. The most important difference between this client and the previous clients is in the following statement:

> request.open("GET","simple_server.php?mydata="+theform.myname.value, **true**);

Note that in this statement, we explicitly set processing of the XMLHttpRequest to be asynchronous by setting the asynchronous parameter to "true."

LISTING 11.5   Asynchronous Client Using XMLHttpRequest

```
<html>
    <body>
        <h1 id="myHeader"> This is an AJAX example</h1>
        <p> This code describes how to do an AJAX example </p>
        <p id="thispart"> This is the part that is updated </p>
        <p id="thatpart"> It cleverly updates only part of a web page </p>
        <form action = "simple_server.php"
            <p> Enter your name: <input type="text" name="myname" />
                <button type = "button"  onclick = "doAJAXstuff(this.form)">
                    Paint part of the web page
                </button>
            </p>
        </form>
        <script type = "text/javascript">
            function doAJAXstuff(theform) {
                request = new XMLHttpRequest();
                request.open("GET","simple_server.php?mydata="+theform.myname.value,
                    true);
                request.onreadystatechange = function () {
```

```
                        if (request.readyState == 4)
                            my_callback();
                    }
                    request.send();
                    document.getElementById("thatpart").style.font = "bold 30px Times New
                        Roman sans-serif";
                }
                function my_callback() {
                    if (request.status == 200) {
                        document.getElementById("thispart").innerHTML = request.
                        responseText;
                        document.getElementById("thispart").style.font = "italic bold
                        20px arial, serif";
                        alert("There wasn't an error, just wanted to let you see
                        how an alert works.
                                Received from the server:\n"+request.responseText);
                    }
                    else if (request.status=404) {
                        alert("Server was not found: data returned is :\n"+request.responseText);
                    }
                }
            </script>
        </body>
</html>
```

The first web page view produced by running this Client is shown in Figure 11.6. Note that this is the same that was earlier shown in Figure 11.1.

Now we will look at what happens in this example after we select the button "Paint part of the web Page." In this example, we are using font, bold, and italics on different parts of the web page to indicate that certain kinds of processing are happening. This is shown in Figure 11.7.

In Figure 11.7, we see that the font, font size, and boldness have been changed of the line:

"It cleverly updates only part of a web page."

If you look back at Listing 11.5, you can see that this was done by the following line:

document.getElementById("thatpart").style.font = "bold 30px Times New Roman sans-serif";

FIGURE 11.6 First web page produced by asynchronous client.

FIGURE 11.7   Asynchronous processing by client.

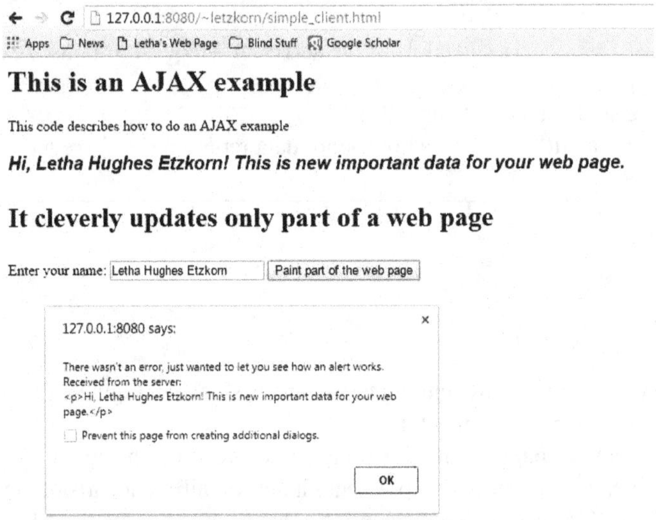

FIGURE 11.8   Asynchronous processing by client.

This line represents the work that the Client was doing when it continued on processing after calling XMLHttpRequest. That is, the Client continues its own work while the server is doing its processing separately. This is an example of asynchronous operation.

The alternative would have been for the Client to block and do nothing while waiting for the Server to finish. (This alternative would have been an example of synchronous processing.)

Now we will look at Figure 11.8, this shows what has happened to the web page after the callback function my_callback (see Listing 11.5) was called by the server after the server ended its processing. When you run this yourself, you will see that we had to wait a little while for this to happen (5 seconds, because the server did a sleep for 5 seconds). This gave us time to see the intermediate work done by the Client while the server was working independently (see Figure 11.7) before the final processing occurred.

So to summarize, the difference between asynchronous processing and synchronous processing is:

- In synchronous processing, a client calls a server and then blocks and waits until the server responds.
- In asynchronous processing, the client calls the server but the client continues doing independent work until the server responds.

SIDEBAR 11.1 CROSS-DOMAIN REQUESTS

However, you can potentially run into problems using XMLHttpRequest if you want to access a server on a different domain that the one where your code is running, this is called a *cross-domain request*. JavaScript calls from one domain to another have been used in hacker attacks, so browsers don't generally permit this.

If you need to do this, there are three common ways:

- Web proxy, you access a local web server (proxy server) with your XMLHttpRequest and the proxy server accesses the remote website—you may need to do this for legacy browsers
- Use JSONP (JavaScript with Padding)—you may need to do this for legacy browsers
- Cross Origin Resource Sharing (CORS)—supported in most modern web browsers

SIDEBAR 11.2 JSONP

JSONP makes use of the fact that when you use the "script" tag in JavaScript, the script tag is not subject to the same origin policy.

First of all, let's remember what the "src" attribute in the script tag in HTML does. For example:

```
<script src=URL>
    ...
</script>
```

Here the "src" attribute can access a different website, or it can access a JavaScript file on the current website, such as mywebsite/myscript.js.

Next, we are assuming that the remote website will normally pass back JSON-type data (this is common with AJAX).

What you are going to do (since we are using JSONP) is have the remote web site wrap its JSON data in a call to a local callback function that you define yourself.

```
<script}
function myCallbackFunction(JSON text) {
    ...
}
</script>
<script src="url of server?jsoncallback=myCallbackFunction>
</script>
```

So here when the "src" attribute calls the server, it would return something like this: myCallbackFunction({ "item": "value", "item2:"value2" })

Remember that the JSON format is syntactically the same as a JavaScript Object, but JSON is text only. You can convert the JSON to a JavaScript object by using the JavaScript function JSON.parse(JSON text). So your code in myCallbackFunction would look something like:

```
var myobj = JSON.parse(text);
```

So on the client side you need:

- Callback function defined
- "src" attribute on a <script> tag that calls the remote URL, this by convention should include the name of the callback function

The server will return a JavaScript function call that is passing the text of the JavaScript object.
So when the "src" attribute executes the script, it will call the local callback function.

SIDEBAR 11.3   CROSS ORIGIN RESOURCE SHARING (CORS)

The Cross Origin Resource Sharing standard provides a methodology for allowing HTTP requests from one domain to another domain. This can apply to RESTful type HTTP web services in general, however, in particular, this standard is used to allow XMLHttpRequests between domains.

We will examine two common scenarios using XMLHttpRequest with CORS:

- A simple cross-site request
  - Uses GET, HEAD, or POST (POST with Content-Type of text/plain, multipart/form-data, or application/x-www-form)
  - No custom headers in the HTTP request
  - Normally, a simple cross-site request would be expected to include credentials in the HTTP request
- Preflighted requests—a preflighted request is a request from client to server to ask for permission to perform a particular cross-domain request
  - Uses method *other than* GET, HEAD, or POST (POST with Content-Type *other than* text/plain, multipart/form-data, or application/x-www-form)
  - There are custom headers in the HTTP request
  - For example, a preflighted request could have POST with a Content-Type of application/xml. As an alternate example, it could use a PUT

To perform cross-site requests, CORS employs various headers in HTTP packets. Some headers used (among several others) are:

- Request Headers include:
  - Origin
  - Access-Control-Request-Method
- Response Headers include:
  - Access-Control-Allow-Origin
  - Access-Control-Allow-Methods

For XMLHttpRequest to work cross-site, the browser must support an XMLHttpRequest that uses CORS.

In a simple cross-site request, an XMLHttpRequest could be used to send a simple HTTP GET request. However, the HTTP GET request would include an Origin header listing the current web site:

Origin: www.myWebsite.com

If the server wishes to allow access, then the server (let's assume it's at www.theRemote Website.com) could send an HTTP response with the header:

Access-Control-Allow-Origin: www.myWebsitecom

The server could also reply with:

Access-Control-Allow-Origin: *

which means that the content on the remote website is freely available to anyone in the world.

A preflighted request occurs when the client must do an initial HTTP exchange with the server to see whether sending the actual HTTP request is allowed.

Here, the preflight HTTP request (let's assume the real request that you want to eventually send is a POST with Content-Type of application/xml) would contain the headers:

Origin: www.myWebsite.com
Access-Control-Request-Method

The preflight HTTP response would contain:

Access-Control-Allow-Origin: http://mywebsite.com
Access-Control-Allow-Methods: POST, GET

After receiving permission in the preflight HTTP response, the client can then send the real HTTP request.

11.2   TECHNOLOGY REVIEW: JAVA SERVLETS

A Java Servlet is a method for adding dynamic content to a server. *Dynamic content* here means that the servlets change at runtime what the user sees come back from the server, and the way the server behaves.

There are two main packages that are used: javax.servlet and javax.servlet.http. If you're using the HTTP protocol, which is what nearly everyone does, then you extend javax.servlet.http with your own servlet code.

Similar to what we saw in Chapter 8 with Enterprise Java Beans (EJBs), servlets have to run in a container, usually called a *servlet container* or perhaps a *web container*. A well-known open source example of a servlet container is Apache Tomcat. Another open source example is Glass-Fish. We will be using GlassFish for our examples (similar to what we did in Chapter 8 with EJBs). GlassFish, as you will recall from Chapter 8, is a reference implementation for Java EE 7. (At one time Tomcat was a reference implementation for Java Servlets.) Tomcat is more limited in scope than GlassFish since GlassFish provides an application server for all of Java EE. Both the GlassFish and Tomcat implementations use the Catalina servlet container. Other popular open source web servers that also support Java Servlets include Apache TomEE (this is a Java EE application server) and Wildfly (formerly JBoss).

11.2.1   Are Servlets RESTful

Are Servlets an example of a RESTful architecture or a RESTful web service? The answer is, they can be, it depends partly on how the servlets are implemented—or one could alternately say that it depends on how loose your definition of "RESTful" is.

The Representational State Transfer (REST) architectural style is defined relative to distributed hypermedia systems. A *hypermedia* system is a system that is a combination of audio, video, graphics, text, and hypertext. For example, the World Wide Web is the prime example of a hypermedia system.

If you recall from Section 9.2, the primary ideas behind a RESTful architectural style are that it would possess the following constraints:

- *Client/server:* Separation of concerns, exemplified by a client/server architecture. The idea is that different components can evolve independently—the user interface in the client can evolve separately from the server, and the server is simpler.
- *Stateless:* The client–server interaction is stateless. There is no stored context on the server. Any session information must be kept by the client.
- *Cacheable:* Data in a response (a response to a previous request) is labeled as cacheable or non-cacheable. If it is cacheable, the client (or an intermediary) may reuse that for the same kind of request in the future.
- *Uniform interface:* There is a uniform interface between components. In practice, there are four interface constraints:
  - Resource identification—requests identify the resources they are operating on (by a URI, for example)
  - Resource manipulation through the representation of the resource—when a client or server has access to a resource, it has enough information based on understanding the representation of the resource to be able to modify that resource
  - Messages are self-descriptive—the message contains enough information to allow a client or server to handle the message; this is normally done through the use of internet media types (MIME types)
  - Use of hypermedia to change the state of the application—for example, the server provides hyperlinks that the client uses to make state transitions
- *Layered system:* Components are organized in hierarchical layers, the components are only aware of the layer within which the interaction is occurring. Thus, a client connecting to a server is not aware of any intermediate connections.
  - Intermediate filter components can change the message while it is in transit: because the message is self-descriptive and the semantics are visible, the filter components understand enough about the message to modify it
- Code on demand: This is optionally supported, that is, clients can download scripts that extend their functionality.

So for a servlet implementation of a web service to be considered RESTful, it has to meet the RESTful architecture standards.

The servlet must adhere to the client/server paradigm. This is clearly the case.

Also, to meet the strict idea of RESTful, the servlet must also be acting in a stateless manner. This depends on how your servlet is written. Previously in Section 8.4.5.4, we briefly discussed how it is possible for session state (as well as potentially other kinds of state information) to be stored in a servlet (we will discuss this again in Section 11.3.7). Since it is possible to save state on the server side, a server that is implemented in that way would not meet the strict definition of RESTful.

In regard to the uniform interface constraint, a servlet that extends the HttpServlet interface (extends the interface defined in javax.servlet.http) is RESTful because it has handlers for each of the HTTP methods, and because the data sent in Requests and Responses can contain Internet Media Type (MIME types) data:

- doGet (HttpServletRequest request, HttpServletResponse response)
- doPost (HttpServletRequest request, HttpServletResponse response)

- doPut (HttpServletRequest request, HttpServletResponse response)
- doDelete (HttpServletRequest request, HttpServletResponse response)
- doHead (HttpServletRequest request, HttpServletResponse response)
- doTrace (HttpServletRequest request, HttpServletResponse response)
- doOptions (HttpServletRequest request, HttpServletResponse response)

Also in regard to Uniform Interface, a servlet must control a resource (typically accessed via a URI). Since a servlet can implement the Create, Read, Update, Delete (CRUD) operations that would be used on persistent storage (an example of a resource), this is usually easy to do.

The hierarchical layer constraint together with the intermediate filter constraint are met with servlets because they employ the HTTP protocol for communication, typically running on top of TCP/IP over a standard internet connection.

However, servlets have often been considered to be the *assembly language* of RESTful middleware, that is, they're very low level compared to some other RESTful middleware options.

11.2.2 Java Servlet Lifecycle

The lifecycle of a typical servlet that handles HTTP requests is specified in the following interfaces:

- Javax.servlet.Servlet
- Javax.servlet.GenericServlet
- Javax.servlet.http.HttpServlet

The servlet container controls the servlet lifecycle using the following methods from the Servlet API:

- Void init (ServletConfig config)
  - Calls init() on the servlet and passes the servlet the configuration information
- Void service (ServletRequest request, ServletResponse response)
- Void destroy()
- (There's also a method called getServletInfo, which the servlet can use to provide information about itself)

The servlet container first initializes the servlet:

- Maps the URL to the servlet in the servlet container
- Instantiates the servlet
- Calls init() on the servlet and passes the servlet the configuration information

When the initialization is complete, then:

- When client requests are received by the servlet container, the servlet container calls the service method:
  - The service method is defined as an abstract method in javax.servlet.GenericServlet, and is overridden in javax.servlet.http.HttpServlet
  - The service method spawns a new thread:
    - A ServletRequest object is passed into the servlet
    - A ServletResponse object is received back from the servlet, and the information in this object is returned by the servlet container to the client
  - The service method then calls the appropriate HTTP request handler (as specified by javax.servlet.http.HttpServlet):
    - DoGet (HttpServletRequest request, HttpServletResponse response)
    - DoPost (HttpServletRequest request, HttpServletResponse response)

- DoPut (HttpServletRequest request, HttpServletResponse response)
- DoDelete (HttpServletRequest request, HttpServletResponse response)
- DoHead (HttpServletRequest request, HttpServletResponse response)
- DoTrace (HttpServletRequest request, HttpServletResponse response)
- DoOptions (HttpServletRequest request, HttpServletResponse response)
- (alternately, instead of using the service method, the various handlers can be called direct)

When a servlet instance is to be removed from the servlet container, the servlet container calls destroy() on the servlet:

- This allows the servlet to release resources prior to being terminated
- Typical times when the servlet container would call destroy would be:
  - When the servlet container is about to shut down
  - When the servlet has timed out
  - When the servlet container needs the memory being taken up by the servlet

11.2.3 SIMPLE SERVLET EXAMPLE USES WEBSERVLET

In this section, we will look at a very simple servlet example. This example, which is shown in Listing 11.6, provides only a "doGet" handler. This servlet extends HttpServlet, which is why it can use a doGet handler that receives an object (HttpServletRequest object) that contains an HTTP Request as input, and returns an object (HttpServletResponse object) that contains an HTTP response as output.

This is a very simple servlet, it returns a tiny little web page in the HTTP response object that contains the following data as the payload:

<html><body><i>Happily working</i><b> myservlet</b> using @WebServlet</body></html>

Note that this example sets the media type (often known as MIME type) to "text/html" before sending the response. We're going to do a good bit in the next few sections here regarding media types. If you don't already understand media types, then you should read Section 4.6 before proceeding.

Note that the output from the statement:

System.out.println("Inside myservlet in doGet method");

will show up in the GlassFish server log file. We talked previously about how to view the Server log file in Section 4.11.2, and we saw some examples of the server log being used in Section 8.4.5.

That's about all there is related to what this servlet is actually doing. Now let's look at how the servlet is deployed and accessed from a container.

This example uses the @WebServlet annotation to tell the container how to access this servlet. It gives it a URL pattern consisting of "/myservlet." (There's a different way to do this, called a web.xml file, we'll look at that later on.) Being able to use @WebServlet annotation was initially provided in Servlet 3.0 (released in 2009), prior to that a web.xml file had to be used.

The way to deploy and run this is as follows:

First, you compile the servlet into a class file, and put the class file in a directory "classes" that is a subdirectory of another directory called "WEB-INF." The WEB-INF directory is how the container knows how to find the servlet information.

In this particular case, given the package name from the following statement:

package example.myservlet;

and knowing the file name is the same as the class name, which is:

myservlet

then the WEB-INF directory will contain the following:

/WEB-INF/classes/example/myservlet/myservlet.class

The directory "example/myservlet" is set by the package name example.myservlet, whereas the file name myservlet.class comes from the name of the Java class.

We could have had a different package name. For example, if we had used "anexample/someservlet" as the package name (while keeping the class name the same), then the WEB-INF would instead have contained the following:

/WEB-INF/classes/anexample/someservlet/myservlet.class

but we didn't do this, so we will be using the earlier directory structure inside the WEB-INF directory.

To deploy a servlet, we have to put it in a .war file (*Web* application *AR*chive file). Jar files and war files are both compressed files created using the Java jar archive tool. Most commonly there's a WEB-INF directory inside a war file.

To create the war file, we would do:

jar -cvf myservlet.war WEB-INF

Note that we've used the "myservlet" name again as the name of the war file. This is important because it will become part of the URL we use to access this servlet.

We saw previously in Section 4.11.2 how to deploy a .jar file on GlassFish. To deploy a .war file, you do the same procedure, just deploy the .war file instead of the .jar file.

After we deploy the myservlet.war file on GlassFish, we can now access the servlet using a web browser at the following URL:

http://localhost:8080/myservlet/myservlet

In this URL, the first "myservlet" came from the name of the war file: this term serves as the base portion of the URL, the "context root." The second "/myservlet" came from the @WebServlet annotation. Yes, I should probably have used different names for these to differentiate one from another, so you can figure out which to use when you do variations of this, but it gets so boring to think up names for very simple examples. ☺ I hope I have explained it well enough. If not, sigh. Please read it again, or else run the examples from the textbook and vary things until you get it. Doing it that way is the best way to learn, anyhow.

LISTING 11.6   Servlet Implemented Using WebServlet

```
package example.myservlet;
import java.io.*;
import javax.servlet.annotation.WebServlet;
import javax.servlet.*;
import javax.servlet.http.*;

@WebServlet (
  urlPatterns="/myservlet"
)
public class myservlet extends HttpServlet {
```

```
    public void doGet (HttpServletRequest request,
             HttpServletResponse response)
      throws ServletException, IOException
  {
        // Following output will show up in GlassFish log file
        // because System.out is standard output it will show up
        // on the console

        System.out.println("Inside myservlet in doGet method");
        // put a text/html header in the HTTP
        response.setContentType("text/html");

        // Write a small simple web page into the HTTP response
        PrintWriter myout = response.getWriter();
        myout.println("<html><body><i>Happily working</i><b> myservlet</b> using
        @WebServlet</body></html>");

  }
}
```

11.2.4   How to Pass Parameters to a Web Servlet (Still Using WebServlet)

In this example, we're going to see how you can pass parameters to a Web Servlet. We'll start by passing only one parameter—that is a string value—this is shown in Listing 11.7.

Here we retrieve the data parameter as follows:

```
String mystring;
// Get the data items from the HTTP post, by name
mystring=request.getParameter("mystring");
```

and we write it to the Response as follows:

```
// Prepare a writer to the response
PrintWriter myout = response.getWriter();
// Write the data you just received to the response
myout.println("received data is "+mystring);
```

LISTING 11.7   Pass One String Parameter to a doPost

```
package example.myservlet;
import java.io.*;
import java.util.*;
import javax.servlet.annotation.WebServlet;
import javax.servlet.*;
import javax.servlet.http.*;

@WebServlet (
  urlPatterns="/myservlet"
)
public class myservlet extends HttpServlet {
```

```
        @Override
        public void doPost(HttpServletRequest request,
                    HttpServletResponse response)
            throws ServletException, IOException
        {
                // Following output will show up in GlassFish log file
                System.out.println("Inside myservlet in doPost method");

                String mystring;

                // Get the data items from the HTTP post, by name
                mystring=request.getParameter("mystring");

                // Prepare a writer to the response
                PrintWriter myout = response.getWriter();

                // Write the data you just received to the response
                myout.println("received data is "+mystring);
        }
}
```

To call this, you need something a little more complicated than a simple URL access through a browser. You could use an html form perhaps with some JavaScript, or something like that, similar to what we saw previously in AJAX. However, in the examples in the text, I went a different way, I used cURL commands. We previously discussed cURL in Section 4.12. However, as you recall, cURL is a command-line utility that sends various protocols, including HTTP.

I used the following cURL command:

    curl--request POST http://localhost:8080/myservlet/myservlet --data 'mystring=hithere'

Now let's look at how you would send multiple parameters. Take a look at Listing 11.8. Here we read the parameters as follows:

    String mystring;

    // Get the data items from the HTTP post, by name
    mystring=request.getParameter("mystring");

    int myint;

    // Get the data items from the HTTP post, by name
    myint=Integer.parseInt(request.getParameter("myint"));

It's very similar to how we did it in the previous example, except that this time we have to convert the "myint" parameter to an integer.

We write it to the Response very similarly to the previous example:

    // Prepare a writer to the response
    PrintWriter myout = response.getWriter();

```
// Write the data you just received to the response
myout.println("received data is "+mystring+" and "+myint);
```

LISTING 11.8   Pass One String Parameter and One Int parameter to a doPost

```
package example.myservlet;
import java.io.*;
import java.util.*;
import javax.servlet.annotation.WebServlet;
import javax.servlet.*;
import javax.servlet.http.*;

@WebServlet (
  urlPatterns="/myservlet"
)
public class myservlet extends HttpServlet {

    @Override
    public void doPost(HttpServletRequest request,
             HttpServletResponse response)
       throws ServletException, IOException
    {
        // Following output will show up in GlassFish log file
        System.out.println("Inside myservlet in doPost method");

        String mystring;
        // Get the data items from the HTTP post, by name
        mystring=request.getParameter("mystring");

        int myint;

        // Get the data items from the HTTP post, by name
        myint=Intcgcr.parseInt(request.getParameter("myint"));

        // Prepare a writer to the response
        PrintWriter myout = response.getWriter();

        // Write the data you just received to the response
        myout.println("received data is "+mystring+" and "+myint);
    }

}
```

There are two cURL commands we can use to send these two parameters. The first one is similar to our earlier parameter passing example:

```
curl--request POST http://localhost:8080/myservlet/myservlet --data 'mystring=hithere&myint=105'
```

However, the other is a little different, and looks a lot like a cURL GET (except of course we're using a POST):

```
curl--request POST "http://localhost:8080/myservlet/myservlet?mystring=hithere&myint=105"
```

11.2.5 SLIGHTLY MORE COMPLICATED SERVLET EXAMPLE USES WEBSERVLET

In the example shown here in Listing 11.9, we're going to see a few additional things that a servlet can do. First of all, in Section 11.2.2 in our discussion of the servlet lifecycle, we talked about the "service" routine. In Listing 11.9, you can see that a service routine is present, but has been commented out. If this is commented out, then the various handler routines (doGet, doPut, etc.) are called direct. However, if you uncomment the service routine, it will run and the HTTP calls will go through it. This gives you a way to add additional processing around the HTTP request/response handling.

Note also that there are various routines for:

- Init
- Destroy
- GetServiceInfo

which we also previously saw in Section 11.2.2.

The various calls to System.out.println will result in text being written to the Server log, so we can trace through the server log what happens when this runs.

There are also routines for doGet, doPost, doPut, and doDelete.

The doGet here is only providing a simple web page (text/html) output, it's not reading any input parameters. It's pretty well the same as the doGet we previously saw in Listing 11.6.

The doPost is getting various parameters, by name, from the HTTP request, using the following code:

```
data1=request.getParameter("data1");
data2=request.getParameter("data2");
data3=request.getParameter("data3");
data4=request.getParameter("data4");
```

In the following cURL command, we see a POST with data items named: data1, data2, data3, and data4.

```
curl--request POST http://localhost:8080/myservlet/myservlet --data
'data1=hithere&data2=student&data3=from&data4=yourteacher'
```

After you deploy this servlet, you can call the above command and get the following response:

```
data1 is hithere
data2 is student
data3 is from
data4 is yourteacher
```

The doPut reads a file that was sent in the HTTP request, using the following code:

```
// Get the file data from the HTTP PUT request
InputStream filedata = request.getInputStream();
```

It then echoes the data from this file back to the client.

You can send a Put as in the following cURL command that sends the file named "readme.txt" to the server.

```
curl-T readme.txt  http://localhost:8080/myservlet/myservlet
```

The output that is echoed back is just the contents of the readme.txt file. It's a little long and boring so I won't show what it looks like here. ☺

The other routines provided (init, destroy, getServletInfo, and doDelete) do various calls to System.out.println that will show up in the GlassFish server log. In the case of getServletInfo and doDelete, they also return a snappy little message ☺ to the client.

LISTING 11.9   Slightly More Complicated Servlet Implemented Using WebServlet

```java
package example.myservlet;
import java.io.*;
import java.util.*;
import javax.servlet.annotation.WebServlet;
import javax.servlet.*;
import javax.servlet.http.*;

@WebServlet (
urlPatterns="/myservlet"
)
public class myservlet extends HttpServlet {

    @Override
    public void init(ServletConfig config)
        throws ServletException
    {
            // Following output will show up in GlassFish log file
            System.out.println("Inside myservlet in init method");
    }

/**** commented service out to let the specific routines (doGet, etc.)
        handle the HTTP messages.
    @Override
    public void service(HttpServletRequest request,
                HttpServletResponse response)
        throws ServletException, IOException
    {
            // Prepare a writer to the response
            PrintWriter myout = response.getWriter();
            String current_request= request.getMethod();

            myout.println("current request method is "+current_request);
            // Find out which HTTP method is being called
            if (current_request.equals("GET"))
                    doGet(request,response);
            else if (current_request.equals("POST"))
                    doPost(request,response);
            else if (current_request.equals("PUT"))
                    doPut(request,response);
            else if (current_request.equals("DELETE"))
                    doDelete(request,response);
            else
                    myout.println("oops didn't recognize the request");
```

```java
}

************/
  @Override
  public void doGet(HttpServletRequest request,
              HttpServletResponse response)
    throws ServletException, IOException
  {
      // put a text/html header in the HTTP response
      response.setContentType("text/html");

      // Following output will show up in GlassFish log file
      System.out.println("Inside myservlet in doGet method");

      // Write a small simple web page into the HTTP response
      PrintWriter myout = response.getWriter();
      myout.println("<html><body><i>Happily working</i><b> myservlet</b> using
      @WebServlet</body></html>");
  }

  @Override
  public void doPost(HttpServletRequest request,
              HttpServletResponse response)
    throws ServletException, IOException
  {
      // Following output will show up in GlassFish log file
      System.out.println("Inside myservlet in doPut method");

      String data1,data2,data3,data4;

      // Get the data items from the HTTP post, by name
      data1=request.getParameter("data1");
      data2=request.getParameter("data2");
      data3=request.getParameter("data3");
      data4=request.getParameter("data4");

      // Prepare a writer to the response
      PrintWriter myout = response.getWriter();

      // Write the data you just received to the response
      myout.println("data1 is "+data1);
      myout.println("data2 is "+data2);
      myout.println("data3 is "+data3);
      myout.println("data4 is "+data4);
  }
  @Override
  public void doPut(HttpServletRequest request,
              HttpServletResponse response)
    throws ServletException, IOException
```

```
{
    // Following output will show up in GlassFish log file
    System.out.println("Inside myservlet in doPost method");

    // Prepare a writer to the response
    PrintWriter myout = response.getWriter();

    // Get the file data from the HTTP PUT request
    InputStream filedata = request.getInputStream();
    // Write the length of the file to the response
    myout.println("content length is "+request.getContentLength());

    // Write the file's data back to the response
    myout.println("File data received by servlet is : ");

    int data;
    data = filedata.read();
    while (data != -1)
    {
        myout.print( (char) data);
        data = filedata.read();
    }
    myout.println();
}


@Override
public void doDelete(HttpServletRequest request,
            HttpServletResponse response)
    throws ServletException, IOException
{
    // Following output will show up in GlassFish log file
    // because System.out is standard output it will show up
    // on the console
    System.out.println("Inside myservlet in doDelete method");

    // Write to the response
    PrintWriter myout = response.getWriter();
    myout.println("I got the delete but I refuse to delete anything :-)");
}

@Override
public String getServletInfo()
{
    // Following output will show up in GlassFish log file
    System.out.println("Inside myservlet in getServletInfo method");
    return "slightly_more_complicated_servlet_by_Etzkorn";
}
```

```
@Override
public void destroy()
{
    // Following output will show up in GlassFish log file
    // because System.out is standard output it will show up
    // on the console
    System.out.println("Inside myservlet in destroy method");
}
}
```

Let's look at the GlassFish server log to see various messages that were put there using the System.out.println calls. In this we see where the server "myservlet" was created. Then we see a call from the container to "init," a call to "doGet," a call to "doPost," two calls to doPut, and a call to doDelete. See Figure 11.9.

11.2.6 Simple Servlet Uses web.xml

If you look at the servlet shown here in Listing 11.10, the only difference between it and the servlet in Listing 11.6 is that here the @WebServlet annotation is not used. Instead, a separate file called "web.xml" is used as a deployment descriptor.

As you recall from Section 11.3.3, being able to use @WebServlet annotation was initially provided in Servlet 3.0 (released in 2009), prior to that a web.xml file had to be used. The biggest advantage to using the @WebServlet annotation is that with the annotation there is no chance of your Java class name being changed to no longer match the name in the web.xml file. It's also easier to use annotation because everything is in one file, you don't have to go back and forth between the Java file and the web.xml file.

However, web.xml does have some advantages. For example, if you ever need to change the configuration without recompiling the Java class then you must use web.xml.

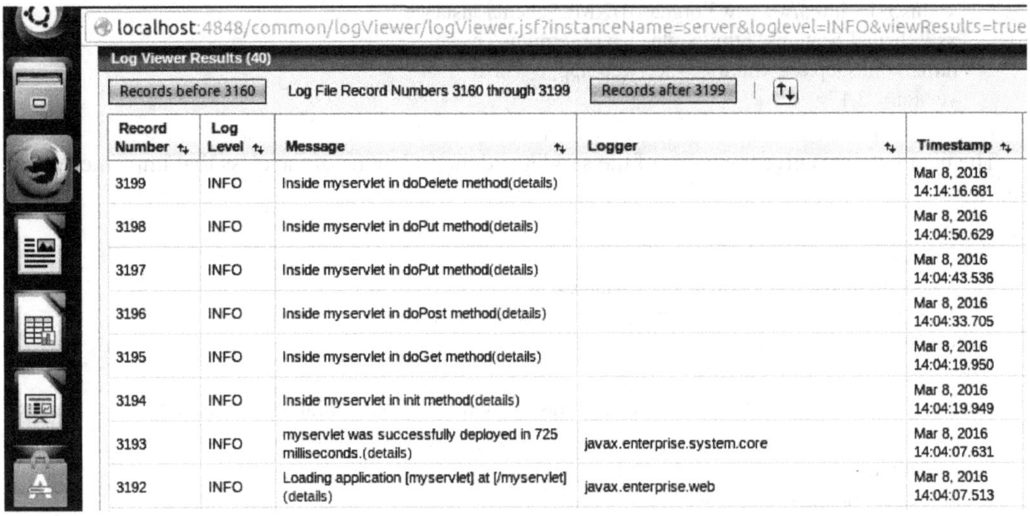

localhost:4848/common/logViewer/logViewer.jsf?instanceName=server&loglevel=INFO&viewResults=true				
Log Viewer Results (40)				
Records before 3160	Log File Record Numbers 3160 through 3199	Records after 3199		
Record Number	Log Level	Message	Logger	Timestamp
3199	INFO	Inside myservlet in doDelete method(details)		Mar 8, 2016 14:14:16.681
3198	INFO	Inside myservlet in doPut method(details)		Mar 8, 2016 14:04:50.629
3197	INFO	Inside myservlet in doPut method(details)		Mar 8, 2016 14:04:43.536
3196	INFO	Inside myservlet in doPost method(details)		Mar 8, 2016 14:04:33.705
3195	INFO	Inside myservlet in doGet method(details)		Mar 8, 2016 14:04:19.950
3194	INFO	Inside myservlet in init method(details)		Mar 8, 2016 14:04:19.949
3193	INFO	myservlet was successfully deployed in 725 milliseconds.(details)	javax.enterprise.system.core	Mar 8, 2016 14:04:07.631
3192	INFO	Loading application [myservlet] at [/myservlet] (details)	javax.enterprise.web	Mar 8, 2016 14:04:07.513

FIGURE 11.9   GlassFish server log after a few cURL commands.

LISTING 11.10   Servlet Implemented Using web.xml

```
package example.myservlet;
import java.io.*;
import javax.servlet.annotation.WebServlet;
import javax.servlet.*;
import javax.servlet.http.*;


public class myservlet extends HttpServlet {

  public void doGet(HttpServletRequest request,
            HttpServletResponse response)
     throws ServletException, IOException
  {
     // put a text/html header in the HTTP response    response.setContentType("text/html");
     // Following output will show up in GlassFish log file
     System.out.println("Inside myservlet in doGet method");
     // Write a small simple web page into the HTTP response
     PrintWriter myout = response.getWriter();
     myout.println("<html><body><i>Happily working</i><b> myservlet</b> using web.xml
         file</body></html>");
  }
}
```

In Listing 11.11, we see a web.xml deployment descriptor that we can use to deploy the servlet from Listing 11.10. This web.xml file would be placed in the WEB-INF directory, and the war file created and deployed as before.

The first few lines of this particular web.xml file show that it is using Servlet 3.1 as part of Java EE:

```
<web-app xmlns="http://xmlns.jcp.org/xml/ns/javaee"
   xmlns:xsi="http://www.w3.org/2001/XMLSchema-instance"
   xsi:schemaLocation="http://xmlns.jcp.org/xml/ns/javaee
   http://xmlns.jcp.org/xml/ns/javaee/web-app_3_1.xsd"
   version="3.1">
```

The next few lines give the name of the servlet and the full name of the class that implements that servlet:

```
<servlet>
    <servlet-name>myservlet</servlet-name>
    <servlet-class>example.myservlet.myservlet</servlet-class>
</servlet>
```

The last few lines provide the url pattern that go with that particular servlet name:

```
<servlet-mapping>
    <servlet-name>myservlet</servlet-name>
    <url-pattern>/myservlet</url-pattern>
</servlet-mapping>
```

As in the previous examples, the name of the war file is the base portion (context root) of the URL, and the URL pattern comes immediately following the war file name. As before, it would be accessed in a browser as follows:

http://localhost:8080/myservlet/myservlet

LISTING 11.11   web.xml Deployment Descriptor

```xml
<web-app xmlns="http://xmlns.jcp.org/xml/ns/javaee"
    xmlns:xsi="http://www.w3.org/2001/XMLSchema-instance"
    xsi:schemaLocation="http://xmlns.jcp.org/xml/ns/javaee http://xmlns.jcp.org/xml/
    ns/javaee/
    web-app_3_1.xsd"
    version="3.1">
    <servlet>
        <servlet-name>myservlet</servlet-name>
        <servlet-class>example.myservlet.myservlet</servlet-class>
    </servlet>
    <servlet-mapping>
        <servlet-name>myservlet</servlet-name>
        <url-pattern>/myservlet</url-pattern>
    </servlet-mapping>
</web-app>
```

11.2.7 ASYNCHRONOUS SERVLET

The servlet example we see in Listing 11.12 illustrates how servlets can handle asynchronous communication. In this case, the servlet starts a separate thread running (the doWork class that implements the Runnable interface is the thread). I'm going to assume you know at least a little bit about threads. I like to explain as much as I can but this textbook has been suffering from requirements creep. ☺

The original process in the servlet fires off the doWork thread using the following command:

```
new Thread (new doWork(ac) ).start();
```

Before the original process in the servlet fires off the doWork thread, it sets up an asynchronous listener. This listener is waiting for various events to occur in the doWork thread:

- OnComplete
- OnTimeout
- OnStartAsync
- OnError

The only event that is ever going to happen in this particular example, however, would be the onComplete event. If you look at the doWork thread, it sleeps for 20 seconds to simulate doing some real work, then it creates an HTTP response with a string that says it's been doing some really useful stuff. ☺ After that it says that it's complete, as follows:

```
ac.complete();        // when hard work is done, signify completion
```

LISTING 11.12   Asynchronous Servlet

```
package example.myservlet;
import java.io.*;
import java.lang.Thread;

import javax.servlet.annotation.WebServlet;
import javax.servlet.*;
import javax.servlet.http.*;
import javax.servlet.http.HttpServlet;
import javax.servlet.http.HttpServletRequest;
import javax.servlet.http.HttpServletResponse;

import javax.servlet.AsyncContext;
import javax.servlet.AsyncEvent;
import javax.servlet.AsyncListener;
import javax.servlet.ServletException;

import javax.servlet.http.HttpServlet;

class doWork implements Runnable {
    private AsyncContext ac;

    public doWork(AsyncContext the_ac) {
        // set the context of the thread to the original context
        this.ac=the_ac;
    }
    public void run() {
        System.out.println("inside doWork thread");
        // do a lot of hard work
        try {
            Thread.sleep(10000);  // sleep for 10 sec to simulate hard work

            // Put some stuff in the response so it get done after completion
            PrintWriter myout = ac.getResponse().getWriter();
            myout.println("this is really useful stuff");
            System.out.println("just wrote some stuff into response");

        } catch (Exception e)  {
            System.out.println("Some kind of Exception");
        }
        ac.complete();        // when hard work is done, signify completion
    }
}

@WebServlet (
urlPatterns="/myservlet",asyncSupported = true
)
```

```
public class myservlet extends HttpServlet {
  public void doGet(HttpServletRequest request,
            HttpServletResponse response)
      throws ServletException, IOException
  {
  // Following output will show up in GlassFish log file
  System.out.println("Inside myservlet in doGet method");

  AsyncContext ac = request.startAsync();
  ac.addListener(new AsyncListener()
    {
      @Override
      public void onComplete(AsyncEvent event) throws IOException {
        System.out.println("onComplete: Asynchronous task is now done");
      }
      @Override
      public void onTimeout(AsyncEvent event) throws IOException {
        System.out.println("onTimeout");
      }
      @Override
      public void onStartAsync(AsyncEvent event) throws IOException {
        System.out.println("onStartAsync");
      }
      @Override
      public void onError(AsyncEvent event) throws IOException {
        System.out.println("onError");
      }

    }
  );
  System.out.println("just before thread start");

  new Thread (new doWork(ac) ).start();

  System.out.println("just after thread start");
  System.out.println("very end of doGet");

  }
}
```

There are various System.out.println statements that write into the GlassFish System log. The system log from a run of this asynchronous servlet is shown in Figure 11.10.

Note that you can also use a web.xml file to deploy an asynchronous servlet. To do so, you would just remove the @WebServlet annotation and add the web.xml file from Listing 11.11 to the WEB-INF directory, with an additional tag to the web.xml file to make it asynchronous:

```
<async-supported>true</async-supported>
```

A separate directory with this asynchronous servlet using a web.xml file is provided in the code that comes with this textbook.

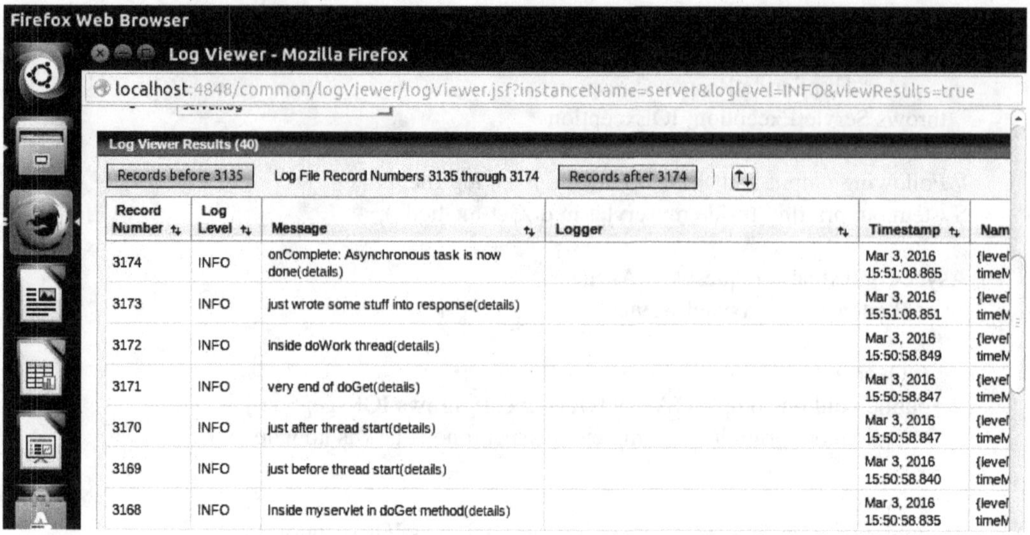

FIGURE 11.10 Server log for asynchronous servlet.

11.2.8 SERVLET STORAGE BETWEEN HTTP REQUEST/RESPONSE CALLS AND SERVLET SESSIONS

In this section, we're going to discuss how data can be stored inside a servlet. Using this information, you can create a Session that can be used to associate different HTTP Request/Response Calls with each other. You should remember that a RESTful architecture includes *stateless* as one of its criteria. Thus, using a session like this in your servlet would mean you do not have a RESTful architecture by the strictest definition.

Let's look at how data can be stored in a servlet. Note: I went over a lot of this earlier in an example related to EJBs, that you can see in Section 8.4.5.4. In that example, I used a servlet to store a bunch of EJBs, so as to force the container to run out of memory. ☺ It's a good example, and a practical example, please go look at it, it will be a good way for you to learn how to store data in a servlet. However, for completeness I've included some of the discussion here as well, although not the example.

A servlet has a convenient thing called an *attribute*, that makes it easy to store resources inside the servlet (and thus inside the container). (Attributes can also be used to pass information between servlets.)

Attributes and parameters in a Java EE web application are related to the *servlet scope* that specifies where that attribute or parameter is available for use. The scope of the servlet is how the servlet maintains a state.

To use attribute information within a scope, these are the routines that one could call:

- SetAttribute(name, object) saves the object along with its name
- GetAttribute(name) returns the object associated with the specified name
- RemoveAttribute(name) removes the object from the context
- GetAttributeNames() returns an enum containing the names of all attributes
  - Could do:
    - Enumeration the_names=request.getAttributeNames();

Servlets have three scopes:

1. Application (Context) scope—the lifetime of a web application. The data in this scope is available while a web application is in service, from start to finish (or reload). It is valid during interaction of all users with a particular web application.

2. Request Scope—the duration of the Request. The data in this scope is valid from when an HTTP request is received by the servlet until an HTTP response is generated by the servlet. It is valid during a single user's interaction with a web application during a single HTTP request.
3. Session scope—the lifetime of the Client. The data in this scope is valid from when a client establishes a connection with the application until the connection is closed. It is valid across multiple HTTP requests from a single user.

Application (Context) scope employs the javax.servlet.ServletContext interface, which defines methods used by a servlet to communicate with the servlet container. There is one context for each web application in a Java Virtual Machine. To access this, you can do:

- ServletContext mycontext = getServletContext();

Or:

- ServletConfig myconfig = getServletConfig();
  ServletContext mycontext=myconfig.getServletContext();

Request scope employs the javax.servlet.http.HttpServletRequest interface, which provides HTTP requests to HTTP servlets. When using this scope an HttpServletRequest object is created by the servlet container and passed to doGet, doPut, etc. in the servlet. To access this scope, you can call getAttribute(name), etc., on the request object passed into doGet (from inside doGet()), etc.

Session scope employs the javax.servlet.http.HttpSession interface—used to create a session from an HTTP client (one user) to an HTTP server that persists for a specified period of time. To use this scope, you can call;

- HttpSession session = request.getSession();
  - GetSession()—gets the session, if there isn't already an HttpSession object, it creates one.

The way the getSession routine works is as follows:

- If cookies are enabled:
  - It generates a JSESSIONID cookie and value that is used to identify this session when further requests arrive from this client. This JSESSIONID cookie is sent to the client in a response, the client uses it in future requests.
  - The HTTP header, if displayed, would include:
    - Set-Cookie: JSESSIONID=..long messy hex value...; Path=/example; Expires= ..date.. ; Secure
- If cookies are not enabled, it uses URL rewriting:
  - A JSESSIONID is added at the end of the URL, and the request is redirected to this URL
    - www.mstuff.com/hello becomes www.mystuff.com/hello/jsessionid=...long messy hex value...

URL rewriting consists of telling the server to redirect a request from one URL to a different URL. Typically URL rewriting is done so a more readable URL can be the one the client accesses first, then that url is redirected to a less readable internal URL (the domain name is the same in both cases, but the rest of the URL would need to be redirected). In this particular case, however, URL rewriting is used to establish a session, so the more readable URL is rerouted to a less readable URL.

11.3   TECHNOLOGY REVIEW: JAVA API FOR RESTFUL WEB SERVICES (JAX-RS)

Java API for RESTful Web Services (JAX-RS) is a Java-based middleware that allows creating a RESTful web service, that is, a web service that obeys the characteristics expected of a RESTful architecture. We previously discussed what is meant by a RESTful architecture and a RESTful web service in Section 9.2.

However, briefly, a RESTful architecture consists of resources that are accessed and manipulated by well-defined operations in a stateless manner. The World Wide Web is considered to be an example of a RESTful architecture, where each resource is represented by a URL, and the well-defined operations that access these resources are defined by the HTTP protocol.

So JAX-RS provides a way to use Java to employ HTTP to manipulate and access resources located on the web, where the location of these resources is specified by a URL, and that JAX-RS operates in a stateless manner.

The reference implementation of JAX-RS is jersey (jersey also provides additional features). Other implementations of JAX-RS include RESTeasy (from Wildfly), Apache CXF (Apache CXF also handles many other standard middlewares, including CORBA as well as other web services standards such as JAX-WS), among several others. We will be using jersey for the examples in this textbook.

JAX-RS is commonly deployed in a servlet container, either a container obeying the Servlet 2.X specification, or a container obeying the Servlet 3.X specification. However, there are other ways that JAX-RS can be deployed, such as within an EJB container (perhaps to provide a RESTful interface to the EJB) or within an OSGi implementation (one OSGi implementation is Apache Felix, which is the OSGi shell that is used by GlassFish).

Our examples in this textbook were done assuming deployment in a Servlet 3.X container, although we will briefly also examine deployment in a Servlet 2.X container.

11.3.1   JAX-RS BASICS INCLUDING JAX-RS ANNOTATIONS

JAX-RS uses annotations on Java class definitions to define resources and to define the associated actions that can be performed on these resources.

A class that JAX-RS would consider to be "resource" class is a class that can be accessed via a URL. A resource class is specified using annotations similar to what we see in Listing 11.13 (the annotations are shown in bold).

LISTING 11.13   JAX-RS Resource Class

```
@Path("/hello")
public class Hello {
    @GET
  public String method_that_handles_GETs() {
  ...useful stuff...
  }
}
```

The class in Listing 11.13 is a resource class because it is accessible via a URL and because it provides either some kind of useful data or some kind of useful functionality ("functionality" means that it does some kind of work) that is accessed through a method that is annotated using a *resource method annotation* (a method annotation associated with an HTTP message).

Note that the default life cycle of a root resource class in JAX-RS is per-request. What this means is that every time the URI path in an HTTP request matches the root resource, a new instance of the root resource class is created. Thus, JAX-RS is stateless.

This particular example provides a @GET resource method annotation. The associated method, method_that_handles_GETs(), is called a "resource method." This method is called when an HTTP GET message is received by the servlet container (or EJB container or OSGi shell). For the rest of the discussion in this chapter we will assume deployment in a servlet container. In general, resource method annotations indicate which resource methods are called when the servlet container has received HTTP requests.

Annotations on these resource methods indicate which HTTP command accesses each method. The most basic resource method annotations are below (we'll see a few others later):

- @GET—handles HTTP GET requests
- @POST—handles HTTP POST requests
- @PUT—handles HTTP PUT requests

Each one of these basic resource method annotations may result in parameters being sent to the annotated handler method. Some parameters are generally pretty well expected when you're sending a POST or a PUT.

On a GET, a parameter is not always expected, but it's pretty common to send one, although it's often a bad idea. The query string parameters that are sent with GETs are commonly logged in many locations (such as web server logs, history caches in browsers, etc.) and thus represent a security risk. A query string parameter would be appended to a URL, as in the following example:

- http://example.com/mystuff?paramA=2000&paramB=3000

There are other annotations that specify how the parameter(s) of a resource method are bound to the parameters within an HTTP request, these are called "parameter annotations." This is a form of "injection"—you may remember the discussion of dependency injection in Section 8.4. Basically "injection" grabs the particular information you need from where it came from and stuffs it where you need it.

Some of the most basic parameter annotations are:

- @PathParam—specifies one or more parameters that are included in the URL, for example: my.example.com/mypath/myparametervalue
- @QueryParam—specifies one or more parameters that are in query string format, for example: myexample.com?myparametername=myparametervalue
- @FormParam—specifies one or more parameters that are in urlencoded format (application/x-www-form-urlencoded), such as would occur when sent from an HTML form

Later in this chapter, we will look at how to use these parameter-based annotations.

Note that both of these also require an @Path annotation on the associated method.

You can also receive and send different Internet Media Types (MIME types) using these basic method annotations. These can specify the kinds of Internet Media Types that your method expects to receive when called, using the following annotation:

- @Consumes

These can also specify the kinds of Internet Media Types that your method will produce and send back in a response, using the following annotation:

- @Produces

See Section 4.6 for a description of Internet Media Types. To accept a particular kind of Internet media type, you would annotate the method similar to what is shown in Listing 11.14 (the annotation associated with Internet Media Types is shown in bold).

LISTING 11.14   Simple Internet Media Type (MIME type) Annotation Example

```
@Path("/hello")
public class Hello {
    @POST
    @Consumes(MediaType.TEXT_XML)
    public String method_that_handles_POSTs() {
    ...useful stuff...
    }
}
```

Note that Internet Media Types can be used to differentiate between the methods that are called. See Listing 11.15: in this example, if an HTTP POST is received that contains a header specifying that data with an Internet Media Type of text/xml is included in the HTTP request (Content-Type is text/xml) then the method named "method_that_handles_POSTs_for_TEXT_XML()" will be called, whereas if the HTTP POST contained a header specifying that data with an Internet Media Type of text/plain is included in the HTTP request (Content-Type: text/plain) then the method named "method_that_handles_POSTs_for_TEXT_PLAIN()" will be called.

LISTING 11.15   Simple Internet Media Type (MIME Type) Annotation Example

```
@Path("/hello")
public class Hello {
    @POST
    @Consumes(MediaType.TEXT_XML)
    public String method_that_handles_POSTs_for_TEXT_XML() {
    ...useful stuff...
    }
    @POST
    @Consumes(MediaType.TEXT_PLAIN)
    public String method_that_handles_POSTs_for_TEXT_PLAIN() {
    ...useful stuff...
    }
}
```

It works similarly if your code uses an @Produces annotation. Consider a case where you used the following annotations on a resource method in a resource class:

```
@POST
@Produces(MediaType.TEXT_PLAIN)
```

Then if an HTTP POST request is received with a header (Accept: text/plain) specifying that the client is expecting to receive a response containing data with an Internet Media Type of text/plain, then this resource method would be called. Note that an HTTP POST request with an Accept: text/xml header would not result in this resource method being called—another method would have to handle that request.

We will discuss more about how Internet Media Types are handled by JAX-RS later on in this chapter. A few other definitions you need to know to have a fairly wide view of JAX-RS:

- Entity—encapsulates a message and also includes information about Internet Media Type, language, and encoding. We're going to see some library functions that access entities later on in this chapter.
- Filters—can modify requests and responses, including headers, entities, and parameters.

Other JAX-RS resource method annotations are:

- @DELETE—handles HTTP DELETE requests
- @HEAD—handles HTTP HEAD requests
- @Provider—a way to programmatically extend how JAX-RS operates (kind of like a plugin). There are three kinds of providers:
  - Entity providers—which map data representations (JSON, XML, etc.) to Java objects
    - This allows you to examine the raw XML, JSON, etc. data of a message.
  - Context providers—control the context that resources can access using an @Context annotation.
  - Exception providers—map Java exceptions to a Response object.
- Other parameter annotations include:
  - @CookieParam—extracts information from cookie-related HTTP headers.
  - @MatrixParam—extracts information from URL path segments (see below)
  - @Context—can inject a variety of components into your web service.
    - This can include: HTTP headers, HTTP URI information, Request, Resource Context, Security Context, Configuration, and providers, among others.
    - For example, although the @HEADER annotation is useful to inject header information, you must identify the header by name in this annotation To iterate over several headers, you could use @Context.

A URL Matrix parameter has the form:

http://myexample.com/mystuff;paramA=2000;paramB=3000

whereas a query parameter (as we saw earlier) has the form:

http://myexample.com/mystuff?paramA=2000&paramB=3000

However, the main difference between a query parameter and a matrix parameter is that a query parameter applies to the request taken as a whole, whereas the matrix parameter applies to a particular path element within the request. An example of a query parameter might be:

http://myexample.com/mystuff?studentname=Smith&professorname=Etzkorn

whereas an equivalent matrix parameter might be:

http://myexample.com/mystuff/students;name=Smith/professors;name=Etzkorn

11.3.2 Simple JAX-RS Example

We will now look at several JAX-RS examples. In this section, we start by looking at a simple example that handles a GET, a POST, and a PUT, while distinguishing between different Internet Media Types (MIME types) in regard to what kind of data (Internet Media Type/MIME type) is Produced and in regard to what is Consumed.

As you will recall from Section 11.4.1, "Produced" refers to the kind of data (which Internet Media Type) the resource method will send back in a response. The annotation @Produces specifies the Internet Media Type that the resource method produces, and the header Accept: *internet media type (example: text/plain)* in the HTTP request is used to map the HTTP request to the appropriate resource method to handle it.

Similarly, from Section 11.4.1, "Consumed" refers to the kind of data (which Internet Media Type) the resource method expects to receive in a request. The annotation @Consumes specifies the Internet Media Type that the resource method expects to receive, and the header Content-Type: *internet media type (example: text/plain)* in the HTTP request is used to map the HTTP request to the appropriate resource method to handle it.

In this example, we use various cURL commands to send different HTTP messages and Internet Media Types (MIME types) to exercise the different resource methods provided in Listing 11.16.

LISTING 11.16   Simple JAX-RS Example Showing Produces and Consumes Internet Media Types (MIME Types)

```
package example.restful;
import javax.ws.rs.GET;
import javax.ws.rs.POST;
import javax.ws.rs.PUT;
import javax.ws.rs.Path;
import javax.ws.rs.PathParam;
import javax.ws.rs.core.Response;
import javax.ws.rs.Produces;
import javax.ws.rs.Consumes;
import javax.ws.rs.core.MediaType;


@Path("/hello")
public class Hello {
    // called when request has accept text/plain header
    @GET
    @Produces(MediaType.TEXT_PLAIN)
    public String return_plaintext() {
        return "Hello World\n\n";
    }
    // called when request has accept text/html header
    @GET
    @Produces(MediaType.TEXT_HTML)
    public String return_html() {
      return "<html> " + "<body>" + "<h1>" + "Hello" +"</h1>"+"<h2>"+"to" + "</h2>"
      + "<h2>" + "all the World" + "</h2>"+"</body>" + "</html> "+"\n";
    }
    // called when request has accept text/xml header
    @GET
```

```
@Produces(MediaType.TEXT_XML)
public String return_XML() {
    return "<?xml version=\"1.0\"?>" + "<thedata> Hello World" + "</thedata>"+"\n";
}
// called when request sends a POST with data in format "variable=value"
@POST
public String received_POST(String msg) {
    return "POST: got a string "+msg+"\n";
}
// called when request sends a PUT with JSON data
@PUT
@Consumes(MediaType.APPLICATION_JSON)
public String received_JSON_PUT(String msg) {
    return "PUT: got a JSON file "+msg+"\n";
}
// called when request sends a POST with JSON data and
// must return more interesting response
@POST
@Consumes(MediaType.APPLICATION_JSON)
public Response received_JSON_POST(String msg) {
  if (!msg.isEmpty())
    {
      String mymessage = "POST: got a JSON file " + msg + "\n";
      return Response.status(200).entity(mymessage).build();
    }
  else {
    return Response.status(Response.Status.NOT_FOUND).entity("Null String Received\n
      \n").build();
    }
  }
}
```

Let's look first at the following resource method:

```
@GET
@Produces(MediaType.TEXT_PLAIN)
public String return_plaintext()
```

It is called by the cURL command shown in Listing 11.17, and it produces the output that is also shown in Listing 11.17. See that the header "Accept: text/plain" maps to the annotation:

@Produces(MediaType.TEXT_PLAIN)

**LISTING 11.17   cURL Command GET Accept Media Type text/plain (Maps to
                  Produces text/plain)**

curl --request GET -H "Accept: text/plain" http://localhost:8080/myrestful/restful/hello

Output produced is:

Hello World

Next let's look at the following resource method:

```
@GET
@Produces(MediaType.TEXT_HTML)
public String return_html()
```

It is called by the cURL command shown in Listing 11.18, and it produces the output that is also shown in Listing 11.18. See that the header Accept: text/html maps to the annotation:

@Produces(MediaType.TEXT_HTML)

LISTING 11.18 cURL Command GET Accept Media Type text/html (Maps to Produces text/html)

```
curl --request GET -H "Accept: text/html" http://localhost:8080/myrestful/restful/hello
```

Output produced is:

```
<html> <body><h1>Hello</h1><h2>to</h2><h2>all the World</h2></body></html>
```

Next let's look at the following resource method:

```
@GET
@Produces(MediaType.TEXT_XML)
public String return_XML()
```

It is called by the cURL command shown in Listing 11.19, and it produces the output that is also shown in Listing 11.19. See that the header Accept: text/xml maps to the annotation:

@Produces(MediaType.TEXT_XML)

LISTING 11.19 cURL Command GET Accept Media Type text/xml (Maps to Produces text/xml)

```
curl --request GET -H "Accept: text/xml" http://localhost:8080/myrestful/restful/hello
```

Output produced is:

```
<?xml version ="1.0"?><thedata> Hello World</thedata>
```

Next let's look at the following resource method:

```
@POST
public String received_POST(String msg)
```

It is called by the cURL command shown in Listing 11.20, and it produces the output that is also shown in Listing 11.20.

Note that when you use the "—data" parameter with a cURL command and the media type is not otherwise specified, cURL sends the data in the HTTP request the same way it would if you used an HTML form and pressed a Submit button, it includes the data as payload and includes (by default) the content-type "application/x-www-form-urlencoded." However, when there is no MediaType annotation on the resource method, it accepts this request.

LISTING 11.20   cURL Command POST Default myvariable=value Format Uses Content-Type application/x-www-form-urlencoded (Maps to POST with no MediaType Annotation)

curl -X POST --data "mystuff=32" http://localhost:8080/myrestful/restful/hello

    Output produced is:

POST: got a string mystuff=32

Next let's look at the following resource method:

```
@PUT
@Consumes(MediaType.APPLICATION_JSON)
public String received_JSON_PUT(String msg)
```

It is called by the cURL command shown in Listing 11.21, and it produces the output that is also shown in Listing 11.21, assuming the mydata file specified in the cURL command is the mydata file shown in Listing 11.22. See that the header Content-Type: application/json maps to the annotation:

```
@Consumes(MediaType.APPLICATION_JSON)
```

LISTING 11.21   cURL Command PUT Uses Content-Type application/json (Maps to Consumes application/json)

curl -X PUT -H "Content-Type: application/json" -d @mydata
http://localhost:8080/myrestful/restful/hello

Output produced is:

PUT: got a JSON file { "firstName":"Joe", "lastName":"Blow",
"education":{"bachelors":"BSCS","masters":"MSCS"}, "employer":"ACME Software" }

Finally let's look at the last resource method in this example:

```
@POST
@Consumes(MediaType.APPLICATION_JSON)
public Response received_JSON_POST(String msg)
```

It is called by the cURL command shown in Listing 11.23, and it produces the output that is also shown in Listing 11.23, assuming the mydata file specified in the cURL command is the mydata file shown in Listing 11.22. This cURL command is a little different, in that it employs the "-i" parameter. The "-i" parameter specifies that the HTTP header of the response will be included in the output.

LISTING 11.22   Example mydata JSON File

```
{
        "firstName":"Joe",
        "lastName":"Blow",

        "education":
            {
                "bachelors":"BSCS",
                "masters":"MSCS"
            },
        "employer":"ACME Software"
}
```

Note that the output response header showed "Content-Type: text/plain." This is because this particular resource method is returning a string. See where this resource method produced a response:

```
String mymessage = "POST: got a JSON file " + msg + "\n";
return Response.status(200).entity(mymessage).build();
```

It specifically built a response with a status 200. As you should recall from Section 4.2, the HTTP status code 200 means OK, the request was handled successfully. Then it created an "entity." You should remember from Section 11.4.1 that an entity encapsulates a message and also includes information about Internet Media Type, language, and encoding. Here the entity encapsulated was a string, and so the Internet Media Type used was text/plain.

LISTING 11.23   cURL Command POST Uses Content-Type application/json (Maps to Consumes application/json)

```
curl -i -X POST -H "Content-Type: application/json" -d @mydata
http://localhost:8080/myrestful/restful/hello
```

Output produced is:

```
HTTP/1.1 200 OK
Server: GlassFish Server Open Source Edition 4.1.1
X-Powered-By: Servlet/3.1 JSP/2.3 (GlassFish Server Open Source Edition 4.1.1 Java/Oracle
        Corporation/1.7)
Content-Type: text/plain
Date: Sat, 12 Mar 2016 18:57:30 GMT
Content-Length: 142
POST: got a JSON file { "firstName":"Joe", "lastName":"Blow",
"education":{"bachelors":"BSCS","masters":"MSCS"}, "employer":"ACME Software" }
```

Still looking at the last resource method, let's see what happens when we send an empty file to it. This situation is shown in Listing 11.24, and the output produced by this cURL command is also shown in Listing 11.24. The cURL command in Listing 11.24 is the same as the cURL command shown in Listing 11.23, except that the file is called "mydata1" instead of "mydata" and in this case the "mydata" file is an empty file.

Here the resource method executes the following code:

```
return Response.status(Response.Status.NOT_FOUND).entity("Null String Received\n\n").build();
```

As you can see from Listing 11.24, an HTTP 404 status code was included in the response header. This is the status code that means the resource was not found. The code "Response.Status.NOT_FOUND" in the code is what set this status code. Again, the entity that was created encapsulated a string, in this case "Null String Received."

LISTING 11.24   cURL Command POST Uses Content-Type application/json (Maps to Consumes application/json)

```
curl -i -X POST -H "Content-Type: application/json" -d @mydata1
http://localhost:8080/myrestful/restful/hello
```

Output produced is:

```
HTTP/1.1 404 Not Found
Server: GlassFish Server Open Source Edition  4.1.1
X-Powered-By: Servlet/3.1 JSP/2.3 (GlassFish Server Open Source Edition  4.1.1  Java/
Oracle
    Corporation/1.7)
Content-Type: text/plain
Date: Sat, 12 Mar 2016 19:15:38 GMT
Content-Length: 22
Null String Received
```

This simple example gives you most of what you need to get started with JAX-RS. However, there are a *few* other things, such as how to deploy the JAX-RS service, how to pass different kinds of parameters to a JAX-RS server, how to use a client to call a JAX-RS server (instead of just using cURL commands like we have so far), and how to implement an asynchronous JAX-RS server. We'll look at these issues in the following sections.

11.3.3   HOW TO DEPLOY A JAX-RS SERVER

As you recall from Section 11.4, JAX-RS is commonly deployed in a servlet container, either a container obeying the Servlet 2.X specification, or a container obeying the Servlet 3.X specification. However, there are other ways that JAX-RS can be deployed, such as within an EJB container (perhaps to provide a RESTful interface to the EJB) or within an OSGi implementation (one OSGi implementation is Apache Felix, which is the OSGi shell that is used by GlassFish).

Our examples in this textbook were done assuming deployment in a Servlet 3.X container, although we will briefly also examine deployment in a Servlet 2.X container. When deploying in a Servlet container, one must also choose between using web.xml and using an ApplicationConfig class with an ApplicationPath annotation to specify how deployment should occur. We will look at both methods.

The way to deploy a JAX-RS server (in our case, on GlassFish) is similar to how a servlet is deployed (we previously saw how to deploy a servlet in Section 11.2.3). This is reasonable because we're deploying a JAX-RS server in a servlet container. ☺

The procedure for how to do this is as follows. First, you compile the JAX-RS server into a class file, and put the class file in a directory "classes" that is a subdirectory of another directory called "WEB-INF." The WEB-INF directory is how the container knows how to find the JAX-RS information.

If you decide to use web.xml for deployment, then the WEB-INF directory also includes a file called web.xml that specifies how the container handles the JAX-RS server/how the JAX-RS server will be accessed. The web.xml file is known as a *deployment descriptor*. Note that we previously discussed how to deploy a servlet using a web.xml file in Section 11.2.6. We will look at the web.xml file later on below. (The alternative is to use an ApplicationConfig class, we will also look at that later on below.)

Let's look at how we would deploy the example from Listing 11.16. In this particular case, we are given the package name from the following statement:

    package example.restful;

and knowing the file name is the same as the class name, which is:

    Hello

then the WEB-INF directory will contain the following:

    /WEB-INF/classes/example/restful/Hello.class

The directory "example/restful" is set by the package name example.restful, whereas the file name Hello.class comes from the name of the Java class.

We could have had a different package name. For example, if we had used "anexample/somerestful" as the package name (while keeping the class name the same), then the WEB-INF would instead have contained the following:

    /WEB-INF/classes/anexample/somerestful/Hello.class

but we didn't do this, so we will be using the earlier directory structure inside the WEB-INF directory.

If you are using a web.xml deployment descriptor (again, we'll discuss what this looks like below), then it is located in the WEB-INF directory, as follows:

    /WEB-INF/web.xml

To deploy a JAX-RX server, we have to put it in a .war file (**W**eb application **AR**chive file). Jar files and war files are both compressed files created using the Java jar archive tool. Most commonly there's a WEB-INF directory inside a war file.

To create the war file, we would do:

    jar -cvf myrestful.war WEB-INF

Note that we've used the "myrestful" name again as the name of the war file. This is important because it will become part of the URL we use to access this servlet.

We saw previously in Section 4.11.2 how to deploy a .jar file on GlassFish. To deploy a .war file, you do the same procedure, just deploy the .war file instead of the .jar file.

11.3.3.1 Using a web.xml File to Deploy a JAX-RS Server

The web.xml file that I used for the example in Listing 11.16 is shown in Listing 11.25. The first few lines of this particular web.xml file show that it is using Servlet 3.1 as part of Java EE:

```
<web-app xmlns="http://xmlns.jcp.org/xml/ns/javaee"
     xmlns:xsi="http://www.w3.org/2001/XMLSchema-instance"
     xsi:schemaLocation="http://xmlns.jcp.org/xml/ns/javaee
http://xmlns.jcp.org/xml/ns/javaee/web-app_3_1.xsd"
     version="3.1">
```

The text between the "<!" and the "-->" is a comment.

The text between <servlet> and </servlet> say that this is a JAX-RS application that is being loaded into the servlet container:

```
<servlet-name>javax.ws.rs.core.Application</servlet-name>
<load-on-startup>1</load-on-startup>
</servlet>
```

The "load-on-startup" says that this servlet (including the JAX-RS core application) should be instantiated and initialized when the web application is started. If it's a negative value or there is no integer here, then the container makes the decision about when to load the servlet, but when the value is 0 or a positive number, it must be loaded when the web application starts. The integer value itself says the order in which this particular servlet is loaded, servlets with lower numbers are loaded before servlets with higher numbers. For servlets have the same number, then the container chooses which of those to load first.

The last few lines provide the URL pattern that go with that particular servlet name:

```
<servlet-mapping>
        <servlet-name>javax.ws.rs.core.Application</servlet-name>
        <url-pattern>/restful/*</url-pattern>
    </servlet-mapping>
```

LISTING 11.25   web.xml Deployment Descriptor for Servlet 3.X Container

```
<web-app xmlns="http://xmlns.jcp.org/xml/ns/javaee"
        xmlns:xsi="http://www.w3.org/2001/XMLSchema-instance"
        xsi:schemaLocation="http://xmlns.jcp.org/xml/ns/javaee
        http://xmlns.jcp.org/xml/ns/javaee/web-app_3_1.xsd"
        version="3.1">
        <!-- load application class
        all @Path and @Provider classes included in application will be
        automatically registered in the application -->
        <servlet>
                <servlet-name>javax.ws.rs.core.Application</servlet-name>
                <load-on-startup>1</load-on-startup>
        </servlet>
        <servlet-mapping>
                <servlet-name>javax.ws.rs.core.Application</servlet-name>
                <url-pattern>/restful/*</url-pattern>
        </servlet-mapping>
    </web-app>
```

As in the servlet examples in Section 11.3, the name of the war file is the base portion (context root) of the URL, and the URL pattern comes immediately following the war file name. It would be accessed using the following URL (which is what we did using the various cURL examples we discussed in Section 11.4.2):

http://localhost:8080/myrestful/restful/hello

So in the above url, "myrestful" was the name of the war file, "restful" was specified in the <servlet-mapping> portion of the web.xml file, and the "hello" comes from the @Path("/hello") annotation that was used to annotate the Hello resource class shown in Listing 11.16.

In Listing 11.26, we see part of a web.xml file that employs the notation needed to deploy our JAX-RS server in a Servlet 2.X container. This example assumes that you're using jersey. Here, you have to declare you're using the Jersey container servlet, then your own server is passed in as a parameter—in this case, "jersey.config.server.provider.packages" defines packages that contain application-specific resources and packages, which are scanned for JAX-RS root resources and providers. Otherwise, it is very similar to our previous web.xml example.

The reason I only included "part of" the web.xml file is that this notation will work in Servlet 3.X containers as well as Servlet 2.X containers. So in the examples provided with this textbook, I just kept using my Servlet 3.X selection statements at the beginning of the file.

LISTING 11.26 (Part of) web.xml Deployment Descriptor for Servlet 2.X Container

```
<servlet>
    <servlet-name>Jersey RESTful Service</servlet-name>
    <servlet-class>org.glassfish.jersey.servlet.ServletContainer</servlet-class>
    <init-param>
        <param-name>jersey.config.server.provider.packages</param-name>
        <param-value>example.restful</param-value>
    </init-param>
    <load-on-startup>1</load-on-startup>
</servlet>
<servlet-mapping>
    <servlet-name>Jersey RESTful Service</servlet-name>
    <url-pattern>/restful/*</url-pattern>
</servlet-mapping>
</web-app>
```

11.3.3.2 Using an ApplicationConfig Class to Deploy a JAX-RS Server

This example shows how to use an ApplicationConfig class to deploy a JAX-RS server, rather than using a web.xml file. See Listing 11.27.

JAX-RS provides a generic abstract class called "Application" that a web service can extend to declare root resource and provider classes. ApplicationConfig can be used (instead of web.xml) to define all the JAX-RS services associated with the current application, and to tell JAX-RS (and Jersey) where the services are located.

The @ApplicationPath annotation specifies part of the URL that is used to access the root resource class. In this case, it's taking over the URL specification that was originally done by the web.xml file. So when we have the URL that we were using before:

http://localhost:8080/myrestful/restful/hello

Here "myrestful" is the name of the war file, and the "hello" comes from the @Path("/hello") annotation that was used to annotate the Hello resource class shown in Listing 11.16, but the "restful" is specified in @AnnotationPath instead of in the <servlet-mapping> portion of the web.xml file.

Note that the AnnotationConfig class can be used for many configuration activities, for example, it could be used to instantiate various web service resource classes. However, in simple deployments such as this, an empty class can be specified.

LISTING 11.27 ApplicationConfig File

```
package example.restful;
import javax.ws.rs.ApplicationPath;
import javax.ws.rs.core.Application;
@ApplicationPath("/restful")
public class ApplicationConfig extends Application
{
    // empty class

}
```

11.3.4 PASSING PARAMETERS TO A JAX-RS SERVER

You should recall the "parameter notations" that we previously discussed in Section 11.4.1. In JAX-RS, parameter annotations are used to specify how the parameter(s) of a resource method are bound to the parameters within an HTTP request.

This is a form of "injection"—you may remember the discussion of dependency injection in Section 8.4. Basically, "injection" grabs the particular information you need from where it came from and stuffs it where you need it.

Some of the most basic parameter annotations are:

- @PathParam—specifies one or more parameters that are included in the URL, for example: my.example.com/mypath/myparametervalue
- @QueryParam—specifies one or more parameters that are in query string format, for example: myexample.com?myparametername=myparametervalue
- @FormParam—specifies one or more parameters that are in urlencoded format (application/x-www-form-urlencoded), such as would occur when sent from an HTML form

In this section, we will look at various examples using each of these parameter notations.

11.3.4.1 @PathParam Parameters

In this section, we will look at parameters that are passed as part of the URL. These are called "path parameters" because they're passed as part of the path that makes up the URL.

The first, simplest example is shown in Listing 11.28. Here we pass a single string parameter to a function that handles a POST request.

In this example, we see that the URL path itself has been extended, using a variable as the extension. This is done as follows:

```
@Path("{mystring}")
```

LISTING 11.28   Simple Path Parameter Example Using POST

```
package example.restful;
import javax.ws.rs.POST;

import javax.ws.rs.Path;
import javax.ws.rs.PathParam;
import javax.ws.rs.core.Response;

@Path("/hello")
public class Hello {
    @POST
    @Path("{mystring}")
    public String received_POST(@PathParam("mystring") String mystring) {
            System.out.println("Data received was "+mystring+"\n");
            return "data received was "+mystring+"\n";


    }
}
```

Here the "mystring" is the name of a variable. You know that because it's enclosed in curly brackets. If it weren't enclosed in curly brackets then "mystring" would just be a string that is a portion of the URL.

To find what the data type of the mystring variable is, you look at the parameter list of the resource method:

```
@PathParam("mystring") String mystring
```

The basic way to call the code in Listing 11.28 is the cURL command shown in Listing 11.29, along with its output.

In this, the basic path is:

```
http://localhost:8080/myrestful/restful/hello
```

and the "hithere" is the string value being sent into mystuff.

LISTING 11.29   cURL Command for Simple Path Parameter Example

```
curl --request POST http://localhost:8080/myrestful/restful/hello/hithere
    Output produced is:

    data received was hithere
```

For this particular example, a cURL command that sends the data as –data "hithere" would also work, but calling it that way is not the way a path parameter is supposed to work.

Next let's look at an example, shown in Listing 11.30, where we send multiple path parameters to a resource method. As before, an @Path statement defines the variables:

```
@Path("{mystring}/{myint}")
```

In this case, there are two variables, named "mystring" and "myint."
The data types associated with these two variables are shown in the parameter list:

```
@PathParam("mystring") String mystring,
@PathParam("myint") int myint)
```

This shows that the variable "mystring" is of type string, and the variable "myint" is of type integer.

LISTING 11.30   Path Parameter Example with Multiple Parameters Using POST

```
import javax.ws.rs.POST;
import javax.ws.rs.Path;
import javax.ws.rs.PathParam;

@Path("/hello")
public class Hello {
    @Path("{mystring}/{myint}")
    @POST

    public String received_POST( @PathParam("mystring") String mystring,
                                 @PathParam("myint") int myint ) {
    System.out.println("Data string received was "+mystring+"\n");
    System.out.println("Data int received was "+myint+"\n");
    return "data received was: "+mystring+" and "+myint+"\n";


    }
}
```

The basic way to call the code in Listing 11.30 is the cURL command which is shown in Listing 11.31, along with its output.

LISTING 11.31   cURL Command for Path Parameter Example with Multiple Parameters

```
curl --request POST http://localhost:8080/myrestful/restful/hello/hithere/105
```

Output produced is:

```
data received was: hithere and 105
```

11.3.4.2 @QueryParam Parameters

In this section, we look at passing one or more parameters that are in a query string format to a JAX-RS server.

We previously discussed query string parameters in Section 11.4.4.2. A typical query string parameter would be appended to a URL, as in the following example (this example shows two query string parameters):

http://example.com/mystuff?paramA=2000&paramB=3000

One tends to think of query string parameters as being sent as part of an HTTP GET request, but they can also be sent with a POST or PUT. The example JAX-RS server we will see in Listing 11.32 expects to receive a single string query parameter along with a POST request.

In this example, the @QueryParam notation in the parameter list is how the QueryParam is specified:

@QueryParam("mystring") String mystring

Note that, unlike the path parameter examples we saw in the previous section, the @Path("/postpath") notation has really nothing to do with the query parameters, it's simply part of the overall URL path.

LISTING 11.32   Simple Query Parameter Example Using POST

```
package example.restful;
import javax.ws.rs.POST;
import javax.ws.rs.Path;
import javax.ws.rs.QueryParam;

@Path("/hello")
public class Hello {
    @POST
    @Path("/postpath")
    public String received_POST(@QueryParam("mystring") String mystring) {
        System.out.println("Data received was "+mystring+"\n");
        return "data received was "+mystring+"\n";
    }
}
```

The basic way to call the code in Listing 11.32 is the cURL command which is shown in Listing 11.33, along with its output.

LISTING 11.33   cURL Command for Simple Query Parameter Example

```
curl --request POST http://localhost:8080/myrestful/restful/hello/postpath?mystring=hithere
```

Output produced is:

data received was hithere

Our next example, which we see in Listing 11.34, will pass multiple query parameters to a JAX-RS server using an HTTP POST request.

In this example, the two query parameters are passed as follows, as shown in the parameter list of the resource method:

```
@QueryParam("mystring") String mystring,
@QueryParam("myint") String myint)
```

Here we are passing one query parameter named "mystring" that has a string value, and another query parameter named "myint" that has an integer value.

LISTING 11.34   Query Parameter Example with Multiple Parameters Using POST

```
package example.restful;
import javax.ws.rs.POST;
import javax.ws.rs.Path;
import javax.ws.rs.QueryParam;


@Path("/hello")
public class Hello {
    @POST
    @Path("/postpath")

    public String received_POST(@QueryParam("mystring") String mystring,
                                @QueryParam("myint") String myint) {
    System.out.println("Data string received was "+mystring+"\n");
    System.out.println("Data int received was "+myint+"\n");
    return "data received was "+mystring+" and "+myint+"\n";
    }
}
```

The basic way to call the code in Listing 11.34 is the following cURL command, including multiple query parameters:

```
curl --request POST http://localhost:8080/myrestful/restful/hello/postpath?mystring=hithere&myint=107
```

The output produced by this cURL command is:

```
data received was hithere and 107
```

11.3.4.3   @FormParam Parameters

In this section, we are going to look at how to pass parameters to a JAX-RS server that are in urlencoded format (application/x-www-form-urlencoded), such as would occur when sent from an HTML form.

The example JAX-RS server we will see in Listing 11.35 expects to receive a single string form parameter along with a POST request.

The way the form parameter is specified is in the parameter list of the resource method as follows:

LISTING 11.35   Simple Form Parameter Example Using POST

```
@FormParam("mystring") String mystring
package example.restful;
import javax.ws.rs.POST;
import javax.ws.rs.Path;
import javax.ws.rs.FormParam;

@Path("/hello")
public class Hello {

    @POST
    @Consumes("application/x-www-form-urlencoded")
    public String received_POST(@FormParam("mystring") String mystring) {
    System.out.println("Data received was "+mystring+"\n");
    return "data received was "+mystring+"\n";
    }
}
```

The basic way to call the code in Listing 11.35 is the HTML form which is shown in Listing 11.36.

LISTING 11.36   HTML form for Simple Form Parameter Example

```
<html>
    <body>
        <h1 id="myHeader"> This is a JAX-RS example</h1>
        <form action = "http://localhost:8080/myrestful/restful/hello" method="POST">
            <p> Enter data to send: <input type="text" name="mystring" /> </p>
        </form>
    </body>
</html>
```

Figure 11.11 shows the user interface produced by the HTML form. When the string "Letha" is entered into this form, and the Submit button is clicked, the output shown in Listing 11.37 is produced.

LISTING 11.37   Output Produced by Simple Form Parameter Example

data received was Letha

11.3.4.4   Expanded Parameter Example Shows Need for @Consumes/@Produces

There are two reasons for the example shown in Listing 11.38. One is to allow you the student to see a few more examples of parameter passing. The specific purpose of the examples provided for each resource method in Listing 11.38 are summarized in Table 11.1.

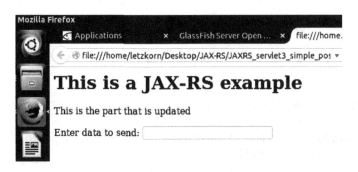

FIGURE 11.11   User interface produced by HTML form shown in Listing 11.36.

LISTING 11.38   Need for @Consumes/@Produces When Using Parameters

```java
import javax.ws.rs.GET;
import javax.ws.rs.POST;
import javax.ws.rs.PUT;
import javax.ws.rs.Path;
import javax.ws.rs.PathParam;
import javax.ws.rs.QueryParam;
import javax.ws.rs.core.Response;
import javax.ws.rs.Produces;
import javax.ws.rs.Consumes;
import javax.ws.rs.core.MediaType;


@Path("/hello")
public class Hello {
 // called when GET is sent to url with no parameters, Response return type
 @GET
    public Response return_plaintext_no_params() {

            return Response.status(200).entity("GET no params \n\n").build();
    }
    // called when GET is sent to url with query parameter (?id=45 for example)
    @GET
    @Produces(MediaType.TEXT_HTML)
    public Response return_html_query_param(@QueryParam("id") int id) {

            return Response.status(200).entity("GET query parameter "+id+"\n\n").build();
    }
    /* called when GET is sent to URL with multiple query parameters (?id=45&thestuff=hello
    for example) */
    @GET
    @Produces(MediaType.TEXT_XML)
    public Response return_html_query_param(@QueryParam("id") int id,
                                @QueryParam("thestuff") String thestuff) {

        return Response.status(200).entity("GET multiple query parameters: id is "+ id + " and
            thestuff
```

```
                        is " +thestuff+"\n\n").build();
    }
    // called when GET is sent to url with parameter
    @GET
    @Path("{id}")
    public Response return_plaintext_single_param(@PathParam("id") String id) {

            return Response.status(200).entity("GET short path: value passed is
                "+id+"\n\n").build();
    }
    // called when GET is sent to url with parameter, path more fully specified
    @GET
    @Path("/more/{id}")
    @Produces(MediaType.TEXT_PLAIN)
    public Response return_plaintext_multiple_params(@PathParam("id") String id) {
            return Response.status(200).entity("GET longer path: value passed is
                "+id+"\n\n").build();
    }
    // called when POST is sent to url with parameter
    @POST
    @Path("{id}")
     public Response received_POST_single_param(@PathParam("id")  String id) {
            return Response.status(200).entity("POST: value passed is "+id+"\n\n").build();
    }
    // called when GET is sent to url with multiple parameters
    @GET
    @Path("{id}/{thestuff}")
    public Response return_plaintext_single_param(@PathParam("id")         int id,
                                        @PathParam("thestuff")  String thestuff) {

        return Response.status(200).entity("GET multiple path parameters: id is "+ id + " and
            thestuff is " +thestuff+"\n\n").build();
    }

}
```

The other purpose for the example in Listing 11.38 is to illustrate that the Internet Media Types (MIME types) that are associated with each resource method via either a @Consumes or @Produces annotation are primarily what JAX-RS uses to route a particular HTTP request to a particular resource method.

In fact, without the Internet Media Types being specified, GlassFish won't load the war file that is created from this example. Although this file would compile without the @Produces and @Consumes annotations, upon trying to load the file GlassFish will produce an error saying that it couldn't determine which method to send a GET request to. Exercise for the student ☺: selectively delete the @Produces or @Consumes statements associated with the GET methods and see at what point this fails to load into GlassFish. This indicates that the query parameters being different themselves are not enough to distinguish between one resource method and another.

TABLE 11.1

Summary of Examples Shown in Each Resource Method in Listing 11.38

HTTP Method	Parameter(s) Passed	Internet Media Type
GET	No parameter	no @Produces or @Consumes (defaults to accepting application/x-www-form- urlencoded)
GET	One query parameter	text/html
GET	Multiple query parameters	text/xml
GET	One path parameter	no @Produces or @Consumes, (defaults to accepting application/x-www-form-urlencoded)
GET	One path parameter, (longer path specified)	text/plain
POST	One path parameter	no @Produces or @Consumes, (defaults to accepting application/x-www-form-urlencoded)
GET	Multiple path parameters	no @Produces or @Consumes, (defaults to accepting application/x-www-form-urlencoded)

11.3.5 JAX-RS Client API

The JAX-RS Client API can be used to access any RESTful resources. It is not limited only to accessing JAX-RS RESTful resources.

In this section, we're going to look at two different ways to implement a JAX-RS Client. First, we're going to see a "generic" invocation. A generic invocation is one where the creator of a request and the (eventual) invoker (submitter) of the request could be separate. In this case, the invoker of the request doesn't have to know most of the details about what is inside the request (the invoker only has to know whether the request is synchronous or asynchronous). I've set up this particular JAX-RS Client to run inside the servlet container and obey JAX-RS style annotations, thus it can be called by your browser. The purpose of this is to show you that you can invoke one RESTful interface from inside another RESTful interface.

In our second example, we're going to use specific separate routines for Get, Put, and Post to build and invoke the request at the same time. This is easier for someone reading the code to understand and more convenient for the programmer, but it does not separate the invoker of the request from the original creator of the request. I've made this example a JAX-RS client that runs as a separate Java application. (We'll also do a very brief introduction to the JSON API in this section.)

The JAX-RS server, we will be accessing in this example, is the server originally shown in Listing 11.16.

11.3.5.1 JAX-RS Client Using Generic Invocation—Runs Inside Servlet Container

In this example, we do a generic invocation where we build the request and then separately invoke it.

We first create a client and a target (endpoint) URL that will be accessed:

```
Client client=ClientBuilder.newClient();
WebTarget theURL = client.target("http://localhost:8080/myrestclient/restclient/hello");
```

We use the JAX-RS ClientBuilder interface and the JAX-RS WebTarget interface to do this.

Next, we build the invocation object, and set it with all information that will be needed to invoke the desired request:

```
final String mediaType=MediaType.TEXT_PLAIN;
Invocation theInvoke = theURL.request(mediaType).buildGet();
```

We're using the InvocationBuilder interface to do this. Note that we have set the request to be a GET request using buildGet. We could instead have used:

- BuildPost()
- BuildPut()
- BuildDelete()

Or we could have used an arbitrary request method name.

Note that we have placed a string containing the Internet Media Type in the request. This sets it to accept text/plain. We could similarly have set it to accept any other Internet Media Type.

We could have added an arbitrary header as follows:

```
Invocation theInvoke = theURL.request(mediaType).header("my","stuff").buildGet();
```

We could have put cookies in the request through a call to:

```
.cookie("my","stuff")
```

The request defaults to a synchronous request, but we could have set it to asynchronous through a call to:

```
.async()
```

**LISTING 11.39   JAX-RS Client Using Generic Invocation—Runs Inside
                   Servlet Container**

```
package example.restclient;
import javax.ws.rs.GET;
import javax.ws.rs.Path;
import javax.ws.rs.core.Response;
import javax.ws.rs.Produces;
import javax.ws.rs.Consumes;
import javax.ws.rs.client.Entity;
import javax.ws.rs.core.MediaType;

import javax.ws.rs.client.Client;
import javax.ws.rs.client.ClientBuilder;
import javax.ws.rs.client.Invocation;
import javax.ws.rs.client.WebTarget;
import javax.ws.rs.core.UriBuilder;


@Path("/theclient")
public class myClient {
        // called when request has accept text/plain header
```

```
@GET
@Produces(MediaType.TEXT_PLAIN)
public String return_plaintext() {
    //  a "generic invocation"

    // Create a Client and a target URL
    Client client=ClientBuilder.newClient();
    WebTarget theURL = client.target("http://localhost:8080/myrestclient/restclient/hello");

    // Build the request
    final String mediaType=MediaType.TEXT_PLAIN;
    Invocation theInvoke = theURL.request(mediaType).buildGet();

    // Do actual invocation
    // this invocation could have been done much later
    Response theresponse = theInvoke.invoke();

    String thestuff = theresponse.readEntity(String.class);
    System.out.println(thestuff);

    return thestuff;
}
}
```

Note that the object in which we stored the invocation that we built is called "theInvoke." We could save that object off in an array or hash table somewhere and save it for later.

Because we didn't need any delay right now ☺ what we did instead is invoke it immediately, by calling"invoke" (on the object where we had stored the invocation) as follows:

```
Response theresponse = theInvoke.invoke();
```

So this is pretty powerful, but perhaps just a bit difficult to understand, primarily in cases where the actual invocation is separate from where you built the invocation object, it might be a little hard to follow.

To run this particular client, you use the browser URL in Listing 11.40, the output is also shown in Listing 11.40.

LISTING 11.40   Call to JAX-RS Client Inside Servlet Container Plus Output

Open in browser:

http://localhost:8080/myrestclient/restclient/theclient

Output Produced is:
Hello World

The output shown in Listing 11.40 was produced because the Client from Listing 11.39 called the following resource method from Listing 11.16:

```
@GET
@Produces(MediaType.TEXT_PLAIN)
public String return_plaintext()
```

This is because the client used a buildGet and an Internet Media Type of text/plain. Exercise for the student ☺: try varying buildGet with buildPost and buildPut and different internet media types, see what you get for output.

11.3.5.2 JAX-RS Client Using Specific Invocations—Runs as Separate Java Application

In this example, shown in Listing 11.41, we use specific separate routines for Get, Post, and Put to build and invoke the request at the same time. This is easier for someone reading the code to understand and more convenient for the programmer, but it does not separate the invoker of the request from the original creator of the request. I've made this example a JAX-RS client that runs as a separate Java application, it will show you that this kind of client can run at the command line just like a cURL command does, and can do the same kind of things (relative to HTTP anyway) that a cURL command does.

We'll also do a very brief introduction to the JSON API in this section that will be continued in the following section.

In this example, we begin by building a Client and a target (endpoint) the same way we did in the previous Client API example:

```
Client client=ClientBuilder.newClient();
WebTarget theURL = client.target("http://localhost:8080/myrestful/restful/hello");
```

After that, this particular Client example allows you to choose between Get, Put, and Post at runtime. For the Get, it allows you to choose between text/plain, text/html, and text/xml at runtime.

Let's look at one of the Get paths through this client code, the one that uses text/plain:

```
mediaType=MediaType.TEXT_PLAIN;
Response theGetResponse=theURL.request(mediaType).get();
```

So this is building a request using .get() in the same code statement where the request is sent. It does not separate building the request from sending the request, the way it did in the previous generic Client API example.

LISTING 11.41   JAX-RS Client Using Specific Invocations—Runs as Separate Java Application

```
import java.io.*;

import javax.ws.rs.core.Response;
import javax.ws.rs.core.MediaType;

import javax.json.Json;
import javax.json.JsonObject;

import javax.ws.rs.client.Client;
import javax.ws.rs.client.ClientBuilder;
```

```java
import javax.ws.rs.client.Invocation;
import javax.ws.rs.client.Entity;
    // This entity class encapsulates message entities
import javax.ws.rs.client.WebTarget;
import javax.ws.rs.core.Response;
import javax.ws.rs.core.UriBuilder;
import javax.ws.rs.core.MediaType;

public class myClient {

    public static void main(String [] args) throws Exception {
      Client client=ClientBuilder.newClient();
      WebTarget theURL = client.target("http://localhost:8080/myrestful/restful/hello");
      InputStreamReader r = new InputStreamReader(System.in);
      BufferedReader br = new BufferedReader(r);
      String mediaType="";
      String thestuff= "";
      System.out.println("Enter (G)ET,(P)UT,or P(O)ST");
      String message=br.readLine();
      if (message.equals("G") )
        {
            System.out.println("Enter (P)lainText, (H)tml, (X)ML");
            message=br.readLine();
            if (message.equals("X") ) // XML
                    mediaType=MediaType.TEXT_XML;
            else if (message.equals("H")  )  // HTML
                    mediaType=MediaType.TEXT_HTML;
            else // default to plain text
            {
                    mediaType=MediaType.TEXT_PLAIN;
            }
            Response theGetResponse=theURL.request(mediaType).get();
            thestuff = theGetResponse.readEntity(String.class);
        }
      else if ( message.equals("P") )
      {   // PUT
                // The following shows two different ways to send JSON data.
                // Send it as a string, or create a JsonObject (using the
                // JSON API) and send it that way. Comment out whichever
                // you don't need
                // String payload = "{ \"firstName\":\"Joe\", \"lastName\":\"Blow\", \"education\":
                {\"bachelors\":\"BSCS\",\"masters\":\"MSCS\"}, \"employer\":\"ACME Software\"
      }";
            JsonObject payload = Json.createObjectBuilder().add("hi","there").build();
            mediaType=MediaType.APPLICATION_JSON;
            // Create a message entity containing the payload data and
            // the media type
```

```
            Entity myentity = Entity.entity(payload,mediaType);
            Response thePutResponse=theURL.request().put(myentity);
            thestuff = thePutResponse.readEntity(String.class);
        }
        else if ( message.equals("O") )
        {   // POST
                File f = new File("./mydata");
                mediaType=MediaType.APPLICATION_JSON;

                // Create a message entity containing the file and
                // the media type
                Entity myentity = Entity.entity(f,mediaType);

                Response thePostResponse=theURL.request().post(myentity);
                thestuff = thePostResponse.readEntity(String.class);
        }
        else
        System.out.println("error in input\n");
        System.out.println(thestuff);
    }
}
```

Now let's look at the code in this example that handles a POST. This code POSTs a file, so first it reads the file:

```
File f = new File("./mydata");
```

Then it creates an Entity that encapsulates the file together with its Internet Media Type (in this case it's a JSON file with an application/json media type):

```
mediaType=MediaType.APPLICATION_JSON;

// Create a message entity containing the file and
// the media type
Entity myentity = Entity.entity(f,mediaType);
```

After this, it creates and sends a POST request in the same statement, using the Entity that was already created:

```
Response thePostResponse=theURL.request().post(myentity);
```

Finally, let's look at how a PUT command is handled. In this case, JSON data is going to be sent. This can be done with a string or else the JSON API can be used to create the JSON data. (In the code shown, the JSON API is used, because the JSON string that is the alternative is commented out.)
Let's look first at the string method:

```
String payload = "{ \"firstName\":\"Joe\", \"lastName\":\"Blow\", \"education\":{\"bachelors\":\"BSCS
\",\"masters\":\"MSCS\"}, \"employer\":\"ACME Software\" }";
mediaType=MediaType.APPLICATION_JSON;
Entity myentity = Entity.entity(payload,mediaType);
```

Response thePutResponse=theURL.request().put(myentity);

So what happened in this code is a string containing the JSON data was created as a payload (that is, the data) in the HTTP request packet. Then an Entity is created that encapsulates this string with the Internet Media Type application/json. Finally a PUT request is built and sent in the same statement using the put() routine.

Now let's look (briefly) at the JSON API. Here the JSON data is created in a JsonObject as follows:

JsonObject payload = Json.createObjectBuilder().add("hi","there").build();

(it's not the same data as before, you notice, I just wanted to differentiate the two examples a little.) After that the request is built and sent immediately exactly as before:

```
 mediaType=MediaType.APPLICATION_JSON;
// Create a message entity containing the payload data and
// the media type
Entity myentity = Entity.entity(payload,mediaType);
Response thePutResponse=theURL.request().put(myentity);
```

The code I used to create the Java Application Client is shown in Listing 11.42. It requires linking in the client libraries. I recommend putting this in a script so you can rerun it easily (this is what I did in the code examples provided for the instructor with this textbook).

LISTING 11.42   How to Call Java Application Client

```
export GLASSFISH_HOME=/home/letzkorn/glassfish4
export JAR_FILE_TWO=$GLASSFISH_HOME/glassfish/lib/gf-client.jar
export JAR_FILE_THREE=$GLASSFISH_HOME/glassfish/modules/*
java -classpath ".:$JAR_FILE_TWO:$JAR_FILE_THREE" myClient
```

The output of a call to the Client where PUT is selected, and the JSON API is used is shown in Listing 11.43.

LISTING 11.43   Output of Call to Client Using PUT and JSON API Shown

```
Enter (G)ET, (P)UT,or P(O)ST
P
PUT: Got a JSON file {"hi", "there"}
```

11.3.6   JSON API

We briefly introduced the JSON API in Section 11.3.5.2. You may find the JSON API useful, because RESTful web services have largely moved to using JSON instead of XML, so we'll continue to look at it just a little longer. (If you do this, put it all on one line. I split it up for readability.)

In Listing 11.44, we see a short example of how to use the JSON API, this example shows you how to create a nested object.

LISTING 11.44   Using JSON API to Build Nested JSON Object

```
JsonObject myobject =
    Json.createObjectBuilder()
        .add("hi","y'all")
            .add("location",
                Json.createObjectBuilder()
                    .add("city","Huntsville")
                    .add("state","Alabama"))
        . build();
```

You can read a JsonObject as follows:

```
JsonReader myjsonReader = Json.createReader(some input file stream);
JsonObject myobject = myjsonReader.readObject();
myjsonReader.close();
```

Now let's do a small example of extracting the data from a JSON object. Suppose you had a class that contained a greeting from a rock star to his audience, and you wanted to read the JSON information we created just above into that Greeting. The code to do this is shown in Listing 11.45.

Note first that the code previously shown in Listing 11.44 is used to build a JSON object.

LISTING 11.45   Code Using JSON API for Rock Star Greeting Example

```
package myJSONAPIexample;

public class Location {
    public String city;
    public String state;
}
package myJSONAPIexample;
public class Greeting {
    public String whogreeted;
    public Location thelocation;
}
package myJSONAPIexample;
import java.io.*;

import javax.json.Json;
import javax.json.JsonObject;
public class myClient {

    public static void main(String [] args) throws Exception {
        JsonObject myobject =
            Json.createObjectBuilder().add("hi","y'all").add("location",Json.createObject
            Builder().add("city","Huntsville").add("state","Alabama")). build();

        Greeting currentGreeting = new Greeting();
        currentGreeting.whogreeted=myobject.getString("hi");
```

```
            JsonObject innerLocation=myobject.getJsonObject("location");

            Location mylocation = new Location();
            mylocation.city=innerLocation.getString("city");
            mylocation.state=innerLocation.getString("state");

            currentGreeting.thelocation=mylocation;
            System.out.println("Greeting is : hi "+ currentGreeting.whogreeted+" "+curren-
            tGreeting.thelocation.
            city+" "+currentGreeting.thelocation.state+"\n");
        }
    }
```

Next, we see that a new Greeting object is created, and that the JSON API function getString is used to extract the first greeting value (it will extract the "y'all," which is the who is being greeted value associated with the "hi").

```
Greeting currentGreeting = new Greeting();
currentGreeting.whogreeted=myobject.getString("hi");
```

Next the location data will be extracted into a separate JsonObject, using the JSON API call getJsonObject().

```
JsonObject innerLocation=myobject.getJsonObject("location");
```

The Location object is a sub-object of the Greeting object. So that object has to be created and its data extracted from the JsonObject named innerLocation, using two getString() calls:

```
Location mylocation = new Location();
mylocation.city=innerLocation.getString("city");
mylocation.state=innerLocation.getString("state");
```

Finally, we set the location sub-object in the Greeting object to our new Location object:

```
currentGreeting.thelocation=mylocation;
```

11.3.7 ASYNCHRONOUS JAX-RS EXAMPLE

Now we've finished with that ☺ we're going to look at how to add asynchronous operations to JAX-RS.

One of the major things to remember when you're doing asynchronous work with JAX_RS:

The web.xml is different from in the earlier servlet3 web.xml files. To do asynchronous operation, you have to add:

```
<async-supported>true</async-supported>
```

If you forget to put this line in the file, you'll get an error message something like:

Server encountered an internal error that prevented it from fulfilling this request.</p><p><b>exception</b>
<pre>javax.servlet.ServletException: javax.ws.rs.ProcessingException: Attempt to suspend a connection of an
asynchronous request failed in the underlying container
Ask me how I know this. ☺

11.3.7.1   Very Simple Asynchronous JAX-RS Example

Let's look at our first very simple asynchronous example; it's shown in Listing 11.46.

LISTING 11.46   Very Simple Asynchronous Example

```
package example.restful;
import javax.ws.rs.GET;
import javax.ws.rs.Path;

import javax.ws.rs.core.Response;
import javax.ws.rs.container.AsyncResponse;
import javax.ws.rs.container.Suspended;
import java.util.concurrent.BlockingQueue;
import java.util.concurrent.ArrayBlockingQueue;

@Path("/hello")
public class Hello {

    @GET
    public void asyncGet(@Suspended final AsyncResponse asyncResponse) {
        new Thread (
                new Runnable()
                {
                    @Override
                    public void run() {
                        String result = "Received the GET, doing asynchronous response";
                        asyncResponse.resume(result);
                    }
                }
        ).start();
    }
}
```

Then you can send a cURL command to call it as follows:

```
curl -X GET http://localhost:8080/myrestful/restful/hello
```

(or you can access that URL in your browser).

What is happening in this example is, the client continues working on the original thread, while the
JAX-RS asynchronous server starts off in a new thread, and does its work there. When it finally gets
finished (in this particular example it gets finished immediately), it sends a resume() to the client who
is still running (and doing its own work) on the original thread (in this particular example the client
didn't happen to have any other work to do).

Here, the code:

```
@Suspended final AsyncResponse asyncResponse
```

specifies the connection to the client on the original thread; this connection has been suspended. The variable "asyncResponse" contains the information about how to restart this suspended connection. Note that it's only the *connection* to the client that was suspended, the client itself is *not* suspended, it's executing and doing whatever it needs to do while waiting for the server to finish.

Note that the return type of the asyncGet() is void, as the code does not really return a value directly, rather the result is returned when the resume() is (eventually) executed.

So when the server eventually gets finished with its processing, it would send the following to restart that suspended connection and return the result to the client:

```
asyncResponse.resume(result);
```

11.3.7.2   Asynchronous JAX-RS Example—Multiple Clients

In the code shown in Listing 11.47, we see an attempt to simulate independent processing by the Server; this simulation is done by a Sleep for 5 seconds. Other than that, this is the same asynchronous server example that we saw before in Listing 11.46.

LISTING 11.47   Asynchronous JAX-RS Server, Illustrates Extended Processing Before Resume Client

```
package example.restful;
import javax.ws.rs.GET;
import javax.ws.rs.Path;
import javax.ws.rs.core.Response;
import javax.ws.rs.container.AsyncResponse;
import javax.ws.rs.container.Suspended;
import java.util.concurrent.BlockingQueue;
import java.util.concurrent.ArrayBlockingQueue;

@Path("/hello")
public class Hello {

    @GET
    public void asyncGet(@Suspended final AsyncResponse asyncResponse) {
    new Thread (new Runnable() {
    @Override
    public void run() {

            try {
                    Thread.sleep(5000);
                    // Sleep 5 seconds to pretend to be some long drawn out processing
            }
            catch (InterruptedException e) {
                    e.printStackTrace();
            }
```

```
                              String result = "Received the GET, doing asynchronous response";
                              asyncResponse.resume(result);
                  }
          } ).start();
      }
}
```

Now we're going to look at three different clients to access this asynchronous server; all three are implemented as Java Applications, and use the Client API that we saw earlier in Section 11.4.5.

Of course, the very simplest client we could use would be a web browser that accesses the URL, or a cURL command that sends a simple Get request.

However, our simplest client that uses the Client API is shown in Listing 11.48. This client is not itself asynchronous, it uses a blocking Get, so it's not able to do any work while waiting for the server to finish, it just has to wait until it is done.

LISTING 11.48   Simplest Client that Uses Client API

```java
import java.io.*;

import javax.ws.rs.core.Response;
import javax.ws.rs.core.MediaType;

import javax.json.Json;
import javax.json.JsonObject;

import javax.ws.rs.client.Client;
import javax.ws.rs.client.ClientBuilder;
import javax.ws.rs.client.Invocation;
import javax.ws.rs.client.Entity;
      // This entity class encapsulates message entities
import javax.ws.rs.client.WebTarget;
import javax.ws.rs.core.Response;
import javax.ws.rs.core.UriBuilder;
import javax.ws.rs.core.MediaType;
public class simplestClient {

    public static void main(String [] args) throws Exception {

        Client client=ClientBuilder.newClient();
        WebTarget theURL = client.target("http://localhost:8080/myrestful/restful/hello");
            InputStreamReader r = new InputStreamReader(System.in);
        BufferedReader br = new BufferedReader(r);

        String mediaType=MediaType.TEXT_PLAIN;
        Response theGetResponse=theURL.request(mediaType).get();
      // This is doing a blocking get, it waits for the server
      // to finish
```

```
                    String thestuff = theGetResponse.readEntity(String.class);
                    System.out.println(thestuff);
        }

}
```

When you run this simplest client, the only difference between the output in the previous section and the output now is that the server pauses for 5 seconds during processing to pretend that it took a while to create the result. But the result itself is the same:

Received the Get, doing asynchronous response.

Now let's look at another client, shown in Listing 11.49. This client uses the Java Future interface. We saw the Future interface before in Section 8.3.5.2. The Future interface is used for asynchronous operations. It provides methods to check if the asynchronous work on the server has been completed yet, and to retrieve the result of the computation when the server has completed.

This client calls the Future interface as follows:

```
Future<Response> responseFuture = asyncInvoker.get();
```

Then while the JAX-RS server is doing its work, the Client is doing useful work, while repeatedly polling to see if the server has finished yet:

```
while (!responseFuture.isDone())
{
        System.out.println("doing useful work while waiting");
}
```

Note that the isDone() interface is part of the Future interface.
When the JAX-RS server is finally done, the future interface grabs the result:

```
Response response = responseFuture.get();
```

The results from calling this client are shown in Listing 11.50.

LISTING 11.49   Asynchronous Client Uses Future Interface–Polling

```
import java.io.*;

import javax.ws.rs.core.Response;
import javax.ws.rs.core.MediaType;

import javax.ws.rs.client.Client;
import javax.ws.rs.client.ClientBuilder;

import javax.ws.rs.client.Invocation;
import javax.ws.rs.client.Invocation.Builder;
import javax.ws.rs.client.Entity;
        // This entity class encapsulates message entities
```

```
import javax.ws.rs.client.AsyncInvoker;
import java.util.concurrent.Future;
public class futureClient {

    public static void main(String [] args) throws Exception {

        Client client=ClientBuilder.newClient();
        AsyncInvoker asyncInvoker =
                    client.target("http://localhost:8080/myrestful/restful/hello").request
                    ().async();

            System.out.println("Just about to do asynchronous call");
        String mediaType=MediaType.TEXT_PLAIN;

        Future<Response> responseFuture = asyncInvoker.get();

        while (!responseFuture.isDone())
        {
            System.out.println("doing useful work while waiting");
        }

        Response response = responseFuture.get();

        final String thestuff = response.readEntity(String.class);
        System.out.println("Finally done, message received from remote is: ");
        System.out.println(thestuff);

        client.close();
        System.exit(1);
    }
}
```

**LISTING 11.50   Results from Calling Asynchronous Client Uses Future
                   Interface–Polling**

Just about to do asynchronous call
doing useful work while waiting
doing useful work while waiting
doing useful work while waiting
…continues printing this for a long time, possibly 80000+ times …
doing useful work while waiting
doing useful work while waiting
doing useful work while waiting
Finally done, message received from remote is:
Received the Get, doing asynchronous response

Lastly, let's look at a Client that employs a callback function, shown in Listing 11.51. That is, instead of having to repeatedly poll the JAX-RS server, the Client can simply wait until the server finishes, when the server finishes it will call the callback function. (This is similar to how AJAX behaves; we saw AJAX in Section 11.2)

We're still using the Future interface, but now we're passing a callback function to it that will be called when the server completes.

LISTING 11.51   Asynchronous Client Uses Callback Function

```java
import java.io.*;

import javax.ws.rs.core.Response;
import javax.ws.rs.core.MediaType;

import javax.json.Json;
import javax.json.JsonObject;
import javax.ws.rs.client.Client;
import javax.ws.rs.client.ClientBuilder;
import javax.ws.rs.client.Invocation;
import javax.ws.rs.client.Invocation.Builder;
import javax.ws.rs.client.Entity;
    // This entity class encapsulates message entities
import javax.ws.rs.client.WebTarget;
import javax.ws.rs.core.Response;
import javax.ws.rs.core.UriBuilder;
import javax.ws.rs.client.AsyncInvoker;
import javax.ws.rs.client.InvocationCallback;

import java.util.concurrent.Future;

public class callbackClient {

    public static void main(String [] args) throws Exception {
        Client client=ClientBuilder.newClient();

        AsyncInvoker asyncInvoker =
                client.target("http://localhost:8080/myrestful/restful/hello").request
                ().async();

        System.out.println("Just about to do asynchronous call");

        String mediaType=MediaType.TEXT_PLAIN;

        Future<Response> responseFuture = asyncInvoker.get(
            new InvocationCallback<Response> ()
        {
            @Override
                    public void completed(Response theresponse)
```

```
            {  // This callback function is called back when call succeeds
                    System.out.println("Response received");
                    System.exit(1);
            }

            @Override
                    public void failed(Throwable thethrowable)
            {  // This callback function is called back when call fails
                    System.out.println("call failed, here comes stack trace:");
                    thethrowable.printStackTrace();
                    System.exit(1);
            }

        }
        );

        while (1==1)
        {
                System.out.println("doing useful work while waiting");
    // Give a little space between print statements so you can
    // see the response received
                try {
                        Thread.sleep(2000);
                }
                catch (Exception e) { }
        }
    }
}
```

The callback function is defined and set as a callback function in the following code, at the same time the GET is sent to the JAX-RS server. Note that the callback function is passed as a .get() parameter:

```
Future<Response> responseFuture = asyncInvoker.get(
    new InvocationCallback<Response> ()
{
    @Override
            public void completed(Response theresponse)
    {  // This callback function is called back when call succeeds
        System.out.println("Response received");
        System.exit(1);
    }
    @Override
            public void failed(Throwable thethrowable)
    {  // This callback function is called back when call fails
        System.out.println("call failed, here comes stack trace:");
        thethrowable.printStackTrace();
        System.exit(1);
    }
}
);
```

The results from the client from Listing 11.51 are shown in Listing 11.52. Note that there are only three "doing useful work while waiting" print statements. This is because I wised up and did a two-second sleep in between each time I printed out that useful work was being done. ☺

LISTING 11.52   Results from Calling Asynchronous Client Uses Callback Function

```
Just about to do asynchronous call
doing useful work while waiting
doing useful work while waiting
doing useful work while waiting
Response received
```

11.3.8   WHY DO YOU NEED JAX-RS WHEN YOU'VE GOT SERVLETS?

The annotation @GET may remind you of a servlet doGet, and @POST of a servlet doPost, etc.

So given that JAX-RS can run in a servlet container, why—doggone it ☺*—do you have to learn a whole new technology to do RESTful web services in Java?

The answer is, you *don't* have to. However, there are some advantages in using JAX-RS instead of servlets. If you recall from our discussion in Section 11.2.1, servlets have often been considered to be the "assembly language" of RESTful middleware, that is, they're very low level compared to some other RESTful middleware options. So if you think in those terms, you'll realize JAX-RS can do things using fewer code statements than what is necessary for servlets. Granted, in this situation much of the additional code that is required to do work in servlets is boilerplate code, that is, it's very little different each separate time you use it. However, it does tend to obfuscate (render obscure or unclear) your view of what is happening in the code.

To illustrate the differences between JAX-RS and a servlet, I've provided code that does the same thing using each of the two middlewares, that is, the code handles a POST HTTP method request with a query parameter. The servlet code is in Listing 11.53 and the JAX-RS code is in Listing 11.55. Two cURL commands to call the servlet code are shown in Listing 11.54, and a cURL command to call the JAX-RS code is shown in Listing 11.56.

First let's note that there is a little difference between the two: As you can see by comparing the cURL commands in Listing 11.54 with the cURL command in Listing 11.56, the servlet code is a little less restricted in how parameters can be passed to it than the JAX-RS code. This is (presumably) because the JAX-RS query parameter handling is done through injection, which is looking for a particular input format to use to grab the data. In this case, it is grabbing the data off the URL string.

Note that when you use the "—data" parameter with a cURL command, it sends the data the same way it would if you used an HTML form and pressed a Submit button—it includes the data as payload and includes (by default) the content-type "application/x-www-form-urlencoded." (We saw this behavior before when we looked at JAX-RS with one form parameter, and also in our original simple JAX-RS example in Section 11.3.2).

LISTING 11.53   Simple Servlet with One Query-Style Parameter

```
package example.myservlet;
import java.io.*;
import java.util.*;
import javax.servlet.annotation.WebServlet;
import javax.servlet.*;
import javax.servlet.http.*;
```

```
@WebServlet (
    urlPatterns="/myservlet"
)
public class myservlet extends HttpServlet {

 @Override
    public void doPost(HttpServletRequest request,
            HttpServletResponse response)
    throws ServletException, IOException
    {
        // Following output will show up in GlassFish log file
        System.out.println("Inside myservlet in doPost method");
        String mystring;
        // Get the data items from the HTTP post, by name
        mystring=request.getParameter("mystring");

        // Prepare a writer to the response
        PrintWriter myout = response.getWriter();
        // Write the data you just received to the response
        myout.println("received data is "+mystring);
    }
}
```

**LISTING 11.54   Two cURL Commands to Access Simple Servlet with One
                  Query-Style Parameter**

```
curl --request POST http://localhost:8080/myservlet/myservlet --data 'mystring=hithere'
```

or

```
curl --request POST http://localhost:8080/myservlet/myservlet?mystring=hithere
```

However, otherwise, from the standpoint of succinctness and readability, the JAX-RS code is superior. Let's look at why.

First of all, we see that the servlet code method signature itself (the method definition header, including parameters) gives you less information about what's going on than does the JAX-RS method signature. Here is the servlet's method signature:

```
public void doPost(HttpServletRequest request,
        HttpServletResponse response)
```

while here is the JAX-RS method signature:

```
@POST
@Path("/postpath")
public String received_POST(@QueryParam("mystring") String mystring)
```

Note that in the servlet's method signature, you don't see what kind of parameters are being passed, plus you don't find out in the servlet method signature what the data type of the eventual response will be. Both of these are clear in the JAX-RS method signature.

Now let's look at how we read the query parameters. In the servlet code in Listing 11.53, this is how you read the query parameter:

```
String mystring;

// Get the data items from the HTTP post, by name
mystring=request.getParameter("mystring");
```

Note that the servlet code is in addition to the servlet's method signature whereas in the JAX-RS code, the query parameter passing is done as part of the annotation in the method signature itself, and does not require any additional code within the body of the method:

```
@POST
@Path("/postpath")
public String received_POST(@QueryParam("mystring") String mystring)
```

LISTING 11.55   Simple JAX-RS POST with One Query Parameter

```
package example.restful;
import javax.ws.rs.POST;
import javax.ws.rs.Path;
import javax.ws.rs.QueryParam;


@Path("/hello")
public class Hello {
    // called when request sends a POST with data in format "variable=value"
    @POST
    @Path("/postpath")
    public String received_POST(@QueryParam("mystring") String mystring) {
        System.out.println("Data received was "+mystring+"\n");
        return "data received was "+mystring+"\n";
    }
}
```

Finally, let's consider how the response is returned to the Client. In the servlet code, we see:

```
// Prepare a writer to the response
PrintWriter myout = response.getWriter();

// Write the data you just received to the response
myout.println("received data is "+mystring);
```

whereas in the JAX-RS code we see:

```
return "data received was "+mystring+"\n";
```

In the servlet code, you have to create a writer to write the response, and then you write the data to the response, whereas in the JAX-RS code you simply return the data.

**LISTING 11.56   cURL Command to Access Simple JAX-RS POST with One
                   Query parameter**

curl --request POST http://localhost:8080/myrestful/restful/hello/postpath?mystring
    =hithere

So clearly, even in a very simple example, we can see that the servlet code is less succinct and more wordy than is JAX-RS code (for the same level of functionality).

AJAX EXERCISES

1. AJAX stands for Asynchronous JavaScript and XML. When we talk of AJAX now, do we always mean XML?
2. Where is the call to XMLHttpRequest most commonly implemented?
3. With AJAX, you call XMLHttpRequest to connect to a web page. Why is calling a function considered RESTful?
4. When using XMLHttpRequest to do an asynchronous call, does this work using polling?
5. How does XMLHttpRequest know when the server is done?
6. When XMLHttpRequest is sent to the server, does the server respond by downloading an entire web page?
7. What could be bad about using XMLHttpRequest to access a server on a different domain than the one where your code is running?
8. What is Cross Origin Resource Sharing (CORS) for, and how does it work?
9. Does a web server have to service a CORS request?
10. What is a preflighted request?

JAVA SERVLETS EXERCISES

1. How does a servlet maintain a state?
2. What is the lifetime of session scope in a servlet?
3. Set an attribute named "myattrib" to the value "Hi" in session scope.
4. What is the purpose of a JSESSIONID cookie?
5. Is it dangerous in regard to security to use URL rewriting instead of a JSESSIONID cookie?
6. What are the advantages or disadvantages over using @WebServlet versus a WEB-INF directory containing a web.xml file?
7. Do you package a servlet in a jar file like EJBs?
8. Why can cURL be useful to test RESTful web services?

JAX-RS EXERCISES

1. How is JAX-RS normally deployed?
2. What is the default lifecycle of a root resource class in JAX-RS?
3. Why is JAX-RS stateless?
4. Why is using parameters on a GET request often a bad idea?
5. How does JAX-RS specify which Internet Media Types a particular function will handle?
6. How does, say, @Consumes(MediaType.TEXT_XML), correspond to the contents of an HTTP request?
7. Create a cURL command that will send a POST with a Content-type of text/xml.

8. Use the JSON API to create a JSON object that contains the following name/value pairs: Description of horse with name, weight, height, color, address (similar to the SOAP example previously shown in Listing 10.3, but only do one horse)

9. When using asynchronous JAX-RS, how does the deployment change?

10. Why do you need JAX-RS when you've got servlets?

CONCEPTUAL QUESTIONS

1. In regard to various Internet Media Types (MIME types): why do you think JAX-RS uses those to distinguish between different resource methods to handle a request? What would the alternatives be?

2. We talked in depth about asynchronous communication in regard to AJAX because that's one of the most important functions of AJAX. We also talked about asynchronous communication in Servlets and in JAX-RS>.

   a. What are the advantages of asynchronous communication compared to synchronous communication and how does that apply to the technologies in this chapter: AJAX, Java Servlets, JAX-RS?

   b. What are some situations where you might want to use asynchronous communication? Would these situations be different for any of the technologies in this chapter?

3. In what ways do JavaScript/PHP/AJAX, Java Servlets, and JAX-RS conform to the Service-Oriented Architectures paradigm (we discussed Service-Oriented Architectures in Chapter 9)? In what way do JavaScript/PHP/AJAX, Java Servlets, and JAX-RS *not* conform to the Service-Oriented Architectures paradigm?

4. What are the primary advantages of RESTful web services compared to non-RESTful web services such as JAX-WS or non-RESTful WCF. Give specific technology-related examples.

5. What are the primary advantages of RESTful web services compared to object-oriented middlewares such as CORBA or EJB? What are the disadvantages? Give specific technology-related examples.

BIBLIOGRAPHY

ApacheFelix. 2015. Welcome to Apache Felix. http://felix.apache.org/ (accessed March 10, 2016).

Bien, A. 2013. Java EE 7 and JAX-RS 2.0. http://www.oracle.com/technetwork/articles/java/jaxrs20-1929352. html (accessed March 2, 2016)

cURL. 2015. Command Line Tool and Library. http://curl.haxx.se/ (accessed July 13, 2015)

Daityari, S. 2014. *Working with and around the Same Origin Policy*. Sitepoint. http://www.sitepoint.com/working-around-origin-policy/ (accessed September 27, 2015).

Garrett, J.J. 2005. Ajax: A New Approach to Web Communications. http://adaptivepath.org/ideas/ajax-new-approach-web-applications/ (accessed September 27, 2015).

Gupta, A. 2015. Thinking in Java EE (at least trying to!). https://abhirockzz.wordpress.com/2015/05/03/using-context-in-jax-rs-part-1/ (accessed March 11, 2016).

Huston, V. 2001. Design Patterns. http://www.vincehuston.org/dp/ (accessed July 30, 2016).

IBM. 2011. Implementing RESTful Views of EJB Applications Using JAX-RS. WebSphere Application Server Network Deployment. IBM Knowledge Center. https://www.ibm.com/support/knowledgecenter/SSAW57_8.0.0/com.ibm.websphere.nd.doc/info/ae/ae/twbs_jaxrs_ejb.html?cp=SSAW57_8.0.0%2F1-3-0-35 (accessed March 10, 2016).

Israel, A. 2013. What's the Difference between GlassFish and Apache Tomcat? Quora. https://www.quora.com/Whats-the-difference-between-Glassfish-and-Apache-Tomcat (accessed March 4, 2016).

Java Community Process. 2013. Java Specification Release JSR-340 Java Servlet 3.1. https://jcp.org/en/jsr/detail?id=340 (accessed March 12, 2016).

Java EE 6 Tutorial. 2013. Creating a RESTful Root Resource Class. http://docs.oracle.com/javaee/6/tutorial/doc/gilik.html (accessed March 12, 2016).

Java EE 6 Tutorial. 2013. Using Scopes. http://docs.oracle.com/javaee/6/tutorial/doc/gjbbk.html (accessed February 9, 2016).

Java Interface. 2013. AsyncResponse. http://docs.oracle.com/javaee/7/api/javax/ws/rs/container/AsyncResponse.html (accessed March 13, 2016).

Java Jasks. 2015. Async Operation Throws Processing Exception. http://java.jasks.org/async_operation_throws_processingexception (accessed March 2, 2016).

JavaTpoint. 2016. Attribute in Servlet. http://www.javatpoint.com/attribute (accessed February 7, 2016).

Jersey. 2015. Chapter 11. Asynchronous Services and Clients. Jersey 2.22.2 User Guide. https://jersey.java.net/documentation/latest/async.html (accessed March 2, 2016).

Jersey. 2016. Appendix A. Configuration Properties. Jersey 2.22.2 User Guide. https://jersey.java.net/documentation/latest/appendix-properties.html (accessed March 12, 2016).

Jersey. 2016. Chapter 3. JAX-RS Application, Resources, and Sub-resources. Jersey 2.22.2 User Guide. https://jersey.java.net/documentation/latest/jaxrs-resources.html#d0e2193 (accessed March 11, 2016).

Jersey. 2016. Chapter 4. Application Deployment and Runtime Environments. Jersey 2.22.2 User Guide. https://jersey.java.net/documentation/latest/deployment.html (accessed March 12, 2016).

Jersey. 2016. Chapter 5. Client API. Jersey 2.22.2 User Guide. https://jersey.java.net/documentation/latest/client.html#d0e4257www.oracle.com/technetwork/articles/java/jaxrs20-1929352.html (accessed March 12, 2016).

Jersey. 2016. RESTful Web Services in Java. https://jersey.java.net/ (accessed March 10, 2016).

JournalDev. 2013. Java JSON Processing API Tutorial. http://www.journaldev.com/2315/java-json-processing-api-example-tutorial (accessed March 13, 2016).

Marshall, A. 2015. Top 10 Open Source Java and Java EE Application Servers. IDR Solutions. https://blog.idrsolutions.com/2015/04/top-10-open-source-java-and-javaee-application-servers/ (accessed March 4, 2016).

Mikic, M. 2014. GlassFish vs. Tomcat. Stack Overflow. http://stackoverflow.com/questions/23563340/glassfish-vs-tomcat Tomcat (accessed March 4, 2016).

Mkyong. 2011. JAX-RS @PathParam Example. http://www.mkyong.com/webservices/jax-rs/jax-rs-pathparam-example/ (accessed March 9, 2016).

Mozilla Developer Network (MDN). 2015. HTTP Access Control (CORS). https://developer.mozilla.org/en-US/docs/Web/HTTP/Access_control_CORS (accessed September 29, 2015).

NowSecure. 2014. Avoid Query String for Sensitive Data. https://www.nowsecure.com/resources/secure-mobile-development/coding-practices/avoid-query-string-for-sensitive-data/ (accessed March 11, 2016).

Oracle. 2013. Accessing REST Resources with the JAX-RS Client API. https://docs.oracle.com/javaee/7/tutorial/jaxrs-client.htm (accessed March 13, 2016).

Oracle. 2013. Class ClientBuilder. http://docs.oracle.com/javaee/7/api/javax/ws/rs/client/ClientBuilder.html (accessed March 13, 2016).

Oracle. 2013. Interface Future<V>. https://docs.oracle.com/javase/7/docs/api/java/util/concurrent/Future.html (accessed March 13, 2016).

Oracle. 2013. Interface Invocation.Builder. https://docs.oracle.com/javaee/7/api/javax/ws/rs/client/Invocation.Builder.html (accessed March 13, 2016).

Oracle. 2013. Interface WebTarget. https://docs.oracle.com/javaee/7/api/javax/ws/rs/client/WebTarget.html (accessed March 13, 2016).

Oracle. 2013. javax.servlet.http.HttpServlet. https://docs.oracle.com/javaee/7/api/javax/servlet/http/HttpServlet.html (accessed March 4, 2016).

Oracle. 2013. javax.servlet.GenericServlet. Java EE 7 Documentation. http://docs.oracle.com/javaee/7/api/javax/servlet/GenericServlet.html (accessed March 4, 2016).

Oracle. 2013. javax.servlet.Servlet. Java EE 7 Documentation. https://docs.oracle.com/javaee/7/api/javax/servlet/Servlet.html (accessed March 4, 2016).

Oracle. 2013. javax.ws.rs.client. http://docs.oracle.com/javaee/7/api/javax/ws/rs/client/package-summary.html (accessed March 13, 2016).

Oracle. 2013. The Java EE 6 Tutorial. http://docs.oracle.com/javaee/6/tutorial/doc/gilik.html (accessed March 9, 2016).

Oracle. 2016. java.util.concurrent.interface Future<V>. https://docs.oracle.com/javase/7/docs/api/java/util/concurrent/Future.html (accessed March 2, 2016).

Ranganathan, A. 2015. CORS In Action. http://arunranga.com/examples/access-control/ (accessed September 29, 2015).

Schock, J. 2013. So How Does JSONP Really Work? http://schock.net/articles/2013/02/05/how-jsonp-really-works-examples/ (accessed September 27, 2015).

Stack Overflow. 2009. What Does the Servlet <load-on-startup> value Signify. http://stackoverflow.com/questions/809775/what-does-the-servlet-load-on-startup-value-signify (accessed March 12, 2016).

Stack Overflow. 2010. URL Matrix Parameters vs. Request Parameters. http://stackoverflow.com/questions/2048121/url-matrix-parameters-vs-request-parameters (accessed March 11, 2016).

Stack Overflow. 2011. How to Access Parameters in a RESTful POST Method. http://stackoverflow.com/questions/8194408/how-to-access-parameters-in-a-restful-post-method (accessed March 11, 2016).

Stack Overflow. 2011. Java War vs Jar—What Is the Difference. http://stackoverflow.com/questions/5871053/java-war-vs-jar-what-is-the-difference (accessed March 8, 2016).

Stack Overflow. 2011. Servlet vs. RESTful. http://stackoverflow.com/questions/7874695/servlet-vs-restful (accessed February 10, 2016).

Stack Overflow. 2012. How to Set Up JAX-RS Application Using Annotations Only (No web.xml). http://stackoverflow.com/questions/9373081/how-to-set-up-jax-rs-application-using-annotations-only-no-web-xml (accessed March 12, 2016).

Stack Overflow. 2012. What Does Provider in JAX-RS Mean? http://stackoverflow.com/questions/13557442/what-does-provider-in-jax-rs-mean (accessed March 11, 2016).

Stack Overflow. 2014. What Is the Benefit of Using Java Based Config Instead of web.xml for Servlet 3.X. http://stackoverflow.com/questions/26848057/what-is-benefit-of-using-java-based-config-instead-of-web-xml-for-servlet-3-x (accessed March 8, 2016).

Staudacher, H. 2011. Step by Step: How to bring JAX-RS and OSGi Together. EclipseSource Developerhttp://eclipsesource.com/blogs/2014/02/04/step-by-step-how-to-bring-jax-rs-and-osgi-together/ (accessed March 10, 2016).

Stenberg, D. 2016. cURL. https://curl.haxx.se/ (accessed March 12, 2016).

Watrous, D. 2012. RESTful Java Servlet. http://software.danielwatrous.com/restful-java-servlet/ (accessed March 10, 2016).

W3C. 2014. XMLHttpRequest: Snapshot Specification for the XMLHttpRequest Living Standard: Editor's Draft. https://dvcs.w3.org/hg/xhr/raw-file/tip/Overview.html (accessed September 27, 2015).

W3C. 2014. Cross Origin Resource Sharing. http://www.w3.org/TR/cors/ (accessed September 29, 2015).

W3Schools. 2015. HTML script <src> Attribute. http://www.w3schools.com/tags/att_script_src.asp (accessed September 27, 2015).

Web Hypertext Application Technology Working Group (WHATWG). 2015. XMLHttpRequest: Living Standard. https://xhr.spec.whatwg.org/ (accessed September 27, 2015).

Wikipedia. 2016. Hypermedia. https://en.wikipedia.org/wiki/Hypermedia (accessed March 10, 2016).

12 RESTful Web Services in .NET

As we saw earlier in Section 9.2, there are some differences of opinion as to what "RESTful" and "non-RESTful" mean. We already looked at "non-RESTful" in Chapter 10, and then in the introduction to Chapter 11 we summarized again exactly what is meant by RESTful web services. Please review these sections again before reading the rest of this chapter.

In this chapter, we're going to examine some of the RESTful web services provided by the Microsoft .NET libraries. We're going to look first at how Windows Communication Foundation (WCF) can be used to implement RESTful web services, then we're going to look at ASP.NET MVC, and finally at ASP.NET CORE 1.0. With regard to ASP.NET Core 1.0, we're focusing on the same kinds of examples we used in ASP.NET MVC. We're not going to look at earlier technologies such as web forms. The reasoning behind these choices is described later on in Section 12.2.

For RESTful WCF, there are larger practical examples provided in Chapter 17, available in online resources.

12.1 TECHNOLOGY REVIEW: WINDOWS COMMUNICATION FOUNDATION—RESTful

We introduced you to what is meant by a RESTful architecture in Chapter 9. This section will show you how WCF can implement a RESTful web service.

We previously saw a general description of WCF in Section 10.5. Nearly everything in that section was non-RESTful, except for the example of a client to read Web Services Description Language (WSDL) by directly using HTTP. That client was included in Section 10.4 because it is so useful! Note that although the client that reads WSDL was implemented by directly using HTTP, and thus that client itself can be considered RESTful that makes use of the WSDL interface is non-RESTful. Note, however, that in order to understand this section, you will find it beneficial to have previously read Section 10.5—I have made each separate technology review section in this textbook as independent as possible; however, there are numerous basic WCF concepts that it was just too wordy to reproduce here.

As in Section 10.5, in all cases here I've provided the programmatic way of handling WCF rather than the configuration way. I did this because the programmatic way provides a better comparison to the other, non-Microsoft technologies we examine in this textbook. It should be relatively easy to convert these to a configuration type programming.

12.1.1 RESTful BINDINGS AND BEHAVIOR

WCF uses WebHttpBinding together with WebHttpBehavior to provide a RESTful web service (Microsoft tends to call these *Web style* services in their online documentation). WebHttpBinding is pretty straightforward (once you understand the overall RESTful architecture concept). It uses HTTP commands directly to transfer data, rather than running some other protocols (SOAP and WSDL for example) on top of HTTP. Similarly, it uses plain XML (plain old XML) as its default data format (note that JSON is also supported) as the format of the data it sends and receives.

12.1.2 SELF-HOSTED RESTful WEB SERVICE

Microsoft provides a special version of a Self-Host to be used to self-host web services. This class (derived from ServiceHost) is called WebServiceHost. It defines a web endpoint automatically.

This web endpoint is automatically configured with WebHttpBinding and WebHttpBehavior. An example of an extremely simple Self-Host using WebServiceHost is shown in Listing 12.1.

Note that the class library project that generates the .dll file is the same here as it was in Chapter 10. Note that the ServiceContract together with the OperationContract define a remote procedure call. However, now, instead of using, for example, WSDL/SOAP (assuming WSHttpBinding was chosen) to implement the remote procedure call itself on top of HTTP, instead with this RESTful code the remote procedure call is handled by HTTP commands themselves, such as GET, PUT, etc.

LISTING 12.1   Extremely Simple RESTful Self-Hosting using WebServiceHost

```csharp
using System;
using System.Collections.Generic;
using System.Linq;
using System.Text;
using System.Threading.Tasks;
using System.ServiceModel;
using System.ServiceModel.Description;
using System.ServiceModel.Web;
using SelfHost;

  class Program
  {
    static void Main(string[] args)
    {
      Uri baseAddress = new Uri("...your url ... /HelloWorldService");

      WebServiceHost host = new WebServiceHost(typeof(myHelloWorldService), base
        Address);
      try {

        host.Open();

        foreach (ServiceEndpoint current_endpoint in host.Description.Endpoints)
        {
          Console.Write("endpoint name is {0}\n," current_endpoint.Name);
          Console.Write("endpoint address is {0}\n," current_endpoint.Address);
          Console.Write("endpoint binding is {0}\n," current_endpoint.Binding);
          Console.ReadLine();
        }

        Console.WriteLine("The service is running and is located at \n {0}. \n Call it and
          pass it your name: {1} \n," baseAddress, "someone's name");
        Console.WriteLine("To stop the service hit enter");
        Console.ReadLine(); // Keep the console window from disappearing so you can see
          it (by making it wait for input)

        // Close the ServiceHost.
        host.Close();
```

```
        }
    catch (CommunicationException ce_exception)
    {
        Console.WriteLine("Exception {0} occurred.  Will abort\n," ce_exception.Message);
        Console.ReadLine();
        host.Abort();
    }
  }
}
```

12.1.3 EXTREMELY SIMPLE RESTFUL WEB SERVICE CLIENT

Now in Listing 12.2, we see a very simple RESTful web client that can be used to call the Self-Hosted web service that we just saw in Listing 12.1. This example uses a ChannelFactory to create a channel between the client and the server. The only difference between this code and the code we saw in Chapter 10, is that now we use WebChannelFactory to create the channel, instead of ChannelFactory itself. WebChannelFactory is a derived class of ChannelFactory that creates channels that are configured to use WebHttpBinding and WebHttpBehavior.

LISTING 12.2   Extremely Simple RESTful Web Service Client Created Using Channel Factory

```
using System;
using System.Collections.Generic;
using System.Linq;
using System.Text;
using System.Threading.Tasks;
using System.ServiceModel;
using System.ServiceModel.Description;
using System.ServiceModel.Web;
using SelfHost;
namespace client_using_ChannelFactory
{
  class Program
  {
    static void Main(string[] args)
    {
        Uri baseAddress = new Uri("http://localhost:8731/Design_Time_Addresses/Hello
            WorldService");
        WebChannelFactory<ImyHelloWorldService> mychannelFactory =
            new WebChannelFactory<ImyHelloWorldService>(baseAddress);

        ImyHelloWorldService current_channel = mychannelFactory.CreateChannel();
        string msg;
        msg = "Hi to all, just received:  " + current_channel.HelloWorld("Both John Doe and
            Joe Blow") + "\n";

        Console.WriteLine(msg);
```

```
        Console.ReadLine(); // Make console pause so we can read it
    }
  }
}
```

12.1.4 WEB SERVICE CONTRACT SPECIFYING WHICH HTTP COMMANDS TO USE

The Service Contract example shown in Listing 12.3 uses the WCF Web HTTP programming model to implement the interface. The Web HTTP Programming model provides a web service that can be accessed by many different kinds of clients. For example, if you specify an Operation as being accessed by using a WebGet (as shown in Listing 12.3), then you can use a browser as a client to access this web service.

The example shown in Listing 12.3 can use a Self-Host that is exactly the same as the Self-Host shown in Listing 12.1.

Note that this example uses a static variable as a "pretend database" consisting of one value. A static variable stays around between calls, its value doesn't disappear at the end of a call. Here the remote procedure call "HelloWorld" sets the value of the "pretend database" variable to the passed-in string. The remote procedure call "getHelloWorld" then reads the "pretend database" variable and returns its value.

Therefore, for this code to work, you have to call "HelloWorld" *before* you call "getHelloWorld." That's because "HelloWorld" sets the pretend_database static variable to a value. Otherwise there would be no value to read.

In the below examples, assume the URI where the service is located is:

> http://localhost:8731/ HelloWorldService

How to access this web service using a browser:

> If you use the
> [WebGet(UriTemplate = "HelloWorld/{yourname}")]
> then you can call "HelloWorld" in your browser as follows:

> http://localhost:8731/ HelloWorldService/HelloWorld/myname

> and you can call "getHelloWorld" in your browser as follows:
> http://localhost:8731/ HelloWorldService/getHelloWorld

You can see from this, that the statements:

> [OperationContract]
> [WebGet(UriTemplate = "HelloWorld/{yourname}")]

sets the URI that accesses the HelloWorld remote procedure call and passes in the string "myname" to:

> ...HelloWorldService/HelloWorld/myname

Similarly, the statements:

> [OperationContract]
> [WebGet (UriTemplate="getHelloWorld")]

set the URI that accesses the getHelloWorld remote procedure call to:

...HelloWorldService/getHelloWorld

Also, we note that in this particular case, these two remote procedure calls are accessed by an HTTP "GET" operation. That is, the client (a web browser or any other client) sends a "GET" message. In the first case of the HelloWorld operation, the client would send an HTTP GET message to the specified address, and also append the "myname" string to the GET. In the second case of the getHelloWorld operation, the client would simply send a GET to the specified address.

LISTING 12.3   Service Contract That Uses the WCF Web HTTP Programming Model

```
using System;
using System.Collections.Generic;
using System.Linq;
using System.Text;
using System.Threading.Tasks;
using System.ServiceModel;
using System.ServiceModel.Description;
using System.ServiceModel.Web;
namespace SelfHost
{
    [ServiceContract]
    public interface ImyHelloWorldService
    {

        // Have to call HelloWorld FIRST, and only THEN can you call getHelloWorld!!!!!

        // Get it
        [OperationContract]
        [WebGet (UriTemplate="getHelloWorld")]

        string getHelloWorld();

        // Set it
        [OperationContract]
        [WebGet(UriTemplate = "HelloWorld/{yourname}")]

        string HelloWorld(string yourname);
    }

    public class myHelloWorldService : ImyHelloWorldService
    {
        static string pretend_database;  // pretends to be an (external) database
        public string getHelloWorld()
        {
            string mymsg = "and a very simple Hello, world to whoever it may concern";
            mymsg = pretend_database;
            return mymsg;
        }

        public string HelloWorld(string yourname)
```

```
        {
            string mymsg = "Hello, world, especially hello to " + yourname;
            pretend_database = yourname;
            return mymsg;
        }
    }
}
```

Note that WebGet is not the only available HTTP operation format that can be specified in the WCF HTTP programming model. For example, if you did [WebInvoke] instead of WebGet, then the Operation Contract would default to expecting the client to send an HTTP POST message.

Alternately, if instead of WebGet you did:

[WebInvoke(UriTemplate = "HelloWorld/{yourname}," Method="PUT")]

then the OperationContract would expect the client to send an HTTP PUT message.

Note that since the cURL utility can send HTTP commands, cURL can be used to access the web service whose contract is shown in Listing 12.3.

You can also use a client that is extremely similar to the simple client shown in Listing 12.2. You would have to call current_channel.HelloWorld("myname") to set the value of the "pretend_database" variable, and current_channel.getHelloWorld() to retrieve (consume) the value of the "pretend_database" variable.

12.1.5   WCF-RESTful Web Service That Returns JSON Data

As mentioned earlier, the WebHttpBinding defaults to using plain old XML as its data format. However, the JSON format is a desirable format for web services, since it is less wordy/more efficient than plain old XML (or SOAP either, for that matter).

In the example from Listing 12.4, you will be sending your data back in JSON format.

LISTING 12.4   WebGet Specifying JSON Format

[WebGet(UriTemplate = "HelloWorld/{yourname}," ResponseFormat=WebMessage
Format.Json)]

However, a simple name passed from client to server, as was done in Listing 12.3, does not adequately illustrate the JSON format. Therefore, let's look at the Service Contract shown in Listing 12.5. This Service Contract provides a user-defined data type named "PersonBeingGreeted" that contains both a greeting string and a name string.

A client that can access the service in Listing 12.5 is shown in Listing 12.6. However, you can't really see inside this client that the data it consumed had really been in JSON format. All you can see is how the client chose to write it out to the screen, the actual format it was transmitted in is invisible to you.

To see the data in JSON format, go to your browser and enter:

http://localhost:8731/HelloWorldService/HelloWorld/joe

Or you can access it with cURL as follows:

curl http://localhost:8731/ HelloWorldService/HelloWorld/joe

Your output will look like this:

{"greeting":"Hello to the Person ,""theName":"joe"}

**LISTING 12.5   Service Contract That Uses the RESTful WCF Web HTTP
                  Programming Model with JSON**

```csharp
using System;
using System.Collections.Generic;
using System.Linq;
using System.Text;
using System.Threading.Tasks;
using System.ServiceModel;
using System.ServiceModel.Description;
using System.ServiceModel.Web;

namespace SelfHost
{
  public class PersonBeingGreeted
  {
     public string greeting { get; set; }
     public string theName { get; set; }
  }

  [ServiceContract]
  public interface ImyHelloWorldService
  {

     // Set it
     [OperationContract]

     [WebGet(UriTemplate = "HelloWorld/{yourname},", ResponseFormat=WebMessage
     Format.Json)]
     PersonBeingGreeted HelloWorld(string yourname);
  }
  public class myHelloWorldService : ImyHelloWorldService
  {
     public PersonBeingGreeted HelloWorld(string yourname)
     {
        PersonBeingGreeted the_current_person;

        the_current_person = new PersonBeingGreeted();

        the_current_person.greeting = "Hello to the Person ";
        the_current_person.theName = yourname;
```

```
        return the_current_person;
    }
  }
}
```

**LISTING 12.6   Client to Access RESTful WCF Web HTTP Programming Model
                 with JSON**

```
using System;
using System.Collections.Generic;
using System.Linq;
using System.Text;
using System.Threading.Tasks;
using System.ServiceModel;
using System.ServiceModel.Description;
using System.ServiceModel.Web;
using SelfHost;

namespace client_using_ChannelFactory
{
  class Program
  {
    static void Main(string[] args)
    {
      Uri baseAddress = new Uri("http://localhost:8731/Design_Time_Addresses/
            HelloWorldService");
      WebChannelFactory<ImyHelloWorldService> mychannelFactory =
            new WebChannelFactory<ImyHelloWorldService>(baseAddress);

      ImyHelloWorldService current_channel = mychannelFactory.CreateChannel();

      string msg;
      msg = "Just set value in pretend_database, echoed value is " + current_channel.
            HelloWorld("All people of the world") + "\n";
      Console.WriteLine(msg);
      msg = "Get value from pretend_database, value is" + current_channel.getHelloWorld()
            + "\n";
      Console.WriteLine(msg);
      Console.ReadLine(); // Make console pause so we can read it

    }
  }
}
```

12.2 TECHNOLOGY REVIEW: ASP.NET MODEL–VIEW–CONTROLLER AND ASP.NET CORE

12.2.1 THE MODEL–VIEW–CONTROLLER PATTERN

According to Reenskaug (2010), Trygve M.H. Reenskaug invented the Model–View–Controller (MVC) design pattern while at Xerox Parc in 1978.

Model–view–controller is sometimes called a design pattern, sometimes called an architecture pattern, sometimes called a software architecture, sometimes called a *separation of concerns*. Some people can get argumentative about exactly what it means, see StackOverflow (2008) and Programmers Stack Exchange (2011).

So let me give my own definition. You can argue about it afterwards as much as you want. ☺

A model refers to some organized data store. Note that the "model" in MVC is not *required* to be associated with a database per se. It could be a file, individual data objects, or even an interface accessing remote data (and perhaps you don't know how the data is stored in the remote server). Of course the model *can* be associated with a database and that is a very common situation. In all cases, however, the data must always be stored *through* the model, that is, the model is responsible for organizing and retrieving the data. For example, it's wrong to store the data inside the controller, that doesn't match the MVC pattern.

A view is a description of the model. Different views would show different aspects of the model, so it's making choices about which data is important to describe what it wants to describe. The view has to interact with the model and understand the model in order to retrieve the correct data.

The controller handles interactions between the user, the model, and the view. The controller is responsible for interacting with the user in order to update the data, it is also responsible for controlling which view is seen. Sometimes the controller is responsible for selecting or even generating particular data items that are used by a view. When a particular view is seen by a user, the user can employ that view to call the controller in order to update the data in the model.

This is called a "separation of concerns" because it's trying to break data-handling and viewing into loosely coupled pieces (model, view, and controller) that can vary independently without affecting each other too much.

There is some overlap with other well-known design patterns. For example, according to Huston (2001):

> The Observer pattern captures the lion's share of the Model–View–Controller architecture that has been a part of the Smalltalk community for years.

Huston (2001) further states that the Observer pattern is:

> The 'View' part of Model–View–Controller.

Huston's argument about Observer serving as a "View" is reasonable in terms of Observer describing events that occur on an observed object, but Observer doesn't include a part of "View" that is often discussed, which is, the View can interact with the controller to cause the model to be changed. The Observer design pattern is relatively passive, the only way in which it is not passive is that in some versions it can pull data from the observed object rather than simply waiting for the observed object to push events to it.

And *that's* enough argument about *that* for now anyway. Now we're going to look at what the ASP.NET RESTful technology called ASP.NET MVC (in the most recent versions of ASP.NET, this is included in ASP.NET Core) means by MVC. ASP.NET MVC has a fairly specific meaning in its own world of what this is.

12.2.2   What Are ASP.NET, ASP.NET MVC, and ASP.NET Core, Anyway?

First of all, the .NET framework is a framework with an associated class library that is used by software that runs in the Common Language Runtime (CLR) environment on Microsoft Windows. This is a powerful library that does many different things, including database access, user interfaces, communications, etc. The .NET framework has always been meant to be used on Microsoft Windows. There is a separate project called Mono that supports the .NET framework on other operating systems, especially variations of Linux or Android. My experience with having some of my students use Mono is that it has not always been completely compatible with the .NET framework on Windows itself, there have always been certain kinds of software that wouldn't port from .NET itself to Mono. Also, there has always been an issue that Mono might be infringing some Microsoft patents. However, Microsoft recently purchased Xamarin, the primary supporter of Mono, so this may no longer be an issue, see Microsoft (2016).

ASP.NET is a framework for building websites that is associated with and employs the .NET framework (it can be thought of as part of the .NET framework). It is a server-side technology that is intended to create dynamic web pages, that is, web pages that change and update at runtime.

There was an earlier server-side technology provided by Microsoft, called Active Server Pages (ASP), dating back to 1998 that was later replaced by ASP.NET.

ASP.NET Web Forms is a programming model that uses ASP.NET to build web pages, and that provides dynamic web pages. Although there is a single page model, typically with ASP.NET Web Forms, the markup (the html and associated visual controls) on one page (with file extension .aspx), and the "code behind" is C# code (with file extension .cs) or Visual Basic code (with file extension .vb). Web development is normally done using visual programming. For example, when using Visual Studio, the developer drags and drops images representing user controls, for example a button, to a "designer" view. This would create a Button image on the designer view (represented in a file with extension .aspx) and it would create a template of C# (or Visual Basic) code in the code behind (the C# files in the code behind would have extensions ".cs"). However, with ASP.NET web forms, there is a fairly tight coupling between the .aspx markup file and the "code behind" .cs (or .vb) file. The markup (the view) is chosen first, so this typically means that the code behind must be fairly complex so as to handle different situations, where the final view that the user needs to see is different from the originally selected view.

In recent times, ASP.NET MVC technology has become popular. This combines ASP.NET with the MVC pattern, and works by responding to HTTP messages, which makes its operation somewhat RESTful. After you understand this technology better, we'll discuss later on, in Section 12.2.13, the degree to which ASP.NET MVC is truly RESTful. One of the primary advantages of ASP.NET MVC compared to ASP.NET web forms is that the action to be performed is chosen first, and the action can be used with different views. So the view and the action are not so tightly coupled as occurred with ASP.NET web forms. Also, to make flexible views, ASP.NET MVC employs the Razor technology, which we will examine briefly in the next section. Razor mixes markup (HTML) and calls to C# code (or Visual Basic code) in the same file.

There is another technology produced by Microsoft called "Web API" that is similar to ASP.NET MVC in some ways, but has a different focus. A Web API is intended to be consumed by another application, whereas ASP.NET MVC is intended to create websites. Web API returns HttpMessageResponse instead of ActionResponse (we'll see what these are later on in this section), and MVC has some other files needed by a website that are not typically used in Web API.

In ASP.NET Web Forms, the aspx markup pages specify the view the user sees. In ASP.NET MVC, the controller decides which view the user sees. But Web API is not intended to render a web page to the user, it is more oriented toward calls from other applications than for user views.

ASP.NET Core 1.0 is a new framework released by Microsoft in 2016. It is open source, freely available, and cross platform which is an example of Microsoft moving further away from their previous history of mostly proprietary Windows-based software. ASP.NET Core combines ASP.NET

MVC and Web API into a single model, and is a complete rewrite/new write, but has many similarities to ASP.NET MVC.

In this section, we will examine ASP.NET MVC and then we will move on to a similar example in ASP.NET Core. I've already got too many different technologies in this textbook—don't you agree, students? ☺ So we're not going to focus on the Web API differences from ASP.NET MVC.

12.2.2.1 Razor

Razor is a way to access ASP.NET, using a simplified syntax compared to earlier methods, that embeds calls to C# (or VisualBasic) and ASP.NET *inside* HTML code. Another way of saying this is to say that Razor is a "view engine." A view engine is a method for embedding server code in a web page, such that the HTML provides a template for that web page (the overall flow of the web page), and the embedded server code modifies that web page to produce the specific, desired web page. Output is the (specific, desired) web page (usually in HTML format) that is then rendered (shown appropriately to the user) by a browser.

A few syntax rules when using Razor with C# (see W3Schools 2016):

- C#/Razor files have the extension .cshtml
- C# code blocks inside the HTML are enclosed in @{ ... }
- All inline expressions inside the HTML (variables and functions) start with @
  - Note that for, while, etc. begin with @, and need not be embedded within @{ ... }
- Code statements end with a semicolon
- The "var" keyword is used to declare variables
- C# code is case sensitive

We're going to be using some Razor code in our examples; what you need to know will be explained when we go through it. We'll also see a few examples of calls to various ASP.NET HTML helpers from inside Razor, later on. However, we're not going to go over too much display type code in this textbook, as our primary focus is distributed connections through middleware from one computer to another computer. It's just that sometimes, especially with web services, we need a little information about displaying the data in order to make it all work, so we're looking at the minimum required.

12.2.2.2 Roadmap for Examining ASP.NET MVC and ASP.NET CORE

One good way to illustrate how to use the MVC pattern in general is to use a database. That's because the "model" in MVC is very often in practice associated with a database (although as you should recall from our earlier discussion, according to the MVC design pattern it's not required to be a database), so using a database is a good way to show in a practical way how MVC works. For example, if you examine the basic Microsoft tutorials on ASP.NET MVC (see Anderson 2012) and ASP.NET CORE MVC (see Anderson 2016), you will note that both employ a database.

In the other technologies in this textbook, I used the Marina project, which employs a database, as the last, more comprehensive example to illustrate the technology. However, here we're sort of going back to front to our usual way of doing things by doing the Marina project first instead of last. The reason for this is, with ASP.NET MVC and ASP.NET CORE MVC, since those two technologies are very focused on the "model" part of the pattern, it makes sense to examine the Marina project first, that is, go ahead and do the database accesses first, and then afterward look at the various methodologies in the ASP.NET MVC and ASP.NET CORE MVC technologies.

As we walk through our project creation, we're going to do it in the most straightforward way for the Marina project that we are focusing on. Relative to this, contrary to the flow of the basic Microsoft tutorials, when we create our Marina project, we will begin by creating our Model first, and only afterward will we learn how to create our Controller and View. If you get lost in the Marina project creation, it might be helpful for you to go back and read those basic Microsoft tutorials.

12.2.3 THE MARINA PROJECT

As I mentioned previously in Section 1.5, the Marina project is a web-based application that is used to manage a large sailboat marina that employs a database to keep track of sailboats, owners, whether the owners have paid their sailboat rental, and handling any sailboat maintenance requests that come in from owners.

In this project, our database item refers to *sailboat model*—it is only coincidental that we have a "model" *inside* an ASP.NET MVC-type "model." ☺ This oddity arose because I originally created this example to be implemented in different technologies that did not include a model as part of the technology, in those situations it was sufficient to call a *sailboat model* simply a "model." (I've been using this particular example in my middleware course for years, just like it is.) It looks perhaps a little weird here but since I'm using the word "model" to mean *sailboat model* for several other technologies in this book, I didn't want to make it different for one technology, and for the other technologies the word "model" is just simpler. So suffer through it. ☺ It would have been more confusing I believe if I had changed the name, since I am assuming you're reading more than just the ASP.NET MVC/ASP.NET CORE portion of the textbook. You are, aren't you? Don't disappoint me!

12.2.4 ASP.NET MVC4 IN VISUAL STUDIO 2012

In this section, first we will create a basic Marina project. Then in the following section, we will add an asynchronous controller to the Marina project (RequestMaintenance).

After we implement our controller that requests maintenance, in the section after that we will look at how scheduling maintenance could be handled in a separate website implemented using PHP.

Then we will look at how scheduling maintenance could be handled in the same ASP.NET MVC project.

In this section, we're going to see how to implement the Marina project in ASP.NET MVC4 in Visual Studio 2012. As we do this, we're going to discuss how a model, a view, and a controller can really be used, in general but also specifically in a database-type project, and particularly for the Marina project.

12.2.4.1 Create MVC Project

The first two steps are very basic. Create a new project, and select ASP.NET MVC4 Web Application (see Figure 12.1). Then select Internet Application, the View Engine Razor, and pick your project name and directory (see Figure 12.2).

12.2.4.2 Create Model

Now we are going to create a Model. The Model represents the data that is stored in the database. In this particular technology, we are going to create the model first. After we create the model, then later on (but not too much later) we will use the Model to automatically generate the database and the various Create, Read, Update, Delete (CRUD) operations to access the database. Using the model to create the database and associated operations is called *scaffolding*. This gets your database running quickly; then you can modify the operations, and add additional operations, as needed. Many different frameworks use scaffolding, and of course ASP.NET MVC and ASP.NET CORE MVC do so.

First we create the model and give it a name (see Figures 12.3, 12.4).

We see the blank model that we have created in Figure 12.5.

In Figure 12.6, we see how to add our database items: name, model, slip, begin_date, end_date. You just replace the blank model code with this code.

FIGURE 12.1 Step 1: Create MVC project.

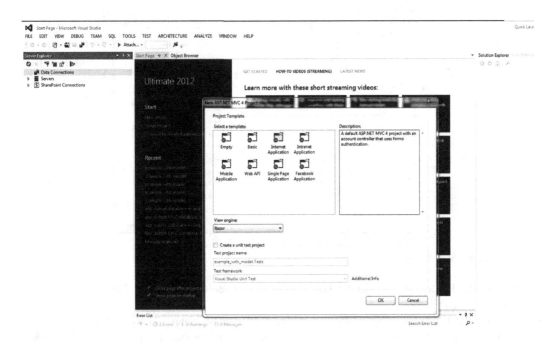

FIGURE 12.2 Step 2: Select project template.

Notice the "get" and "set," those are just accessor functions that allow you to get and set the database values. Remember that we're using an object as a model of the database.

We also have a value named "id." This is how the database distinguishes one database record from another database record (set of associated values: name, model, slip, begin_date, end_date). In Figure 12.19, later on, we will see the id numbers associated with each database record.

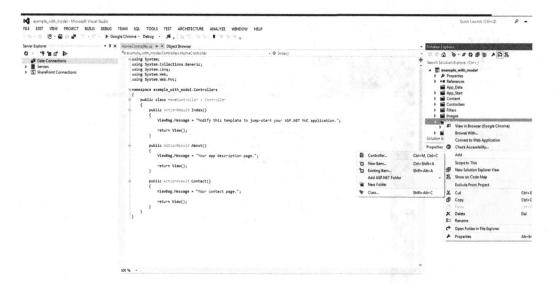

FIGURE 12.3   Step 1: Create the model itself.

FIGURE 12.4   Step 2: Enter model name.

In Figure 12.20, later on, we will see how an id can be used to display the database record that is associated with it.

We also added code for a Context class, in this case, MarinaDBContext. This class is responsible for connecting to the database, and for mapping between records in the database and the objects in the Model.

Next we will tell the MarinaDBContext how to access the Marina database. We have to modify the Web.Config file to do this. In Figure 12.7, we see how this is done, by adding the following code to the connectionStrings section:

```
<add name="MarinaDBContext"
  connectionString=
  "Data Source=(LocalDB)\v11.0;AttachDbFilename=|DataDirectory|\Marinas.mdf;Integrated
```

FIGURE 12.5   Step 3: Prior to adding model content.

FIGURE 12.6   Step 4: Add model content: methods to access database items.

FIGURE 12.7   Step 5: Access Marina database from Web.Config file.

```
Security="True"
   providerName="System.Data.SqlClient"
/>
```

The connectionStrings section of the Web.Config file is tasked with connecting to databases. It specifies the name of the connectionString (in this case, MarinaDBContext), the server where the database is located, the name of the database, and the appropriate security credentials that a user must employ to access the database.

Here you can see that we are using the LocalDB. That is, we are using the version of SQL Server Express that is installed by default in Visual Studio 2012 (see MSDN 2016e). Here, Data Source gives the server name and the desired instance, running on the server, of SQL Server, in the format ServerName\Instancename. Here, the Data Source is LocalDB)\v11.0.

AttachDbFilename gives the name of the database file and the path to it. In this case, the database file is named "Marinas.mdf." Since this uses the |DataDirectory| variable, that means that the Marinas.mdf file is located in the AppData folder in your Visual Studio 2012 Marina project.

Integrated Security=True means that we will use Windows integrated security to log in to our database. Windows integrated security is also known as Windows Authentication or Integrated Windows Authentication. This is more complicated than I want to go into here (see Microsoft 2014) for a discussion. The alternative is to employ a username and password to access the database, which you would do by setting the Integrated Security variable to false.

When we use providerName="System.Data.SqlClient," we are selecting the default .NET Framework data provider for SQL Server. A data provider is used to connect the SqlDataSource control to a data source.

12.2.4.3 Create Controller

The next step is to create the controller. This is shown in Figure 12.8. The name comes up as defaultController, and we replace that with Marinas controller.

FIGURE 12.8   Step 5. Create Marina controller.

FIGURE 12.9   Step 6: Look at automatically generated code in the Marina controller.

The code in the Controller is automatically generated, based on the model. This automatically generated code can be seen in Figure 12.9. See that a class named MarinasController has been created that is of type Controller. A database context named db is defined at the top of this class, this database context will allow us to access the database that will shortly be created.

As mentioned before, the various Create, Read, Update, Delete (CRUD) operations to access the database have been automatically generated and are located in the Controller. You can see the "Create" operation at the bottom of Figure 12.9. Some other useful operations have been created, we can see two of them here:

1. The Index controller operation will give a list of database items. Index is called by default when you access the Marina controller, or it can be called specifically.
2. The Details controller operation, with a parameter of "id," will list all the data inside one database record.

There are several others, we'll look at some in detail later on.

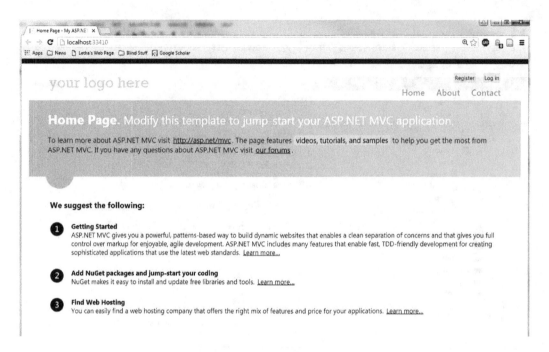

FIGURE 12.10   Step 8: See home page after start without debugging.

12.2.4.4   Do a Build Followed by Start without Debugging

Step 7 is the following: Now that you've created the model and controller, simply do a build and then select start without debugging. This will perform the scaffolding and create your database. As part of this, it will create files called Marinas.mdf and Marinas_log.ldf in the App_Data directory, which is one of the subdirectories of your project directory (your project directory shown here is called "example_with_model").

When you select start without debugging, your browser will come up at localhost on an arbitrary port number that is selected by Visual Studio (see Figure 12.10). You can do things in Visual Studio to force this port number to a particular port number instead of an arbitrarily chosen/random port number. Please just google for how to do that, or Bing if you're like that. For this version of Visual Studio, I googled for:

   visual 2012 asp.net mvc set port number

12.2.4.5   Examine Default Views of Marina Database

As it happened, when your scaffolding occurred, it created default views as well. See Figure 12.11 to see the Default views for the Marina database. These are in files of type cshtml. These are Razor files, which means they mix HTML with calls to C#. We're going to see how these views (using Razor) work, in a practical way, later on. If you recall, way back in Figure 12.2 you chose to use Razor views. So it's your fault!

Actually this is a good way to do views.

12.2.4.6   Enter Data in Database

Finally and at last we're ready to enter data in the database. To do this, we will select start without debugging, which will take us to the localhost with an arbitrary port number. In this particular situation, shown in Figure 12.12, we are at "localhost:33410." Now we need to select the Marinas

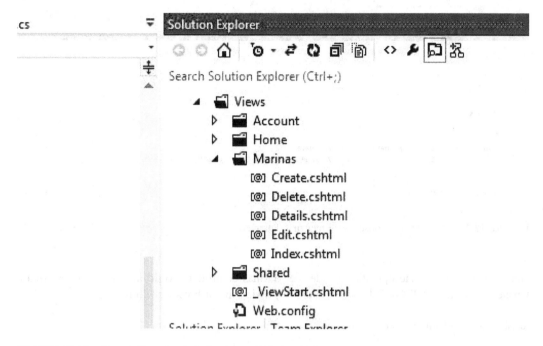

FIGURE 12.11 Step 9: Examine default views of Marina database.

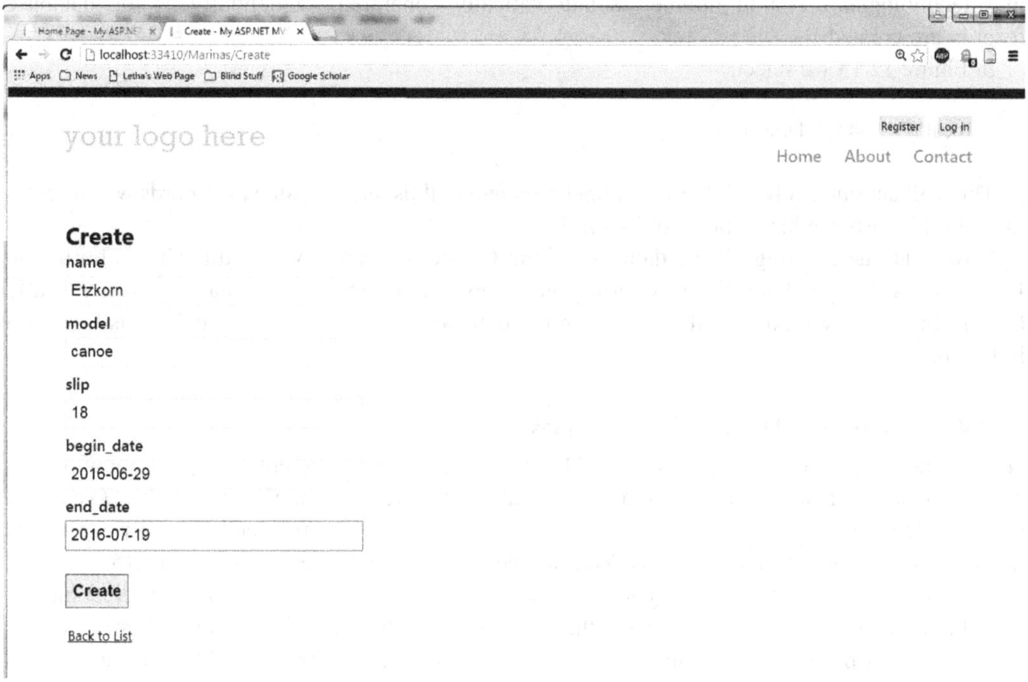

FIGURE 12.12 Step 10: Enter data in database.

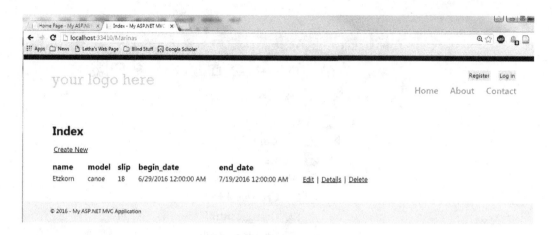

FIGURE 12.13   Step 11: Response after Enter first data record.

controller and the Create operation inside the Marinas controller. To do this, we add "/Marinas/ Create" to "localhost:33410." The total address showing in our browser will be:

localhost:33410/Marinas/Create

When we're doing this, we're really doing "routing" which is a way of mapping our calls to the correct controller. There's a lot more to "routing"—we're going to go into it more later on.

The Create operation is one of the automatically generated "CRUD" operations, and it allows us to enter one database record, that possesses one id number. In Figure 12.12, we see that we enter our standard data (we've been entering this same data all through the textbook in the various technologies). The id number is automatically generated, sequentially as the database records are created.

In Figure 12.13 we select:

localhost:33410/Marinas

This will automatically call the Index operation and will list all the database records we currently have. In this case, we have one record so far.

Now continue entering all the data by calling Create over and over again. This is boring so I won't show it to you here. I'll only show you the result of calling the Marina's controller (really Calling Index) so we can see all the data in the database after you've entered it. This is shown in Figure 12.14.

12.2.4.7   Show Data Directly from Database

Now we're going to look at the data in the Marina's database in a different way. Do a View servers explorer. Click on data connections. Show all the database contexts you have connected to. Then click on MarinaDBContext as that's the one we're working with (it's also conveniently the only one shown here). Click on Tables, then on Marinas. You can see the various data items in Figure 12.15: id, name, slip, begin_date, end_date (at least, you can sorta see them, they're partly behind the select menu). Note the little key symbol shown beside the id field, this indicates that this is the primary key of this database. A primary key has to have a unique value for each record in a table in a database, so it can be used to uniquely identify any particular record. Note that "slip" might be another possibility for primary key here, since typically in a Marina you can have only one sailboat in a particular slip.

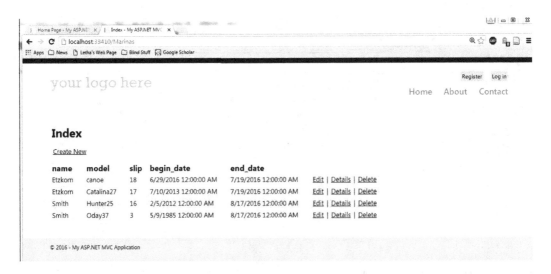

FIGURE 12.14 Step 12: Response after Entering all data.

FIGURE 12.15 Step 13: Select Show Table Data.

However, I'm not going to explain primary key further here, read your database textbooks, we're focusing on middleware! What we're using the id field for here will become clear soon enough.

Do a right click on Marinas, this will bring up the select menu that's shown in Figure 12.15, and select Show Table Data.

In Figure 12.16, we see all the data in this particular table in this database. (Loosely speaking, I've been calling this table [Marinas] our database.) Here you can see the id fields too, which you couldn't see earlier in Figure 12.2 when we did an index. (You could modify the Index controller to show you the id field, if you wanted to, but the automatically generated version doesn't do that.)

12.2.4.8 Use Other Default Views of Marina Database

Now we're going to examine how to use some of the other default views in the Marina database. We'll look at the Details view first. To see this, we access the Details controller. As you recall, this was automatically generated, see Listing 12.7.

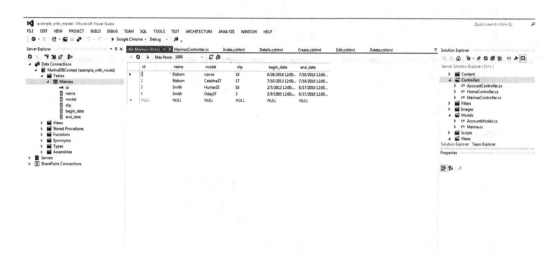

FIGURE 12.16   Step 14: Results showing the data.

LISTING 12.7   Details Controller

```
// GET: /Marinas/Details/5

public ActionResult Details(int id = 0)
   {
      Marina marina = db.Marinas.Find(id);
      if (marina == null)
         {
            return HttpNotFound();
         }
      return View(marina);
   }
```

As you can see from Listing 12.7, the routing path to reach this controller is done by sending an HTTP GET to "/Marinas/Details/5." Of course this has to be appended to the base URL, in our case this would be "1ocalhost:33410." Another way to do it would be to send an HTTP GET to "/Marinas/Details?id=5" which is what I generally do (see Figure 12.17). As you probably know by now from reading the earlier parts of this book, sending a GET is what your browser does best.☺ So we'll use our browser here (I'm using Chrome for these examples).

The Details controller returns an ActionResult data type.

Strictly speaking, the method that I tend to call the "Details controller" (lots of other people do this too) is really called an "Action Method" that is attached to a controller, in this case the MarinasController.

Action methods return ActionResults. There are several different possible ActionResults; for a complete list, see MSDN (2016a) and MSDN (2010a). However, a few of the important ones include those shown in Table 12.1.

The ViewResult class renders (that is, displays appropriately) a given View. An example of this is seen in Listing 12.7, where it calls:

```
return View(marina);
```

Details
name
Etzkorn
model
canoe
slip
18
begin_date
6/29/2016 12:00:00 AM
end_date
7/19/2016 12:00:00 AM

Edit | Back to List

FIGURE 12.17   Step 15: See details of an entry.

TABLE 12.1

Selected ActionResult Types and Associated Helper Methods

ActionResult Type	Associated Helper Method
ViewResult	View
RedirectResult	Redirect
JsonResult	Json
FileResult	File
HttpStatusCode	(none)

What it's doing here is returning an appropriate display (according to the appropriate Razor View) of a particular record in the database. The View() routine passes back an item of type ViewResult, which appropriately matches the ActionResult return type.

Other things it could return would be a RedirectResult, that is, a new web page that it will be redirected to immediately (we'll see an example of this later on), a JsonResult (as you might expect, this returns a result in JSON format) or a FileResult which returns a specified file. All of these map into the ActionResult return type, and are produced by the appropriate helper.

The HttpStatusCode is simply an indication of what happened relative to servicing an HTTP message. In this case, we have the code:

```
if (marina == null)
{
    return HttpNotFound();
}
```

So as you can see, if the particular item specified in the id variable does not exist in the database, it would return the HTTP 404, or not found, error message.

In Figure 12.18, we call the Index view explicitly. We've already seen this view, of course, it's the default, that is, it's what happens when you call the Marinas controller itself (we saw that back in Figure 12.14). This is just another way.

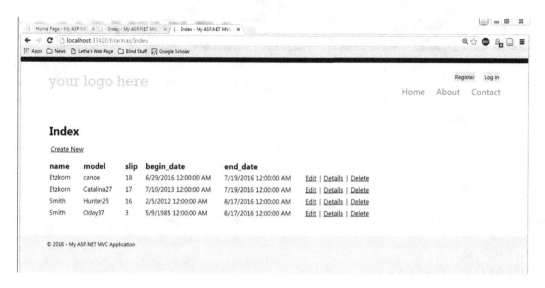

FIGURE 12.18   Step 16: See index of all entries.

FIGURE 12.19   Step 17: See Layout page.

12.2.4.9   Change Layout in Shared View

Now we're going to look at how to change something that applies across all the views. We'll do this by changing the layout view, which sets stuff that applies to all the other views. See Figure 12.19 to see the original Layout view before we change anything. You can see from the layout view that each web page will have clickable links called Home, About, and Contact, that can help the user navigate. You can also see a little item called "your logo here" about a third of the way

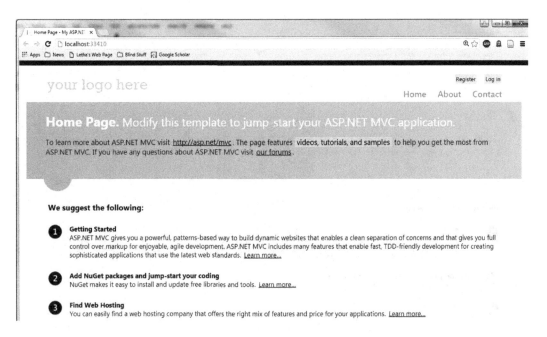

FIGURE 12.20 Step 18: See original home page, note logo area.

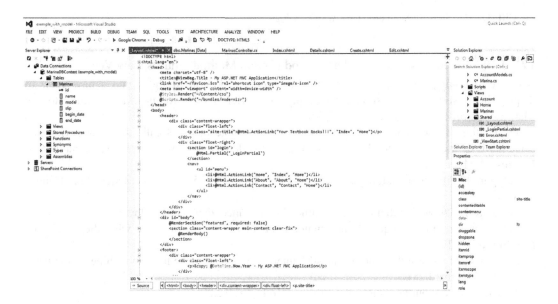

FIGURE 12.21 Step 19: Change logo in Layout page.

down the page. We're going to change that! Before we change it, however, look at Figure 12.20, it shows the original home page. See the "Your Logo Here" in big characters at the top.

Now we're going to change the logo to say "Your Textbook Rocks!!!" By changing this logo on the layout view, we're going to say "Your Textbook Rocks!!!" on all the pages, because of course, your textbook does rock.☺ You can see how we did this in Figure 12.21.

In Figure 12.22, we can see that, indeed, your textbook is now rocking. It says so!

If you check the other pages, you'll see that they also say your textbook rocks.

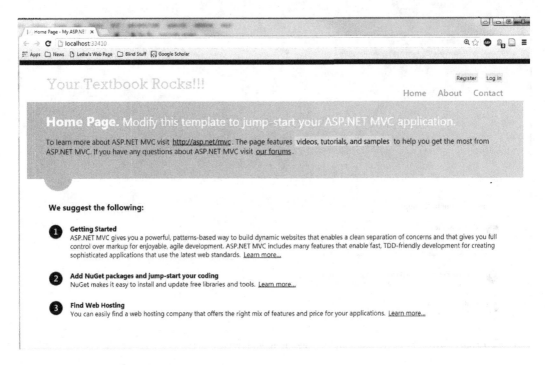

FIGURE 12.22   Step 20: See home page with new logo.

12.2.4.10   Create a New Controller Method (Action Method) and Its New View

Now we're going to create a new Controller Method (Action Method) and a new view to display it. First we will just add an empty controller named RequestMaintenance to the MarinasController.

We do this just by typing it in (see Figure 12.23). Note that this calls the default view the same name as the Controller Method, so we have to add a new view with that same name (see Figures 12.24 and 12.25).

In Figure 12.24, we start adding a new view, and in Figure 12.25 we add the RequestMaintenance view.

In Figure 12.26, we see that the new RequestMaintenance view really is there.

Let's run our simple RequestMaintenance controller and view and see what they look like (see Figure 12.27).

Now let's add some stuff to our RequestMaintenance view to make it do something a little more useful (see Figure 12.28).

Now let's look at our new view after it runs (see Figure 12.29).

12.2.5   Add Asynchronous Controller to Marina Project in ASP.NET MVC4

Okay, we're done with simply getting started with our Marina project in ASP.NET MVC using Visual Studio 2012. Now we'll add the asynchronous RequestMaintenance controller.

12.2.5.1   Scheduling Maintenance Using PHP Server

Our first example assumes that a separate PHP server is running to handle our asynchronous request. (Note: when I tested this, I used the Apache Web Server to run the PHP code.) The PHP code does sleep in the middle. This is meant to simulate a delay in finding the appropriate

FIGURE 12.23 Step 21: Add RequestMaintenance to controller.

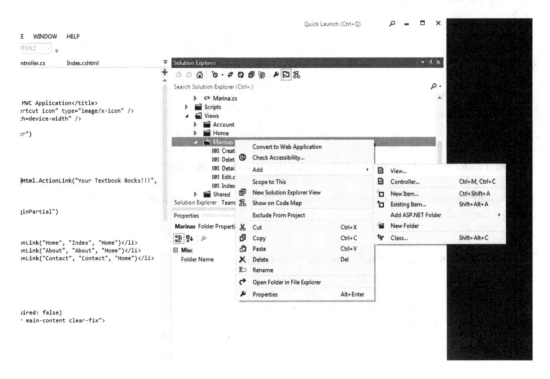

FIGURE 12.24 Step 22: Create a new view.

FIGURE 12.25   Step 23: New view will be RequestMaintenance view.

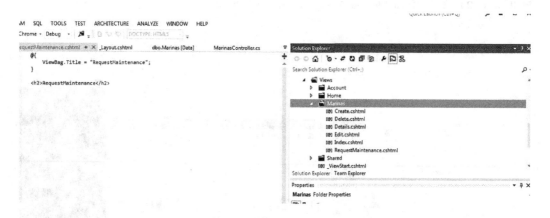

FIGURE 12.26   Step 24: See RequestMaintenance view is added to Marina DB views.

maintenance person. I've put this in seconds, but in practice in a real marina it would more likely be days (or weeks).

LISTING 12.8   **Simple PHP Schedule Maintenance Server**

```php
<?php
    $mydata = $_REQUEST["mydata"];
    sleep(5);
    print "Hi, $mydata! Your maintenance person will be George. He is available next
    Tuesday.";
?>
```

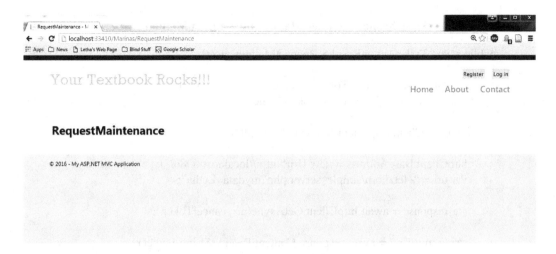

FIGURE 12.27   Step 25: Run original RequestMaintenance view.

FIGURE 12.28   Step 26: Change RequestMaintenance view.

Now in Listing 12.9, I show an asynchronous controller (of course this really is an Action Method but we'll continue loosely to call these controllers) that calls the PHP server to schedule maintenance.

Note first that it is specified as an "async" task. (It has to do that in order to do an "await." We'll talk about "await" in just a minute. Also note that instead of returning an ActionResult, it returns a task that operates on an ActionResult data type.

Note that here we're not looking at how asynchronous calls really really work, instead we're looking more at the syntax of asynchronous calls. Later, in Section 12.2.6, we'll look at how asynchronous calls really work when using ASP.NET MVC.

In Listing 12.9, we first define a Cancellation Token. This will contain information about what failed, if the HTTP call to the PHP server doesn't go through.

LISTING 12.9   Asynchronous RequestMaintenance Action Method

```
public async Task<ActionResult> RequestMaintenance()
{
    CancellationToken cancelToken = default(CancellationToken);
    var cancelToken = CancellationToken.None;

    using (HttpClient httpClient = new HttpClient())
    {
        httpClient.BaseAddress = new Uri("http://localhost:8080/");
        var uri = "~letzkorn/simple_server.php?mydata=Letha";

        var response = await httpClient.GetAsync(uri, cancelToken);

        string mystring = await response.Content.ReadAsStringAsync();
        ViewBag.myHtml = mystring;
    }
    return View();
}
```

Then we create an Http client. This is used to send HTTP messages to a server. We set the base address of the PHP server. Then we set the URI that is the specific address of the server. To run this, you'll have to change this URI to be your own URI, based on where your Apache web server (assuming you use the Apache web server to run your PHP file like I did) is set up.

Here the PHP code from Listing 12.8 is stored in a file named simple_server.php. We'll be using an HTTP GET. I passed it my own name, "Letha." Please pass your own name instead. ☺ We don't need a lot of Letha's whizzing around the ether.

In the next statement, we're going to do an "await" on an asynchronous GET:

    var response = await httpClient.GetAsync(uri, cancelToken);

The "await" here will block the current thread until the GetAsync returns, so in terms of asynchronous operation it's kind of useless. However, note that we don't set a particular data type on the "response"

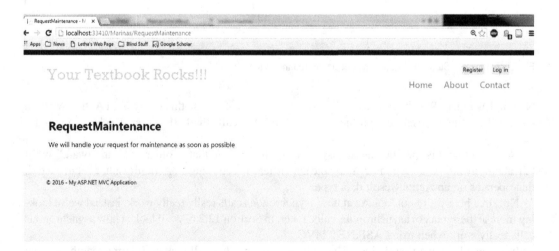

FIGURE 12.29   Step 27: Run new RequestMaintenance view.

variable, instead we're using a general "var" without a particular specified type. Using a "var" together with an "await" can save you a lot of effort in figuring out the particular return types of functions. That's one good reason sometimes to use "awaits" even if you're not really doing asynchronous work. In this case, the GetAsync is going to return a Task<HttpResponseMessage>, but I didn't have to specify the type for the response.

In the next statement:

    string mystring = await response.Content.ReadAsStringAsync();

"Content" is a property of HttpResponseMessage that returns the value in the message. ReadAsStringAsync will then return that content as a string.

Next we're stuffing this string into a ViewBag variable:

    ViewBag.myHtml = mystring;

A ViewBag is a way to send a small amount of data from a controller to a view. (There's another related item called ViewData but for our purposes we can focus on ViewBag.)

We're going to use this data item named "myHtml" to send data from our new RequestMaintenance controller to our new RequestMaintenance view, see Listing 12.10.

LISTING 12.10   New RequestMaintenance View Using ViewBag

```
@{
    ViewBag.Title = "RequestMaintenance";
}
<h2>RequestMaintenance</h2>
    <p>@ViewBag.myHTML</p>
    <p>@Html.ActionLink("Home," "Index," "Home")</p>
```

In Figure 12.30, we see the results after we access our new RequestMaintenance controller.

12.2.5.2 Scheduling Maintenance Using Internal ASP.NET MVC4 Server

Next we're going to move the Scheduling Maintenance server back inside ASP.NET MVC. The code to do this is shown in Listing 12.11.

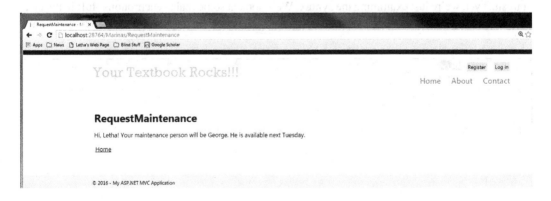

FIGURE 12.30   After Run New RequestMaintenance view for Async PHP.

LISTING 12.11   Scheduling Maintenance Server Inside ASP.NET MVC

```
public async Task<string> mystuff(string myname)
{
    await Task.Delay(5000);
    string mystring = "! Your maintenance person will be Sabrina. She is available next
        Friday.";
    mystring = "Hi, " + myname + mystring;
    return mystring;
}

public async Task<ActionResult> RequestMaintenance()
{
    string myname = "Letha";
    var response = mystuff(myname);
    var mystring = await response;
    ViewBag.myHtml = mystring;
    return View();
}
```

Here, the code in the RequestMaintenance controller (action method) is much simpler than in the previous example, because it's calling a local action method rather than a remote server.

I called the local action method "mystuff." By the way, note that by convention (established by Microsoft) all asynchronous methods are supposed to end in the characters "async." Well, that kind of convention is important when you have some routines that are the same except one is run async and the other is run synchronously. Since we're not doing that here, I allowed myself to rebel. ☺

There's a nice big delay in mystuff. It's attempting to simulate the asynchronousness of it all. (By the way, the await on the Task.Delay is blocking the current thread until the Task.Delay returns.) Note that mystuff is returning Task<string>. It has to return a Task because it's async but it returns a string because it only needs a simple value returned.

You can actually access the mystuff controller direct via the web (see Figure 12.31), you don't have to necessarily go through RequestMaintenance.

In the RequestMaintenance controller itself, the line:

```
var mystring = await response;
```

blocks the current thread waiting on the mystuff to return. So we're not doing a lot of really asynchronous stuff yet, we're just examining the syntax. We'll look at some real asynchronous stuff in the next section. See Figure 12.32 where we access RequestMaintenance using the web browser.

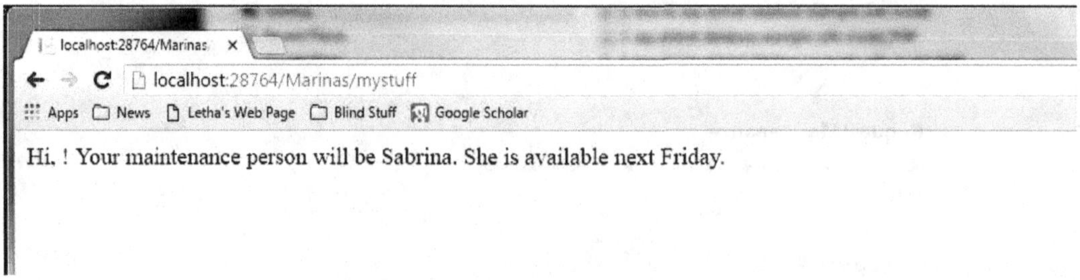

localhost:28764/Marinas   ×

← → C   localhost:28764/Marinas/mystuff

Apps   News   Letha's Web Page   Blind Stuff   Google Scholar

Hi, ! Your maintenance person will be Sabrina. She is available next Friday.

FIGURE 12.31   Access mystuff controller (Action Method) direct.

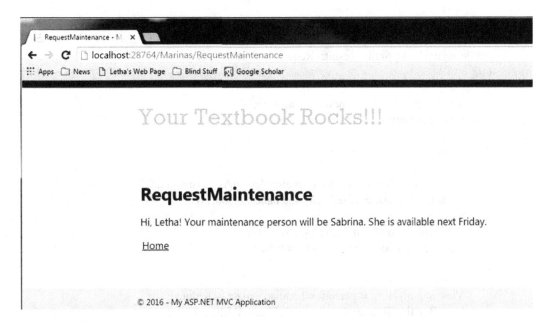

FIGURE 12.32   Access RequestMaintenance direct.

12.2.6   How Asynchronous Calls Really Work in ASP.NET MVC

Okay, now we've looked at the syntax and flow for asynchronous calls. Let's look at some examples that really illustrate asynchronous operation.

12.2.6.1   Simple Asynchronous Example

In Listing 12.12, I've broken the maintenance server task into two separate Action Methods, one to choose which person will do the maintenance, and one to schedule that person. This will make for a slightly more interesting set of operations.

Note that choosing a maintenance person delays for 2 seconds and scheduling a maintenance person delays for 5 seconds. These are important because we are going to compare asynchronous operation to synchronous operation by how their timing works.

LISTING 12.12   **Separate ChooseMaintenance and ScheduleMaintenance Action Methods**

```
public async Task<string> chooseMaintenancePersonAsync(string myname)
{
    await Task.Delay(2000);
    string mystring = "! Your maintenance person will be Sabrina. ";
    mystring = "Hi, " + myname+ mystring;
    return mystring;
}

public async Task<string> scheduleMaintenancepersonAsync()
{
    await Task.Delay(5000);
    string myotherstring = "She is available after 3pm next Friday.";
    return myotherstring;
}
```

LISTING 12.13   Asynchronous RequestMaintenance

```
public async Task<ActionResult> RequestMaintenanceAsync()
{

     Stopwatch mywatch = new Stopwatch();
     mywatch.Start();

     string myname = "Letha";

     var chooseTask = chooseMaintenancePersonAsync(myname);
     var scheduleTask = scheduleMaintenancepersonAsync();

     var person_scheduled = await chooseTask;
     var date_scheduled = await scheduleTask;

     mywatch.Stop();
     ViewBag.myHtml = person_scheduled + date_scheduled;
     ViewBag.timeRequired = mywatch.ElapsedMilliseconds;

     return View();
}
```

LISTING 12.14   Synchronous RequestMaintenance

```
public ActionResult RequestMaintenanceSync()
{
     Stopwatch mywatch = new Stopwatch();
     mywatch.Start();

     string myname = "Letha";

     var person_scheduled= chooseMaintenancePerson(myname);
     var date_scheduled = scheduleMaintenanceperson();

     mywatch.Stop();

     ViewBag.myHtml = person_scheduled + date_scheduled;
     ViewBag.timeRequired = mywatch.ElapsedMilliseconds;

     return View();
}
```

The Views for RequestMaintenanceSync and RequestMaintenanceAsync are shown in Listings 12.15 and 12.16. They're the same, but are in separate views to make the two RequestMaintenance action methods simpler.

LISTING 12.15 RequestMaintenanceAsync View

```
@{
   ViewBag.Title = "RequestMaintenance";
}
@model string
<h2>RequestMaintenance</h2>
      <p>@ViewBag.myHTML</p>
      <p>The Time Required in milliseconds was: @ViewBag.timeRequired</p>
      <p>@Html.ActionLink("Home", "Index", "Home")</p>
```

LISTING 12.16 RequestMaintenanceSync View

```
@{
   ViewBag.Title = "RequestMaintenance";
}
<h2>RequestMaintenance</h2>
      <p>@ViewBag.myHTML</p>
      <p>The Time Required in milliseconds was: @ViewBag.timeRequired</p>
      <p>@Html.ActionLink("Home", "Index", "Home")</p>
```

In both our synchronous and asynchronous RequestMaintenance action methods we are going to use a stopwatch. We create and start the stopwatch as follows:

```
Stopwatch mywatch = new Stopwatch();
mywatch.Start();
```

We stop the stopwatch as follows:

```
mywatch.Stop();
```

Then we grab the results from the watch timing as follows:

```
ViewBag.timeRequired = mywatch.ElapsedMilliseconds;
```

For completeness, note that there is another stopwatch action that we'll use later on, it resets the watch (a Stop() won't reset the watch), but we won't be using this in this particular example:

```
mywatch.Reset();
```

We're going to time the calls to the chooseMaintenance action method and the scheduleMaintenance action method.

Let's look first at the synchronous RequestMaintenance. We're calling the chooseMaintenance action method and the scheduleMaintenance action method as follows:

```
var person_scheduled = chooseMaintenancePerson(myname);
var date_scheduled = scheduleMaintenanceperson();
```

Note that we're not using any "await"s (of course we're not using the "async" keyword anywhere either). So this is all synchronous. So we call "chooseMaintenancePerson(myname)" first and then call "scheduleMaintenanceperson()" afterward. Since "chooseMaintenancePerson(myname)" takes about 2 seconds to run and "scheduleMaintenanceperson" takes about 5 seconds to run, so the whole thing will take about 7 seconds. This is what happened—see Figure 12.33.

Now let's look at the Asynchronous RequestMaintenance. In this we first call:

```
var chooseTask = chooseMaintenancePersonAsync(myname);
var scheduleTask = scheduleMaintenancepersonAsync();
```

The calls start asynchronously, and pass back Task<ActionResult> tasks.
Then we do an "await" on the results of those passed-back tasks:

```
var person_scheduled = await chooseTask;
var date_scheduled = await scheduleTask;
```

The results of running the asynchronous RequestMaintenance are shown in Figure 12.34. Whooptedo! We finished in about 5 seconds this time! So clearly the chooseMaintenance action method and the scheduleMaintenance action method were running at the same time. The longer of the two was the scheduleMaintenance action method, which required 5 seconds, so that's the one that dominated the time.

12.2.6.2 (Async or Sync?) Example Using Two PHP Servers

Now let's expand our original PHP example. Here we have two separate PHP servers, one to choose a maintenance person and one to assign that maintenance person. Each takes 5 seconds.

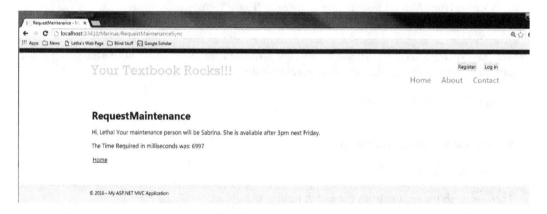

FIGURE 12.33 Results of running synchronous RequestMaintenance.

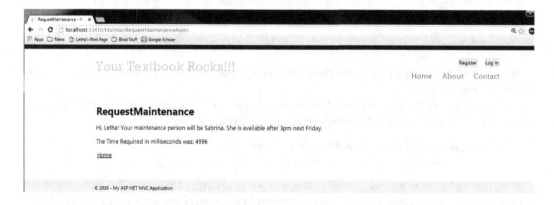

FIGURE 12.34 Results of running asynchronous RequestMaintenance.

LISTING 12.17 Separate PHP ChooseMaintenance Action Method

```php
<?php
  $mydata = $_REQUEST["mydata"];
  sleep(5);
  print "Hi, $mydata! Your maintenance person will be Julie.";
?>
```

LISTING 12.18 Separate ScheduleMaintenance Action Method

```php
<?php
  $mydata = $_REQUEST["mydata"];
  sleep(5);
  print " She is available after 2pm next Tuesday.";
?>
```

LISTING 12.19 RequestMaintenance Action Method

```csharp
public async Task<ActionResult> RequestMaintenance()
  {
    CancellationToken cancelToken = default(CancellationToken);
    using (HttpClient httpClient = new HttpClient())
    {
      httpClient.BaseAddress = new Uri("http://localhost:8080/");
      var uriA = "~letzkorn/chooseMaintenancePerson.php?mydata=Letha";
      var uriB = "~letzkorn/scheduleMaintenancePerson.php";
      Stopwatch mywatch = new Stopwatch();
      Stopwatch myotherwatch = new Stopwatch();
      myotherwatch.Start();
      mywatch.Start();
      var response = await httpClient.GetAsync(uriA, cancelToken);
      mywatch.Stop();
      ViewBag.timeRequiredA = mywatch.ElapsedMilliseconds;
      mywatch.Reset();
      mywatch.Start();
      var scheduleTask = await httpClient.GetAsync(uriB, cancelToken);
      mywatch.Stop();
      ViewBag.timeRequiredB = mywatch.ElapsedMilliseconds;
      mywatch.Reset();
      myotherwatch.Stop();
      ViewBag.timeRequiredE = myotherwatch.ElapsedMilliseconds;
      mywatch.Start();
      var person_scheduled = await response.Content.ReadAsStringAsync();
      mywatch.Stop();
      ViewBag.timeRequiredC = mywatch.ElapsedMilliseconds;
      mywatch.Reset();
```

```
            mywatch.Start();
            var date_scheduled = await scheduleTask.Content.ReadAsStringAsync();
            mywatch.Stop();
            ViewBag.timeRequiredD = mywatch.ElapsedMilliseconds;
            mywatch.Reset();

            ViewBag.myHtml = person_scheduled + date_scheduled;

        }

        return View();
    }
```

What we're doing in Listing 12.19 is we're calling two PHP servers:

```
        var response = await httpClient.GetAsync(uriA, cancelToken);
        var scheduleTask = await httpClient.GetAsync(uriB, cancelToken);
```

Then we're waiting for the response from both servers:

```
        var person_scheduled = await response.Content.ReadAsStringAsync();
        var date_scheduled = await scheduleTask.Content.ReadAsStringAsync();
```

It's just we're measuring each call separately. The timeRequiredA measures the first GetAsync. The timeRequiredB measures the second GetAsync. The timeRequiredC measures the first ReadAsStringAsync, while the timeRequiredD measures the second ReadAsStringAsync.

The timeRequiredE measures both of the GetAsync calls taken together.

The results are shown in Figure 12.35.

It required 10+ seconds to run the two PHP servers. So this was not asynchronous!

Can you figure out why? (*Hint*: I think there were some extra "awaits" there.)

12.2.7 REDIRECT

Now we're going to look at a few other things related to ASP.NET MVC. We're going to look at how to do a Redirect (you remember we briefly mentioned redirect before in Section 12.2.4).

As you recall, when a web page redirects, what it does it open a different web page at a different URL.

LISTING 12.20   Action Methods to Illustrate Redirect

```
    public async Task<ActionResult> RedirectExampleOne()
    {
        return RedirectToAction("Index");
    }

    public async Task<ActionResult> RedirectExampleTwo()
    {
        return RedirectToAction("mystuff," new { myname = "Letha" });
    }
```

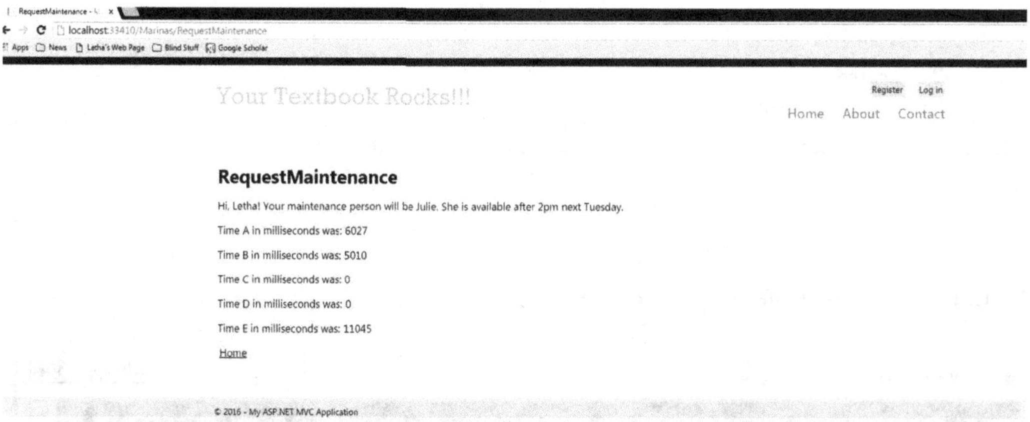

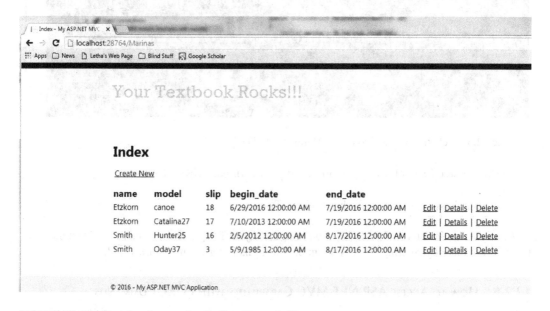

FIGURE 12.35   Results from two PHP server example.

FIGURE 12.36   Results after running RedirectExampleOne.

Note that several of the automatically generated action methods in the Marina controller already do a Redirect. However, the code around the Redirect in those methods was extraneous to our main discussion here, and possibly could confuse the issue, so I made a couple of simplified calls to redirect in two new action methods. These are called RedirectExampleOne() and RedirectExampleTwo() and are shown in Listing 12.20.

The first action method here (RedirectExampleOne) redirects to the Index page. In the second action method here (RedirectExampleTwo) it redirects to the action method "mystuff" that you previously saw in Listing 12.11.

To call RedirectExampleOne, you do (insert your own base URL here):

http://localhost:28764/Marinas/RedirectExampleOne

After you run RedirectExampleOne you're back at the Index page, and you can't see from the URL that you got there by running RedirectExampleOne, this is shown in Figure 12.36.

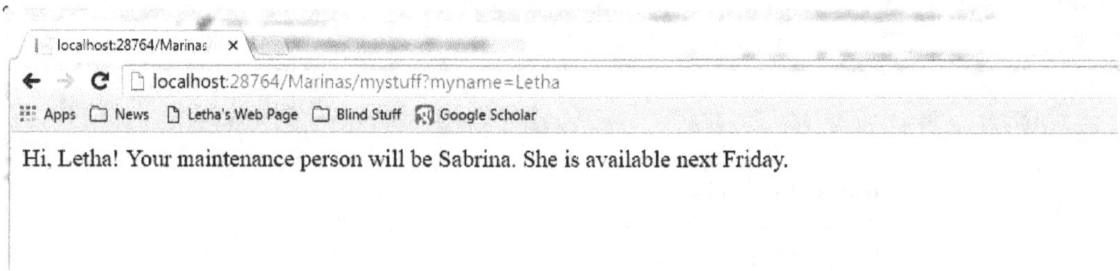

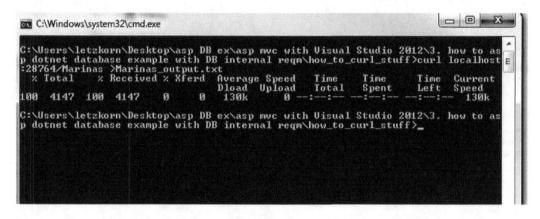

The browser shows:

localhost:28764/Marinas/mystuff?myname=Letha

Apps News Letha's Web Page Blind Stuff Google Scholar

Hi, Letha! Your maintenance person will be Sabrina. She is available next Friday.

FIGURE 12.37   Results after running RedirectExampleTwo.

FIGURE 12.38   cURL command to access Marina controller.

To call RedirectExampleTwo, you do (insert your own base URL here):

http://localhost:28764/Marinas/RedirectExampleTwo

After you run RedirectExampleTwo you're at the mystuff page, and you can't see from the URL that you got there by running RedirectExampleTwo, this is shown in Figure 12.37.

12.2.8 How to Access ASP.NET MVC Capabilities with cURL Commands

We've been using a browser (in my case Chrome) so far to access our ASP.NET MVC code. However, it's possible to use many other clients. We want to look at how to send other HTTP commands than GET to our ASP.NET MVC code, so we really need something different from a simple browser. It's possible to install browser extensions to do this, and it's also possible to do it in Java-Script (remember XMLHttpRequest?). However, since we've used cURL commands before for this purpose (see Section 4.12), let's use cURL now. (Getting some practice with cURL with also help you understand the cloud computing sections in this textbook.)

Let's first look at simple use of cURL to access our already existing controllers/action methods/ associated views. We will access the Marina controller itself first, using the following cURL command (remember that the cURL command sends an HTTP GET by default):

curl localhost:28764/Marinas >Marinas_output.txt

What this looks like when we run it is shown in Figure 12.38. The results from this command were placed in the Marinas_output.txt file, this is shown in Listing 12.21. As you can see, this is simply the web page that was rendered by the View. (Remember that the Index view is the default view when you call Marinas.) This can be a good debugging technique in that you can see exactly what HTML your web page is created. Note that the output is in HTML5, we can tell that from the "<!DOCTYPE html>" line at the top.

LISTING 12.21   Contents of Marinas_output.txt File after running cURL Command

```
<!DOCTYPE html>
<html lang="en">
  <head>
    <meta charset="utf-8" />
    <title>Index - My ASP.NET MVC Application</title>
    <link href="/favicon.ico" rel="shortcut icon" type="image/x-icon" />
    <meta name="viewport" content="width=device-width" />
    <link href="/Content/site.css" rel="stylesheet"/>
    <script src="/Scripts/modernizr-2.6.2.js"></script>
  </head>
  <body>
    <header>
      <div class="content-wrapper">
        <div class="float-left">
          <p class="site-title"><a href="/">Your Textbook Rocks!!!</a></p>
        </div>
        <div class="float-right">
          <section id="login">
            <ul>
                <li><a href="/Account/Register" id="registerLink">Register</a></li>
                <li><a href="/Account/Login" id="loginLink">Log in</a></li>
            </ul>
          </section>
          <nav>
            <ul id="menu">
                <li><a href="/">Home</a></li>
                <li><a href="/Home/About">About</a></li>
                <li><a href="/Home/Contact">Contact</a></li>
            </ul>
          </nav>
        </div>
      </div>
    </header>
    <div id="body">

      <section class="content-wrapper main-content clear-fix">

  <h2>Index</h2>
    <p>
  <a href="/Marinas/Create">Create New</a>
</p>
<table>
  <tr>
    <th>
```

```
            name
        </th>
        <th>
            model
        </th>
        <th>
            slip
        </th>
        <th>
            begin_date
        </th>
        <th>
            end_date
        </th>
        <th></th>
    </tr>
    <tr>
        <td>
            Etzkorn
        </td>
        <td>
            canoe
        </td>
        <td>
            18
        </td>
        <td>
            6/29/2016 12:00:00 AM
        </td>
        <td>
            7/19/2016 12:00:00 AM
        </td>
        <td>
            <a href="/Marinas/Edit/1">Edit</a> |
            <a href="/Marinas/Details/1">Details</a> |
            <a href="/Marinas/Delete/1">Delete</a>
        </td>
    </tr>
    <tr>
        <td>
            Etzkorn
        </td>
        <td>
            Catalina27
        </td>
        <td>
            17
        </td>
```

```
      <td>
          7/10/2013 12:00:00 AM
      </td>
      <td>
          7/19/2016 12:00:00 AM
      </td>
      <td>
          <a href="/Marinas/Edit/2">Edit</a> |
          <a href="/Marinas/Details/2">Details</a> |
          <a href="/Marinas/Delete/2">Delete</a>
      </td>
  </tr>
  <tr>
      <td>
          Smith
      </td>
      <td>
          Hunter25
      </td>
      <td>
          16
      </td>
      <td>
          2/5/2012 12:00:00 AM
      </td>
      <td>
          8/17/2016 12:00:00 AM
      </td>
      <td>
          <a href="/Marinas/Edit/3">Edit</a> |
          <a href="/Marinas/Details/3">Details</a> |
          <a href="/Marinas/Delete/3">Delete</a>
      </td>
  </tr>
  <tr>
      <td>
          Smith
      </td>
      <td>
          Oday37
      </td>
      <td>
          3
      </td>
      <td>
          5/9/1985 12:00:00 AM
      </td>
      <td>
          8/17/2016 12:00:00 AM
```

```
        </td>
        <td>
          <a href="/Marinas/Edit/4">Edit</a> |
          <a href="/Marinas/Details/4">Details</a> |
          <a href="/Marinas/Delete/4">Delete</a>
        </td>
     </tr>
  </table>
        </section>
        </div>
        <footer>
          <div class="content-wrapper">
            <div class="float-left">
               <p>&copy; 2016 - My ASP.NET MVC Application</p>
            </div>
          </div>
        </footer>
        <script src="/Scripts/jquery-1.8.2.js"></script>

     </body>
  </html>
```

Now use the following cURL command to access the "mystuff" action method in the MarinasController:

> curl localhost:28764/Marinas/mystuff?myname=Letha

Please do substitute your own name, or we'll just have too many "Letha"s in the ether. Sigh. The results of running this cURL command are shown in Figure 12.39.

12.2.9 Access Controller Using HTTP Commands Other than GET

Okay, now that we know how to use cURL commands to access the Marina controller and all its action methods, let's look at how to send different kinds of HTTP commands and have them handled in the controller.

A simple controller action method set up to receive HTTP Put messages is shown in Listing 12.22. The "[HttpPut]" here is an example of an annotation. We could instead have done "[HttpPost]" or "[HttpDelete]" if we had needed to handle those kinds of HTTP commands.

FIGURE 12.39   cURL command to access mystuff action method and its results.

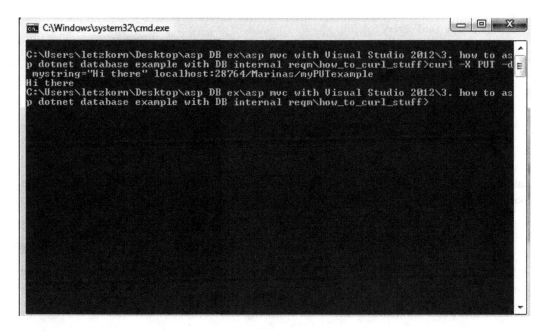

FIGURE 12.40   cURL command to send PUT to Marina's controller.

LISTING 12.22   Controller Action Method Annotated with HttpPut

```
[HttpPut]
public string myPUTexample(string mystring)
{
    return mystring;
}
```

We now use the following cURL command to send a PUT to this controller action method:

    curl –X Put –d mystring="Hi there" localhost:28764/Marinas/myPUTexample

This cURL command and its results are shown in Figure 12.40.

Note that there are some [HttpPost] examples in the automatically generated controller code. For example, there's an Edit action method that is accessed using an Http GET and there's another Edit action method that is accessed using a POST. Play around with these, and see how they differ.

One of these automatically generated action methods is shown in Listing 12.23. Note the annotation "ActionName("Delete")" associated with this.

**LISTING 12.23   Automatically Generated Action Method for Delete Receiving
                Http Post**

```
//
// POST: /Marinas/Delete/5

[HttpPost, ActionName("Delete")]
```

```
[ValidateAntiForgeryToken]
public ActionResult DeleteConfirmed(int id)
{
    Marina marina = db.Marinas.Find(id);
    db.Marinas.Remove(marina);
    db.SaveChanges();
    return RedirectToAction("Index");
}
```

Earlier in the file, there was an action method for a Delete that was accessed using a Get. Its header looked like this:

```
// GET: /Marinas/Delete/5
public ActionResult Delete(int id = 0)
```

So the action method in Listing 12.23 must have a different name "DeleteConfirmed." But you want to always access all your delete routines using the same URL, something like:

http://localhost:28764/Marinas/Delete

So to allow the code in Listing 12.23 to be accessed using this URL, the "DeleteConfirmed" action method is given an alias using "ActionName." But the code in Listing 12.23 is called only when an HttpPost is used.

While we're looking at Listing 12.23, let's discuss the "[ValidateAntiForgeryToken]." This is trying to prevent cross-site request forgery, in which malicious code is sent using a trusted user's credentials, often by convincing the user to click on a form containing the malicious code, or by loading that form when the page loads. The antiforgery token is a cookie that is generated in the trusted user's original form. Then if a different form is submitted, the cookie value doesn't match the trusted user's cookie, and an error is raised.

12.2.10   ROUTING IN ASP.NET MVC

"Routing" in the ASP.NET MVC world refers to mapping incoming requests to a resource, in the case of ASP.NET MVC, the resource would be an action method on a controller. It's often compared to "URL rewriting" (URL rewriting is often used to map messy looking cryptic URLs to URLs that can easily be remembered).

The basic idea of routing, in regard to what we've been seeing so far in ASP.NET MVC, is that instead of having to use the actual name of the controller and action method in a URL, you can use a different URL that is more descriptive of what you're trying to do. Or you can use multiple different URLs. There's more to it than this, and routing applies to all ASP.NET and not just ASP.NET MVC, but in this textbook we're sticking with the basic concepts only as they apply to ASP.NET MVC.

In a specified URL, you can use specific names of controllers and action methods, as we've been doing:

http://1ocalhost:33410/Marinas/RequestMaintenance

Here our base URL is: http://localhost:33410
And our controller/action method is: /Marinas/RequestMaintenance
When you specify URL patterns, as they apply to how an action method on a controller is called, you can do a specific URL like this. Or you can use variables called "placeholders" that can match

more than one controller, more than one action method, or more than one id parameter, such as the following:

{controller}/{action}/{id}

The default routes are configured in the RouteConfig.cs class, which is in the App_Start folder. This class from the current example is shown in Listing 12.24.

LISTING 12.24   RouteConfig Class

```
using System;
using System.Collections.Generic;
using System.Linq;
using System.Web;
using System.Web.Mvc;
using System.Web.Routing;
namespace example_with_model
{
    public class RouteConfig
    {
        public static void RegisterRoutes(RouteCollection routes)
        {
            routes.IgnoreRoute("{resource}.axd/{*pathInfo}");
            routes.MapRoute(
                name: "Default,"
                url: "{controller}/{action}/{id},"
                defaults: new { controller = "Home," action = "Index," id = UrlParameter.Optional }
            );
        }
    }
}
```

What the code in Listing 12.24 does is register the default routes. Here, we see that the default route is the Index page. You can modify this code to add your own routes. Just add additional calls to routes. MapRoute in this class in the RouteConfig.cs file. Add them above the default route in the class.

Each route is evaluated in order, the first route that matches the incoming URL is the one used.

You can do routing through annotations (this is called *attribute routing*), for example:

[Route ("myroute")]

or

[Route ("myroute/mystuff")]

or

[Route ("myroute/mystuff/{id}")]

etc.

These would typically be applied to an action method.

You can apply a route to the controller itself, for example, you could apply the following to the controller:

[RoutePrefix ("mybasicurl")]

If you do this, then all the action methods in the controller would be accessible as follows:

http://baseurl/mybasicurl/actionmethodname

(Of course, you can override the action method name using a Route command.)

You can also put constraints on values. For example, you can specify that an id field (parameter passed in) is an int, or a double, or etc. However, I won't go into that further here.

12.2.11   HTML HELPERS

Our focus in this textbook is the middleware that enables us to connect between distributed computers. However, sometimes we have to do some work with display technologies to allow us to see what is going on, because, especially with some of the web services, the display technologies are so intimately related with the distributing computing technologies being used. This is partly why we had to cover HTML and the like back in Chapter 4.

Here we're going to look at display-related functions that are used heavily in ASP.NET MVC: HTML Helpers. These mirror various basic html tags.

In the Razor views, which mix html and calls to C#, it is arguable that the HTML Helpers aren't all that useful—why not just use the html itself? But prior to Razor they were very important, and in any case it's traditional now to use them in ASP.NET, and besides, they're all over the place in the automatically generated code.

The code in Listing 12.25 is the automatically generated code for the Create view. So far I've been considering that you could just sort of figure out what's going on here. But now let's look at this in more depth.

As you recall, every time we have an "@" sign in Razor that represents a call to C# code. We start out here in Listing 12.25 in the first statement passing our Marina model to the Create view, this is done with the following statement:

@model example_with_model.Models.Marina

Note that there's nothing magical about this particular model. We could pass any model to this view. We could also pass a model consisting of a simple data type such as string to a view. Before we go on and look further at our automatically generated Create view, let's look quickly at how this would work. We could pass a string as a model to a view using the following statement:

@model string

Then instead of using a ViewBag like we did earlier, we can pass this to our RequestMaintenance view (see Figure 12.41). It would work much the same as our earlier ViewBag data.

Now, however, let's get back to our automatically generated Create view in Listing 12.25. You should notice calls similar to the following:

@Html.LabelFor(model => model.name)
@Html.EditorFor(model => model.name)
@Html.ValidationMessageFor(model => model.model)

In fact, these are all over the place in this code!

FIGURE 12.41   Pass a simple string model to a View.

As I mentioned before, these are called HTML Helper functions. Some of these are the same as basic HTML forms, but others do additional work. In any case, it's clear that for you to really understand what these Views in ASP.NET MVC are doing, you'll have to have an understanding of these. We will go through several HTML helpers and describe how they work. We won't do an exhaustive look at all of them, but we'll do enough that you will be functional.

We'll look at these in most cases by adding them to the existing views, it just makes it easier and sidesteps a few Visual Studio type issues here and there.

LISTING 12.25   Automatically Generated Create View

```
@model example_with_model.Models.Marina
@{
    ViewBag.Title = "Create";
}

<h2>Create</h2>
@using (Html.BeginForm()) {
    @Html.AntiForgeryToken()
    @Html.ValidationSummary(true)
    <fieldset>
        <legend>Marina</legend>
        <div class="editor-label">
            @Html.LabelFor(model => model.name)
        </div>
        <div class="editor-field">
            @Html.EditorFor(model => model.name)
            @Html.ValidationMessageFor(model => model.name)
        </div>
        <div class="editor-label">
            @Html.LabelFor(model => model.model)
        </div>
```

```
      <div class="editor-field">
        @Html.EditorFor(model => model.model)
        @Html.ValidationMessageFor(model => model.model)
      </div>
      <div class="editor-label">
        @Html.LabelFor(model => model.slip)
      </div>
      <div class="editor-field">
        @Html.EditorFor(model => model.slip)
        @Html.ValidationMessageFor(model => model.slip)
      </div>
      <div class="editor-label">
        @Html.LabelFor(model => model.begin_date)
      </div>
      <div class="editor-field">
        @Html.EditorFor(model => model.begin_date)
        @Html.ValidationMessageFor(model => model.begin_date)
      </div>
      <div class="editor-label">
        @Html.LabelFor(model => model.end_date)
      </div>
      <div class="editor-field">
        @Html.EditorFor(model => model.end_date)
        @Html.ValidationMessageFor(model => model.end_date)
      </div>
      <p>
        <input type="submit" value="Create" />
      </p>
   </fieldset>
}
<div>
   @Html.ActionLink("Back to List," "Index")
</div>
@section Scripts {
   @Scripts.Render("~/bundles/jqueryval")
}
```

12.2.11.1 EditorFor versus TextBoxFor

We'll start by looking at the Html.EditorFor and compare it to TextBoxFor, which is an alternative way to enter data. We'll do this by modifying the original Edit View in our example. We show the original web page created by the Edit View in Figure 12.42, for later comparison.

The LabelFor shows the name of the item, "slip," and the EditorFor shows the value of the slip for the item with id=1.

Note that instead of using "LabelFor" and "EditorFor," we could have instead used "@Html.Label("name"), and @Html.Editor("slip") and we would have achieved basically the same thing.

The LabelFor and EditorFor versions are strongly typed. Instead of giving just any arbitrary string name, you have to pass in the model value that you are using. Then you will get compile time checks for some model errors that you wouldn't if you just used the model item name.

LISTING 12.26   Original Code Showing LabelFor and EditorFor with the Slip Data

```
<div class="editor-label">
  @Html.LabelFor(model => model.slip)
</div>

<div class="editor-field">
  @Html.EditorFor(model => model.slip)
  @Html.ValidationMessageFor(model => model.slip)
</div>
```

Instead, however, of just passing in @Html.EditorFor(model.slip), which is what you would at first think would be the appropriate thing to do, instead you pass in @Html.Editorfor(model => model.slip).

When you see "model => model.slip," this is an example of a "lambda" expression. A lambda expression is a C# thing that creates an anonymous function that can be passed as an argument. There's quite a lot to be said about these. Sometime or other, if you plan to become a real heavy duty C# ASP.NET type programmer you'll have to learn this.

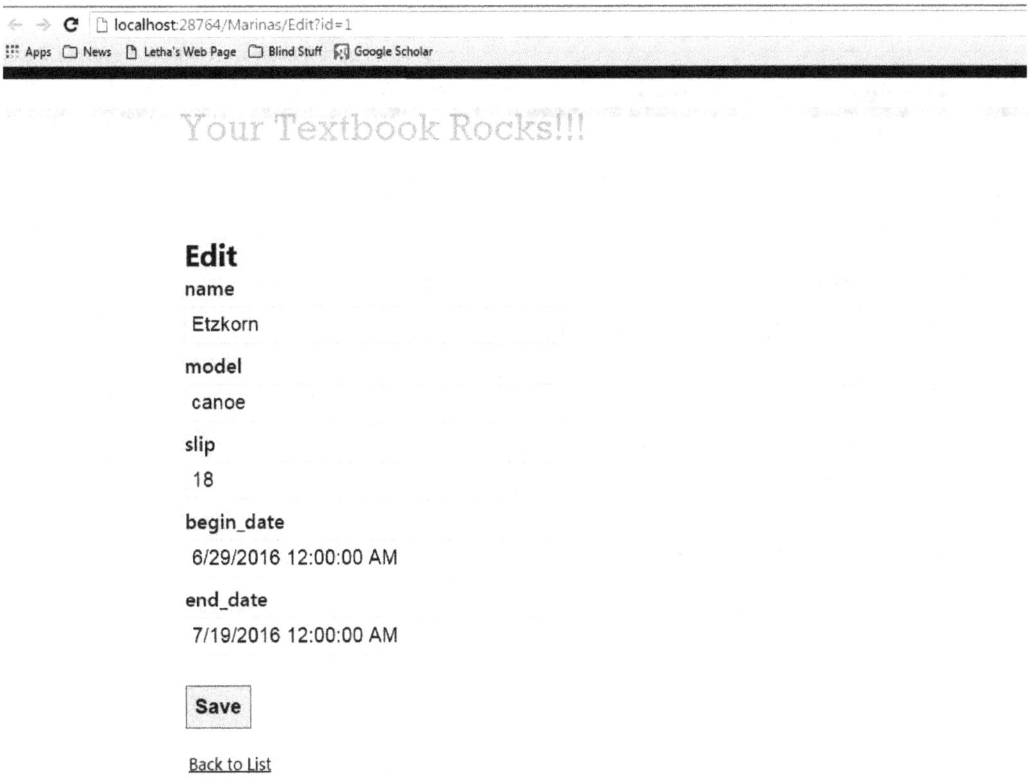

FIGURE 12.42   Results from running original Edit View.

However, for what we're doing here, you can mostly ignore how it works. Just do monkey -see monkey -do.

Now in Listing 12.27, we will replace the original EditorFor with a TextBoxFor.

LISTING 12.27   Updated Code Replacing EditorFor with TextBoxFor

```
<div class="editor-label">
    @Html.LabelFor(model => model.slip)
</div>
<div class="editor-field">
 @*   @Html.EditorFor(model => model.slip) *@
    @Html.TextBoxFor(model=>model.slip,"stuff")
    @Html.ValidationMessageFor(model => model.slip)
</div>
```

We see the results from running this code in Figure 12.43. This looks much the same as the original in Figure 12.42, except we've replaced the tentative value for input with a text string "stuff." (Note that if you hit enter without changing this, the validation won't let it go through.)

The difference between EditorFor and TextBoxFor is that EditorFor is sensitive to the type of data it is operating on (as specified by the model) and will generate appropriate kinds of data input for the model, whereas TextBoxFor always generates simple text-based input.

Your Textbook Rocks!!!

                                                                                    Hor

Edit

name

Etzkorn

model

canoe

slip

stuff

begin_date

6/29/2016 12:00:00 AM

end_date

7/19/2016 12:00:00 AM

Save

Back to List

FIGURE 12.43   Results from Edit View with TextBoxFor handling slip input.

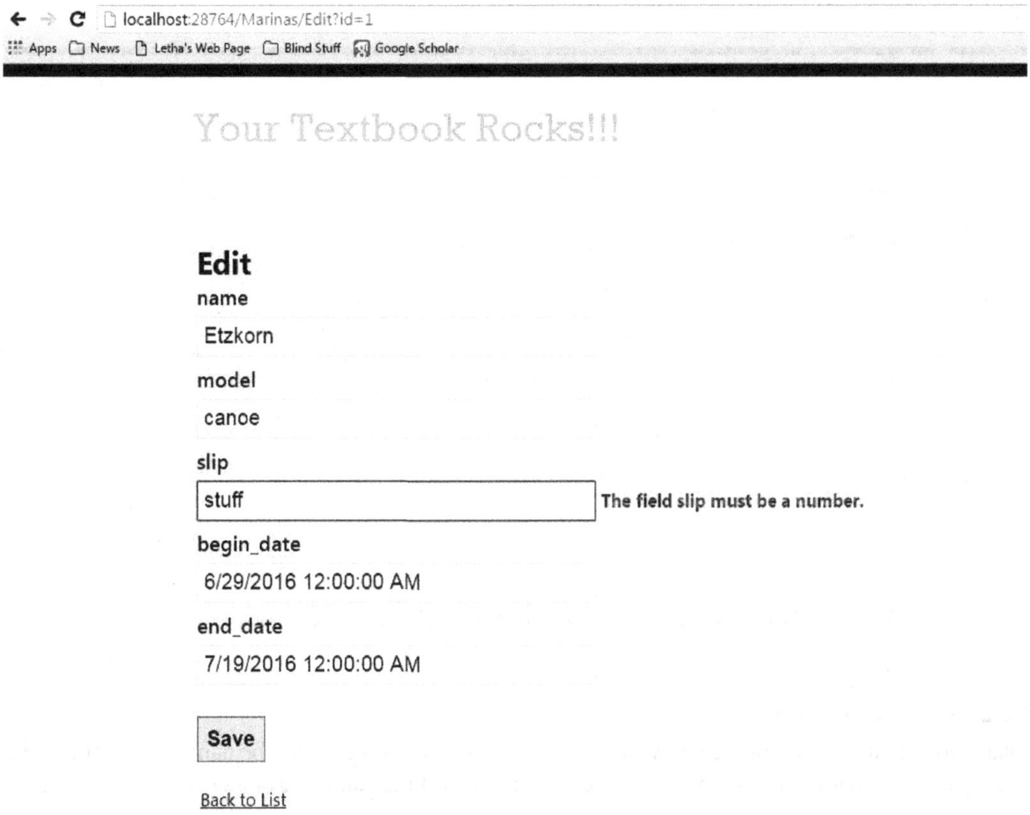

← → C   🗋 localhost:28764/Marinas/Edit?id=1
::: Apps ☐ News 🗋 Letha's Web Page ☐ Blind Stuff 🔍 Google Scholar

Your Textbook Rocks!!!

Edit

name

Etzkorn

model

canoe

slip

| stuff | The field slip must be a number.

begin_date

6/29/2016 12:00:00 AM

end_date

7/19/2016 12:00:00 AM

Save

Back to List

FIGURE 12.44   Submit value "stuff" in Form.

12.2.11.2   ValidationMessageFor

To see what the @Html.ValidationMessageFor does for us, let's look at what happens when we're using @TextBoxFor with the slip parameter set to "stuff," and we go ahead and submit the form. As you can see from Figure 12.44, we get an error.

Now let's comment out the "@Html.ValidationMessageFor" command, as shown in Listing 12.28.

LISTING 12.28   @Html.ValidationMessageFor Commented Out

```
<div class="editor-label">
    @Html.LabelFor(model => model.slip)
</div>
<div class="editor-field">
 @*  @Html.EditorFor(model => model.slip) *@
    @Html.TextBoxFor(model=>model.slip,"stuff")
 @*  @Html.ValidationMessageFor(model => model.slip) *@
</div>
```

The results are shown in Figure 12.45. Well, shucks, that ain't right. We were able to input "stuff" as a value for "slip" but "slip" has to be a number. Looks like our ValidationMessageFor command was doing us a lot of good. Need to put that sucker back in there.

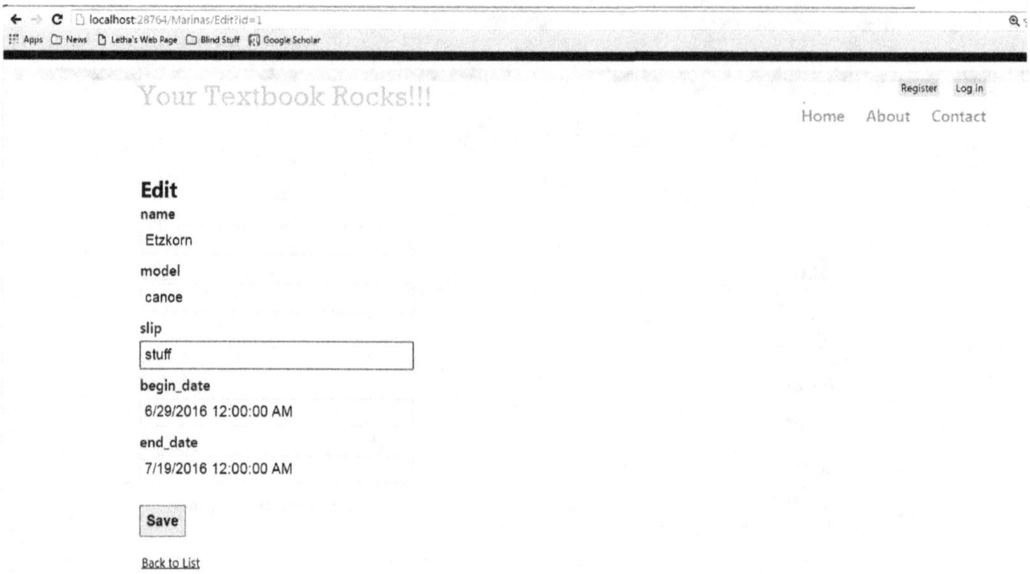

FIGURE 12.45   Input erroneous value with ValidationMessageFor commented out.

12.2.11.3   RadioButton

Okay, now, still working in the edit view, let's add a radio button to enter the name of a boat owner. We'll comment out the name entry with EditorFor and add the RadioButtonFor in Listing 12.29.

LISTING 12.29   Radio Button to Enter Boat Owner's Name

```
<div class="editor-field">
  @*    @Html.EditorFor(model => model.name)
       @Html.ValidationMessageFor(model => model.name)
  *@

  Enter a different name:

  <br />@Html.RadioButtonFor(model=>model.name,"Etzkorn") Etzkorn
  <br />@Html.RadioButtonFor(model=>model.name,"Smith") Smith
  <br />@Html.RadioButtonFor(model=>model.name,"Other") Other
</div>
```

Note that this has only two people's names, and that any boat being owned by anyone other than Etzkorn or Smith is unusual. Well, we'll pretend that either most of the slips aren't suitable for rental (maybe no power run to them), or else that Etzkorn and Smith are millionaires. ☺

In any case, the results are shown in Figure 12.46.

12.2.11.4   TextArea and TextAreaFor Example

We'll add the TextArea and TextAreaFor example to the RequestMaintenance View. This is shown in Listing 12.30.

FIGURE 12.46   Radio button example.

LISTING 12.30   TextArea and TextAreaFor Examples in RequestMaintenance View

```
@model example_with_model.Models.Marina
@{
    ViewBag.Title = "RequestMaintenance";
}
<h2>RequestMaintenance</h2>
    <p>We will handle your request for maintenance as soon as possible</p>
    <p>@Html.TextArea("status,""We are working very very hard. Really!!!,"
        new {rows=1, columns=50} )</p>
    <p>@Html.TextAreaFor(model=>model.name, new {rows=1, columns=50} )</p>
    <p>@Html.TextAreaFor(model=>model.model, new {rows=1, columns=50} )</p>
    <p>@Html.TextAreaFor(model=>model.slip, new {rows=1, columns=50} )</p>
```

The results from running this view is shown in Figure 12.47.

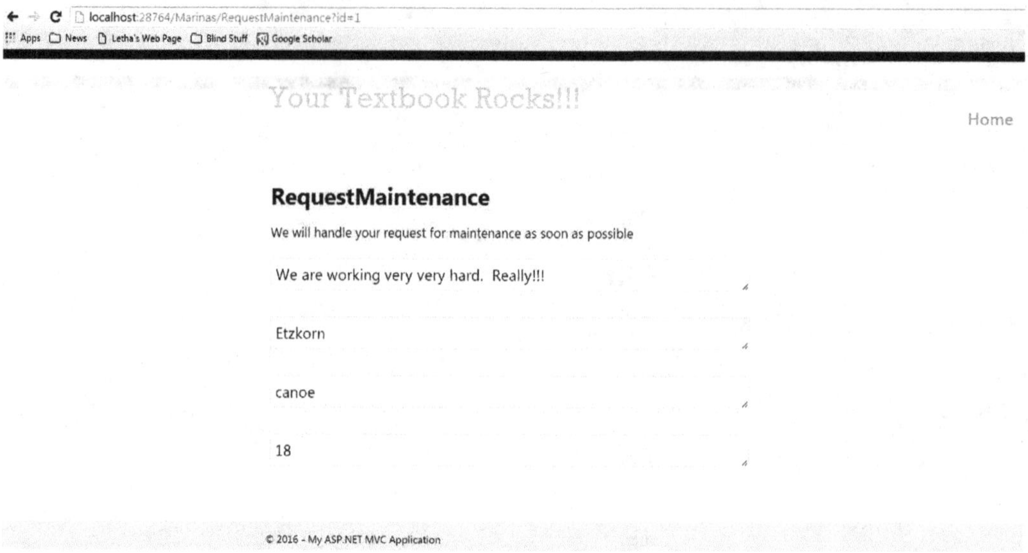

← → C [localhost:28764/Marinas/RequestMaintenance?id=1
::: Apps ☐ News ☐ Letha's Web Page ☐ Blind Stuff 🔍 Google Scholar

Your Textbook Rocks!!!

Home

RequestMaintenance

We will handle your request for maintenance as soon as possible

We are working very very hard. Really!!!

Etzkorn

canoe

18

© 2016 - My ASP.NET MVC Application

FIGURE 12.47   Results using TextArea and TextAreaFor.

12.2.11.5   ListBoxFor

Now we'll look at how to do an Html.ListBoxFor. We'll add this to the Create view. We'll create a ListBox to let us enter the boat's model name.

First we will define the list we are going to use. We'll add this to the top of the Create View, as seen in Listing 12.31.

LISTING 12.31   Define a List

```
@{
    ViewBag.Title = "Create";

    var ListModel = new List<SelectListItem>()
    {
        new SelectListItem() {  Value="Catalina27," Text="Catalina 27" },
        new SelectListItem() {  Value="Oday37," Text="Oday 37" },
        new SelectListItem() {  Value="Hunter25," Text="Hunter 25" },
        new SelectListItem() {  Value="canoe," Text="canoe" },
        new SelectListItem() {  Value="rowboat," Text="rowboat" }
    };
}
```

Then we'll add the list box that uses this list further down in this view, see Listing 12.32. We will comment out the EditorFor to allow us to use ListBoxFor to enter this data.

The Create View using the ListBox is shown in Figure 12.48.

The results after creating the items in the ListBox are shown in Figure 12.49.

12.2.11.6   DropDownList

Now let's add a dropdown list to the same Create View that we just used to do a ListBox.

We will change the top of the Create View to define the list for names as well as the list for boat models. See Listing 12.33.

LISTING 12.32   Call ListBoxFor

```
<div class="editor-label">
  @Html.LabelFor(model => model.model)
</div>

<div class="editor-field">
  @* @Html.EditorFor(model => model.model) *@
  @Html.ListBoxFor(model=>model.model, new MultiSelectList(ListModel,
    "Value,""Text"))
  @Html.ValidationMessageFor(model => model.model)
</div>
```

LISTING 12.33   Define a List for Names and a List for Models

```
@{
  ViewBag.Title = "Create";
  var ListNames = new List<SelectListItem>()
  {
    new SelectListItem() {  Value="Etzkorn," Text="Etzkorn" },
    new SelectListItem() {  Value="Smith," Text="Smith" },
    new SelectListItem() {  Value="Other," Text="Other" }
  };

  var ListModel = new List<SelectListItem>()
  {
    new SelectListItem() {  Value="Catalina27," Text="Catalina 27" },
    new SelectListItem() {  Value="Oday37," Text="Oday 37" },
    new SelectListItem() {  Value="Hunter25," Text="Hunter 25" },
    new SelectListItem() {  Value="canoe," Text="canoe" },
    new SelectListItem() {  Value="rowboat," Text="rowboat" }
  };
}
```

Now we will comment out the EditorFor input for the name, and add a dropdown list instead.

LISTING 12.34   DropDown List

```
<div class="editor-field">
@*      @Html.EditorFor(model => model.name)
    @Html.ValidationMessageFor(model => model.name) *@
  @Html.DropDownListFor(model=>Model.name,ListNames)
</div>
```

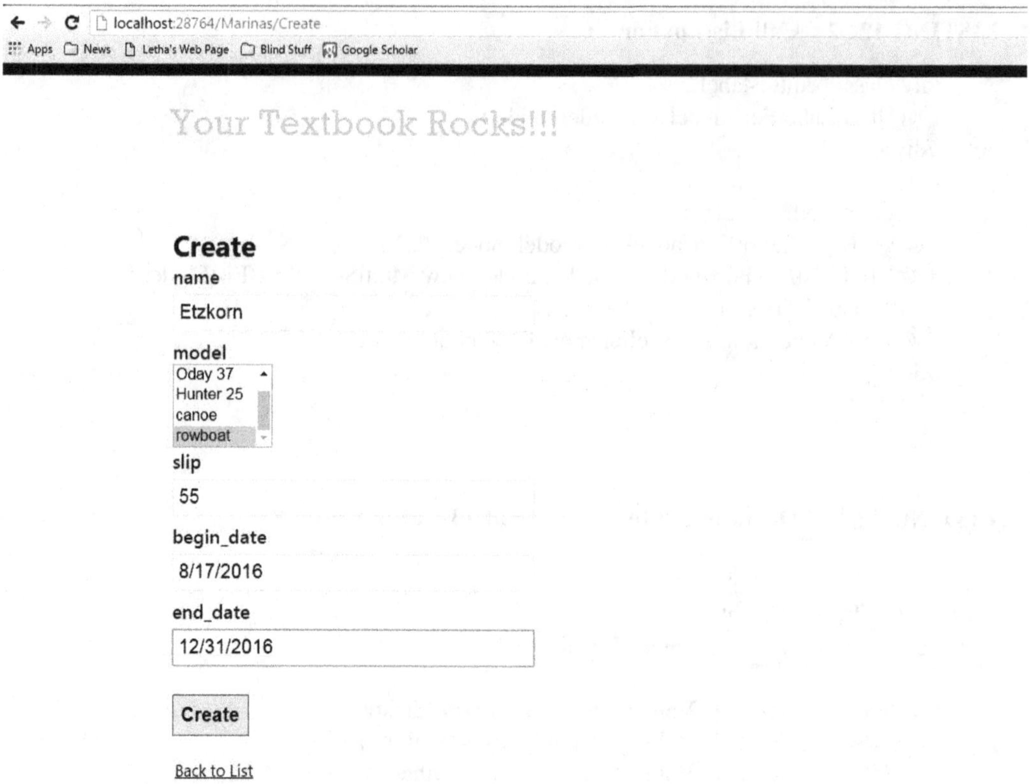

← → C localhost:28764/Marinas/Create

Apps News Letha's Web Page Blind Stuff Google Scholar

Your Textbook Rocks!!!

Create

name

Etzkorn

model

| Oday 37 |
| Hunter 25 |
| canoe |
| rowboat |

slip

55

begin_date

8/17/2016

end_date

12/31/2016

Create

Back to List

FIGURE 12.48   View using ListBoxFor.

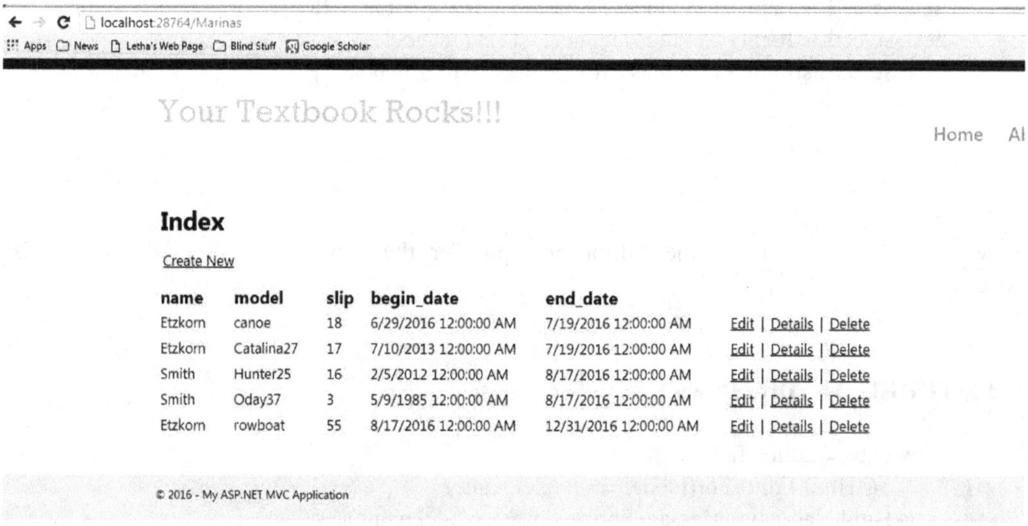

← → C localhost:28764/Marinas

Apps News Letha's Web Page Blind Stuff Google Scholar

Your Textbook Rocks!!!

Home   Al

Index

Create New

name	model	slip	begin_date	end_date			
Etzkorn	canoe	18	6/29/2016 12:00:00 AM	7/19/2016 12:00:00 AM	Edit	Details	Delete
Etzkorn	Catalina27	17	7/10/2013 12:00:00 AM	7/19/2016 12:00:00 AM	Edit	Details	Delete
Smith	Hunter25	16	2/5/2012 12:00:00 AM	8/17/2016 12:00:00 AM	Edit	Details	Delete
Smith	Oday37	3	5/9/1985 12:00:00 AM	8/17/2016 12:00:00 AM	Edit	Details	Delete
Etzkorn	rowboat	55	8/17/2016 12:00:00 AM	12/31/2016 12:00:00 AM	Edit	Details	Delete

© 2016 - My ASP.NET MVC Application

FIGURE 12.49   Results after creating items using ListBoxFor.

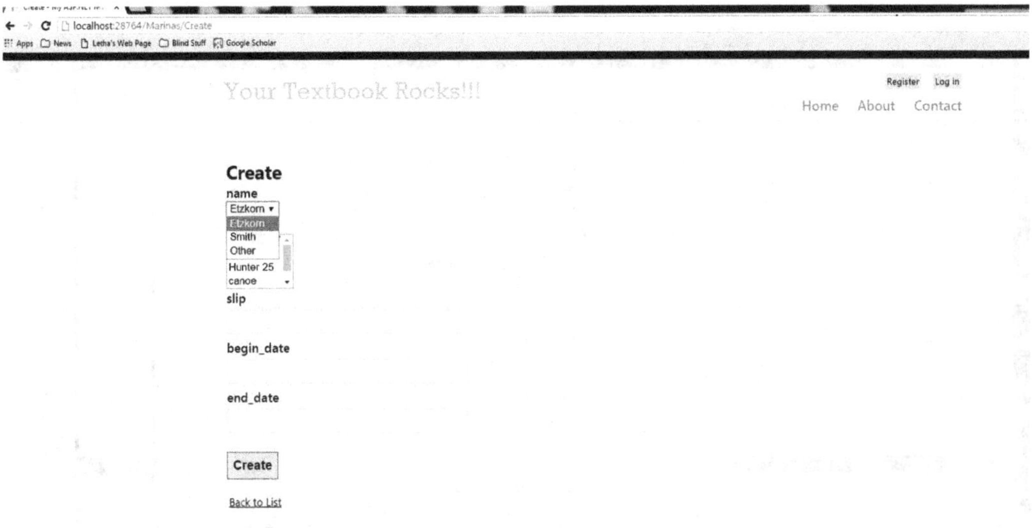

FIGURE 12.50   DropDown list in create View.

When we run the Create View, it now looks like Figure 12.50. This isn't super pretty, as it shows the DropDown List for names on top of the ListBox for models. But I think you'll catch the drift. ☺

12.2.12   ASP.NET CORE 1.0 IN VISUAL STUDIO 2015

In this section, we're going to see how to implement the Marina project in ASP.NET Core 1.0 in Visual Studio 2015. Here, we're going to discuss how a model, a view, and a controller can really be used in general, but also specifically in a database-type project, and particularly for the Marina project.

Note that this sequence of steps may very well change somewhat in later releases of Visual Studio (and even updates of Visual Studio 2015), but hopefully by examining future Microsoft tutorials and comparing them to this sequence of steps, you will be able to modify this sequence of steps so you will still be able to create the Marina project. This is always an issue with moving code. It's impossible to foretell the future, so we all just do the best we can. ☺

12.2.12.1   Create MVC Project

In our first step, we will create the project as shown in Figure 12.51. We'll name it MarinaStuff. Make sure to select ASP.NET CORE.

Next we will select Web Application and we will change our authentication mechanism to Individual User Accounts. According to Anderson (2016), scaffolding (that is, automatically creating the database and associated CRUD (Create, Access, Update, Delete) accessors) requires changing the authentication to Individual User Accounts (see Figure 12.52). They say this is expected to change in the future.

Note: Do NOT host in the cloud, we're not doing that this time. ☺

Next, if desired, you can change the layout page to tailor it for your application; the layout page is shown in Figure 12.53.

Next, as in Figure 12.54, change the title of the Index page to read "Marinas."

12.2.12.2   Create Model

Next, create the model itself by right clicking on Models, then select Add, then select Class (see Figure 12.55).

FIGURE 12.51   Create the project.

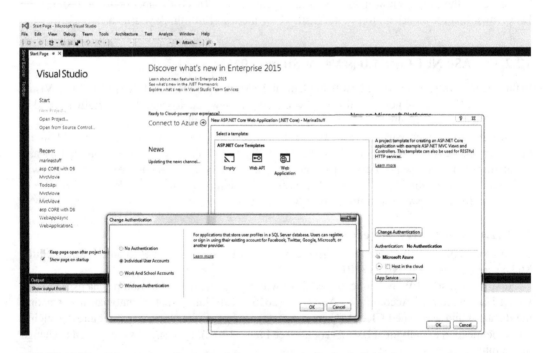

FIGURE 12.52   Select web application and change authentication to individual user accounts.

Now enter the name of the model, as in Figure 12.56. Call it "Marina.cs."
Immediately after you create the model, the empty model will appear as in Figure 12.57.
Now enter the model content for the Marina database, as shown in Figure 12.58.

12.2.12.3   Create Controller

Next we will add a controller, as shown in Figure 12.59. Right click on Controllers, select Add, select
Controller.

FIGURE 12.53 Change Layout page in views.

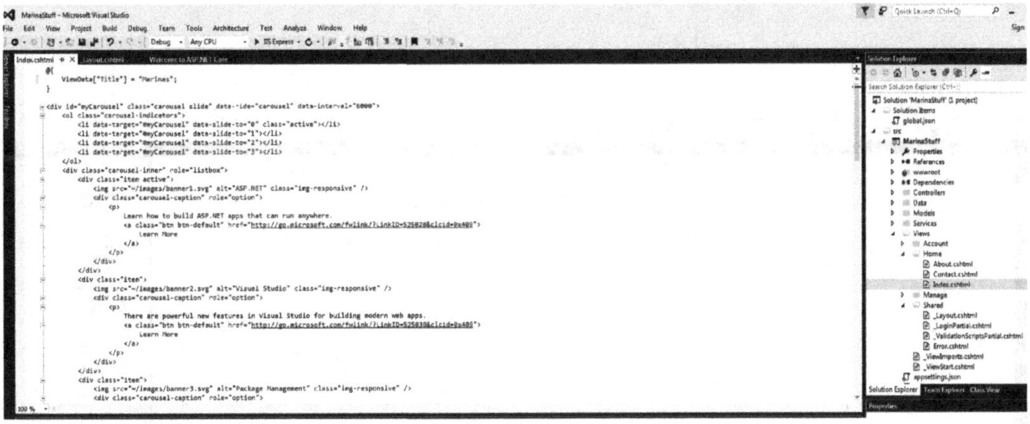

FIGURE 12.54 Change title of Index page in views.

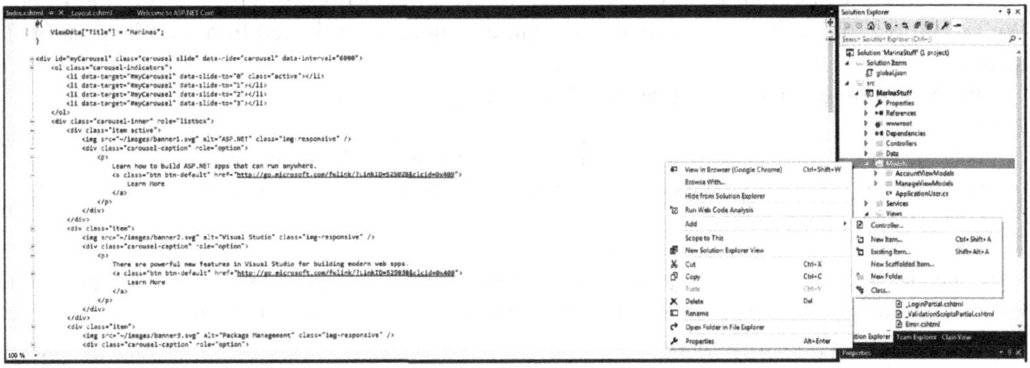

FIGURE 12.55 Create the model itself.

FIGURE 12.56   Enter the model name.

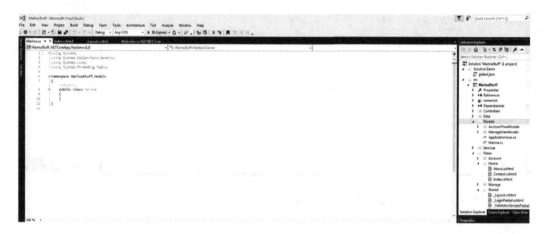

FIGURE 12.57   Model prior to adding content.

Select MVC Controller with views, using Entity Framework as shown in Figure 12.60. We've ignored Entity Framework up to now, but it is an object-oriented front end for relational databases.

MSDN (2015a) defines Entity Framework as follows:

Entity Framework (EF) is an object-relational mapper that enables .NET developers to work with relational data using domain-specific objects. It eliminates the need for most of the data-access code that developers usually need to write.

So the idea behind Entity Framework is, you define and use your data as objects as appropriate for your application. Then Entity Framework accesses the underlying database for you so you don't have to know a lot about how to do that.

Next we will add the controller itself. Its model class will be "Marina," its data context class will be "MarinaStuff," and you will name it "MarinasController." (see Figure 12.61).

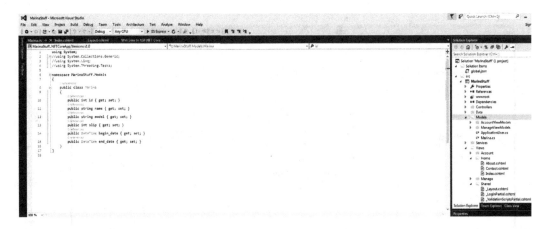

FIGURE 12.58   Enter Model content for Marina database

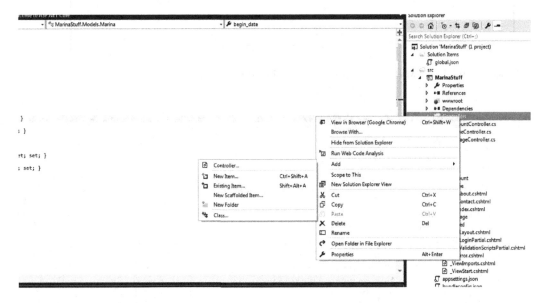

FIGURE 12.59   Create a controller.

Do run without debugging, and you get Figure 12.62.

Next, add "/Marinas" to the "localhost:xxxx" address to select the Marinas controller. You will get the error shown in Figure 12.63.

So to fix this error, exit, and restart Visual Studio. Open a command prompt and cd to your directory ...\MarinaStuff\src\MarinaStuff

Type "dotnet ef migrations add initial" as shown in Figure 12.64.

Then type "dotnet ef database update" as shown in Figure 12.65.

To confirm that this worked correctly, you can look at the files in: yourprojectname\MarinaStuff \src\MarinaStuff\Data\Migrations

They should look something like the files shown in Figure 12.66.

Now do a run without debugging, and select the Marina's Controller. You'll get a nice working Marina's Index page as shown in Figure 12.67. Unfortunately, it doesn't have any data in it, but we'll add that next.

FIGURE 12.60   Select MVC controller views Entity Framework.

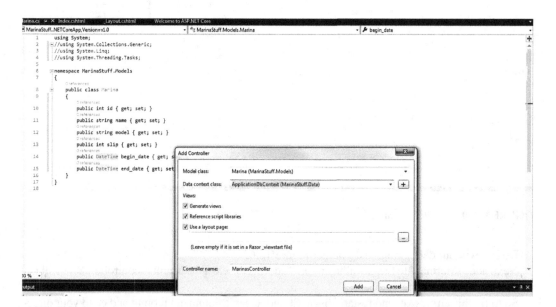

FIGURE 12.61   Add the controller.

Whew! These last few instructions were pretty awful. I bet Microsoft changes these fairly soon, don't you? As I write this, you definitely have to do it this way. Unfortunately.

12.2.12.4   Enter Data

After you do a run without debugging, type in your browser:

localhost:xxxxx/Marinas/Create

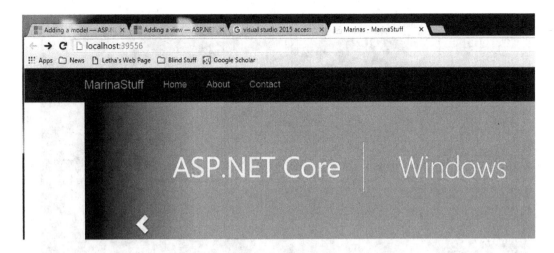

FIGURE 12.62   After run without debugging.

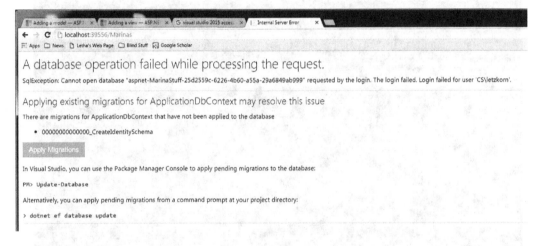

FIGURE 12.63   Error when select Marinas controller in browser.

Remember to replace xxxxx with your own port number; it should be showing in your browser after you do the run.

Now enter a data item as shown in Figure 12.68.

Enter all your data items for the Marina database. After you've entered them all, you can see them in the response. It will look like Figure 12.69.

Now turn on the SQL Server Object Explorer window in Visual Studio 2015. Then select Databases, MarinaStuff, and then dbo.Marina. This will look something like Figure 12.70. You can see all the columns in the database this way.

If you right click on dbo.Marina then you can select Design View (see Figure 12.71, but click two items up from the item highlighted; I'm using this one Figure to show two separate steps), then you can see the Design View. See Figure 12.72. This shows the columns at the top and the associated SQL code at the bottom.

If you want to modify the data types of any column, you can do that from the Design View as shown in Figure 12.73.

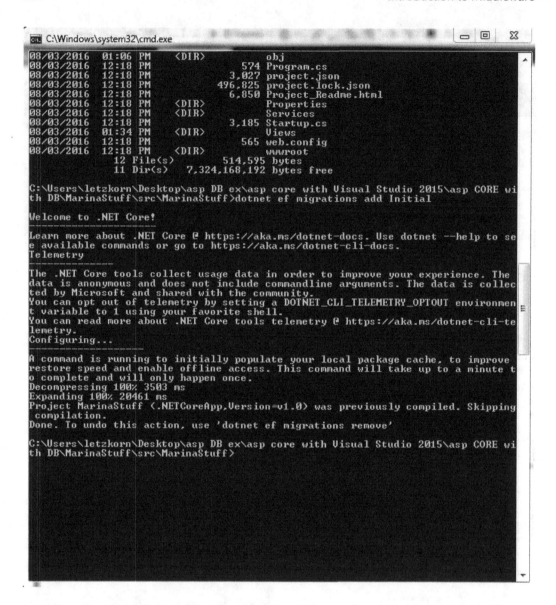

FIGURE 12.64   Add initial using EF migrations.

```
C:\Users\letzkorn\Desktop\asp DB ex\asp core with Visual Studio 2015\asp CORE wi
th DB\MarinaStuff\src\MarinaStuff>dotnet ef database update
Project MarinaStuff (.NETCoreApp,Version=v1.0) will be compiled because Input it
ems added from last build
Compiling MarinaStuff for .NETCoreApp,Version=v1.0

    0 Warning(s)
    0 Error(s)
Time elapsed 00:00:02.3418611

Done.

C:\Users\letzkorn\Desktop\asp DB ex\asp core with Visual Studio 2015\asp CORE wi
th DB\MarinaStuff\src\MarinaStuff>_
```

FIGURE 12.65   Update the database.

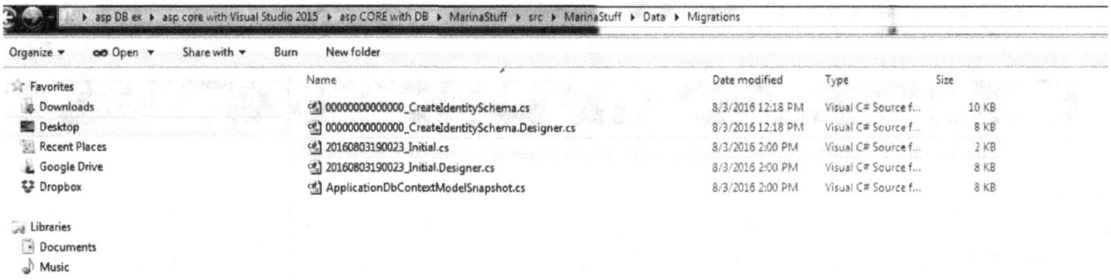

FIGURE 12.66 Files in MarinaStuff\src\MarinaStuff\Data\Migrations.

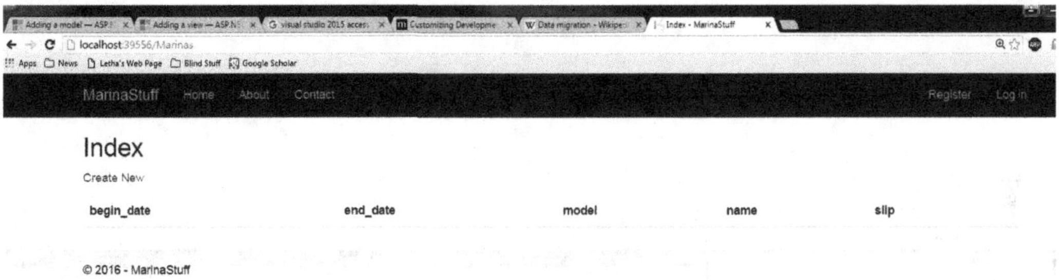

FIGURE 12.67 Working Marina's index.

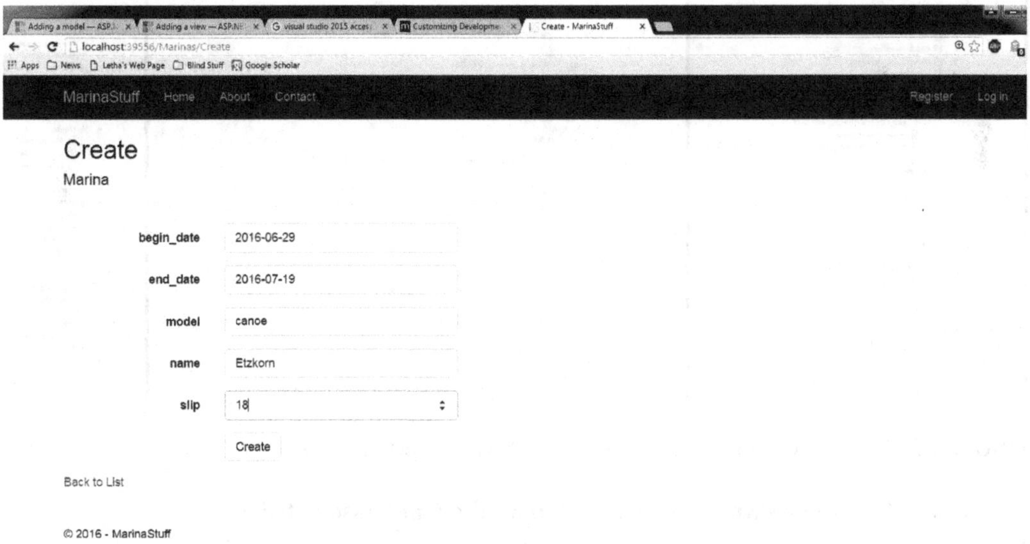

FIGURE 12.68 Enter data item.

Now select View Data—look back up at Figure 12.71. This will allow you to see the data in the database, as shown in Figure 12.74.

12.2.12.5 Use Other Default Views of Marina Database

In this section, as opposed to using the SQL Server Object Explorer, we will use our controllers to look at the data in the Marina database. In Figure 12.75, we see an entry using the Details default view. In Figure 12.76 we see all entries using the Index View.

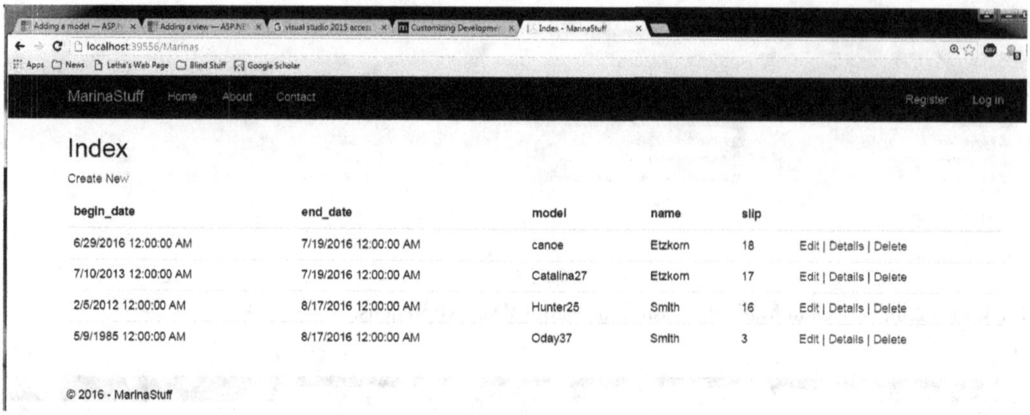

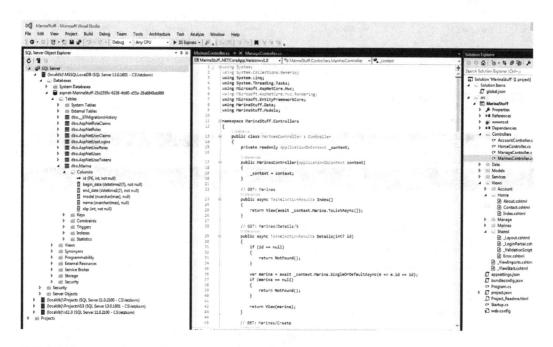

FIGURE 12.69   Response after all data items entered.

FIGURE 12.70   View localdb columns through SQL Server Object Explorer.

12.2.12.6   Add RequestMaintenance Action Method and Associated View

In this section, we will add a new Action Method to our Controller and a new view to display it. Let's first create an empty Action Method. This is shown in Listing 12.35 and in Figure 12.77.

LISTING 12.35   New RequestMaintenance Action Method

```
public async Task<IActionResult> RequestMaintenance()
    {
    }
```

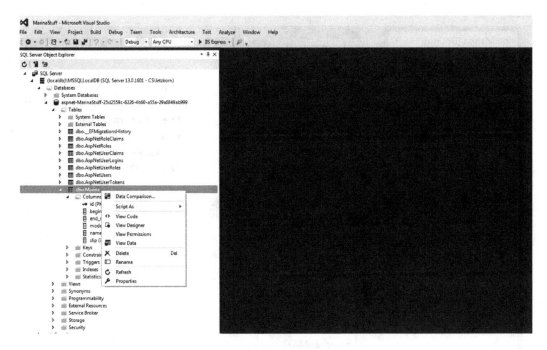

FIGURE 12.71 Select View Data in SQL Server Object Explorer.

FIGURE 12.72 Designer view of dbo.Marina.

Notice that this is quite different from the original RequestMaintenance view that we looked at earlier using Visual Studio 2012 (see Figure 12.23). In Visual Studio 2012, by default, the methods returned "ActionResult" and not "Task<ActionResult>."

The reason ActionResult and not Task<ActionResult> was used in Visual Studio 2012 was the default action methods created using scaffolding were not async, and we originally created our

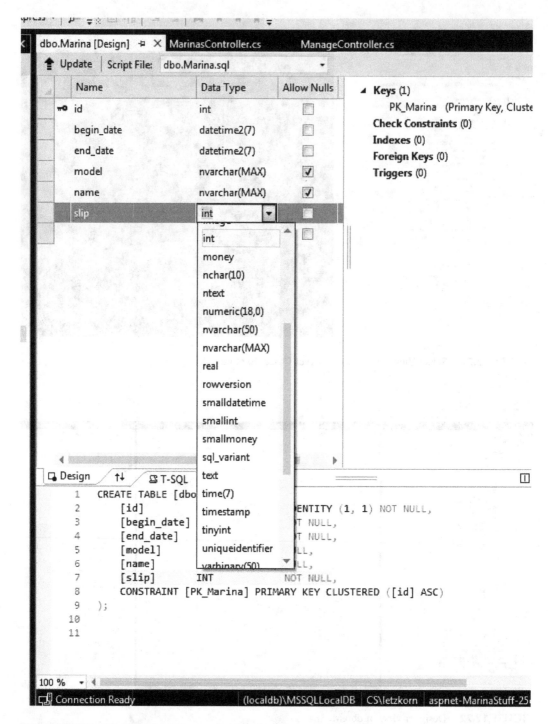

FIGURE 12.73 Modify column data types in Design View.

original Visual Studio 2012 RequestMaintenance action method to behave similarly to the default action methods.

We didn't make our original RequestMaintenance action method asynchronous until Listing 12.9 and Figure 12.30, and at that point we used the keyword "async" and we made RequestMaintenance return "Task<ActionResult> instead of just <ActionResult>.

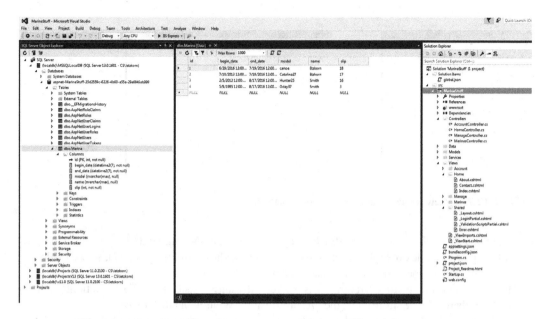

FIGURE 12.74   Data in Marina database shown using SQL Server Object Explorer.

FIGURE 12.75   View one entry using details default view.

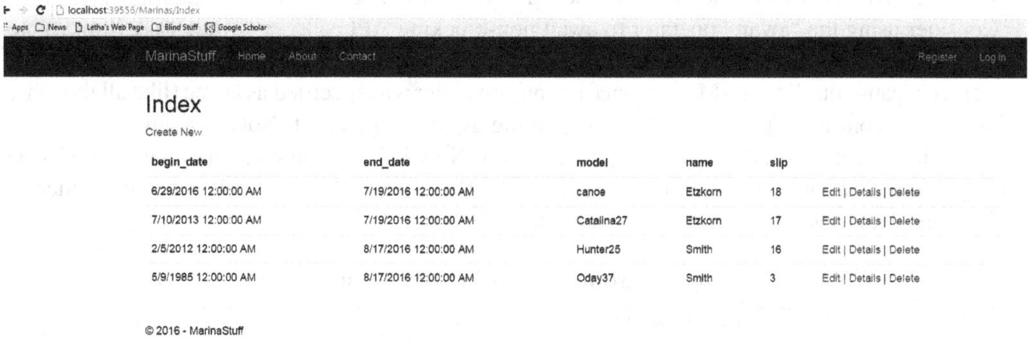

FIGURE 12.76   View all entries in Marina database using index view.

FIGURE 12.77   New RequestMaintenance action method.

Here you can see that in Visual Studio 2015 all the action methods start out as async when they are scaffolded (see the Index default action method that is also shown in Figure 12.77), so we made our RequestMaintenance method also start out as async.

However, here our methods return "Task<IActionResult>" instead of "Task<ActionResult>." Look close, there's an "I" in front of the "ActionResult." What is the difference?

IActionResult is an interface, and ActionResult is an implementation of the IActionResult interface. Using an interface like this allows you to return a lot of different kinds of data types that do not obey the ActionResult interface. One example is HttpStatusCodeResult. So using IActionResult just makes things more generic and flexible.

By the way, the "I" in ASP.NET always means interface. Other interfaces you might see in ASP.NET are "IEnumerable"and "IDisposable." "IEnumerable" is used to represent collections that can be counted (enumerated), that is, that you can iterate though, while "IDisposable" is used to explicitly release unmanaged resources (those not handled by the garbage collector).

Now let's add a RequestMaintenance View to go with our new RequestMaintenance Action method. In Figure 12.78, we see how to right click on Marinas, select Add, then Select View.

In Figure 12.79, we name the view "RequestMaintenance" and we select the Marina model class and the MarinaStuff data context.

The default view we just created is shown in Figure 12.80.

We'll delete most of that stuff and leave only the parts we need, as shown in Figure 12.81.

Now we'll add the nice little maintenance message we currently need, as shown in Figure 12.82.

So run without debugging and we'll get the response shown in Figure 12.83.

Note that you'll get something like the following error:

C:\Users\letzkorn\Desktop\asp DB ex\asp core with Visual Studio 2015\asp CORE with DB\MarinaStuff\src\MarinaStuff\Controllers\MarinasController.cs(22,42):

warning CS1998: This async method lacks "await" operators and will run synchronously.

Consider using the "await" operator to await non-blocking API calls, or "await Task.Run(...)" to do CPU-bound work on a background thread.

This is because our RequestMaintenance action controller was specified as async (like all the other default action controllers) but we didn't do anything asynchronous in it. Not yet anyway.

Well, this was complicated! But we got through it. Now let's do some variations on our Marina project similar to what we did before with ASP.NET MVC. Let's look at asynchronous implementations of the RequestMaintenance action method.

12.2.12.7   Add Asynchronous Controller to Marina Project in ASP.NET CORE

12.2.12.7.1   Scheduling Maintenance Using Simple PHP Server

Here we will use a RequestMaintenance action method that accesses a PHP server that is the same as that seen previously in Listing 12.8. We're using an HttpClient here, as we did previously with

ince()

ic());

I)

defaultAsync(m => m.id == id);

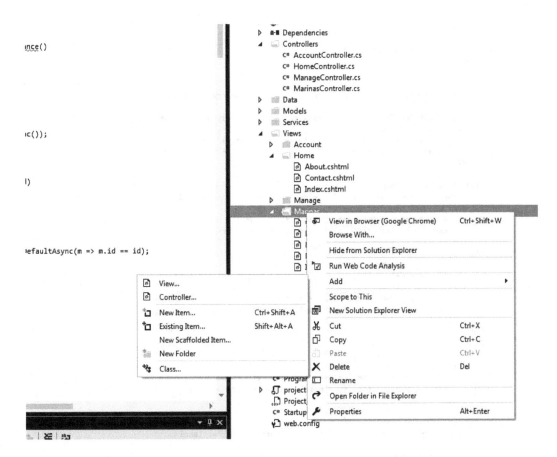

FIGURE 12.78 Add a New View.

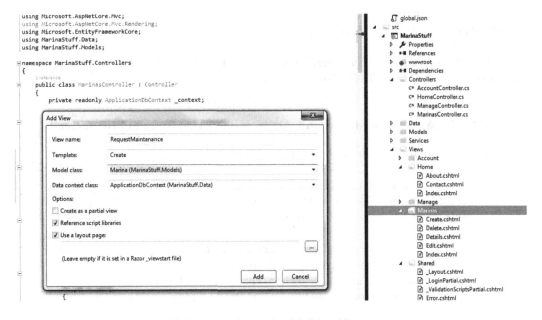

FIGURE 12.79 Name RequestMaintenance view, select Model and Data context.

```
:h2>RequestMaintenance</h2>

form asp-action="RequestMaintenance">
    <div class="form-horizontal">
        <h4>Marina</h4>
        <hr />
        <div asp-validation-summary="ModelOnly" class="text-danger"></div>
        <div class="form-group">
            <label asp-for="begin_date" class="col-md-2 control-label"></label>
            <div class="col-md-10">
                <input asp-for="begin_date" class="form-control" />
                <span asp-validation-for="begin_date" class="text-danger" />
            </div>
        </div>
        <div class="form-group">
            <label asp-for="end_date" class="col-md-2 control-label"></label>
            <div class="col-md-10">
                <input asp-for="end_date" class="form-control" />
                <span asp-validation-for="end_date" class="text-danger" />
            </div>
        </div>
        <div class="form-group">
            <label asp-for="model" class="col-md-2 control-label"></label>
            <div class="col-md-10">
                <input asp-for="model" class="form-control" />
                <span asp-validation-for="model" class="text-danger" />
            </div>
        </div>
        <div class="form-group">
            <label asp-for="name" class="col-md-2 control-label"></label>
            <div class="col-md-10">
                <input asp-for="name" class="form-control" />
                <span asp-validation-for="name" class="text-danger" />
            </div>
        </div>
        <div class="form-group">
            <label asp-for="slip" class="col-md-2 control-label"></label>
            <div class="col-md-10">
                <input asp-for="slip" class="form-control" />
                <span asp-validation-for="slip" class="text-danger" />
            </div>
        </div>
        <div class="form-group">
```

FIGURE 12.80   Default RequestMaintenance view.

ASP.NET MVC4 in Listing 12.9. There's not a lot of difference other than passing back Task
<IActionResult> instead of Task<ActionResult>.

LISTING 12.36   Request Maintenance Action Method That Accesses PHP Server

```
public async Task<IActionResult> RequestMaintenance()
{
    // CancellationToken cancelToken = default(CancellationToken);
    var cancelToken = CancellationToken.None;
    using (HttpClient httpClient = new HttpClient())
    {
        httpClient.BaseAddress = new Uri("http://localhost:8080/");
        var uri = "~letzkorn/simple_server.php?mydata=Letha";
        var response = await httpClient.GetAsync(uri, cancelToken);
        string mystring = await response.Content.ReadAsStringAsync();
```

```
        ViewBag.myHtml = mystring;
    }
    return View();
}
```

12.2.12.7.2 Scheduling Maintenance Using Two PHP Servers

LISTING 12.37   ChooseMaintenance Person PHP Server

```php
<?php
  $mydata = $_REQUEST["mydata"];
  sleep(5);
  print "Hi, $mydata! Your maintenance person will be Julie.";
?>
```

LISTING 12.38   ScheduleMaintenance Person PHP Server

```php
<?php
  $mydata = $_REQUEST["mydata"];
  sleep(5);
  print " She is available after 2pm next Tuesday.";
?>
```

**LISTING 12.39   RequestMaintenance Calling Two PHP Servers (This Version Really
                  Synchronous)**

```
public async Task<ActionResult> RequestMaintenance()
{
    CancellationToken cancelToken = default(CancellationToken);
    using (HttpClient httpClient = new HttpClient())
    {
        httpClient.BaseAddress = new Uri("http://localhost:8080/");
        // Replace port number with the one your Visual Studio happened to use
        string myname = "Letha";
        var uri = "~letzkorn/chooseMaintenancePerson.php" + "?mydata=" + myname;
        var uriA = "~letzkorn/scheduleMaintenancePerson.php";
        Stopwatch mywatch = new Stopwatch();
        mywatch.Start();

        // Calling .Result blocks, same as calling Wait
        // therefore, .Result makes these a synchronous call
        HttpResponseMessage response = httpClient.GetAsync(uri, cancelToken).Result;
        HttpResponseMessage responseA = httpClient.GetAsync(uriA, cancelToken).Result;
```

```
        mywatch.Stop();
        ViewBag.timeRequired = mywatch.ElapsedMilliseconds;
        mywatch.Reset();
        mywatch.Start();
        // Again, note that .Result performs a synchronous call
        string mystring = response.Content.ReadAsStringAsync().Result;
        string mystringA = responseA.Content.ReadAsStringAsync().Result;
        mywatch.Stop();
        ViewBag.timeRequiredA = mywatch.ElapsedMilliseconds;
        mywatch.Reset();
        mywatch.Start();
        //Note that there isn't any new work to be done here now

        mywatch.Stop();
        ViewBag.timeRequiredB = mywatch.ElapsedMilliseconds;
        ViewBag.myHtml = mystring+ mystringA;
    }
    return View();
}
```

In this RequestMaintenance action method, instead of using "await" we're calling ".Result" instead, as in the following:

HttpResponseMessage response = httpClient.GetAsync(uri, cancelToken).Result;

Calling .Result blocks, it's the same as calling Wait. Therefore, calling .Result makes these a synchronous call.

You can see this in the results in Figure 12.84. The time for the first two calls (using GetAsync) to execute is 11017 milliseconds (a bit over 11 seconds). But since each separate PHP program took

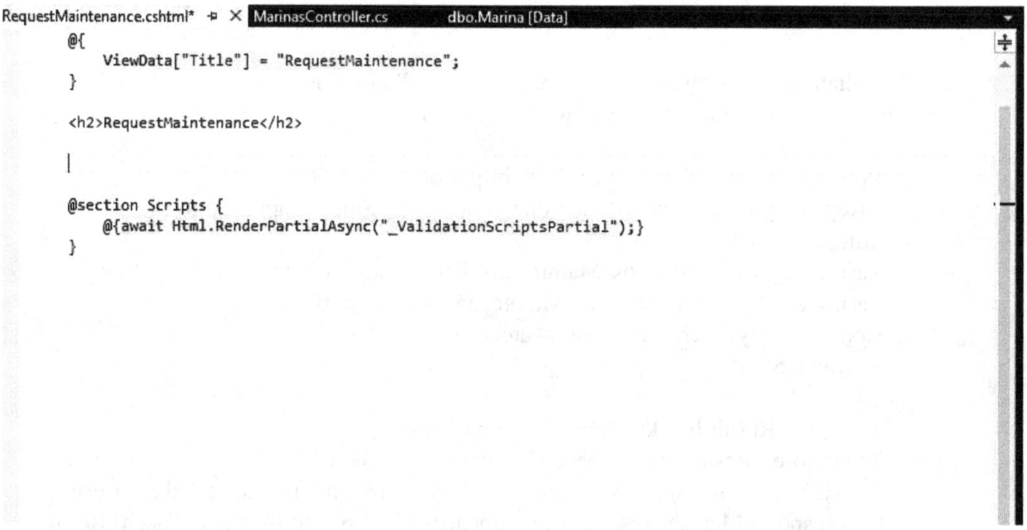

```
RequestMaintenance.cshtml*  ⊕ ✕  MarinasController.cs        dbo.Marina [Data]
    @{
        ViewData["Title"] = "RequestMaintenance";
    }

    <h2>RequestMaintenance</h2>

    |

    @section Scripts {
        @{await Html.RenderPartialAsync("_ValidationScriptsPartial");}
    }
```

FIGURE 12.81   Basic parts of RequestMaintenance view.

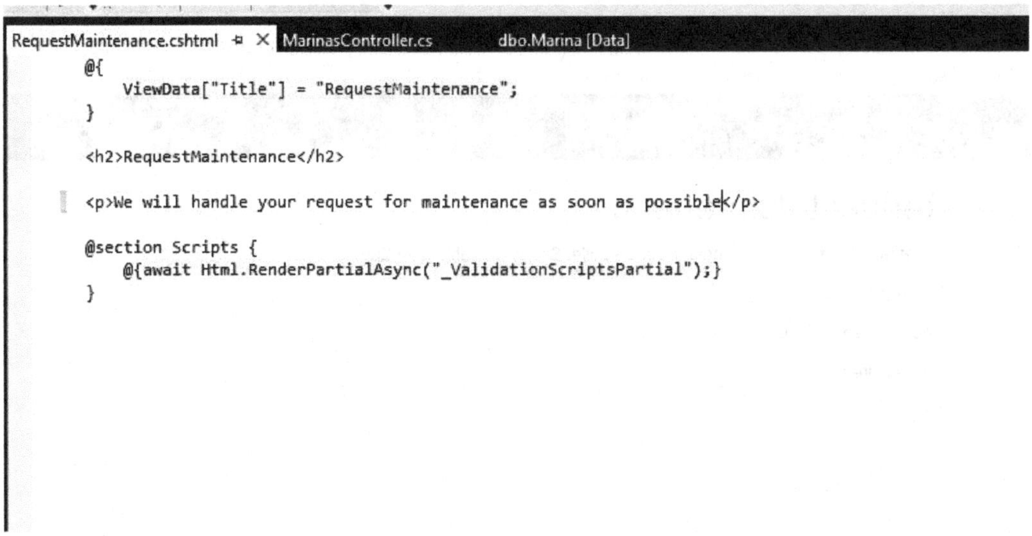

```
RequestMaintenance.cshtml  ⬜ ✕  MarinasController.cs          dbo.Marina [Data]
        @{
            ViewData["Title"] = "RequestMaintenance";
        }

        <h2>RequestMaintenance</h2>

        <p>We will handle your request for maintenance as soon as possible</p>

        @section Scripts {
            @{await Html.RenderPartialAsync("_ValidationScriptsPartial");}
        }
```

FIGURE 12.82   New Simple RequestMaintenance view.

FIGURE 12.83   Response from simple RequestMaintenance view.

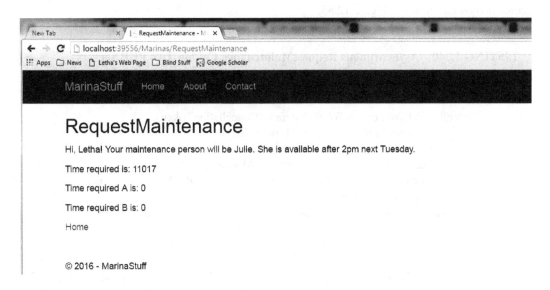

FIGURE 12.84   Results calling two PHP servers synchronous version.

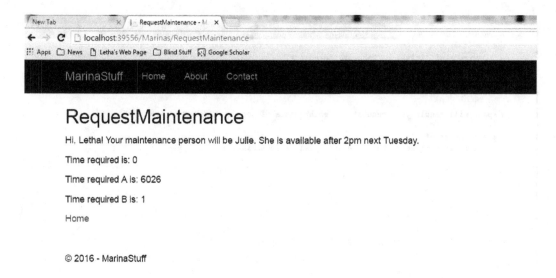

FIGURE 12.85   Results calling two PHP servers asynchronous version.

5 seconds to execute, it's clear the times were added together, and so we're not working in a synchronous way.

If you use "await" instead everywhere you used ".Result" here, you'd get a similar response. I have included this RequestMaintenance code using "await" in Visual Studio 2015 with the code that comes with the textbook, but I'm not going to inflict it on you here, it's too similar to the MVC4 examples we saw before.

12.2.12.7.3 Asynchronous Scheduling Maintenance Using Two PHP Servers

For this example, the PHP servers used are the same as those in Listings 12.36 and Listing 12.37. The difference here is that we will use a truly asynchronous version of the RequestMaintenance action method.

See the RequestMaintenance action method example in Listing 12.40. The results of running this action method are shown in Figure 12.85.

LISTING 12.40   Asynchronous RequestMaintenance Calling Two PHP Servers

```
public async Task<ActionResult> RequestMaintenance()
{
    CancellationToken cancelToken = default(CancellationToken);
    using (HttpClient httpClient = new HttpClient())
    {
        httpClient.BaseAddress = new Uri("http://localhost:8080/");
        // Replace port number with the one your Visual Studio happened to use
        string myname = "Letha";
        var uri = "~letzkorn/chooseMaintenancePerson.php" + "?mydata=" + myname;
        var uriA = "~letzkorn/scheduleMaintenancePerson.php";
        Stopwatch mywatch = new Stopwatch();
        mywatch.Start();
        Task<HttpResponseMessage> response = httpClient.GetAsync(uri, cancelToken);
```

```
                  Task<HttpResponseMessage> responseA = httpClient.GetAsync(uriA, cancelToken);
                  mywatch.Stop();
                  ViewBag.timeRequired = mywatch.ElapsedMilliseconds;
                  mywatch.Reset();
                  mywatch.Start();
                  HttpResponseMessage the_response = response.Result;
                  HttpResponseMessage the_responseA = responseA.Result;
                  mywatch.Stop();
                  ViewBag.timeRequiredA = mywatch.ElapsedMilliseconds;
                  mywatch.Reset();
                  mywatch.Start();
                  string mystring = await the_response.Content.ReadAsStringAsync();
                  string mystringA = await the_responseA.Content.ReadAsStringAsync();
                  mywatch.Stop();
                  ViewBag.timeRequiredB = mywatch.ElapsedMilliseconds;
                  ViewBag.myHtml = mystring+ mystringA;
              }
          return View();
      }
```

As you can see from Figure 12.85, although each of the PHP servers requires 5 seconds to run, the entire run requires only 6026 milliseconds (a bit over 6 seconds) so it's clear we're working asynchronously!

What did we have to do to make this happen? Well, when we call the urls originally we're not using an "await" or a ".Result." Instead, we just call them with the GetAsync alone.

The only nasty part of this is that we have to figure out what the return type from the GetAsync really is. In this case it is "Task<HttpResponseMessage>."

When you use an "await" it cleans up a lot of return type stuff for you. When you don't use "await" you have to do more work figuring out your return types yourself.

We did do an "await" on the ReadAsStringAsync, you do normally have to block *somewhere* just to make sure you return a real value for your result. However, those didn't take much time.

When in doubt about how something is operating in regard to synchronous or asynchronous, it's a good idea to time it.

Remember, by the way, that you have to do a Reset on your stopwatch after you first use it. Otherwise it will continue counting time from where you left off before.

12.2.12.7.4   Other ASP.NET CORE 1.0 Visual Studio 2015 Items

I've included a few other examples with the code provided for the instructor with this textbook that I didn't go through here. The reason is, they're pretty well the same as the ASP.NET MVC4 Visual Studio 2012 examples, except using Visual Studio 2015 instead. So I didn't include them here for fear of boring you to tears.

All the cURL stuff also works pretty well the same, by the way.

12.2.13   Is ASP.NET MVC Really RESTful?

Now that we know about ASP.NET MVC, let's think about the degree to which it is RESTful and the degree to which it is not RESTful.

It's certainly not based on SOAP or WSDL so from that regard we wouldn't classify it as non-RESTful.

It's definitely responding direct to HTTP messages, so in that regard it's RESTful.

Each HTTP message is represented by a web page, generically using URLs in the format:

    controller/action/id

StackOverflow (2010) has a good discussion about why this URL routing that is typically used by ASP.NET MVC is not RESTful by the basics employed by Fielding (see Chapter 2). That is, this kind of controller/action/id routing is not accessing a resource. Rather, it's calling an action which is more functionally-related than resource related. The StackOverflow (2010) argument is that if the URL looked like:

    resource/id

Then ASP.NET MVC would be RESTful. The StackOverflow (2010) discussion goes on to say that the resource/id kind of URL can indeed be created with ASP.NET MVC, so that would be RESTful.

In any case, think about it, using Fielding's criteria from Chapter 2. Exercise for the reader. ☺

WCF-RESTFUL EXERCISES

1. What does WCF use to create RESTful web services?
2. What annotation would you use to specify that a method is called using an HTTP GET?
3. What annotation would you use to specify that a method is called using an HTTP POST?
4. How would you select the use of JSON data instead of XML data?
5. Can WCF self-host a web service?

ASP.NET MVC AND ASP.NET CORE 1.0 EXERCISES

1. Compare .Result to await. What are the differences? What are the similarities?
2. What are the differences between:
     a.   ActionResult and Task<ActionResult>
     b.   Task<ActionResult> and Task<IActionResult>
3. Is ASP.NET MVC RESTful per Fielding's criteria?
4. How does [ValidateAntiForgeryToken] work? (look it up)
5. What are the advantages and disadvantages of using ViewBag to transfer data between controller and view versus using a model to transfer data between controller and view?
6. What happens if you're doing timing studies and you don't reset your stopwatch in between timing different items?
7. Why did I employ two separate PHP servers in the example in Section 12.2.12.7.3? What did this enable me to illustrate, and how did this work?
8. Play with using "await" on the GetAsync in Listing 12.40. What kinds of return types can you use?
9. Why wasn't the code in Listing 12.19 asynchronous? (*Hint*: Compare it to the example in Section 12.2.12.7.3)
10. Give an example of how to pass a model consisting of a simple data type to a view.

CONCEPTUAL QUESTIONS

1. In regard to various Internet Media Types (MIME types): Why doesn't WCF make use of Internet Media Types in a similar manner to JAX-RS (see Chapter 11 for JAX-RS)?
2. What are the advantages of asynchronous communication compared to synchronous communication and how does that apply to the technologies in this chapter: RESTful WCF, ASP.NET MVC?
     a.   What are some situations where you might want to use asynchronous communication? Would these situations be different for any of the technologies in this chapter?

3. In what ways do, RESTful Windows Communication Foundation, and ASP.NET MVC applications conform to the Service-Oriented Architectures paradigm (we discussed Service-Oriented Architectures in Chapter 9)? In what way do RESTful Windows Communication Foundation, and ASP.NET MVC *not* conform to the Service-Oriented Architectures paradigm?

4. What are the primary advantages of RESTful web services compared to non-RESTful web services such as JAX-WS or non-RESTful WCF. Give specific technology-related examples.

5. What are the primary advantages of RESTful web services compared to object-oriented middle-wares such as CORBA or EJB? What are the disadvantages? Give specific technology-related examples.

6. Are there any advantages or disadvantages of the RESTful .NET web services (RESTful WCF, ASP.NET MVC, ASP.NET CORE 1.0) compared to the RESTful web services we previously saw in Chapter 11 (JavaScript/PHP/AJAX, servlets, JAX-RS)?

BIBLIOGRAPHY

Anderson, R. 2012. Intro to ASP.NET MVC 4. http://www.asp.net/mvc/overview/older-versions/getting-started-with-aspnet-mvc4/intro-to-aspnet-mvc-4 (accessed July 29, 2016).

Anderson, R. 2016. Getting Started with ASP.NET Core MVC and Visual Studio. https://docs.asp.net/en/latest/tutorials/first-mvc-app/start-mvc.html# (accessed August 13, 2016).

cURL. 2015. Command Line Tool and Library. http://curl.haxx.se/ (accessed July 13, 2015).

Dusted Codes. 2016. Understanding ASP.NET Core 1.0 (ASP.NET 5) and Why It Will Replace Classic ASP.NET. https://dusted.codes/understanding-aspnet-core-10-aka-aspnet-5-and-why-it-will-replace-classic-aspnet (accessed September 2, 2016).

Egozi, K. 2013. Attribute Routing in ASP.NET MVC 5. https://blogs.msdn.microsoft.com/webdev/2013/10/17/attribute-routing-in-asp-net-mvc-5/ (accessed August 21, 2016).

Huston, V. 2001. Design Patterns. http://www.vincehuston.org/dp/ (accessed July 30, 2016).

Koirala, S. 2014. Webforms vs MVC and Why MVC Is Better? CodeProject. http://www.codeproject.com/Articles/821275/Webforms-vs-MVC-and-Why-MVC-is-better (accessed September 2, 2016).

Microsoft. 2014. Windows Authentication Overview. https://technet.microsoft.com/en-us/library/hh831472(v=ws.11).aspx (accessed August 13, 2016).

Microsoft. 2016. Microsoft to Acquire Xamarin and Empower More Developers to Build Apps on Any Device. https://blogs.microsoft.com/blog/2016/02/24/microsoft-to-acquire-xamarin-and-empower-more-developers-to-build-apps-on-any-device/#sm.00006mclo3wd5eumsru1cp2yoj4p7 (accessed September 2, 2016).

Microsoft Forum. 2015. What Is Difference between Actionresult and IActionresult. http://forums.asp.net/t/2071936.aspx?What+is+difference+between+Actionresult+and+IActionresult (accessed August 28, 2016).

MSDN. 2008. A Guide to Designing and Building RESTful Web Services with WCF 3.5. https://msdn.microsoft.com/en-us/library/dd203052.aspx (accessed March 16, 2016).

MSDN. 2010a. Controllers and Action Methods in ASP.NET MVC Applications. https://msdn.microsoft.com/en-us/library/dd410269(v=vs.100).aspx (accessed August 20, 2016).

MSDN. 2010b. WCF REST vs. WCF SOAP. https://msdn.microsoft.com/library/hh273094(v=vs.100).aspx (accessed March 16, 2016).

MSDN. 2015a. Entity Framework. Data Developer Center. https://msdn.microsoft.com/en-us/data/ef.aspx (accessed August 28, 2016).

MSDN. 2015b. WCF Web HTTP Programming Model. https://msdn.microsoft.com/en-us/library/bb412169(v=vs.110).aspx (accessed March 16, 2016).

MSDN. 2015c. <WebChannelFactory<TChannel> Class. https://msdn.microsoft.com/en-us/library/bb908674(v=vs.110).aspx (accessed July 13, 2015).

MSDN. 2015d. <webHttpBinding>. https://msdn.microsoft.com/en-us/library/bb412176(v=vs.110).aspx (accessed July 13, 2015).

MSDN. 2015e. <webHttpBehavior>. https://msdn.microsoft.com/enus/library/system.servicemodel.description.webhttpbehavior(v=vs.110).aspx (accessed July 13, 2015).

MSDN. 2016a. ActionResult Class. https://msdn.microsoft.com/en-us/library/system.web.mvc.actionresult(v=vs.118).aspx (accessed August 20, 2016).

MSDN. 2016b. HttpResponseMessage. Content Property. https://msdn.microsoft.com/en-us/library/system.net. http.httpresponsemessage.content(v=vs.118).aspx (accessed August 20, 2016).

MSDN. 2016c. IDisposable Interface. https://msdn.microsoft.com/en-us/library/system.idisposable(v=vs.110). aspx (accessed August 28, 2016).

MSDN. 2016d. IEnumerable Interface. https://msdn.microsoft.com/en-us/library/system.collections.ienumerable (v=vs.110).aspx (accessed August 28, 2016).

MSDN. 2016e. SQL Server Connection Strings for ASP.NET Web Applications .NET Framework 4.5. https:// msdn.microsoft.com/en-us/library/jj653752.aspx#datasource (accessed August 13, 2016).

Programmers Stack Exchange. 2011. What Is MVC, Really? http://programmers.stackexchange.com/questions/ 127624/what-is-mvc-really (accessed August 28, 2016).

Stack Overflow. 2008. What Is MVC (Model View Controller)? http://stackoverflow.com/questions/129921/ what-is-mvc-model-view-controller (accessed August 28, 2016).

Stack Overflow. 2010. What's so RESTful about ASP.NET MVC? http://stackoverflow.com/questions/ 3730777/whats-so-restful-about-asp-net-mvc (accessed August 28, 2016).

Stack Overflow. 2011. Servlet vs. RESTful. http://stackoverflow.com/questions/7874695/servlet-vs-restful (accessed February 10, 2016).

Stack Overflow. 2012. Is MVC RESTful by Design. http://stackoverflow.com/questions/9275613/is-mvc-restful-by-design (accessed July 29, 2016).

Stack Overflow. 2012. ValidateAntiForgeryToken Purpose, Explanation and Example. http://stackoverflow. com/questions/13621934/validateantiforgerytoken-purpose-explanation-and-example (accessed August 21, 2016).

Stack Overflow. 2014. Difference between MVC 5 Project and Web Api Project. http://stackoverflow.com/questions/22589245/difference-between-mvc-5-project-and-web-api-project (accessed September 2, 2016).

Stack Overflow. 2015. MVC Pattern, No Database, Where to Store Objects? http://stackoverflow.com/questions/ 29275878/mvc-pattern-no-database-where-to-store-objects (accessed August 21, 2016).

Stack Overflow. 2015. Purpose of ActionName. http://stackoverflow.com/questions/6536559/purpose-of-actionname (accessed August 21, 2016).

Stenberg, D. 2016. cURL. https://curl.haxx.se/ (accessed March 12, 2016).

TutorialsTeacher. 2016. Routing in MVC. http://www.tutorialsteacher.com/mvc/routing-in-mvc (accessed August 21, 2016).

W3Schools. 2015. HTML script <src> Attribute. http://www.w3schools.com/tags/att_script_src.asp (accessed September 27, 2015).

W3Schools. 2016. ASP.NET Web Pages—Adding Razor Code. http://www.w3schools.com/aspnet/webpages_ razor.asp (accessed September 2, 2016).

Wikipedia. 2016. Hypermedia. https://en.wikipedia.org/wiki/Hypermedia (accessed March 10, 2016).

Section V

Middleware for the Cloud

13 Introduction to the Cloud and Introduction to the OpenStack Cloud

13.1 JUST WHAT IS A CLOUD, ANYWAY?

As we saw previously in Section 1.3.6, IBM (2016) defines cloud computing as follows:

> Cloud computing, often referred to as simply "the cloud," is the delivery of on-demand computing resources—everything from applications to data centers—over the Internet on a pay-for-use basis.

So the idea with a cloud is that instead of doing your own computing and storing your data on the computer on your desktop yourself, you hire a company to do the computing and store the data on their big computer servers that you access via the web. This is the idea of a *public cloud*.

A company can also implement its own *private cloud*. That is, instead of having computing and data storage on employees' desks, the company can buy its own big servers, then the employees do their computing and store their data on those servers.

Hybrid clouds are also possible, where part of a company's computing is provided by a separate cloud company, and part is done in house.

There are three service models for cloud computing:

1. Infrastructure as a Service (IaaS)
2. Platform as a Service (PaaS)
3. Software as a Service (SaaS)

For Infrastructure as a Service, the cloud provider "rents out" infrastructure, including servers, storage, networking. They can offer pools of virtual machines (or can be physical computers), data storage either as block storage that is attached to a virtual machine directly or through a network drive or as object storage that is accessible via a web interface, as well as firewalls, etc. In this model, users provide their own operating system images and their own application software, these are used to create instances of the virtual machines. For the most part, users are in charge of maintaining their own operating system and application software. One well-known example of IaaS is the Amazon Elastic Compute Cloud (EC2).

For Platform as a Service, the cloud provider offers a complete computing platform, including: operating system, web server, database, etc., and also includes other services such as block storage that is attached to a virtual machine directly or through a network drive or as object storage that is accessible via a web interface. In this model, the user manages the application software whereas the cloud provider manages the computing platform and underlying hardware. Some well-known examples of PaaS are the Amazon Web Services Elastic Beanstalk and Google App Engine.

For Software as a Service (sometimes known as *Software-on-demand*), software is "rented" rather than purchased. The cloud provider offers the application software and databases. The cloud providers manage and operate the application software. Some examples of SaaS are Microsoft Office 365, DropBox, Google Docs, Citrix GoToMeeting, and various Salesforce.com offerings: Sales Cloud, Service, Cloud, etc.

Sometimes this SaaS offering can be run on top of some other cloud provider's IaaS or PaaS offering. For example, originally DropBox ran its offerings on top of the Amazon cloud.

13.2 WHY THE CLOUD? WHY NOT THE CLOUD? AND WHO ARE THE CLOUDS?

However, this brings up another issue. Under what circumstances should a company move its application(s) or general IT services to the cloud? When is it better for applications and IT services to stay separate? Or perhaps a company should run its own private cloud. Or perhaps a hybrid cloud.

Note that sometimes moving to a cloud makes sense, and sometimes moving away from a cloud makes sense. Many startup companies begin by hosting their applications on a cloud, for example, this is what DropBox did—see Metz (2016). I'm one of the founders of a new startup company myself—we do process capture and teamwork analysis—and we hosted our application on a cloud. Because I did it, it makes all kinds of sense. ☺ But it really does make a lot of sense for startup companies because then they don't have to buy servers and hire IT staff themselves, and it saves their capital to spend on development or marketing more directly related to making money.

But sometimes it also makes sense to move away from a cloud. For example, Metz (2016) discusses how DropBox decided that it was financially worth their while to create their own cloud, in that the cost of using Amazon services was higher than what they could achieve by setting up their own servers and hiring their own system administrators (cloud administrators). According to Butler (2016a), Akhil Gupta, vice president of Infrastructure for Dropbox, decided that the huge scale of DropBox in terms of quantities of data and number of users (500 petabytes and 500 million respectively as of March 2016) justified creating their own internal cloud. Also, creating their own internal cloud enabled DropBox to have end to end control so that they could improve a user's experience along with performance and reliability. There was one situation, however, discussed by both Metz (2016) and Butler (2016) of a mobile app company named Zynga, who started on Amazon Web Services, then as their business grew they created their own Z-cloud, but later still their business dropped off greatly and they returned to the Amazon Web Services cloud.

So what are some benefits for having your company's software on a cloud?

- If you don't have a huge quantity of users, data, or processing, then your costs are probably lower if you use a cloud:
  - You won't have to pay for as many system administrators
  - You won't have to buy big servers
  - You don't have to manage big networks
- You can have scalability, that is, if you have a sudden increase in users then the cloud infrastructure can handle it (of course, at a price).
  - To be able to do this yourself you would have to pay for and maintain extra infrastructure in terms of servers, networks, and system administrators
- Your data may be backed up at a different location, such that it can survive a large natural disaster. Possibly even a war.
- There are some security advantages:
  - The cloud provider has a big incentive to keep all its software up to date with security patches
    - Whereas you would have to have a good staff of system administrators, as well as regular update procedures, to make sure this is done in your own company
  - The cloud most likely provides some sort of physical security for its servers
    - If you do the same in your company, this requires locked rooms with access control, and additional procedures that must be followed. For example, who gets a key? and If someone is fired, do you change all the locks?
  - The cloud provider has a big incentive to hire good system administrators who have been background-checked

- There are some advantages in regard to data privacy
  - There are some expensive certifications that can be difficult for a small company to acquire
    - Wood and Tracy (2011) say that certification can be expensive for the healthcare industry to comply with the Health Insurance Portability and Accountability Action (HIPAA) and for the federal government organizations to comply with the Federal Information Security Management Act (FISMA)

What are some negatives for having your company's software on a cloud?

- Your particular application may not benefit from added scalability, particularly if it is a traditional monolithic application architecture for which a stable demand is expected
- It may be difficult to organize or rewrite your application such that it would run well when located on a cloud. There is some literature that says that an application must have a Service-Oriented Architecture in order to be able to be hosted on a cloud; we discussed this previously in Section 9.1.2
  - Even if it is possible to move your application to the cloud such that its performance is good, there will probably be some cost involved in making this happen. Perhaps significant cost.
- There may be security disadvantages associated with being on a cloud:
  - The cloud provider has a big incentive to have good security, however, if you onboard your software to a cloud, you give up control of its security.
    - You can perhaps specify in your Service Level Agreement that certain security measures be taken
      - But how do you know this is actually being done?
- There can be data privacy disadvantages associated with being on a cloud:
  - Your data would be managed by the cloud provider, not by you.
    - The system administrators would be vetted (given background checks) by the cloud provider, not by you
  - In large cloud companies with data centers located in other countries (maybe not that friendly to your own country), then physical location of the data can be a big issue.
  - How do you know the cloud provider is not mining your private data for its own purposes—see Winkler (2012)—and perhaps selling this information to a third party?
  - How do you ensure that your cloud provider is, indeed, meeting legal security requirements for your data, in cases where data privacy is legally required?
    - What is your company's liability if the cloud provider does this incorrectly?
  - There are cases where, by law or by privacy agreement, an individual wishes to delete his/her private information. How can you ensure the cloud provider actually does this?
  - What is your cloud provider's policy on notifying you if there has been a data breach? How long will this take?—see Winkler (2012)
  - What is your responsibility for notifying the cloud provider if your data has been breached? Do you have any liability?
- There may be performance disadvantages associated with being on a cloud:
  - It could be that the cloud's internal technologies are not well-tuned to how your application runs
    - Perhaps the cloud's infrastructure has been tuned to work well for a bigger customer
    - Thinking in a sneaky or maybe paranoid way, how do you know that "bigger customer" isn't your major competitor? After all, both companies can buy services from the same cloud provider.

There has been considerable discussion on whether your application must be in the form of a service-oriented architecture in order to move to the cloud. See Section 9.1.2 for a discussion of this.

13.2.1   WHO ARE THE CLOUDS?

According to Darrow (2015) of *Fortune* magazine, as of May 2015, far and away the largest cloud was Amazon Web Services, which according to the Gartner Magic Quadrant report, supplied more than 10 times the computing power to customers than the combined other 14 top cloud providers (of the top 15). (The Gartner, Inc. Magic Quadrant report is a market research into a specific technology industry.)

The remaining cloud providers in the top 15 (see Tsidulko 2015) are Microsoft Azure (the second biggest cloud provider), Google Compute Engine, CenturyLink, VMWare vCloud Air, IBM SoftLayer, Rackspace, Verizon Terremark, Virtustream, CSC, Fujitsu, Joyent, NTT Communications, Interoute, and Dimension Data.

Of these top 15 cloud providers, several provide proprietary cloud implementations, which include Amazon Web Services, Microsoft Azure, Google, VMWare vCloud Air, Verizon Terremark, Joyent.

Several employ an open source cloud: IBM SoftLayer, Rackspace, CSC BizCLoud, NTT Communications, and Fujitsu Cloud employ the OpenStack open source cloud computing platform, whereas Interoute employs the CloudStack open source cloud computing platform. We'll talk about open source cloud computing platforms shortly. ☺

Cantrill, CTO of Joyent, said that Joyent wanted to use OpenStack as an example of what *not* to do, according to Butler (2015). Joyent employs Triton containers instead of virtual machines. According to Cantrill:

> Triton lets you run secure Linux containers directly on bare metal via an elastic Docker host that offers tightly integrated software-defined networking.

A Docker container, Docker (2016a), is different from a virtual machine in that an operating system is not included in the container. Instead, according to Opensource.com (2016), a Docker container uses the same Linux kernel as the system it's running on. This gives a Docker container higher performance than a virtual machine. Also, Docker containers only need to contain software that the host computer doesn't already have.

13.2.2   OPEN SOURCE SOFTWARE TO SUPPORT PLATFORM AS A SERVICE (PaaS)

Since we've just talked about Docker containers, let's go a little further in that area and examine software that is used to support Platform as a Service (PaaS) offerings before we go on to the open source cloud computing platforms.

Butler (2016) mentioned some PaaS technologies that are being integrated with the OpenStack cloud computing platform. The purpose of these PaaS services are to allow developers to quickly create and deploy code on the infrastructure (in this case OpenStack infrastructure). He listed Kubernetes, which is being used or experimented with by 42% of OpenStack users, Cloud Foundry, which is being used by 24% of OpenStack users, and also Apache Mesos and RedHat OpenShift.

Kubernetes, made by Google, is used to automate the deployment of application containers across clusters of hosts. According to StackOverflow (2015):

> Kubernetes is a cluster orchestration system inspired by the container orchestration that runs at Google. Built by many of the same engineers who built that system. It was designed from the ground up to be an environment for building distributed applications from containers. It includes primitives for replication and service discovery as core primitives, whereas such things are added via frameworks in Mesos. The primary goal of Kubernetes is a system for building, running and managing distributed systems.

Kubernetes can be compared to Docker Swarm. Docker Swarm makes a pool of Docker hosts look like a single, virtual Docker host, that is, it makes a cluster of Docker hosts look like a single

Docker Application Programming Interface (API). In comparing Kubernetes to Docker, Farcic (2015) says:

> Kubernetes and Docker Swarm are probably [the] two most commonly used tools to deploy containers inside a cluster. Both are created as helper tools that can be used to manage a cluster of containers and treat all servers as a single unit.

Cloud Foundry is an open source PaaS technology that is used to build and deploy applications on public and private clouds; providing scalability is one of its abilities. To provide lifecycle management (release engineering, etc.), CloudFoundry uses an open source tool called BOSH. Cloud Foundry was originally created by VMWare, it became owned by Pivotal when VMWare and its parent company EMC spun off Pivotal in 2013.

Babcock (2015) says CloudFoundry is:

> ...still trying to find its standing somewhere between the public cloud and the enterprise data center.

Babcock also says that CloudFoundry supplies data services, including MySQL-as-a-Service, and also supplies RabbitMP messaging (we will talk briefly about RabbitMQ later on). It also provides a lightweight application server called Spring Boot that can be included with an application. (The Spring framework is an application framework for Java, and Spring Boot is a method for creating a stand-alone, easy-to-run Spring framework-based application.) CloudFoundry can also be integrated with Apache Tomcat. CloudFoundry supports Java, PHP, Python, Ruby, Node.js, Perl, and Google's Golang (Go).

There is a separate commercial product that belongs to Pivotal, called Pivotal Cloud Foundry. There is also a Cloud Foundry Foundation (2016), whose purpose is:

> ...to make Cloud Foundry the leading application platform for cloud computing worldwide.

The Cloud Foundry Foundation has 50+ members, including, as of 2016: Pivotal, VMWare, IBM, Accenture, Docker, Verizon, Cisco, Fujitsu, SUSE, among many others. Several companies offer PaaS services implemented using Cloud Foundry, these include IBM BlueMix and HP Helion among several others.

Apache Mesos (previously called Nexus), originally developed at the University of California in Berkeley, is an open source cluster manager. It provides abstractions of compute resources (CPU, storage, etc.) away from both physical computers and virtual machines. Distributed systems running on top of Mesos are called frameworks. Mesos decides what resources to give to a framework, then the framework decides how resources are allocated within its distributed system. Mesos supports C/C++, Java, Scala, Python, Perl, Haskell, and Go, see Vivien (2015).

OpenShift is the name of a PaaS offering by RedHat that uses the open source OpenShift Origin (2016a and 2016b) application container platform. OpenShift Origin is used to build, test, deploy, and manage cloud applications. It also provides lifecycle management. It is built on Docker containers and Kubernetes cluster management. OpenShift Origin has "cartridges," which provide the functionality required to run an application. These cartridges can include programming language support, database support, etc., and are extensible so any programming language or tool can be added.

13.2.3   OPEN SOURCE CLOUD PLATFORMS THAT SUPPORT INFRASTRUCTURE AS A SERVICE

According to Kleman (2015) arguably the major open source cloud platforms in the market that provide Infrastructure as a Service (IaaS) support are:

- OpenStack
- Apache CloudStack
- Eucalyptus
- OpenNebula

TABLE 13.1

Comparison of Open Source Clouds

Cloud	History	License	Governance Model	Language Written in	Installation Difficulty
OpenStack	Founded by Rackspace and NASA in 2010	Apache v2.0	Foundation	Python	Difficult
CloudStack	Released by Citrix into Apache in 2011	Apache v2.0	Technical Meritocracy	Java, C	Medium
Eucalyptus	Began at Rice Univ. and UCSB, now sponsored by HP. Has a formal compatibility agreement with AWS (close Amazon ties)	GPLv3.0	Benevolent Dictator	Java, C	Medium
OpenNebula	Sponsored OpenNebula Systems (formerly C12G)	Apache v2.0	Benevolent Dictator	C++, C, Ruby, Java, shell script, lex, yacc	

Which is the most likely to become the defacto standard? According to Burns (2013):

> While most independent sources interviewed for this story contend that OpenStack is a likely front runner, they all refused to pick an ultimate winner.

When comparing open source cloud platforms, OpenStack is by far the most widely used at the present time. Kleman (2015) mentioned that as of 2015 more than 150 companies were contributing to OpenStack development. Kleman says:

> Let's face facts: OpenStack is a more mature and more widely adopted platform. But that doesn't mean it's not facing the heat of other players in the market. There is a lot of money being pumped into platforms like CloudStack and even Eucalyptus.

According to Butler (2016), OpenStack can be used to create a public cloud or a private cloud, but 65% of the OpenStack users have used it for private clouds, and 16% have used it to create public clouds. Another 12% hire a service provider to host deployment of a dedicated OpenStack.

A brief comparison of the major open source cloud platforms is shown in Table 13.1.

Eucalyptus was purchased by HP in 2014. Now there is an HP Helion OpenStack cloud and an HP Helion Eucalyptus cloud.

In terms of security, according to Burns (2013), OpenStack's security, which is token-based, is strong. CloudStack provides baseline security with VLAN/Firewall, and Eucalyptus' security is key managed, and all five Eucalyptus components must register with each other.

In terms of architecture, OpenStack has a distributed architecture with several components, and a massively scalable storage system. CloudStack's architecture is monolithic. Eucalyptus has a limited graphical user interface (GUI), with a distributed five-part architecture that is similar to Amazon Web Services. OpenNebula has a monolithic architecture.

13.3   OPENSTACK CLOUD

The OpenStack Cloud is not a single monolithic unit. It is broken into several different services. This number of services tends to grow and change with time. ☺ I've listed a few current ones in Table 13.2. I haven't listed all of them, just the ones you're more likely to (kind of) understand. We won't look at

TABLE 13.2

Some Component OpenStack Services (Among Others)

	Service	Description
Nova	Compute	Manages and automates computing resources, controls virtual machines
Glance	Image	Stores disk images and snapshots of virtual machines
Keystone	Identity	User authentication for all OpenStack services, role-based access
Horizon	Dashboard/GUI	Allows provisioning and automating services
Neutron	Networking	Manages the networking of the cloud. IP addresses, VLANS, etc.
Cinder	Block Storage	Allows blocks of storage to be assigned to compute instances.
Swift	Object Storage	Object storage, accessed through web API
Heat	Orchestration	Allows a virtual machine's compute, networking and storage to be automatically configured
Trove	Database	Handles databases
Ceilometer	telemetry	Monitoring and Billing system
Sahara	Elastic Map Reduce	Handles Hadoop clusters
Zaqar	Multiple Tenant Cloud Messaging	Can be used in SaaS to send messages between multiple components of the SaaS
Manila	shared file system service	API includes primitives to create, delete, and give/deny access to a share of a file system
Searchlight	search service	Allows search across different OpenStack services
Barbican	security API	Secure storage and management of passwords, encryption keys, and certificates

TABLE 13.3

Some OpenStack Supported Public Clouds as of January 2015

Internap's Agile Cloud (Netherlands, Canada)	IO Cloud (USA)
Rackspace (USA, China, UK, Australia)	City Cloud (Sweden)
DreamCompute (USA)	HP Helion Public Cloud
teutoStack Public cloud (Germany)	DataCentred Public Cloud (UK)
OVH Group RunAbove (Canada, France)	Numergy Cloud (France)
UOS Cloud (China)	KLOUD (Mexico)
Dualtec Public Cloud (Brazil)	Elastx (Sweden)
Anchor OpenCloud (Australia)	Cloudwatts Cloud Services (France)
Auro Enterprise Public Cloud (Canada)	

all of these in this textbook, just a few of the most important. Remember that there are yet more OpenStack components that I didn't even list!

As we saw in the previous section, OpenStack is the most widely used open source cloud platform. Some examples of OpenStack supported public clouds are shown in Table 13.3.

Some examples of OpenStack supported private clouds are shown in Table 13.4.

The OpenStack cloud was originally created by combining the Nebula cloud computing project from NASA with the Swift Object storage project from Rackspace. Llewellyln (2012) quotes the former Nebula project manager, Ray O'Brien from NASA, as follows:

> … on the first open source release of our Nova controller, we found that Rackspace had taken a strikingly similar technical approach to their storage systems and were set to begin the construction of a compute controller just as we were preparing to focus on storage. Given our technical alignment and with the

TABLE 13.4

Some OpenStack Supported Private Clouds as of January 2015

IBM Cloud Openstack Services	Rackspace Private Cloud
(Netherlands, USA, China, UK, Australia, Singapore, Canada)	(China, USA, UK, Australia)
Metacloud OpenStack (China, Netherlands, UK, USA, Singapore)	Blue Box Cloud Private Cloud (USA, Switzerland)
Mirantis Openstack Express (Netherlands, USA, Singapore)	AURO Enterprise Private Cloud (Canada)
BlueBox Cloud (USA)	UOS Managed Private Cloud (China)
Morphlabs Enterprise Cloud (Philippines)	DataCentred Private Cloud (UK)

open source release of Rackspace's Swift storage software, we joined forces to create OpenStack. Our hope was that a community would form around these two pieces of software toward the construction of an open source cloud operating system. To say that our greatest hopes in this regard were met would be an understatement. OpenStack today has the support of hundreds of individuals and organizations around the world, all set on realizing the original vision for the project.

In the next few sections, 13.3.1 through 13.3.3, we will do an overview of how to use OpenStack the easiest way, using the OpenStack graphical user interface (GUI) (the Dashboard). First we'll look briefly at some hints as to how you might do an OpenStack installation. Next we'll look at how to control OpenStack with the Dashboard. We'll use the Dashboard to create an instance of a virtual machine. Then we will secure shell (SSH) to that virtual machine—so we can use it. ☺

Note that it's a little dangerous to go through the Dashboard interfaces in detail—dangerous based on the cloud changes so quickly, who knows how long these interfaces will be current. ☺ But even if the OpenStack Dashboard (Horizon) interface were to change considerably, it's still worth it to you, the reader, to read through this section. Going through basic cloud "stuff" using a GUI like this to do commands and to track the results of commands is the best way to get a new student started on the cloud. After you go through this, you'll have a much better idea of what a cloud is all about.

After you the student have a good idea as to the kinds of things that can happen in the OpenStack cloud, then we'll look in depth at some of the components that make up the OpenStack cloud. We will look at Keystone, OpenStack's Identity (authentication) service. Then we will look at OpenStack Nova, the compute node for OpenStack, which is the heart of the OpenStack cloud. Finally, we will look at Software-Defined Networking (SDN) and how that is implemented in OpenStack Neutron.

After we examine these components in depth, we will look at the OpenStack RESTful interface. We will look at how to authenticate and then how to start an instance of a virtual machine. We will do this first using cURL commands, then with Python, and finally using the OpenStack command-line clients.

Before we get started thinking about installation, there are two suggested minimal installation architectures for OpenStack. If you use Neutron, there is a three-node minimal installation:

- Controller node—runs Keystone Identity Service, Glance image service, Horizon dashboard, message queue, and supporting SQL database, as well as management portions for the Compute node, Networking node. Also runs Networking plugins.
- Compute node (can be more than one)—runs portion of the hypervisor that operates virtual machines (the KVM hypervisor is the default). It also runs the Networking plugin and an agent to connect project (tenant) networks to VMs and to provide firewall and security group services.
- Networking node—runs agents to handle internet connectivity for VMs. Also provisions project (tenant) networks and provide switching, routing, Dynamic Host Configuration Protocol (DHCP), and Network Address Translation services.

If you don't use Neutron but instead use nova-network (which has been deprecated):

- Controller node—runs Keystone Identity Service, Glance image service, Horizon dashboard, message queue and supporting SQL database, as well as management portion of the Compute node.
- Compute node (can be more than one)—runs portion of the hypervisor that operates virtual machines (the KVM hypervisor is the default). It provisions project (tenant) networks and provides firewall and security group services.

13.3.1 OpenStack Installation Tips

Installing OpenStack can be difficult. One who has recently gone through the OpenStack installation process might be tempted to add a few expletives in front of the word "difficult."

One of the major reasons an OpenStack install is so difficult is that OpenStack consists of numerous sub-applications, each with its own issues (see Table 13.2).

You also have to choose which hypervisor you're going to work with, and install that. According to Butler (2016), 93% of OpenStack clouds use the Kernel Virtual Machine (KVM) hypervisor.

OpenStack sits alongside the hypervisor, and gives you control over it, it basically gives an administrator interface to the hypervisor to start up virtual machines and make changes to virtual machines.

As I mentioned in the Preface to this textbook, I also created a course, CS454/CS554, Cloud Computing—I first taught a version of that as a selected-topics course in Spring 2015, and then taught the regular course in Spring 2016. I and my students, along with our CS department system administrators, have managed to achieve several different kinds of OpenStack installs. In fact, installing OpenStack was one of the projects in the Cloud Computing course. What I'm going to provide you here are some of our lessons learned, to hopefully help you when you try to install OpenStack.

First of all, make sure you have enough RAM!!!!! The absolute smallest quantity of RAM that we've been able to make OpenStack really work in terms of running virtual machine instances containing a real operating system was 16 Gigabytes, and you really need 32 Gigabytes. With 16 Gigabytes, OpenStack will be able to run a "real" operating system, such as Ubuntu or Fedora. When we tried OpenStack with 8 Gigabytes, we were able to get it to install, but we could only run the test Cirros operating system in the virtual machine instances. With 4 Gigabytes of RAM, OpenStack flatly will not install, it thrashes and repeatedly hits the disk. The DevStack documentation claims that some versions of the install will work with only 4 Gigabytes of RAM but we have not found this to be the case.

We did our first installs using the KVM hypervisor. We have also managed to get OpenStack to work with the Xen hypervisor, of those with Xen, the install using XenServer was the easiest. Right now our best installs have been done with KVM, but we think that's just because we've been using KVM longer and we understand it better.

Our easiest installs have been achieved using DevStack:

http://docs.openstack.org/developer/devstack/

A DevStack install, however, is not intended to be a full production install of OpenStack. DevStack is not a general OpenStack installer. However, for using OpenStack for academic purposes it works *fairly* well. Note that you may end up with the occasional unexpected thing—in the middle of the Spring 2016 semester, we found that the DevStack install didn't have OpenStack's Amazon Web Services EC2 interface enabled, we had to reconfigure our installs so we could use that interface—our previous DevStack installs had the EC2 interface enabled, so this change surprised us. It's best to make your own copy of the DevStack version you want to use, so you can keep working on that particular version. That's what we have done.

Our most stable DevStack install, that we had the least trouble with, was the single machine install:

http://docs.openstack.org/developer/devstack/guides/single-machine.html

The single machine install, installed with static IP addresses, is the install I have used the most during my class lectures. We've installed it both on top of minimal Ubuntu, and on top of standard Ubuntu. If you're a student without a lot of sysadmin background (or alternately you don't have sysadmin help) then I recommend doing this install.

However, for the purpose of teaching cloud computing I wasn't really happy with this one, as it puts the cloud management and the cloud virtual machines ON THE SAME computer. Which seemed Mickey Mouse to me, as we of course are trying to teach what happens in a cloud, with many different servers running many different virtual machines.

So we tried the Multi-Node lab DevStack installation that assumes you'll have multiple physical machines. We weren't able to get this working well in our environment; it tended to interact poorly with our campus network. As of writing this, we are still working on getting this installation to work well on our campus network, along with some other work we're doing to install our own SDN (using Open vSwitch and OpenFlow). (Note that OpenStack Neutron is currently somewhat in flux.) Behind a router, so it's not conflicting with our campus network, we have managed to achieve a full Open-Stack production install, and we're working on getting that to a central server on the campus network.

What we ended up with, due to our problems with the campus network, for teaching purposes, was a different kind of configuration, where we create two virtual machines, and store an OpenStack manager node in one virtual machine and an OpenStack compute node in the other virtual machine. That way, we "pretend" we have a two physical machine environment. We are using the DevStack install for manager and compute node. This works, and it is what I have used to teach my classes.

In our procedure that we used in Spring 2016, first we installed Ubuntu Server (version 14.04). Then we installed virt-manager, and libvirt with KVM/QEMU. Then we created a virtual machine that we named "manager." We loaded a minimal Ubuntu onto the manager virtual machine (Ubuntu 14.04 Trusty Tahr, 64-bit). Then inside the manager virtual machine we did a DevStack install of OpenStack. Next we created a virtual machine that we named "compute." We loaded a minimal Ubuntu onto the compute node virtual machine (Ubuntu 14.04 Trusty Tahr, 64-bit). Then we did a DevStack install of OpenStack on the compute virtual machine. The local.conf file of the manager virtual machine is set as one would do for a cluster controller on a physical multi-node install, whereas the local.conf file of the compute virtual machine is set basically as one would do for a compute node on a physical multi-node install.

If you don't want to mess with DevStack, descriptions of a production level install of OpenStack are online. They can be quite difficult.

13.3.2 How to Use OpenStack

The OpenStack Dashboard is a GUI that allows control of the various OpenStack components. The Dashboard is implemented as a separate application, called Horizon.

After you have done an OpenStack DevStack install, when you bring up OpenStack, you will get a login screen. I recommend logging in as admin (with whatever password you gave yourself during the install). After you log in, you will see the screen shown in Figure 13.1.

As you can see in Figure 13.1, this came up in the Projects panel. The Projects panel here shows you that you have a project named demo and a project named admin, these are the ones you would use. The basic DevStack install gives you a project and login named demo, and a project and login named admin. You can, of course, add additional projects. In this textbook, however, we will stick to these two.

At the top of this page, will be a menu where you can select which project you are currently using. This is shown in Figure 13.2.

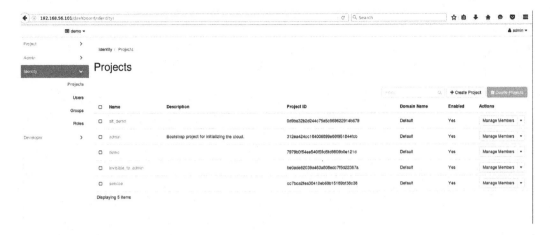

FIGURE 13.1 OpenStack projects panel.

FIGURE 13.2 Select project in OpenStack.

Let's move to the admin project while we walk through the dashboard some more. Start by opening the admin project tab, so you can look at what the admin project is doing itself. This is shown in Figure 13.3.

Now select the instances tab. This is shown in Figure 13.4. You can see in Figure 13.4 that I previously (3 days ago, as I am writing this) created an instance of an operating system. The instance is called "anewinstance." It is running the toy operating system (the image that is assigned to the instance) that comes with OpenStack (cirros), in this case it is running cirros-0.3.2-x86_64-uec (that would usually show under the image name, but due to the way this was created it unfortunately doesn't show). It has the m1.nano size, which gives it a particular amount of memory and etc., and it has a keypair named tryitout that I previously created and assigned to it.

Let's discuss these various items.

First of all, an instance is what OpenStack calls a running OpenStack virtual machine. An image is a copy of an operating system. When an instance (virtual machine) is started, it must be given some kind of operating system to run. OpenStack can run many different versions of Linux (including Ubuntu, RedHat, Fedora, SUSE, Debian) and it can run Windows. Several tested images are available, or you can create your own image.

FIGURE 13.3   Admin project tab.

FIGURE 13.4   Instances in admin project.

The CirrOS image (shows up as cirros on the Dashboard) is a small test version of Linux that is included with OpenStack. Its primary advantage is that it doesn't require a lot of memory to run.

The keypair associated with an OpenStack instance consists of a public key and a private key. You can use the OpenStack dashboard to create these credentials, or you can create them other ways (you can use SSH-keygen, for example). If you plan to use SSH (secure shell) to log into your instance, you will need a keypair in most cases (there are username/password options for some images). When you create a keypair using the OpenStack dashboard, it will register the public key with the OpenStack instance, and it will allow you to download the private key so you can keep it safe.

Let's create a new keypair that we can assign to a new instance that we will also create. Select the Access & Security tab on the Dashboard. It will come up with Security Group selected as default. We're going to continue to use the Default security group, since this is an introductory textbook, we just don't have time to get into everything!

However, we have to configure the Default security group (to allow us later on to connect to the instance that we're going to create). You must set your security group to allow SSH access and also to allow Internet Control Message Protocol (ICMP) access (we're going to pretty well ignore what is meant by ICMP here, see Section 3.5.1 for a discussion of what it does). See the Manage Rules button in Figure 13.5. After you click on this, you will see the screen shown in Figure 13.6.

FIGURE 13.5 Access and security tab, default security group.

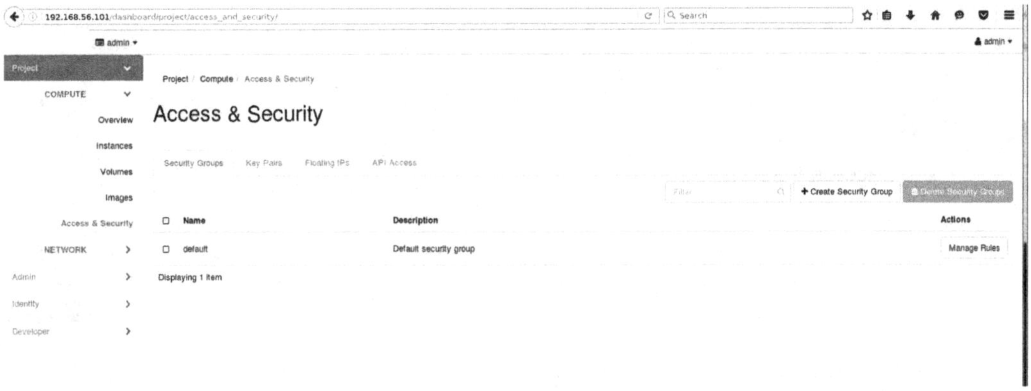

FIGURE 13.6 Manage security group rules.

See the Add Rule button in Figure 13.6? Click that and we move on to selecting rules. The first rule we must select is the All ICMP rule, see this in Figure 13.7. You select All ICMP from the dropdown menu and click the Add button.

We don't have a screenshot for it here, but you must similarly select SSH from the drop down menu and click the Add button for that as well.

Now select the Key Pairs tab. You will see the screen shown in Figure 13.8. Note that this has a Create Key Pair button (you could also import a key pair that you previously created in a different way, that's another option).

Select Create Key Pair, and name it "myveryownkeypair." You will get the screen we show in Figure 13.9.

You can then download "myveryownkeypair.pem." This .pem file will contain your private key. Take care of it! (The file extension ".pem" specifies a container file that can store private keys, public keys, or digital certificates. It originally stood for Privacy Enhanced Email—that particular email technology was never heavily used, but the .pem files remain.) Anybody who has access to this file can log into all your virtual machines. It's like having your password.

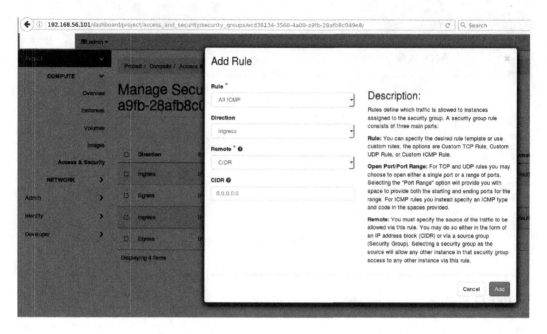

FIGURE 13.7   Add Rule all ICMP.

FIGURE 13.8   Key Pairs tab.

So now you have your own keypair associated with the Default security group. So when you create an instance using that security group, you can specify that that instance will be accessible using this particular keypair.

Let's go start an instance. First, select the demo project from the menu at the top (we showed you this menu previously in Figure 13.3). Now select the Project tab, then the Instances tab. There should be a "Launch Instance" tab toward the right-hand side of the screen. Click on the Launch Instance tab. You will get the screen shown in Figure 13.10.

For instance name, type in "myveryowninstance."

Click Next to go to the Source tab. For "Select Boot Source" click "Image." For "Create New Volume" click "No." Then on the available images at the bottom, click the + button beside cirros. CirrOS is the small test operating system. This is the safest! Because hopefully you have enough RAM to allow it to run. We're using the "-uec" version of cirros ("uec" stands for Ubuntu Enterprise Cloud, which was an Ubuntu cloud solution that has been replaced) which is all that shows up on this screen (if you look at the Images screen you would also see other cirros images). Note that

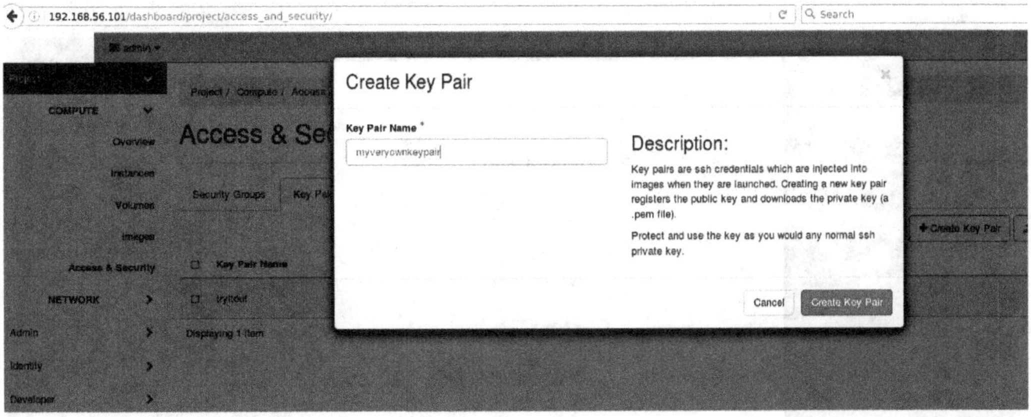

FIGURE 13.9 Create Key Pairs.

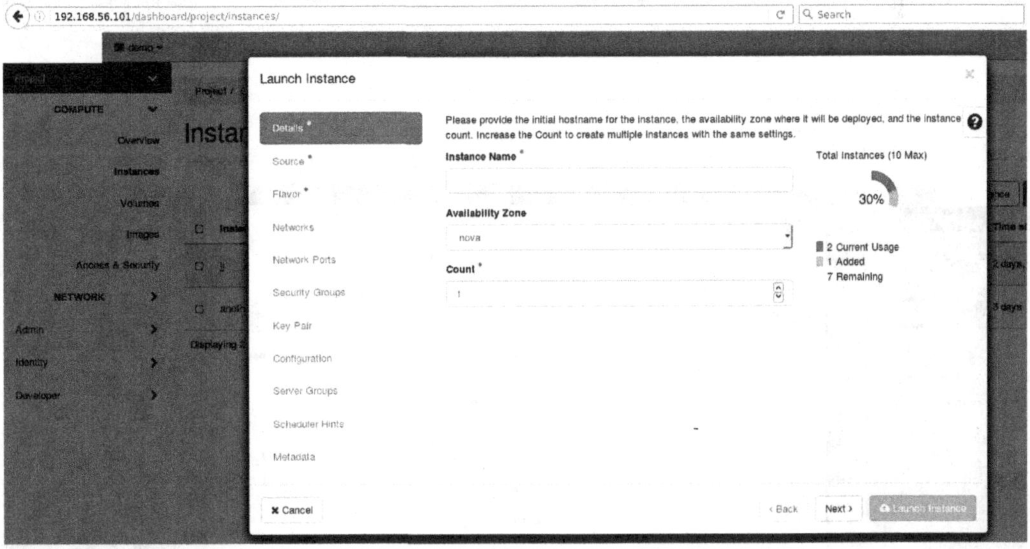

FIGURE 13.10 Launch instance.

we selected "No" for Create New Volume (when we do this, the image name will show up on our Instances screen).

This will give you the screen in Figure 13.11.

Click Next to go to the Flavor tab. This corresponds to various choices about the number of virtual CPUs, how much disk memory you're allowing this instance to use (various kinds of disks), and how much RAM you're allowing this instance to use. This starts out with m1.nano, which is the smallest. Let's use m1.nano because maybe that will be small enough to fit into the quantity of RAM we have. The characteristics of this flavor are shown in Figure 13.12.

If you're using OpenStack on a server with lots and lots of RAM, then the amount of RAM you assign to an instance is not that big a deal. However, if you have an OpenStack install on a computer with not too much RAM, this can be a big issue. By trial and error, we found that the DevStack version of OpenStack (as of 2015) requires a minimum of 8 Gigabytes of RAM just to install and to run a few cirros instances. To really run real instances using Ubuntu or Fedora images, you need at least

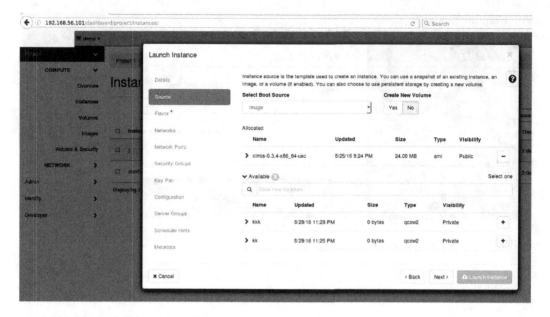

FIGURE 13.11   Select Image to be used in a new instance.

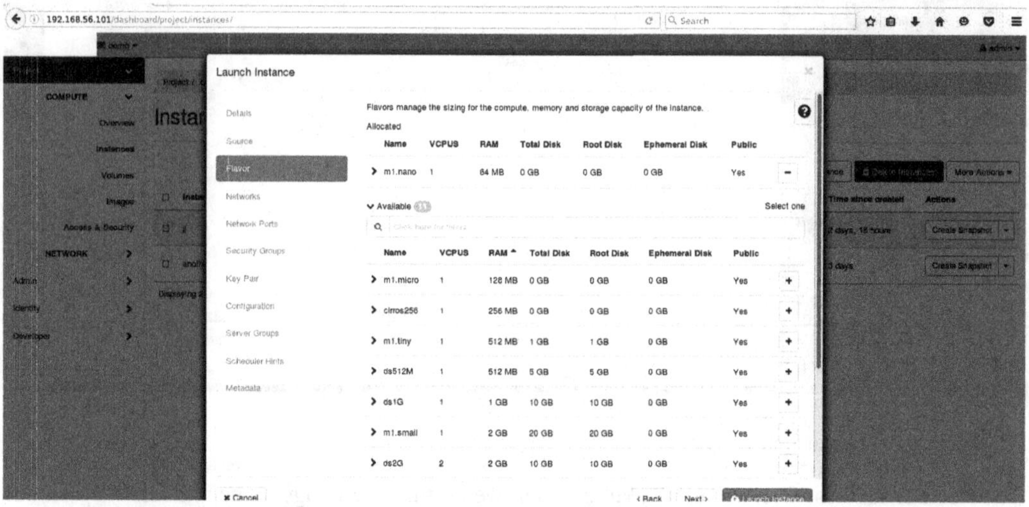

FIGURE 13.12   Characteristics of Flavor m1.medium.

16 Gigabytes of RAM. (Note that with only 4 Gigabytes of RAM, we weren't able to get OpenStack to even install. It apparently starts disk thrashing.)

Now BEFORE you select Launch, select the Access & Security tab. On this tab, select the keypair you created "myveryownkeypair." This is shown in Figure 13.13.

Now select the Launch button in the bottom right-hand corner. This will start up your instance, and include the correct keypair. See your running instance in Figure 13.14.

If you forgot to create the keypair, then this running instance will have an empty spot where the keypair name should have been.

FIGURE 13.13   Launch instance with Key Pair.

FIGURE 13.14   Running instance.

13.3.3   How to Log into OpenStack Instance with SSH

We will now secure shell (SSH) into the instance that you previously created. To avoid networking issues, because our network might be different from whatever network you're using, we will "cheat" in that we will do all our work from where the OpenStack Manager was previously installed (we called it the controller node in Section 13.3). That is, we will log direct onto the computer where the OpenStack Manager was installed. This could be a virtual machine, or a separate computer, depending on how you did the install. The OpenStack Manager will be running on Linux.

First, you must have some version of secure shell (SSH) on the machine where you have the OpenStack Manager installed. If for some reason your machine doesn't already have this, and you haven't used this before, google for "SSH," there is a lot of documentation about it on the web, and you can download it and install it for free.

First you are going to type:

ssh -i myveryownkeypair.pem cirros@10.0.0.4

Note that according to the Instance page on the Dashboard, myveryowninstance was running at local IP address 10.0.0.4. So that is the IP address we use here.

If you look back at the OpenStack images, this cirros image has "cirros" as its username. That's why we use cirros@10.0.0.4. You do NOT use myveryowninstance@10.0.0.4, this won't work.

If you go to the OpenStack documentation page that talks about images, it will give the usernames for login for several of the images that come with OpenStack. Of course for CirrOS, the username is "cirros." For the Ubuntu images, the username is "ubuntu." For the Fedora images, the username is "fedora."

The "-i" option with SSH says that a private key will be read from the given file.

The first time you do this, with this key, SSH will ask you if you want to add the remote host to a list of known hosts. That is, it will tell you that the authenticity of the remote host cannot be established and asks if you want to continue connecting. Type "yes." At this point, the remote host will be added to the list of known hosts.

There are a few problems that can happen, however. One such problem is shown in Listing 13.1. Here you see a situation where you already had the key in the known–hosts file.

LISTING 13.1   Key Already in known_hosts

```
letzkorn@letzkorn:~/testitout$ ssh -i myveryownkeypair.pem cirros@10.0.0.5
@@@@@@@@@@@@@@@@@@@@@@@@@@@@@@@@@@@@@@@@@@@-
@@@@@
@         WARNING: REMOTE HOST IDENTIFICATION HAS CHANGED!         @
@@@@@@@@@@@@@@@@@@@@@@@@@@@@@@@@@@@@@@@@@@@-
@@@@@

IT IS POSSIBLE THAT SOMEONE IS DOING SOMETHING NASTY!
    Someone could be eavesdropping on you right now (man-in-the-middle attack)!
    It is also possible that a host key has just been changed.
    The fingerprint for the RSA key sent by the remote host is fe:3b:d3:8e:3a:ad:11:1d:0a:a7:
af:80:ad:43:bd:fa.
    Please contact your system administrator.
    Add correct host key in /home/letzkorn/.ssh/known_hosts to get rid of this message.
    Offending RSA key in /home/letzkorn/.ssh/known_hosts:1 remove with: ssh-keygen
-f "/home/letzkorn/.ssh/known_hosts" -R 10.0.0.5
    RSA host key for 10.0.0.5 has changed and you have requested strict checking.
    Host key verification failed.
letzkorn@letzkorn:~/testitout$ rm /home/letzkorn/.ssh/known_hosts
```

This could be a man in the middle attack, as the warning says. However, since you've been playing around starting up instances with different key pairs, the chances are this is just you having changed things. As the message says, you can remove the host from the known_hosts file as follows:

ssh-keygen -f "/home/letzkorn/.ssh/known_hosts" -R 10.0.0.5

Or, alternately, you can just delete the known_hosts file from the .ssh directory using the "rm" command.

Another problem you might have is shown in Listing 13.2.

LISTING 13.2   Wrong Permissions for Keypair File

letzkorn@letzkorn:~/testitout$ ssh -i myveryownkeypair.pem cirros@10.0.0.5
   The authenticity of host "10.0.0.5 (10.0.0.5)" can't be established.
   RSA key fingerprint is fe:3b:d3:8e:3a:ad:11:1d:0a:a7:af:80:ad:43:bd:fa.
   Are you sure you want to continue connecting (yes/no)? Yes
   Warning: Permanently added "10.0.0.5" (RSA) to the list of known hosts.

   @@-
   @@@@@@@
   @   WARNING: UNPROTECTED PRIVATE KEY FILE!   @
   @@-
   @@@@@@@

   Permissions 0644 for "myveryownkeypair.pem" are too open.
   It is required that your private key files are NOT accessible by others.
   This private key will be ignored.
   bad permissions: ignore key: myveryownkeypair.pem
   cirros@10.0.0.5's password:

Here it tells you that your permissions are too open for your private key file. This is bad, you don't want other people to be able to read your private key. Do the following:

   chmod 600 myveryownkeypair.pem

This sets permissions on the private key such that only the owner (you) can read it and write it.

So now, if you do this command, you will get what is shown in Listing 13.3. That is, it will give you a $ prompt. To make sure you are actually inside cirros, type "pwd." It will return /home/cirros, as shown in Listing 13.3.

LISTING 13.3   Inside Cirros Instance

   letzkorn@letzkorn:~/testitout$ chmod 600 *.pem
   letzkorn@letzkorn:~/testitout$ ssh -i myveryownkeypair.pem cirros@10.0.0.5
   $ pwd
   /home/cirros
   $

So you have now logged into your instance!

13.3.4   OPENSTACK KEYSTONE

Keystone is a common authentication system used by all the OpenStack services. Keystone is accessed using the OpenStack Identity API, and must be configured before use.
   Keystone services include:

1. Identity
   - Credential validation (username/password)
   - Maintains users, groups, projects, domains, roles

2. Token
   - After credentials have been verified, tokens for authentication are generated/validated/ managed
3. Catalog
   - An endpoint registry used for endpoint discovery
4. Policy
   - Rule-based authorization, rule management

Data types recognized by Keystone are:

- User—has account credentials, has project or domain
- Group—collection of users, has project or domain
- Project (earlier called "Tenant")—unit of ownership, has one or more Users
- Domain—unit of ownership, has Users, Groups, Projects
- Role—a descriptive metadata item, with User/Project pair
- Token—identifying credential, used with User or User/Project
- Rule—a set of requirements for performing an action
- Also key/value metadata, used with User/Project pair

In order to focus on the more simple situations, to help us get started, we'll mostly ignore Domains. They're a higher level concept that comes into play when you have multiple users and projects and groups. We're going to stick with one or two users and one or two projects and one or two groups. No point in going too far too fast or you the student will get lost. ☺

Note that early versions of OpenStack referred to "Tenants" then somewhere along the way there was a decision made to change this to "Project." The OpenStack online documentation tends to use these terms interchangeably. ☺

13.3.4.1 Security Groups

A security group contains a set of rules to allow it to filter IP packets. You can have security groups that are specific to your project. If you don't create a security group, the default security group will be used.

To be able to SSH into your instance, you have to set the security group you are using to allow SSH and ICMP access. How to do this using the dashboard was shown previously in Section 13.3.2. You can also do this with various other methods: cURL commands, nova command-line tool, neutron command-line tool, etc. However, I didn't include these in this textbook for fear of making it all too complicated and thus confusing you the student. ☺ For now, just plan on setting your security groups with the dashboard as specified in Section 13.3.2. If you need to use the other commands later, it's all online. The OpenStack references related to security groups in the bibliography provided for this chapter will give you what you need.

13.3.4.2 Tokens

Keystone allows different kinds of authentication; these include:

- Username/password
- Token-based
  - Universally Unique Identifier (UUID) tokens
  - Public Key Infrastructure (PKI)/ Public Key Infrastructure Compressed (PKIZ) tokens
  - Fernet tokens
- Amazon Web Services

Also, Keystone allows plugins to extend authentication mechanisms.

One way to authenticate is to employ username/password. However, you would have to supply them in every separate command to an API, which means that each command sent is a chance for your username and password to be stolen. It also means that you have to store the username and password locally, or you will have to re-enter them (type them in) for every separate command! It can be dangerous to store them locally, since someone might steal them, but re-entering them every time is just too much in a situation where you have multiple commands.

An alternative is to use tokens. A token is valid only for a limited time, which means that even if a token is stolen when it is being sent across the network in a command to an API, it is a short time until the thief can no longer use it. Similarly, if you store (cache) a token locally, even if it is stolen in the case when your local account is hacked, it is a short time until the thief can no longer use it.

By the way, a brief parenthetical comment: normally we use the word *hacker* rather than "thief" when we're thinking about break-ins to a computer. There's a bit of a traditional tendency for computer folks to think of hackers as being clever, outwitting the authority figures who run big computer systems. However, let's think about what can happen when someone hacks your computer and acquires your password or private key or token that you use to connect to a big public cloud. That person can then run software on your account and your credit card will be charged for it. That hacker can potentially run up thousands of dollars on your account. How is that different from a thief taking your wallet and using your credit card? Think about it.

One big reason for making this point right now, before you get started using clouds—if you do log onto a big public cloud, be careful about your credentials. Even if your credentials aren't stolen, you can lose a lot of money if you're not careful with them. There's a market for stolen computing power. For example, one reason people steal computing time is to run bitcoin miners.

There's one case of a guy named Ryan Hellyer who made his Amazon-hosted website's code open source. Unfortunately, he had stored his Amazon credentials in a config file on the website. Amazon sent him an urgent email telling him to check his EC2 virtual machine usage. He checked his billing and it was okay, but when he checked his virtual machine usage, there were huge numbers of virtual machines running and being charged to him. He had to delete each separately, which took several hours. He ended up owing $6000 to Amazon. Note also that his Amazon bill wasn't updated in real time so it took a few hours for the charges to show up on the bill.

Another dude named Joe Moreno accidentally included his Amazon credentials in some code he uploaded to GitHub. He ended up owing more than $5000 to Amazon.

It's not just Amazon this happens to, many public clouds have these kinds of accidentally publicized credentials cases. Sometimes the public clouds forgive these kinds of accidental charges. Do you want to take the chance?

The size of tokens is a major issue, since performance degrades when huge amounts of token data are transmitted across a network and also when huge amounts of token data are stored in a persistent token database, since authentication requests require searching for the token in persistent storage, and can take a very long time. This can result in the need to repeatedly flush the persistent token database (some token formats, such as the Fernet tokens, don't have this problem). Note that some token formats are larger than others, which exacerbates the problem.

Before we get into how different kinds of tokens work in terms of generating and validating the tokens, let's first look at what happens when a token is revoked.

First of all, why would one wish to revoke a previously created token? I mean, it's going to expire soon enough, right?

Fisher (2015) gives the following reasons for intentionally revoking tokens:

- A user has been deleted
- A role has been removed from a user
- A user has been removed from a project
- A user has logged out of the OpenStack Dashboard (Horizon)
- A user has switched to a different project in the OpenStack Dashboard (Horizon)

Obviously with some of these it is very inappropriate to just wait for the token to expire. For example, perhaps a user has been removed from a project for bad behavior, or a user is no longer allowed to use a particular role because the user is no longer associated with that business function. Clearly in both situations there could be repercussions for a user being allowed continued access—even potential financial repercussions.

Of course, this naughty behavior would have to happen fairly fast because a token has a limited lifetime, although it varies based on configuration settings. For example, the default token expiration time that is set in the Keystone configuration file, according to OpenStack (2016f) is 3600 seconds (or 1 hour). But some evildoers are super speedy. ☺

The way OpenStack handles this is, a revocation event is stored in a revocation event list on Keystone. Everytime a token is validated with Keystone, Keystone must check this revocation list. If the token is there, then Keystone must reject it, even if the token is otherwise valid. Keystone also does some cleanup every time a token is checked, it removes any expired tokens from the revocation list. See Fischer (2015) and Desai and Pokorny (2015) for more information.

13.3.4.2.1   Universally Unique Identifier Tokens

When configured to use UUID tokens, Keystone generates tokens in UUID 4 format. See Section 3.6 for an in-depth description of UUID. However, briefly, a UUID is an identifier that is most likely different from all other identifiers in the area where you're looking at them. That is, the way a UUID is generated makes it unlikely that two separately generated UUIDs are the same.

UUID tokens are 128 bits (16 bytes) long.

The way that UUID tokens work on Keystone is as follows:

First stage—user acquires a token:

- The user sends a username/password to Keystone to request a token
- Keystone generates a UUID token (in UUID 4 format) and sends it back to the user
- Keystone keeps a copy of this token, together with user identification information, in its database

Subsequent stages—user uses the token:

- User sends a request to some other OpenStack component service (such as Nova or Glance) including the token
- The OpenStack component service sends the token to Keystone for authentication
- If the token is in the Keystone database and has not expired and has not been revoked, then Keystone tells the other OpenStack component service, okay go ahead. Otherwise Keystone tells the other OpenStack component service, nope, I don't recognize that token.

Keystone must periodically prune tokens from its token database, those expired, and any users whose user privileges have been revoked.

One problem with the way Keystone uses UUID tokens is that every user of any OpenStack component service must send a validation message to Keystone. This can make a lot of network traffic to Keystone.

When a UUID token is created on one instance of Keystone, it would have to be passed around to other instances of Keystone before they could recognize it. In the meantime, a user who received a token from one instance of Keystone but then tried to access another instance of Keystone in the same cloud would find that token denied.

We will look at an example of how to use UUID tokens later in Section 13.4. As a little bit of a peek ahead, however, in the example in Section 13.4, OpenStack was configured to use UUID tokens, so we generated a UUID token (we'll see this again later):

- 12ea1917464149dcad68d0dc1eb30842

As we recall from Section 3.6, UUID 4 (Random) format has the following general format:

- Xxxxxxxx-xxxx-4xxx-axxx-xxxxxxxxxxxx

So dividing it up according to the above UUID4 template, you can see it follows UUID 4 format:

- 12ea1917-4641-49dc-ad68-d0dc1eb30842

13.3.4.2.2 Public Key Infrastructure Tokens

Another option is for Keystone to use PKI tokens. To really understand how Keystone uses PKI tokens, you should first read Section 5.5 that explains PKI.

However, briefly, when Entity A wishes to connect to Entity B on a network, a third party that is trusted by both entities verifies Entity A's credentials so Entity B will know that Entity A is who it says it is. The trusted third party is called a *Certification Authority*.

After checking out Entity A's credentials, the Certification Authority issues a certificate, that it digitally signs, that says that Entity A is who it says it is. Entity A can then pass this certificate on to Entity B. Entity B recognizes the Certification Authority's digital signature on the certificate, so it accepts the certificate and is willing to talk to Entity A.

When using PKI tokens, Keystone acts as a Certification Authority. At the time Keystone is installed, a Certificate Authority private key, a Certificate Authority certificate, a Signing Private Key, and a Signing Certificate are generated.

Now let's look at what is included in the PKI tokens. When you're using either PKI or PKIZ tokens (we'll look at PKIZ tokens shortly), then the entire normal Keystone validation response is included as part of the token. Part of a typical Keystone validation response is shown in Listing 13.8. This response is fairly long and provides a lot of information, such as the identifiers for various OpenStack interfaces, and the URL and port numbers for these OpenStack interfaces. OpenStack calls this interface information in the Keystone response the *service catalog*. You can see that the project information is also included.

(Note that the example in Listing 13.8 was generated when we were using UUID tokens, with PKI tokens this information is included in the token itself.)

In addition to the service catalog and the project information the PKI tokens also include the user's roles, the user's public key, and the token expiration date.

This information is now converted into Cryptographic Message Syntax (CMS) and signed with the Certificate Authority Signing Key. CMS is described in detail in Section 5.8. The recipient will of course have to convert it back from CMS and verify the signature before processing it further.

When a user sends a request including a PKI token to an OpenStack component service via its API, the OpenStack component service/API has a local copy of the Signing Certificate, the Certificate Authority Certificate, and the Certification Revocation List (CRL). If the OpenStack API has not previously downloaded this information from Keystone, then it does it immediately before processing the user's request. (I haven't mentioned CRLs before in this section, see Section 5.5 for a description of how a CRL works. Briefly, however, tokens are checked versus this list to see if they have been formally revoked by the Certification Authority.)

Assuming the PKI token has not been revoked (does not appear on the CRL), then the OpenStack API checks the token versus the Certificate Authority Certificate and the Signing Certificate. If this is valid, and the token has not yet expired, then the OpenStack API will process the user's request.

These PKI tokens can be humongous. A basic token with a single endpoint is approximately 1700 bytes. The PKI token sizes increase proportionally as regions and services are added to the catalog, and sometimes can be over 8KB.

PKIZ tokens try to fix this problem by compression—PKIZ tokens are just PKI tokens compressed using zlib compression, and except for that PKIZ works the same as PKI.

Since the OpenStack component service (endpoint/API) has local copies of the certificates, it doesn't have to go back to Keystone to ask if the token is valid every time it receives a user request. It only has to download the Signing Certificate and the Certificate Authority Certificate once, at the time they are first needed. However, periodically each OpenStack component service must update the CRL by requesting it from Keystone. This must be done frequently, once per second is the number that Kupidura (2013) mentions.

PKIZ tokens, even though compressed, are still quite long. Young (2014) says:

> The packaging for a PKIZ token has a lower bound based on the signing algorithm. An empty CMS document of compressed data is going to be no less than 650 bytes. An unscoped token with proper compression comes in at 930 bytes.

So based on certificate checking being done locally to the OpenStack component service (endpoint), the PKI and PKIZ token implementations result in reduced network traffic compared to UUID tokens. However, since the PKI and PKIZ tokens themselves are very long, network traffic due just to sending these long tokens can still be a problem.

13.3.4.2.3   Fernet Tokens

Fernet tokens use symmetric (secret) Key Encryption. With Fernet tokens, the data in a message (its payload) is encrypted using the Advanced Encryption Standard (AES) Cipher Algorithm in Cipher Block Chaining (CBC) Mode (AES–CBC), then the whole Fernet token is signed using a SHA256 HMAC, and finally the whole is base 64 URL encoded. See Section 5.3 for a discussion of hash functions, and Section 5.4 for message authentication codes. See Sections 4.7 and 4.8 for a discussion of base 64 encoding, URL (percent) encoding, and base 64 URL encoding.

For HMAC on Fernet tokens, the Key used is the Signing Key. The hash function used is SHA-256.

The block size the algorithm works on is 512 bits. Output size is 256 bits (32 bytes).

The contents of a Fernet token are shown in Tables 13.5 and 13.6. Table 13.5 shows the major fields, while Table 13.6 shows the format of the payload/ciphertext.

If the token is project scoped, then the User Identifier and the Project Identifier are globally unique. Note that a domain-scoped token will have a domain identifier instead of a project identifier, etc.

An example of a project-scoped Fernet token, given by Mathews (2016), is

gAAAAABU7roWGiCuOvgFcckec0ytpGnMZDBLG9hA7Hr9qfvdZDHjsak39YN98HXxoYLIqV-
m19Egku5YR3wyI7heVrOmPNEtmrfIM1rtahudEdEAPM4HCiMrBmiA1Lw6SU8jc2rPLC7FK7nB-
Cia_BGhG17NVHuQu0S7waA306jyKNhHwUnpsBQ%3D

TABLE 13.5
Fernet Token Contents

Field	Info about Contents	Size
0x80	Fernet token version	8 bits
Current timestamp	In UTC	64 bits
Initialization vector	Random number	128 bits
Payload/ciphertext		Variable size, a multiple of 128 bits, padded as necessary
HMAC		Signed using Signing Key —SHA256

TABLE 13.6
Payload/Ciphertext Format

Field	Info about Contents
• Version	Possible values: • unscoped=0 • domain scoped=1 • project scoped=2 • trust scoped=3 • federated unscoped=4 • federated domain scoped=6 • federated project scoped=5
User Identifier	UUID
Methods	oauth1, password, token, external
Project identifier	UUID
Expiration time	In UTC
Audit Identifier	Serves as a Token Identifier (URL safe random number)

TABLE 13.7
Fernet Key File Format

First 128 Bits (16 Bytes)	Last 128 Bits (16 Bytes)
Signing Key— key that will be used to do HMAC SHA256 signing of token contents	Encrypting Key— encryption key that will be used to encrypt token payload using AES

According to Mathews (2016):

Fernet tokens should always weigh in under 255 bytes (unlike PKI tokens which sometimes exceed 8,192 bytes—thus breaking the Internet)

Each Keystone instance will maintain a key repository, typically in the directory:

/etc/keystone/fernet-keys/

In this directory, various Fernet key files are kept. Each key file's name is an integer number: 0, 1, 2, etc. By default three key files are maintained (max_active_keys=3 in config file). The format of a Fernet key file is shown in Table 13.7.

The contents of a Fernet key file is 256 bits (32 bytes) total. It is base 64 URL encoded.

Fernet tokens don't have the problem that UUID tokens had with replicating tokens between different instances of Keystone in a large cloud. This is because you just pass the keys around, not the tokens themselves. This is a lot less information that must be sent than thousands of individual tokens, and it's also a lot less token information that Keystone must store.

One advantage of Fernet tokens compared to UUID tokens is that token pruning per se is not necessary, as keys are stored instead of tokens. There is the issue that the keys must be periodically updated, but the problem of updating the keys across multiple instances of Keystone is ameliorated through key rotation. That is, using key rotation allows the operator to distribute the new key over a span of time.

There are three types of key files:

1. Primary Key (Signing Key):
   - The key that does all encryption
   - Can also do decryption
   - The key with the highest index number
2. Staged Key:
   - Will be the next signing key, after rotation occurs
   - Each new key starts out as the Staged Key
   - The key with index 0
3. Secondary Key:
   - Used to be the Primary Key
   - Now can only do decryption
   - All keys in between the Staged Key (key 0) and the Primary key (key with the highest index number) are Secondary Keys

An example of Fernet key rotation for three keys is shown in Table 13.8, also see Fischer (2015), Bragstad (2015a and 2015b), and Desai and Pokorny (2015).

To see this in the actual code, at initial state, do:

```
ls /etc/keystone/fernet-keys
```

then you would get something like:

```
0 1 2
```

After you explicitly do a rotate, do again:

```
ls /etc/keystone/fernet-keys
```

then you will get:

```
0 2 3
```

Note that if you are using four or more key files, you would just have additional secondary keys. With four keys, for the example in Table 13.8, Key 1 would not be deleted after the first rotation, rather, it would be copied into another secondary key—it wouldn't be deleted until you ran out of additional secondary keys.

To setup a new key repository, do this:

```
keystone-manage fernet_setup
```

TABLE 13.8

Fernet Key Rotation, Three Key Files

State	Staged Key	Secondary Key	Primary Key (Signing Key)
Initial Post	0	1	2
Rotation	New Key 0	2	3
		(Key 1 was deleted)	(Was old Key 0)

To do a manual rotate, you can do this (will also create a new Key 0 to take part in the rotation):

```
keystone-manage fernet_rotate
```

Bragstad (2015b) notes that if the number of key files (max_active_keys in the config file) is set to a low number and if your Keystone tokens have a long lifespan, or else if you do a key rotation too often, it is possible to revoke a key that is still in use. He gives the example: If you plan to rotate your primary key every 30 minutes and each Keystone token has a lifespan of 6 hours, max_active_keys should be set to 12 or more.

Note that initially Mathews (2015) found that Fernet tokens were faster to generate and to validate than either UUID tokens or PKI/PKIZ tokens. PKI and PKIZ tokens were generally the slowest. However, a later study—also see Mathews (2015)—showed that although Fernet tokens were faster to generate than UUID tokens, they were slower to validate. Note that Fischer (2015) also determined that a large number of token revocations can greatly diminish the performance of token validation.

13.3.4.3 Open Standard for Authorization (OAuth) in Keystone

If you noticed in Table 13.6, Fernet tokens support OAuth.

OAuth (Open Standard for Authorization) in general is a way for a user to employ their Google, Facebook, Twitter, etc. accounts to log on to a third-party website, so that they can do so without that website getting their username/password information.

With Keystone, what happens is a third party (a Consumer) is given access to OpenStack services by permission from a Keystone user.

This works as follows: The Keystone user has a username/password that works on Keystone. The Keystone user requests that Keystone allow a third party (the Consumer) access to OpenStack. Keystone sends an identifier for this consumer, and a secret key for this consumer, back to the Keystone user.

The Keystone user then sends the consumer identifier and the secret key to the Consumer (this is done in some way totally unrelated to OpenStack, this is called an out-of-band message). The Consumer then uses this information to ask for a Request token from Keystone (this Request token, after various approval steps, will eventually result in the Consumer being given permission to create an Access token).

After the Consumer receives the Request token, it requests authorization from the Keystone user. The Keystone user then sends its approval of the authorization to Keystone. Keystone will then send an OAuth verifier code to the Keystone user. The Keystone user sends the OAuth verifier code (out of band) to the Consumer.

Finally, the Consumer can ask Keystone to create an Access token for it. When Keystone sends back the Access token, the Consumer can finally use this Access token to request a regular Keystone API token. Whew. ☺

The steps of this interaction are shown in Figure 13.15.

13.3.4.4 Keystone Trusts

In Keystone, a user called a *trustor* can delegate a "trust" consisting of specified rights (one or more "Roles") to a user called "trustee." A "trust" is stored as an object. A token can have a trust associated with it.

There are two default roles in OpenStack:

1. Member—a typical user
2. Admin—a typical superuser

Other roles can be defined. However, the most likely use of a role would be for a member to be allowed to be an admin for a particular project for a particular length of time.

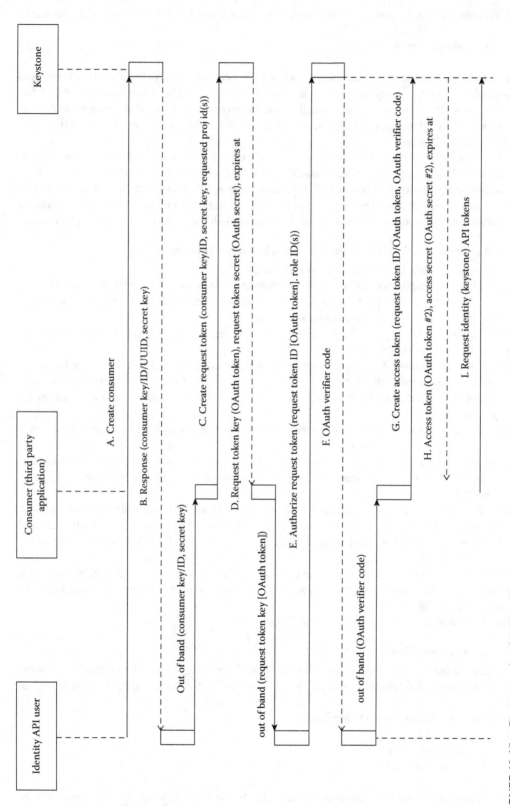

FIGURE 13.15   Consumer using OAuth in Keystone.

TABLE 13.9
Trust Object Information

Object Attribute	Description
impersonation	Allows the trustee to impersonate the "trustor"
project_id	Identifies project for which the trust was delegated
expires_at	Time at which the trust expires
remaining_uses	Number of times a trust may be exercised
trustor_user_id	User who created the trust (trustor)
trustee_user_id	User who receives the trust (trustee)
roles	List of roles to be granted to the trustee

The Keystone Trust Interface works as follows:

Step 1. User A requests a token from Keystone:
• Send HTTP Get to http://localhost:355357/v3/auth/tokens
Step 2. User A sends a POST to Keystone to create a trust at the /OS-TRUST/trusts interface
• Includes trust object in JSON format
• Includes User A token originally received from Keystone
Step 3. Keystone trusts interface responds
• Response includes a trust identifier for the trust that was created
Step 4. User A gives trust identifier to User B
Step 5. User B requests a token from Keystone
Step 6. User B performs a request for a Trust token
• Includes User A's token
• Includes trust identifier

A trust object in Keystone contains the information in Table 13.9.

13.3.5 OpenStack Nova

Nova is the component within OpenStack that is intended to provide computing resources to users. Nova provisions and manages Virtual Machines (VMs). It was part of the original 2010 OpenStack Austin release, which included Nova and Swift (if you recall, Swift is the OpenStack object storage).

Nova was NASA's contribution to the OpenStack project, and included (some version of) all aspects needed to implement a cloud controller. Parts of this since have split off into Cinder (block storage) and Glance (image management). Nova-network has remained as a part of nova, but at this point it is deprecated in favor of OpenStack Neutron (Neutron was previously known as Quantum).

OpenStack Nova can work with several different hypervisors. (The hypervisors we've used Nova with here at UAH are KVM and Xen.)

Nova consists of several components, which can typically run on different servers:

• Message Queue—central hub for passing messages between components. Uses Advanced Message Queuing Protocol (AMQP). By default uses RabbitMQ, can use Apache Qpid
• Nova API—handles OpenStack RESTful API, EC2, and admin interfaces. Provides an endpoint, initiates running and instances, enforces some policies

- Authorization manager—provides APIs for users, projects, roles, communicates with Keystone for details. Actual user store can be a database or LDAP back end
- Nova-objectstore—replicates S3 API to do image storage and retrieval, facilitates interaction with euca2ools. Can be useful to test features that will eventually run on S3. Normally replaced with OpenStack Glance
- Nova-network (deprecated in favor of neutron)—accepts network tasks from the queue, responsible for IP forwarding, VLANs, and bridges
- Nova-database—SQL database (SQLAlchemy compatible) that stores build time and run time state. Includes instances in use, instance types available for use, projects, networks
- Nova-conductor—a stateless RPC server. Acts as a proxy to the database. For example, inside nova-compute, when making a Virtual Machine (VM) update in the database, do an RPC to nova-conductor
- Nova-scheduler—allocates VMs to hosts. Takes VM instance requests from the queue and determines which compute host it should run on. Allows plugins for different scheduling algorithms
- Nova-compute—handles interface between VMs and hypervisor. Creates and terminates VM instances—accepts actions from the queue then performs system commands to implement these actions while updating state in the database

See Figure 13.16 for a basic view of how Nova internals interact.

OpenStack communicates between internal components using a Message Queue and AMQP. This uses a publish/subscribe message paradigm. We will see more about publish/subscribe in Chapter 15, Message-Oriented Middleware. However, briefly, in the publish/subscribe message paradigm, messages can be distributed from one producer to many consumers, or from many producers to many consumers. For example, all consumers that subscribe to a particular topic (channel) will receive the message.

With Nova, an AMQP message broker handles communication between any two Nova components and messages are queued. This means that the Nova components are only loosely coupled,

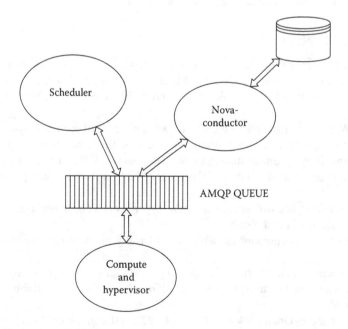

FIGURE 13.16   Basic view of Nova internals.

which is a good thing in this situation. If you recall the discussion of synchronous versus asynchronous communication from Section 1.3.1 (and our various implementations of synchronous and asynchronous communication in various middleware technologies since then), synchronous communication and the associated blocking of one component to wait on another component could be very bad from a performance standpoint. When you consider that a cloud includes multiple users, each with his/her own agenda and each not knowing—and probably not caring ☺—about the other cloud users, it is clear that it would be bad for one user to block another. So asynchronous communication through a message broker is clearly the way to go. Nova implements both request/response and one-way communication between Nova components.

Note that it is possible to configure Nova to work without nova-conductor, which means that each compute node would access the database directly. However, without nova-conductor, if any nova-compute node is successfully attacked, then the attacker also has full database access. However, even with nova-conductor running, an attacker with control of a compute node could still list all instances in the database and destroy them or update their state, see Mao (2013).

Also, according to Mao (2013) using nova-conductor allows the database schema to be easily upgraded, and improves performance because by default a database call in Nova is blocking. Also Mao (2013) says that you can start as many instances of nova-conductor as needed.

The nova-scheduler handles scheduling for virtual machine instances based on filtering and weighing. The filter scheduler (nova.scheduler.filter_scheduler.FilterScheduler) is the default scheduler for scheduling virtual machine instances. It supports filtering and weighting to make informed decisions on where a new instance should be created. When it receives a resource request, it first applies filters to determine which host is eligible—the host is either accepted or rejected by a filter, there is no "maybe" result. ☺ Example filters include (among others):

- AvailabilityZoneFilter—in the requested availability zone
- ComputeFilter—passes all hosts that are running and enabled
- DiskFilter—is there sufficient disk space?
- CoreFilter—are there sufficient CPU cores available?
- RamFilter—does the host have sufficient RAM available?

By default, virtual machine instances are spread evenly across all available hosts, and hosts for new instances are chosen randomly from a set of the N best available hosts. Various options can change how this works, for example, one option in the nova.conf (configuration) file allows virtual machine instances to be stacked on one host until that host's resources are used up (set ram_weight_multiplier in the config file to a negative number). Another option (scheduler_host_subset_size) selects the value N used to select the N best available hosts.

The filter scheduler weights each host in the list of available hosts. By default, it uses the RAM Weigher to determine which host to place the instance on. Using the RAM Weigher, the hosts with large quantities of RAM will be selected first, until you exceed a maximum number of VMs per node. If you disable the RAM Weigher, then VMs will be randomly distributed among available hosts (note that each host already was checked by a filter to determine that it had sufficient RAM to run the VM).

As mentioned earlier, nova-network has been deprecated in favor of Neutron. Before we get into this discussion, note first that with networking in the cloud, we are concerned not only with physical networks between devices but also with virtual networks that connect virtual machines.

Nova-network does not support as many network topologies as Neutron. The three network topologies supported by nova-network are:

- Flat—all VMs share the same network (same subnet and bridge). The subnet and bridge are specified beforehand by the network administrator. Each VM receives a fixed IP address from a pool of available addresses.

- Flat DHCP—a DHCP server allocates IP addresses to VM instances on the specified subnet. These IP addresses are not assigned to host network interfaces but only VM interfaces.
- VLAN—a VLAN and bridge are created for each project (tenant). Each project has a range of private IPs that can only be accessed from inside the VLAN. Each project has its own VLAN, Linux networking bridge, and subnet.

With nova-network, the project (tenant) does not have control over the network topology, and there is no way to insert advanced networking services (firewalls, for example). Nova-network only supports simple Linux bridges, and does not support monitoring, access control, or advanced quality of service.

13.3.6 OPENSTACK NEUTRON

Neutron provides considerable functionality that was not provided by nova-network. Neutron allows users to configure their own network topology including multi-tier networks (web tier, application tier), and their own network (how to assign IP addresses, etc.). It also allows use of advanced network services, including services intended to improve security and quality of service.

When Neutron is being used (and not nova-network), there is a portion of Neutron (that we previously referred to in Section 13.3.6 as a "management portion" of Neutron) that runs on the controller node as a Python daemon (see Section 12.2 for a discussion of the controller node in a minimal Neutron configuration). It provides network APIs and passes messages to Neutron plugins.

In Figure 13.17, you see an overview of Neutron internals. There is a block called Software-Defined Network. This was previously described in Section 7.4. However, briefly, a loose definition ☺ of a SDN is that it is a programmatically configured network that includes both virtual networks and physical networks. It can create a network connection from one virtual switch to another virtual machine, or to a physical network interface.

OpenStack Neutron components communicate with each other using AMQP and a message queue.

Neutron uses various plugin agents to implement different protocols or functions. There are two kinds of plugins:

1. Core plugins
2. Service plugins

Core plugins implement basic network management including IP address management (DHCP agent) and L2 networking (Modular Layer 2 [ML2] plugin), whereas service plugins implement additional services including load balancing (Load Balancing as a Service or LBaaS), VPNs (VPNaaS), firewalls (FWaaS), metering, etc.

The ML2 plugin is a core Neutron plugin that allows Neutron to work with different kinds of layer 2 networks. A diagram of the ML2 plugin is shown in Figure 13.18. In Figure 13.18, you see that ML2 has *types* and *mechanisms*. The *type* is the type of network being used, and the *mechanism* is the technology being used to implement the network.

In Figure 13.18, we see three kinds of network types listed (other kinds can be added), these are:

1. GRE (Generic Routing Encapsulation)
2. VLAN (Virtual Local Area Network)
3. VXLAN (Virtual Extensible Local Area Network)

Generic Routing Encapsulation (GRE) is a tunneling protocol used across an IP network to encapsulate many other protocols. Tunneling protocols are often used to allow a different (foreign) protocol to run over a network that does not support that particular protocol. They are also often used to provide services that the underlying network does not support.

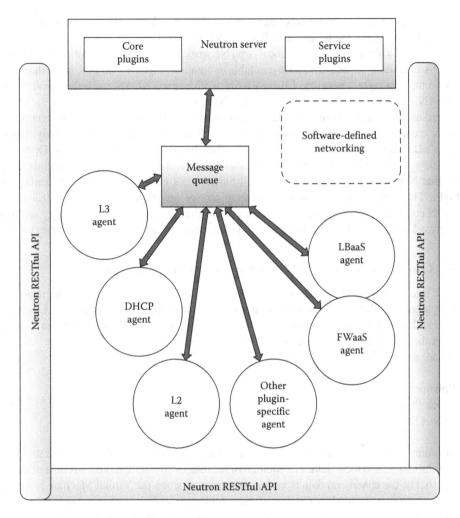

FIGURE 13.17 Overview of OpenStack Neutron.

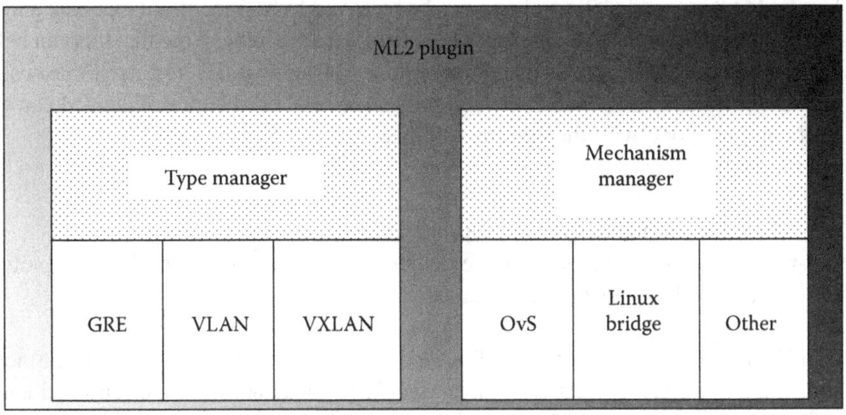

FIGURE 13.18 Modular Layer 2 plugin.

A Virtual Local Area Network allows partitioning of a network such that users (in this case, VMs) on one VLAN cannot see the traffic on a different VLAN.

The purpose of a Virtual Extensible Local Area Network is to improve scalability of networking in the cloud by extending the address space available to create VLANs. To do this, it overlays a layer 2 network on top of a layer 3 network. Like a VLAN, a VM on a VXLAN can only see other VMs on that VXLAN, they can't see the traffic on other VXLANs.

In regard to ML2 mechanisms, OvS stands for Open vSwitch, which is a well-known open source method for creating virtual switches to connect to VMs in a SDN. Open vSwitch employs Openflow, which is a SDN standard. See Section 7.4 for a further discussion of SDN including Open vSwitch and Openflow. Linux bridges are an alternative method to create a virtual switch to connect to a VM.

Note that Neutron allows connecting to full-blown SDN controllers, such as OpenDaylight or Floodlight. This can be done either as a separate service plugin, or through the ML2 plugin (or both). SDN controllers can be used to provide a view of the complete network topology and to monitor the network state, both physical and virtual. SDN controllers can also manage changes to the SDN.

13.3.7   OpenStack Block Data Storage and Object Data Storage

Let's look briefly at OpenStack data storage. We could spend a lot of time here, but using these is somewhat more straightforward (at least, in my opinion) than the previous OpenStack components we looked at (Keystone, Nova, Neutron, and of course Horizon), so I've chosen not to go into as much depth with these. Using them is an exercise for the reader. ☺

There are three kinds of storage with OpenStack:

1. Ephemeral
2. Block Storage
3. Object Storage

Each running Virtual Machine receives some ephemeral storage, it's used to store the operating system of the image, and local data. The lifetime of the data in this storage is the lifetime of the Virtual Machine, that is, the ephemeral data is no longer preserved when the Virtual Machine is terminated.

Block storage is performed by Cinder, whereas Object Storage is performed using Swift.

Cinder was originally part of Nova (called nova-volume). Cinder attaches storage volumes to a virtual machine. A storage volume is a storage area with its own file system. The server that is running Cinder can have storage volumes located on physical disks attached to the Cinder server itself, or can be located on other physical disks.

A volume can only be attached to one virtual machine at any one time. However, a volume can outlive a Virtual Machine, and also a volume can be removed from one virtual machine and attached to another virtual machine without losing any of the data in the volume. Note that this can help recovery if a Virtual Machine crashes, or if its compute node crashes—if the VM itself crashes it can be restarted with the current volume, and if the compute node crashes, then a similar VM can be started on a different compute node with the current volume.

Cinder has three basic services:

1. Cinder-scheduler—schedules the appropriate volume service
2. Cinder-volume—manages block storage devices—does load balancing between volumes
3. Cinder-backup—allows backup of volumes

OpenStack Swift (originally created by Rackspace, and part of the original OpenStack Austin release) stores data as binary objects (can have associated metadata) that are retrieved and written using HTTP commands (GET, PUT, etc.). Swift stores objects on object servers. Swift is best used for storing unstructured data, such as email, images, audio, and video, etc.

Swift organizes object data into a hierarchy. Your account is the top level of the hierarchy, and you own the information associated with that account (project or tenant). Inside the account (project or tenant) can be containers (namespace for objects). Within one account, the names of containers must be unique. The containers may have associated Access Control Lists (ACLs) that specify who can have access to the objects within the container (individual objects do not have associated ACLs).

Swift has the concept of a "ring." A ring keeps track of where data is stored in the cluster, it is used to map names to the physical locations of objects (physical device on physical node). There is a ring for accounts (projects or tenants), a ring for containers, and a ring for each separate storage policy.

For data backup, rings are divided into zones, within which data is replicated. By default, three replicas of data objects are created and stored in a separate zone (to protect against hardware failures). A zone can consist of a single disk drive or a server in either the local data center or a different data center.

13.4 TECHNOLOGY REVIEW: OPENSTACK RESTFUL INTERFACE

OpenStack consists of several different components, as previously discussed among several other components, these include:

- Nova, the Compute service—manages computer resources, in particular virtual machines, through working with various hypervisors such as Xen, KVM, and VMWare, among others
- Keystone, the Identity Service—provides centralized authentication for all OpenStack components
- Horizon, the Dashboard—a GUI to access and control cloud resources

We are going to focus in on these components for now, as these are the components we access in our description of the OpenStack RESTful interface.

In order to explore this interface, we are going to do the steps required to start up our own virtual machine (VM) (otherwise known as a server, or an instance, in OpenStack terminology) that runs a Linux-type operating system: In this case, we will run CirrOS. The CirrOS image (shows up as cirros on the Dashboard) is a small test version of Linux that is included with OpenStack. Its primary advantage is that it doesn't require a lot of memory to run. We will choose a beginning amount of disk and RAM to be assigned to this instance/server/VM. Finally, we will secure shell (SSH) to this instance to show that it is truly running.

Obviously, there are numerous other things that we *could* do, such as create new disk images (this would require access to Glance, the OpenStack image service), or set up internal user networks connecting the user's VMs (through Neutron, the OpenStack networking service), or allocate Block storage to a virtual machine (through Cinder), etc. However, once you have the basics down pat you should be able to read the OpenStack online documentation and do the other things as well. Plus, we need to leave time in your life for all the other technologies we explore in this book. ☺

There are several different ways to access the OpenStack RESTful interface. Four of the most popular are:

1. The OpenStack Dashboard. I discussed this elsewhere in Section 13.3.2. That section will get you started, then if you just play around with the Dashboard some, you should learn that fairly well
2. Using cURL to send appropriate HTTP commands
3. Using Python with the Python libraries provided with OpenStack
4. Using the command-line clients

We will look first at using cURL and then we will look at how to use Python to access the OpenStack RESTful interfaces. Finally, we will look at using the command-line clients.

TABLE 13.10

Some Important OpenStack Port Numbers

OpenStack Component	API	PORT #
Keystone (Identity)	Public Port	5000
	Admin Port	35357
Nova (Compute)	EC2 API	8788 or 8773
	OpenStack RESTful API	8774
	OpenStack Metadata	8775
Cinder (Block Storage)	Public port & Admin Port	8776
Swift (Object Storage)	Object Server	6000
	Container Server	6001
	Account Server	6002
Neutron (Networking)	Public Port & Admin Port	9696
Glance (Images)	Glance Registry	9191
	Glance API	9192

13.4.1 THE VARIOUS OPENSTACK INTERFACES AND PORT NUMBERS

Different OpenStack RESTful interfaces are listening at different port numbers on the Open-Stack URL. These interfaces start listening when OpenStack is installed and starts running. See Table 13.10.

There are two versions of the Keystone interface commonly used today, version 2 and version 3. I will use version 3 in some examples, and version 2 in other examples. Hopefully, it won't be too difficult for you to swap from one to another. For example, when I use the URL:

http://localhost:5000/v3

then I'm using version 3. When I use the URL:

http://localhost:5000/v2.0

then I'm using version 2.

The Keystone version 2 interface is going to be deprecated, but you see it around a lot, so it made sense to use it occasionally. Version 3 is a superset of version 2. (Keystone version 3 requires you to set a user domain, or at least requires setting it to default. This will be shown in the examples below.)

13.4.2 ACCESSING THE OPENSTACK RESTFUL INTERFACE USING cURL

Whenever accessing any kind of OpenStack interface, the first step is to authenticate with Keystone. It would be helpful to review Section 4.12 on cURL and Section 4.5 on JSON before beginning this section.

13.4.2.1 Authentication Using Keystone

Our basic cURL command will be as shown in Listing 13.4.

LISTING 13.4   CURL Command Accessing Keystone for Authentication

```
curl -i -H "Content-Type: application/json" \
-d @my_credentials \
http://localhost:5000/v3/auth/tokens
```

This will send a JSON file containing the appropriate credentials to the OpenStack Keystone public port. The -H "Content-Type: application/json" tells Keystone that we are working with JSON format.

The JSON file containing the credentials (called mycredentials.json in Listing 13.4) can have somewhat different formats. The format shown in Listing 13.5 shows the JSON file that one would use to specify default scope (not specifying a particular project). Here the username is **admin** and the admin password is **mypassword**. The rest of this JSON file contains commands to OpenStack Keystone.

LISTING 13.5   Credentials JSON File Specifying Default Scope

```
{
  "auth": {
    "identity": {
      "methods": [
        "password"
      ],
      "password": {
        "user": {
          "name": "admin",
          "domain": {
            "id": "default"
          },
          "password":"mypassword"
        }
      }
    }
  }
}
```

The JSON credentials file shown in Listing 13.6 specifies a particular project, in this case the admin project. Here the username is **admin** and the admin password is **mypassword**, while the project name is **admin**. The rest of the JSON file contains commands to OpenStack Keystone.

LISTING 13.6   Credentials JSON file Specifying Scope of the Admin Project

```
{
    "auth":{
        "identity": {
            "methods": [
                "password"
            ],
            "password": {
                "user": {
                    "name": "admin",
```

```
                              "domain": {
                                   "id": "default"
                              },
                              "password": "mypassword"
                         }
                    }
               },
               "scope": {
                    "project": {
                         "name": "admin",
                         "domain": {
                              "id": "default"
                         }
                    }
               }
          }
     }
}
```

LISTING 13.7   Top Portion of Response from Keystone after Receipt of Admin Project JSON

Date: Wed, 29 Jul 2015 17:19:46 GMT
Server: Apache/2.4.7 (Ubuntu)
X-Subject-Token: **12ea1917464149dcad68d0dc1eb30842**
Vary: X-Auth-Token
Content-Length: 6816
Content-Type: application/json

Listing 13.7 shows part of the response from Keystone, which in this case will consist of a file that is mostly in JSON format, but that has a header in the format shown in Listing 13.7. The value in X-Subject-Token, shown in bold here, is the authorization token that is provided by Keystone. This token provides the authorization you require in order to work more with OpenStack.

For this example, OpenStack was configured to use UUID tokens, so this particular token is in UUID 4 (Random) format. As we recall from Section 3.6, UUID 4 (Random) format has the following general format:

- Xxxxxxxx-xxxx-4xxx-axxx-xxxxxxxxxxxx

This particular token is as follows:

- 12ea1917464149dcad68d0dc1eb30842

So dividing it up according to the above UUID4 template, you can see it follows UUID 4 format:

- 12ea1917-4641-49dc-ad68-d0dc1eb30842

Assume for the unix/linux examples in this textbook that we are using the bash shell.

To proceed, we need to put this token in an environment variable. So our first step would be:

```
export CURRENT_TOKEN=12ea1917464149dcad68d0dc1eb30842
```

You can do:

```
echo $CURRENT_TOKEN
```

to see that this worked.

Note that in the code examples provided for the instructor with this textbook, there are several unix/linux scripts that will do a lot of this housekeeping for you. Multiple scripts were provided rather than one big script so when you use the code you can walk bit by bit through the procedure and better understand what is happening. For this textbook discussion here, however, I am discussing the code that is *inside* the provided unix/linux scripts.

The first part of the response was in Listing 13.7, but the remainder of the response will be in JSON format: portions of this are shown in Listing 13.8. The response here is a fairly long file and provides a lot of information, such as the identifiers for various OpenStack interfaces, and the URL and port numbers for these OpenStack interfaces. For example, the endpoints for the Amazon EC2 nova (compute) interface are shown in Listing 13.8. (We didn't show the endpoints for the other interfaces due to space considerations.)

It also gives the project ID for the admin project, which is what we specified before (this is shown in bold in Listing 13.8). We need this project ID for later use, but we won't grab it from here from this response, we'll grab it in a different way later on (that will allow us to illustrate other OpenStack interfaces).

(Our later methods work because you're using the "admin" username, not another username such as "demo." If you're using the "demo" username, then go ahead and get the project ID here, put it in an environment variable called "PROJECT_ID" and skip to Section 13.4.2.2.)

Note that this response also gives a time limit during which the authorization token is valid. We also didn't show this here due to space considerations.

LISTING 13.8   Various Portions of Response from Keystone after Receipt of Admin Project JSON

```
...
    {
        "endpoints": [
            {
                "id": "bd130670250c4cb0bba1750a54b66be0",
                "interface": "internal",
                "region": "RegionOne",
                "region_id": "RegionOne",
                "url": "http://146.229.233.30:8773/services/Cloud"
            },
            {
                "id": "d265e0d952e2448a9b526d11358a5d9e",
                "interface": "public",
                "region": "RegionOne",
                "region_id": "RegionOne",
                "url": "http://146.229.233.30:8773/services/Cloud"
            },
```

```
                    {
                        "id": "d42457653d964f379ca76bbeb3785e25",
                        "interface": "admin",
                        "region": "RegionOne",
                        "region_id": "RegionOne",
                        "url": "http://146.229.233.30:8773/services/Admin"
                    }
                ],
                "id": "a8ed22e51fa64843be94a113e5516db8",
                "name": "ec2",
                "type": "ec2"
            },
    ...
        "project": {
            "domain": {
                "id": "default",
                "name": "Default"
            },
            "id": "8db4c730ab654955afda3eab32108cd8",
            "name": "admin"
        },
```

Next, we are going to list all projects that are associated with the current token.

You can only list projects if you're an administrative user, so this works because you're using the "admin" username and password, not another username such as "demo."

If you're using the "demo" username, then you probably should have acquired the project ID from the response to the original code shown in Listing 13.4. (If this is the case, then skip to Section 13.4.2.2.) You actually CAN get the demo project ID from the output of the list projects command; however, you have to have previously authenticated yourself as an administrative user in order to have done a list projects command.

So to list all projects associated with the current token, we do:

    curl -s -H "X-Auth-Token:$CURRENT_TOKEN" http://localhost:5000/v3/projects

Note that the port number is 5000, so we are still working with the Keystone interface.

Part of the response to this command is shown in Listing 13.9. It's describing the various projects. The project ID for the admin project is shown in bold. So it can be grabbed from here and put in the PROJECT_ID environment variable.

LISTING 13.9   Various Portions of Response from Keystone to List Projects Command

```
"projects": [
    {
        "description": null,
        "domain_id": "default",
        "enabled": true,
        "id": "7837ae0d4b2e47fd86134337567f027f",
        "links": {
            "self": "http://146.229.233.30:5000/v3/projects/7837ae0d4b2e47fd86134337567f027f"
        },
```

```
        "name": "demo"
    },
    {
        "description": null,
        "domain_id": "default",
        "enabled": true,
        "id": "889bede5a5424ec29f642c40532a331a",
        "links": {
            "self": "http://146.229.233.30:5000/v3/projects/889bede5a5424ec29f642c40532a331a"
        },
        "name": "alt_demo"
    },
    {
        "description": null,
        "domain_id": "default",
        "enabled": true,
        "id": "8db4c730ab654955afda3eab32108cd8",
        "links": {
            "self": "http://146.229.233.30:5000/v3/projects/8db4c730ab654955afda3eab32108cd8"
        },
        "name": "admin"
    },
    ...
]
```

13.4.2.2 Starting an Instance (Server) Using Nova

We are thoroughly authenticated now, we have the $CURRENT_TOKEN environment variable set to the authentication token we received from Keystone, and we have the $PROJECT_ID environment variable set to the current project we want to work on. So we can proceed with the rest of our task of starting up an instance of a virtual machine (server) using the OpenStack Nova compute node.

Important point: If you have a delay anytime in this process, it is possible you may have to re-authenticate! Authentication tokens are good only for a certain time period.

In order to start an instance of a virtual machine and have it do anything useful at all, that instance must be running some kind of an operating system. The way OpenStack starts an operating system running is to copy a system image of an operating system into the virtual machine instance. A system image is a copy of the entire state of a running Operating System. OpenStack has a few canned images that you can use: Major Operating Systems such as Ubuntu Linux or RedHat Linux provide releases that can be used for this, plus OpenStack provides a small test Linux version called CirrOs. We will be using CirrOs in the virtual machine instance we create here.

In addition to images already accessible through OpenStack, you can use OpenStack to create an image from a file: this is typically done through the Glance component, can be controlled through the Dashboard (Horizon component). You can also make a snapshot of your own currently running virtual machine instance. Then this image, stored in the snapshot, can be used to create duplicate virtual machine instances.

First we will list the images accessible (for the purpose of creating an instance of a virtual machine) by the current project. We do this using the code in Listing 13.10. Here we are accessing the Nova RESTful API, located at port 8774. We send it an HTTP GET command. We tell it we want all images associated with $PROJECT_ID, and we pass it our $CURRENT_TOKEN to show that we previously went through authentication. The " -H "Accept: application/json" tells Nova that we're expecting to receive data in JSON format.

Note "X-Auth-Project-Id: admin" which tells it we were authorized as an admin project. This really is optional in this case. I'm including it because it's in the code examples provided for the instructor with the textbook and I don't want to change them because they're working and I don't want to mess them up. ☺

Note the:

python --mjson.tool

This is a pretty print tool, it just makes the JSON output readable.

LISTING 13.10   cURL Command Listing Images Accessible from the Current Project

curl -s http://localhost:8774/v2/$PROJECT_ID/images -X GET -H "X-Auth-Project-Id: admin" -H "Accept: application/json"   -H "X-Auth-Token: $CURRENT_TOKEN" | python --mjson.tool

---

Part of the output from the cURL command in Listing 13.10 is provided in Listing 13.11. This shows the description of the image containing a version of Fedora Linux. It also shows the description of the image containing CirrOS that we're going to use. The ids of the images are shown in bold, and so are the names of the images.

Note that the ID in both cases comes first, so if you're scrolling through it, you don't find which OS the ID goes with until several statements later. I assume this was because some programmer stored it in a data structure in a way that made this the easiest way to write it out. Luckily, there are various libraries to deal with it; we'll see that when we get to the Python interface later. But it's sure aggravating when you're working in cURL and especially when you're doing manual cut/pastes. To make things easier, in the code that is provided for the instructor with this textbook, I've provided various cute little scripts to extract all these items.

Once you've found the ID that corresponds to your chosen image, put this in an environment variable called IMAGE_ID.

LISTING 13.11   Various Portions of Response from Nova to List Images Command

```
{
    "id": "0c95691a-1062-4940-a39e-40b6adfdf498",
    "links": [
        {
            "href": "http://localhost:8774/v2/8db4c730ab654955afda3eab32108cd8/images/
                0c95691a-1062-4940-a39e-40b6adfdf498", "rel": "self"
        },
        {
            "href": "http://localhost:8774/8db4c730ab654955afda3eab32108cd8/images/
                0c95691a-1062-4940-a39e-40b6adfdf498",
            "rel": "bookmark"
        },
        {
            "href": "http://146.229.233.30:9292/images/0c95691a-1062-4940-a39e-
                40b6adfdf498",
            "rel": "alternate",
            "type": "application/vnd.openstack.image"
        }
    ],
```

```
      "name": "Fedora-x86_64-20-20140618-sda"
},
{
    "id": "da413111-80f7-4496-95a6-8c4315f4c6d8",
    "links": [
      {
        "href": "http://localhost:8774/v2/8db4c730ab654955afda3eab32108cd8/images/
            da413111-80f7-4496-95a6-8c4315f4c6d8",
        "rel": "self"
      },
      {
        "href": "http://localhost:8774/8db4c730ab654955afda3eab32108cd8/images/
            da413111-80f7-4496-95a6-8c4315f4c6d8",
        "rel": "bookmark"
      },
      {
        "href": "http://146.229.233.30:9292/images/da413111-80f7-4496-95a6-
            8c4315f4c6d8",
        "rel": "alternate",
        "type": "application/vnd.openstack.image"
      }
    ],
    "name": "cirros-0.3.2-x86_64-uec"
}
```

Next, you need to pick a flavor. A flavor assigns a quantity of RAM, total amount of disk, number of virtual CPUs. You can see the available flavors from the Dashboard if you try to launch an instance from there. There is also considerable documentation about various flavors in the online OpenStack documentation. However, if you want to list the flavors using a cURL command, use the command shown in Listing 13.12.

LISTING 13.12   cURL Command Listing Available Flavors

```
curl -s http://localhost:8774/v2/$PROJECT_ID/flavors -X GET -H "X-Auth-Project-Id:
admin" -H "Accept: application/json" -H "X-Auth-Token: $CURRENT_TOKEN" | python
--mjson.tool
```

Listing 13.13 shows the response for m1.large (ID #4) and m1.nano (ID #42). Names and their associated ID numbers are shown in bold. We need to know that m1.nano corresponds to ID #42, before we go try to create an instance of a virtual machine. We certainly did find that out from using this command, however, we could also have just paged through OpenStack documentation to figure out which ID number goes with which flavor.

We will choose the m1.nano flavor, because this is nice and small and works well with our choice of the CirrOS operating system. Choosing a flavor such as m1.large to run CirrOS is definitely overkill. However, note that m1.nano is far too small to run an OS like, say, Fedora.

LISTING 13.13   Various Portions of Response from Nova to List Flavors Command

```
{
    "id": "4",
    "links": [
        {
            "href": "http://localhost:8774/v2/8db4c730ab654955afda3eab32108cd8/flavors/4",
            "rel": "self"
        },
        {
            "href": "http://localhost:8774/8db4c730ab654955afda3eab32108cd8/flavors/4",
            "rel": "bookmark"
        }
    ],
    "name": "m1.large"
},
{
    "id": "42",
    "links": [
        {
            "href": "http://localhost:8774/v2/8db4c730ab654955afda3eab32108cd8/flavors/42",
            "rel": "self"
        },
        {
            "href": "http://localhost:8774/8db4c730ab654955afda3eab32108cd8/flavors/42",
            "rel": "bookmark"
        }
    ],
    "name": "m1.nano"
}
```

Before we get going on the next steps (creating a keypair and using SSH to access our instance), let's recall what we know about security groups. Remember from Section 13.3.3, to be able to SSH into your instance, you have to set the security group you are using to allow SSH and ICMP access. How to do this using the dashboard was shown previously in Section 13.3.2. You can also do this with various other methods: cURL commands, nova command-line tool, neutron command-line tool, etc. However, I didn't include these in this textbook for fear of making it all too complicated and thus confusing you the student. ☺

So we will use the default security group that has its rules set up for SSH and ICMP access using the dashboard as previously shown in Section 13.3.2. If you need to use the other commands later, it's all online. The OpenStack references related to security groups in the bibliography provided for this chapter will give you what you need.

For our next step, we have to create a keypair. That is to say, we will be using Asymmetric Key Cryptography, which employs a public key and a private key. See Section 5.2 for an explanation of what this means.

One easy way to create a key pair is through the OpenStack dashboard. Go to Access & Security on your current project. Select the Key Pairs tab. Select Create Key Pair. This will start an automatic download of the private key (OpenStack will have the public key). Put the private key in your directory.

Before you can use your private key to SSH to your OpenStack instance, you will have to change its permissions, for example:

chmod 600 mykey.pem

(See Section 13.3.3 for more information on this.)

Note that you could also use SSH-keygen, as follows (these steps are shown on the OpenStack Dashboard, at Access & Security, select Key Pairs tab, Import Key Pair):

. ssh-keygen –t rsa – f cloud.key

Then the public key is in the file cloud.key.pub and the private key is in the file cloud.key.

(GitHub [2016] has more information about how to do this.)

If you used SSH-keygen, then you would have to import your public key to OpenStack. One way to do this is to go to Access & Security, select Key Pairs tab, then Import Key Pair.

After completing this step, OpenStack will have your public key, stored in some security group in OpenStack. You can see it when you go to the Access & Security tab, Key Pairs tab.

You will also have your own private key. Let's call our private key: *mykey.pem*

Finally, we are ready to create the instance.

First, create a file. Let's call it myInstanceInfo.json. Contents of this file are shown in Listing 13.14. You will have to write the contents of your environment variable IMAGE_ID in the imageRef location in this file. You will write the number 42 into the flavorRef location, because that's the flavor number for m1.nano. Put the name of your private key in key_name; here we've named it "mykey" because we previously created a private key that we named mykey.pem. We have named this virtual machine instance "myname," substitute whatever name you want here.

LISTING 13.14   File myInstanceInfo.json Containing Information Needed to Start a Virtual Machine Instance

```
{
    "server": {
        "flavorRef": "42",
        "imageRef": "da413111-80f7-4496-95a6-8c4315f4c6d8",
        "key_name": "mykey",
        "max_count": 1,
        "min_count": 1,
        "name": "myname",
        "security_group": "default"
    }
}
```

After you create the file myInstanceInfo.json, then execute the cURL command shown in Listing 13.15.

LISTING 13.15   cURL Command to Start a Virtual Machine Instance

```
curl -i http://localhost:8774/v2/$PROJECT_ID/servers -X POST -H "X-Auth-Project-Id:
admin" -H "Content-Type: application/json" -H "Accept: application/json" -H "X-Auth-
Token: $CURRENT_TOKEN" -d @myInstanceInfo.json
```

Congratulations!!! You have started a new instance of a virtual machine.

You can see this on your Dashboard. Go to your project, select the Instances tab, and there it will be. You can now SSH to this instance. Section 13.3.3 tells you in detail how to do this.

13.4.3 ACCESSING THE OPENSTACK RESTFUL INTERFACE USING PYTHON

As in the previous cURL example, in order to explore how to access the OpenStack RESTful interface using Python, we are going to do the steps required to start up our own virtual machine (VM) (otherwise known as a server, or an instance, in OpenStack terminology) that runs a Linux-type operating system: In this case, we will run CirrOS. The CirrOS image (shows up as cirros on the Dashboard) is a small test version of Linux that is included with OpenStack. Its primary advantage is that it doesn't require a lot of memory to run. We will choose a beginning amount of disk and RAM to be assigned to this instance/server/VM. Finally, we will secure shell (SSH) to this instance to show that it is truly running.

13.4.3.1 Authentication Using Keystone

First we have to authenticate.

The very first step is to type:

```
python
```

to enter the Python runtime environment. After this, your prompts will likely look something like this:

```
>>>
```

You will type the remainder of your commands inside this environment. To exit the environment, type control-D. However, once you exit the environment you will have to start over again!

The next steps to authenticate are shown in Listing 13.16. First you import the Keystone Python client.

Next we will call the Client function on the Keystone client. We will pass it the various variables to enable authentication: domain names (user and project), username, password, project, and the Keystone URL (see that we are using port 5000, the Keystone public port). The username, password, domain, and project names are shown in bold in Listing 13.16. After this command, the variable Keystone will be authenticated, and can be used to access the Keystone component.

LISTING 13.16   Access Keystone Using Python

```
from keystoneauth1.identity import v3
from keystoneauth1 import session
from keystoneclient.v3 import client
auth = v3.Password(
          user_domain_name='default',
          username='admin',
          password='mypassword',
          project_domain_name='default',
          project_name='admin',
          auth_url='http://localhost:5000/v3'
          )
mysess=session.Session(auth=auth)
keystone=client.Client(session=mysess)
return keystone
```

Note that this example used the v3 interface. When you're using the v3 interface with Python now, you should use sessions. As of early summer 2015, the DevStack install didn't require sessions, but beginning in late summer it apparently requires sessions to be used.

When using sessions, a session object stores your credentials. The session object is passed to a client so the client can do appropriate OpenStack-related actions.

After a session is established, the session object is responsible for handling authentication. When a request that needs authentication is sent to the session, then the session is responsible for requesting a token from the authentication plugin (or using an existing token).

An OpenStack *authentication plugin* is an implementation of a method of authentication. *Identity plugins* are those associated with Keystone. The two basic ones that are currently shipped with Keystone are the v3 and v2.0 plugins.

Next, do the following:

```
type(keystone)
```

to see if this authentication procedure worked. If it returns something like this:

```
<class 'keystoneclient.v3.client.Client'>
```

then the authentication worked!

Now that we have an authenticated Keystone client (in the Keystone variable), we can use it to call various Keystone functions. To list all projects, type:

```
keystone.projects.list()
```

You can also do various other things. For example, to list all users, type:

```
keystone.users.list()
```

To list all endpoints, type:

```
keystone.endpoints.list()
```

13.4.3.2 Starting an Instance (Server) Using Nova

We are Keystone authenticated now, so we can proceed with the rest of our task of starting up an instance of a virtual machine (server) using the OpenStack Nova compute node.

Important point: If you have a long delay, for example, a day anytime in this process, it is possible you may have to re-authenticate! Authentication tokens are good only for a certain time period.

Our first step now, is we have to set ourselves up with a client that talks to Nova. You should already be in Python now, so you type the commands in Listing 13.17 at the Python prompt.

First you import the Nova Python client. Then you set up variables with the parameters you need in order to authenticate this client. This contains username, password, project, and URL as before. This time, the URL passed in is the Keystone admin port, 35357 (shown in bold), and we're using Keystone's version 2 interface. Remember that all OpenStack authentication goes through Keystone. We are setting up this time to have a client that accesses uses the v2.0 interface instead of the v3 interface (we used the v3 interface in the previous section).

LISTING 13.17   Access v2.0 Interface Using Python

```
from novaclient  import client
my_version='2'
my_username='admin'
my_password='mypassword'
my_project='admin'
my_auth_url='http://localhost:35357/v2.0'
mynova=client.Client(version=my_version,project_id=my_project,username=my_
username, api_key=my_password,auth_url=my_auth_url)
```

After this you can do:

```
mynova.servers.list()
```

to see the virtual machine instances (servers) associated with the selected project.

Now we need to select an image. Type:

```
mynova.images.list()
```

Results will look like Listing 13.18.

LISTING 13.18   Results of Nova Images List

```
>>> myclient.images.list()
[<Image: my_own_snapshot>, <Image: Fedora-x86_64-20-20140618-sda>, <Image:
cirros-0.3.2-x86_64-uec>, <Image: cirros-0.3.2-x86_64-uec-ramdisk>, <Image:
cirros-0.3.2-x86_64-uec-kernel>]
```

Pick the complete image name (cirros-0.3.2-x86_64-uec) from the list of images, and copy it for later pasting. Note: Don't get any extra spaces or other extra characters!!!

You will paste this name (shown in bold) into a find command, the results of the find command are stored into the "myimage" variable in Listing 13.19.

We will again select a flavor of m1.nano. This time we put in "m1.nano" itself rather than "42" (we previously had to use 42 with cURL). The name m1.nano is in bold in Listing 13.19. Again, we put it into a find command, the results of the find command are stored in the "myinstance" variable in Listing 13.18.

You must also select a name for the virtual machine instance ("myserver" shown in bold in Listing 13.16) and the name of your key ("mykey" shown in bold in Listing 13.19).

(See the section on cURL for how to create a key pair. GitHub (2016) also has more information about this.)

LISTING 13.19   Python Commands to Start a Virtual Machine Instance

```
myimage=myclient.images.find(name= cirros-0.3.2-x86_64-uec)
myflavor=myclient.flavors.find(name=m1.nano)
myinstance=myclient.servers.create(name="myserver",image=myimage,flavor=myflavor,
key_name=mykey)
```

After you have completed the commands in Listing 13.19, then:

Congratulations!!! You have started a new instance of a virtual machine.

You can see this on your Dashboard. Go to your project, select the Instances tab, and there it will be.

You can now SSH to this instance. Section 13.3.3 tells you in detail how to do this.

13.4.4 ACCESSING THE OPENSTACK RESTFUL INTERFACE USING COMMAND-LINE CLIENTS

There are two sets of command-line clients. There is a newer way, using the common client, that is to say, the openstack command line client (OSC) and there is the older way, using the separate Keystone and nova command-line clients.

We will go over both sets.

13.4.4.1 Using the Common Client—The OpenStack Command Line Client (OSC)

Here I will do two examples, one using the Keystone Version 3 API, and one using the Keystone Version 2 API.

13.4.4.1.1 Example Using Keystone V3 API

In this example, I'm using the Keystone version 3 API.

To authenticate, set the environment variables as follows:

```
export OS_AUTH_URL=http://localhost:5000/v3export OS_USERNAME=admin
export OS_PASSWORD=mypassword
export OS_USER_DOMAIN_NAME=default
export OS_IDENTITY_API_VERSION="3"
export OS_PROJECT_NAME="admin"
```

Then type:

```
openstack image list
```

you can cut and paste the CirrOS image name from this output.

Then type:

```
openstack server create –flavor m1.nano –image "cirros-0.3.2-x86_64-uec" –key-name myveryownkeypair
theserver
```

Congratulations!!! You have started a new instance of a virtual machine.

You can see this on your Dashboard. Go to your project, select the Instances tab, and there it will be.

Instead of using your dashboard, if you want to see if the instance is there, do:

openstack server list

If it shows up on the list of instances, then it has been created!

You can now SSH to this instance. Section 13.3.3 tells you in detail how to do this.

13.4.4.1.2 Example Using Keystone V2 API

In this example, I'm using the Keystone Version 2 API.

To authenticate, set the environment variables as follows:

```
export OS_TENANT_NAME=admin
export OS_USERNAME=demo
export OS_PASSWORD=mypassword
export OS_AUTH_URL=http://localhost:5000:/v2.0
```

Then type:

   openstack image list

you can cut and paste the CirrOS image name from this output.

Then type:

   openstack server create –flavor m1.nano –image "cirros-0.3.2-x86_64-uec" –key-name myveryownkeypair tt

Congratulations!!! You have started a new instance of a virtual machine.

You can see this on your Dashboard. Go to your project, select the Instances tab, and there it will be.

Instead of using your dashboard, if you want to see if the instance is there, do:

openstack server list

If it shows up on the list of instances, then it has been created!

You can now SSH to this instance. Section 13.3.3 tells you in detail how to do this.

13.4.4.2   Using Separate Keystone and Nova Clients

In this section, we are going to look at using the separate command-line clients.

13.4.4.2.1   Authenticate Using Separate Keystone Client

Easy way to access various command-line clients:

Go to the devstack directory. (I am assuming you have done a DevStack install. For more discussion of this, go to Section 13.3.1.)

In the devstack directory is a file called openrc.

Type:

   source openrc

This will set various environment variables to default values so that you can access the openstack stuff. This includes environment variables such as OS_USERNAME, OS_PASSWORD, etc.

   OS_USERNAME=demo
   OS_PASSWORD=mypassword
   OS_TENANT_NAME=demo
   OS_AUTH_URL=http://localhost:5000/v2.0
   (or whatever IP address has been internally assigned.)
   (this is the Keystone port on localhost, port 5000 tells us that. It's using version 2.0 of the Keystone API)
   OS_REGION_NAME=RegionOne

You can see these by doing an echo, for example:

   echo $OS_USERNAME

Alternately, if you want to set these individually without using openrc, you can do that. It would work like this:

   export OS_USERNAME=demo

In order to log in as admin instead of as demo, do the following:

   export OS_USERNAME=admin
   export OS_PASSWORD=mypassword
   export OS_TENANT_NAME=admin

OpenStack tends to use the name "tenant" and "project" interchangeably. So pick whichever strikes your fancy. In commands, however, sometimes OpenStack uses one term and sometimes OpenStack uses the other term.

You will have to log in as admin instead of as demo in order to do a few commands like the following: To view all tenants (projects):

keystone tenant-list

To display all current users:

keystone user-list

To display all current users for a particular tenant, you would do the following:

keystone user-list –tenant-id *tenantID*

However, you would have to find the tenantID (project ID). One way to do this is:

keystone token-get | grep tenant | awk '{print $4}'

Note that if you happen to be using OS_USERNAME=admin, then the above command will return the tenantID (project ID) that is associated with admin. If you happen to be using OS_USERNAME=demo, then the above command will return the tenantID (project ID) that is associated with demo.

13.4.4.2.2 Create Instance Using Separate Nova Client

First you will have to create a public key/private key keypair that you can later use to access your instance. We have seen other ways to do this elsewhere in this document. Another way to do it is to type:

nova keypair-add jj4 >jj4.pem

Set permissions on this keypair so it can be used:

chmod 600 jj4.pem

Now, to find an image you can use, do:

nova image-list

It will give a list of images. Do a copy of the ID name of whichever image you chose, so you can paste it in a later command that we will see below.

Another way to do this would be to do:

glance image-list

But then I'd have to talk about glance image service and I said I wasn't going to do that here. ☺ You need to find available flavors, so do:

nova flavor-list

To find the available flavors.

Now you can create the instance. Do:

nova boot – -flavor 1 – -image (insert the ID you copied in the previous statement) –security-groups default –key-name jj4   theCirrosServer

Congratulations!!! You have started a new instance of a virtual machine.
You can see this on your Dashboard. Go to your project, select the Instances tab, and there it will be. Instead of using your dashboard, if you want to see if the instance is there, do:

nova   list

If it shows up on the list of instances, then it has been created!
You can now SSH to this instance. Section 13.3.3 tells you in detail how to do this.

EXERCISES

1. Under what circumstances might it be reasonable for a company to move its applications off a public cloud and onto its own servers?
2. What are advantages and disadvantages of using, say, a Triton container instead of a virtual machine? (*Hint*: see Bisson, C. 2015. Comparing Triton containers to VMs and bare metal servers, https://www.joyent.com/blog/understanding-triton-containers) (accessed October 9, 2016).
3. Why is the size of OpenStack Keystone tokens important?
4. Why is it important to be able to revoke tokens?
5. What kind of Keystone token is the following?
   12ea1917-4641-49dc-ad68-d0dc1eb30842
6. What kind of Keystone token is the following?
   gAAAAABU7roWGiCuOvgFcckec0ytpGnMZDBLG9hA7Hr9qfvdZDHjsak39YN98HXxoYLIqV-m19Egku5YR3wyI7heVrOmPNEtmrfIM1rtahudEdEAPM4HCiMrBmiA1Lw6-SU8jc2rPLC7FK7nBCia_BGhG17NVHuQu0S7waA306jyKNhHwUnpsBQ%3D
7. List one advantage of Fernet tokens compared to UUID tokens.
8. Inside Nova, how is communication between Nova components handled?
9. In Nova, what is the purpose of a RAM filter?
10. How does Nova RAM Weigher work?
11. What is the Modular Layer 2 plugin, and what is it used for?
12. What is the difference between OpenStack Cinder and OpenStack Swift?
13. How does Swift keep track of where data is stored?
14. In the response from Keystone to an authentication request, on what line in the response file is the token specified?
15. Is the response file that Keystone provides to an authentication request truly a JSON file?
16. Is the OpenStack RESTful interface really RESTful?
17. When using PKI tokens, what entity serves as the Certificate Authority?

CONCEPTUAL QUESTIONS

1. Originally Nova (from NASA) and Cinder (from Rackspace) were the two software projects that were combined to form OpenStack. We went into detail in this textbook about how nova-network is being replaced with Neutron. What are the advantages of breaking off pieces of a cloud into separate services? Are there any disadvantages? Speaking more generally, what would be the advantages and disadvantages of a monolithic cloud (everything done in one big package) as opposed to the OpenStack approach which employs several different services?
2. OpenStack stands alongside the hypervisor and uses the hypervisor, rather than building its own hypervisor. Most OpenStack installs use the KVM hypervisor but the Xen hypervisor (among others) is also

heavily used. What are the advantages and disadvantages of having OpenStack use outside hypervisors rather than implementing its own?

3. We've read some about cloud and virtualization security, both here and previously in Chapter 6. Do you feel safe putting your own precious private information (for example, your tax forms for the IRS that include your social security number and birthdate) on a cloud? Why or why not?

4. To what degree does using Software as a Service or Platform as a Service trap you into always having to use the same provider? In addition to the information provided in this textbook, do some googling to see how hard it would be to change from one provider to a competitor. Use this to justify your answer.

5. Is it a good thing, based on security, privacy, performance, and independence of a person that so much computing is moving to the cloud? Why or why not?

6. In relation to security, privacy, performance, and independence of a person, how does cloud computing compare to the previous time computing was centralized, back in the old mainframe days? (And does this comparison makes sense?)

7. Set up an application that is implemented using a Service-Oriented Architecture. Do this using one or more of the technologies we've examined in this textbook (for example, you could implement one server in PHP and a different server using JAX-RS or just a servlet). Move this application to a cloud—if you don't have an OpenStack or CloudStack cloud installed locally, then buy time on a public cloud. This will require multiple virtual machines, and you will have to have a web server on each virtual machine, so if you do this on your own local cloud make sure you have plenty of memory. What kinds of issues arose when using a cloud to host this SOA application compared to hosting it on several of your own computers?

BIBLIOGRAPHY

Apache. 2016. Mesos. http://mesos.apache.org/ (accessed April 26, 2016).

Babcock, C. 2015. Cloud foundry pros & cons, Information Week. http://www.informationweek.com/cloud/platform-as-a-service/cloud-foundry-pros-and-cons/d/d-id/1320427 (accessed April 26, 2016).

Bragstad, L. 2015a. Fernet tokens and key distribution. http://lbragstad.com/fernet-tokens-and-key-distribution/ (accessed May 3, 2016).

Bragstad, L. 2015b. Fernet Tokens and Key Rotation. http://lbragstad.com/fernet-tokens-and-key-rotation/ (accessed January 25, 2016).

Bregman, A. 2016. OpenStack neutron: Introduction. http://abregman.com/2016/01/04/openstack-neutron-introduction/ (accessed May 6, 2016).

Bryant, C. 2014. Open source compute clouds (IaaS). A guide to open source cloud computing software. Tom's IT Pro. http://www.tomsitpro.com/articles/open-source-cloud-computing-software,2-754-4.html (accessed April 25, 2016).

Burns, C. 2013. Stack wars: OpenStack v. CloudStack v. Eucalyptus. Network World. http://www.networkworld.com/article/2166407/cloud-computing/stack-wars–openstack-v–cloudstack-v–eucalyptus.html (accessed April 26, 2016).

Butler, B. 2014. OpenStack 101. The parts that make up the project. Network World. http://www.networkworld.com/article/2176963/cloud-computing/openstack-101–the-parts-that-make-up-the-project.html (accessed April 23, 2016).

Butler, B. 2015. The anti-OpenStack. https://www.joyent.com/about/press/the-anti-openstack (accessed April 25, 2016).

Butler, B. 2016a. Why DropBox dropped Amazon's cloud: And what it means for the cloud market. Network World. http://www.networkworld.com/article/3045570/cloud-computing/why-dropbox-dropped-amazons-cloud.html (accessed April 23, 2016).

Butler, B. 2016b. OpenStack by the numbers: Who's using open source clouds and for what? Network World. http://www.networkworld.com/article/3060339/open-source-tools/openstack-by-the-numbers-who-s-using-open-source-clouds-and-for-what.html (accessed April 25, 2016).

Cantrill, B. 2015. Triton: Docker and the "best of all worlds." Joyent. https://www.joyent.com/blog/triton-docker-and-the-best-of-all-worlds (accessed April 25, 2016).

Cloud Foundry Foundation. (2016). What will you create with Cloud Foundry? https://www.cloudfoundry.org/foundation/ (accessed April 26, 2016).

Darrow, B. 2015. Shocker! Amazon remains the top dog in cloud by far, but Microsoft, Google make strides. Fortune. http://fortune.com/2015/05/19/amazon-tops-in-cloud/ (accessed April 25, 2016).

Desai, P., and Pokorny, B. 2015. Deep dive into Keystone tokens and lessons learned. http://www.slideshare.net/priti_desai/deep-dive-into-keystone-tokens-and-lessons-learned (accessed May 4, 2016).

Docker. 2016a. What is Docker. https://www.docker.com/what-docker (accessed April 25, 2016).

Docker. 2016b. Docker swarm overview. https://docs.docker.com/swarm/overview/ (accessed April 26, 2016).

Evans, C. 2014. OpenStack storage: Cinder and Swift explained. Computer Weekly. http://www.computer-weekly.com/feature/OpenStack-storage-Cinder-and-Swift-explained (accessed May 6, 2016).

Farcic, V. 2015. Docker clustering tools compared: Kubernetes vs Docker Swarm, Technology Conversations. https://technologyconversations.com/2015/11/04/docker-clustering-tools-compared-kubernetes-vs-docker-swarm/ (accessed April 26, 2016).

Fischer, M. 2015. Keystone token revocation cripple validation performance. http://www.mattfischer.com/blog/?p=672 (accessed May 4, 2016).

Flux7. 2014. (Tutorial) What is Nova and how to Install & use it? OpenStack. http://blog.flux7.com/blogs/openstack/tutorial-what-is-nova-and-how-to-install-use-it-openstack (accessed May 5, 2016).

Gagné, M. 2015. Reducing Keystone PKI token size. http://blog.mgagne.ca/reducing-keystone-pki-token-size/ (accessed February 1, 2016).

Gartner. 2016. Gartner Magic Quadrant. http://www.gartner.com/technology/research/methodologies/research_mq.jsp (accessed April 25, 2016).

GitHub. 2016. Generating SSH keys. https://help.github.com/articles/generating-ssh-keys/ (accessed April 22, 2016).

Gooding, S. 2014. Ryan Hellyer's AWS nightmare: Leaked access keys result in a $6,000 bill overnight. WP Tavern. http://wptavern.com/ryan-hellyers-aws-nightmare-leaked-access-keys-result-in-a-6000-bill-overnight (accessed April 30, 2016).

Hui, K. 2013. Laying Cinder Block (Volumes) in OpenStack, Part 1: The basics. Cloud Architect Musings. https://cloudarchitectmusings.com/2013/11/18/laying-cinder-block-volumes-in-openstack-part-1-the-basics/ (accessed May 6, 2016).

Huin, M. 2013. Role delegation in Keystone: Trusts. RDO. http://blogs.rdoproject.org/5858/role-delegation-in-keystone-trusts (accessed January 28, 2016).

IBM. 2016. What is cloud computing?. https://www.ibm.com/cloud-computing/what-is-cloud-computing (accessed April 19, 2016).

IETF. 2003. The AES-CBC cipher algorithm and its use with IPsec. RFC 3602. https://tools.ietf.org/html/rfc3602 (accessed May 3, 2016).

IETF. 2009. Cryptographic Message Syntax (CMS). RFC 5652. https://tools.ietf.org/html/rfc5652 (accessed April 30, 2016).

Jackson, J. 2013. Pivotal launched from VMware, EMC technologies. PCWorld. http://www.pcworld.com/article/2036305/pivotal-launched-from-vmware-emc-technologies.html (accessed April 26, 2016).

Kashaba, S. 2012. OpenStack cloud storage services: First look at Folsom's Cinder project. Mirantis. https://www.mirantis.com/blog/openstack-cinder-first-look/ (accessed May 6, 2016).

Kerner, S.M. 2014. Verizon Terremark CTO tells how company built its own cloud. eWeek. http://www.eweek.com/cloud/verizon-terremark-cto-tells-how-company-built-its-own-cloud.html (accessed April 25, 2016).

Kinder, N. 2014. OpenStack identity API v3 OS-TRUST extension. GitHub. https://github.com/openstack-attic/identity-api/blob/master/v3/src/markdown/identity-api-v3-os-trust-ext.md (accessed January 28, 2016).

Kleman, B. 2015. Understanding CloudStack, OpenStack, and the cloud API. http://www.datacenterknowledge.com/archives/2015/02/23/openstack-vs-cloudstack-the-platforms-and-the-cloud-apis/ (accessed April 26, 2016).

Kupidura, B. 2013. Understanding OpenStack authentication: Keystone PKI, OpenStack Unlocked. Mirantis. https://www.mirantis.com/blog/understanding-openstack-authentication-keystone-pki/ (accessed May 3, 2016).

Lawson, A. 2015. Understanding OpenStack Neutron ML2 Plugin1037. AQORN. http://aqorn.com/understanding-openstack-neutron-ml2-plugin/ (accessed May 6, 2016).

Llewellyn, A. 2012. Nebula, NASA, and OpenStack. openNASA. https://open.nasa.gov/blog/nebula-nasa-and-openstack/ (accessed May 5, 2016).

Mao, Y. 2013. Understanding nova-conductor in OpenStack Nova. Cloudy Stuff Happens. http://cloudystuff-happens.blogspot.com/2013/04/understanding-nova-conductor-in.html (accessed May 5, 2016).

Mardesh, J. 2014. Developers, check your amazon bills for bitcoin miners. http://readwrite.com/2014/04/15/amazon-web-services-hack-bitcoin-miners-github/ (accessed April 30, 2016).

Mathews, D. 2015. Benchmarking OpenStack Keystone token formats. http://dolphm.com/benchmarking-openstack-keystone-token-formats/ (accessed May 4, 2016).

Mathews, D. 2016. OpenStack Keystone Fernet tokens. http://dolphm.com/openstack-keystone-fernet-tokens/ (accessed May 4, 2016).

Metz, C. 2016. The epic story of dropbox's exodus from the amazon cloud empire. Wired. http://www.wired.com/2016/03/epic-story-dropboxs-exodus-amazon-cloud-empire/ (accessed April 23, 2016).

Mirantis. 2012. Under the hood of Swift. http://www.openstack.org/blog/2012/02/1997/ (accessed May 6, 2016).

OpenBSD. 2016. ssh—OpenSSH SSH client (remote login program). http://man.openbsd.org/OpenBSD-current/man1/ssh.1 ssh (accessed April 22, 2016).

OpenShift Origin. 2016a. OpenShift OrigIn: The open source application container platform. https://www.openshift.org/ (accessed April 26, 2016).

OpenShift Origin. 2016b. OpenShift Origin system architecture guide. https://docs.openshift.org/origin-m4/oo_system_architecture_guide.html (accessed April 26, 2016).

Opensource.com. 2016. What is Docker, introduction to Docker. https://opensource.com/resources/what-docker (accessed April 25, 2016).

OpenStack. 2010. AMQP and Nova. http://docs.openstack.org/developer/nova/rpc.html (accessed May 5, 2016).

OpenStack. 2013. OpenStack services and port. https://ask.openstack.org/en/question/6433/openstack-services-and-port/ (accessed April 23, 2016).

OpenStack. 2014. Chapter 1. Architecture. http://docs.openstack.org/juno/install-guide/install/yum/content/ch_overview.html (accessed May 6, 2016).

OpenStack. 2016a. Object Storage API overview. http://docs.openstack.org/developer/swift/api/object_api_v1_overview.html (accessed May 6, 2016).

OpenStack. 2016b. Appendix B. firewalls and default ports. http://docs.openstack.org/kilo/config-reference/content/firewalls-default-ports.html (accessed April 22, 2016).

OpenStack. 2016c. Chapter 9. Managing projects and users. http://docs.openstack.org/openstack-ops/content/projects_users.html (accessed May 5, 2016).

OpenStack. 2016d. OpenStack virtual machine image guide. http://docs.openstack.org/image-guide/index.html (accessed April 22, 2016).

OpenStack. 2016e. Compute API v2.1 (CURRENT), http://developer.openstack.org/api-ref-compute-v2.1.html (accessed April 22, 2016).

OpenStack. 2016f. Configuring Keystone. http://docs.openstack.org/developer/keystone/configuration.html (accessed April 30, 2016).

OpenStack. 2012. Create a security group. Occi. https://wiki.openstack.org/wiki/Occi#Create_a_Security_Group (accessed April 30, 2016).

OpenStack. 2016a. Creating a security group cURLing nova v1.1 api. https://ask.openstack.org/en/question/18052/creating-a-security-group-curling-nova-v11-api/ (accessed April 30, 2016).

OpenStack. 2016b. DevStack. https://wiki.openstack.org/wiki/DevStack (accessed April 22, 2016).

OpenStack. 2016c. DevStack. http://docs.openstack.org/developer/devstack/ (accessed April 22, 2016).

OpenStack. 2016d. Human interface guide. http://docs.openstack.org/developer/python-openstackclient/humaninterfaceguide.html (accessed April 22, 2016).

OpenStack.2016e. Identity service configuration file. http://docs.openstack.org/juno/config-reference/content/keystone-configuration-file.html (accessed May 4, 2016).

OpenStack. 2016f. OpenStack installation guide for Ubuntu 12..0.4/14.04 LTS/Icehouse. http://docs.openstack.org/icehouse/install-guide/install/apt/content/ (accessed April 22, 2016).

OpenStack. 2016g. Releases. https://wiki.openstack.org/wiki/Releases (accessed April 22, 2016).

OpenStack. 2016h. Swift architectural review. http://docs.openstack.org/developer/swift/overview_architecture.html (accessed May 6, 2016).

OpenStack. 2016i. Keystone command line utility (pending deprecation). http://docs.openstack.org/developer/python-keystoneclient/man/keystone.html (accessed April 22, 2016).

OpenStack. 2016j. v3 examples using cURL. Keystone. http://docs.openstack.org/developer/keystone/api_curl_examples.html (accessed April 22, 2016).

OpenStack. 2016k. OpenStackClient. http://docs.openstack.org/developer/python-openstackclient/ (accessed April 23, 2016).

OpenStack. 2016l. Security groups. http://docs.openstack.org/openstack-ops/content/security_groups.html (accessed April 30, 2016).

Rackspace. 2013. Three OpenStack myths to consider as we close out 2013. http://www.rackspace.com/blog/three-openstack-myths-to-consider-as-we-close-out-2013 (accessed April 22, 2016).

Rao, S. 2015. OpenDaylight is one of the best controllers for OpenStack—Here's how to implement it. The New Stack. http://thenewstack.io/opendaylight-is-one-of-the-best-controllers-for-openstack-heres-how-to-implement-it/ (accessed May 6, 2016).

Rao, S. 2015. SDN's scale out effect on OpenStack Neutron. The New Stack. http://thenewstack.io/sdn-controllers-and-openstack-part1/ (accessed May 6, 2016).

Redhat. 3.3. Networking with nova-network, 3. Compute. OpenStack Platform. https://access.redhat.com/documentation/en-US/Red_Hat_Enterprise_Linux_OpenStack_Platform/5/html/Cloud_Administrator_Guide/section_networking-nova.html (accessed May 5, 2016).

ReleaseNotes/Austin. 2010. Release Notes, Austin. https://wiki.openstack.org/wiki/ReleaseNotes/Austin#Release_Notes.2C_Austin (accessed May 5, 2016).

StackExchange UNIX & LINUX, SSH key-based authentication: known_hosts vs. authorized_keys, http://unix.stackexchange.com/questions/42643/ssh-key-based-authentication-known-hosts-vs-authorized-keys (accessed July 14, 2015).

StackOverflow. 2015. What is the difference between Docker Swarm and Kubernetes/Mesophere? http://stackoverflow.com/questions/27334934/what-is-the-difference-between-docker-swarm-and-kubernetes-mesophere (accessed April 26, 2016).

SUSO Support Site. 2009. SSH tutorial for linux. http://support.suso.com/supki/SSH_Tutorial_for_Linux (accessed April 23, 2016).

Tsidulko, J. 2015. Here's who made gartner's 2015 cloud IaaS magic quadrant. CRN. http://www.crn.com/slide-shows/cloud/300076877/heres-who-made-gartners-2015-cloud-iaas-magic-quadrant.htm (accessed April 25, 2016).

Vivien, V. 2015. Building massively-scalable distributed systems using Go and Mesos. DZone/DevOps Zone. https://dzone.com/articles/building-massively-scalable (accessed April 26, 2016).

Young, A. 2014. Minimal token size, Adam Young's web log. http://adam.younglogic.com/2014/11/minimal-token-size/ (accessed May 3, 2016).

Wentland, D. 2012. Introduction to OpenStack Quantum. http://www.slideshare.net/danwent/openstack-quantum-intro-os-meetup-32612 (accessed May 6, 2016).

Winkler, V. 2012. Cloud computing: Data privacy in the cloud. TechNet Magazine. https://technet.microsoft.com/en-us/magazine/jj554305.aspx (accessed April 23, 2016).

Wood, J., and Tracy, R. 2011. Security advantages of cloud computing. Modern DC Business. http://www.moderndcbusiness.com/security-advantages-of-cloud-computing.html (accessed April 23, 2016).

14 Introduction to Amazon Web Services and Introduction to the CloudStack Cloud

In this chapter we're going to look at two other big clouds: Amazon Web Services (AWS) from Amazon.com, Inc. and the Apache open source CloudStack cloud.

Make no mistake, as of this writing in 2016, the AWS cloud is the biggest cloud around. According to the Synergy Research Group (2016):

> For full-year 2015 AWS share of the worldwide market was 31%, followed by Microsoft (9%), IBM (7%), Google (4%) and Salesforce (4%).

Synergy divides the cloud marketplace into the first tier (they call the first tier "the big four"), which consists of Amazon, Microsoft, IBM, and Google, and the second tier, which includes (among others) Salesforce, Rackspace, Oracle, NTT, Fujitsu, Alibaba, and HPE.

So, since AWS is the 800-pound gorilla of cloud computing we're going to cover the AWS cloud here. Note, however, that AWS is a proprietary cloud; it's not based on open source cloud software such as OpenStack or CloudStack. So the view that we can get into how the AWS cloud works internally is fairly limited. However, according to Vaughn-Nichols (2012), Elastic Compute Cloud (EC2) is based on the Xen hypervisor, also see Xen Project (2016), and its base operating system is a version of Red Hat Enterprise Linux.

Therefore, we will have to focus primarily on AWS service offerings and APIs. There are oodles of free Kindle books that Amazon provides that already talk about AWS, see Amazon Web Services (2013a, 2013b), and Amazon Web Services (2016b, 2016f). We'll get you started, and then you have lots of additional reading material available. ☺

Apache CloudStack is the second most widely used open source cloud, after OpenStack, although by all accounts it's pretty far behind OpenStack in market share, see Linthicum (2014) and Deutscher (2015). The cloud market, however, is quite volatile, it's hard to keep up. For example, Citrix has been a big backer of CloudStack (although they also work with OpenStack, see Deutscher 2015) but recently, as of this writing, Citrix in January 2016 sold its products based on CloudStack, Citrix Cloud Platform, and CloudPortal Business Manager, to Accelerite (owned by Persistent Systems). Note that Citrix Cloud Platform is really the Citrix commercial version of CloudStack, see Panietteri (2016). Still, CloudStack remains the second most widely used open source cloud, and as such is worthy of discussion.

We will first look at the Amazon Web Services cloud and its service offerings, including how to use the AWS EC2 Dashboard to create a virtual machine instance, and how to SSH to that instance.

Then we will look at the AWS EC2 RESTful interface. Note that OpenStack and CloudStack both implement versions of the AWS RESTful interface—partly, of course, to help capture customers away from AWS. ☺ We will look first at the OpenStack version of the AWS RESTful interface, then we will look at how to use the AWS EC2 RESTful interface on AWS itself (we'll also look very briefly at the AWS S3 RESTful interface).

Lastly, we will look at the CloudStack cloud.

14.1   AMAZON WEB SERVICES CLOUD

The AWS cloud provides a huge quantity of services. AWS breaks its services into the following categories—see Amazon Web Services (2016) products list, each with sub-products (typically several sub-products):

- Compute
- Storage and Content Delivery
- Database
- Networking
- Analytics
- Enterprise Applications
- Internet of Things
- Mobile Services
- Developer Tools
- Management Tools
- Security and Identity
- Application Services
- Software (maintenance)

Some of these are largely functions that support other areas of AWS, rather than public offerings themselves—this seems to be the case with the Security and Identity offerings, for example. Others are Platform as a Service offerings or Software as a Service offerings—such as Amazon Mobile SDK (under the Mobile Services category) or Amazon WorkMail (under the Enterprise Applications category).

There's certainly no way we can cover all of these in one middleware textbook!

Besides, with some of these we're getting well away from the main topic of this textbook, which is middleware and how distributed computers interact with each other. So let's focus in on the categories that are most associated with the concept of middleware: Compute, Networking, and to a lesser degree Storage and Content Delivery. (Database is also related, in that one primary use for middleware is to connect to databases, but addressing the specifics of this here is getting outside our main middleware area.)

Even though we've narrowed it down to three categories, it's still far too much for this textbook. So, let's select just a few products in these categories to examine. We choose to examine:

From the Compute category:
- Amazon Elastic Compute Cloud (EC2)
- Amazon EC2 Container registry
- Amazon EC2 Container service
- AWS Elastic Beanstalk
- Auto Scaling

From both the Compute category and the Networking category:
- Amazon Elastic Load Balancing (ELB)
- Amazon Virtual Private Cloud (VPC)

From the Storage and Content Delivery:
- Amazon Simple Storage Service (S3)
- Amazon Elastic Block Store (EBS)

Amazon EC2 runs virtual machine instances, using various operating systems as the guest operating systems in the instances. EC2 is an IaaS offering, in that the users manage their own instances and deployments. In terms of actual code, we're primarily going to look at code to connect with, and we use Amazon EC2 because that's the basis for most other cloud computing on AWS, and will keep us quite busy (although we'll also look briefly at code to access Amazon S3). But we'll also do an overview of these other services so as to get a feel for the basic offerings of the AWS cloud.

The Amazon EC2 Container registry and the Amazon EC2 Container service support Docker containers. We saw these previously in Sections 13.2.1 and 13.2.2. As you may recall from those sections, a Docker container, Docker (2016) is different from a virtual machine in that an operating system is not included in the container. Instead, according to Opensource.com (2016), a Docker container uses the same Linux kernel as the system it's running on. This gives a Docker container higher performance than a virtual machine. Also, Docker containers only need to contain software that the host computer doesn't already have.

Auto scaling has two purposes, it monitors your EC2 virtual machine instances to make sure they're running, and if not automatically replaces them. It can also automatically increase the number of EC2 instances running your application during demand spikes. Then it automatically decreases the number of EC2 instances when demand goes down, to save costs to the owner of the EC2 instances.

Amazon Elastic Load Balancing (ELB) is an IaaS offering, it automatically distributes incoming application traffic across multiple Amazon EC2 instances. Since ELB is IaaS, you have to manage your own instances and deployments (see Suchman 2012).

AWS Elastic Beanstalk handles deploying and scaling web services, this includes load balancing and automatic scaling. Elastic Beanstalk is a PaaS; you give it your web service and it does the work. According to Suchman (2012), Elastic Beanstalk uses Amazon Elastic Load Balancer internally.

Amazon Virtual Private Cloud (VPC) allows a user to create a logically isolated section of the AWS cloud. This is done by allocating (configuring) pools of computing resources such that they are isolated from other users. This isolation is achieved through use of a VLAN.

Amazon Elastic Block Store (EBS) allows a volume (block storage), typically containing a file system, to be attached to a virtual machine instance. Amazon EBS volumes are automatically backed up to provide fault tolerance. Block storage allocated can increase and decrease as needed.

Amazon Simple Storage Service (S3) provides object storage (can be a file), with the objects accessible through a web API: there is a RESTful API and a non-RESTful (SOAP-based) API, however, the SOAP-based API has been deprecated, see Amazon Simple Storage Service (2016). Objects are organized into *buckets*. There is an access control list (list of permissions for who is allowed to access an object) associated with each bucket and with each object.

14.1.1 HOW TO USE AMAZON WEB SERVICES

Here, we're going to examine using the EC2 API on AWS including how to create a virtual machine instance, and how to SSH to that instance. Unfortunately, what AWS looks like will probably change fairly soon, remember AWS is "pushing new features into production at a breathtaking pace" (Bias 2013). AWS has a pretty good tutorial on their web page, with figures, so plan to look at that and we'll talk you through it here. As you go through this, be thinking about how this compares to the OpenStack Dashboard. I think you'll agree there are several similarities in the general flow of how things work, but that the look and feel at each step is different.

First you need to get an AWS account. They have free-tier accounts that last for a year, see Amazon Web Services (2016). Be careful! If you exceed the free-tier limits you will be charged. Also, be careful with your credentials!!! Don't embed them in software and put the software out in the world. You will be charged!

Log in using your AWS account. Select the EC2 Dashboard.

We want to launch an instance—you can see the big Launch Instance button. But there are a few things we have to do first.

Before you do anything else, select your region. This is in the upper right-hand corner of the screen. I selected US East. If you recall from Chapter 13, OpenStack also had regions show up, but since we were pretty well using the defaults, we used Region One without having to set anything.

Scroll down until Security Groups shows up on the left-hand side menu. Click on Security Group. Select the default security group. Then select Actions. Select Edit Inbound Rules.

Click on Add Rule, and add SSH. Then click on Add Rule and add ALL ICMP. So far it's a lot like OpenStack, if you remember how that worked from Section 13.3.2. Or rather, OpenStack is a lot like this. ☺

Note that in this particular security group we're allowing SSH and ICMP to come from anywhere. If you do it this way, do NOT let your instances run too long, because anybody can try to connect, so it's not as secure as it might be. You could put your IP address in it instead, that would be safer.

Next, scroll down until you get to Key Pairs on the menu on the left hand side. Select that, then select Create Key Pair. Wow, this is what we did in OpenStack as well.

Give your key pair the name "thekey." Download the thekey.pem file and keep it in a safe place. We're using public key encryption, see Section 5.2 for a discussion of this. When you download the .pem file you will have downloaded a private key. The AWS cloud will keep track of your public key. You use the private key to access your virtual machine instances.

Note that you can have multiple keypairs and that all of them have to be kept safe, anyone who has access to any one of these can log into one of your running instances (that is associated with that particular keypair), and charge all cloud use to *your very own credit card*.

When I did this, I had previously similarly created another keypair, called mine.pem. You presumably have this one stored away in a safe place as well. ☺ I hope so! Because the "mine" keypair is the one we're going to use, not the one you just created. ☺

Now look back where we started at the Launch Instance button. Click on that button and you will get a list of possible operating system images. Some are part of the free tier and some cost money.

Select the top free-tier image available. In this screen, it will look something like:

Amazon Linux AMI 2016.03.1 (HVM), SSD Volume Type - ami-f5f41398

We previously saw these AMI images back in Section 7.2.

Next you will be taken to a screen that allows you to select the instance type.

Select t2.micro because it's free-tier eligible. The instance type is similar to what we're used to calling a "flavor" in OpenStack. It gives you a set of predefined resources. Note that as of this writing, a t2 instance gives you, according to BluePi (2015):

High Frequency Intel Xeon Processors with Turbo up to 3.3GHz
Burstable CPU, governed by CPU Credits, and consistent baseline performance
Lowest-cost general purpose instance type, and Free Tier eligible (t2.micro only)
Balance of compute, memory, and network resources

A "burstable" instance gives you a baseline CPU performance level but allows you to "burst" above this baseline level. The "micro" gives you one vCPU, 6 CPU credits per hour, and only allows you to use Elasic Block Store (EBS). If you recall, EBS provides blocks of storage that can be attached to an instance and typically accessed like a filesystem.

By the way Amazon vCPUs are a little difficult to figure out, see Babcock (2015). Fielding (2014) claimed that:

A vCPU in an AWS environment actually represents only half a physical core.

Next click Review and Launch in the lower right-hand corner of the screen. You will get a confirmation screen that gives a description of the instance, and details about the image. If you previously set up your security group to allow all SSH and all ICMP, you will get a warning message that your security is open to the world.

After you have reviewed the instance and are happy with its settings, click Launch. It will ask you to select a keypair to use. Select the "mine" keypair—because of course you were careful and kept track of it, right?

Then click Launch Instances and you will have a running instance! This will remind you a lot about the OpenStack list of running instances, in that it includes the state of the instance, its instance type (flavor in OpenStack), and its IP addresses.

14.1.2   How to Log into AWS EC2 Instance with SSH

These instructions assume you are going to log onto Linux on some computer (but not on the AWS cloud)—maybe your laptop or desktop. You have to have secure shell (SSH) installed.

You previously downloaded the file mine.pem; you should have it still available (stored in a safe place). Put it in the directory you're currently working in. Fix the permissions of this file so that only the owner can access it (this means only the owner can read and write it):

```
chmod 600 mine.pem
```

Now you can SSH to either the IP address (when I did it, I got 54.90.160.116) or you can SSH to the public DNS address (when I did it, I got ec2-54-90-160-116.compute-1.amazonaws.com).

EC2 instances on Amazon have the username ec2-user.

So now we will SSH to our running instance as follows (we will use the public DNS address):

```
ssh –i mine.pem ec2-user@ec2-54-90-160-116.compute-1.amazonaws.com
```

We have successfully SSHed to our instance! Now do a "pwd" command to see what directory we're in, inside our instance. This comes up as:

```
/home/ec2-user
```

14.2   TECHNOLOGY REVIEW: AMAZON WEB SERVICES EC2 RESTFUL INTERFACE

Because of Amazon's market share in the cloud world, other clouds find it useful to provide the same web interfaces as Amazon, trying to steal Amazon's customers ☺ but also for technological reasons. Bias (2013) says:

> … Amazon has continued to push new features into production at a breathtaking pace. They are, quite simply, in control of the innovation curve in public cloud. Every public cloud feature added by an AWS competitor is measured directly against what AWS has already built.

However, in addition to keeping up with the Joneses (the Joneses here are Amazon), which is what Bias (2013) is advocating, there are also other good technological reasons for why developers might want different clouds to support the same or very similar APIs. The reason is simply the difficulty of moving applications from one cloud to another, if your company decides to change cloud providers. If it's too difficult, the cost of changing your application to work with the new cloud might make swapping clouds prohibitively expensive, even if there are otherwise good business and technological reasons to do so.

However, Scoble (2013) argues that OpenStack does not have to support AWS APIs. He says first that he talked with many startup companies, and that none of them said that OpenStack supporting other APIs was important to whether they choose OpenStack. He said:

> If you think Cloud innovation is finished, or that only Amazon can innovate (i.e., do new things for new markets) then by all means you should drop everything and make OpenStack 100% compatible with Amazon's APIs.
> But, if you believe, like I do, that we're entering into a new age that demands new technologies … then you must dismiss Randy Bias' advice and get back to work on building the future.

However, Orozco (2013) says, in order to swap APIs, it's not the syntax of the API that is so important, that is, the order of calls and parameters within the calls, it's the API semantics:

> The more subtle level is API semantics. Two semantically compatible APIs allow you to manipulate equivalent objects and relationships, at a commensurate level of abstraction.

Orozco claims that the regular OpenStack APIs are mostly semantically compatible with the AWS EC2 API, although with a few incompatibilities.

More recently, CloudScaling (where Bias works) has released a drop-in replacement for OpenStack's EC2 API—see Bias (2015) and Robles (2015).

Now we're going to look here at the AWS EC2 interface (API). There are numerous other APIs, of course, but the EC2 API is the starting point for most other work, as it's where you start virtual machine instances. We'll also look briefly at the S3 API on AWS.

In any case, we are going to look here first at the EC2 API plug-in for OpenStack. This seemed like a good way to get you students into the EC2 API, since you're already used to OpenStack from the previous chapter. Then we'll mosey on over into using the AWS EC2 API itself. We'll be using Python to access the EC2 API in both cases.

For both OpenStack and EC2 we will be using the Boto library. The Boto library is a library for use with Python that makes it easy for programmers to access an EC2 API. There is also a library called Boto3. According to Boto CloudHackers (2016), going forward the Boto3 library is recommended, although it can be used side by side with Boto. So we will look first at Boto examples, and then at Boto3 examples, first with OpenStack and then with Amazon EC2 itself.

We'll also look briefly at the AWS S3 API using Boto3.

14.2.1 OpenStack Amazon Web Services EC2 Interface

First of all, you have to download the EC2 credentials. These are in a file called admin-x509.zip. You download this file by going to the Access and Security tab on the dashboard, click API access. Then click Download EC2 Credentials.

(The other tab, Download OpenStack RC file, is also used to set credentials. We previously saw a version of this file in the /devstack directory when we installed OpenStack.)

Unzip the file, then do:

    source ec2rc.sh

This will set your environment variables appropriately, including your access key and secret key. Note that you can also see the EC2 base URL on the screen in Figure 14.1.

A recent version of /devstack did not automatically enable the nova EC2 API in the install. We had to use the EC2 API plugin, see GitHub (2015).

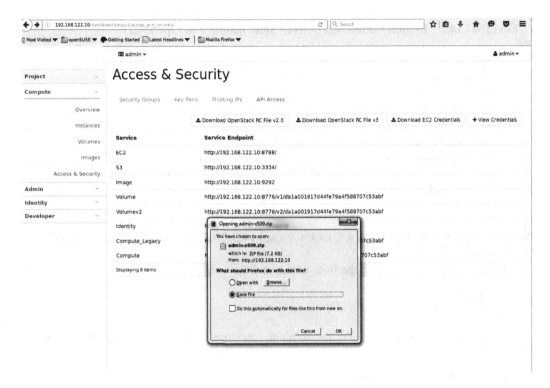

FIGURE 14.1   Download OpenStack EC2 credentials.

When we did this, we also had to use a different URL:

export EC2_URL=http://146.229.233.30:8788/services/Cloud

Whereas the original URL for the EC2 API that was part of nova was:

export EC2_URL=http://146.229.233.30:8773/services/Cloud

14.2.1.1   Access OpenStack EC2 API Using Boto

The Python code using the Boto library to instantiate a virtual machine instance in OpenStack, talking to the main OpenStack EC2 API is shown in Listings 14.1 and 14.2. Note that the myendpoint is explicitly set to the OpenStack EC2 API plugin URL.

To make the code in Listing 14.2 work, I put the code in Listing 14.1 in a file called auth_proj.py.

LISTING 14.1   Python Function to Connect to EC2 API in OpenStack

```
def authfunc(boto):
    import os
    myendpoint='http://localhost:8788/services/Cloud'
    my_access_key=os.getenv("EC2_ACCESS_KEY")
    my_secret_key=os.getenv("EC2_SECRET_KEY")
    ec2 = boto.connect_ec2_endpoint(myendpoint, aws_access_key_id=my_access_key,
        aws_secret_access_key=my_secret_key)
    return ec2
```

LISTING 14.2   Python Code Uses Boto to Start Instance in OpenStack

```python
python
import boto
import auth_proj
myconn=auth_proj.authfunc(boto)
myconn.get_all_images()
myimage=myconn.get_image('ami-00000001')
myimage.name
myconn.run_instances(key_name='mykey',image_id='ami-00000001', instance_
    type='m1.nano')
```

Before we run the code in Listing 14.2, look at Figure 14.2. This shows the Dashboard immediately before running this Python code.

In Listing 14.2, first we import the Boto library and the auth_proj.py file.

```
import boto
import auth_proj
```

Then we create a connection using the authfunc (previously defined in Listing 14.1) from the auth_proj.py file.

```
myconn=auth_proj.authfunc(boto)
```

Then we get all the images available:

```
myconn.get_all_images()
```

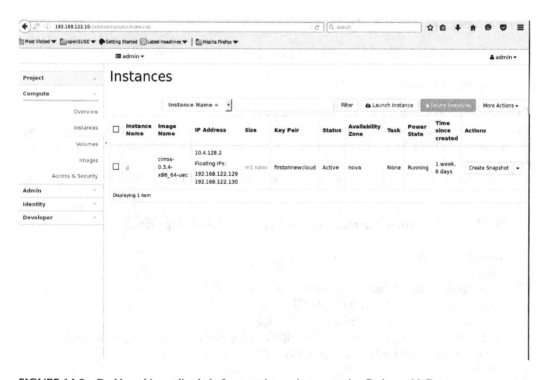

FIGURE 14.2   Dashboard immediately before creating an instance using Python with Boto.

This last will return various images, the output will look something like
[Image:aki-00000002, Image:ami-00000001, Image:ari-00000003, Image:ami-00000004]

Next we select one of the images (this is the cirros image in the version of OpenStack where these examples were created):

myimage=myconn.get_image('ami-00000001')

To check this, we use the following statement:

myimage.name

This will return something like:

u'cirros-0.3.2-x86_64-uec'

and you can see if you got the right image.

Then the next statement starts an image:

myconn.run_instances(key_name='mykey',image_id='ami-00000001', instance_type='m1.nano')

You should be able to see the new instance on the dashboard!!!

You can see a screenshot of the running Python code in Figure 14.3.

In Figure 14.4, we see the Dashboard immediately after the Python code created a new instance.

Now SSH to that instance; you previously learned how to do this in Section 13.3.3.

In Figure 14.5, we see the console immediately after SSHing to the instance. Note that we did the SSH from the same machine where the OpenStack manager node (controller node) was installed.

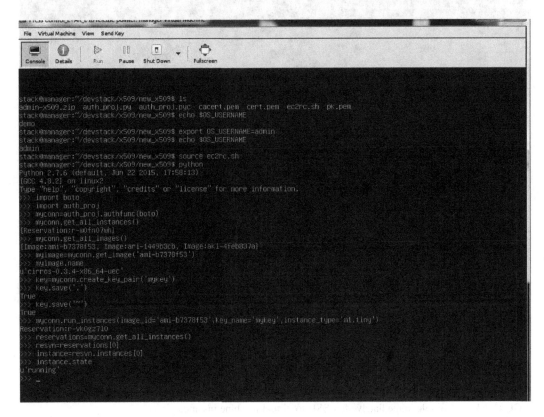

FIGURE 14.3 Running Python Boto code.

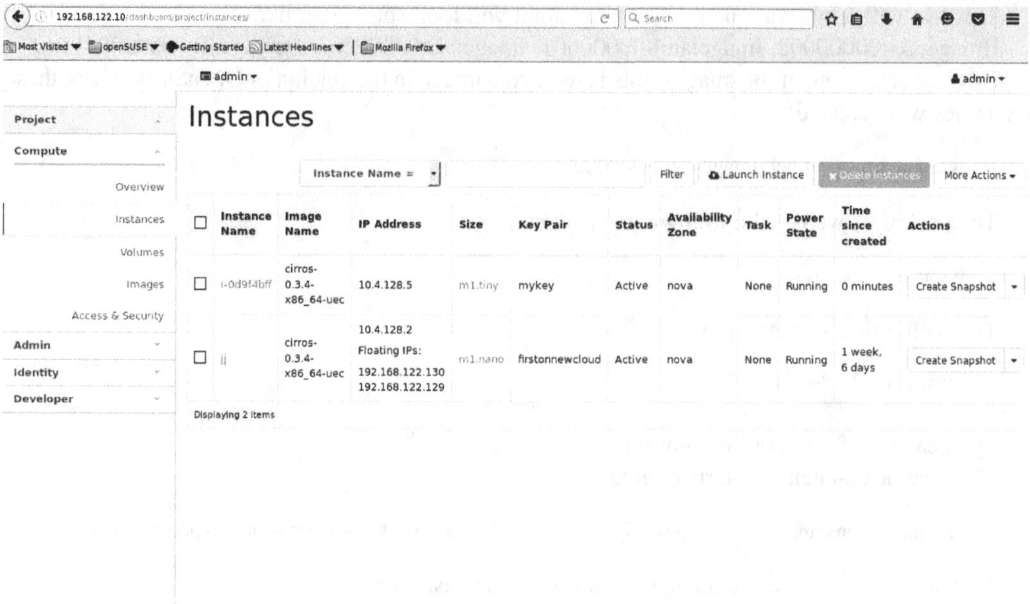
192.168.122.10/dashboard/project/instances/
Most Visited
openSUSE
Getting Started
Latest Headlines
Mozilla Firefox
admin
admin
Project
Compute
Overview
Instances
Volumes
Images
Access & Security
Admin
Identity
Developer
Instances
Instance Name =
Filter
Launch Instance
Delete Instances
More Actions
Instance Name
Image Name
IP Address
Size
Key Pair
Status
Availability Zone
Task
Power State
Time since created
Actions
i-0d9f4bff
cirros-0.3.4-x86_64-uec
10.4.128.5
m1.tiny
mykey
Active
nova
None
Running
0 minutes
Create Snapshot
jj
cirros-0.3.4-x86_64-uec
10.4.128.2
Floating IPs:
192.168.122.130
192.168.122.129
m1.nano
firstonnewcloud
Active
nova
None
Running
1 week, 6 days
Create Snapshot
Displaying 2 items

FIGURE 14.4 Dashboard immediately after creating an instance using Python with Boto.

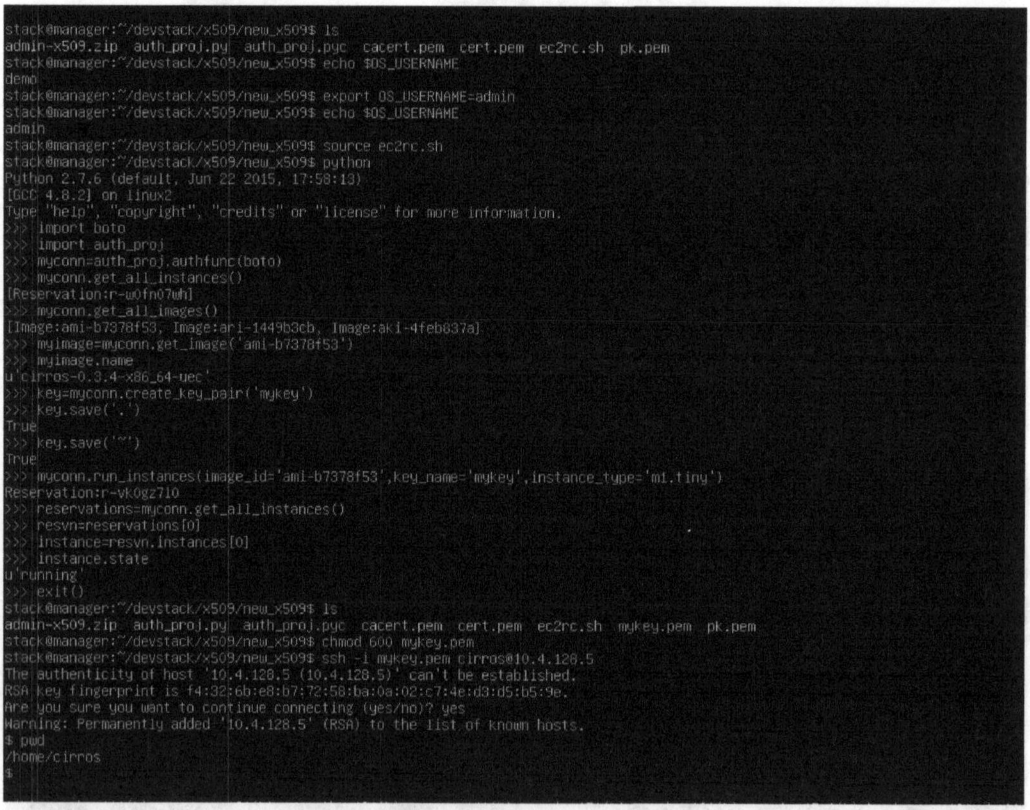
stack@manager:~/devstack/x509/new_x509$ ls
admin-x509.zip auth_proj.py auth_proj.pyc cacert.pem cert.pem ec2rc.sh pk.pem
stack@manager:~/devstack/x509/new_x509$ echo $OS_USERNAME
demo
stack@manager:~/devstack/x509/new_x509$ export OS_USERNAME=admin
stack@manager:~/devstack/x509/new_x509$ echo $OS_USERNAME
admin
stack@manager:~/devstack/x509/new_x509$ source ec2rc.sh
stack@manager:~/devstack/x509/new_x509$ python
Python 2.7.6 (default, Jun 22 2015, 17:58:13)
[GCC 4.8.2] on linux2
Type "help", "copyright", "credits" or "license" for more information.
>>> import boto
>>> import auth_proj
>>> myconn=auth_proj.authfunc(boto)
>>> myconn.get_all_instances()
[Reservation:r-w0fn07wh]
>>> myconn.get_all_images()
[Image:ami-b7378f53, Image:ari-1449b3cb, Image:aki-4feb837a]
>>> myimage=myconn.get_image('ami-b7378f53')
>>> myimage.name
u'cirros-0.3.4-x86_64-uec'
>>> key=myconn.create_key_pair('mykey')
>>> key.save('.')
True
>>> key.save('~')
True
>>> myconn.run_instances(image_id='ami-b7378f53',key_name='mykey',instance_type='m1.tiny')
Reservation:r-vk0gz710
>>> reservations=myconn.get_all_instances()
>>> resvn=reservations[0]
>>> instance=resvn.instances[0]
>>> instance.state
u'running'
>>> exit()
stack@manager:~/devstack/x509/new_x509$ ls
admin-x509.zip auth_proj.py auth_proj.pyc cacert.pem cert.pem ec2rc.sh mykey.pem pk.pem
stack@manager:~/devstack/x509/new_x509$ chmod 600 mykey.pem
stack@manager:~/devstack/x509/new_x509$ ssh -i mykey.pem cirros@10.4.128.5
The authenticity of host '10.4.128.5 (10.4.128.5)' can't be established.
RSA key fingerprint is f4:32:6b:e8:b7:72:58:ba:0a:02:c7:4e:d3:d5:b5:9e.
Are you sure you want to continue connecting (yes/no)? yes
Warning: Permanently added '10.4.128.5' (RSA) to the list of known hosts.
$ pwd
/home/cirros
$

FIGURE 14.5 Console immediately after SSH to virtual machine instance.

14.2.1.2 Access OpenStack EC2 API Using Boto3

Now we will access the OpenStack EC2 API using Boto3. Boto3 has two main ways of looking at things, resources and clients. A resource is a "higher level abstraction" than a client, whereas clients provide a low-level interface whose methods map closely with service APIs, according to Boto 3 1.3.1 (2016). One easy way to think of it is to think of a service such as EC2 or S3 as a resource. You can do many higher level application type things by accessing the resource directly. Then if you need to you can create a client on EC2 or a client on S3 or etc., to do some low-level things.

We will begin by using a Boto3 resource to access the EC2 interface. The code to do this is shown in Listing 14.3.

LISTING 14.3   Using Boto3 to Access OpenStack EC2 API

```
import boto3
ec2=boto3.resource('ec2',aws_access_key_id='..insert your access key here..',
aws_secret_access_key='…insert your secret key here…', region_name='RegionOne',
endpoint_url='http://192.168.122.10:8788')
instances=ec2.instances.all()

for w in instances:

    print w
    images=ec2.images.all()

for w in images:

    print w
    image=ec2.Image('ami-b7378f53')
    image.name
    ec2.create_instances(ImageId='ami-b7378f53', InstanceType='m1.nano', Keyname=
    'mykey', MinCount=1, MaxCount=1)
    instances=ec2.instances.all()

for w in instances:

    print w
```

Before we begin running this Python code, the OpenStack Dashboard immediately prior to running it is shown in Figure 14.6.

In the code in Listing 14.3, we begin by importing the Boto3 library. Then we create a resource object that corresponds to the EC2 API, using the following statement:

```
ec2=boto3.resource('ec2',region_name='RegionOne',endpoint_url='http://192.168.122.10:8788')
```

Note that in the original Boto code in Listing 14.1, we did not require a region name. This does require a region name. RegionOne is the default region.

We had to specify the endpoint_url. If we hadn't, the Boto3 libraries would have assumed we were using the actual AWS url—it would have failed, however, because RegionOne is not a valid AWS region; it wouldn't have gotten to the point of having the credentials themselves fail. Ask yourselves how I know this. ☺

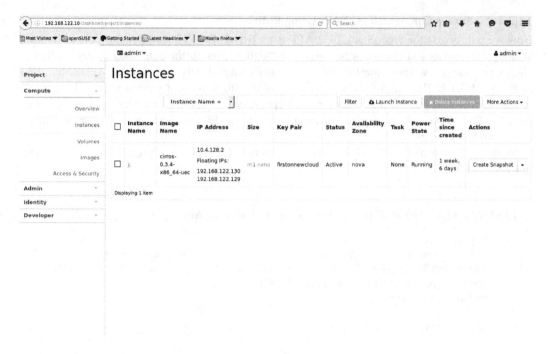

FIGURE 14.6   Dashboard immediately before creating an instance using Python with Boto3.

Next we print all the instances currently recognized by the EC2 resource; we're doing this so we can compare later after we create a new instance:

```
instances=ec2.instances.all()
for w in instances:
  print w
```

Next, we have to select an image to use in order to create our new virtual machine instance. We find out which images are available as follows:

```
images=ec2.images.all()
for w in images:
  print w
```

Then we pick out one of those images to see if it really is the image we want:

```
image=ec2.Image('ami-b7378f53')
image.name
```

Next we create the instance, using the following code:

```
ec2.create_instances(ImageId='ami-b7378f53', InstanceType='m1.nano', Keyname='mykey',
MinCount=1, MaxCount=1)
```

This code could have created multiple instances, but we set it to create only one instance by setting MinCount=1 and MaxCount=1.

(Note that we select the flavor by using the parameter name "InstanceType." Later on when we connect directly to the AWS EC2 interface, we'll use "instance_type" instead. The Boto3 library wouldn't let me use "instance_type" here when I tried to do that.)

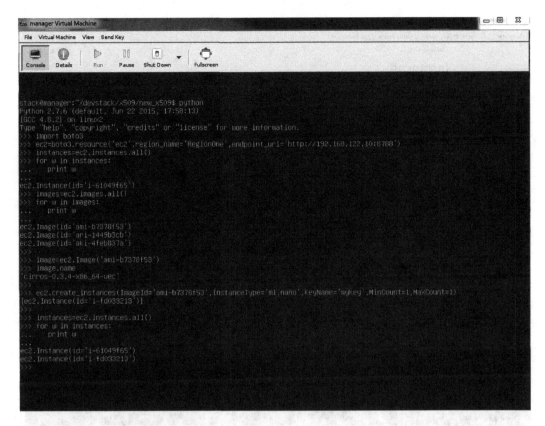

FIGURE 14.7   Running Python Boto3 code.

Finally, we print out all the instances again, the same way we did the first time, just to make sure that our new instance was created.

Results from the running Python code that uses the Boto3 libraries are shown in Figure 14.7.

The dashboard immediately after the Python code is run is shown in Figure 14.8.

Now we SSH to the instance The Console immediately after we SSH to the instance is shown in Figure 14.9.

14.2.1.3   Use Boto3 Client

Let's briefly look at a Boto3 client. We will describe regions using a Boto3 client in Listing 14.4, and the results are in Figure 14.10. We will describe volumes using a Boto3 client in Listing 14.5, the results are in Figure 14.11.

LISTING 14.4   Python Boto3 Code to Describe Regions

```
import boto3
ec2=boto3.client('ec2', aws_access_key_id='..insert your access key here..',
aws_secret_access_key='...insert your secret key here...', region_name='RegionOne',
endpoint_url='http://192.168.122.10:8788')
ec2.describe_regions()
```

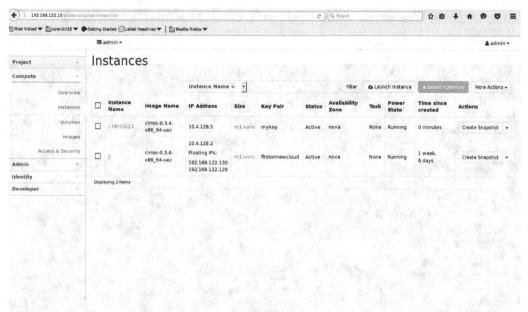

FIGURE 14.8 Dashboard immediately after creating an Instance using Python with Boto3.

```
ec2.Image(id='ami-b7378f53')
ec2.Image(id='ari-1449b3cb')
ec2.Image(id='aki-4feb837a')
>>>
>>> image=ec2.Image('ami-b7378f53')
>>> image.name
'cirros-0.3.4-x86_64-uec'
>>>
>>> ec2.create_instances(ImageId='ami-b7378f53',InstanceType='m1.nano',KeyName='mykey',MinCount=1,MaxCount=1)
[ec2.Instance(id='i-fd033213')]
>>>
>>> instances=ec2.instances.all()
>>> for w in instances:
...     print w
...
ec2.Instance(id='i-61049f65')
ec2.Instance(id='i-fd033213')
>>> quit()
stack@manager:~/devstack/x509/new_x509$ ssh -i mykey.pem cirros@10.4.128.5
@@@@@@@@@@@@@@@@@@@@@@@@@@@@@@@@@@@@@@@@@@@@@@@@@@@@@@@@@@@
@    WARNING: REMOTE HOST IDENTIFICATION HAS CHANGED!    @
@@@@@@@@@@@@@@@@@@@@@@@@@@@@@@@@@@@@@@@@@@@@@@@@@@@@@@@@@@@
IT IS POSSIBLE THAT SOMEONE IS DOING SOMETHING NASTY!
Someone could be eavesdropping on you right now (man-in-the-middle attack)!
It is also possible that a host key has just been changed.
The fingerprint for the RSA key sent by the remote host is
d9:fc:d8:9f:66:9a:58:2e:6e:f9:b4:86:35:58:2c:82.
Please contact your system administrator.
Add correct host key in /opt/stack/.ssh/known_hosts to get rid of this message.
Offending RSA key in /opt/stack/.ssh/known_hosts:7
  remove with: ssh-keygen -f "/opt/stack/.ssh/known_hosts" -R 10.4.128.5
RSA host key for 10.4.128.5 has changed and you have requested strict checking.
Host key verification failed.
stack@manager:~/devstack/x509/new_x509$ ssh-keygen -f "/opt/stack/.ssh/known_hosts" -R 10.4.128.5
# Host 10.4.128.5 found: line 7 type RSA
/opt/stack/.ssh/known_hosts updated.
Original contents retained as /opt/stack/.ssh/known_hosts.old
stack@manager:~/devstack/x509/new_x509$
stack@manager:~/devstack/x509/new_x509$
stack@manager:~/devstack/x509/new_x509$ ssh -i mykey.pem cirros@10.4.128.5
The authenticity of host '10.4.128.5 (10.4.128.5)' can't be established.
RSA key fingerprint is d9:fc:d8:9f:66:9a:58:2e:6e:f9:b4:86:35:58:2c:82.
Are you sure you want to continue connecting (yes/no)? yes
Warning: Permanently added '10.4.128.5' (RSA) to the list of known hosts.
$ pwd
/home/cirros
$
$(L) n-sch  11$(L) n-novnc  12$(L) n-cauth  13$(L) n-cpu  14$(L) c-api  15$(L) c-sch  16$(L) c-vol  17-$(L) horizon  18$ shell-
```

FIGURE 14.9 Console immediately after SSH to virtual machine instance.

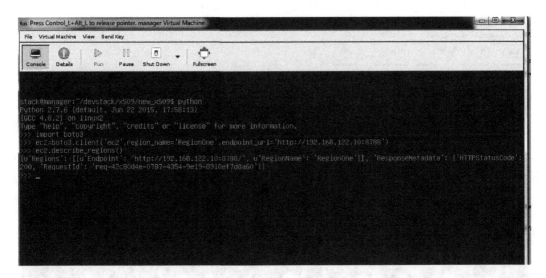

FIGURE 14.10 Execution of code from Listing 14.4.

LISTING 14.5 Python Boto3 Code to Describe Volumes

```
import boto3
ec2=boto3.client('ec2', aws_access_key_id='..insert your access key here..',
aws_secret_access_key='...insert your secret key here...', region_name='RegionOne',
endpoint_url='http://192.168.122.10:8788')
ec2.describe_volumes()
```

I chose these solely and only because the results would all show up on one screen. ☺ All the other "describe" type client examples I tried had too much output, so it was difficult to see. You can do a lot more than just describe things with a client, however, it can do just about anything. See Boto 3 Docs. 1.3.1 (2016a) for a description of all the EC2 Client calls.

14.2.2 AMAZON WEB SERVICES EC2 RESTFUL INTERFACE ON THE AWS CLOUD

First you have to get your AWS credentials, the Access Key and the Secret Key. These are called *root account credentials* because they are associated with your AWS account itself. These will be used to sign your requests that you send using Python to AWS. In your main AWS home screen (the screen that shows when you first log in), go to the upper right-hand corner, and select your name. You will get a drop down menu. Select the Security Credentials menu item. This will take you to the Security Credentials page.

Now click on Select New Access Key. After you do this, on the next screen, click Download Key File.

When you download the key file, it will be named rootkey.csv. You can read this file in a text editor, or you can read it in Excel.

The rootkey.csv file will have contents:

AWSAccessKeyId=*theaccesskeyitself*
AWSSecretKey=*thesecretkeyitself*

Take the access key itself from the rootkey.csv file and put it in a file named "aa." Take the secret key itself from the rootkey.csv file and put it in a file named "bb." Then type:

export AWS_ACCESS_KEY_ID='cat aa'
export AWS_SECRET_ACCESS_KEY='cat bb'

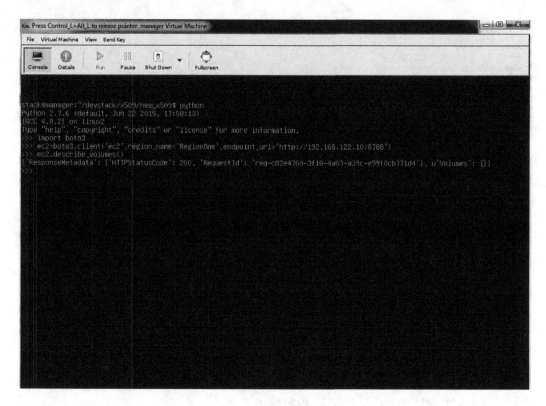

FIGURE 14.11   Execution of code from Listing 14.5.

In the code that is provided for the instructor with this textbook, I've put the two Linux export commands in a file called:

   create_env_variables_credentials

So if you want to, instead of typing the two export commands separately, after you split the access key into the "aa" file and the secret key into the "bb" file, you can type:

   source   create_env_variables_credentials

To see if your environment variables are set correctly, do:

   echo $AWS_ACCESS_KEY_ID

and

   echo $AWS_SECRET_ACCESS_KEY

Note: with all these files, if you send them in from a Windows system, you'll have to convert them to Linux format. If you have the dos2unix utility, then use that. For example:

   dos2unix create_env_variables_credentials

or just

```
dos2unix *
```

(the second one will convert all files in the current directory).
If you don't have dos2unix installed, if you're an administrator you can install it.
If not, you can do the following:

```
tr -d "\r" < create_env_variables_credentials >junk_file
mv      junk_file create_env_variables_credentials
```

The Boto and Boto3 libraries are supposed to pick these environment variables up automatically. It worked for me with Boto but not with Boto3. There's an alternative way to configure for these credentials, however. Instead of putting your access key and secret key in environment variables, put them in a config file as follows:

Make a directory called ".aws." Note that it has to have the "." in front of the "aws."
Make a text file called "credentials." The credentials file should contain:

```
[default]
aws_access_key_id=…put your very own access key here…
aws_secret_access_key=…put your very own secret key here…
```

14.2.2.1 Access EC2 API Using Boto

We will now look at how to access the AWS EC2 API using Boto. We are going to use Boto to launch an instance of a virtual machine. First go back and look at the list of running instances prior to executing our Python/Boto code.

The first thing to do is to SSH into our instance that we created previously using the AWS graphical user interface (GUI). You should have learned how to do this before in Section 14.1.2. We'll be running our Python code out of our own AWS instance.

Our Python code initially will be as shown in Listing 14.6. Note that we're assuming that Python has already been installed and that the Boto library has already been installed in our AWS instance. This was the case when I logged in to create these examples. ☺ We're using Python 2 (you can see this later on in Figure 14.12).

In the code in Listing 14.6, we first import the Boto libraries. Then we connect to the appropriate region, in this case "us-east-1." Remember, back in Section 14.1 we selected this as our region using the AWS GUI.

Next we get an image using an image id. The image I chose was:

```
'ami-f5f41398'
```

How did we know to pick that particular image id? We previously saw it when we launched an instance using the EC2 Dashboard. It's the id of the first free tier HVM image shown.

We check this by printing out the image name after we get it, to make sure we got the right one—because we don't want to accidentally choose the wrong one because we don't want to have to pay to use a non-free tier image. ☺

Next we choose the instance_type "t2.micro". Why did we pick that particular instance type? As it happens, it's the one we chose previously when we launched an instance using the EC2 Dashboard. (Note that not all instance types will work with this image.)

Finally, we launch the instance using the call to run_instances.

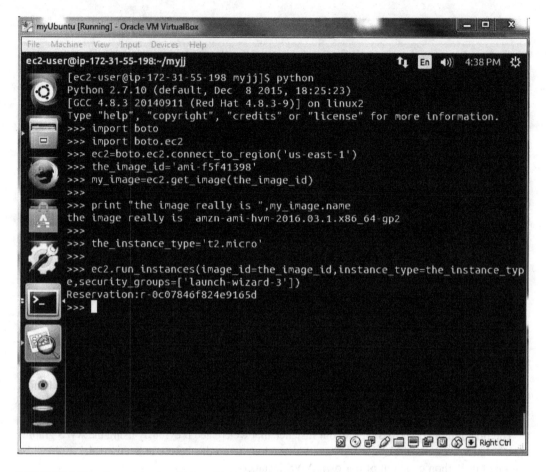

FIGURE 14.12 Execution of code from Listing 14.6.

LISTING 14.6   Python Boto Code for AWS EC2—Not Quite Working

```
import boto
import boto.ec2
ec2=boto.ec2.connect_to_region('us-east-1')
the_image_id='ami-f5f41398'
my_image=ec2.get_image(the_image_id)
print "the image really is ",myimage.name
the_instance_type='t2.micro'
ec2.run_instances(image_id=the_image_id,instance_type=the_instance_type, security_
    groups=['launch-
wizard-3'])
```

A screenshot showing the code in Listing 14.6 as it executes is shown in Figure 14.12. Note that this shows that we really did use the correct image id, that is, the one we wanted (one of the free ones).

But wait! It worked, didn't it? We didn't get any errors. Using the AWS GUI, take a look at the list of running instances. It's got a new instance, right?

Look closer. Oh, no, we forgot the key name! So we can't SSH into it. So we'll have to fix that. See the fixed code in Listing 14.7.

LISTING 14.7   Python Boto Code for AWS EC2—It Works!!!

```
import boto
import boto.ec2
ec2=boto.ec2.connect_to_region('us-east-1')
the_image_id='ami-f5f41398'
my_image=ec2.get_image(the_image_id)
print "the image really is ",my_image.name
the_instance_type='t2.micro'
ec2.run_instances(image_id=the_image_id,instance_type=the_instance_type, key_
    name='mine',
security_groups=['launch-wizard-3'])
```

The only difference in the code in Listing 14.7 and the code in Listing 14.7 is "key_name='mine'" in the call to run_instances.

A screenshot showing the code in Listing 14.7 as it executes is shown in Figure 14.13.

It looks an awful lot like the running of the code from Listing 14.6. Only this time, we get the correct answer. Use the AWS GUI to check again on the list of running instances. Our new instance has a key!

Using the AWS GUI, you can compare the two instances we created, one has a key and the other does not. (Our original instance that we're running out of is also still there.)

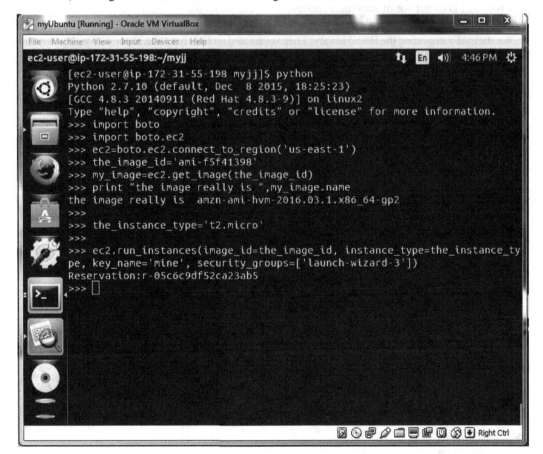

FIGURE 14.13   Execution of code from Listing 14.7.

And you can SSH into this one!!!

Note, try SSHing into it from the computer where you SSHed into your original AWS instance, rather than SSHing from one amazon instance to the other. You have to worry about outgoing rules in your security group if you do that, and I didn't want to have to go into that in this textbook.

14.2.2.2 Access EC2 API Using Boto3

Now we'll do the same thing except this time we'll use Boto3. To make the Boto3 code work when I ran it, I had to put the access key and secret key in the /.aws/credentials file, as previously shown in Section 14.2.

Before we run the Boto3 Python code, use the AWS GUI to look again at our view of running instances.

Let's start by SSHing into our one running Python instance. We're going to do all our Python work here from inside an AWS instance. You should have learned how to do this before in Section 14.1.2.

We'll be using Python 2. This came installed on this image when I used it. However, it came with the Boto library pre-installed, but not Boto3. So you may have to install Boto3.

To do this, do (inside your AWS instance):

```
sudo bash
pip install boto3
```

then type ctrl-D to get out of superuser mode.

Our Python code to start a virtual machine instance using Boto3 is shown in Listing 14.8.

We started by importing the Boto3 library. Then we created an EC2 resource in our region. If you recall from Section 14.2.1.2, Boto3 has two main ways of looking at things, resources and clients. A resource is a *higher level abstraction* than a client, whereas clients provide a low-level interface whose methods map closely with service APIs, according to Boto 3 1.3.1 (2016).

For example, we can use an EC2 resource to create virtual machine instances (which is what we do in Listing 14.8). We can use an EC2 resource to create key pairs, or to create security groups, or numerous other things. We can do many similar things in an EC2 client (for example, an EC2 client has a create_security_group method). It's just lower level more specific calls when you're using the client. We'll look at a couple of simple client calls a bit later on.

After we create the ec2 resource, we'll get a list of all the instances on that resource by calling ec2.instances.all(), and by printing out the instances returned.

Finally, we will start a virtual machine instance by calling ec2.create_instances. Note that we have to pass it an image id (we're using the same one we used when we looked at Boto), and an instance type and key name. We also have to tell it how many instances we want created (MinCount to MaxCount). In this case, we want one instance.

LISTING 14.8   Python Boto3 Code for AWS EC2

```
import boto3
ec2=boto3.resource('ec2',region_name='us-east-')
instances=ec2.instances.all()
for w in instances:
.....print w
ec2.create_instances(ImageId='ami-f5f41398', instance_type='t2.micro', KeyName='
    mine',
MinCount=1,MaxCount=1)
```

What happens while we're executing the code from Listing 14.8 is shown in Figure 14.14.

In Figure 14.14, look at the instance ids printed out by in the for loop. Compare these to the instance ids in that you can see using the AWS GUI. They're the same!

The AWS GUI now shows the new instance we created.

Before we do anything else though, let's print out the new set of instances using a Python for loop. See this in Figure 14.15. It's there, and it matches the dashboard. ☺

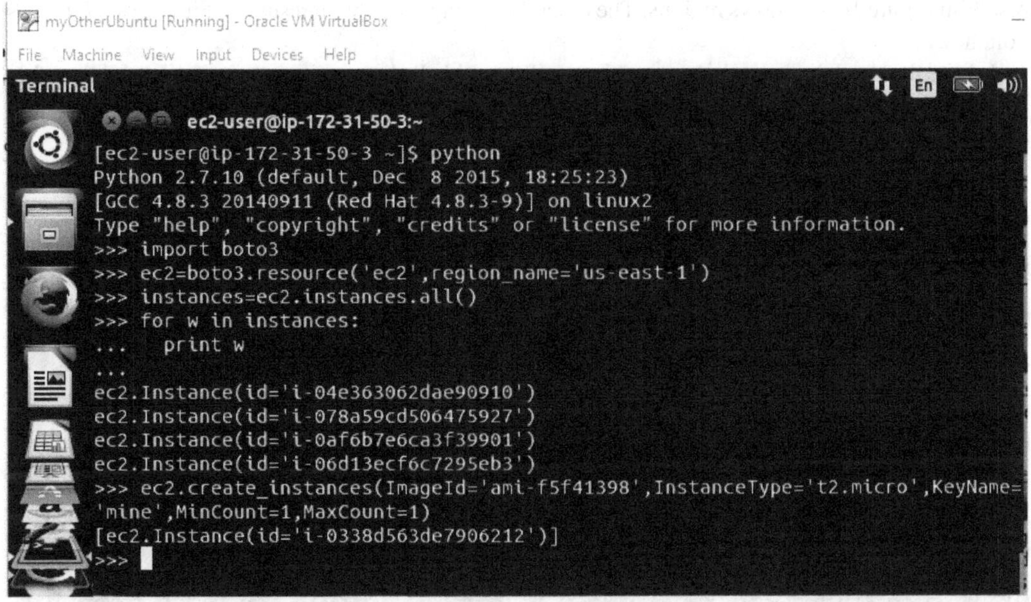

FIGURE 14.14 Execution of code from Listing 14.8.

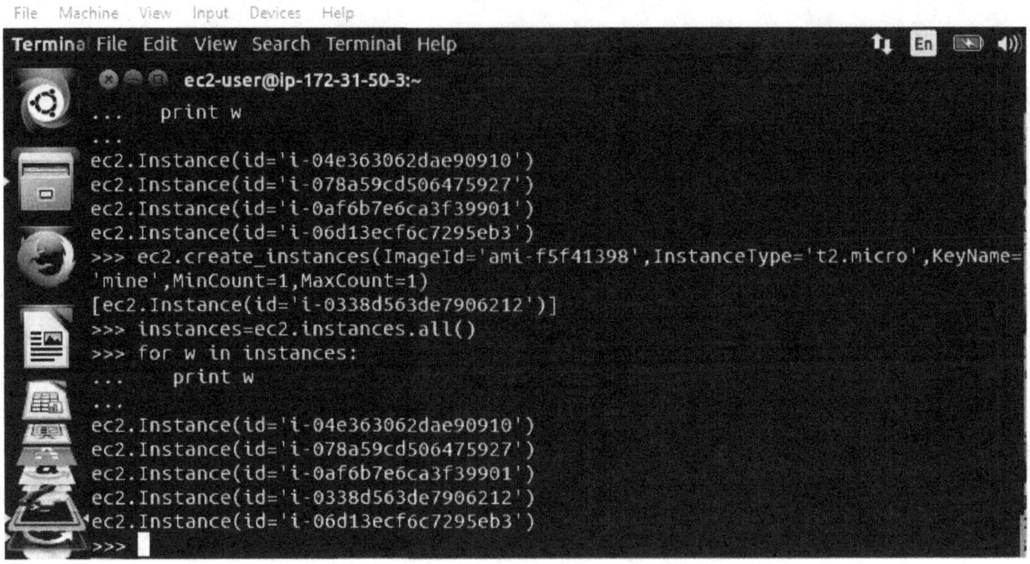

FIGURE 14.15 Print out instances using Python after a new instance has been added.

Now you can SSH into it from the computer where you SSHed into your original AWS instance. (Do this rather than SSHing from one Amazon instance to the other. You have to worry about outgoing rules in your security group if you do that, and I didn't want to have to go into that in this textbook.)

14.2.2.2.1   Use Boto3 Client

Before we go on about our business, let's use a Boto3 client, just to see one, or in this case, two.

I'm giving two short examples of using a Boto3 EC2 client. One, shown in Listing 14.9 with its results in Figure 14.16, shows regions. The other, in Listing 14.10 with results in Figure 14.17, shows volumes.

I chose these solely and only because the results would all show up on one screen. ☺ All the other "describe" type client examples I tried had too much output; it was difficult to see. You can do a lot

FIGURE 14.16   Execution of code from Listing 14.9.

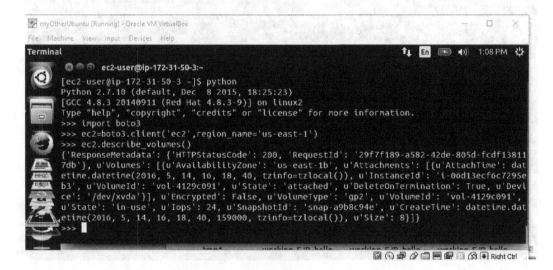

FIGURE 14.17   Execution of code from Listing 14.10.

more than just describe things with a client; however, it can do just about anything. See Boto 3 Docs. 1.3.1 (2016) for a description of all the EC2 Client calls.

LISTING 14.9   Python Boto3 Code to Describe Regions

```
import boto3
ec2=boto3.client('ec2',region_name='us-east-1')
ec2.describe_regions()
```

LISTING 14.10   Python Boto3 Code to Describe Volumes

```
import boto3
ec2=boto3.client('ec2',region_name='us-east-1')
ec2.describe_volumes()
```

14.2.2.2.2   Use Boto3 to Access S3

Note that accessing Amazon S3 using resources in Boto3 is very similar to what we saw using Boto3 with EC2, see Boto3 Docs. 1.3.1 (2016).

In S3, a "bucket" is used to store objects. Inside a bucket, you have a key and then the object that is associated with that key. You can choose a region where the bucket will be located.

Code to manipulate buckets, keys, and associated file objects is shown in Listing 14.11.

LISTING 14.11   Python Boto3 Code to Control Objects and Buckets

```
import boto3
s3=boto3.resource('s3',region_name='us-east-1')
s3.create_bucket(Bucket='longnastyname')
s3.Bucket('longnastyname').upload_file('testy.txt','thetestyfile')
bucket=s3.Bucket('longnastyname')
for theobject in bucket.objects.all():
 print theobject
s3.Bucket('longnastyname').download_file('thetestyfile','kk.txt')
for key in bucket.objects.all():
 key.delete()
bucket.delete()
```

In the code in Listing 14.11, first we import the Boto3 library, then we set up a resource object that points to the S3 interface for region 'us-east-1':

```
s3=boto3.resource('s3',region_name='us-east-1')
```

Next, we use that resource to create a bucket, the bucket will be located in the region the resource pointed to:

```
s3.create_bucket(Bucket='longnastyname')
```

The bucket has the name "longnastyname." It needs a long nasty name because it has to be a unique name across all buckets stored in AWS. Amazon recommends prefixing your bucket name with the name of your company to avoid collisions with pre-existing bucket names. When I tried this, surprisingly the name 'longnastyname' had not previously been used. ☺ But keep in mind, all the students who use this textbook will look at this code. So you may very well need a different name. But do make it long and nasty so you don't collide with pre-existing bucket names.

Then we upload a file called "testy.txt" to the bucket and give it the key named "thetestyfile":

```
s3.Bucket('longnastyname').upload_file('testy.txt','thetestyfile')
```

Then we get a pointer to the bucket, and we print out all the objects in the bucket, just to make sure the object really got into the bucket:

```
bucket=s3.Bucket('longnastyname')
for theobject in bucket.objects.all():
    print theobject
```

Then we download the file into a different file name just to show that we can retrieve that file whenever we want to:

```
s3.Bucket('longnastyname').download_file('thetestyfile','kk.txt')
```

Here, we used the keyname "thetestyfile" to retrieve the object, and we wrote the data into the file named "kk.txt."

Next, we want to get rid of the bucket and the object it contains. First, we have to get rid of all the keys in the bucket, because you can't delete a bucket if it still has any keys in it:

```
for key in bucket.objects.all():
.....key.delete()
```

And finally, we delete the bucket:

```
bucket.delete()
```

Figure 14.18 shows the running Python code for Listing 14.11, so you can see what it looks like as it executes.

14.3 CLOUDSTACK CLOUD

In this section, we will take a brief look at the CloudStack cloud. As we discussed previously in section 13.2.3, CloudStack is a well-known open source cloud, although its market share is far behind that of OpenStack.

CloudStack has a monolithic architecture, which may have some advantages over OpenStack's distributed architecture, in terms of installation and maintenance, although the jury is still out on these issues.

According to Apache CloudStack (2016a) CloudStack was originally started in 2008 by a company named first VMOps and then Cloud.com. Citrix bought Cloud.com in 2011. In 2012,

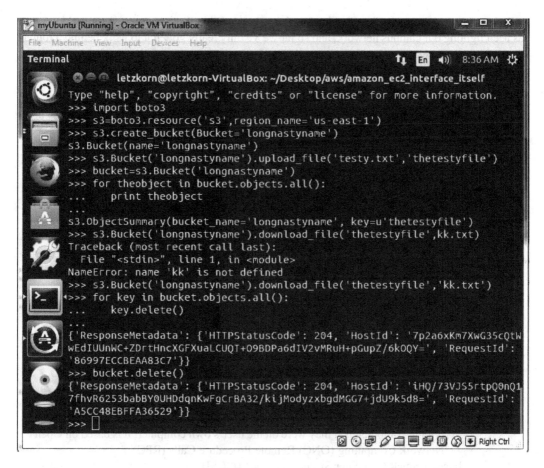

FIGURE 14.18   Running Python code for Listing 14.11.

Cirix released CloudStack to the Apache Incubator under the Apache software license. In 2013, CloudStack was released from the Apache Incubator.

Note that CloudStack also supports the AWS EC2 API, and can also support AWS S3.

14.3.1   CLOUDSTACK DEPLOYMENT

The Apache CloudStack Management server runs in an Apache Tomcat container. (We previously met Apache Tomcat in Sections 4.10 and 11.2.) It is responsible for allocating virtual machines to host computers, for assigning IP addresses, and for allocating and managing storage. It also provides all APIs.

The minimum deployment for two machines would consist of one machine running the Cloud-Stack Management server and a second, separate machine running hypervisor software. The second machine would be the cloud itself, that is, where the virtual machines (VMs) (mostly) run and where the data is (mostly) stored.

It is possible to do an install on a single machine, which in that case would run both the Management server and the hypervisor.

Of course, a more typical install would consist of multiple management servers and multiple host machines running hypervisors. Perhaps thousands of host machines.

We've managed to install CloudStack a few times, but the CloudStack suggested networking setup has been fighting our campus network, and so far we've only really gotten it to work behind a router, where the campus network requirements don't interfere with it.

In CloudStack deployment, the following terms are used:

- Region
  - A collection of one or more zones (geographically near each other) that is managed by at least one management server
  - The largest organizational unit in a CloudStack cloud
- Zone
  - Represents one data center
  - Consists of one or more pods plus secondary storage
  - Secondary storage is zone wide, contains disk templates, ISO images, snapshots
    - Secondary storage is always accessed using NFS
  - Note that primary storage is normally cluster wide
    - However, if using either the KVM hypervisor or the VMware vSphere hypervisor, primary storage can be done per zone
- Pod
  - Rack (or row of racks) + layer2 switch and one or more clusters
- Cluster
  - One or more hosts plus primary storage
    - If using only local disk for an installation, can skip separate primary storage
  - Primary storage is basically virtual hard drives, used to actually run instances
  - At least one primary storage server is required per cluster
    - Network File System (NFS)
      - NFS allows a computer user to treat a file system and its files that are located on a remote computer as if they were on the user's own computer. It is based on Open Network Computing (ONC) Remote Procedure Calls (RPC)
    - Internet Small Computer System Interface (iSCSI)
      - ISCSI emulates SCSI commands over an IP network. SCSI is a standard for connecting computers to peripherals
- Host
  - A single compute node, often a hypervisor

14.3.2 CloudStack Accounts and Domains

Now let's look at how the CloudStack cloud handles accounts. An account represents a customer.

It is possible for an account to have multiple users although normally an installation would associate one user with one account. Users in the same account are not isolated from each other; however, users in one account are isolated from users in a different account.

Resources belong to the account, not to an individual user within the account.

Domains contain multiple logically related accounts.

There are three types of accounts:

1. Root administrator
   a. Has complete access to the system
2. Domain administrator
   a. Can access the current domain, but cannot see into physical servers or other domains
3. User
   a. Username is unique across accounts in a domain

Note that a user *within* an account is not a root administrator or a domain administrator. Rather, the account *itself* is a root administrator or a domain administrator.

The root administrator can dedicate resources to a domain or to an account. For example, a zone, cluster, pod, or host can be dedicated to an account.

A project in CloudStack is associated with both people and resources. A project is located within a single domain, that is, a project cannot be associated with more than one domain. An administrator can set global limits to control the quantity of resources that each project can own. A project administrator can add people to a project, or, alternately, an invitation can be sent to a person that the person could then accept (or decline).

14.3.3 CLOUDSTACK AUTHENTICATION PLUS AN EXAMPLE OF A COMMAND

The different methods for authentication in CloudStack:

- CloudStack login API
- Access key and secret key method
- External LDAP server
- SAML 2.0 identity provider plugin

We will talk about each below, but we will look in depth at an example that uses the access key and secret key method to authenticate, and afterward performs a CloudStack command.

14.3.3.1 CloudStack Login API

When authentication is done through the CloudStack login API, the user receives a JSESSIONID cookie, which the user includes with all messages (until the session times out).

We previously saw JSESSIONID in Section 8.4.5.4. However, briefly, a JSESSIONID cookie is generated by a Servlet container such as Tomcat (remember that the CloudStack Management server runs in an Apache Tomcat container). Since HTTP is stateless, there is no way within HTTP itself to connect multiple request/response pairs into an ongoing session. However, this can be done by the use of cookies. Any HTTP request or HTTP response that includes the JSESSIONID cookie is considered to be part of the session.

Weber (2014) on the CloudStack-users mailing list archives gives the following example of how to use the CloudStack login API with cURL:

Begin quoted material: "
Remember that parameters has [sic] to be encoded if they contain any kind of special characters.
curl -i '
http://localhost:8080/client/api?command=login&user=admin&password=MyPassword&response=json
returns a snippet like this:
Set-Cookie: JSESSIONID=07CA185081E6A476775ECA9D190EF1F8; Path=/client
{ "loginresponse" : { "timeout" : "1800", "lastname" : "cloud",
"registered" : "false", "username" : "admin", "firstname" : "admin",
"domainid" : "6f920fbd-94fc-11e3-b2e0-0050568c15a3", "type" : "1", "userid"
: "d68e7072-94fc-11e3-b2e0-0050568c15a3", "sessionkey" :
"WxjAu9zZzbmrBGDarnW1cVfm+/g=", "account" : "admin" } }
Then you take the JSESSIONID and sessionkey and pass them as Ove said.
List Zones example using above
curl -i -H "Cookie: JSESSIONID=07CA185081E6A476775ECA9D190EF1F8;
Path=/client" '
http://localhost:8008/client/api?command=listZones&sessionkey=WxjAu9zZzbmrBGDarnW1cVfm%2B

%2Fg%3D&response=json'
    ": End quoted material

(NOTE: Ove was the author of a previous response on the mailing list.)

14.3.3.2 Access Key and Secret Key Authentication Plus an Example Using CloudStack Commands

First it is necessary to acquire your Access Key and your Secret Key from CloudStack. The easiest way to do this is to download it using the CloudStack GUI. How to do this is shown in Figure 14.19.

In Listing 14.12, we see a CloudStack script that authenticates using the Access Key and Secret Key method. After authenticating, it performs a call to the CloudStack API that was passed in as a parameter to the script.

The format used by CloudStack commands using access key and secret key is in the following format:

> http://localhost:8080/client/api?apikey=… &command=… &response=json&signature=…

So the different sub-parts of this format is:

- Baseurl:8080/client/api?
- &apikey-…the api key that was previously downloaded…
- &command=…a command that corresponds to a method on the CloudStack API…
- &response=json
- &signature=…

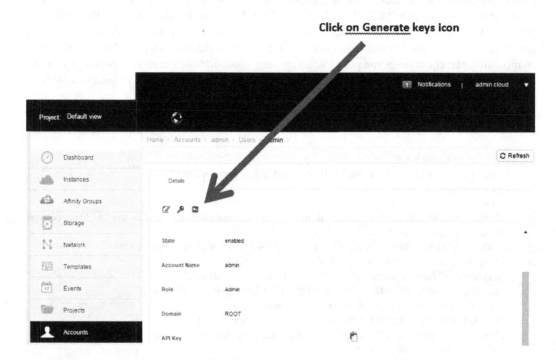

FIGURE 14.19 Download access key and secret key from CloudStack GUI.

LISTING 14.12   CloudStack Script Authenticates Using Access Key and Secret Key, then Performs Selected Command

```
# This is a script to access the CloudStack API

# This script uses one parameter, the selected command.
# call it like this: ./call_any_command.sh listUsers
#(this example calls the listUsers command)

# set up the base URL

baseurl='http://localhost:8080/client/api?'

# IMPORTANT: remember to put in your own api key and secret key
api_key=HmIyrn_8ZITJuIELjbLRhh_uCaKHVHmbxuUlvlvaVfum0_U2rv60MXzAL105l-
WetgNj5hBcYnbmAVezP_-H_mQ

secret_key=zYxTsoXoYl-sNvHUVfOzETcyJmc9aR8hMn-ONyklH2mNeoQMNMFff-
taM3S8d5e9Xhh1uBh7F8PPVtwf19uvO_w

# Start building pieces of the request, start with selecting the api key
request1=apikey=
request1=$request1$api_key

# Continue building pieces of the request, select the command
request2="&command="$1

# Continue building pieces of the request, select a response in JSON format
request3="&response=json"

# Put the request all together
request_so_far=$request1$request2$request3

#Now we have to get an hmac hash of the request. By the CloudStack
#rules, this has to be done on a lower case version of the request.
#So now turn the request into lower case
lowercasecommand=$(echo $request_so_far | tr 'A-Z' 'a-z')
#Make an extra copy of the lowercase command. We went through a lot
#to get to it, so we want to make sure we don't lose it :-)
signature=$lowercasecommand

#Do the hmac hash using OpenSSL. The result in $tmpsignature will be
#in binary so you won't be able to see it using echo.
tmpsignature=$(echo -n $signature | openssl sha1 -binary -hmac $secret_key)

#Now do the base64 encoding. This puts the binary in an ASCII format so it
#can be sent via an HTTP Get
finalsignature=$(echo -n $tmpsignature | openssl base64)

#Now build one more part of the request, a selection of the signature
```

```
signature_selection='&signature='

#Now build the final request
myrequest=$baseurl$request_so_far$signature_selection$finalsignature

# Now use cURL to send the request. cURL defaults to using a GET.
curl $myrequest
```

The signature that is attached to the command is generated using the earlier parts of the command as input:

- Apikey=… &command=… &response=json

Then it turns this to lowercase. Then it does an HMAC-SHA1 hash on the lowercased earlier parts of the command, using the secret key to do the hash. Then it does a base64 encode of the hashed value. Then it appends this to the rest of the command as:

- &signature=…the base64 encoded, HMAC-SHA1 hash of the earlier parts of the command…

Now let's look at the script itself. First, the script sets up the baseURL:

```
baseurl='http://localhost:8080/client/api?'
```

Next, it creates variables consisting of the access key (api key) and the secret key (you will have previously had to cut/paste those here into the script):

```
api_key=…access key itself…
secret_key=…secret key itself…
```

Then it builds the pieces of the request that will next be used to create the digital signature:

```
# Start building pieces of the request, start with selecting the api key
request1=apikey=
request1=$request1$api_key
# Continue building pieces of the request, select the command
request2="&command="$1
# Continue building pieces of the request, select a response in JSON format
request3="&response=json"
# Put the request all together
request_so_far=$request1$request2$request3
```

What we have when we're done with this part of the code is that the variable request_so_far contains:

- Apikey=… &command=… &response=json

Next we convert the request_so_far into lowercase:

```
lowercasecommand=$(echo $request_so_far | tr 'A-Z' 'a-z')
```

Then we make a copy of it in the signature variable:

```
#Make an extra copy of the lowercase command. We went through a lot
#to get to it, so we want to make sure we don't lose it :-)
signature=$lowercasecommand
```

It's not really to make sure we don't lose it. What it's for is to put the value in a variable that's got a name that reflects what we're going to use this value for (signature). Before, it was convenient for me to have it in a variable named lowercase because that reminded me what it was for. I didn't have all the comments in place when I originally wrote this script. ☺ It's more accurate to say, we don't want to "lose track" of it.

Next we do an HMAC-SHA1 hash with the secret key. We use OpenSSL to do this:

```
#Do the hmac hash using OpenSSL. The result in $tmpsignature will be
#in binary so you won't be able to see it using echo.
tmpsignature=$(echo -n $signature | openssl sha1 -binary -hmac $secret_key)
```

Then we base64 encode it so we can send it in HTTP GETs:
Now do the base64 encoding. This puts the binary in an ASCII format so it

```
#can be sent via an HTTP Get
finalsignature=$(echo -n $tmpsignature | openssl base64)
```

Finally, we append it as a digital signature to the full request:

```
#Now build one more part of the request, a selection of the signature
signature_selection='&signature='
#Now build the final request
myrequest=$baseurl$request_so_far$signature_selection$finalsignature
```

And last of all, we send it on to CloudStack:

```
# Now use cURL to send the request. cURL defaults to using a GET.
curl $myrequest
```

Note that all command parameters must be in alphabetical order, and also to work in all cases the signature should be url encoded.

14.3.3.3 External LDAP Server

The Lightweight Directory Access Protocol (LDAP) is a protocol that runs on an IP network and provides directory look up services, see IETF (2006). There are variations that run on TCP/IP and others that run on UDP over IP.

With CloudStack, you use an external LDAP server to implement username/password lookup. According to CloudStack (2016):

To set up LDAP authentication in CloudStack, call the CloudStack API command addLdapConfiguration and provide Hostname or IP address and listening port of the LDAP server.

14.3.3.4 SAML 2.0 Identity Provider Plugin

CloudStack allows use of Security Assertion Markup Language (SAML) 2.0 for authentication, through use of a SAML 2.0 identity provider plugin.

SAML 2.0 is an example of trusted third-party authentication. The general concept should be familiar to you from Public Key Infrastructure (PKI), which we saw in Section 5.5. However, SAML 2.0 is different from PKI. For one thing, SAML is an Organization for the Advancement of Structured Information Standards (OASIS) standard, see OASIS (2009).

Single Sign On in SAML uses third-party authentication and basically works as follows, see IBM (2016):

> The SAML web SSO flow includes three actors: the end user, the identity provider (IdP), and the service provider (SP). The user always authenticates to the IdP, and the SP relies on IdP assertion to identify the user.

In CloudStack, the identity provider is the SAML plugin and the service provider is CloudStack itself.

The SAML 2.0 plugin is implemented using OpenSAML (an opensource Java library), see Yadav (2014).

14.3.4 CLOUDSTACK NETWORKING

In CloudStack, each new Virtual Machine (VM) receives its very own public IP address. Static Network Address Translation (NAT) maps the private IP address assigned to the VM to that VM's public IP address (at a router). If instead a VM is using Elastic IPs, then whenever an elastic IP is acquired, the VMs public IP address is returned to the public IP address pool.

A zone can have either basic networking or advanced networking. A zone must use one or the others, that is, a particular zone is either basic or advanced for its entire lifetime. However, within a cloud, different zones can use different networking models: that is, one zone may use advanced networking and another basic networking.

Basic networking in a zone (a basic zone) has the following characteristics:

* Supports only one physical network
* In a basic zone, you do not have VLANs, but you can split traffic across multiple
* Physical NICs
  * CloudStack uses a separate NIC (called storage NIC) for storage network traffic
  * Recommend separate NICs for management traffic and guest traffic
* Each VM is assigned an IP directly from the network
* Each pod is a broadcast domain
* Each pod has a unique CIDR (see Section 3.3.3 for a discussion of CIDR)
  * CloudStack will assign IP addresses in the CIDR associated with a pod to guests in that pod
* Has Domain Name System (DNS) 1 and DNS 2 for use by guest VMs. These are accessed by public IP addresses
* Has internal DNS 1 and DNS 2, accessed by the management traffic network. Used by system VMs (virtual routers, console proxies, secondary storage VMs, etc.). Private IP addresses for the pods must have a route to these internal DNS servers
* Optional guest isolation via layer 3 means allows use of security groups (for example, filtering of IP addresses)
* Possible traffic types are: management, public, guest, and storage

Advanced networking in a zone (advanced zone) has the following characteristics:

* Supports multiple networks
* Supports both physical and virtual networks
* Allows the use of tagged VLANs
* Networks defined by VLAN identifier, IP range, and gateway
  * Good practice involves setting different CIDRs for different zones
  * Guest network can be isolated or shared
  * In isolated network, VLANs ranges assigned to each CloudStack account
  * Administrator can create additional networks for use by guests

  – Can be associated with a single account, or
  – Can be available to all accounts
- Has DNS 1 and DNS 2 for use by guest VMs. These are accessed by public IP addresses.
- Has internal DNS 1 and DNS 2, accessed by the management traffic network. Used by system VMs (virtual routers, console proxies, secondary storage VMs, etc.). Private IP addresses for the pods must have a route to these internal DNS servers.

In each zone, the management network has a range of reserved IP addresses. These reserved IP addresses must be unique across the entire cloud. Hosts in a pod are assigned private IP addresses.

It is possible to configure secondary storage traffic to travel over a separate storage network. However, by default, CloudStack storage traffic travels over the management network.

Management network handles traffic between Management servers and Hosts, System VMs, and (optionally) storage.

Guest traffic can go only between VMs inside one zone. For virtual machines in different zones to communicate with each other, they must communicate with each other using a public IP address.

CloudStack uses System Virtual Machines to perform certain tasks in the cloud. A system virtual machine is a special kind of virtual machine with system privileges. All System VMs come from a single template, see Apache CloudStack (2016).

A "Virtual Router" is a type of System Virtual Machine. A virtual router runs in a virtual machine on the hosts. Typically the Management Service automatically creates a virtual router for each network. Networking features are provided for guest traffic by using a virtual router. The virtual router serves as a DHCP server for the local network, and assigns IP addresses to the guest VMs.

There is an Open vSwitch plugin for CloudStack. Open vSwitch is the native software-defined network (SDN) implementation for OpenStack. It employs Generic Routing Encapsulation (GRE) tunnels between hosts as a way to encapsulate traffic and create a virtual network.

GRE creates a connection that looks to the endpoints as if it were a private point-to-point connection. It does this by sending an outside protocol as data inside an IP packet. Since the outside protocol is not aware of being carried by IP, it can ignore any intermediate stages in the IP routing, and treat the connection as if it were truly point to point.

Security group rules can be mapped to a CIDR or to another account/security group.

14.3.5 CloudStack Object Storage

In CloudStack, Object Storage is provided as plugins, this includes:

- Swift from OpenStack
  - With Swift, still must have NFS-based secondary storage enabled per zone, it serves as staging area in that artifacts from swift are copied to NFS shares and from there to primary storage
- Amazon S3
  - Has to be available within an entire region, is not per zone
  - Data cannot be copied between different regions

EXERCISES

1. What are the names of the EC2 Credentials that we used on OpenStack and CloudStack?
2. Is the EC2 interface automatically enabled in OpenStack?
3. What is the difference between using port 8788 and port 8774 in OpenStack Nova?
4. What are the two main paradigms in Boto3? And what's the difference?

5. What is a bucket for in S3?
6. What is one issue to remember relative to bucket names on AWS?
7. What is the main difference between CloudStack's architecture and OpenStack's architecture?
8. What Container does CloudStack run inside?
9. How do sessions work using CloudStack?
10. With the CloudStack code we saw, what credentials did we use to authenticate?

CONCEPTUAL QUESTIONS

1. Compare the methods of authentication that we examined in OpenStack, Amazon Web Services, and CloudStack. Are there any advantages or disadvantages in regard to authentication methods between the different clouds?
2. In general, compare the RESTful APIs that we saw for OpenStack, Amazon Web Services, and Cloud-Stack (you will have to do this mostly for OpenStack and AWS as we didn't look as heavily at Cloud-Stack). Are these "semantically equivalent," that is, are there several things you can do in one that you couldn't do in another?
3. Talk about the ease of use of OpenStack, Amazon Web Services, and CloudStack, to the degree to which you are able—that is, if you have been able to access all three, then discuss this from your personal experience. If not, then compare any subset. Alternately, discuss this based on the information in this textbook and any other information you can acquire through either a web search or a formal literature review.
4. What are the advantages of Object Storage compared to, say, NFS type storage? What are the disadvantages? *Hint*: think about migrating virtual machines.
5. In what ways can you consider OpenStack, Amazon Web Services, and CloudStack to be examples of middleware? And in what ways are they examples of distributed operating systems? And in what ways are they examples of applications?
6. Use an OpenStack virtual machine instance and call a web application in a CloudStack virtual machine instance. Or use a CloudStack virtual machine instance and call a web application in an AWS virtual machine instance. Or other variations. What are the difficulties that arose in each case?

BIBLIOGRAPHY

Amazon Simple Storage Service. 2016. Appendix: SOAP API. http://docs.aws.amazon.com/AmazonS3/latest/API/APISoap.html (accessed May 15, 2016).

Amazon Web Services. 2013a. Amazon Elastic Compute Cloud (EC2) user guide for Linux instances (free on Kindle). https://www.amazon.com/Kindle-Store/b?ie=UTF8&node=133140011 (accessed March 24, 2017).

Amazon Web Services. 2013b. Amazon Simple Storage Service (S3) getting started guide (free on Kindle). https://www.amazon.com/Kindle-Store/b?ie=UTF8&node=133140011 (accessed March 24, 2017).

Amazon Web Services. 2016a. Amazon EC2 instance types. https://aws.amazon.com/ec2/instance-types/ (accessed May 12, 2016).

Amazon Web Services. 2016b. Amazon Virtual Private Cloud (free on Kindle). https://www.amazon.com/Kindle-Store/b?ie=UTF8&node=133140011 (accessed March 24, 2017).

Amazon Web Services. 2016c. AWS free tier. https://aws.amazon.com/free/ (accessed May 12, 2016).

Amazon Web Services. 2016d. Connecting to your Linux instance using SSH. http://docs.aws.amazon.com/AWSEC2/latest/UserGuide/AccessingInstancesLinux.html (accessed May 11, 2016).

Amazon Web Services. 2016e. Finding a Linux instance using the Amazon EC2 console. http://docs.aws.amazon.com/AWSEC2/latest/UserGuide/finding-an-ami.html#finding-an-ami-console (accessed May 11, 2016).

Amazon Web Services. 2016f. Getting started with AWS: Deploying a web application (free on Kindle). https://www.amazon.com/Kindle-Store/b?ie=UTF8&node=133140011 (accessed March 24, 2017).

Amazon Web Services. 2016g. Getting started with the AWS SDK for Python (Boto). https://aws.amazon.com/developers/getting-started/python/ (accessed May 11, 2016).

Amazon Web Services. 2016h. Products. https://aws.amazon.com/products/ (accessed May 15, 2016).

Amazon Web Services. 2016i. Troubleshooting connecting to your instance. http://docs.aws.amazon.com/AWSEC2/latest/UserGuide/TroubleshootingInstancesConnecting.html (accessed May 11, 2016).

Angus, P. 2013. Understanding CloudStack's physical networking architecture. http://www.shapeblue.com/understanding-cloudstacks-physical-networking-architecture/ (accessed May 18, 2016).

Apache CloudStack. 2016a. CloudStack's history. https://cloudstack.apache.org/history.html (accessed May 19, 2016).

Apache CloudStack. 2016b. Domain Admin API, Apache CloudStack API documentation (v4.8.0). http://cloudstack.apache.org/api/apidocs-4.8/TOC_Domain_Admin.html (accessed May 18, 2016).

Apache CloudStack. 2016c. Managing accounts, users and domains, administration guide. http://docs.cloudstack.apache.org/projects/cloudstack-administration/en/4.8/accounts.html (accessed May 18, 2016).

Apache CloudStack. 2016d. Managing networks and traffic, Administration Guide. http://docs.cloudstack.apache.org/projects/cloudstack-administration/en/4.8/networking_and_traffic.html (accessed May 18, 2016).

Apache CloudStack. 2016e. Root Admin API, Apache CloudStack API Documentation (v4.8.0). http://cloudstack.apache.org/api/apidocs-4.8/TOC_Root_Admin.html (accessed May 18, 2016).

Apache CloudStack. 2016f. User API, Apache CloudStack API Documentation (v4.8.0). http://cloudstack.apache.org/api/apidocs-4.8/TOC_User.html (accessed May 18, 2016).

Apache CloudStack. 2016g. Using an LDAP server for user authentication, Administration Guide. http://docs.cloudstack.apache.org/projects/cloudstack-administration/en/4.8/accounts.html#using-an-ldap-server-for-user-authentication (accessed May 19, 2016).

Apache CloudStack. 2016h. Using projects to organize users and resources, Administration Guide. http://docs.cloudstack.apache.org/projects/cloudstack-administration/en/4.8/projects.html (accessed May 18, 2016).

Apache CloudStack. 2016i. Working with system virtual machines. Administration Guide. http://docs.cloudstack.apache.org/projects/cloudstack-administration/en/4.8/systemvm.html# (accessed May 18, 2016).

Apache Cloudstack wiki. 2013. S3-based secondary storage. https://cwiki.apache.org/confluence/display/CLOUDSTACK/S3-based+secondary+Storage (accessed May 18, 2016).

Babcock, C. 2015. Amazon's "Virtual CPU"? You figure it out. Information Week. http://www.informationweek.com/cloud/amazons-virtual-cpu-you-figure-it-out/a/d-id/1323652 (accessed May 12, 2016).

Bias, R. 2013. OpenStack's future depends on embracing Amazon. Now. CloudScaling. http://www.cloudscaling.com/blog/cloud-computing/openstack-aws/ (accessed May 12, 2016).

Bias, R. 2015. The future of OpenStack's EC2 APIs. CloudScaling. http://cloudscaling.com/blog/openstack/the-future-of-openstacks-ec2-apis/ (accessed May 12, 2016).

BluePi. 2015. Different types of AWS instances. https://bluepiit.com/blog/different-types-of-aws-instances/ (accessed October 9, 2016).

Boto. 2014. An introduction to Boto's EC2 interface. http://boto.cloudhackers.com/en/latest/ec2_tut.html (accessed May 11, 2016).

Boto. 2014. Boto.ec2. http://boto.cloudhackers.com/en/latest/ref/ec2.html (accessed May 11, 2016).

Boto CloudHackers. 2016. Boto: A Python interface to Amazon Web Services. http://boto.cloudhackers.com/en/latest/ (accessed May 14 2016).

Boto 3 Docs. 1.3.1. 2016a. EC2, client. http://boto3.readthedocs.io/en/latest/reference/services/ec2.html#client (accessed May 14, 2016).

Boto 3 Docs. 1.3.1 2016b. Quickstart. http://boto3.readthedocs.io/en/latest/guide/quickstart.html (accessed May 15, 2016).

Boto 3 Docs. 1.3.1. 2016c. Resources. http://boto3.readthedocs.io/en/latest/guide/resources.html (accessed May 14, 2016).

Butler, B. 2016. Shakeup at Citrix continues: CloudStack products sold off. NetworkWorld. http://www.networkworld.com/article/3021057/cloud-computing/shakeup-at-citrix-continues-cloudstack-products-sold-off.html (accessed May 12, 2016).

Deutscher, M. 2015. What CloudStack? After three years, Citrix moves back into OpenStack's embrace. http://siliconangle.com/blog/2015/04/23/what-cloudstack-after-three-years-citrix-moves-back-into-openstacks-embrace/ (accessed May 12, 2016).

Docker. 2016. What is Docker. https://www.docker.com/what-docker (accessed April 25, 2016).

Fielding, M. 2014. Virtual CPUs with Amazon Web Services. Pythian. https://www.pythian.com/blog/virtual-cpus-with-amazon-web-services/ (accessed May 12, 2016).

Frommel, O. 2015. Controlling Amazon cloud with Boto. http://www.admin-magazine.com/Articles/Integrating-AWS-Cloud-Services-with-Your-Custom-Apps (accessed May 11, 2016).

GitHub. 2015. OpenStack/ec2-api. https://github.com/openstack/ec2-api (accessed May 18, 2016).

IBM. 2016. SAML 2.0 web browser single-sign-on. https://www.ibm.com/support/knowledgecenter/SSEQTP_8.5.5/com.ibm.websphere.wlp.doc/ae/cwlp_saml_web_sso.html (accessed May 18, 2016).

IETF (Internet Engineering Task Force). 2006. Lightweight Directory Access Protocol (LDAP): The protocol, RFC 4511. https://tools.ietf.org/html/rfc4511 (accessed May 19, 2016).

Linthicum, D. 2014. CloudStack, losing to OpenStack, takes its ball and goes home. InfoWorld. http://www.infoworld.com/article/2608995/openstack/cloudstack–losing-to-openstack–takes-its-ball-and-goes-home.html (accessed May 12, 2016).

OASIS (Organization for the Advancement of Structured Information Standards). 2009. SAML V2.0. https://www.oasis-open.org/standards#samlv2.0 (accessed May 19, 2016).

Opensource.com. 2016. What is Docker, introduction to Docker. https://opensource.com/resources/what-docker (accessed April 25, 2016).

Orozco, T. 2013. Why do developers care about cloud API compatibility? http://www.scalr.com/blog/why-do-developers-care-about-cloud-api-compatibility (accessed May 12, 2016).

Panettieri, J. 2016. Citrix Systems exits CloudStack versus OpenStack cloud war. Channele2e. https://www.channele2e.com/2016/01/11/citrix-systems-exiting-cloudstack-vs-openstack-war/ (accessed May 12, 2016).

Pope, M. 2014. A new and standardized way to manage credentials in the AWS SDKs. Amazon Web Services Security Blog. https://blogs.aws.amazon.com/security/post/Tx3D6U6WSFGOK2H/A-New-and-Standardized-Way-to-Manage-Credentials-in-the-AWS-SDKs (accessed May 11, 2016).

Robles, P. 2015. OpenStack gets drop-in replacement for Amazon's EC2 API. ProgrammableWeb. http://www.programmableweb.com/news/openstack-gets-drop-replacement-amazons-ec2-api/2015/02/16 (accessed May 12, 2016).

Scoble, S. 2013. My own letter to OpenStack management. https://plus.google.com/+Scobleizer/posts/HQ7Wi4WCQse (accessed May 12, 2016).

Scott's Weblog. 2013. Using GRE Tunnels with Open vSwitch. http://blog.scottlowe.org/2013/05/07/using-gre-tunnels-with-open-vswitch/ (accessed May 18, 2016).

Suchman, P. 2012. What is the difference between Amazon's Elastic Beanstalk and Elastic Load Balancer products? Quora. https://www.quora.com/What-is-the-difference-between-Amazons-Elastic-Beanstalk-and-Elastic-Load-Balancer-products (accessed May 15, 2016).

Synergy Research Group. 2016. AWS remains dominant despite Microsoft and Google growth surges. https://www.srgresearch.com/articles/aws-remains-dominant-despite-microsoft-and-google-growth-surges (accessed May 12, 2016).

TechTarget. 2016. Generic Routing Encapsulation (GRE). http://searchenterprisewan.techtarget.com/definition/Generic-routing-encapsulation-GRE (accessed May 19, 2016).

Vaughn-Nichols, S.J. 2012. Amazon EC2 cloud is made up of almost half-a-million Linux servers. ZDNet. http://www.zdnet.com/article/amazon-ec2-cloud-is-made-up-of-almost-half-a-million-linux-servers/ (accessed May 15, 2016).

Weber, E. 2014. Problem when using Cloudstack Login API. Cloudstack-users mailing list archives. http://mail-archives.apache.org/mod_mbox/cloudstack-users/201406.mbox/%3CCAMO1gsDHtwf8P0w6Q6sRwrtd1kdonqzun7pisK-rCWCAhsAQtg@mail.gmail.com%3E (accessed May 19, 2016).

Xen Project. 2016. Amazon Web Services. http://www.xenproject.org/project-members/141-amazon-web-services.html (accessed May 15, 2016).

Yadav, R. 2014. SAML2 In Apache CloudStack, ShapeBlue. http://www.shapeblue.com/saml2-cloudstack/ (accessed May 19, 2016).

Section VI

Message-Oriented Middleware

15 Introduction to Message-Oriented Middleware

15.1 JUST WHAT IS MESSAGE-ORIENTED MIDDLEWARE, ANYWAY?

In Message-Oriented Middleware (MOM), one or more Producers creates messages and sends them to a queue. Then one or more Consumers retrieve messages from the queue. The queue, however, can actually be a message broker that can do value-added analyses on the messages, for example, can implement quality-of-service techniques based on priorities. The use of this intermediary message broker (queue) allows the Producers and Consumers to work asynchronously with respect to each other. Also, the use of this intermediary message broker allows loose coupling, which can help when it is necessary to have heterogeneous systems communicate.

Curry (2004) said:

A client of a MOM system can send messages to, and receive messages from, other clients of the messaging system. Each client connects to one or more servers that act as an intermediary in the sending and receiving of messages. MOM uses a model with a peer-to-peer relationship between individual clients; in this model, each peer can send and receive messages to and from other client peers.

Curry (2004) further states that the message queue is a fundamental concept associated with MOM.

Löwis (2008) characterized Message-Oriented Middleware as:

- focuses on non-blocking communication, where a producer gives a message to the middleware and a consumer receives the message from the middleware
- provides store-and-forward reliability
- provides loose coupling in many senses: syntax, semantics, space, and time
- a message broker can change the format of the message

15.2 POINT-TO-POINT VERSUS PUBLISH/SUBSCRIBE

Liu and Gorton (2005) said:

MOM typically supports two forms of messaging: point-to-point and publish/subscribe (Pub/Sub). In the PTP model, the message producer posts a *message* to a *queue* and the message consumer retrieves the message from the queue. In the Pub/Sub model, a message producer publishes a message to a *topic*, and all consumers subscribing to the same topic retrieve a copy of the message. MOMs also define a set of reliability attributes for messaging, including non-persistent or persistent and non-transactional or transaction queues.

We previously discussed Gomaa's (2011) group message communication patterns in Chapter 1: There are two communication patterns for group messaging: the broadcast message communication pattern, and the subscription/notification message communication pattern. With the broadcast message pattern, an unsolicited message is sent to all recipients. The subscription/notification message pattern uses a selective form of group communication where the same message is sent to members of a group. A component can subscribe and unsubscribe from a group, and can belong to more than one group.

In the point-to-point messaging paradigm, one or more producers sends a message through a message broker (in the simplest case, this would be a queue) to a single consumer. The consumer receives this message only once.

In the publish/subscribe message paradigm, messages can be distributed from one producer to many consumers, or from many producers to many consumers. All consumers that subscribe to a particular topic (channel) will receive the message.

15.3 WHEN WOULD YOU WANT TO USE MESSAGE-ORIENTED MIDDLEWARE?

Curry (2004) said:

> If the distributed systems will be geographically dispersed deployments with poor network connectivity and stringent demands in reliability, flexibility, and scalability, then MOM is the ideal solution.

MOM may also be used when a service it provides is useful. Curry (2004) lists some common MOM services:

- Message filtering—messages that are of interest are selected
  - Some possible filters include:
    - Channel-based
      - Events are categorized into predefined groups
      - Consumers subscribe to groups of interest
    - Subject-based
      - Messages contain a tag field that says what their subject is
      - Subscribers receive messages with selected subjects
    - Content-based
      - Querying languages are used to examine the data in the message
    - Content-based with patterns (composite events)
      - Querying languages are used to examine data in multiple messages
- Transactions—Tasks are grouped into a single unit of work
  - Transactional messaging
    - Used when several messages are sent, but the tasks from all messages must all succeed or else all must fail.
      - If any one message fails, then the results of all the other messages must be rolled back.
  - Transaction roles—the roles of message producer, message consumer, and message broker are defined as follows:
    - Message producer interacting with message broker:
      - Send a message or a set of messages to the message broker
      - The broker stores the messages and then sends them when it receives a commit from the producer
      - The broker disposes of all messages when it receives a Rollback from the producer
    - Message consumer interacting with message broker:
      - The consumer receives a message or set of messages from the message broker
      - The broker disposes of all messages when it receives a commit from the consumer (this is because the messages have been correctly handled so they're no longer needed).
      - The broker resends all messages to the consumer when it receives a Rollback from the consumer (this is because the remaining messages that have taken effect must be known so they can be reversed).

- Reliable message delivery. Message delivery can be configured to take place in different ways:
  - At most one time
  - At least one time
  - Only one time
  - Number of retries on delivery failure
- Guaranteed message delivery
  - Consumer must acknowledge message receipt.
  - Messages that have not been acknowledged are retransmitted after a time period (how this is done is settable according to reliable message delivery).
- Message formats
  - One message format may be converted into another message format.
  - Possible plug-ins to do format changes.
- Load balancing
  - The workload of the system is spread over several different servers. There are two main methods for balancing the load:
    – Push—the message broker uses some algorithm to balance the load over multiple servers.
    – Pull—when a server has need of input, it pulls a message from the queue (the argument here is that the server itself knows best when it is not busy and needs more to do).
- Clustering—replicating the state of a server across several other servers to help with fault tolerance.
  - In this way, if a server fails, the client can be sent to a different server in a seamless manner.

15.4 WHAT MIDDLEWARE TECHNOLOGIES CAN BE DESCRIBED AS MESSAGE-ORIENTED MIDDLEWARE?

Curry (2004) said:

To date, a number of MOM standardizations have emerged such as the CORBA Event Service [25], CORBA Notification Service [26] and most notably the Java Message Service (JMS).

Liu and Gorton (2005) said:

Messaging services are implemented by message-oriented middleware (MOM) such as Microsoft MSMQ, IBM WebSphere MQ, CORBA Notification Services and Sun's JMS (Java Messaging Service).

Tarkoma (2012) said:

Message-oriented Middleware and Event Notification are becoming more popular in the industry with the advent of the CORBA Notification Service and DSS[sic], the Java Messaging Service, and other related specifications and products from many vendors.

Another well-known Message-Oriented Middleware is the Advanced Message Queueing Protocol (AMQP) from Organization for the Advancement of Structured Information Standards (OASIS) and the International Standards Organization.

The Enterprise Service Bus can also be considered a Message-Oriented Middleware, although its features go beyond what is normally expected from a MOM. Also, the Enterprise Service Bus could use some kind of web services instead of a Message-Oriented Middleware, so the kind of implementation might affect whether it truly meets the definition of MOM.

We're going to look at a few of the more commonly known Message-Oriented Middlewares below. We're not doing this in as much depth as previous middlewares we've looked at, that is, we're not going to dig down into the software and actually try to write code. This is a bit more of an advanced concept, and we've already looked at a lot for an introductory textbook. ☺

15.5   CORBA EVENT SERVICE AND CORBA NOTIFICATION SERVICE

McHale (2007) says that the CORBA Event Service provides a basic form of publish–subscribe, whereas the CORBA Notification service greatly extends the Event Service to provide a richer version of publish–subscribe. McHale notes that the CORBA terminology is different from normal MOM technology. In CORBA, the term *supplier* is used instead of *publisher* and the term *consumer* is used instead of *subscriber*. The term *topic* becomes *event channel*.

The CORBA Event Service provides a PushConsumer IDL that (in part) is defined as follows:

```
interface PushConsumer {
    void push(in any data);
    void disconnect_push_consumer();
};
```

Then you provide servant code on the Consumer side that would handle this IDL interface. (Of course, the IDL skeleton code.)

When the Event service receives a message from the supplier that is for you, the Event Channel that has been defined on the Event Service would call "Push" and your CORBA code would handle it:

Supplier → Push message to Event Service, which puts message in a queue.
When message moves at front of queue, Event service → Push message to CORBA Server.

Note that there can be several suppliers and several consumers.

The CORBA Event Service provides a PullSupplier IDL that (in part) is defined as follows:

```
interface PullSupplier {
    any pull();
    any try_pull(out boolean has_event);
    void disconnect_pull_supplier();
};
```

The difference between pull and try_pull is that pull is blocking but try_pull is non-blocking. If there is an event when try_pull is called, then the boolean has_event is set true. This works as follows:

Supplier → Push message to Event Channel
Consumer → Pull message from Event Channel

What we have seen here are the Canonical Push Model and the Hybrid Push/Pull model of Event Service operation. I showed you these first because I think they're the easiest to understand.

There are actually four models of operation:

The Canonical Push Model:

Active Suppliers call Push on the Event Channel to push a message to the Event Service.
Passive Consumers receive a push call from the Event Channel.

The Canonical Pull Model:

Active consumers call Pull on the Event Channel to ask the Event Service for a message.
The Event Channel then calls Pull on the Passive Supplier.

The Hybrid Push/Pull Model:

An active supplier calls Push on the Event Channel, which then queues the message.
The active consumer calls Pull on the Event Channel to receive the message.

The Hybrid Pull/Push Model:

> The Event Channel calls Pull on a Passive Supplier.
> The Event Channel calls Push on a Passive Consumer.
> (This model requires the Event Service to be somewhat intelligent.)

The CORBA Notification Service is a super set of the Event Service. It provides Quality of Service as well as other additional functionality. Some of the functionality provided:

- Filter objects can be attached to event channels
  - These filter objects provide constraints as to the messages that can be passed
    - This is intended to:
      - reduce work at the server, throwing away inappropriate messages
      - reduce network traffic due to inappropriate messages
  - A constraint language is provided to write these constraints
    - This constraint language is an extension of the constraint language used by the old CORBA Trading Service
- Additional control over when to deliver messages is provided. This includes (among many other items):
  - Expiration times for event messages
  - Maximum number of events accepted per consumer
  - Priority of events
- Structured Events
  - Has headers that include fixed and variable portions
  - Can specify specific event types
  - Can specify event domains (telecommunications, health care, etc.)

15.6   JAVA MESSAGE SERVICE AND MESSAGE BEANS

The Java Message Service (JMS) provides queue- and topic-based messaging. It provides two messaging models:

1. Point to point
2. Publish/subscribe

With point to point, a queue is used, with publish/subscribe a topic is used.
The JMS components are:

- JMS client—produces or consumes messages
- Non-JMS clients—use a messaging system's native Application Programming Interface (API) instead of JMS
- Messages—defined by an application, used to send information between clients
- Service provider—implements the JMS interfaces. Examples of providers include (among many others):
  - OpenJMS
  - Apache ActiveMQ
- Administered objects—clients connect to these using Java Naming and Directory Interface (JNDI), use them to establish connections:
  - Destination—the object a client uses to specify the target of messages produced or consumer. When using point to point, destinations are queues, in publish/subscribe, destinations are topics.
  - Connection factories—used to establish a Connection between a JMS client and a service provider

After a Connection is established, a Session is then created. A Session is single threaded. A message producer associated with a session sends messages to a destination, and a message consumer associated with a session receives messages from a destination. A Message Selector associated with a session is used to filter messages.

A JMS message consists of (only the header is required):

- Header—used for routing
- Additional properties
- Body, message types include:
  - Text (string data)
  - Byte (byte data)
  - Map (key/value pairs)
  - Stream (stream of primitive values)
  - Serializable Object

There are two ways a Consumer can handle messages with JMS:

1. Synchronously—subscriber calls receive method, to fetch the message from the associated destination. Receive blocks until message arrives or timeout
2. Asynchronously—a message listener is registered with a consumer. When a message arrives, the JMS provider calls "onMessage" on the listener.

JMS provides some quality-of-service mechanisms, these include (among others):

- Message expiration time
- Priority
- Persistence

15.6.1 MESSAGE BEANS ACCESSED BY JAVA MESSAGE SERVICE

There are two major kinds of Enterprise Java Beans (EJBs) normally discussed:

1. Session Beans
2. Message Beans

Both qualify as EJBs because they both are server-side components that run in an EJB container in an application server. However, Message Beans operate as a Message-Oriented Middleware.

(We previously looked at Session Beans in Section 8.4.)

Message Beans are typically called using the Java Messaging Service (JMS). Message Beans can support any messaging protocol (queue-based as just described), but by default they support the JMS. In this case, a Message Bean would act as a JMS message listener.

Unlike a Session Bean, a Message Bean does not have an interface that a client looks up in order to call a method on the interface. Rather, a Message Bean is not coupled directly to a client. A Session Bean would normally have an interface class and a bean class, whereas a Message Bean only has a Bean class.

In the case of a Message Bean, the client sends messages to a queue. The Message Bean listens for messages on the queue.

A Message Bean is similar in some ways to a Stateless Session Bean. A Message Bean is stateless. The container can call any Message Bean instance to handle a message, so there can be pools of Message Beans in a container.

A Message Bean might more accurately be called a "message driven" bean. Message Beans are annotated with "@MessageDriven." Message Beans receive messages from:

javax.jms.MessageListener, which has one method:

    void onMessage(Message inMessage)

See Listing 15.1 for an outline of a Message Bean (Message-Driven Bean). This is just an outline, to give you the flavor. We're not going to look at enough here to really do coding.

At the beginning, the term "mappedName" is the JNDI name of the location from which the Message Bean will consume messages. The destinationType says what kind of destination we're working with: the choices are javax.jms.Queue or javax.jms.Topic. Here we're using a queue so we select that one.

Note that for this code to work, some code somewhere must have previously created a queue, annotated as @Resource, with a mappedName of "theQueue."

The idea here is that when the queue receives a message, the EJB container invokes the onMessage method of the MessageListener interface, which then calls onMessage, which then does the appropriate work.

LISTING 15.1   Outline of Java Message Bean

```
@MessageDriven(
  mappedName = "theQueue",
  activationConfig = {
            @ActivationConfigProperty(      propertyName = "destinationType",
                                            propertyValue = "javax.jms.Queue")
              }
)
public class theMessageBean implements MessageListener {

  public void onMessage(Message message) {
        … put very important stuff here…
  }
}
```

Note that with Java Messaging Service, the API is specified, but the format of messages is not, so every JMS broker can implement messages in a different format.

15.7   OBJECT MANAGEMENT GROUP (OMG) DATA DISTRIBUTION SERVICE (DDS)

The OMG Data Distribution Service is intended to provide real-time, scalable, dependable publish/subscribe.

Corsaro (2010a) compares DDS to Java Message Service and AMQP:

One way of comparing DDS to JMS and AMQP is to measure what they standardize. JMS standardizes an API while AMQP standardizes a wire-protocol – DDS standardizes both. DDS is fully distributed and does not require the presence of any broker mediating communication between producers and consumers. On the other hand, both JMS and AMQP have a broker-based architecture where one or more brokers mediate the distribution of information from sources to destinations.

A wire protocol is defined by PCMagazine Encyclopedia (2016) as follows:

In a network, a wire protocol is the mechanism for transmitting data from point a to point b. The term is a bit confusing, because it sounds like layer 1 of the network, which physically places the bits "onto the wire." In some cases, it may refer to layer 1; however, it generally refers to higher layers, including Ethernet and ATM (layer 2) and even higher layer distributed object protocols such as SOAP, CORBA or RMI. See OSI model, communications protocol, data link protocol and distributed objects.

Corsaro (2010a) also says that DDS provides more extensive Quality-of-Service control than either JMS or AMQP, and provides more extensive querying of messages while providing low latencies.

DDS is language, operating system, and hardware independent.

In DDS, a topic is a unit of information that a Publisher and a Subscriber exchange. A topic has a name, a type, and a quality-of-service setting.

A DDS topic type is described in a struct in IDL, and may contain primitive types, sequences, arrays, structs, etc. It's like what you would see in a CORBA IDL interface, except it focuses on data and not method calls. Here is an example:

```
struct myDataType {
        string thename;
        float thevalue;
        long anothervalue;
        short yetanothervalue;
};
```

A topic type is associated with a list of keys. A key identifies a particular piece of data within a topic (an instance of a topic type).

Topics are registered with a DDS implementation. Then data is written to a topic using a data writer and read from a topic using a data reader. A listener on a topic uses a data reader to read the data from the topic.

When a data reader is created, it can be associated with a Content Filtered Topic. A Content Filtered Topic is associated with a particular topic and filters the data in that topic. Thus, a Data Reader that is associated with a Content Filtered Topic will only be able to read data that the filter allows through.

A pre-existing Data Reader can be called with a Query Condition (created specifically for that particular Data Reader) as an argument. Then the Data Reader will only be able to read data that matches the Query Condition.

Various quality-of-service properties may be specified: reliability, availability, priority, etc. When a publisher is matched to a subscriber, the quality of service provided by the publisher must match the quality of service needed by the subscriber. Specific kinds of quality of service are specified in DDS, this includes (among others):

- Reliability
  - All data guaranteed delivered, or
  - Best effort
- Deadline
  - Maximum inter-arrival time between data items may be specified
- Latency Budget
  - Maximum delay from when data is written until data given to the receiver

15.8 ADVANCED MESSAGE QUEUEING PROTOCOL (AMQP)

Advanced Message Queueing Protocol (AMQP) is an ISO/IEC Standard (ISO/IEC 19464) and an OASIS standard. According to an OASIS press release at the time AMQP became a standard (see Geyer 2012), AMQP can be described as:

> AMQP is a wire-level messaging protocol that offers organizations an efficient, reliable approach to passing real-time data and business transactions with confidence. AMQP provides a platform-agnostic method for ensuring information is safely transported between applications, among organizations, within mobile infrastructures, and across the Cloud.

Geyer (2012) says further:

> AMQP supports common interaction patterns: one way, request/response, publish/subscribe, transactions, and store-and-forward. It does this with flow-control, multiplexing, security, recovery and a portable data representation that enables message filtering. AMQP is capable of being used in both point-to-point and hub-and-spoke (broker-based) topologies.

If you recall from Chapter 13, AMQP is used for messaging between individual components of OpenStack. The Microsoft Azure Service Bus cloud service also supports AMQP. According to Microsoft Azure:

> The Azure Service Bus is a generic, cloud-based messaging system for connecting just about anything—applications, services, and devices—wherever they are.

AMQP is designed to work on any language or operating system.

AMQP has exchanges, routes, queues, and bindings. An Exchange receives messages and then routes them to appropriate queues. Bindings are rules for how messages are sent from exchanges to queues.

A producer publishes a message to an exchange. Routing rules then determine which queues will receive a message. Then one or more consumers that subscribe to that queue will receive a message. Most commonly, one subscriber (consumer) is associated with a queue. If there is more than one subscriber then the messages are sent round-robin to the consumers.

The different kinds of exchanges are as follows (a routing key is a string that contains routing information):

- Fanout exchange—Any message sent to the exchange is sent to all queues bound to that exchange, no routing keys involved.
- Direct exchange—A queue is bound to the exchange to request messages that exactly match a routing key.
- Topic exchange—A queue is bound to the exchange to request messages that match a routing key pattern.
- Headers exchange—It uses additional headers for routing rather than using routing key strings. This enables different types of data (other than strings) to be used for routing. However, otherwise the operation is similar to direct exchange.

Before publishing can take place, an exchange, a queue, and bindings must first be defined.

Spring (2016) provided a comparison of AMQP and Java Messaging Service. They say that AMQP has only queues whereas JMS supports queues and topics. With AMQP, a message from a producer is published to an exchange, then various bindings (routing rules) select which queues receive the message. However, only one consumer receives messages from an AMQP queue. With JMS, multiple consumers may consume a message on a topic, but only one consumer can receive a message on a queue. Thus although AMQP and JMS work quite differently, they are very similar in actual results for sending messages from producers to consumers.

JMS and AMQP both have message headers that allow message routing, and with both, brokers are responsible for message routing.

EXERCISES

1. How is the CORBA Notification Service related to the CORBA Event Service?
2. How are the constraints that provide filtering/quality of service for the CORBA Notification service programmed?
3. How do Java Message Beans receive messages?
4. What is one major difference between the architecture of Data Distribution Service (DDS) and Java Message Beans and also between the architecture of DDS and AMQP?
5. What is an "Exchange" in AMQP? How does it work?
6. How are AMQP and JMS similar? How are they different?

CONCEPTUAL QUESTIONS

1. Consider the purposes of Message-Oriented Middleware. Could you do the same thing with a more basic middleware such as CORBA, EJB, or one of the web services? What would be the advantages and disadvantages?
2. Is AMQP a good choice to be used in OpenStack? Why or why not?
3. According to the CloudStack description of Event Notification, see Apache CloudStack (2016):

    An event bus is introduced in the Management Server that allows the CloudStack components and extension plugins to subscribe to the events by using the Advanced Message Queuing Protocol (AMQP) client. In CloudStack, a default implementation of event bus is provided as a plugin that uses the RabbitMQ AMQP client.

    Considering that CloudStack is often said to have a "monolithic" architecture, that is, one Management Server running on one machine (with another machine running the hypervisor) can implement a minimal two-machine cloud, does the use of AMQP surprise you? Why or why not? (*Hint*: How many components does CloudStack really consist of?)
4. Do you see any advantages or disadvantages between the different terminology and methods used in the different paradigms? For example, the CORBA Event Service has "event channels," JMS has queues and topics, AMQP has exchanges and queues.
5. Let's say you are developing a brand new cloud for your company, let's call it AVeryGoodCloudIndeed, Inc. If you tend toward a few components in your cloud, largely monolithic, which Message-Oriented Middleware would you choose, of the ones you have seen in this chapter? If you tend toward numerous components in your cloud, which Message-Oriented Middleware would you choose, of the ones you have seen in this chapter? Justify your answer.

BIBLIOGRAPHY

Advanced Message Queueing Protocol. 2016. About. https://www.amqp.org/about/what (accessed May 22, 2016).
Apache CloudStack. 2016. Event Notification. http://docs.cloudstack.apache.org/projects/cloudstack-administration/en/4.8/events.html (accessed May 22, 2016).
CoderPanda. 2013. JMS Tutorial. http://www.coderpanda.com/jms-tutorial/ (accessed May 22, 2016).
Corsaro, A. 2009. The DDS Tutorial: Part I. OMGWiki. http://www.omgwiki.org/dds/sites/default/files/Tutorial-Part.I.pdf (accessed May 21, 2016).
Corsaro, A. 2010a. The Data Distribution Service for Real-Time Systems: Part 1. *Dr. Dobbs' Journal*. http://www.drdobbs.com/architecture-and-design/the-data-distribution-service-for-real-t/222900238 (accessed May 21, 2016).
Corsaro, A. 2010b. The DDS Tutorial: Part II. http://www.slideshare.net/Angelo.Corsaro/the-dds-tutorial-part-ii (accessed May 21, 2016).
Curry, E. 2004. Message Oriented Middleware. In *Middleware for Communications*. Wiley, Chichester, England, pp. 1–28. http://www.edwardcurry.org/publications/curry_MfC_MOM_04.pdf (accessed January 31, 2016).

Digital Ocean. 2014. An Advanced Message Queuing Protocol (AMQP) Walkthrough. https://www.digitalocean. com/community/tutorials/an-advanced-message-queuing-protocol-amqp-walkthrough (accessed May 22, 2016).

Geyer, C. 2012. *Press Release: Advanced Message Queuing Protocol (AMQP) 1.0 Becomes OASIS Standard.* OASIS. http://www.amqp.org/node/102 (accessed May 22, 2016).

Gomaa, H. 2011. *Software Modeling and Design: UML, Use Cases, Patterns, and Software Architectures.* Cambridge University Press, New York.

JavaTpoint. 2016. JMS Tutorial. http://www.javatpoint.com/jms-tutorial (accessed May 22, 2016).

Liu, Y. and Gorton, I. 2005. Performance Prediction of J2EE Applications Using Messaging Protocols. Component-Based Software Engineering. 8th International Symposium (CBSE) St. Louis, MO, USA, 2005. In *Lecture Notes on Computer Science 3489.* Heineman, G.T., Crnkovic, I., Schmidt, H.W., Stafford, J.A., Szyperski, C., Wallnau, K. (Eds.). Springer-Verlag. Berlin.

Löwis, M.v. 2008. Message Oriented Middleware. Lecture Notes for Middleware and Distributed Systems Course. Hasso-Plattner Institut, Universitat Potsdam. http://www.dcl.hpi.uni-potsdam.de/teaching/mds_08/mds04_mom.pdf (accessed January 31, 2016).

Mchale, C. 2007. *Publish and Subscribe Services.* http://www.ciaranmchale.com/corba-explained-simply/publish-and-subscribe-services.html#toc105 (accessed February 2, 2016).

Microsoft Azure. 2016. Azure Service Bus. https://azure.microsoft.com/en-us/services/service-bus/ (accessed May 22, 2016).

Object Management Group. 2004. CORBA Event Service. http://www.omg.org/spec/EVNT/ (accessed May 21, 2016).

Oracle. 2013. Basic JMS API Concepts. In *The Java EE 6 Tutorial.* http://docs.oracle.com/javaee/6/tutorial/doc/bncdx.html (accessed January 31, 2016).

Oracle. 2013. Javax.jms.MessageListener. https://docs.oracle.com/javaee/7/api/javax/jms/MessageListener.html (accessed May 21, 2016).

Oracle. 2013. The Message-Driven Bean Class. In *Java EE 6 Tutorial.* http://docs.oracle.com/javaee/6/tutorial/doc/bnbpo.html (accessed May 21, 2016).

Oracle. 2013. What Is a Message Driven Bean. In *The Java EE 6 Tutorial.* https://docs.oracle.com/javaee/6/tutorial/doc/gipko.html (accessed February 2, 2016).

PCMagazine Encyclopedia. 2016. Wire Protocol. http://www.pcmag.com/encyclopedia/term/54750/wire-protocol (accessed May 22, 2016).

Spring. 2016. Understanding AMQP, Pivotal Software, Inc. https://spring.io/understanding/AMQP (accessed May 22, 2016).

StackOverflow. 2013. Message Oriented Middleware vs. Enterprise Service Bus. http://stackoverflow.com/questions/309374/message-oriented-middleware-mom-vs-enterprise-service-bus-esb (accessed May 21, 2016).

Tarkoma, S. 2012. *Publish/Subscribe Systems: Design and Principles.* Wiley, Hoboken, NJ.

Vasudevan, N. 2012. Java Message Service (JMS) API. *The Open Tutorials.* http://theopentutorials.com/post/uncategorized/java-message-service-jms-api/ (accessed May 22, 2016).

Willbanks, M. 2010. The Art of Message Queues. http://www.slideshare.net/mwillbanks/the-art-of-message-queues-tekx (accessed May 22, 2016).

Section VII

Comparison of Middlewares

16 Introduction to Comparing Middlewares

16.1 HOW CAN DIFFERENT MIDDLEWARES BE COMPARED, ANYWAY?

There are a few things to think about in terms of choosing a middleware technology. First, can it do every kind of architecture you might need to implement? We can look at that by comparing architectural style/patterns that a particular technology can support. Second, how efficient is a particular middleware technology compared to other middleware technologies, how high quality a solution can a particular middleware produce, and how easy is the middleware to learn? Third, how does one go about developing a middleware solution, and how does one choose which middleware to use (and at what point during the software development process does one do that)?

So let's first compare various middleware technologies according to the architectural styles they support. To do this, we will use the Architectural Styles/Patterns we saw in Chapter 2. We will first look critically at the lists of styles/patterns by Gomaa, Fielding, Schmidt, and Staal from Chapter 2, and develop a final list of Architectural Styles/Patterns that removes any overlap and that also is in places improved by combining different but related information from multiple lists. We'll use this list later in this chapter to compare different middleware technologies in terms of what they support. We'll also use it later on to examine different project scenarios where we need to select different architectural styles to design them.

Now let's begin.

Gomaa's call/return pattern is defined as: Assuming distributed object-oriented software, a caller operating in the calling object invokes a called operation in the called object (located on another node), with input parameters passed to the called object, and output parameters and return value returned to the called object at the end of the operation.

Fielding's Distributed Objects style is defined as:

- Objects possess encapsulated data and have a well-defined interface, the interfaces define operations that may be used to invoke an object
- An operation on one object may invoke operations on other objects
- For one object to interact with another, it must know the identity of the other object
  - When the identity of an object changes, all objects that invoke it must be modified

Let us combine these two into one pattern:

Name: Call Specific Distributed Object
Description:

- The calling object and called object may be located on different computers
- A calling object invokes an operation on a specific called object (the object has a specific identity)
- The called object has a well-defined interface, that defines operations, input and output parameters, and a return value

Gomaa's Broker patterns are defined as follows:

- Broker patterns—A broker is an intermediary between client and server.
  - Service registration pattern
    - The service must register with the broker, including name, description, and location.

- Broker forwarding pattern
  - The client sends a message to the broker, and the broker forwards the request on to the server.
- Broker handle pattern
  - Instead of always forwarding each client message to the service, after the first message from the client, the broker returns a service handle to the client. Then for all subsequent messages, the client calls the server directly.

Fielding's Brokered Distributed Objects style is defined as follows:

- These include name resolvers that accept a service name from a client and return the specific name of an object that will satisfy the request.
- He gives CORBA as an example of a brokered distributed object system.

If you take Fielding's comment that CORBA is an example of a brokered distributed object system, what he must have been talking about, in light of his definition, was the CORBA Naming Service. The CORBA Naming service accepts a name from a client, maps that name to an IOR, and returns the IOR to the client. In the future, the client uses the IOR to contact the server directly (doesn't have to go through the CORBA Naming Service every time).

So Gomaa's pattern and Fielding's style, at one level, mean the same thing. At a different level, however, Gomaa's pattern could also apply to the JNDI which can be used both for Enterprise Java Beans (EJBs) (distributed object components) or for web services. (Remember that Fielding's patterns were done when web services were still fairly new.) So Gomaa's pattern is more general.

So let's use Gomaa's Broker pattern exactly as it is, but including three sub-patterns as part of the main pattern that we're going to use:

Name: Broker Pattern
Description:

- A broker is an intermediary between client and server.
  - Service registration pattern
    - The service must register with the broker, including name, description, and location.
  - Broker forwarding pattern
    - The client sends a message to the broker, and the broker forwards the request on to the server.
  - Broker handle pattern
    - Instead of always forwarding each client message to the service, after the first message from the client, the broker returns a service handle to the client. Then for all subsequent messages, the client calls the server directly.

Gomaa has:

- Synchronous message communication with reply
  - A client sends a request to a server and waits for a response.
  - Since several clients may send requests to the same server, a queue of messages can form at the server.
- Asynchronous message communication
  - The client and the server proceed at different speeds.
  - A client sends a message to the server and does not wait for a reply.
  - When the server receives the message, if it is busy, it queues the message.
    - The server alternately could request a message from the client, if there is no message available, the server would suspend itself until a message becomes available.
  - When the server completes handling the message, the client is notified.

- Asynchronous message communication with callback
  - This is a variation on the asynchronous message communication.
  - When the client sends a message to the server, the client includes a handle to a callback routine.
  - When the server completes the message, the server calls the callback routine on the client to pass its information to the client and thus complete its response.

Fielding has:

- Client/server
  - A server listens for requests, a client sends requests to the server.
  - The basic form of client/server is often called *remote procedure call.*

So Gomaa's version has more specific patterns than Fielding's, but also has wider application because it isn't specifically restricted to remote procedure calls per se (for example, it could apply to RESTful web services). We'll go with Gomaa's but rename each pattern as being specifically client/server, because each is really a separate architectural style, and we don't want to lose track of the main concept (client/server) while we're focusing on the variations (synchronous vs. asynchronous). We'll drop one thing, however, that Gomaa talked about: The server alternately could request a message from the client, if there is no message available, the server would suspend itself until a message becomes available. We're dropping this because in asynchronous communication we don't want to talk about *blocking* at all. Remember that in Chapter 2, we were not using Gomaa's original notation. He originally talked about *producers* and *consumers* but in Chapter 2 since we were just getting started, I called the producer of a message the "client" and the consumer of the message the "server" just to make things easier for you. In terms of a client/server architecture, however, it's entirely possible for the server to be a producer. The easiest thing to do here is just to think that your server could also serve as a client in some regards (at some points the server could be a producer and the client a consumer, using Gomaa's notation).

Name: Synchronous client/server
Description:

- A client sends a request to a server and waits for a response.
- Since several clients may send requests to the same server, a queue of messages can form at the server.

Name: Asynchronous client/server without callback
Description:

- The client and the server proceed at different speeds.
- A client sends a message to the server and does not wait for a reply.
- When the server receives the message, if it is busy, it queues the message.
- When the server completes handling the message, the client is notified.

Name: Asynchronous client/server with callback
Description:

- This is a variation on the asynchronous message communication.
- When the client sends a message to the server, the client includes a handle to a callback routine.

Now let's pick up a couple of items from Fielding that don't appear in Gomaa:

- Client-stateless-server
  - Like client/server except that the server is not allowed to retain an application state
    - A request from the client to the server is interpreted only in the context of the information included in that request, and is not interpreted using information stored on the server.
  - Any session state is stored on the client.
- Remote session
  - The state of the application interaction is stored on the server.
- Remote data access
  - The application state is spread across both client and server.

We will go with Fielding's definitions but again rename each pattern as being specifically client/ server, because each is really a separate architectural style, and we don't want to lose track of the main concept (client/server).

Name: Stateless client/server
Description:

- The server is not allowed to retain an application state
  - A request from the client to the server is interpreted only in the context of the information included in that request, and is not interpreted using information stored on the server.
- Any session state is stored on the client

Name: Stateful client/server
Description:

- The state of the application interaction is stored on the server.

Name: Shared state client/server
Description:

- The application state is spread across both client and server.

Now let's look at another style that Fielding has but Gomaa doesn't have:

- Layered system and layered client/server
  - Lower protocol levels are hidden from the main level.
  - Enhanced basic client/server style with proxy and gateway components.
    - A proxy forwards requests from one or more client components to a server component.
    - A gateway appears to the client to be a normal server, but is actually forwarding the requests, which it may modify (for security, etc.), on to the server.

To my way of thinking, this one is actually two separate patterns. The first is that lower protocol levels are hidden from the main level. I think for the purposes of this textbook, we can ignore that one, it's mostly the way things work on the internet.

The second is the idea of a proxy. A proxy can mean many things. It can be an internal proxy, such as a client would have (automatically created) in CORBA, or it could be a whole intermediate external system, as an intermediary between beginning client and final server, this intermediate system has a server facing the original client, and a client facing to the final server.

Before we start naming our own patterns here, let's look at a couple more of Fielding's patterns and a couple more of Gomaa's patterns.

The Fielding patterns are:

- Event-based integration
  - Instead of invoking a component directly, a component can broadcast events.
  - Components register interest in an event, and the system invokes the registered components.
- C2 (see Taylor et al. (1996); was called C2 because was based on experience with the Chiron-1 user interface)
  - Combines event-based integration with layered-client–server
  - A connector between components routes, broadcasts, and filters messages
    - Receives asynchronous notification messages—notifications are announcements of a state change within a component
    - Sends asynchronous event messages

The Gomaa patterns are his Group communication patterns

- Broadcast pattern
  - An unsolicited message is sent to all recipients.
- Subscription notification pattern
  - This is a selective form of group communication where the same message is sent to members of a group. A component can subscribe and unsubscribe from a group, and can belong to more than one group.

So what we are seeing are the following concepts:

- Proxy
- Broadcast
- Publish/subscribe

If you were to combine Proxy with Broadcast and add in the idea of a message queue, then one starts thinking Message-oriented middleware (MOM). Especially if you add in publish/subscribe.

Of course, you can do Proxy (in terms of an intermediate server instead of a lower level proxy such as inside a CORBA client) without a message broker and without using MOM, for example, a gateway to allow CORBA to go through a firewall leaps to mind. Also, broadcast without use of an intermediary is likely useful in many cases, although we have seen the advantages to an intermediary in MOM. So let's go forward with the following patterns:

Name: Proxy without message queue
Description:

- An intermediate node between beginning client and final server
- Can add, remove, or filter messages between client and server

Name: Broadcast without message queue

- An unsolicited message is sent to all recipients

Before we go on, however, let's remember our background related to Message-Oriented Middleware. Liu and Gorton (2005) said:

MOM typically supports two forms of messaging: point-to-point and publish/subscribe (Pub/Sub). In the PTP model, the message producer posts a *message* to a *queue* and the message consumer retrieves the message from the queue. In the Pub/Sub model, a message producer publishes a message to a *topic*, and all consumers subscribing to the same topic retrieve a copy of the message. MOMs also define a set of reliability attributes for messaging, including non-persistent or persistent and non-transactional or transaction queues.

We'll use these concepts in our own list of styles:

Name: Point-to-point
Description:

- Acts as a proxy using a message queue
  - Asynchronous
  - An intermediate node between beginning client and final server
  - Can add, remove, or filter messages between client and server
  - Messages can be:
    - Posted to queue by client (producer) and removed by server (consumer)
    - Posted to queue by server (producer) and removed by client (consumer)

Name: Publish/subscribe
Description:

- Asynchronous
- Acts as a proxy using one or more message queues (called topics)
  - With one or more subscribers receiving notifications

Note that we could also use Canonical push, Canonical pull, hybrid push/pull, hybrid pull/push. But this all is getting very heavily into MOM and we didn't go heavily into that in this textbook.

Now let's look at a few more patterns, this time the patterns that Schmidt and Buschmann (2003) examined in regard to Distributed Object Middleware:

- The Reactor pattern
  - The server must be able to handle new events while waiting for other events to occur—a server shouldn't block indefinitely waiting on one kind of event
  - Multithreading would work, but if not the Reactor pattern could be used:
    - Each service should have its own separate event handler.
    - Each event handler registers itself with an initiation dispatcher.
    - A separate synchronous event demultiplexer waits for events to occur.
    - When a particular event occurs, the synchronous event demultiplexer tells the initiation dispatcher about the event.
    - The initiation dispatcher then calls the appropriate event handler.
- The Acceptor–Connector pattern
  - Separates the work of establishing connections from the work of handling a service.
  - To do this, three components are used:
    - Acceptor
      - The acceptor waits for connection requests (in a passive way), then establishes the connection and starts up the service handler.
    - Connector
      - The connector works actively to establish a connection with a remote acceptor, and starts up a service handler on its side.

- – Service handler
  - – After the connection is established, the two service handlers talk to each other without talking any more to the connector or acceptor.
- • The Component–Configurator pattern
  - • Allows linking and unlinking of separate components at runtime without a need for static compilation or linking.
    - – Using Component–Configurator, you might run a script that contains directives for how to link and unlink different components at runtime.
- • The Proxy pattern (originally from Gamma et al. 1994; we already looked at this one in terms of Gomaa's proxy so we will ignore it here)
- • The Adapter pattern (originally from Gamma et al. 1994)
  - • Used to convert the interface of an object to an interface that the caller desires.
    - – There is a run-time version of Adapter and a compile time version.

Let's expand how we look at these in terms of service-oriented architectures and web services, instead of just focusing on distributed objects, as did Schmidt and Buschmann (2003). The Reactor pattern could be handled by a web server/application server). Also note that a component container, such as an EJB container, can handle the Reactor pattern (particularly one accessing a pool of stateless Session Beans). The Acceptor/Connector reminds one either of a web server/application server, or else of a separate publisher class and implementation class, such as we saw in JAX-WS.

Component–Configurator and Adapter should remind a person of SOAs in general. An SOA can call any needed components at runtime, no need for static linking. The Adapter pattern also represents SOAs, if a new interface is needed then that can be defined and the original interfaces called.

So these are important concepts, but come free (perhaps *included* is a better word), so to speak, when considering components in a container, web services, or SOAs (depending) as compared to true distributed objects, because in distributed objects (such as CORBA), additional handling is required.

So basically if a project really needed some of these, it might be better to move over to web services and/or an SOA, or at least a container-based solution to handle them. So I think we're better off not considering these separately, but rather including them as part of an overarching architecture such as web SOA architecture or component container.

Question: Can an appdomain in .NET Remoting be considered to be a container in terms of what we're talking about here? We'll think about this later on.

Before we define our own patterns to use here, let's look again at Staal's (2006) SOA patterns, which we previously saw in Chapter 2, to check for any overlap or additional information.

Staal's (2006) requirements for an SOA (you could call these aspects of an architectural style) included:

- • Gamma et al.'s Bridge pattern
  - • Let interface and implementation vary independently
- • Gamma et al.'s Proxy pattern (we've seen this before with Gomaa, we will ignore it here)
- • Interface implemented such that different technologies can be used to implement it
- • Explicitly defined interface
- • Messages must be represented in a standard format
- • Stateless interaction between client and server is preferred
- • Service composition must be coordinated

I believe we need Gamma et al.'s Bridge pattern; we haven't talked about that explicitly elsewhere, and it applies to many technologies, not just SOAs.

So let's define that as:

Name: Bridge
Description:

- Let interface and implementation vary independently

What about: Interface implemented such that different technologies can be used to implement it? I think we need that, it could be important in many places, not just in SOAs, so let's define that as:

Name: Independent interface
Description:

- Interface implemented such that different technologies can be used to implement it

We haven't talked about messages in a standard format, but that could be important in many places, not just in SOAs:

Name: Standard message format
Description:

- Messages must be represented in a standard format

We've already got a pattern for stateless operation.
So, instead of using some of these separate lower-level patterns, here we define our overarching architectural styles:

Name: Distributed Objects
Description:

- One object accesses a remote object through a direct call to a method defined on that object

Name: Distributed Components
Description:

- Remote object accessed through calls to a container rather than direct calls to a method

Name: Web Services
Description:

- Use interfaces to the World Wide Web to provide application services
- Interfaces provided through use of a web server/application server

Name: Service-Oriented Architectures
Description:

- A service does part of its own particular task by calling other services (sub-services) to do sub-tasks
  - The service may do additional work
  - The service may also include code to glue sub-services together
- All services have well-defined interfaces
- Service composition must be coordinated
- Messages must be represented in a standard format

Fielding had a few other architectural styles that were related to Mobile code: Virtual Machine, Remote Evaluation, Code on Demand, and Mobile Agent. We'll do a separate evaluation of Cloud Computing with these in the next section. However, they won't be part of our overall Middleware comparison plan, we'll treat that as a separate issue.

Oooo-kaay, I think we can stop! We have a reasonable set of architectural styles/patterns to look at.

Is there anything magic about this? Is this the best thing ever in a collection of architectural styles/ patterns?

Doubtful. It clearly doesn't define everything; for example, we explicitly left out anything to do with cloud computing. We also didn't talk about anything at all to do with databases, and that's a big thing for middleware to access, as you hopefully have figured out.

However, it's fairly comprehensive in regard to the kinds of things we've been talking about in this textbook, and we based it off formal literature by some well-known researchers. So, it's a start.

When you need to do this yourself for your company, you can use this as a starting point to do a better job. ☺ Or at least one that's more directly targeted toward the kind of work your company is doing right now.

16.2 HOW DO MIDDLEWARE TECHNOLOGIES MAP TO OUR SELECTED ARCHITECTURAL STYLES/PATTERNS?

In this section, we will look at whether the technologies we examined in this textbook *directly support* the various architectural styles

Some tricky things: You probably didn't see a lot about asynchronous calls in the section on CORBA. It was mentioned in passing when talking about the narrow() routine. I didn't include it because the CORBA section was already huge, bigger than the other sections. However, there is a way to do an asynchronous call in CORBA: if you mark a method in the Interface Description Language with the keyword "oneway" then that method won't block. Additionally, asynchronous calls are possible through the CORBA Event Service/CORBA Notification service, as we saw in Chapter 15.

I listed .NET Remoting as not supporting the Bridge pattern because you can make a separate DLL file that contains the interface and then use reflection on the DLL file to determine the interface, similarly for WCF. However, if being very strict about what is included in the technology itself, I suppose one could argue that .NET Remoting itself doesn't allow this, it's strictly looking at what shows in reflection; the mode of operation occurs based on the design of the particular project. There is a similar situation with EJB, where we could possibly argue that EJB wouldn't have to have a separate interface file defined. It could do it with the class file. In these kinds of situations, I feel these were intended to be normal operation from the beginning, so I count them here as being part of the technology.

In regard to a standard format for EJBs, the data in EJB is serialized into a Java byte stream. We discussed that briefly in this textbook but did not go into specifics; it is explained in detail in JavaTips (2009). Also, in regard to EJBs implementing web services, as we discussed in Section 8.4, a Stateless Session Bean and a Singleton Session Bean can implement a web service endpoint, but a Stateful Session Bean cannot.

With SOAs, most people think in terms of web services, which is why I listed the distributed object/components as not supporting that architectural style. However, as you should recall from Chapter 9, many people do claim that distributed objects can be used to create an SOA. What we discussed in Chapter 9 is that this kind of SOA should be better done behind a firewall, at an individual company.

In terms of the MOM patterns—point-to-point and publish/subscribe—these are met in CORBA by the CORBA Event Service/Notification Service. They are met in the Java technologies through the use of the Java Messaging Service. They are met in the Microsoft world through the use of Microsoft Message Queueing (MSMQ), although we haven't talked about that service before.

When talking about calling a specific distributed object, this is possible in EJB through the use of a Stateful Session Bean but it is not required—consider pools of Stateless Session Beans.

In regard to Broadcast without message queue, any middleware can be used to do this, simply by keeping a list of recipients, and sending messages to all those recipients. This isn't built into the middleware per se but this kind of operation is quite common.

When discussing the Broker pattern, for CORBA that would be the Naming Service. For EJBs, JAX-WS, and JAX-RS that would be the JNDI. For WCF and .NET Remoting, I'm counting the Windows Active Directory Domain Service, although it's not a good one-to-one comparison with JNDI or the CORBA Naming Service.

I marked JAX-WS and JAX-RS as *not* being related to the Distributed Object pattern, even though both are implemented using Java classes, because they are accessed via a web interface and not strictly an object interface. Similarly for WCF and WCF-RESTful. But I could be convinced otherwise with these. ☺

In terms of independent interface, where one can use different middleware technologies to talk to each other, I'm thinking of the various web services technologies as a definite *yes* on this, and the object-oriented/component-oriented technologies as a *yes* but with more difficulty. Note that CORBA allows practically any programming language/operating system combination to talk to each other and also allows different CORBA ORBs to talk to each other, but each side should normally be running CORBA. There are some ORBs that allow access to .NET Remoting and EJBs, but it requires a good bit of fiddling, from what I've seen. Also, .NET Remoting under the Mono project should be able to talk to Windows .NET Remoting but both sides should normally be .NET Remoting. However, it has been possible for .NET Remoting to talk to EJBs as well as to CORBA.

As you should recall from Chapter 8, the distinction between objects and components can sometimes be arguable. Here I'm using the definition we developed earlier in Section 8.1: A component is a remote object accessed through calls to a container rather than direct calls to a method. As you recall from Chapter 8, many other definitions of a component are possible. In regard to this particular definition, EJBs definitely fit it, but .NET Remoting is arguable. To the best of my understanding, an appdomain acts more like a native process than it does a container similar to the EJB understanding of a container. I believe the main difference between an appdomain and a native process is that the appdomain provides greater isolation. I would be open to other arguments about this. ☺

In regard to having an independent interface and having different technologies connect to each other, if one is using WSDL/SOAP then it should be possible. This should allow JAX-WS to connect to WCF (non-RESTful). If one is using RESTful then it should also be possible, for that means that one should be able to connect between AJAX, JAX-RS, and WCF (RESTful). However, the degree to which this is actually practical is not something I have studied myself. Various web references claim some of these are doable, see Zaikin (2012), StackOverflow (2010a), and Kumar (2014).

In regard to stateful versus stateless for the various web services (JAX-WS, WCF, AJAX, servlets, JAX-RS, WCF-RESTful): WCF supports sessions, which are stateful. Also, I went ahead and marked the rest as being able to be stateful, because one can do that by just passing a state value back and forth in a cookie, or by using URL rewriting. Also, there is some specific support for this, for example, JAX-WS can use sessions through HttpSession (see Oracle 2016), as can Java servlets (see javax.servlet.http 2012). However, most people seem to believe it is better when possible for web services to be stateless, largely because it makes scalability easier (see Hadlow 2013; Letizi 2008; StackOverflow (2010b)).

Note that EJBs support sessions through a JSESSIONID cookie or through URL rewriting.

It's possible to do stateless operation on CORBA through, say, use of a servant manager. Also, a default servant could be used to implement a stateless CORBA object—it's handling all the clients so it's not considered to be dedicated to a single client, so the session concept relative to any individual client is considerably diminished. (Note that using a single CORBA object, the default servant, to handle all clients is not really scalable, so it kind of goes against a lot of the reason one normally would want a stateless connection.) However, statelessness is not really one of the strengths of CORBA.

For .NET Remoting, of course Server-Activated Single Call can be used to implement a stateless session. Or instead, you could save a state to some database or perhaps a file and implement a stateful session even when using Server-Activated Single Call.

WCF does support asynchronous operation, although we didn't really go in depth, see MSDN (2016a). Also, a RESTful WCF can be made asynchronous but it's perhaps not the most straightforward thing to do (see StackOverflow 2011; Zabir 2011).

In regard to web services, I listed EJBs as supporting web services because it's possible to define a web interface to an EJB.

Okay, so! You might argue about my individual ratings in Table 16.1, or even several of them. (Please, do feel free to argue this. You may have some knowledge about individual technologies that I don't, or perhaps you don't accept my reasoning in some situations.) In any case, unless you argue with the whole table, I think it's safe to say that nearly anything can be done with any one of these middleware technologies.

So if we're choosing one versus the other, we have to choose based on different issues.

TABLE 16.1

Middleware Technologies Mapped to Our Selected Architectural Styles/Patterns

Architectural Style/Pattern	CORBA	.NetR	EJB	JAX-WS	WCF	AJAX	Serv.	JAX-RS	WCF-Rest
Asynchronous client/server with callback	Y	Y	Y	Y	Y	Y	Y	Y	Y
Asynchronous client/server without callback	Y	Y	Y	Y	Y	Y	Y	Y	Y
Bridge	Y	Y	Y	Y	Y	Y	Y	Y	Y
Broadcast without message queue	Y	Y	Y	Y	Y	Y	Y	Y	Y
Broker Pattern	Y	N	Y	Y	Y	Y	Y	Y	Y
Call-Specific Distributed Object	Y	Y	Y	N	N	N	N	N	N
Distributed Components	N	N	Y	N	N	N	N	N	N
Distributed Objects	Y	Y	Y	N	N	N	N	N	N
Independent interface (different technologies)	Y	Y	Y	Y	Y	Y	Y	Y	Y
Point-to-point	Y	Y	Y	Y	Y	Y	Y	Y	Y
Proxy without message queue	Y	Y	Y	Y	Y	Y	Y	Y	Y
Publish/subscribe	Y	Y	Y	Y	Y	Y	Y	Y	Y
Service-Oriented Architectures	N	N	N	Y	Y	Y	Y	Y	Y
Shared state client/server	Y	Y	Y	Y	Y	Y	Y	Y	Y
Standard message format	Y	Y	Y	Y	Y	Y	Y	Y	Y
Stateful client/server	Y	Y	Y	Y	Y	Y	Y	Y	Y
Stateless client/server	Y	Y	Y	Y	Y	Y	Y	Y	Y
Synchronous client/server	Y	Y	Y	Y	Y	Y	Y	Y	Y
Web Services	N	N	Y	Y	Y	Y	Y	Y	Y

16.2.1 ARCHITECTURAL STYLES/PATTERNS RELATED TO THE CLOUD

Now the other styles that Fielding had were related to Mobile code:

- Virtual machine
  - The code is executed within a controlled environment.
  - When combined with remote evaluation, it is part of a network-based style.
- Remote evaluation
  - A client possesses code to perform a service but lacks the resources.
  - The client sends the code to perform a service to a remote server that possesses the necessary resources, which then executes the code (in a controlled environment, one possible environment is a virtual machine).
  - The server then sends the results back to the client.
- Code on Demand
  - A client has access to the resources needed to perform a service, but does not possess the code to perform the service.
  - The client requests a remote server to send it the code to perform the service, then the client executes the code locally.
- Mobile agent
  - An entire computational component that contains the code needed to perform a service is moved to a location that possesses the necessary resources to perform a service, along with its state.
    - This can be considered a derivation of either Remote Evaluation or Code on Demand, since the computational component can be moved from client to server or from server to client.
    - The computational component can be in the middle of processing when it is moved to the remote site.

If you combine some of these together, then you get cloud-like operation. What Fielding is calling a "virtual machine" here, I might be more likely to call a *sandbox*, in that he's focusing on the isolation rather than on virtual machine migration. He *does* discuss how it could be combined with remote evaluation, which is one aspect related to virtual machine migration. He's distinguishing two other concepts: Code on Demand and Mobile Agent based on whether or not the code is moved in its entirety and executed separately (mobile agent) or whether the code is downloaded and executed under the control of a local entity (Code on Demand).

One could consider that a cloud uses Virtual Machine together with Remote Evaluation and Mobile Agent (Code on Demand is more like an old Java applet than it is cloud-related).

16.3 MIDDLEWARE PERFORMANCE, QUALITY, AND EASE OF LEARNING COMPARISONS

You should recall from Chapter 2, Fielding also describes architectural properties that will allow one to differentiate between architectural styles.

A summary of Fielding's architectural properties is as follows:

1. Performance, consists of three sub-categories:
   - Network performance, which consists of:
     - Throughput
       - Rate of transfer of information between components (includes both application data and overhead required by communication)

- Overhead
  - Consists of initial setup overhead and per-interaction overhead
    - This distinction is important when you consider that some communications can share setup overhead over several connections.
- Bandwidth
  - Maximum available throughput on a particular network link
- Usable bandwidth
  - The portion of the overall bandwidth that the application can actually use
- User-perceived performance, this is how a user individually perceives performance as he or she waits for an application to get done. This consists of:
- Latency
  - Time between initiation of a command and when the response arrives. In this context, latency consists of:
    a. Time required for the application to recognize the command
    b. Time required to set up a communication between a client and a server
    c. Time required to send a message from client to server (and separately the Time to send the response back from server to client)—this involves actual network interaction
    d. Time to process a message on the client, and time to process a message on the server
    e. Time to complete sufficient message transfer and processing so as to render a usable result—this involves actual network interaction
- Completion time—amount of time taken to fully complete a user action. This is different from latency because it is related to whether (and to what degree) the data is being reported to the user in chunks. That is, does the middleware wait until the entire quantity of data being transferred has arrived before it is reported to the user? Or are parts of the data reported as they come in. The user would likely feel that things are going better if s/he were getting some early results. That is, the early results represent a reduction in latency to the user. However, if on-the-fly processing is going on in order to present early results to the user, the completion time of the whole user action could actually be worse (because the on-the-fly processing required more time than after-the-whole transmission processing).
- Network efficiency
  - What is the distance and network complexity between the client and the server? If they're in the same process it's a lot faster than if they're at widely separated spots on the internet.
  - Caching data can improve efficiency by reducing the amount of data that must be transferred over a network. Finding ways to reduce the number of network interactions can also improve efficiency.
2. Scalability—suppose suddenly the server must handle huge numbers of clients, how easy is it for the server to handle this suddenly large number of connections?
   - The amount of coupling between components affects this. So can a decentralized style as opposed to a centralized style.
   - How frequent the interactions are is an issue.
   - Synchronous operation versus asynchronous operation is also important.
3. Simplicity
   - Can small software components be created? If the software components are small, then they can be more easily understood and verified.
   - How easy to understand are the middleware connections between software components? If they are well defined in a general way, and you don't have to define a lot of specialized connections between particular software components, then the overall connectivity is simpler and thus more easily understood and verified.

4. Modifiability
  - How easy is it to make changes in your distributed system? Is it possible to change components without stopping the whole distributed system from running?
  - How hard is it to configure your distributed system to run in the first place?
5. Evolvability
  - Do you have to change multiple software components in order to change one component? If so, how many of these do you have to change?
6. Extensibility
  - How hard is it to add new functionality to an existing, running system?
7. Customizability
  - How hard is it to (temporarily) extend the functionality of an existing component?
8. Configurability
  - How hard is it to change your configuration when the system is running?
9. Reusability
  - Can software components (or connections) be reused in other software components (or connections) without modification?
10. Visibility
  - How easy is it to monitor the interactions between software components?
11. Portability
  - Can the software run in different environments?
12. Reliability
  - How likely is the software to fail?
    - Are there single points of failure, or is there some redundancy?
  - Can recoverable actions be implemented?

Whew! It can be hard to compare one technology with another technology for some of these quality factors. So much depends on how the code in a particular project is written, compared to the middleware that was used.

Also, in terms of throughput and latency and such, so much depends on how fast the network is between client and server and how busy it is the particular day when you're doing the comparisons. So for throughput, bandwidth, usable bandwidth, latency, and completion time, we really can't say a lot. The best thing to do for these would to be create benchmark applications that are typical of the kinds of things you are really using, and then do measurements while running these: at traffic peak times of day and times of week, at traffic minimum times of day and times of week, etc. To do a real comparison between middlewares you'd have to implement the same benchmarks in multiple middlewares and measure all of those so you can compare. It's a daunting prospect. Some studies are done like this from time to time—exercise for the reader, look up a few!

We can talk about overhead, however:

- Consists of initial setup overhead
- Per-interaction overhead

One aspect of initial setup overhead would be the number of messages required to set up a connection. This would be more if something like a CORBA Naming Service were used, rather than a client being given upfront the location of the server, but I don't see any major differences between middlewares on this.

One big different, however, is the per-interaction overhead. All these middleware technologies are running on top of TCP/IP (except for rare occasions when they're on top of UDP). They mostly require another protocol to run on top of TCP/IP—in the case of CORBA this is IIOP, in the case of the various web services this is (usually) HTTP, note that HTTP is really required for the RESTful web services. .NET Remoting can support an HTTP channel, a TCP channel, or a Named Pipes channel.

WCF also allows a choice of HTTP versus TCP. It's also possible for JAX-WS to run over a TCP connection. If a TCP channel is chosen, then this can improve efficiency because one less protocol layer is used, but it also means that it's difficult to go through firewalls—firewalls work better with HTTP.

Note that .NET Remoting, WCF, and JAX-WS normally use SOAP as the format for the messages. SOAP is a fairly wordy XML-based protocol and data format, you should remember it from Section 10.2. XML is text-based, because it's supposed to be human readable, but this means actual data is sent as characters. This can result in much heavier data traffic than if binary were used.

Note that CORBA always uses binary, .NET Remoting and WCF can use binary. So those would be your first choice if you had some situation where the amount of data sent, or the speed of transmission, are very important. However, it won't go well through a firewall.

If you're considering an SOA, then this can help reusability—what an SOA does is reuse existing services in a new way. One can think of object-oriented type reusability through inheritance, as well, this would apply to most of the technologies we examined (because WCF and JAX-WS, for example, uses classes to implement web services). However, this is reusability at a much smaller granularity level than one would achieve with an SOA. So for reusability, an SOA is much preferred.

Scalability we discussed earlier, one way to help your scalability is to have a stateless design.

In terms of Simplicity, Modifiability, Evolvability, Extensibility and so forth, at base the major thing you're talking about is how hard the code is to understand. How difficult the middleware is to understand factors heavily into this. CORBA in particular has had some problems in this area. According to Henning (2006):

> The platform had a steep learning curve and was complex and hard to use correctly, leading to long development times and high defect rates.

Henning also said:

> In addition, developers who had gained experience with CORBA found that writing any nontrivial CORBA application was surprisingly difficult. Many of the APIs were complex, inconsistent, and downright arcane, forcing the developer to take care of a lot of detail.

On the other hand, back in 2001 time frame, I did a study of CORBA interoperability (see Ironside et al. 2001 and Etzkorn et al. 2002). (Interoperability wasn't one of Fielding's quality factors, but Presson et al. from Boeing RADC used it (see Chapter 2), so let's use it too.) According to our study, CORBA was able to connect and run between different ORB vendors, different programming languages, and different operating systems.

We'll leave the other quality factors as exercises for the student, although these are generally fairly heavy workload studies as benchmarks that you implement in different middlewares and examine according to the quality factor you're concerned with—that would be the best way to do this. If you do a web search, you can find a few previous studies such as these.

16.4   ARCHITECTURE TRADEOFF ANALYSIS

Next, let's look at how to begin developing a middleware project, and at what point to choose which middleware technology to use. A good way to start with this is to choose a particular architectural style, and consider how the particular style chosen will affect the quality of your software.

We're going to look at a fairly heavyweight methodology for doing this. Keep in mind that you could do a lighter-weight version of this methodology; we'll discuss some ways to do that as we go. Also, the methodology that we'll be looking at was proposed in the context of the Spiral software process model (and alternately the Waterfall model). We'll discuss as we go how this kind of thing might be applied as part of an agile process, maybe Scrum.

Kazman et al. (1998a and 1998b) from the Carnegie Mellon Software Engineering Institute say:

> Quality attributes of large software systems are principally determined by the system's software architecture. That is, in large systems, the achievement of qualities such as performance, availability, and modifiability depends more on the overall software architecture than on code-level practices such as language choice, detailed design, algorithms, data structures, testing, and so forth.

They go on to say that the quality attributes of a system interact with each other: Security impacts performance, performance affects modifiability, and so forth. For this reason, any software design must do tradeoffs. To do this they develop a methodology for analyzing tradeoffs related to the architecture chosen. They say their methodology should be performed iteratively, over the life-cycle of the software system being analyzed. Their tradeoff methodology consists of the following steps:

- Step 1—Collect Scenarios
  - Collect examples of system usage from stakeholders
- Step 2—Collect Requirements/Constraints/Environment
  - In relation to quality attributes:
    - Identify requirements
    - Identify constraints
    - Identify environment
  - This includes revisiting scenarios from the previous step to make sure important quality attributes have been considered
- Step 3—Describe Architectural Views
  - Look at competing architectures
    - The different architectures that can be considered here may be limited based on:
      - Legacy systems
      - Interoperability
      - Successes or failures of previous projects
- Step 4—Attribute-Specific Analyses
  - Each quality attribute is analyzed *all by itself, in isolation*, relative to each candidate architecture.
  - At this point, attributes are *not* compared individually against requirements.
  - At this point, any interaction between attributes is not considered.
- Step 5—Identify Sensitivities
  - Sensitivity points, that is, attributes that are affected significantly by a change in the architecture are identified.
- Step 6—Identify Tradeoffs
  - Tradeoff points, that is, changes in elements of the architecture that affect multiple attributes, are identified. They give the following example:
    - "For example, the performance of a client-server architecture might be highly sensitive to the number of servers (performance increases, within some range, by increasing the number of servers). The availability of that architecture might also vary directly with the number of servers. However, the security of the system might vary inversely with the number of servers (because the system contains more potential points of attack). The number of servers, then, is a tradeoff point with respect to this architecture. It is an element, potentially one of many, where architectural tradeoffs will be made, consciously or unconsciously."

Kazman et al. (1998a and 1998b) analyze a remote temperature sensor system and look at the following architecture solutions:

1. Client/server with 1 server and 16 simple clients.
2. Client/server with 2 identical servers and 16 simple clients.
3. Client/server with 1 server and 16 clients. Each client has an intelligent cache in between it and the server (we'll look at the operation of the intelligent cache below).

The temperature sensor system is described as follows:

- The temperature of a set of furnaces is monitored with a sensor and reported to an operator.
  - There are 16 furnaces.
  - It is assumed there will be one client per furnace.
- The operator is at a different location from the furnaces.
  - The operator is located at a host computer.
- The host computer sends control commands to the temperature sensor to tell it how often to send periodic updates.
  - Different furnaces have different reporting frequencies.
- The temperature sensor periodically sends temperature readings to the host computer.
- The computer that is responsible for performing remote temperature sensing, called the Remote Temperature Server:
  - Has attached a hardware component (described as an Analog to Digital Converter, ADC) that can read the temperature of one furnace at a time
    - Requests for temperature readings are queued for the ADC.
    - The ADC reads the temperature of each furnace at the frequency specified in the most recent request.
  - Furnace tasks schedule themselves to run for some time period.
  - An ADC task that is associated with the ADC hardware:
    - Accepts requests from furnace tasks
    - Measures temperature on the physical furnaces
    - Passes the result back to the appropriate furnace task
  - A Communication task responsible for connecting from individual furnace tasks to individual external clients.

Kazman et al. (1998a and 1998b) wish to analyze the system based on the quality factors availability, security, and performance. (They treated security largely separately, so we won't look at that here.)

The intelligent cache in architecture solution 3 above intercepts updates to its associated client, builds a collection or history of these updates, and every so often passes this information on to the client. If there is an interruption in service connection to the furnace, the intelligent cache uses past history to model what the temperature values should be.

Let's go through each step of the methodology, from Kazman et al. (1998a and 1998b). In each step they consider availability and performance.

Step 1—Collect Scenarios
Here they collected availability and performance scenarios (they did a security analysis that was separate from this process). One scenario related to performance was:

   The client sends a control request and receives the first periodic update

One scenario related to availability was:

   A server suffers a software failure and was rebooted

Note that these scenarios might be user stories as collected during the Scrum agile process.

Step 2—Collect Requirements/Constraint/Environment
One performance requirement was:

Client must receive a temperature reading within F seconds of sending a control request

One availability requirement was:

System must not be unavailable for more than 60 minutes per year

These may also be a user story, or more likely attached to a user story.

Step 3—Describe Architectural Views
This is where they looked at the architecture candidates, these appeared to be somewhat arbitrarily selected (here the clients connect to the server(s) over a network):

1. Client/server with 1 server and 16 simple clients
2. Client/server with 2 identical servers and 16 simple clients
   - Each server has its own ADC task, furnace tasks, and communication module
     - Note that there appears to be only one ADC hardware component, it's just that now two ADC tasks can talk to it
   - Each server handles eight clients, and is backup for the other eight
     - When a server is down for a certain period of time, the clients swap to the other server (they know its location)
3. Client/server with 1 server and 16 clients. Each client has an intelligent cache in between it and the server (we'll look at the operation of the intelligent cache below)

Step 4—Attribute-Specific Analyses
They analyzed Performance and Availability (see Barbacci et al. 1998). Their Performance analysis was done in a very time-consuming way; they created a latency model for each candidate architecture where they mathematically analyzed the different paths through the different architectures. Their Availability model was hardware-oriented and looked at failure rates of the computers and ADC. (This ignored the possibility of software failure due to bugs, unfortunately).

Once they had equations based on these analyses, they were able to compare the candidate architectures over Performance and then separately over Availability.

Well, it's still reasonable to do this kind of heavyweight analysis sometimes. Another fairly heavyweight alternative would be to do a full-scale simulation. A somewhat less heavyweight alternative would be to take a UML-based approach and implement these high level architectures in UML, then do executable UML analyses (using a tool such as IBM Rhapsody).

If you're working in an agile process, such as Scrum, you can start measuring performance as soon as you have working code. However, even in a highly iterative process such as Scrum, which is targeted toward making changes easy, it might be a little difficult to change your high-level architectural styles at that point. So let's look at a third method that can be done even if you're doing one or more of the other methods, which is pretty simple: Talk the situation through with your team and consider your options intellectually.

Of course, Barbacci et al. (2008) did do a discussion based on their equations. However, for example, skipping the equations, they also discussed how under heavy load, in a situation where all reports happen to be scheduled at the same time, the server must work very hard to read the thermometer (using the ADC) and queue up the reports, which then are transmitted to the clients only after 64 readings have been queued. (Why 64? Read Barbacci.)

Here comes a brief additional discussion of our own:

We've tentatively allocated one very simple client per furnace task, then multiple furnace tasks talk to a single piece of hardware (the ADC). Is that a reasonable thing to do, since there is only one piece of hardware (ADC) to measure temperature, and each furnace has to take its turn? Would it possibly be better to allocate one somewhat smarter task to the ADC and have one smart client talk to it?

Based on all we've been told in this scenario, there's only one operator at one host computer expecting to receive this information anyway.

They say that requests for temperature readings are collected in a queue and fed to the ADC task one at a time. So it's an asynchronous connection. It looks as if the assumption is that the clients are connecting synchronously to the furnace tasks, which then connect asynchronously to the ADC task. Does this make sense? Could furnace tasks plus ADC task all be replaced by one ADC task that the clients connect to asynchronously? Wouldn't this do the same thing? And it's not clear we need more than one client, since there's only one operator at one host computer. However, each furnace should be on a different period for reporting, if multiple furnace tasks are there, how is that handled?

At this point, I think I'd go back and modify the list of candidate architectures to include the following:

- Client/server with one server directly controlling the ADC, one client connecting to the operator/host computer
  - Some kind of MOM running on server computer, connecting from client to server
  - Server keeps track of frequencies related to how often each furnace should be read and sends information back to client

In any case, let's move on to the next step.

Step 5—Identify Sensitivities
Perform variations in the architecture and look again at the performance and availability.

For example, does it matter if we increase the number of servers, with 2 servers in architecture 2, or maybe more servers? If we think of each client connecting synchronously to an individual furnace task that forms part of a server, then yes, it might, because at that point every individual furnace task is taken up by a client, and it takes time to establish a new connection with each furnace task. This would improve both performance and availability.

However, if we're thinking asynchronously when a client calls, sends a message quickly, then drops off, the number of servers may not matter much.

Also, when we remember we only have one piece of hardware (ADC) to read the temperature on the servers (!) then other than for connectivity, the scalability of the servers doesn't seem to be an issue—there's really no point in acquiring too many servers to talk to only one piece of hardware.

This kind of sensitivity analysis could be done for every iteration (at least in the early stages where you're settling on an architecture) of an agile process.

Step 6—Identify Tradeoffs
Our thought process so far does sort of trend me toward an architecture, at least it makes me think more of using MOM asynchronously. And one client and one server. (Unless I'm missing something in their description. But in any case this is a good exercise.)

What are the tradeoffs with this versus the three original architectural styles?

Well, an intelligent cache as in architecture 3 might be useful in cases when the server went down. We could add that to our client. The negative compared to the original model where there were 16 clients is in this case the intelligent cache on the 1 client would have to extrapolate data for 16 different furnaces.

If we use a single server instead of multiple servers as in architecture 2, then one kind of backup is gone. However, how likely is it that one of two identical servers would crash and the other not crash? The only likely scenario I can think of would be that one was hacked. But if they could get one, likely they could get its twin as well.

Note that this kind of tradeoff analysis could also be done in every iteration (at least in the early stages where you're settling on an architecture) of an agile process.

16.4.1 Analysis of Which Middleware(s) We Should Choose

Let's take an extra step now on this architecture and tentatively identify specific middleware technologies we might use:

- It doesn't seem all that data intensive, so it would probably be okay to use SOAP or something similar instead of needing binary.
  - That has advantages in that the data would be human-readable
- We do need some kind of MOM to connect to the ADC server
  - Which one?
    - If we choose MSMQ, then practically speaking that could mean we would have to use Microsoft technologies otherwise.
    - If we choose Java Message Service, then practically speaking that could mean we would have to use Java technologies otherwise.
    - CORBA Event/Notification Service moves us toward CORBA (could be any programming language then)—but then again, we don't need binary, and we haven't discussed firewalls yet
    - AMQP—*hmmm*. Doesn't seem to constrain us to a particular programming environment, has been shown to work with Python (OpenStack) and with Java implementations (CloudStack)
- We were never given any information as to where the operator was located relative to the furnaces, except it was at a different location
  - So we don't know whether we will have to go through firewalls or not
  - However, again, the need for speed doesn't seem that high, that is, we're not transmitting that much data that fast
    - So it would be okay to use a web service if we wanted to
    - Alternately, we could use an EJB with a web interface
    - That would protect us if the company decided to move the operator later on to another, further-away location.

16.4.2 Would Cloud Computing Make Sense? Is This an Internet of Things?

Before we tie ourselves down to specific middlewares, let's consider first: Does it make sense to put any of this in the cloud?

- Well, the temperature sensor can't be in the cloud, neither can its server
- We could access one or more clients through the cloud, however
- If we ever thought we would expand this project to read multiple furnaces at many different locations, with many different operators, then this begins to look like an Internet of Things:
  - Which might work well in a cloud environment

So before making our final decisions here, we need to go back to the stakeholders of the project to determine if it's a possibility the project would ever go bigger, like to an Internet of Things connected to the cloud. Because if so, there are cloud-based MOMs we could use. For example, Microsoft Azure provides an Azure Queue service for message queues in the cloud (but then, how much smarts do we have to have on our final computer that maps to the ADC? *Could* the message queue be located in the cloud?)

Assuming that we don't go to the cloud, then the following selection of technologies might make sense:

- Java Message Service, possibly with ApacheActiveMQ, to be used to do message queueing on a server connected with the ADC hardware

- EJBs with a web service interface to implement connectivity between a single server and a single client at the operator/host computer

This doesn't constrain us to be inside a firewall (which would be the case with CORBA) and allows possible future expansion because of the web service interface.

A similar collection of Microsoft Technologies would make sense.

Assuming we might someday want to go to the cloud and implement a full Internet of Things, then the following technologies might make sense:

- AMQP
- JAX-WS or WCF or if we prefer RESTful (which seems to be more common lately in new interfaces) then JAX-RS or WCF-RESTful. Or AJAX—or for that matter we could just do a simple HTTP command-based interface.

This would allow fairly easy expansion to the cloud, because we could use the web service interfaces (if well designed) to implement an SOA that would allow for expansion.

EXERCISES

1. Why could multithreading be used instead of the Reactor pattern?
2. What's the difference between our usual concept of client/server interaction and the components of the Acceptor–Connector pattern?
3. In Enterprise Java Beans, is it *required* for a client to connect to a particular distributed object?
4. Is an appdomain in .NET equivalent to a container in Enterprise Java Beans?
5. Why is it often better for web services to be stateless?
6. Is it possible to do stateless operation in CORBA?
7. Why is it difficult to compare different middleware technologies in terms of throughput, bandwidth, usable bandwidth, latency, and completion time?
8. Are the different middlewares similar in terms of the learning curve required?
9. Why might CORBA have limitations for its use in the cloud?
10. Does an Internet of Things need to be hosted on a cloud?

CONCEPTUAL QUESTIONS

1. Consider a high-performance embedded systems project, in this case a missile system. It has 20 sensors on all sides of the missile sending back large quantities of image data. Two separate microprocessor systems share these sensors. One system does image analysis to determine where the missile is going and to look for targets. The other system does analysis of the surrounding environment looking for other attacking missiles so it can take evasive action. The microprocessors are fairly small and underpowered because, of course, they blow up when they get to their destination.

    What is a good architectural style and what middlewares should you select? Does any of this make sense to do in the cloud?
2. You have 1000 small sensors that have been thrown into the middle of an enormous forest fire, their microprocessors are underpowered (they're expected to burn up) but they are sending back sensor data as fast as they can. They are all connecting to the central server that is located in your firetruck. Other image data is coming in continuously from helicopters that are circling the fire in the air. This can be considered a large Internet of Things.

    What is a good architectural style and what middlewares should you select? Does any of this make sense to do in the cloud?
3. You have a central grocery store server, it handles the inventory database for 15 grocery stores. As items are checked out at the grocery store cash registers (each grocery store has 10 cash registers), they must be automatically be removed from the inventory database. Also, the central grocery store server monitors 1000 refrigerators of customers who have paid to have the grocery store monitor their refrigerator contents and automatically order certain items, which must then be packaged, their

delivery scheduled, and the items removed from the inventory database. This can be considered a huge Internet of Things.

What is a good architectural style and what middlewares should you select? Does any of this make sense to do in the cloud?

4. You are in control of a no-kill animal shelter. You have hundreds of kennels for dogs and cats, but then you also have hundreds of dogs and cats. Your dogs and cats are traced by small transmitters on their collars. Some dogs can have playtime in the dog play yard at the same time because they are friends or at least get along. Other dogs are aggressive and can never be allowed in the dog play yard but must be walked separately, and this walk must be scheduled with animal shelter personnel. Similarly, some cats may be allowed in the cat outdoor area with other cats, but some cats are aggressive with other cats. You also must keep track of grooming schedules and feeding schedules. As dogs and cats are adopted, the schedules must be changed.

The software to do this could be considered a large Internet of Things—let's consider the "things" to be the collars because dogs and cats are our little buddies. ☺

What is a good architectural style and what middlewares should you select? Does any of this make sense to do in the cloud?

5. You are a city manager, in charge of all traffic in a city. This is the year 2040 so nearly all the cars are self-driving cars. You have to keep track of all cars that are broken down, how fast cars are going on all expressways, all cars that have been ordered to stop in awkward places. Also, you must monitor for anything that looks like someone hacking your car systems.

The software to do this could be considered a huge Internet of Things.

What is a good architectural style and what middlewares should you select? Does any of this make sense to do in the cloud?

BIBLIOGRAPHY

Barbacci, M. Carriere, J., Kazman, R., Klein, M., Lipson, H., Longstaff, T., Weinstock, C. 1998. Steps in an Architecture Tradeoff Analysis Method: Quality Attribute Models and Analysis. Technical Report CMU/SEI-97-TR-029/ESC-TR-97-029.   http://www.dtic.mil/cgi-bin/GetTRDDoc?AD=ADA343692 (accessed March 24, 2017).

Etzkorn, L., Sherrill, J., O'Guin, R. 2002. The CORBA Notification Service: Applicability in a Real Time, Embedded Environment. *Embedded Systems Programming* (renamed Embedded Systems Design). http://www.embedded.com/Home/PrintView?contentItemId=4024457 (accessed February 20, 2017).

Fielding, R. 2000. Architectural Styles and the Design of Network-based Software Architectures. Ph.D. Dissertation, University of California, Irvine, CA. https://www.ics.uci.edu/~fielding/pubs/dissertation/top.htm (accessed April 2, 2016).

Gamma, E., Helm, R., Johnson, R., Vlissides, J. 1994. *Design Patterns: Elements of Reusable Object-Oriented Software*. Addison-Wesley, Reading, MA.

Gomaa, H. 2011. *Software Modeling and Design: UML, Use Cases, Patterns, and Software Architectures*. Cambridge University Press, New York.

Hadlow, M. 2013. *How to Write Scalable Services*. http://mikehadlow.blogspot.com/2013/02/how-to-write-scalable-services.html (accessed May 23, 2016).

Henning, M. 2006. The rise and fall of CORBA. *ACM Queue Magazine* 4(5): 28–34.

Henningsson, K., Wohlin, C. 2002. Understanding the Relations between Software Quality Attributes: A Survey Approach. *Proceedings of the 12th International Conference in Software Quality (ICSQ)*. American Society for Quality, Milwaukee, WI.

IBM. 2016. Implementing Static JAX-WS Web Services Clients. https://www.ibm.com/support/knowledgecenter/was_beta/com.ibm.websphere.base.doc/ae/twbs_devwbsjaxwsclient.html (accessed May 23, 2016).

Ironside, E., Etzkorn, L, Zajac, D. 2001. Examining CORBA Interoperability. *Dr. Dobbs' Journal*: 111–122.

JavaTips. 2009. *The Java serialization algorithm revealed*. JavaWorld. http://www.javaworld.com/article/2072752/the-java-serialization-algorithm-revealed.html (accessed May 23, 2016).

javax.servlet.http. 2012. HttpSession. https://tomcat.apache.org/tomcat-5.5-doc/servletapi/javax/servlet/http/HttpSession.html (accessed May 23, 2016).

Kazman, R., Klein, M., Barbacci, M., Longstaff, T., Lipson, H., Carriere, J. 1998a. The Architecture Tradeoff Analysis Method. In *Proceedings of the International Conference on Software Engineering*. IEEE Computer Society Press, Washington, D.C.

Kazman, R., Klein, M., Barbacci, M., Longstaff, T., Lipson, H., Carriere, J. 1998b. The Architecture Tradeoff Analysis Method. Technical Report. CMU/SEI-98TR-008/ESC-TR-98-008. http://resources.sei.cmu.edu/library/asset-view.cfm?assetid=13091 (accessed February 20, 2017).

Kumar, R. 2014. *Calling WCF Services Using jQuery*. C# Corner. http://www.c-sharpcorner.com/UploadFile/rohatash/calling-wcf-services-using-jquery/ (accessed May 23, 2016).

Letizi, O. 2008. Stateful Web Applications That Scale Like Stateless Ones. *Dr. Dobb's Journal*. http://www.drdobbs.com/tools/stateful-web-applications-that-scale-lik/208403462 (accessed May 23, 2016).

Liu, Y., Gorton, I. 2005. Performance prediction of J2EE applications using messaging protocols. Component based software engineering. 8th International Symposium (CBSE). *In:* Lecture notes on computer science 3489. Eds. Heineman, G.T., Crnkovic, I., Schmidt, H.W., Stafford, J.A., Szyperski, C., Wallnau,K. 327–334. Springer-Verlag, Berlin.

McCall, J., Richards, P.K., Walters, G.F. 1977. *Factors in Software Quality: Concept and Definitions of Software Quality*. RADC-TR-77-369. Vol. I. http://www.dtic.mil/dtic/tr/fulltext/u2/a049014.pdf (accessed April 2, 2016).

McClure, T. 2012. *What Is the Role of Serialization in EJB?* JGuru. http://www.jguru.com/faq/view.jsp?EID=301817 (accessed May 23, 2016).

MSDN. 2016a. How to: Call WCF Service Operations Asynchronously. https://msdn.microsoft.com/en-us/library/ms730059(v=vs.110).aspx (accessed May 24, 2016).

MSDN. 2016b. Message Queuing (MSMQ). https://msdn.microsoft.com/en-us/library/ms711472(v=vs.85).aspx (accessed May 24, 2016).

Musser, D.R. 2006. *Invocation Semantics for IDL Operations*. http://www.cs.rpi.edu/~musser/dsc/idl/idl-overview_6.html (accessed May 23, 2016).

Oracle. 2016. Programming Stateful JAX-WS Web Services Using HTTP Session. https://docs.oracle.com/cd/E14571_01/web.1111/e13734/stateful.htm#WSADV234 (accessed May 23, 2016).

Presson, P.E., Tsai, J., Bowen, T.P., Post, J.V., Schmidt, R. 1983. *Software Interoperability and Reusability Guidebook for Software Quality Measurement*. RADC-TR-83-174. Vol. II. Boeing Company, Rome Air Development Center, Air Force Systems Command, Griffiss Air Force Base, NY.

Shaw, M., Clements, P.A. 1997. Field Guide to Boxology: Preliminary Classification of Architectural Styles for Software Systems. *Proceedings of the Twenty-First Annual International Computer Software and Applications Conference (COMPSAC '97)*. IEEE Computer Society Press, Washington, D.C.

Shaw, M., DeLine, R., Klein, D.V., Ross, T.L., Young, D.M., Zelesnick, G. 1995. Abstractions for Software Architecture and Tools to Support Them. *IEEE Transactions on Software Engineering* 21(4): 314–335.

StackOverflow. 2010a. Java JAX-WS Service with WCF Client. http://stackoverflow.com/questions/4111013/java-jax-ws-service-with-wcf-client (accessed May 23, 2016).

StackOverflow. 2010b. Webservices Are Stateless? http://stackoverflow.com/questions/2312969/webservices-are-stateless (accessed May 23, 2016).

StackOverflow. 2011. How to Make a WCF REST Method Entirely Asynchronous with the Task Parallel Library? http://stackoverflow.com/questions/8040002/how-to-make-a-wcf-rest-method-entirely-asynchronous-with-the-task-parallel-libra (accessed May 24, 2016).

Taylor, R.N., Medvidovic, N., Anderson, K.M., Whitehead, E.J. Jr., Robbins, J.E., Nies, K.A., Oreizy, P., Dubrow, D.L. 1996. A component- and message-based architectural style for GUI software. *IEEE Transactions on Software Engineering* 22(6): 390–406.

Thelin, J.A. 2003. *Comparison of Service-Oriented, Resource-Oriented, and Object-Oriented Architecture Styles*. Cape Clear Software, Inc. http://research.microsoft.com/pubs/117710/3-arch-styles.pdf (accessed April 2, 2016).

Zabir, O. 2011. *Tweaking WCF to Build Highly Scalable Async REST API*. CodeProject. http://www.codeproject.com/Articles/234085/Fixing-WCF-to-build-highly-scalable-async-REST-API (accessed May 24, 2016).

Zaikin, M. 2012. Use Ajax to Access a JAX-RS Resource, Oracle Certified Expert, Java Platform, Enterprise Edition 6 Web Services Developer Study Guidec. http://java.boot.by/ocewsd6-guide/ch07s04.html (accessed February 20, 2017).

Index

Printed in the United States
by Baker & Taylor Publisher Services